Professional Eclipse 3 for Java™ Developers

Professional Eclipse 3 for Java™ Developers

Berthold Daum

WILEY

Other Wiley Editorial Offices

John Wiley & Sons Inc., 111 River Street, Hoboken, NJ 07030, USA

Jossey-Bass, 989 Market Street, San Francisco, CA 94103-1741, USA

Wiley-VCH Verlag GmbH, Boschstr. 12, D-69469 Weinheim, Germany

John Wiley & Sons Australia Ltd, 33 Park Road, Milton, Queensland 4064, Australia

John Wiley & Sons (Asia) Pte Ltd, 2 Clementi Loop #02-01, Jin Xing Distripark, Singapore 129809

John Wiley & Sons Canada Ltd, 22 Worcester Road, Etobicoke, Ontario, Canada M9W 1L1

Wiley also publishes its books in a variety of electronic formats. Some content that appears in print may not be available in electronic books.

British Library Cataloguing in Publication Data

A catalogue record for this book is available from the British Library

ISBN: 0-470-02005-9

Typeset in Indianapolis, IN USA
Printed and bound by Malloy printing in Ann Arbor, MI USA
This book is printed on acid-free paper responsibly manufactured from sustainable forestry in which at least two trees are planted for each one used for paper production.

Credits

Author
Berthold Daum

Executive Editor
Gaynor Redvers-Mutton

Production Editors
Felicia Robinson
Juliet Booker

Book Producer
Ryan Publishing Group, Inc.

Copy Editor
Linda Recktenwald

Compositor
Gina Rexrode

Illustrator
Nathan Clement

Vice President & Executive Group Publisher
Richard Swadley

Vice President & Publishing Director
Sarah Stevens

Vice President and Publisher
Joseph B. Wikert

Editorial Manager
Kathryn Malm

About the Author

Berthold Daum has a Ph.D. in Mathematics and is a professional Java and XML developer who has been using Eclipse since it was first developed. Mr. Daum specializes in innovative electronic business technology and electronic content production; his clients include SAP Integrated Services AG and Software AG. His experience in software training and ability to anticipate the needs of professional developers has been demonstrated in his previous books, including *Eclipse 2 for Java Developers* (Wiley) and *Modeling Business Objects with XML Schema* (Morgan-Kaufmann).

Mr. Daum studied photography in Melbourne and has both exhibited and published his images of Australia's natural beauty.

Introduction

The first version of Eclipse was released in November 2001. Eclipse was announced by IBM as a $40 million donation to the Open Source community. The first reactions to this gift, however, were mixed. While many Java programmers hailed the release of Eclipse enthusiastically (when would one not be enthusiastic about a $40 million present?), Sun Microsystems was initially less than amused.

In the meantime, Eclipse has taken the Java world (and not only the Java world) by storm, despite the fact that Sun Microsystems is still not onboard. Eclipse is now completely managed by eclipse.org, an independent, nonprofit organization in which, however, IBM plays a major role. Despite the fact that the membership fee is quite hefty ($250.00 per year) and commitment is asked in the form of staff members working actively toward the development of Eclipse, the membership circle is not at all small: the Eclipse consortium has about 150 member companies, and people from Ericsson, Genuitec LLC, IBM, Hewlett Packard, Intel, MontaVista Software, QNX Software Systems Ltd., SAP AG, SAS, Serena Software, and the University of Washington belong to the board (Microsoft, you guessed it, is not a member).

So, the question is, what is Eclipse? Is it a Java IDE? Is it a new GUI for Java applications? Is it an application platform or framework?

Eclipse.org refers to Eclipse as a platform for "everything and nothing in particular." That we can use Eclipse to develop Java programs (in fact, it is one of the finest Java IDEs) is just a special application of this platform. But its real application domain reaches far beyond Java development. Because of its plug-in architecture, Eclipse is as adaptable as a chameleon and can find a habitat in quite different environments. The Eclipse Java IDE is, in fact, only an eminent example of an Eclipse plug-in. A large number of other plug-ins have already been developed for Eclipse by various companies and developers or are currently in development (see Appendix A for a small selection of such developments). For example, there is a plug-in for a C++ IDE, while plug-ins for other programming languages such as RPG and COBOL are in preparation. In this book, however, we will concentrate on Java development with Eclipse.

Eclipse is more than a pure development environment. With its SWT and JFace libraries it provides an alternative to Sun's Java libraries, AWT and Swing. SWT and JFace allow the creation of Java applications that closely match native applications (i.e., applications written in C or C++) in both "look and feel" and in responsiveness. In contrast, applications implemented on the basis of Swing often lack responsiveness and sometimes differ—despite the possibility to switch skins—from the "look and feel" of a native application. Such applications are notoriously hard to sell, because end users expect applications that fulfill the standards of the host platform. SWT and JFace could therefore be a breakthrough for Java applications on the desktop. No wonder, therefore, that there is a heated debate for and against SWT/JFace in the respective discussion forums (for example, www.javalobby.com) and that the SWT was voted as the "most innovative Java component."

Finally, Eclipse provides a large framework for implementing Java applications. Besides the GUI libraries SWT and JFace, we find higher-level components such as editors, viewers, resource management, task and problem management, a help system, and various assistants and wizards. Eclipse uses all these components to implement features such as the Java IDE or the workbench, but they can also be used for your own applications. In particular, the Rich Client Platform that was introduced with Eclipse 3 provides a generic framework for a wide class of applications. The Eclipse license model allows users to embed these components into their own applications, to modify them, and to deploy them as part of their own applications—all without paying a cent in license fees. The complete Eclipse code is available as source code, can be browsed online, and can be used within you own projects.

The Eclipse Culture

Of course, Eclipse was not just "invented": it has a history. The author of this book, who has used Visual Age for Java for years, can detect many of the Visual Age construction elements within Eclipse. In fact, the same company that stood behind the development of Visual Age is also responsible for the development of Eclipse. This company is OTI (`www.oti.com`). As long ago as 1988, OTI developed a collaborative development environment for Smalltalk called ENVY, which was later licensed to IBM under the name Visual Age. What followed was the development of Visual Age for Java, but this was still implemented in Smalltalk. Now, OTI has started the next generation of development tools with Eclipse. Of course, we find many of the design elements of Visual Age in Eclipse. The difference is, however, that Eclipse is implemented in Java and that it features a much more open architecture than Visual Age.

Eclipse was licensed by IBM and than donated to the Open Source community. This was not done without self-interest: Eclipse basically is nothing more than the community edition of IBM's WebSphere Studio Application Developer (WSAD). The core platform and the core plug-ins are all the same. The main difference is that Eclipse 3.0 consists of about 90 plug-ins, while WSAD features about 500–700 plug-ins, thus offering greatly extended functionality, such as plug-ins for developing web and database applications.

About This Book

It is practically impossible to write a single book about Eclipse. The sheer complexity of Eclipse would require quite a few books. I have tried to emphasize those topics where Eclipse makes significant contributions to the Java world. In particular, these are the new GUI libraries (SWT and JFace) and the use of Eclipse as a platform and framework for desktop applications. What had to be excluded from this book are WebSphere-specific topics such as J2EE and servlet development. Developing desktop applications is currently one of the strong points of Eclipse.

This book is not an introduction to Java programming. We assume that readers have a good knowledge of Java and of object-oriented programming concepts. Most of the examples used in this book are not trivial. Two examples come from the multimedia area. Here, readers have the possibility of "getting their feet wet" with cutting-edge Java technology such as speech processing and MP3 (all in pure Java!). In the third example, we do something useful and implement a spell checker plug-in for Eclipse. I am sick and tired of bad orthography in Java comments! The last example is a board game implemented on the basis of the Rich Client Platform, just to burn some of the programmer's spare time gained by productivity enhancements of the Eclipse IDE.

This book, therefore, addresses Java programmers—from the student to the professional—who want to implement their own desktop applications with the help (or on the basis) of Eclipse. You will learn all the techniques that are required to create applications of professional quality.

How This Book Is Organized

The novice to Eclipse—or even an experienced Java programmer—is at first overwhelmed by the sheer number of functions. But the functions visible to the user are only the tip of the iceberg. If we start to explore the inner workings of Eclipse, its API, we can get lost easily. Currently the Eclipse download has a size of 83 MB.

Faced with this huge amount of information, this book uses a pragmatic approach. Following the motto that "perception works from the outside to the inside," I first investigate how Eclipse presents itself to the end user. The benefit is twofold: first, each programmer is an end user of the Eclipse Java IDE; second, the various components of the Eclipse workbench, such as editors, views, menus, dialogs, and much more, can also be used in personal applications. Experienced programmers, however, may find an introduction into the Java IDE trivial and superfluous. Nevertheless, it is useful to get well acquainted with the Eclipse user interface, because many of the concepts and details can be later utilized when designing you own applications.

In Chapters 1 through 7 of this book I first introduce practical work with Eclipse, in particular with the Java development environment. Eclipse presents itself as a very powerful Java IDE that continues the positive traditions of Visual Age for Java but also introduces new concepts such as code completion, strong refactoring facilities, assistants that make intelligent proposals for fixing program errors, and a local history that allows a return to previous code versions.

In these chapters I also discuss the organization of the workbench, the resources of the Eclipse workspace such as projects, folders, and files, how these resources are related to the native file system, and the tools for navigation. I explain what perspectives are and how they can be used effectively. The Eclipse Java debugger and the integration of JUnit into Eclipse are discussed, and a short introduction about Eclipse's support for working in a team is given.

The examples used in this part are still all based on AWT and Swing.

However, this will quickly change in the second part of the book, Chapters 8 through 10. Here, I introduce the secrets of the SWT and JFace libraries. For SWT, event processing is discussed, along with the various GUI elements such as text fields, tables, buttons, and trees; the various layout options; graphics operations and how Java2D can coexist with the SWT; and printer output. I also explain the specialties of thread and resource management in the context of the SWT and the integration of SWT widgets with Swing facilities.

In the case of the JFace library, I present the higher user interface levels such as windows, dialogs, viewers, actions, menus, text processing, wizards, and preferences. As an example, an MP3 player that can be deployed independently of the Eclipse platform is implemented completely with SWT and JFace. An interesting detail in this example is how the SWT library is used in a multithreaded application.

In Chapters 11 through 16 I explain how to develop your own products on the basis of the Eclipse platform: either as a plug-in to Eclipse or as a stand-alone application under the Rich Client Platform. Since Eclipse consists more or less only of plug-ins, I first introduce the plug-in architecture of Eclipse. The requirements for a minimal platform are discussed, and I show how workspace resources are used in Eclipse and how plug-ins are declared via a manifest. Then the various components of the Eclipse workbench such as editors, views, actions, dialogs, forms, wizards, preferences, perspectives, and the help system are introduced. All these components are available to the application programmer as building blocks, a fact that can speed up application development considerably.

Then, I show how your own products can be packaged for deployment. Eclipse offers integrated support for all tasks here, too: from the creation of a feature, to the creation of nation language fragment and the definition of an update site, to the automated installation of updates. As an example, a universal and fully functional plug-in for spell checking on Eclipse platforms is implemented.

Finally, I discuss the Rich Client Platform (RCP) that was introduced with Eclipse 3 and serves as a generic platform for a wide range of applications. The board game Hex is implemented as an example of such an RCP application.

In Appendix A some more interesting third-party plug-ins are listed. In Appendix B I discuss the migration to another version of the Eclipse platform. Appendix C contains download addresses for the third-party software and the source code used in the examples.

Acknowledgements

Books are always teamwork, even if only the author's name appears below the title. This is also the case with this book, and here is the place to acknowledge the contribution of all the other team members.

Special thanks go to the publisher John Wiley & Sons and Wrox, in particular to Gaynor Redvers-Mutton who acted as the publishing editor. Thanks go also to the publisher of the original German edition, dpunkt verlag, and the responsible editor there, René Schönfeldt.

Thanks also to Tim Ryan's group who handled the production of this book, especially Linda Recktenwald for copyediting, Gina Rexrode for composition, and Nathan Clement for his technical illustrations.

Many important tips that found their way into this book came from the (anonymous) reviewers but also from developers and employees of OTI who had looked at the first manuscript version. Many thanks! And of course, without the development of Eclipse this book would not have been written, and Eclipse is indeed a tool that I wouldn't want to miss. Thanks again!

Berthold Daum
June 2004
berthold.daum@bdaum.de

Contents

Contents

Contents

Contents

Contents

Contents

Contents

Contents

Contents

Contents

Contents

Introduction to Eclipse

In this chapter you install and configure Eclipse. I then use the classical HelloWorld example to show how to effectively create Java programs under Eclipse. I first discuss the most important workbench preferences and then introduce various utilities for code creation.

Installing Eclipse

Installing Eclipse is very easy. In most cases, the only thing to do is to unpack the downloaded ZIP file onto a disk drive with sufficient free space. What do you need to run Eclipse? The following list shows what is required:

❑ **A suitable platform.** Eclipse 3.0 runs on a wide variety of platforms: Windows, Linux, Solaris, QNX, AIX, HP-UX, and Mac OS X. However, in this book I mostly refer to the Windows platform and occasionally give hints for the Linux platform.

❑ **Sufficient disk space.** 300 MB should be enough.

❑ **Sufficient RAM.** 256 MB should be fine.

❑ **Java SDK 1.4.** If this SDK is not installed on your machine, you can download it from www.javasoft.com and install it by following the instructions given on this site. You should specify the bin subdirectory of the SDK in your PATH environment variable so that you can call the Java Virtual Machine (JVM) by issuing the command java from the command prompt.

❑ **Eclipse SDK 3.0 for your platform.**

❑ The Eclipse example files (**eclipse-examples-3.0**) for your platform.

To install Eclipse, follow these steps:

1. Unpack the Eclipse SDK into the target directory. For example, on Windows that could be the root directory C:\. In effect, the Eclipse libraries will be contained in directory C:\eclipse. Under Linux you could use the /opt/ directory so that the Eclipse files would be stored under /opt/eclipse/.

2. Immediately afterwards, unpack the Eclipse example files into the same root directory. By doing so, the example files are automatically placed into the just-created eclipse subdirectory.

3. That's all. Under Windows you can now invoke Eclipse by clicking the icon with the darkened sun (in the eclipse subdirectory). Under Linux you would issue the shell command /eclipse under the directory /opt/eclipse/.

Eclipse then prompts you with the *Workspace Launcher*. Here you can select the location of the Eclipse workspace. This workspace will later contain all of your Eclipse projects. Usually the \workspace\ folder is located in the Eclipse root directory \eclipse\. However, it makes more sense to install the workspace in a location separate from the Eclipse installation. This makes later upgrades to new Eclipse version easier (see also Appendix A). In addition, it becomes easier to back up the workspace.

For example, you may want to specify ...\Own Files\eclipse-workspace under Windows and /root/eclipse-workspace under Linux. The Eclipse Workspace Launcher is shown in Figure 1.1. Note that later when running Eclipse you can easily switch to a different workspace by invoking the function File > Open workspace.

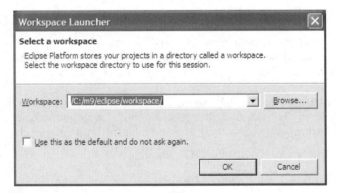

Figure 1.1

Important: When backing up the Eclipse workspace you should always create complete backups—never incremental backups. Eclipse treats the archive attribute of files in a somewhat unconventional way, which can lead to a corrupt workspace when restoring a workspace from an incremental backup. This is a known bug in Eclipse that has not been fixed with the release of Eclipse 3.0.0.

4. After a short while you should see the Welcome screen. Here you have the choice of various information sources such as help pages, tutorials, sample programs, and others:

- ❑ In the Overview section you will find relevant chapters from the various user guides in the Eclipse help system.

- ❑ In the Tutorials section you can learn how to create a simple Java program, a simple SWT application, and an Eclipse plug-in, and you will learn how to create and deploy an Eclipse feature. These tutorials come in form of *Cheat Sheets* that can be followed in a step-by-step fashion.

- ❑ The Samples section contains ready-to-run example programs. These include samples for using the SWT and the Eclipse workbench. If you select such an example program, it will automatically be downloaded from www.eclipse.org (provided that you have established a connection to the Internet) and installed into the Eclipse workbench. Depending on your interests and requirements, it may be worthwhile to take a close look at the code of such an example program.

- ❑ In the What's New section you will find a compilation of the new features contained in Eclipse 3 and also a migration guide for converting the Eclipse 2 application into Eclipse 3 (see also Appendix B). Furthermore, there is a link to the Eclipse Community page and a link to the Eclipse Update site, where you can update your Eclipse installation online.

However, for the moment you continue the startup process by pressing the Workbench button. You should then see the Eclipse Welcome screen, as displayed in Figure 1.2. You can return at any time to this screen by invoking the function Help > Welcome. Figure 1.3 shows Eclipse running.

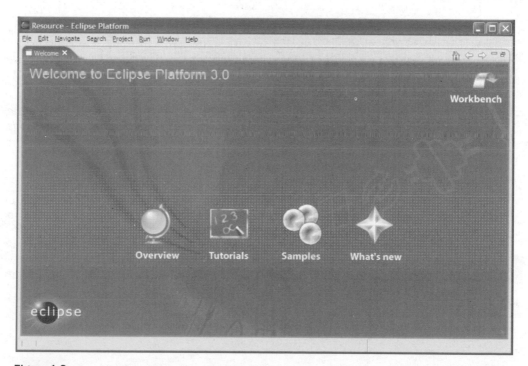

Figure 1.2

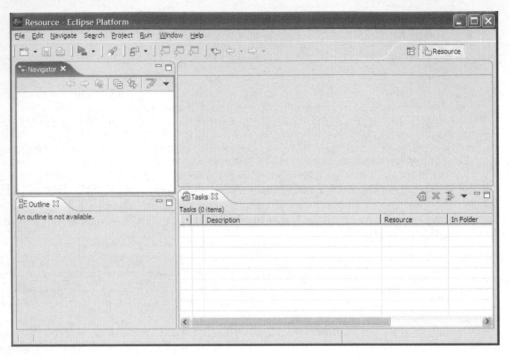

Figure 1.3

5. It is a good idea to create a desktop shortcut for Eclipse. Under Windows simply pull the Eclipse icon onto the desktop by pressing the right mouse button. From the context menu select Create Shortcut Here. Now you can add additional command-line options to this shortcut, for example, the -vm option discussed below. To do so, right-click the shortcut and select Properties from the context menu.

To learn which command-line options are available for Eclipse, check the Eclipse help system by choosing Help > Help Contents. Then select Workbench User Guide, expand the Tasks item, and choose Running Eclipse.

Under Linux you can similarly create a desktop shortcut under KDE or Gnome and add the required command-line options.

A further list of command line options is found at Help > Help Contents > Platform Plug-in Developer Guide > Reference > Other reference information > Runtime options. This section lists all command line parameters and the corresponding System Property keys. (For example, the key osgi.instance.data is equivalent to the command line parameter -data.) These keys can be used to configure Eclipse via the configuration file \eclipse\ configuration\config.ini. Modifying this file allows you starting Eclipse in different configurations without having to use command line parameters.

6. One of the most important command-line options deals with the selection of the Java Virtual Machine (JVM) under which the Eclipse platform is executed. If you don't want to use the standard JVM (the one executed when invoking the `java` command), you can specify a different JVM by using the command-line option `-vm`.

When the Eclipse loader is invoked it uses a three-stage strategy to determine the JVM under which the platform is executed. If a JVM is explicitly specified with the command-line option `-vm`, then this VM is used. Otherwise, the loader will look for a specific Java Runtime Environment (JRE) that was deployed with the Eclipse platform. Such a JRE must be located in the directory `\eclipse\jre\`. If such a JRE does not exist (as in our case), then the location of the VM is derived from the `PATH` environment variable.

By the way, this strategy affects only the JVM under which the platform is executed. Which JVM and which SDK are used for Java development is specified separately in the Eclipse workbench.

The command-line option `-vmargs` can be used to specify parameters for the Java Virtual Machine. For example:

```
eclipse.exe -vm C:\java13\bin\javaw -vmargs -Xmx256M
```

Here Eclipse is started with a specific JVM and sets the JVM heap to 256 MB. With very large projects this can help to prevent instabilities of the workbench.

Another important command-line parameter is the parameter `-data` for specifying the location of the workspace. In this case, the *Workspace Launcher* dialog discussed previously is skipped. This parameter allows you to create different Eclipse desktop shortcuts for different workspaces.

The First Application: Hello World

Until now you haven't seen much of a Java development environment. Eclipse—which is advertised as a platform for everything and nothing in particular—shows, in fact, nothing in particular when invoked for the first time. You are now going to change this radically.

Perspectives

To see something "particular" in Eclipse, you first must open an Eclipse perspective. Perspectives consist of a combination of windows and tools best suited for specific tasks. Perspectives are added to the Eclipse workbench by various Eclipse plug-ins. This is, for example, the case with the user interface of the Java IDE, which is nothing more than a large plug-in for the Eclipse workbench. To start developing Java programs, you therefore must first open the Java perspective. To do so, click the Open Perspective icon, as shown in Figure 1.4.

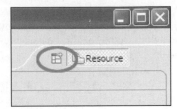

Figure 1.4

Use the Open Perspective icon to open new perspectives. By the way, by clicking the perspective bar with the right mouse button and invoking the function Dock On, you can change the position of the perspective bar. If you were used to Eclipse 2.1, you may want to dock the perspective bar at the left border of the Eclipse workbench.

From the list that appears, select Java. You should then see the screen shown in Figure 1.5.

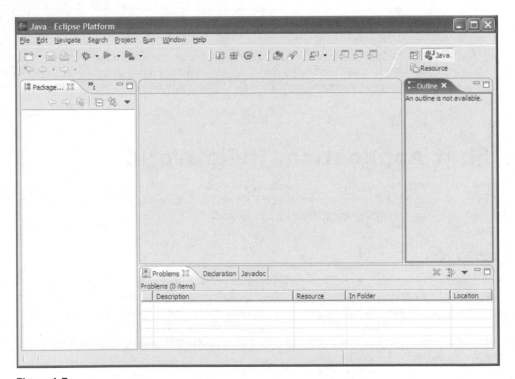

Figure 1.5

The Java perspective shows the windows (Package Explorer, Hierarchy), menu items, and toolbar icons that are typical for Java development. On the left you see a new icon denoting the Java perspective. Above this icon is the icon for the Resource perspective that was active before you opened the Java perspective. You can quickly switch between different perspectives by clicking these icons.

Projects

Now it's time to say Hello to the world and to create your first program. To do so, first create a new Java project. On the toolbar click the Create a Java Project icon, as shown in Figure 1.6. By clicking the icons of this group you can create new Java projects, packages, classes, interfaces, and JUnit Test Cases.

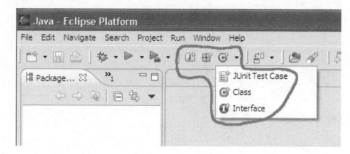

Figure 1.6

In the dialog that appears, name the project with HelloWorld. The Package Explorer now shows an entry for the new project.

Create a New Class

In the next step click the C icon on the toolbar (Create a Java Class). In the following dialog make sure that

❑ The Source Folder is specified as HelloWorld.

❑ The name of the new class is specified as HelloWorld.

❑ public is selected as Modifier.

❑ java.lang.Object is specified as Superclass.

❑ The option to public static void main() is checked.

The Create a New Class Wizard (Figure 1.7) is able to generate some class code. The wizard can generate stubs for the inherited methods, especially if a super class and interfaces are specified.

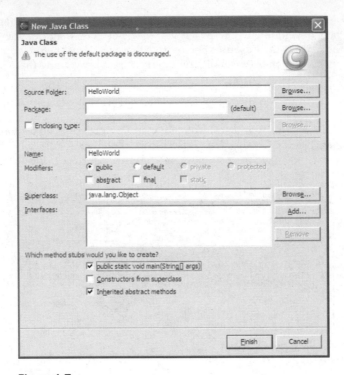

Figure 1.7

After you click the Finish button, the Eclipse workbench looks a bit more like a workbench in use (Figure 1.8).

The Package Explorer shows the contents of the new project, including the libraries of the Java runtime environment. At any time you can open the classes belonging to these libraries and look at their source code. The center window holds the Java source editor, which currently contains the pregenerated code for the HelloWorld class. At the right-hand side you can see the Outline window showing the current class with its methods. You quickly navigate to any method or variable in the source editor by clicking it in the Outline View.

Now you complete the pregenerated code. You change the main() method in the following way:

```java
public static void main(String[] args) {
  System.out.println("Hello World");
}
```

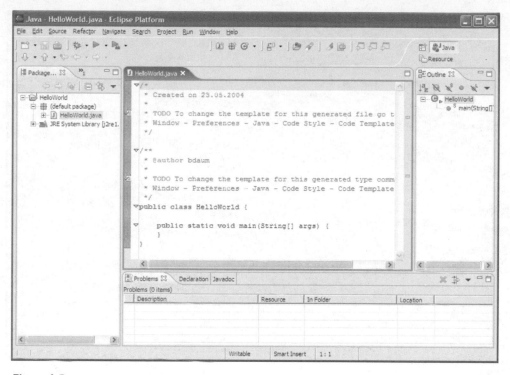

Figure 1.8

By doing this you have finished the programming work for your first project. Save the new class HelloWorld to disk by clicking the floppy disk icon on the toolbar. (Alternatively, you can use the keyboard shortcut Ctrl+S.) This will also compile this class. The program is now ready for execution.

Launch

The Run icon is positioned on the right side of the bug icon. Here, you activate the drop-down menu by clicking the arrow at the right of the Run icon. From this drop-down menu select Run As > Java Application to start program execution. Now, a new tag with the label Console should appear in the Tasks View area. With a click on that tag you can open the Console View (see Figure 1.9), which should display the text "Hello World." Done!

During this first execution, Eclipse creates a new Run Configuration named HelloWorld. A list of all available Run Configurations is found under the arrow on the right side of the Run icon. The Run icon itself is always associated with the Run Configuration that was executed last. To execute the program again, simply click the Run icon.

The console window opens automatically when a program writes to System.out or System.err.

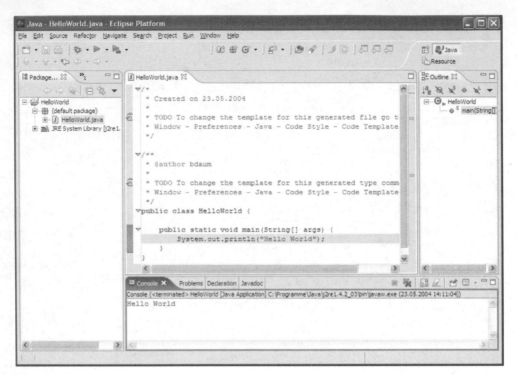

Figure 1.9

The Most Important Preferences for Java Development

Before you continue in your programming efforts, you should first explore your working environment. The Window > Preferences menu gives you access to all Eclipse preferences (see Figure 1.10).

On the left of the Preferences dialog you can select from several preference categories. On the right-hand side of the dialog the details of the selected preference category are shown. All settings made here can be stored into an external file by clicking the Export button or loaded from an external file by clicking the Import button.

Figure 1.10

At first sight, the sheer mass of preferences shown in this dialog may be overwhelming, because each plug-in may contribute its own set of preference categories to this dialog. In this chapter, I will discuss only those preferences that are most relevant in the context of this book. You should take the time to step systematically through all preference categories to get an overview of the possibilities. Some of the categories have subcategories. To expand a category, click the + sign in front of the category name.

Some of the preference settings will make sense only during the discussion of the corresponding Eclipse function. In such cases I will postpone the discussion of the preference settings to the discussion of the corresponding workbench function.

Workbench Preferences

If you previously have worked with Emacs, it may make sense to switch the Key Bindings in Eclipse so you can continue to use the familiar Emacs shortcuts. To do so, expand the Workbench category, select the subcategory Keys, and click the Keyboard Shortcuts tag. In the drop-down list named Active Configuration you can choose between Emacs and Default. You can even define your own keyboard shortcuts. First, go to the Command group and select a command via the Category and Name fields. The existing keyboard shortcut assignments appear in the Assignments list. A keyboard shortcut can consist of a single key combination or a series of key combinations. Edit the sequence of key combinations by placing the cursor into the Name field of the Key Sequence group and pressing the key combination to be added to the sequence. Use the Backspace key to delete entries. To add a new key sequence, don't select an entry in the Assignments list; simply enter the key sequences in the described way, and then press the Add button.

On the Advanced page of the Key Bindings preferences you can enable an assistant that will help you with completing multistroke keyboard shortcuts.

Installed JREs

You probably don't always want to create Java applications that require a Java 1.3 or Java 1.4 platform. In some cases you may need to run on Java 1.2 platforms. Within the preference category *Java*, in the subcategory Installed JREs, you can list all Java Runtime Environments that are installed on the host computer (see Figure 1.11).

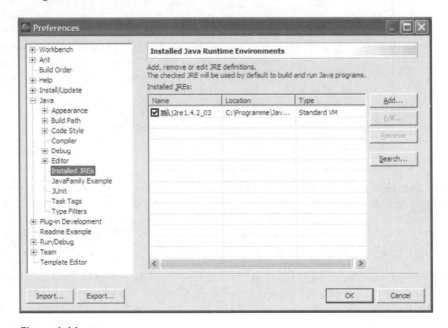

Figure 1.11

In this preference category you can declare all the Java Runtime Environments (SDK or JRE) that are installed on the host computer for Eclipse. Among the JREs listed here, Checkmark One is the default JRE. This JRE will be assigned to all new Java projects. You will learn later how this can be changed in the project settings and how different JREs can be used in different Launch Configurations.

To add a new JRE, just click the Add button (alternatively you can click the Search button to scan a whole directory for a JRE or SDK). Then complete the following dialog (see Figure 1.12).

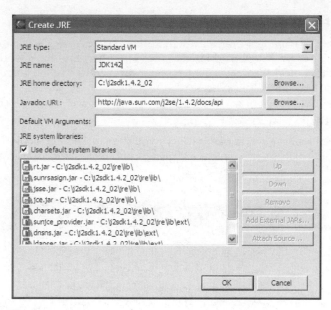

Figure 1.12

A new JRE is added to the Eclipse workbench. I have provided the name and location of the JRE home directory. The location of the corresponding Javadoc is preset by Eclipse and points to the JavaSoft Web site. If the documentation is available locally, you should modify this entry accordingly. The entry Default VM Arguments may specify VM command-line parameters to be used with this VM.

For further customization you could uncheck the Use Default System Libraries item. This would allow you to add further JAR libraries. If any of the JARs does not contain source code, you can attach external source code by pressing Attach Source.

If you want to add a version 1.1 JRE (this is necessary when you want to run your application on a Microsoft VM), you must also change the JRE type to the value Standard 1.1.x VM.

Of course, it is possible to execute an application on a JVM that is different from the JVM under which the application was developed. For example, if you developed an application under Java SDK 1.1.8 and want to test how the application performs under a version 1.3.1 JVM, you must change the runtime environment before executing the program. You can do this by choosing the appropriate JVM in the Eclipse Launch Configurator. You can open the Launch Configurator by invoking the menu function Run > Run.

For the remainder of this book I use the Java 1.4 SDK.

Compiler Preferences

Now take a closer look at the compiler preferences. In the Preferences dialog select the category Java and the subcategory Compiler. Note that all adjustments made here affect the whole workbench. On project level (see the "Project Properties" section in Chapter 4), however, you have the possibility of overriding the global settings made here under Preferences.

Warnings and Errors

On the right-hand side of the Java > Compiler category you see a tabbed notebook. The Style, Advanced, Unused Code, and Javadoc pages show which compiler events create errors or warnings and which compiler events should be ignored (see Figure 1.13).

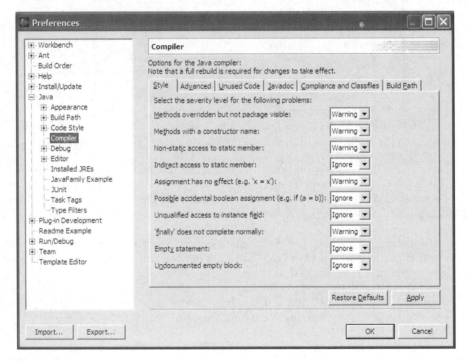

Figure 1.13

Because a lot of third-party code is used in the examples, you need to reset the settings for unused imports, never-read local variables, and never-read parameters on the Unused Code page to Ignore. Otherwise, you could face an overwhelming flood of error messages. But if you develop your own applications, it makes sense to set these settings to Warning because these settings help you to detect and remove garbage from your code. Just try the following: set Parameter Is Never Read to Warning and press OK. The project is recompiled. At the program line

```
public static void main(String[] args) {
```

you now see a warning icon, and in the Problems window you see the entry

```
The argument args is never read
```

Quite right! The HelloWorld program did not make use of the parameter that contains the command-line arguments.

Classfiles and JDK Compliance

On the Compliance & Classfiles page you can specify which symbolic information, such as variable names and line numbers, is to be included in the generated classfiles. This information is required for debugging, and therefore you may want to leave the proposed settings unchanged. However, for a well-tested program it may make sense to remove this information from the classfiles; generated files are much smaller without the symbol tables.

On the same page you can determine whether the compiler must comply with the Java 1.4 or Java 1.3 syntax. With Java 1.4, one new instruction was added to the language: assert. Consequently, the word "assert" can no longer be used as a field or method name. In addition, assert requires support from the JVM. Classes that use this instruction cannot be executed by older JVMs. Since assert is not used in the first example program, leave this setting at the proposed value of Java 1.3.

Formatting Code

Formatting code can be very helpful, because it is easier to detect violations of the control structures of a program (such as open if or while statements) when the program is formatted. In the preference category Java > Code Style > Code Formatter you can configure how the Eclipse code formatter works, as shown in Figure 1.14. The best method is to try some of the settings and to select those that work best for your application. To modify these settings you must first create a new profile (by pressing the New button). Then you can edit this profile by pressing the Edit button. You can create multiple profiles and switch easily among them. When you publish your code, for example, you may use different profiles for different sorts of publications.

But how do you apply code formatting? Very simply: just click with the right mouse button on the source code and select Source > Format from the context menu (Figure 1.14). The key shortcut Ctrl+Shift+F works even faster. Note that it is also possible to select only a portion of the source code to format just that portion.

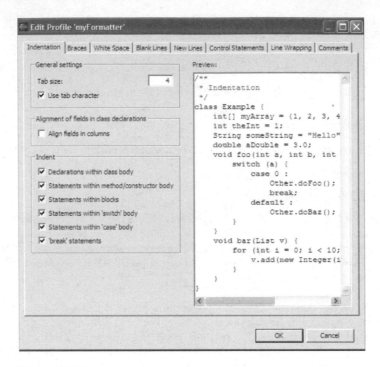

Figure 1.14

Templates

When you created the new `HelloWorld` class, text similar to the following was generated at the top of the new compilation unit:

```
/*
 * Created on 27.04.2004
 *
 * To change this generated comment go to
 * Window - Preferences - Java - Code Style - Code Templates
 */
/**
 * @author Berthold Daum
 *
 * To change this generated comment go to
 * Window - Preferences - Java - Code Style - Code Templates
 */
```

The first comment was generated for the new Java file, and the second comment was created for the new type (`HelloWorld`). You now should follow the advice given in these comments and modify the code generation preferences according to your requirements. Just open the preferences category Java > Code Style > Code Templates (see Figure 1.15).

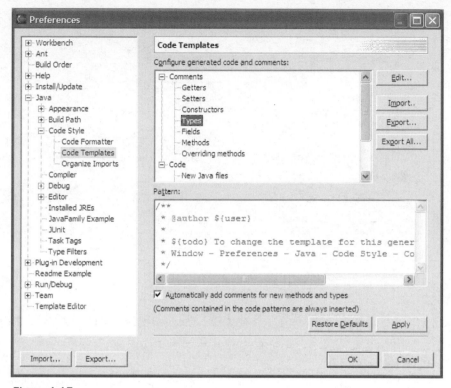

Figure 1.15

For various events, such as the creation of a new type, a new method, or a new constructor, you can specify which code is to be generated.

Select the Types entry and press the Edit button. In the dialog that appears replace the text provided by Eclipse with the string "created first in project." Then press the Insert Variable button. From the list select the variable named `project_name`. The result should look like that shown in Figure 1.16.

After you have committed these changes, new classes and interfaces will be created with a comment containing the user name and the project name.

Figure 1.16 shows the process of editing a code generation template. All variables are prefixed with the $ character and are enclosed in curly brackets. Apart from the template pattern, you can also supply a description (which will appear in the overview) and a template context (Java or Javadoc).

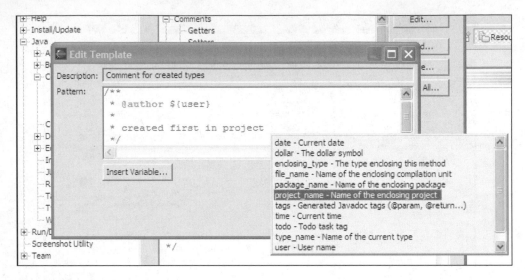

Figure 1.16

Later you may also change the entry for New Java File. The predefined text is shown here:

```
/*
 * Created on ${date}
 *
 * To change the template for this generated file go to
 * Window - Preferences - Java - Code Style - Code Templates
 */
${package_declaration}
${typecomment}
${type_declaration}
```

The variables used here define the sequence of the different code parts. For example, you just specified what happens under `typecomment` in the previous template. Here, delete only the text lines `To change...Code Templates`, and leave everything else as is.

Tasks and Problems

Eclipse uses the *Tasks* and *Problems* views to notify the user about pending tasks. The Problems view lists problems such as errors or warnings. By clicking on such an entry you can quickly navigate to an erroneous program line.

Other task entries are hints about pending development actions and are shown in the Tasks view. Some of these hints are created by Eclipse. For example, when you create a new class or a new method, Eclipse creates a hint that the new construct must still be completed. Programmers may create similar task entries at their own discretion.

Problems, Problems

In the Compiler Preferences section of this chapter, you saw the Problems window in action. The entries in the Problems window correlated to pending problems in the Eclipse workbench. In Figure 1.17 I purposely created a syntax error by inserting a blank into the parameter name args. This resulted in three error messages.

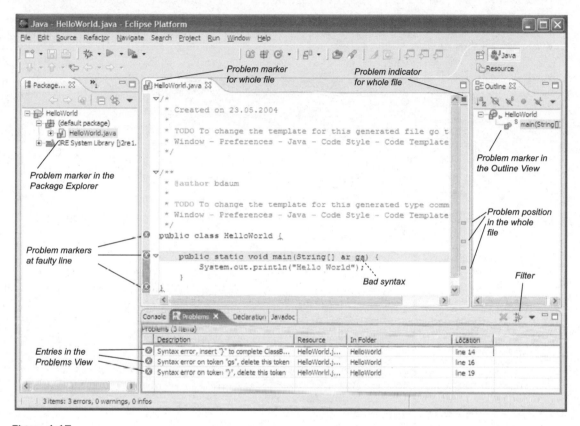

Figure 1.17

After you double-click the problem entries, the faulty expressions are underlined in red. Red error markers on the source editor's left margin mark the faulty lines. The markers on the right margin show the position of the errors relative to the whole file. To scroll to the error position, it is only necessary to pull the scroll bar to the markers. Clicking the markers works just as well.

Error messages are represented by a white cross in a red circle. In contrast, warnings are represented by a yellow triangle. The third problem type is information tasks, which are represented by a blue i character.

Double-clicking the problem entry in the Problems view lets you quickly navigate to the problem location. Should the problem be located in a file that currently is not open, the file will be opened in the editor, and the editor window will be positioned on the error location. Just try it, and click on one of the entries in the Problems view.

As the workbench gets busier, the Problems view often overflows with errors and warnings. At times it can become difficult to find the Problems entries that are related to the current project or file, because the Problems view by default shows all problems and other tasks within the whole workspace. Of course, you can suppress some of the warnings by setting the compiler options accordingly (see the "Compiler Preferences" section). But there is another way to reduce the information overload: by using the Problems Filter (Figure 1.18). You can open the Problems Filter dialog by clicking the Filter button in the toolbar of the Problems window.

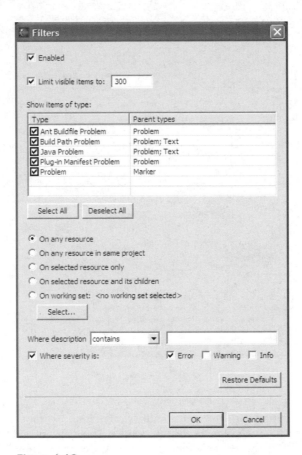

Figure 1.18

The setting shown here allows only entries from the current project to appear in the Problems view. The type of the entry is irrelevant.

Here, in the Problems Filter, you may restrict the entries shown in the Problems view to specific types. For example, you may opt to show only Java problems. The entry types shown in this window depend on the installed plug-ins.

In addition, you can restrict the entries by their origin. The On Any Resource option shows all problems and tasks from the whole workbench. On Any Resource in Same Project shows only problems from the current project. An interesting option is also the definition of a Working Set—a freely configurable and named set of resources. Select On Any Resource in Same Project if you want to see only the tasks and problems of the project on which you are currently working.

You also have the option of filtering problems according their severity. To do so, mark the Where Problem Severity Is check box and also the Error check box. By doing so you can suppress all warnings and information entries.

General Tasks

Task entries generated by the compiler are only a specific type of task entry. In addition, you have the option of creating entries manually. When writing code it often happens that you want to postpone a certain task to a later time. In this case, you can create a task entry that later reminds you of the unfinished work.

Just click with the right mouse button on the left margin of the source editor at the line where you want to create the task marker. Select Add Task from the context menu. In the New Task dialog, enter a task description. The result could look like Figure 1.19.

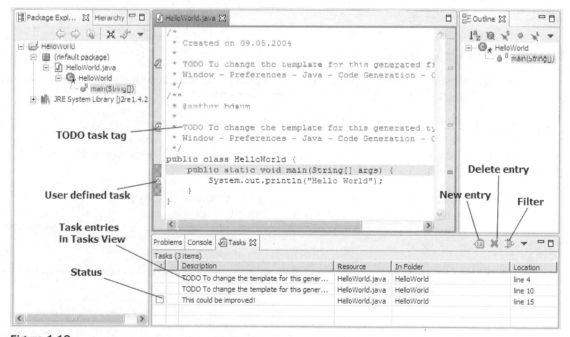

Figure 1.19

This task entry was created by the user. By clicking the status field you can mark the entry as completed. You can click the Delete button to delete one or several selected tasks. You can create task entries that are not related to specific locations with the New Entry button. For example, you could create a task called Don't Forget to Buy Milk!

A function that was introduced with Eclipse 2.1 is even simpler. Just type a comment starting with one of the words TODO, FIXME, or XXX in a new line. This line will automatically appear in the Tasks window as soon as you save the source code. By the way, in Preferences > Java > Task Tags you may define alternative or additional tags such as TUNE, UGLY, etc. Of course, these workbench-wide definitions can be overridden at the project level.

> **If you work in a team, you should always create tasks that are important for other team member, too, in this way (as a comment in the source code) so the tasks can be exchanged as part of the source code.**

Bookmarks

Eclipse also has a construct that is quite similar to tasks: *bookmarks*. In the same way that you created a task entry, you can also create a bookmark. Such a bookmark, however, does not appear in the Tasks view but appears in a separate Bookmark view. Since this view is not a standard part of the Java perspective, you first must open it. Select Window > Show View > Other > Basic > Bookmarks (see also the "Arranging Editors and Views" section in Chapter 4). Bookmarks should be used when you want to mark a specific position in the code but it is not related to a pending task.

The Scrapbook

Eclipse also inherited the *Scrapbook* from Visual Age. A scrapbook page is nothing other than a small file in which you can try out Java expressions or just jot down a new idea.

You can create a new scrapbook page by invoking the function File > New > Other. In the wizard select Java > Java Run/Debug > Scrapbook Page. In the dialog that appears specify a name for the new page and, if necessary, the target folder. The result is the creation of a new empty scrapbook page in the target folder. Scrapbook pages have the file extension .jpage.

Now, how do you use a scrapbook page? You simply type in arbitrary Java expressions. If you use external types in these expressions, you either have to qualify the type names fully or add import statements. The context function Set Imports allows you to add import statements for single types or whole packages.

Then select the expressions that you want to execute and call the Execute context function with the right mouse button (see Figure 1.20).

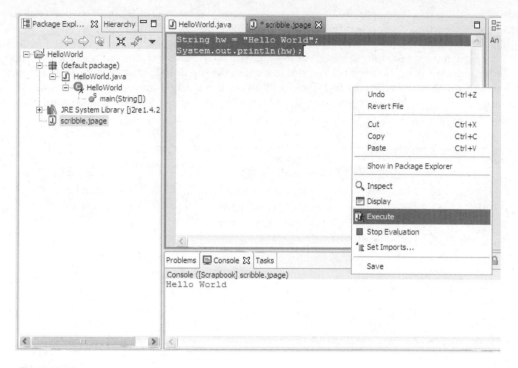

Figure 1.20

The selected expression is executed with the help of the Execute context function. The scrapbook context function appears on the workbench's toolbar at the far right.

It is not necessary to save the scrapbook page before executing the selected code. The selected code is compiled by the Execute function. In the case of a compilation or execution error, Eclipse shows the error message in a pop-up window. You may insert it into the current scrapbook content by pressing Ctrl+Shift+D. You can easily remove it again by applying the Undo function (Ctrl+Z).

Execute is not the only function that you can use to run a Java expression. In cases where you want to know the result of an expression, it would be better to use the Display function. For example, executing the expression

```
6*7
```

with the Display function returns the result

```
(int) 42
```

Eclipse shows the result in a pop-up window. You may insert it into the current scrapbook content by pressing Ctrl+Shift+D. You can easily remove it again by applying the *Undo* function (Ctrl+Z).

A further function for executing selected expressions is Inspect. This function first appears in a pop-up window, but by pressing Ctrl+Shift+I you can move it to the separate Expressions View (see Figure 1.21) that opens automatically when needed. This function is particularly useful when the result of the executed expression is a complex object. In the Expressions window you can open the resultant object and analyze it in detail.

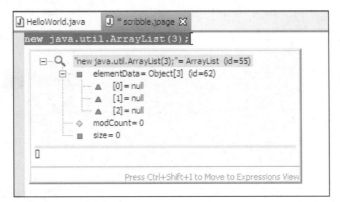

Figure 1.21

The results shown here are displayed in a pop-up window after applying the Inspect function on the expression `new java.util.ArrayList(3);`.

Summary

After this first chapter you should be able to create, compile, and run simple Java program with Eclipse. You should now know how to install Eclipse, create projects, and launch programs. You have become acquainted with the most important preferences and should take some time now to browse through the remaining preferences. However, the purpose of some preferences may become clear only during the course of this book.

Source code annotations such as tasks and problem markers are powerful concepts during the development of a software project. In Chapter 16 you will see that these concepts can be used to adopt a more natural programming style.

Finally, the scrapbook encourages experimenting with Java so that you can try out new program constructs in isolation before integrating them into an application.

In the next chapter I will introduce into the various productivity techniques found in Eclipse.

Effective Programming with Eclipse

2

Eclipse provides the Java programmer with a variety of productivity tools. In this chapter I will present some of these tools such as the various assistants for error correction and automatic code completion, the possibilities for code navigation and code refactoring, and the Local History that allows tracing back changes in the source code to earlier versions.

Little Helpers

Eclipse is equipped with a variety of useful helpers, which—when used correctly—can save a substantial amount of typing and also reduce the number of bugs in your programs. In this section I introduce most of these little helpers.

System Information

Under the Help > About Eclipse Platform menu item you will find some sections that may be important for your daily work. In particular, the Configuration Details button opens a text file that contains all essential information about the current configuration of the Eclipse platform:

❑ The System Properties section contains information about the Java platform under which the Eclipse workbench is executing. In addition, it displays information about the host operating system.

❑ The Features section lists the installed features. A *feature* usually consists of a set of plug-ins that work together to provide specific functionality. For example, the Java IDE is a feature.

❑ The Plug-in Registry section lists all installed plug-ins separately.

❑ The User Preferences section lists the active user preferences under which the platform is running.

❑ The Update Manager Log section lists information about the tasks performed by the Update Manager, such as installing new features or checking existing configurations.

❑ The last section, Error Log, is especially important. Here you find a protocol of all error events that occurred during the execution of the Eclipse platform. If you develop you own plug-ins, this section will prove especially useful. A more comfortable way to view these error messages, however, is with the Error Log View. You can open this view via Window > Show View > Other > PDE Runtime > Error Log. Physically, this error information is stored in the `.metadata/.log` file in the workspace directory.

Help and Hover

Eclipse features a classical help system that is activated on demand. In addition, Eclipse is equipped with a Hover Info that autonomously provides the user with explanations about screen items.

Help

At this stage I don't want to dig too deep into the Eclipse help system. You simply need to know that you can invoke Eclipse help via the Help > Help Contents menu item. Like many other programs, Eclipse uses a client-server solution for its help system. Under the cover, Tomcat works as the help server, and a standard or custom Web browser is used to display the help to the end user.

In a vanilla Eclipse software development kit (SDK), you will find the following help chapters:

1. Workbench User Guide
2. Java Development User Guide
3. Platform Plug-in Developer Guide
4. JDT Plug-in Developer Guide
5. PDE Guide

You can add more chapters by installing additional plug-ins. For chapters 1 – 7 of this book, the first two help chapters are the most relevant. For the remainder of this book, the help chapters 3 and 5 will also become important.

Since Eclipse 2.0, the Eclipse help function has been equipped with a search function. With the Search Scope function you can restrict the search to specific chapters and sections in the help system.

Intro View

The Intro View is the first view you see when you start Eclipse. Initially it covers the whole workbench window, but as you continue it will shrink and take its position to the right of the Outline View. During operation the Intro View will explain the currently active workbench part and offer hyperlinks into the help system. You can manually invoke the Intro View via Help > Welcome.

Context-Sensitive Help

In addition to the explicit help function, you can call help within Eclipse at any time simply by pressing the F1 key—provided the currently active plug-in supports this function. After pressing F1 you get a pop-up window (Infopop), where you can select a relevant help topic and jump directly to it. In this context the Show in Table of Contents button in the help system (the second button to the left of the printer symbol) is useful. It synchronizes the table of contents with the currently displayed help page so that you can see in which context the current help topic is located.

Hover

You probably know hover infos already from other applications: when the mouse hovers over a GUI element, a small pop-up window appears after a short delay that informs you of the purpose and function of the GUI element. Eclipse uses this technique as follows:

- ❑ All buttons on the various toolbars are equipped with hover infos.

- ❑ For files opened in the editor, you can display the full path information by hovering over the tag of the respective editor page.

- ❑ All task and problem markers are equipped with hover infos. You can display the text associated with a particular marker by hovering over the marker, so you don't have to look up the marker in the Tasks window.

- ❑ Finally, hover infos exist for source code as well. Just place the mouse over the type name `String` in our `HelloWorld` example. After a short delay you will see a hover info containing the Javadoc of class `java.lang.String`. Similarly, you will see the Javadoc for method `java.io.PrintStream.println` when you hover over the word `println`. Using this technique, you can quickly find out in which class a certain method is defined, instead of browsing up and down the class hierarchies.

If you press the Ctrl key while hovering over source text, your hover info will show the item's source code instead of the Javadoc!

If the information to be displayed in the pop-up window is too long, you may want to press F2. This will transfer the focus to the pop-up window and equip this window with scroll bars.

Java Information Views

Another possibility to display Javadoc information is the Javadoc View. You can open this view by invoking the function Window>Show View>Other...>Java>Javadoc. The view shows the Javadoc information belonging to the currently selected Java element in human-readable form in a separate scrollable window. I recommendend this view especially for classes containing complex Javadoc comments such as the class `java.util.regex.Pattern`!

You can open another useful window with Window > Show View >Other > Java > Declaration; it shows the declaration of the currently selected Java element.

The call hierarchy of a method can be shown in a separate window also. To do so, select the method name and then apply the context function Open Call Hierarchy.

Figure 2.1 shows the Call Hierarchy View after executing the context function Open Call Hierarchy when method createToolbar() was selected. By clicking one of the hierarchy symbols in the view's toolbar, you can switch between the hierarchy of calling or of called methods.

Figure 2.1

Automatic Code Completion

The functions for automatic code completion in Eclipse are very powerful and include the source menu functions but also the Code Assistant introduced in the following section.

The Code Assistant

One of the most powerful utilities for writing code in Eclipse is the Code Assistant. Tedious typing and searching in Javadoc or source code can be replaced by just a few keystrokes. Try the following:

In the HelloWorld example open under

```
System.out.println("HelloWorld");
```

and enter a new line. In this new line type just three characters

```
Sys
```

and press Ctrl+Spacebar. In the pop-up list that appears, select the class System from the Package java.lang by double-clicking it. Now enter a period. A fraction of a second later, another pop-up list appears. From this list select the field out of type PrintStream. Once again enter a period, and once again you will get a pop-up list; select the method println. The cursor is now positioned within the parentheses for the method parameters. You can now complete this method call by entering the string "Hello Eclipse." All that remains to do is to type the semicolon at the very end of the expression. The new line should now look like this:

```
System.out.println("Hello Eclipse");
```

I expect you get the idea already: the Code Assistant allows you to enter long class and method names with just a few keystrokes. But what is even more important is that it saves you tedious searching and browsing in the documentation. If required, it can automatically insert the necessary import statements as well.

There is an even quicker method, however. Just try the same thing again, but now enter only the letters

```
sy
```

and press Ctrl+Spacebar. From the pop-up list, select the entry sysout. (If you continue typing, the pop-up list will get smaller and smaller, because it displays only entries that match the entered string.) If you select the entry sysout with a single click, another pop-up window appears showing a code proposal for the keyword sysout. You can accept this proposal with a double click or press the Esc key to close both windows.

The code proposal shown is based on a code template that is associated with the keyword sysout. These templates are defined under Preferences > Java > Editor > Templates, where you can also create your own templates. This is done similarly to defining entries for code generation (see the "Templates" section in Chapter 1).

It is worth browsing through all these templates, because they can save you substantial typing. While many templates are named to resemble Java constructs (if, while, catch, etc.), other templates bear the names of design patterns. Take, for example, the lazy template. This template generates the following code:

```
if (name == null) {
    name = new type(arguments);
}
return name;
```

That is a typical pattern for the lazy assignment of a variable. What you have to do with this pattern is just replace the first occurrence of the string name with the name of your own variable, for example, with "myHashMap." This automatically replaces all occurrences of "name" with "myHashMap" throughout the pattern!

In addition to these Java code templates, there are predefined Javadoc templates. For example, if you enter the character @ within a Javadoc comment, a pop-up window appears showing the available Javadoc keywords.

Of course, you can define your own templates. In Chapter 1 you have already modified the typecomment template. Here now is an example for a completely homegrown template. The template generates an if instruction that executes only when the equals() method in the condition is successful. In addition, it make sures that you don't get a null pointer exception.

Template equals:

```
if (${name} != null && ${name}.equals(${cursor})) {
}
```

This template contains the user-defined variable ${name}. When you apply this template, this variable will be replaced with a real field name (just as in the lazy template). In addition, the template contains the system variable ${cursor}. This variable marks the position of the cursor. When applying the template, just replace the first occurrence of "name" with the real field name. Then press the Tab key to jump to the predefined cursor position. There you can enter the argument for the equals() method.

There are two more templates that occasionally prove useful.

Template sconst:

```
public static final String ${name} = "${cursor}";
```

Template iconst:

```
public static final int ${name} = ${cursor};
```

Under Preferences > Java > Editor > Code Assist, you can make adjustments to influence the behavior of the Code Assistant (Figure 2.2).

In particular, the Automatically Add Import Instead of Qualified Name option is very useful. When this option is set, you can in most cases avoid adding import statements manually, simply by using the Code Assistant.

For most of the other options, the default values provided by Eclipse make sense, so you should not need to change these settings. What can be a bit annoying at times is the automatic activation of the Code Assistant after entering a period or a @ character. It could make sense to increase the delay value of this option from 500 msec to 1000 msec.

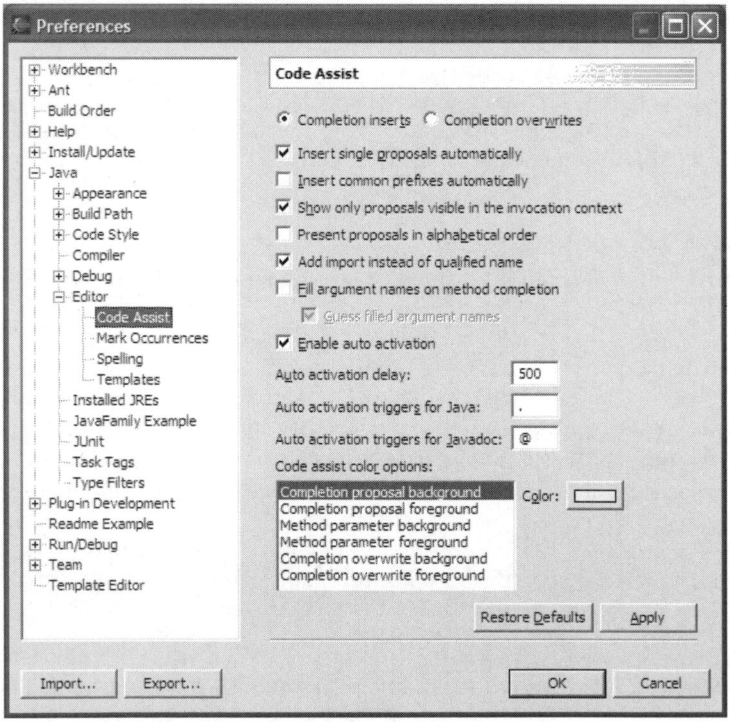

Figure 2.2

Other Functions of Code Completion

Apart from the Code Assistant, which appears either automatically after entering an activation character or when pressing Ctrl+Spacebar, there are a few more context functions for code completion. Take a look at how you can use these functions to create Javadoc comments.

Creating Javadoc

In our `HelloWorld` example program, just place the cursor into the main method and invoke the function Source > Add Javadoc Comment. This will insert the comment lines

```
/**
 * Method main.
 * @param args
 */
```

in front of the method. The only thing that remains to do is to complete this description.

An even simpler method for creating a Javadoc comment is to open a new line in front of the method and to enter the string /** and then press the Enter key.

The Source context submenu contains more useful functions for code completion:

Comment Out Code

❑ **Toggle Comment.** Using this function, you can convert the current line or the selected lines into comment lines (//) or convert comment lines into active code.

❑ **Add/Remove Block Comment.** Using this function, you can convert selected code sections into block comments (/* */) or remove the comment characters around the selected section.

Importing Types

❑ **Organize Imports.** This function analyzes the whole program and inserts the required `import` statements at the beginning of the program. Should this function discover equally named types from different packages during this task, it will prompt you with a list of those packages. You must then select the required type from this list.

❑ **Add Import.** This function inserts an `import` statement for the selected type name at the beginning of the program. Similarly to the Organize Imports function, this function will prompt you for type selection if it discovers equally named types from different packages.

Under Window > Preferences > Java > Code Style > Organize Imports you can specify a threshold value for single type `import` statements. If the program contains more import types from a given package than what were specified under this threshold value, the `import` statements for this package will be combined into a single `import` statement by using wildcards (as in `eclipse.org.*`). The default threshold value is 99.

Overriding Methods

❏ **Override Methods.** This function first shows a selection list for all inherited methods. In this list you can check all methods that you want to override, and Eclipse will generate method stubs for all of them. This function is particularly useful if the class implements one or several interfaces. In such a case, you simply invoke this function and check all the methods of the interface (if they are not already checked). Then simply complete the generated method stubs.

Encapsulating Fields

❏ **Generate Getter and Setter.** This function generates access methods for class fields. For example, if a class contains the field definition

```
private String hi;
```

invoking this function would result in the following generated methods:

```
/**
 * Returns the hi.
 * @return String
 */
public String getHi() {
    return hi;
}
/**
 * Sets the hi.
 * @param hi The hi to set
 */
public void setHi(String hi) {
    this.hi = hi;
}
```

However, this function does not change existing references to the encapsulated field. If you want to change these references, too, you are better off using the Refactor > Encapsulate Field context function.

Alternatively, you may use the Content Assistant to generate a getter or setter. Just type get or set and press Ctrl+Spacebar.

Creating Delegate Methods

❏ **Generate Delegate Methods.** This function can be applied to non-primitive fields and replicates the method of the field's type in the containing type.

Inheriting Constructors

❏ **Add Constructors from Superclass.** This function generates proxies for the inherited constructors. These proxies contain only a super() call. Of course, you can then modify the generated proxies to override the behavior of the constructor.

Generate Constructor

❏ **Generate Constructor Using Fields.** In the dialog that appears you may select from a list of instance fields. The constructor is then generated with the corresponding parameters and assignment statements.

i18n

❏ **Externalize Strings.** This function supports the internationalization of applications. We will discuss this in detail under "Internationalizing Products" in Chapter 12.

❏ **Generate Delegate Methods.** This function can be applied to all non-primitive fields and replicates the methods of the field's type within the class or interface that contains the selected field.

The Correction Assistant

Even before you compile a program by invoking the Save function, the editor tells you how bad a programmer you are. Erroneous expressions are underlined in red—as probably happened to you in school. (The same metaphor is used by some word processors.) So even before compiling a program, you can notice faulty expressions such as a missing bracket or semicolon, so that you can react accordingly.

QuickFix

Depending on the skills of the programmer, you may also occasionally see a yellow lightbulb in the left margin of the source editor. This function is called QuickFix, and it signals that Eclipse has at least one correction proposal for the programmer's mistake. In fact, there are only a few error types where Eclipse loses its wits and is unable to offer a QuickFix proposal. To activate the QuickFix function, click the yellow lightbulb. (The same function can be invoked by pressing Ctrl+1 when the cursor is above the faulty line.)

You try it. Say you purposely make a mistake and write only `print1()` instead of `println()`. Immediately you will see a yellow lightbulb on the left margin (Figure 2.3).

One of the advantages of the Correction Assistant is the fast feedback it gives to the program author. This immediate response to a mistake should trigger a learning effect in the programmer, making the same mistake less likely the next time.

However, you may also use the Correction Assistant to save some typing. For example, when you write some code and refer to a method that has not yet been written, a simple click on the yellow lightbulb that appears allows you to generate a stub for the missing method instantly.

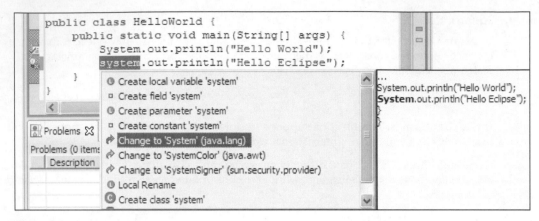

Figure 2.3

In Figure 2.3 you see the Correction Assistant in action. The erroneous class name "system" is underlined in red. On the left you see the yellow lightbulb. Clicking the lightbulb opens a pop-up window with various suggestions. The pop-up window on the right shows what the code will look like if you opt to change the name to "System."

You can switch off the Correction Assistant under Preferences > Java > Editor on the Annotations page.

Quick Assist

Ctrl+1 works even without an error being present. In this case the function is called QuickAssist, and it is a useful function for code transformation and completion. The function depends on the context. For example, if you position the cursor on the parameter of a method declaration and press Ctrl+1 (or click the green lightbulb that mysteriously appeared on the left margin of the editor), various functions will become available for selection, including the function Assign Parameter to New Field. If you select this function, Eclipse will generate an assignment directly after the method header, assigning the parameter to a newly declared field.

In Figure 2.4 you can see that the QuickAssist facility makes a suggestion for assigning parameter args to a static field. Since the field doesn't exist yet, a field declaration is proposed as well.

```
public class HelloWorld {
    public static void main(String[] args) {

...
public class HelloWorld {
private static String[] args;

public static void main(String[] args) {
HelloWorld.args = args;
System.out.println("Hello World");
system.out.println("Hello Eclipse");
...
}
```

□ Assign parameter to new field
☉ Local Rename

Figure 2.4

In the context of an `if`-statement you will, of course, get different proposals, such as to add an `else`-block or to remove the `if`-statement. Similar functions are available for `for`- and `while` blocks.

Convenience Functions of the Java Editor

Eclipse's Java Editor comes with a variety of convenience functions that make code easier to type and to read. In the following sections I will present some of them.

Typing Aids

Under Preferences > Java > Editor on the Typing page, you can activate or deactivate a variety of typing aids. The Java editor is, for example, able to close open parentheses or brackets automatically. It can include string literals in quotes automatically and can wrap the text within Javadoc and other comments.

The function Wrap Java Strings is also nice. In our `HelloWorld` example program, just place the cursor between `Hello` and `World` and press Enter.

The result is the syntactically correct expression

```
System.out.println("Hello " +
  "World");
```

However, these functions are active only when the editor is in the Smart Insert mode. By pressing the Insert key repeatedly, or by clicking the corresponding field in the status line, you can switch among the Smart Insert, Overwrite, and Insert modes. By the way, you can completely switch off the Overwrite mode for the Java editor!

Code Folding

Another nice function of the Java editor is the possibility to collapse code sections and to expand them again. This is achieved with the help of the small arrows at the second vertical ruler at the left of the editor area (see Figure 2.5). An arrow pointing downward indicates an expanded section of code. When you hover with the mouse above this arrow, Eclipse will show how far this section stretches. By clicking the arrow you can collapse this code section. The arrow then changes its shape and points to the right. If you now hover above the arrow, a pop-up window shows the content of the collapsed code section. Click the arrow again, and the code section expands again. Under Window > Preferences > Java > Editor on the Folding page you can enable or disable this function, and you can control which code parts should be displayed in a collapsed state initially.

In this program both the `listAllVoices` and `main()` methods and the group of `import` statements are collapsed. The mouse hovers over the arrow symbol at the `import` group, so that the `import` statements are displayed in a pop-up window.

Figure 2.5

Syntax Coloring

Finally, you should take a look at the options for syntax coloring. Different colors and font styles can be assigned to different elements in Java programs so that the readability of programs is improved. You can configure this feature under Window > Preferences > Java > Editor on the Syntax page. The Enable Advanced Highlighting option lets you switch to a very differentiated syntax coloring mode.

Source Code Navigation

In large projects it is essential to have good navigation tools at hand. Eclipse offers some of them as an editor context function (right mouse click):

❑   **Open Declaration.** This function opens the definition of the selected type in the editor. The shortcut is to press F3.

The alternative to this editor context function is hyperlinks: Just press the *Ctrl* key and move the cursor above the `String` type reference. This type reference now appears in blue and is underlined—it has become a hyperlink. By clicking it you open the definition of `java.lang.String`.

❑ **Open Type Hierarchy.** This function opens a special browser window that will appear in front of the Package Explorer. The new window shows the type hierarchy for the selected type. I will discuss this browser in detail in Chapter 4.

❑ **Open Call Hierarchy**. This function opens a special browser window that will appear in front of the Intro View. The new window shows the call hierarchy for the selected method.

❑ **Open Super Implementation.** This function opens the super implementation of the selected method, i.e., its implementation in the parent class or the next ancestor class.

❑ **Show in Package Explorer.** This function synchronizes the Package Explorer with the current editor window (see the "Packages" section in Chapter 4).

These functions are also available from the workbench's menu bar, under the Navigate title. Here you find additional navigation functions such as:

❑ **Back.** This function works like the Back button in web browsers.

❑ **Forward.** This function works like the Forward button in web browsers.

❑ **Last Edit Location.** This function navigates back to the last location where you modified code.

❑ **Go to Line ... .** This function allows you to jump to a source code line with the specified number.

❑ **Next Annotation.** This takes you to the next source code annotation, such as a syntax error.

❑ **Previous Annotation.** This takes you to the previous source code annotation.

Most of these functions can be invoked via toolbar buttons, too.

Figure 2.6 shows that you can jump to the most recently edited code location with the Last Edit Location button. Two more buttons allow you to step backward and forward in the navigation history of visited code locations. The Show Source of Selected Element button can isolate elements (methods or field definitions) in the editor window.

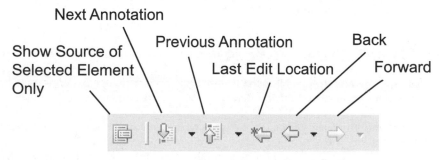

Figure 2.6

Refactoring Code

Modifications of existing programs usually take a lot of time and may introduce new bugs. Even the simple renaming of a type may affect dozens, hundreds, or even thousands of other compilation units. In such cases the computer is superior to the human, and consequently Eclipse offers a rich set of *refactoring* utilities. The purpose of refactoring is to improve the structure of the code without modifying the behavior of the application. Especially in the context of *Extreme Programming* (XP) *refactoring* plays a major role.

In Eclipse, refactoring is achieved by applying Refactor > ... context functions or by using the Refactor > ... menu functions from the main menu. The context functions are context sensitive; that is, only those functions are visible that are applicable in a given context. Eclipse newbies may therefore want to use the Refactor > ... function group from the main menu in order to gain an overview about the available functions.

Modifying Types

Modifications at the type level (classes and interfaces) are best applied in the Package Explorer. The context menu of the Package Explorer offers some functions under the subtitle Refactor, such as Refactor > Move and Refactor > Rename. In addition is it possible to create a copy of a type by using the context function Copy.

❏ **Moving a compilation unit.** Let's assume that you are not happy with the current location of the HelloWorld class in the default package of the project. Instead, you would like to create a new package named HelloPackage and move the class HelloWorld into it.

Just create a new package in the usual way (the Create a Java Package button). Then select the HelloWorld compilation unit in the Package Explorer. From the context menu select the function Refactor > Move…. The dialog that appears contains another small package explorer. Here, you expand the HelloWorld project by clicking the + character, and then select the package HelloPackage as the move target. Once you click OK, the HelloWorld compilation unit is moved into the target package. The source code of HelloWorld now contains the line

```
package HelloPackage;
```

Should other compilation units contain references to the HelloWorld type, these references would be updated accordingly. You can inhibit this by removing the checkmark from UpdateReferences to Moved Element(s). Optionally, you may even update reference in non-Java files.

As a matter of fact, you can also move a compilation unit by a simple drag-and-drop operation with the mouse. You could have just dragged the HelloWorld compilation from the default package into the package HelloPackage and dropped it there. But in larger projects where packages may have a large distance between them, the context function Refactor > Move… usually works better.

❏ **Moving a type.** Similarly, you can move types (classes and interfaces) within a compilation unit. For example, you can drag the class symbol (the green circle with the C) onto another class symbol. The dragged class thus becomes an inner class of the target class. However, in this case the original version of the dragged class remains at its original position, too, so this is a copy function rather than a move.

❑   **Renaming compilation units and types.** Similarly, you can rename compilation units and types by invoking the context function Refactor > Rename….

Figure 2.7 shows the dialog for renaming a compilation unit. In addition to updating references in the code, it is also possible to update references in Javadoc comments, normal comments, and string literals.

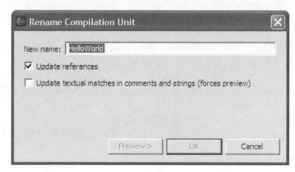

Figure 2.7

Refactoring Code

In addition to classes and interfaces, there are many more possibilities for code refactoring. You can invoke these functions from the source editor's context menu, from the context menu of the Outline view (see the "Outline View" section in Chapter 4), or from the main menu of the workbench.

Methods

❑   **Rename.** Nearly everything can be renamed with the function Refactor > Rename…: classes and interfaces, methods, fields, parameters, and local variables. References to the renamed elements are updated accordingly. If fields are renamed and if the fields have access methods (get....() and set...()), the method names are updated, too.

❑   **Move.** Static methods (and, with some restrictions, also instance methods) can be moved into other classes with the function Refactor > Move… References to these methods are updated accordingly. Public static constants (public static final) and inner classes can be moved, too.

❑   **Pull Up.** Non-static methods and fields can be moved into super classes by applying the function Refactor > Pull up.

❑   **Change Method Signature.** The function Refactor > Change Method Signature allows you to change a method's access modifier, its result type, the order, names, and types of its parameters, and the exception declarations. References to the method are updated accordingly. When new parameters are introduced into the method, it is necessary to define a default value for each new parameter. This default value is inserted as the value for the new parameter when the corresponding method calls are updated.

❑   **Introduce Parameter.** This function can be used to introduce a new parameter into a method declaration. To do so, select an expression within the method declaration and apply the function. In the dialog that appears, enter the name of the new parameter. Eclipse will then replace the selected expression with the parameter name, complete the method head with the new parameter, and expand all method calls with the selected expression.

❑ **Extract Method.** The function Refactor > Extract Method… encapsulates the selected code into a new method definition. Eclipse performs a data flow control analysis for the selected code section. From that it determines the parameters and the result type of the new method. The new method is inserted behind the current method, and the selected code is replaced by a corresponding method call. In some cases, however, it is not possible to apply this function, for example, if there are multiple result values of the selected code section. In cases where the function cannot be applied, Eclipse tells you the reason for the rejection.

Here is an example. In the following method we select the bold line and apply the Extract Method function:

```
public static void main(String[] args) {
   System.out.println("Hello World");
   System.out.println("Hello Eclipse");
}
```

In the dialog that appears, specify helloEclipse as the name for the new method, and you will receive the following:

```
public static void main(String[] args) {
    System.out.println("Hello World");
    helloEclipse();
}
public static void helloEclipse() {
    System.out.println("Hello Eclipse");
}
```

This function detects all occurrences in the current compilation unit where such a substitution can be applied. You can apply the substitution to the current selection only or to all matching occurrences.

Vice-versa, you can resolve methods by applying the function Refactor > Inline.

Factory

❑ **Introduce Factory.** Using the function Refactor > Introduce Factory … you can generate a static factory method from a given constructor. At the same time, all calls to this constructor are replaced by calls to the new factory method.

Types and Classes

❑ **Extract Interface.** With the function Refactor > Extract Interface… you can generate a corresponding interface for an existing class. For example, if you select the class name HelloWorld and invoke this function, you are asked for a name for the new interface. If you enter IHelloWorld and press OK, a Java interface IHelloWorld is generated and the class definition of HelloWorld is completed with the clause implements IHelloWorld. In addition, Eclipse determines which references to HelloWorld can be replaced with a reference to the interface IHelloWorld. As it happens, the interface generated in this example is empty, because the class HelloWorld contains only static methods.

❑ **Generalize Type.** When you select a type name and invoke this function, a dialog with the hierarchy of supertypes appears. You may select one from the tree to replace the originally selected type name.

❑ **Use Supertype.** After creating the interface `IHelloWorld` you can call the function Refactor > Use Supertype Where Possible for class `HelloWorld`. This function offers you a choice between the types `IHelloWorld` and `Object`. Both are supertypes of `HelloWorld`. If you now select `IHelloWorld`, Eclipse will replace all references to `HelloWorld` with references to `IHelloWorld`, provided that this will not result in compilation errors.

❑ **Convert Nested Type to Top Level.** Inner classes and interfaces can be separated into their own compilation unit (`.java` file) by applying the method Refactor > Convert Nested Type to Top Level… to them. The new compilation unit is equipped with the necessary import statements. In the type definition that previously contained the inner type, a new class field is generated whose type declaration refers to the newly generated top-level type. In addition, the constructor of the container type is extended with a new parameter that supplies the new field with an instance of the new top-level type.

❑ **Convert Anonymous Type to Nested Type.** Anonymous classes are used quite often as event listeners. Such anonymous classes can be converted easily into named inner classes by applying the function Refactor > Convert Anonymous to Nested… .

Variables

❑ **Extract Local Variable.** The function Refactor > Extract Local Variable… replaces the selected expression with the name of a new variable. A suitable variable assignment is inserted before the modified expression. For example, in

```
System.out.println("Hello World");
```

select `HelloWorld` and apply the function. In the dialog that appears, specify `hi` for the variable name. The result is:

```
String hi = "Hello World";
System.out.println(hi);
```

Optionally, all occurrences of HelloWorld are replaced with a reference to the variable `hi`.

❑ **Inline method or local variable.** The function Refactor > Inline… works in the opposite way. For example, if you select the variable `hi` and apply this function, all occurrences of `hi` are replaced with the value of `hi` (the string Hello World). Before the replacement is performed, a dialog box shows you the effects of the replacement by comparing the old version with the new version of the compilation unit (see the "Local History" section). Similarly, you can resolve a method by selecting the method name and invoking this function.

❑ **Encapsulate.** The function Refactor > Self Encapsulate… allows you to convert a public variable into a private variable. It generates the access method for this variable (see also Generate Getter and Setter in the "Encapsulating Fields" section) and updates all read and write access to this variable accordingly.

Before:

```
public int status;
public void process() {
  switch (status) {
    case 0 :
```

```
            System.out.println("Status 0");
            break;
        }
    }
}
```

After:

```
private int status;
public void process() {
  switch (getStatus()) {
    case 0 :
      System.out.println("Status 0");
      break;
    }
  }
}
public void setStatus(int status) {
  this.status = status;
}
public int getStatus() {
  return status;
}
```

❑ **Convert Local Variable to Field.** The function Refactor > Convert Local Variable to Field... can convert a local variable that is defined in a method body into an instance field.

Constants

❑ **Extract/Inline Constant.** The extract and inline functions discussed for variables are available for constants, too. For example, select the string `Hello World` and invoke the function Refactor > Extract Constant... In the dialog that appears, assign the name HELLOWORLD to the new constant. Eclipse now inserts the line

```
private static final String HELLOWORLD = "Hello World";
```

and replaces all occurrences of `Hello World` with HELLOWORLD. Vice versa, the function Refactor > Inline... allows you to resolve the names of constants by replacing them with the constant's value.

Undo and Redo

With Edit > Undo (Ctrl+Z) it is possible to revert previous actions. The Undo function can be applied over many steps—no limit seems to exist. Undo can even undo actions across previous *Save* operations.

With Edit > Redo (Ctrl+Y) you can once again execute actions that were previously undone by applying the Undo function.

Undoing the Refactor functions (see the "Refactoring Code" section) is a special case. The normal Undo function can only revert these functions in several steps—and then only partially. To undo a Refactor function, it is better to use the special Undo (Ctrl+Shift+Z) and Redo (Ctrl+Shift+Y) functions in the Refactor submenu.

Local History

The Local History function group belongs to Eclipse's most powerful functionality for maintaining source code. For each compilation unit, Eclipse stores a configurable number of older versions that are updated with each *Save* operation.

You can set the number of stored versions in Preferences > Workbench > Local History. The default value is 50 versions, with a maximum age of seven days and a maximum file size of 1 Mb. If you use the Save key (Ctrl+S) as frequently as I do, it would be better to increase the maximum number of versions a bit.

The Local History functions work for any type of resource, not just for Java source code.

Comparing Resources

The context function Compare > Local History allows you to compare the current version of a compilation unit with previous versions. First, you get a selection list with the previous versions nicely grouped by days. Clicking one of these versions will compare the selected version with the current version.

You can invoke this function from the Package Explorer or from the Resource Navigator. It can also be called from the editor, where it is applied to the selected element only—for example, a method.

In Figure 2.8 I have deleted and modified some comments and extracted the println() statement as a separate method. The comparison shows the deleted lines on the right and the inserted lines on the left-hand side on a gray background. The right vertical ruler shows all modifications to the file: the selected modification has a black border, and all other modifications have a gray border. The window at the top-right corner (Java Structure Compare) allows the comparison of single methods.

Replacing with an Older Version

The function Replace > Local History works very similarly to Compare > Local History. The window is additionally equipped with a Replace button with which you can replace the current version with the version in the right window. In contrast, this function does not have a Java Structure Compare window.

Restore Deleted Resource

Mistakenly deleting a resource is not a tragedy either. The function Restore from Local History provides a selection list for previously deleted resources that can be restored by simply marking their check boxes.

Figure 2.8

Summary

After studying this chapter you should know about the main productivity techniques embodied in the Eclipse platform and the Eclipse Java SDK. Features such as help and hover, and especially the content assistants and templates, allow you to work without constantly searching programming guides and manuals. Instead, the information is provided where and when it is needed. Strong navigation functions allow you to get around in your application quickly. Especially in large applications such functions are essential. Various assistants for source code completion, refactoring, and bug fixes help you to adopt an agile programming style. In Chapter 16 I will discuss how these functions support the Extreme Programming approach. In the next chapter I will introduce the Eclipse Visual Editor.

The Art of (Visual) Composition

One of the more frequently asked questions directed to the Eclipse development team was if and when a visual GUI editor would be available for Eclipse. Eclipse 2 SDK did not provide a visual editor, but after a while several third-party GUI editor plug-ins appeared on the market (see Appendix A). Then, at Christmas 2003, eclipse.org released the first version (0.5) of the Eclipse Visual Editor for Java (VE) that, initially, supports only the design of Swing GUIs under Eclipse 2.1. In May 2004, VE M1 was released for the Eclipse 3 platform. Support of SWT GUIs is planned for version 1.0. What's nice about this tool is that it is completely free and that it is Open Source. But this is not its only advantage

The VE has—like Eclipse—its roots in Visual Age, despite the fact that it was implemented from scratch in Java. One of the main features of the VE is that it supports two-way programming: changes in the visual layout appear immediately in the generated Java code, while changes in the Java code are reflected back to the visual layout as soon as the source code is saved with Ctrl+S. With this feature, the VE completely refrains from using metadata but derives all information from the source code.

Installation

In this task the VE relies on the facilities of the Eclipse Modeling Framework (EMF). Therefore, before installing the VE, you must install the EMF. The EMF can be downloaded from www.eclipse.org/emf/. To install it, just unpack the downloaded archive into the /eclipse root directory. Then start the Eclipse platform and follow the instructions of the Update Manager. After restarting Eclipse, you can install the VE in the same manner. The VE download can be obtained from www.eclipse.org/vep/.

Invocation

After installation, the VE is hard to notice. When you open Eclipse help, you will see a separate chapter for the Visual Editor. After a short browse through the supplied information, you may find out that the VE can be applied to any Java compilation unit. To do so, you must open a closed Java file with the context function Open with > Visual Editor. Afterwards, this file will be always opened with the VE when you double-click it in the Package Explorer.

During your first steps with the VE you will soon notice that a large screen is required to work with the VE efficiently, because the editor area is subdivided into a visual design area and an area for the source code. As a matter of fact, you can maximize the editor area by double-clicking its title bar. Unfortunately, this is not a good solution because the Java Beans View and the Properties View are used frequently during the design process. So, it is better to switch back to the normal workbench mode. Bad news for notebook users, it seems.

A nice feature is that the division of the design area and the source code area is not fixed but can be varied by moving the sash between the areas. By clicking one of the arrows on the sash you can maximize one area or the other. Furthermore, there is a viewing mode switch in the Java Beans View (second button from the left), which you can use to switch this view to a navigator function: the view shows the design area in reduced size, and by moving the gray rectangle you can easily navigate within a large layout.

Preferences

Of course, you can also opt not to use this split-screen editor but use a tabbed folder instead. In this case, both the design area and the source code area completely fill the editor area of the workbench and are activated by selecting the appropriate tab at the bottom of the editor area. This mode is especially useful for smaller screens (notebook users enjoy!). To activate this mode, go to Window > Preference > Java > Visual Editor. On the Appearance page, from the Show the Visual Editor and Source Editor section, select the On Separate Notebook Tabs option.

On the same page you can also determine the skin (Look&Feel) to be used for generated Swing GUIs.

If you own a fast computer, you may also want to shorten the delay for updating the source code after design changes (or vice versa). This is done on the Code Generation page under Source Synchronization Delay. The default value is 500 msec.

Composition

Composing GUIs with the VE is quite simple. On the left margin of the VE you will find a menu with GUI elements. These are organized in groups: Swing Components, Swing Containers, Swing Menus, and AWT Controls. Clicking such a group will expand it and collapse all others. However, clicking the pin at the right-hand side of the group name lets you keep a group open permanently.

To move a GUI element to the design area, first select it with the mouse. Then click the target position in the design area. You don't drag and drop elements, but rather you move them as you would move cards in the card game Freecell.

Try it with a small example. In `HelloWorld` project, just create a new class named `HelloVE` as described in Chapter 1 (with a `main()` method). Then close the Java editor. In the Package Explorer, apply the context function Open with > Visual Editor to `HelloVE`. Now open the Swing Containers group in the GUI element menu of the VE. Select the component `JFrame`. Then click the target position in the design area. The smallest possible `JFrame` instance now appears at the target position. Click the bottom-right corner of this component and drag it to the desired size. As you can see in the Java Beans View, the `JFrame` instance already contains a content pane (`JPanel` instance), which fills the entire area of the `JFrame` instance.

Now click the Swing Components group to open it. Select the `JLabel` component and release the mouse button. Then move the mouse over the (still selected) `JFrame` component in the design area. As you move the mouse, different areas labeled `North`, `Center`, `South`, `East`, and `West` will appear because the content pane is already equipped with a `BorderLayout` (see below in section "Layouts"). Now, click the mouse to place the `JLabel` component into the `Center` area.

In this area you will now see a `JLabel` instance named JLabel.It may well be that this instance appears at a slightly different position because the `BorderLayout` manager performs automatic positioning. Now click the already selected `JLabel` instance once again. A text input area opens, where you can overwrite the text "JLabel" with "Hello VE," as shown in Figure 3.1.

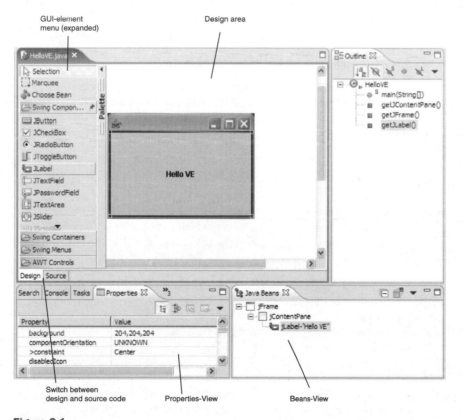

Figure 3.1

47

This figure shows the components of the VE. At the top left you see the selection menu for the GUI elements. Adjoining to the right is the working area, consisting of the design area and the source code editor. On the far left is the Outline View, as already known from the Java editor. At the bottom I have docked the Java Beans View to the right of the Properties View (see the "Arranging Editors and Views" section in Chapter 4), in order to allow for comfortable editing. You may store this arrangement as your own perspective (see the "Managing Perspectives" section in Chapter 4).

As you can see in the Outline View (and in the source code, too), these actions have generated the methods `getJFrame()`, `getJContentPane()`, and `getJLabel()`. All that remains to do is to invoke the method `getJFrame()` from the `main()` method. To do so, modify the `main()` method in the source code area as follows:

```
public static void main(String[] args) {
  HelloVE hello = new HelloVE();
  javax.swing.JFrame frame = hello.getJFrame();
  frame.setVisible(true);
}
```

After saving this code with Ctrl+S, you can execute this program immediately by issuing the command Run > Run As > Java Application.

Beans and Bean Properties

All the components available in the VE's GUI element menu are provided in the form of *Java Beans*. Java Beans are Java classes that follow certain coding standards. For example, a Java Bean must always have a standard constructor without any parameters. The features of such a Java Bean are described in an associated class, a BeanInfo class. The VE uses this information via introspection to display the component in an appropriate form and to generate code.

Generic Beans

The VE is not restricted to AWT and Swing components. In principle, any Java Bean can be placed onto the design area. You may even write your own beans, which then can be used in the VE. You can select such beans by clicking the Choose Bean button in the selection menu. Detailed information about the implementation of Java Beans is found in the book *Java Beans 101* by Steams.

The *Java Beans* View shows the hierarchy of beans used in the design area, so it is easy to keep an overview of the construction of the GUI. The Java Beans View also helps during the selection of components, for example, if a component is hidden in the design area by another component. In this case you can use the Java Beans View to select the component.

Properties

The properties of a bean are displayed in the Properties View and can be modified there. In the above example, the label text is not centered correctly, despite the fact that the `JLabel` component was placed into the `Center` area. The reason is that the component stretches across the whole content pane, and its text content starts to the left of the component. To fix this, select the component jLabel in the Java Beans View. (You may want to rename this component using the context function Rename Field.) In the Properties View, find the property named horizontalAlignment. This property currently has the value LEADING. Select this entry with the mouse. An arrow button appears beside LEADING. Now click this button and select CENTER, and the text is centered.

VE supports almost any of the properties of the Swing components with a few exceptions. For example, you cannot specify client properties (putClientProperty()) in the Properties view, and for JLabel components you cannot specify target components for mnemonic codes (setLabelFor()). Such properties must be set manually in the source code.

Layouts

Now select the component jContentPane in the Java Beans View. Like all Swing containers, this container, too, has a layout. You will find the property layout in the Properties View. As you can see, this container is already equipped with a BorderLayout. Clicking the arrow button gives you a list of the available layout options. At the left of the layout entry is a plus sign. Clicking this sign expands the entry and allows you to make further specifications for this layout manager, such as horizontal gap and vertical gap. Finally, there is an option to work without a layout manager. To do so, select the null option in the list of layout managers. Then you can position the JLabel component freely within the content pane.

Normally, you should change layout settings only after you have filled a container with components. This is because with some layouts, empty containers have a size of zero, and it can become quite tricky to place a component into a container of zero size. However, if something like this should happen, there is always a way out: instead of placing a component into a container within the design area, apply the same operation to the Java Beans View.

If you later want to move components to a different position or even to a different container, this is easy: both the design area and the Java Beans View support moving components by drag and drop. However, the VE does not support cut-and-paste operations for components.

If you need detailed information about Swing and Swing layout managers, please refer to the resources listed in Appendix D, for example to the book *Swing* by Robinson and Vorobiev.

Event Processing

Finally, let's see how event processing can be programmed with the help of the VE. Let's first create one more component, a JButton, in the content pane of the JFrame container. You can select the position freely, for example, the South area (if you are still using the BorderLayout manager). If you are working without a layout manager, reduce the size of the JLabel component somewhat to make room for the new JButton component.

Then, find the entry text in the Properties View and enter "OK" as the button text. Alternatively, you can just click the button in the design area and enter "OK" in the text input area.

Now you can define some event processing for the new button. Right-click the selected button. In the context menu choose Events, and in the cascading submenu select actionPerformed. Now, sit back and watch how the source code for this event is generated:

```
jButton.addActionListener(new java.awt.event.ActionListener() {
  public void actionPerformed(java.awt.event.ActionEvent e) {
    System.out.println("actionPerformed()");
    // TODO Auto-generated Event stub actionPerformed()
  }
});
```

If you now run the program again after saving it, the text actionPerformed() appears in the Console View when you click OK.

The Events submenu, however, lists only the most relevant events for a component. Other event types can be reached via the Add Event function. For example, if you want to react to the resizing of components, you need to invoke the Events > Add Event ... context function. In the dialog that appears, expand the Component class. Then select the componentResized event type. Finally, you may specify whether a subclass of the ComponentAdapter class is to be generated or whether a complete implementation of the ComponentListener interface is to be generated. Afterwards, you can complete the definition of the componentResized() method in the source code area as needed.

This concludes our short introduction into the Eclipse Visual Editor. In Chapter 5 I will demonstrate the VE in the design of a more complex GUI in the context of a larger application.

Summary

This chapter has given you a glimpse of the Eclipse Visual Editor. Novices especially often find it easier to design GUI surfaces visually. Currently the Eclipse Visual Editor supports only Swing GUIs. If you need help creating SWT GUIs (see Chapter 8), you still have to rely on third-party GUI designers, some of which are listed in Appendix A. Another possibility is to use the SWT Layout example plug-in as a code generator.

In the next chapter we will take a more detailed look into the Eclipse workbench.

Organizing Your Code

In this chapter I first discuss the handling of the different components of the Eclipse workbench: editors, views, and perspectives. Then I look at the basic resource types in Eclipse: projects, folders, and files.

Afterwards you will use the new knowledge in a practical example. This time you don't output "Hello World" on the Java console—but on your computer's sound card! In the context of this example I discuss topics such as the import and export of files and archives, the association of source files with binary files, and how to set the project properties correctly.

The Workbench

In the Introduction I mentioned that the Java Development Toolkit (JDT) is merely one of the many possible plug-ins for the Eclipse workbench (which itself is a plug-in to the Eclipse platform). The Eclipse workbench is completely language-neutral—all functions that are specific to development with Java are packaged in the JDT plug-ins.

Switch back to the resource perspective for a moment (see Figure 4.1). Where you previously saw the Package Explorer, you now find the Resource Navigator. The Java packages have vanished, and instead you see a structure of nested folders. The Resource Navigator shows projects, folders, and files. Figure 4.1 shows a project in the Navigator that you will develop in Chapter 5.

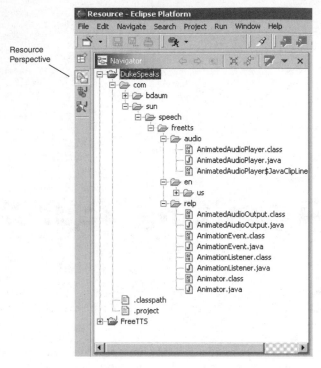

Resource
Perspective

Figure 4.1

Resources

The Resource Navigator shows an overview of the set of resources maintained by the Eclipse workbench (the workspace) and supports navigation within this set of resources.

Resource Types

The workbench understands three different resource types:

❑ **Projects.** A project is always the root node of a resource tree. Projects can contain folders and files. Projects cannot be nested.

❑ **Folders.** A folder can contain files and other (nested) folders.

❑ **Files.** Files are the leaf nodes in a resource tree, i.e., a file cannot contain other resources.

Where Resources Are Stored

All resources are stored directly in the file system of the host platform. This is different from Visual Age, where resources were stored in a repository. In contrast, the structure of projects and folders in the Eclipse workspace directly correlates to the directory structure of the host platform. This has advantages in the case of crashes and for backups. (In Chapter 7 I will discuss how to connect a repository to Eclipse.)

By default, the resources of the Eclipse workbench are stored in the (host) directory `\eclipse\ workspace`. Each project is contained in a corresponding subdirectory. For example, the `AnimationEvent.java` resource shown in the previous figure is stored in the path `\eclipse\ workspace\DukeSpeaks\com\sun\speech\freetts\relp\AnimationEvent.java`. Of course, it is possible to create a workspace directory in a different location by specifying the command-line option `-data` when starting Eclipse

```
eclipse.exe -data C:\myOldWorkSpace
```

or by specifying a different workspace in the Workspace Launcher (see the "Installing Eclipse" section in Chapter 1).

Synchronizing Resources

For each resource in the workbench, Eclipse stores some metadata in the `\eclipse\workspace\ .metadata` directory. Sometimes it happens that the state of a resource in `\eclipse\workspace` does not match the state of the corresponding metadata. In particular, this happens when a workspace file is modified outside Eclipse, for example, by modifying it with an external tool.

This is not a tragedy. All you have to do is select the resource that is out of sync and apply the Refresh context function. This function can be applied not only to single resources but also to folders and projects, so that you can easily resynchronize a whole directory tree.

Navigation

The following context functions and tool buttons in the navigator's context menu and toolbar are available for navigation:

- ❑ **Go Into.** This function reduces the current view to the content of the selected project or folder. This function can be particularly useful when your workspace consists of thousands of resources.

- ❑ **Back.** This button (arrow to the left) returns to the previous view.

- ❑ **Forward.** This button (arrow to the right) reverts the previous Back operation.

- ❑ **Up To.** This button (folder symbol) goes into the next-higher folder or project.

- ❑ **Open in New Window.** This function works similarly to Go Into but opens a new window (with a complete workbench!) in which only the contents of the selected project or folder are shown in the navigator.

The menu of the navigator's toolbar (under the small triangle) offers further functions:

- ❑ The Sort function allows files to be sorted by name or type.

- ❑ The Filters function allows files with specific filename extensions to be excluded from the navigator.

- ❑ The Link with Editor function enables automatic synchronization of the resource selection with the editor content. When you switch editors (by clicking on tags), the selection in the navigator changes accordingly.

- ❑ The Select Working Set function allows you to select a named working set in order to restrict the resources shown in the navigator to the resources belonging to the selected working set. This function also allows you to define new working sets.

- ❑ The Deselect Working Set function removes the working set restrictions from the navigator.

- ❑ The Edit Active Working Set function allows you to modify the current working set.

Associations

In Eclipse the type of a file is usually determined by its filename extension. (It is also possible to assign specific file types to fully qualified filenames.) In the previous figure you saw text-based files such as .java and .html files but also binary files such as the .class files. The file type (and thus the filename extension) controls what happens when a file is opened.

For example, if you click a .java file with the right mouse button, you get a pop-up menu with context functions. When you select the Open With submenu, you get another pop-up menu with editors. In the first menu section you see the editor that was used last for this file (in the current case, the Java source editor). The second section shows all editors that are registered for that filename extension—in the current case these are the Text Editor and the System Editor. The Text Editor is the text editor that is contained in the Eclipse SDK, which can be used for all text-based files. The *System Editor* is the editor that is registered under the host platform for that file type. Eclipse is able to start such editors from the workbench; for example, if you open an HTML file, the host platform's web browser is started.

Most of the file associations (which editor works with which file type) are determined by the Eclipse plug-ins. However, it is also possible to add or modify such associations manually. To do so, just invoke Window > Preferences > Workbench > File Associations (Figure 4.2).

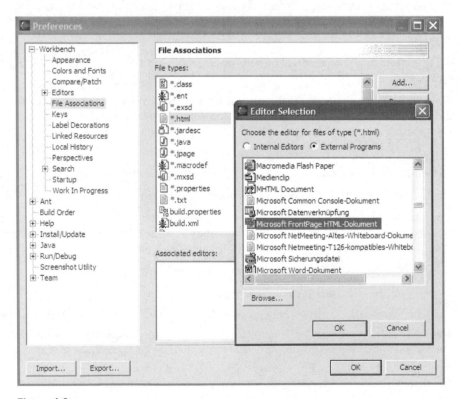

Figure 4.2

In the upper window you see a list of registered file types. By using the Add and Remove buttons, you can add new file types or delete existing ones. In the lower window, the registered editors for the currently selected filename extension are shown. Here, too, you can add new editors or remove existing editors. By using the Default button, you can declare a specific editor as the default editor for that file type.

When you press the Add button, you first get a list of internal editors, i.e., editors that are implemented as Eclipse plug-ins. If you click the External Programs button, you get a list of the applications that are registered in the host operating system for the selected file type. By double-clicking such an application, you can select it as a new editor for this file type.

In Figure 4.2 the file associations are defined. First the filename pattern `* .html` was added, and then Microsoft FrontPage was associated with this file type.

Packages

Switch back to the Java perspective. The picture you see now is quite different: the *Package Explorer* shows the different projects with their package structure and the compilation units.

Folders and Packages

Packages are not real resources but virtual objects. The package structure of a project is derived from the package declaration at the beginning of each Java source file.

The Java specification, however, requires that the package structure of a project be isomorphic to the project's directory structure. For example, all resources of the `com.sun.speech.freetts.relp` package must be stored under the relative path `com/sun/speech/freetts/relp`, as shown in Figure 4.3. In Eclipse, the path is always relative to the project's source code root directory. In our case, the relative path `com/sun/speech/freetts/relp` is equivalent to the host platform path:

```
\eclipse\workspace\DukeSpeaks\com\sun\speech\freetts\relp
```

Each package can be uniquely mapped onto a node in the resource tree. Compilation units, in contrast, can consist of several resources: the source file and one or several binary files. In the case of the AnimatedAudioPlayer class there are two binary files: one for AnimatedAudioPlayer and one for the JavaClipLineListener inner class.

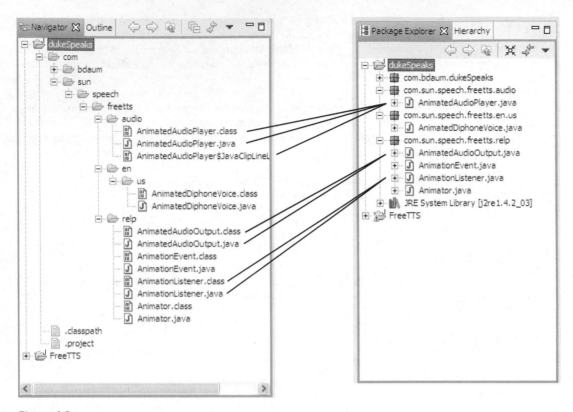

Figure 4.3

Navigation

The Package Explorer is equipped with similar navigation functions to the Resource Navigator. Here, too, are the Go Into and Open in New Window context functions, and in the toolbar there are buttons for the Back, Forward, and Up To functions. Under the toolbar's drop-down menu you can find the same functions for managing working sets and for synchronizing with the editor.

Furthermore, you have the possibility of opening the type hierarchy browser discussed in the next section.

Hierarchy

The type hierarchy shows the super types and subtypes for classes and interfaces. You can restrict the view to super types or subtypes only or show the complete hierarchy. By using the *History* function you can quickly change between the different views, or you can display previously displayed type hierarchies again (see Figure 4.4).

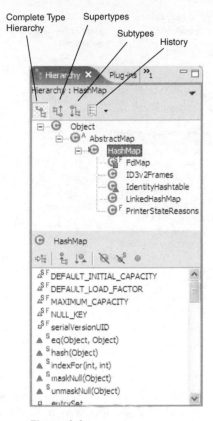

Complete Type Hierarchy · Supertypes · Subtypes · History

Figure 4.4

In the toolbar of the lower window you can find additional functions. The first button affects the upper window. It restricts the view to only those types that implement the field or method selected in the lower window. When you push the second button, the lower window will also show the methods and fields that are inherited by the selected type. The remaining buttons are the same as in the Outline View (see the next section).

The Type Hierarchy Browser can be useful when you want to analyze existing projects and libraries. When creating a new project you will need this browser only when the project becomes bigger.

A faster method for displaying the type hierarchy is pressing the F4 function key, which acts as a shortcut for the Open Type Hierarchy context function. Alternatively, you can use the key combination Ctrl+T to display the type hierarchy in a pop-up window.

The Outline View

The Outline View (Figure 4.5) supports navigation within a source file. In general, the Outline View is not restricted to Java sources but supports—depending on the plug-ins installed—other file types as well.

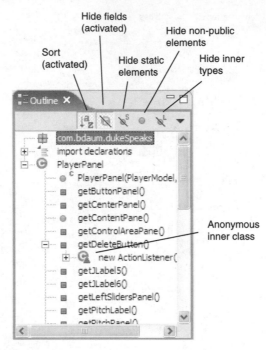

Figure 4.5

For Java programs, the Outline View displays entries for fields and methods and also for `import` statements. If inner classes are defined, these classes also appear in the Outline View; the main type and the inner types form a tree structure. The buttons on the Outline toolbar allow you to restrict the Outline View to specific entry types. Fields and methods can be sorted in alphabetical order by pushing the Sort button (otherwise, their order corresponds to their definition sequence in the source file).

Single-clicking such an entry positions the source editor on the corresponding element. Apart from this facility for quick navigation, the Outline View offers a few more functions. But I'll start with the graphical representation of the entries within the Outline View.

Representation

The first icon in front of an Outline View entry represents the entry type (package, `import` statement, interface, class, method, field) and the visibility (`public`, `protected`, `private`).

Icon	Meaning
	`import` statement
	interface
	class

Icon	Meaning
●	public method
◇	protected method
■	private method
▲	default method (without modifier)
○	public field
◇	protected field
▫	private field
△	default field (without modifier)

In addition to this first icon, additional icons can add information about the entry:

Icon	Meaning
C	constructor
S	static element
F	final element
▲	overridden element

You can change the representation of the Outline View under Window > Preferences > Java > Appearance:

❑ **Show Method Return Types.** Displays the result type of methods in the Outline View.

❑ **Show Override Indicators.** Displays the indicator for methods that override inherited methods.

❑ **Show Member in Package Explorer.** If this option is set, methods and fields are also shown in the Package Explorer as child elements of classes and interfaces. Most of the *Outline* View functions are in this case available in the Package Explorer, too.

Context Functions

The Outline View offers a rich variety of context functions. The most important of these functions are also available as toolbar buttons (see previous figure). Here is an overview of these functions:

❑ **Open Type Hierarchy.** Shows the type hierarchy for the selected element (see Figure 4.5). This function can be applied not only to single types but also to whole packages or projects.

❑ **Open Call Hierarchy.** Shows the call hierarchy for the selected method.

❑ **Open Super Implementation.** This function is available only for elements that override an inherited feature. When applied, the inherited feature is opened in the source editor.

❑ **Cut, Copy, Paste, Delete.** These are the usual copy and delete functions but they are applied to the element selected in the Outline View.

❑ **Refactor > ….** Various functions for refactoring code (see the "Refactoring Code" section in Chapter 2).

❑ **Source > ….** Various functions for automatic source code completion (see the "Automatic Code Completion" section in Chapter 2).

❑ **References > ….** Searches for references to the selected element (see next section).

❑ **Declarations > ….** Searches for definitions of the selected elements (see next section).

❑ **Read Access > ….** Searches for read access to the selected field (see next section).

❑ **Write Access > ….** Searches for write access to the selected field (see next section).

❑ **Occurrences in File.** Lists the occurrences of the selected item in the Search View (see next section).

❑ **Toggle Watchpoint.** This function appears only on field entries and belongs to the debugger's tool set (see Chapter 6).

❑ **Toggle Method Breakpoint.** This function appears only on method entries and belongs to the debugger's tool set (see Chapter 6).

❑ **Compare With > …, Replace With > …, Restore from Local History ….** With these functions you can compare the current version of an element with a previous version from the Local History, or you can restore a previous version (see the "Local History" section in Chapter 2).

Searching

Searching and Finding are different tasks in Eclipse: The Search function performs a search over the whole Eclipse workspace. The Find function, in contrast, searches for a string in the currently active document.

The Search Function

The powerful Eclipse Search function consists of two components: the Search dialog for entering the search criteria and the view containing the search results (see the following two figures).

If the Search function is called from the toolbar of the Eclipse workbench or from the Eclipse main menu, you first get the dialog for entering the search criteria. If you call the function as a context function, this step is omitted, since the search criteria are already defined by the context.

The dialog for entering search criteria has several pages (depending on the installed plug-ins). In Figure 4.6 the dialog contains a page for searching in generic files, a page for searching within the Eclipse help system, a page for Java-specific searching (opened), and a page for searching plug-ins.

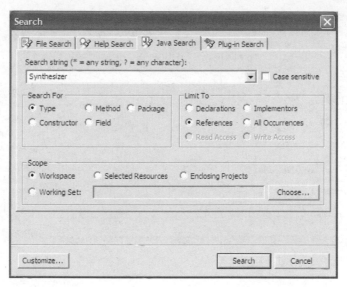

Figure 4.6

In the case of a Java Search you can search for the name of a type, method, package, constructor, or field. You can qualify this name completely or only partially. In addition, you can restrict the search by constraints. You can search only for declarations, only for references, or for both. In case of fields, you can restrict the search to read or write accesses. The search scope can be limited to the selected resources only or to *working sets* (named resource sets).

Besides the Java Search, the Search dialog features additional pages for searching in generic files (this mode also includes a Replace button), for searching in the help system, and for searching plug-ins. With the Customize button you can hide and show specific Search dialog pages.

The results of a search are always shown in the Search View. In the standard Java perspective, the Search View is stacked with the Tasks View. After selecting the Hierarchical Layout option from the view's menu, you can group the search results by project, package, file, or class by pressing the appropriate Search View tool button.

By using the up- and down-arrows in the toolbar of the Search View, you can easily step through all the occurrences of the search item. The corresponding compilation unit is automatically opened in the source editor. The position of the search item is shown on the left margin of the source editor with a yellow arrow.

It is useful to know that the Search View keeps track of the search history. You can recall previous search results by pressing the Previous Search Results button or via the Search Views drop-down menu.

The Search View shows all compilation units in which the sought item was found (Figure 4.7). If this item occurs several times in the same compilation unit, the number of occurrences is shown in parentheses at the end of the entry. Double-clicking an entry in the Search View opens the corresponding compilation unit in the source editor.

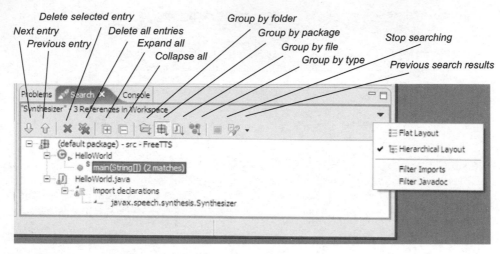

Figure 4.7

Find and Replace

Besides the Search function discussed above, Eclipse, of course, provides a function for finding and replacing strings in text files. With the Edit > Find/Replace function you can obtain a dialog (see Figure 4.8) where you can enter the search string and additional search options. If you call this function while a string is selected, the selected string will be used as the search string.

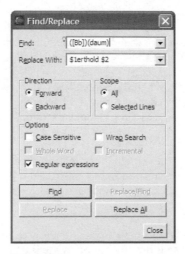

Figure 4.8

The Find/Replace dialog (Figure 4.8) supports searching for character strings and replacing such strings with others. Since Eclipse 3 this function supports regular expressions during finding as well as replacing. When searching, you can search forward or backward and restrict the search to the selected text area. In addition there are further options:

❏ **Case Sensitive.** If this option is checked, the search is performed in case-sensitive mode.

❏ **Wrap Search.** If this option is checked, searching continues at the beginning of the search area when the end is reached (or at the end of the search area when the beginning is reached, in case of searching backward). Otherwise, a message prompt is displayed.

❏ **Whole Word.** If this option is checked, only whole words are searched for.

❏ **Incremental.** If this option is checked, the search begins immediately when the first character of the search string is entered. When more characters are entered, the search operation continues as necessary.

❏ **Regular Expression.** If this option is checked, the search expression is interpreted as a regular expression. Press F1 to obtain help on the syntax of regular expressions, or press Ctrl+Spacebar to obtain a content assistant that helps you with the construction of regular expressions. Capture groups defined in the Find expression are considered, and the results can be used in the Replace expression.

Eclipse offers more *Find* functions that correspond to these options, such as Edit > Find Next, Edit > Find Previous, and Edit > Incremental Find.

Marking Name Occurrences

If you switch on the Mark Occurrences in File option under Window > Preferences > Mark Occurrences, the editor will from then on, when you select a syntactical element, mark all elements in the same file that carry the same name. Since these markers also appear on the right ruler, you can easily navigate to such an element by moving the scrollbar. In many cases this can save a tedious search. Within the Preferences you may, in addition, specify which kind of elements are affected by this option: all types, all methods, all constants, fields, variables, etc. If you mark the Sticky option, the marks will stay around even if the originating element is no longer selected.

This feature can be quickly switched on or off via the Mark Occurrences button.

Arranging Editors and Views

The layout of the different windows in the Eclipse workbench is not fixed and can be configured by the user (with some restrictions). There are essentially three ways in which you can arrange windows within the workbench.

Docked Windows

You can place a window to the left or right of another window or below or above that window. Using this technique, all windows stay visible, but their size shrinks with each new window. You can dock a window to another window by dragging its title area or tag to the edge of the target window. When the cursor changes to a fat arrow, just drop the window.

Stacked Windows

Another option is to stack several windows in front of each other. By clicking the tag of a window you can bring this window to the top. You can stack a window in front of another window by dragging its title area or tag to the target window. When the cursor changes to a stack symbol, release it.

Desktop Windows

A further option is to place a view window as a separate window on the desktop outside the workbench window. However, this option is available only under Windows and Linux GTK. Just grap the view at its tag and pull it over the desktop area.

FastView

FastView can minimize a window in the FastView bar of the workbench: the window is represented by an icon. However, the FastView bar is visible only when it contains at least one view. To convert a view into a FastView, right-click the view's tag and invoke the FastView context function. The FastView bar has context functions, too. With the Orientation function you can determine whether a FastView should be expanded vertically or horizontally. Clicking the FastView function removes the checkmark from it and restores the view to its original state. With the Dock On function you can change the position of the FastView bar: at the bottom of the workbench (the default), at the right, or at the left.

In Figure 4.9 I dragged the Search View to the left edge of the Problems View so that both views are visible side by side.

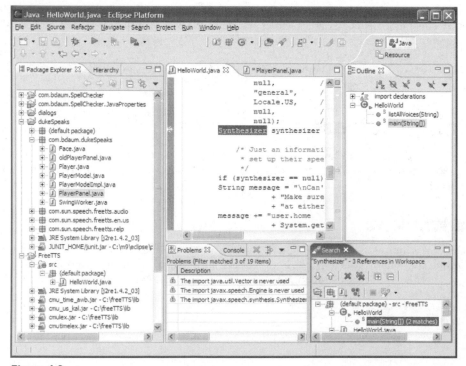

Figure 4.9

Opening and Closing Windows

Closing a window is trivial: clicking the window's Close button in the top-right corner or pressing Ctrl+F4 does the job. But how do you open it again?

❏ For editor windows this is simple: double-clicking the corresponding resource in the Resource Navigator or the Package Explorer will open the resource under the editor previously in use.

❏ For view windows, use the Window > Show View > … function and select the view that you want to open.

By the way, if you want to close all editor windows, just invoke File > Close All or press Ctrl+Shift+F4.

Maximizing Windows

All windows in the workbench can be maximized. Double-clicking the tag of a view or of an editor page or clicking the Maximize icon maximizes the corresponding window, that is, the window occupies all the space in the workbench window. Double-clicking the tag again or clicking the *Restore* icon restores the previous window layout.

Minimizing Views

Views also have a Minimize icon. Clicking this icon will shrink the view (and all views that are stacked in the same area) to the mere title bar. Clicking the Restore icon will bring the view back to its old size and position.

Managing Perspectives

A perspective defines a specific combination of editors, views, and menus within the workbench. In this chapter you already encountered the Resource Perspective and the Java Perspective. In Chapter 6 you will get acquainted with the Debug Perspective.

Defining New Perspectives

Let's assume that you have now arranged all the windows in the Java Perspective to your liking. Is it possible to store these preferences?

You can save this layout with the Window > Save Perspective As function (see Figure 4.10). In the Name field of this function's dialog you can define a name for the new perspective. If you later want to return to the original Java Perspective, you can do so by invoking the Window > Reset Perspective function or by invoking Window > Close Perspective followed by Window > Open Perspective.

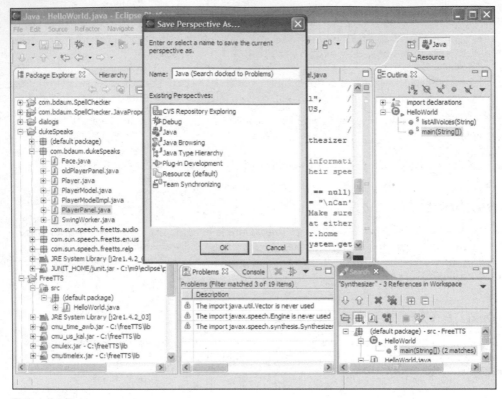

Figure 4.10

The modified workbench configuration shown in the previous figure is stored here as a new perspective under the name Java (Search docked to Problems).

Configuring Perspectives

With the Window > Customize Perspective function (Figure 4.11) you can change certain aspects of the current perspective:

❑ The Shortcuts tab allows you to define which items should be listed directly in a given submenu (otherwise, you would have to click through Others to get to the desired item). Shortcuts can be defined for the File > New, Window > Open Perspective, and Window > Show View submenus.

❑ The Commands tab allows you to define which command groups (action sets) should be visible in the menu bar and toolbar of the current perspective.

You can also invoke this function conveniently by clicking the toolbar with the right mouse button.

With the Window > Customize Perspective > Commands function you can remove whole command groups (action sets) from a perspective or add new command groups. The windows in the middle and at the right show how the selected command group would influence the menu and the toolbar.

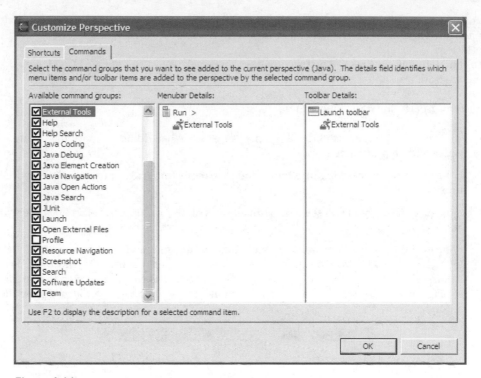

Figure 4.11

In addition, under Window > Preferences > Workbench > Perspectives you can control how to open a new perspective: either in the current workbench window or in a new workbench window. The latter option, however, makes sense only if you are lucky enough to own a very large screen. On smaller screens you may want to use the Eclipse workbench in its maximum size. In this case, the perspective icons on the Perspective bar of the workbench window (top right) are the perfect way to change perspectives.

Another option allows you to create a new perspective automatically when a new project is created, so that each project has its own perspective. Again, you can open the new perspective in the current workbench window or in a new workbench window.

Importing Files

You are now going to teach your `HelloWorld` program to talk. Since version 1.4, Java has contained a speech interface, the Java Speech API (JSAPI). A standard implementation of the interface, FreeTTS, is available for free and can be downloaded from the Internet. FreeTTS has its roots in the speech synthesizer Flite but was ported completely to Java. An interesting fact is that FreeTTS is considerably faster than Flite. Even in terms of speed, Java seems more and more to outperform C++.

FreeTTS (Version 1.2.0) is found at `//sourceforge.net/projects/freetts`. After downloading the binary and source files that amount together to about 24 MB (a real flyweight compared to the Eclipse SDK distribution), unpack the downloaded binaries into an arbitrary directory. In addition, you must unpack the JSAPI (Java Speech API) because it is distributed under a different license model. To do so you just need to execute the jsapi.exe program in the FreeTTS\lib folder.

You could now follow the FreeTTS installation guide and make a test run of FreeTTS. However, don't do that here. Instead, import the system into the Eclipse workbench.

To import third-party software, follow these steps:

1. First, create a new project under the name FreeTTS. When doing so, mark the Create Separate Source and Output Folders option.

2. In the new project select the src folder and invoke the Import Wizard with the Import context function.

3. In the next dialog, you will see a list with all sorts of import sources. Select Filesystem and press the Next button.

4. In the next dialog that appears, press the *Browse* button and navigate to the …\FreeTTS\ demo\JSAPI\HelloWorld folder. This folder now appears in the left window of the dialog. Select it, and at the right-hand side you will see all the files contained in that folder (see Figure 4.12). There, place a checkmark on the HelloWorld.java file and press the Finish button.

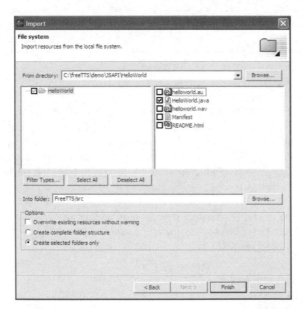

Figure 4.12

If everything has worked correctly, the imported HelloWorld.java program should now be in a default package of the FreeTTS project (Figure 4.13). But there are a lot of error markers, too!

This is to be expected—the FreeTTS runtime system is still missing. You have two options:

❑ **Importing the JAR files of the FreeTTS runtime system into the workbench.** But this would separate you from future version changes. You would need to reimport new versions of these JAR files into the Eclipse workbench.

❑ **Adding the JAR files as external files to the Java Build Path.** This saves you from importing these files. An additional advantage is that you don't have to keep two copies of the files. If the original files are replaced by a new version, the changes will automatically be carried through to your project.

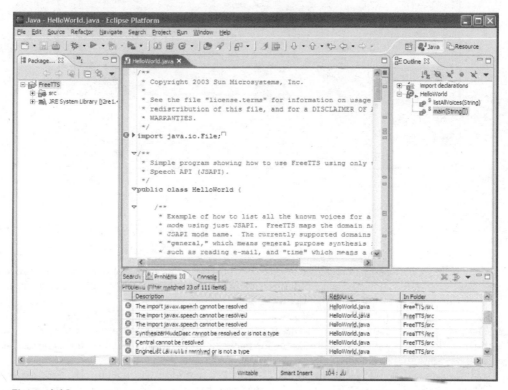

Figure 4.13

Project Properties

In this example I recommend that you use the second option. To add JAR files to the Java Build Path, just invoke the Project > Properties function. In the selection tree choose Java Build Path, and then open the *Libraries* page. Here you see only a single entry: the rt.jar Java 1.4 runtime system.

Press the Add External Jars button and navigate to the directory ...\FreeTTS\lib. From the JAR files now listed in this dialog (cmu_time_awb.jar, ..., jsapi.jar), select all files and then press the *Open* button. These files are now added to the Libraries list (Figure 4.14). Then press the OK button and see what happens. All the error markers should have vanished! (If not, you'll need to rebuild the project by calling the Build Project context function.)

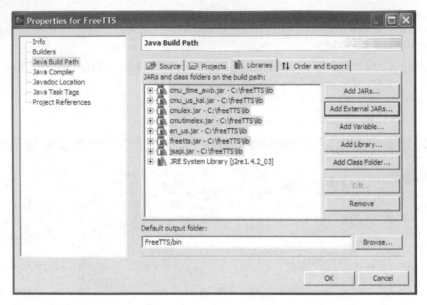

Figure 4.14

Figure 4.14 shows the content of the Libraries page in the Project Properties after adding the FreeTTS JARs.

What is still missing is the source code for the FreeTTS binaries. This code is contained in the downloaded `freetts-srcs-1_2_beta.zip` file. You must associate this file only with the corresponding packages of the FreeTTS project. Here's how it's done.

In the Package Explorer select `freetts.jar` and invoke the Properties context function. In the dialog that appears, select Java Source Attachment for the package properties. Then press the External File button and navigate to the `freetts-srcs-1_2_beta.zip` file. And that's all. If you now open a file from `freetts.jar`, the corresponding source code will appear in the source editor. Of course, this code cannot be edited, only viewed. (You have to repeat this process for the other external JAR files as well.)

Now you should be able to do a test run. Like the very first `HelloWorld` program, execute the new `HelloWorld` program with the same Run > Run As > Java Application function.

However, instead of the expected speech output, you get only the following text on the Java console:

```
Can't find synthesizer.
Make sure that there is a "speech.properties" file at either of these
locations:
user.home : H:\Dokumente und Einstellungen\Berthold Daum
java.home/lib: C:\j2sdk1.4.1\jre\lib
```

Right. Something like this was mentioned in the FreeTTS installation guide. Copy the `speech` `.properties` file from `FreeTTS` into one of the directories mentioned in the error message and execute the program again. You should hear

Hello, World!

provided of course, that your computer is equipped with a sound card and the speakers are connected….

The Java Browsing Perspective

The Java Browsing Perspective delivers a slightly different view of the structure of a Java project and is reminiscent of Visual Age. You can install this perspective by clicking the Open a Perspective button (see the "Hello World" section in Chapter 1). From the list select Java Browsing. The Java Browsing Perspective (Figure 4.15) provides four windows at the top where you can select projects, packages, types, and methods or fields in a hierarchical manner. Since you can easily switch between this perspective and the normal Java Perspective, the Java Browsing Perspective is a good way to avoid losing the overview of a project.

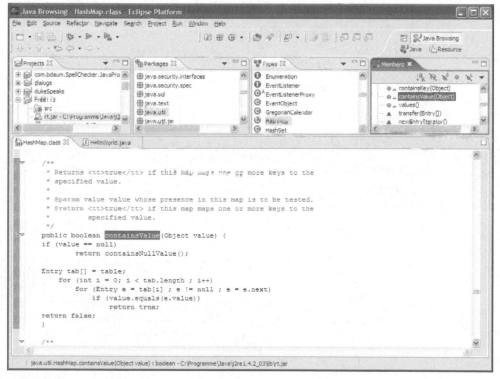

Figure 4.15

Summary

From this chapter you should have acquired a more detailed knowledge of the Eclipse workbench. You should now know what perspectives are and how they are used. You should know the difference between searching and finding, and you should have an understanding of the workspace concept and of Eclipse resources. In the next chapter you will apply this knowledge by implementing a larger example.

5

Project One: Duke Speaks

In this chapter you are going to implement your first major example project. You will learn how to base a new project on an existing project and how to modify and enhance features of the base project. During this task you will use many of the comfortable features of the Eclipse Java IDE.

The example application is based on the FreeTTS speech synthesizer that I have already introduced in Chapter 4. There I implemented the project FreeTTS with a speaking `HelloWorld` program, which communicated with the synthesizer via the JSAPI interface.

In this chapter you will develop a Swing GUI for FreeTTS. This GUI includes an animated face that moves its lips synchronously with the speech output.

Of course, there is also a speech synthesizer manufactured by IBM (ViaVoice) that even comes as an Eclipse plug-in. The Voice Toolkit for WebSphere Studio runs under Eclipse, too, and cooperates with the WebSphere Voice Server SDK. For our purposes, however, FreeTTS is better suited, since it is an Open Source product and supports all platforms supported by Eclipse.

Setting Up the Project

To achieve good lip synchronization, it is necessary to have event notification for single phonemes. The JSAPI, however, supports event notification only at the word level, and this event notification is currently not supported by the FreeTTS JSAPI implementation. The only choice is not to use the JSAPI but to drive FreeTTS via its native API. In addition, you have to create events for each single phoneme. This requires that you modify the FreeTTS runtime system.

Despite these modifications, you can still use the external FreeTTS JARs as a basis. Where necessary you can subclass the FreeTTS classes to apply your modification. These new classes are stored in packages that bear the same name as the parent class but are stored in our new project, `DukeSpeaks`.

First you create the new Java DukeSpeaks project in the usual way. Again, you need to modify the Java Build Path. This time, however, you don't add external JARs but open the Projects page and checkmark the FreeTTS project. This makes the resources of the FreeTTS project available to the DukeSpeaks project as well. This applies, too, to the external JARs that you added to the FreeTTS project. However, these JARs must be marked for export in the FreeTTS project. This is currently not the case.

So you must once again edit the Java Build Path of the FreeTTS project. To do so, select the project in the Package Explorer, right-click, and select the Properties context function. In the dialog that appears, select the Java Build Path category. Then open the Order and Export page. There checkmark all FreeTTS JARs, thus making them available to all projects that build on the FreeTTS project.

To avoid having the example files from Chapter 1 littering the Package Explorer, you should create a new working set. To do so, follow these steps:

1. Click the drop-down button (down-arrow) on the toolbar of the Package Explorer and choose the Select Working Set function. In the dialog that now appears, press the New button.

2. In the next dialog, select Java as the working set type and press the Next button.

3. Finally, enter dukeSpeaks as the name and checkmark the FreeTTS and DukeSpeaks projects. From now on, the Package Explorer displays only these two projects. By invoking the Deselect Working Set function you can restore the original state.

A Short Excursion into Speech Synthesis

Before you start extending the FreeTTS system, you should get acquainted with the basics of speech synthesis and with the architecture of the FreeTTS system.

Speech synthesis works in several steps:

1. A Tokenizer breaks the text into syntactical units (tokens). In general, these are words and numbers, including the punctuation.

2. Some tokens, such as numbers, are converted into words.

3. A Phraser analyzes the word list and organizes it into phrases (sentences and para-sentences). Phrasing establishes the basis for the later decoration of the speech output with pauses and melody.

4. A Segmenter analyzes the words and—with the help of a lexicon—assigns a syllable structure to each word.

5. The Pause Generator inserts a pause in front of each phrase.

6. The Intonator analyzes the syllables and assigns an emphasis and a pitch to each syllable.

7. In a further step and depending on the voice used, some phonemes are replaced by others.

8. The duration for each phoneme is determined.

9. The Contour Generator assigns an envelope curve to each syllable.

10. In a further step, adjoining phonemes are combined into pairs (*diphones*). This allows a better resolution of the text into speech.

11. The PitchMark Generator analyzes the results of the contour generator and generates parameters for the later sound synthesis.

12. The results of the PitchMark Generator and the list of diphones are now used to select and concatenate the corresponding speech samples.

13. Finally, the concatenated samples are replayed with the help of a suitable audio player.

FreeTTS is designed as a modular system. Each of the steps listed above is processed by a specialized Utterance Processor. An *utterance* is the basic data structure in FreeTTS. It may contain the complete text that is to be spoken but may later be broken into individual phrases, which again are represented as Utterance instances.

Each utterance consists of a set of lists (in FreeTTS these are called *relations*). These include the lists of syllables, words, segments (results of the Segmenter), and so on. The various utterance processors perform read and write accesses to these lists.

Detailed information about the architecture of FreeTTS is found in the FreeTTS *Programmer's Guide* (contained in the FreeTTS documentation).

Extending the FreeTTS System

You can derive the information needed for lip synchronization from the durations computed in step 8, where the duration of each single segment (phoneme) was determined. The best point for invoking the lip synchronization, however, is between steps 12 and 13, as close as possible to the audio output.

You can generate the events for lip synchronization by implementing your own utterance processor, called Animator. This processor derives events (AnimationEvent) from the end times stored in each segment and sends these events to an AnimationListener at the right time. You can control this with your own timer.

Animation Events

First, implement the AnimationEvent class and the AnimationListener interface. Both are stored in the com.sun.speech.freetts.relp package. Listing 5.1 shows the code for AnimationEvent.java.

```
package com.sun.speech.freetts.relp;

public class AnimationEvent {

    public int endTime;
    public String phone;

    /**
      * Constructor
```

Listing 5.1 (Continues)

```
    * @param endTime - the end time of the phoneme in msec
    * @param phone - the phoneme string
    */
   public AnimationEvent(int endTime, String phone) {
       this.endTime = endTime;
       this.phone = phone;
   }
}
```

Listing 5.1 (Continued)

Creating a New Class

To create the `AnimationEvent` class,

1. Create the `com.sun.speech.freetts.relp` package in the `DukeSpeaks` project by pressing the Create a Java Package button on the workbench's toolbar.

2. Before creating new classes you should complete the code-generation template for constructors by adding the `Constructor` headline. You do this under Window > Preferences > Java > Code Style > Code Templates > Comments > Constructors.

3. After entering the package name and pressing Finish, create the new class `AnimationEvent`. To do so, click the Create a Java Class button on the workbench's toolbar. Enter the name of the class (`AnimationEvent`) and press the Finish button.

4. Start entering code. You don't have to enter much: you need only create the two fields `endTime` and `phone`, and you must modify the constructor as shown above. When creating comments you can make use of the Source > Add JavaDoc Comment context function. If you apply this function on the constructor, Eclipse will create a Javadoc comment in front of the constructor. (The same function can be invoked by entering the string `/**` in a new line in front of the constructor and then pressing the Enter key.) You only have to complete the text strings after `@param endTime` and after `@param phone`.

Creating a New Interface

Then you can create the `AnimationListener` interface in the same package. This one is also quite simple. Listing 5.2 shows the code for the `AnimationListener.java` interface.

```
package com.sun.speech.freetts.relp;

public interface AnimationListener {

    /**
     * Method processAnimationEvent.
     * @param e AnimationEvent object
     */
    public void processAnimationEvent(AnimationEvent e);
}
```

Listing 5.2

Follow these steps to create the interface:

1. Before creating the interface, you should complete the method code-generation template by adding the `Method ${enclosing_method}` headline. You can do so under Window > Preferences > Java> Code Style > Code Templates > Comments > Methods.

2. Press the Create a Java Interface button on the workbench's toolbar. Here, too, you can use the Source > Add JavaDoc Comment context function when entering comments. If you apply this function on the `processAnimationEvent` method, you only have to complete the text string after `@param e`.

The Animator

Now you can create the `Animator` class, which is also in the `com.sun.speech.freetts.relp` package. This class implements the `com.sun.speech.freetts.UtteranceProcessor` interface with the `processUtterance()` method. The `Animator` receives the `Utterance` instance it needs to process via this method. However, you cannot use this method to start animation, because the startup time needed by FreeTTS and the Java audio system would cause the animation to run ahead of the speech output. To keep the animation fully synchronous, you have to catch the `START` event of the audio system. For this purpose you also need to implement the `javax.sound.sampled.LineListener` interface with the `update()` method. After receiving the `START` event you can use your own timer to generate animation events. To react to the events of this timer, implement the additional `java.awt.event.ActionListener` interface with the `actionPerformed()` method. Once you have generated the animation events, pass them to all `AnimationListener` objects that have registered via the `addAnimationListener()` method.

Creating a Class with Interfaces

You can create this class, too, by clicking the Create a Java Class button, but this time you not only enter the name of the new class into the dialog, you also press the *Add* button to enter the names of the interfaces that this class is going to implement. Usually, it is sufficient to enter just a few characters to qualify the interface. You need to add the following interfaces: `UtteranceProcessor`, `LineListener`, and `ActionListener`. Then press the *Finish* button. Eclipse will now generate a class skeleton that includes all the methods declared in the specified interfaces: `processUtterance()`, `update()`, and `actionPerformed()`. However, this is done only if the Inherited Abstract Methods check box was marked. If you did not do this, you can easily fix the problem and create the new class by applying the Source > Override/Implement Methods context function.

Actually, it didn't matter that you did not have access to the source code of the `LineListener` interface. Eclipse is able to retrieve the required information from the binary object.

Eclipse decorates all generated method stubs with a `TODO` comment. These comments will show up in the Tasks window as entries and will thus remind you to complete the implementation of these methods.

Using the Code Assistant

When entering the code, you should not enter `import` statements and Javadoc comments at this time. Most of the `import` statements are automatically inserted by subsequently using the code assistant (Ctrl+Spacebar) anyway. After you have entered all the code, you can easily add any missing `import` statements by invoking the Source > Organize Imports context function. The Javadoc comments are created with the Source > Add JavaDoc Comment context function or by entering the string /** and pressing Enter. You complete these comments only as required.

When entering method code you can use existing code templates: pri followed by Ctrl+Spacebar generates a stub for a private method; pub followed by Ctrl+Spacebar generates a stub for a public method.

In addition, you don't have to spell out the names of types, methods, and fields. In most cases it is sufficient to type only a few letters and then call the Code Assistant by pressing Ctrl+Spacebar.

The Animator.java Class

The Animator class acts as a controller. Utterances processed by the speech engine are intercepted by the Animator who will produce animation events and post them to registered listeners. A timer object is used to produce the animation events at the correct moment.

```java
package com.sun.speech.freetts.relp;

import java.awt.event.ActionEvent;
import java.awt.event.ActionListener;
import java.util.ArrayList;
import java.util.Iterator;
import java.util.List;

import javax.sound.sampled.LineEvent;
import javax.sound.sampled.LineListener;
import javax.swing.Timer;

import com.sun.speech.freetts.*;

public class Animator
    implements UtteranceProcessor, ActionListener, LineListener {

        // List of AnimationListener instances
        List listeners = new ArrayList(3);
        // Swing Timer object
        Timer timer;
        // Current segment in the segment list
        Item segment;
        // Start time of current segment
        int currentTime = 0;
```

addAnimationListener()

Listeners of type AnimationListener can register with the Animator via method addAnimationListener(). The Animator will post animation events to these listeners.

```java
/**
 * Method addAnimationListener.
 * @param l AnimationListener object
 */
public void addAnimationListener(AnimationListener l) {
    listeners.add(l);
```

```
        }
        /**
         * Method removeAnimationListener.
         * @param l AnimationListener object
         */
        public void removeAnimationListener(AnimationListener l) {
            listeners.remove(l);
        }
```

processUtterance()

Utterances produced by the speech engine are intercepted and processed in method processUtterance(). This method just resets the timer from a previous utterance and retrieves the first segment of the utterance.

```
        /**
         * @see com.sun.speech.freetts.UtteranceProcessor#
         * processUtterance(Utterance)
         */
        public void processUtterance(Utterance utterance)
            throws ProcessException {
                // Reset current time
                currentTime = 0;
                // Stop time if it is still running (previous utterance)
                if (timer != null && timer.isRunning())
                    timer.stop();
                // Fetch first segment of utterance
                segment = utterance.getRelation(Relation.SEGMENT).getHead();
            }
```

actionPerformed()

When the timer expires, and animation event is posted to all registered listeners

```
        /**
         * @see
         * java.awt.event.ActionListener#actionPerformed(ActionEvent)
         */
        // Is executed when the timer expires

        public void actionPerformed(ActionEvent e) {
            // Fire event
            fireAnimationEvent();
        }
```

fireAnimationEvent()

In this case, the end time of the utterance is fetched from the retrieved segment. An AnimationEvent object with this end time is created and posted to all registered listeners. Then a new timer object, which will expire at this end time, is created.

```
/**
 * Method fireAnimationEvent.
 */
private void fireAnimationEvent() {
    // If segment == null we have reached the end of the list
    if (segment != null) {
        // Fetch end time from segment and convert to msec
        int end =
            (int) (1000 * segment.getFeatures().getFloat("end"));
        // Get phoneme from segment
        String phone = segment.getFeatures().getString("name");
        // Advance in segment list
        segment = segment.getNext();
        // Create new AnimationEvent object
        AnimationEvent e = new AnimationEvent(end, phone);
        // Send it to all AnimationListener objects
        Iterator iter = listeners.iterator();
        while (iter.hasNext()) {
            AnimationListener listener =
                (AnimationListener) iter.next();
            listener.processAnimationEvent(e);
        }
        // Create new timer that expires at the end time
        // of the current phoneme.
        timer = new Timer(end - currentTime, this);
        timer.setRepeats(false);
        timer.setCoalesce(false);
        timer.start();
        // Update current time
        currentTime = end;
    }
}
```

update()

The whole animation is started when a START line event arrives. The Animator receives such events because it is registered as a LineListener with the Java Sound System.

```
/**
 * @see javax.sound.sampled.LineListener#update(LineEvent)
 */
public void update(LineEvent event) {
    if (event.getType().equals(LineEvent.Type.START)) {
        // Audio output has started - start animation, too.
        // Fire first event
        fireAnimationEvent();
    }
}

/**
 * @see java.lang.Object#toString()
 */
public String toString() {
    return "Animator";
}
}
```

Embedding into FreeTTS

Because you want to position the animator as close as possible to the audio output, you need to call it from the AudioOutput utterance processor. Of course, you don't want to modify the existing AudioOutput class. Therefore, create a subclass of this class and override the processUtterance() method. Please note the little up-arrow appearing to the left beneath this method. It indicates that this method overrides an inherited definition. By hovering with the mouse above the arrow you can display further information about what was overridden, and by clicking the arrow you can navigate to the over-ridden version, too.

The AnimatedAudioOutput.java class

Listing 5.3 shows the code of the AnimatedAudioOutput class. Please note the call to the Animator in method processUtterance().

```java
package com.sun.speech.freetts.relp;

import com.sun.speech.freetts.ProcessException;
import com.sun.speech.freetts.Utterance;
import com.sun.speech.freetts.UtteranceProcessor;

public class AnimatedAudioOutput extends AudioOutput {

    UtteranceProcessor animator;

    /**
     * Method AnimatedAudioOutput.
     * @param animator Animator object for generating animation events
     */
    public AnimatedAudioOutput(UtteranceProcessor animator) {
        // Initialize animator field
        this.animator = animator;
    }

    /**
     * @see com.sun.speech.freetts.UtteranceProcessor#
     * processUtterance(Utterance)
     */
    public void processUtterance(Utterance u) throws ProcessException {
        // In case we got an Animator we invoke its
        // processUtterance method.
        if (animator != null)
            animator.processUtterance(u);
        // Then proceed as usual
        super.processUtterance(u);
    }
}
```

Listing 5.3

Creating a Subclass

Again, you can create this class with the Create a Java Class button. This time you not only enter the name of the new class, but you also press the Browse button at the right-hand side of the Superclass field. There, select the `AudioOutput` field from the list. Click Finish, and you can start to enter code. In the case of `import` statements and Javadoc comments, just proceed as discussed previously.

When you enter the `processUtterance()` method, the Source > OverrideMethods context function will save you some work. In this function's dialog box mark the `processUtterance()` method below the `AudioOutput` class. Then you need only add the lines for calling the `processUtterance()` method from the `Animator` instance.

Alternatively, you use the Code Assistant to create specific method stubs. For example, to create a stub for the `processUtterance()` method you need only type the letters `pro` and press Ctrl+Spacebar. Then select `processUtterance` from the list.

After you have completed this class, you must tell FreeTTS to use `AnimatedAudioOutput` instead of `AudioOutput`. Which utterance processor is used for audio output is determined in the subclasses of the `com.sun.speech.freetts.Voice` class in the `getAudioOutput()` method. Since you plan to use the voice

```
com.sun.speech.freetts.en.us.CMUDiphoneVoice
```

for your application, you need to extend this class.

For this purpose, create a new `com.sun.speech.freetts.en.us` package in the `DukeSpeaks` project. In this package create a new class named `AnimatedDiphoneVoice`.

The AnimatedDiphoneVoice.java class

When creating the AnimatedDiphoneVoice class, specify `CMUDiphoneVoice` as a super class and check the Constructors from Superclass option. In the generated constructor add the new `animator` parameter and store this parameter in an instance field. See Listing 5.4.

```java
package com.sun.speech.freetts.en.us;

import java.io.IOException;
import java.net.URL;
import java.util.Locale;
import com.sun.speech.freetts.Age;
import com.sun.speech.freetts.Gender;
import com.sun.speech.freetts.UtteranceProcessor;
import com.sun.speech.freetts.relp.AnimatedAudioOutput;

public class AnimatedDiphoneVoice extends CMUDiphoneVoice {

    UtteranceProcessor animator;

/**
 * Constructor
 * @param name - the name of the voice
 * @param gender - the gender of the voice
```

Listing 5.4 (Continues)

```
 * @param age - the age of the voice
 * @param description - a human-readable string providing a
 *              description that can be displayed to users.
 * @param locale - the locale of the voice
 * @param domain - the voice domain, e.g. general, time, wheather
 * @param organization the organization which created the voice
 * @param lexicon - the lexicon to load
 * @param database - a url to the unit database file for this voice
 * @param animator - the animator for lip synchronization
 */
  public AnimatedDiphoneVoice(String name,Gender gender,Age age,
    String description, Locale locale, String domain,
    String organization, CMULexicon lexicon, URL database,
    UtteranceProcessor animator) {
    super(name, gender, age, description, locale, domain,
      organization, lexicon, database);
    this.animator = animator;
  }


  /**
   * @see com.sun.speech.freetts.Voice#getAudioOutput()
   */
  protected UtteranceProcessor getAudioOutput() throws IOException {
      return new AnimatedAudioOutput(animator);
  }
}
```

Listing 5.4 (Continued)

Because you want this class to create an AnimatedAudioOutput, you must override the getAudioOutput() method. Here, too, you can make use of the Source > Override Methods context function. In the dialog that appears, mark the getAudioOutput() method below the CMUVoice class Then, just complete the method as shown above.

Connection with the Java Audio System

What is still missing is the program logic for starting the animator. Here, you must first register the Animator as LineListener with a javax.sound.sampled.Line object. Such an object is created by the com.sun.speech.freetts.audio.JavaClipAudioPlayer player in the end() method in the disguise of a javax.sound.sampled.Clip object.

The correct way to extend JavaClipAudioPlayer would be to subclass it. But unfortunately JavaClipAudioPlayer proves to be a stubborn beast. Too many private fields prevent us from applying the required extensions. Therefore, choose a different path. Simply create a copy of JavaClipAudioPlayer, which you then can modify easily. Theoretically, you could use the Copy function of the Package Explorer, but unfortunately this function cannot be applied to the contents of external JARs. Therefore, you must first create the new com.sun.speech.freetts.audio package in the DukeSpeaks project and create in this package the new AnimatedAudioPlayer class. Then open the JavaClipAudioPlayer class in the FreeTTS package, select the whole text (Ctrl+A), and copy it (Ctrl+C) to the clipboard. Then select the whole text in the new AnimatedAudioPlayer class and replace it with with the contents of the clipboard (Ctrl+V). Now, you can start modifying this class for your requirements. (Modifications are printed in bold type.)

First, create a new private field:

```
private LineListener externalLineListener;
```

In the constructor, insert an equally named parameter and initialize the `externalLineListener` field with the parameter value:

```
/**
 * Constructs a default AnimatedAudioPlayer
 */
public AnimatedAudioPlayer(LineListener externalLineListener) {
    this.externalLineListener = externalLineListener;
    debug = Boolean.getBoolean
        ("com.sun.speech.freetts.audio.AudioPlayer.debug");
    closeDelay = Long.getLong
        ("com.sun.speech.freetts.audio.AudioPlayer.closeDelay",
            150L).longValue();
    setPaused(false);
}
```

Then register `externalLineListener` in the `end()` method with the `Clip` object:

```
...
DataLine.Info info = new DataLine.Info(Clip.class, currentFormat);
Clip clip = (Clip) AudioSystem.getLine(info);
clip.addLineListener(lineListener);
clip.addLineListener(externalLineListener);
clip.open(currentFormat, outputData, 0, outputData.length);
setVolume(clip, volume);
...
```

Finally, apply the Source > Organize Imports function to remove all unnecessary `import` statements.

The User Interface

The user interface is implemented with Swing. Since no Eclipse components are used at all, you can easily execute this application outside of Eclipse.

The other reason for using Swing is that I want to demonstrate the Eclipse Visual Editor (VE), which in its current version (0.5) supports only Swing.

Because the code contains only standard Java programming, there is little to learn about Eclipse APIs in this section. Therefore, I will not discuss the code in detail but provide only a short overview.

The Animated Face

The face with the lip synchronization is implemented as a subclass of the Swing JPanel class. This class has the name Face and is created in the com.bdaum.dukeSpeaks package. The class implements the AnimationListener interface, which was created in the "Animation Events" section. This allows you to register the face as AnimationListener with an Animator instance. It will receive AnimationEvents from the Animator and can then react accordingly to these events.

```
The Face.java class

package com.bdaum.dukeSpeaks;
import java.awt.*;

import javax.swing.JPanel;

import com.sun.speech.freetts.relp.AnimationEvent;
import com.sun.speech.freetts.relp.AnimationListener;

public class Face extends JPanel implements AnimationListener {

  // Relative mouth dimensions, derived from current phoneme
  float mouthWidth = 0.80f;
  float mouthHeight = 0.05f;
  // Relative eye pupil position, derived from current phoneme
  float eyePos = 0.16f;
```

The processAnimationEvent() method receives animation events (AnimationEvent). From the transmitted phoneme it computes the size and shape of the mouth and the position of the eye pupils. The mouth is always drawn as an ellipsoid but with varying positions and diameters. After these values are computed, the repaint() method is called. This enforces the redrawing of the Face component.

```
/**
 * @see com.sun.speech.freetts.relp.AnimationListener
 *                  #processAnimationEvent(AnimationEvent)
 */
public void processAnimationEvent(AnimationEvent e) {
  // Set current phoneme
  String phone = e.phone;
  if (phone.equals("pau")) {
    // In pauses pupils must look upwards
    eyePos = 0.15f;
    // In pauses mouth remains closed
    mouthWidth = 0.80f;
    mouthHeight = 0.05f;
  } else {
    // Otherwise pupils look downwards
    eyePos = 0.4f;
    // Analyze first character of phoneme
    char p1 = phone.charAt(0);
    switch (p1) {
      // Uh's and Oh's
      case 'o' :
```

```
      case 'u' :
        mouthWidth = 0.5f;
        mouthHeight = 0.5f;
        break;
        // Ah's
      case 'a' :
        mouthWidth = 0.75f;
        mouthHeight = 0.75f;
        break;
        // Eh's and Ih's
      case 'e' :
      case 'i' :
        mouthWidth = 1f;
        mouthHeight = 0.1f;
        break;
        // Alles andere
      default :
        mouthWidth = 0.6f;
        mouthHeight = 0.3f;
        break;
    }
  }
  repaint();
}
```

The paintComponent() method is called when the Face component is redrawn. The graphical context is passed as a parameter. Via a type cast (Graphics2D) you convert it into a Java2D context. Then you enable anti-aliasing and employ the usual graphical methods such as fillOval(), drawOval(), or drawPolyline() to draw the face. The size and position of the mouth and the eye pupils depend on the values previously computed from the transmitted phonemes.

```
/**
 * @see javax.swing.JComponent#paintComponent(Graphics)
 */
protected void paintComponent(Graphics cg) {
  super.paintComponent(cg);
  // Cast for Java2D
  Graphics2D g = (Graphics2D) cg;
  // Compute component size
  Dimension d = getSize();
  int width = (int) d.getWidth();
  int height = (int) d.getHeight();
  // Switch off Antialiasing
  g.setRenderingHint(
    RenderingHints.KEY_ANTIALIASING,
    RenderingHints.VALUE_ANTIALIAS_ON);
  // Draw face
  g.setColor(Color.white);
  g.fillOval(0, 0, width, height);
  // Some face dimensions
  int midX = width / 2;
  int midY = height * 3 / 4;
  int eyeDia = height / 10;
```

```
        int eyeInner = eyeDia / 2;
        int eyeY = height / 4;
        int eyeX = midX - eyeDia / 3;
        int eyeOff = width / 6;
        int noseY = height / 3;
        int noseLength = height / 4;
        int noseWidth = width / 12;
        // Draw eyes
        g.setColor(Color.blue);
        g.drawOval(midX - eyeOff - eyeDia / 3, eyeY, eyeDia, eyeDia);
        g.drawOval(midX + eyeOff - eyeDia / 3, eyeY, eyeDia, eyeDia);
        // Draw eye pupils
        int ey = eyeY + ((int) (eyeDia * eyePos));
        g.fillOval(eyeX - eyeOff, ey, eyeInner, eyeInner);
        g.fillOval(eyeX + eyeOff, ey, eyeDia / 2, eyeDia / 2);
        // Draw nose
        g.drawPolyline(
          new int[] { midX, midX + noseWidth, midX },
          new int[] { noseY, noseY + noseLength, noseY + noseLength },
          3);
        // Compute mouth dimensions
        int mw = (int) (width * mouthWidth / 4);
        int mh = (int) (height * mouthHeight / 4);
        int mx = midX - mw / 2;
        int my = midY - mh / 4;
        // Draw mouth
        g.fillOval(mx, my, mw, mh);
    }
}
```

The Control Panel

Now you can begin to construct the control panel. This unit must contain the animated face in its center, below the face a field for text entry, at the left and right of the face sliders for adjusting volume, speed, pitch, and variation.

Two new classes and one interface are needed to implement this control unit:

❑   The PlayerModel interface specifies the interface of the control panel's domain model.

❑   This interface is implemented by the PlayerModelImpl class.

❑   The PlayerPanel class implements the presentation of the data and the various control instruments with the help of Swing.

So, the typical MVC design pattern (Model-View-Controller) is used here. PlayerPanel acts as both a viewer and a controller.

The Model

When implementing the domain model you have the choice of writing the implementation class first or starting with the definition of the interface. In fact, you could omit the interface altogether, but having a separate interface adds some flexibility:

❏   When you opt to create the `PlayerModel` interface first, you can specify the interface later when you create the `PlayerModelImpl` class. Eclipse will then generate all the method stubs for you. This method is particularly interesting if you already have a clear idea of the domain model's API.

❏   Otherwise, when you opt to create the `PlayerModelImpl` implementation first, you can later easily generate the `PlayerModel` interface from the implementation with the help of the Refactor > Extract Interface context function. This technique is recommended when the API of the model is shaped during the implementation. Actually, in the beginning you can work without an interface entirely. You simply use the methods of the implementation. Later, when your domain model has matured and is stable, you can derive the interface with the mentioned context function. This function will also replace all implementation methods' references with references to interface methods, provided this does not lead to compilation problems.

The main task of a `PlayerModel` instance (Listing 5.5) is to encapsulate a FreeTTS `Voice` and to provide access methods to control volume, speed, pitch, and variation. In addition, there is a `play()` method that runs the `speak()` method of the `Voice` instance in a separate thread. For this task you can use a `SwingWorker` instance, so that the speech process does not lock up the GUI.

The `SwingWorker` class that is called from the `play()` method does not belong to the `javax.swing` packages, but you can obtain it from `http://java.sun.com/docs/books/tutorial/uiswing/ misc/ threads.html` or as part of this example's source code from `www.wrox.com`.

```
The PlayerModel.java interface

package com.bdaum.dukeSpeaks;
public interface PlayerModel {

  /**
   * Returns the volume.
   *
   * @return the volume, or -1 if unknown, or an error occurred
   */
  public float getVolume();

  /**
   * Sets the volume.
   *
   * @param volume set the volume of the synthesizer
   */
  public void setVolume(float volume);

  /**
   * Returns the speaking rate.
   *
   * @return the speaking rate, or -1 if unknown or an error occurred
   */
  public float getSpeakingRate();

  /**
   * Sets the speaking rate in the number of words per minute.
   *
   * @param wordsPerMin the speaking rate
   */
```

Listing 5.5 (Continues)

```java
    public void setSpeakingRate(float wordsPerMin);

    /**
     * Returns the baseline pitch for the current synthesis voice.
     *
     * @return the baseline pitch for the current synthesis voice
     */
    public float getPitch();

    /**
     * Sets the baseline pitch for the current synthesis voice.
     *
     * @param pitch the baseline pitch
     */
    public void setPitch(float pitch);

    /**
     * Returns the pitch range for the current synthesis voice.
     *
     * @return the pitch range for the current synthesis voice
     */
    public float getRange();

    /**
     * Sets the pitch range for the current synthesis voice.
     *
     * @param range the pitch range
     */
    public void setRange(float range);

    /**
     * Performs text-to-speech on the given text.
     *
     * @param text the text to perform TTS
     */
    public void play(String text);
}

The PlayerModelImpl.java class

package com.bdaum.dukeSpeaks;

import com.sun.speech.freetts.Voice;

public class PlayerModelImpl implements PlayerModel {

    // The Voice instance used in this model
    private Voice voice;
    // Semaphore for inhibiting double playing
    private boolean playing = false;

    /**
     * Method PlayerModelImpl.
     * @param voice a FreeTTS voice object.
     */
    public PlayerModelImpl(Voice voice) {
      this.voice = voice;
```

Listing 5.5 (Continues)

```
    }

    /**
     * @see PlayerModel#play(String)
     */
    public void play(final String text) {
      // do nothing if player runs already.
      if (playing)
        return;
      // Set semaphore to true
      playing = true;
      // The speech process runs in a separate thread
      // that is managed by the SwingWorker instance worker
      final SwingWorker worker = new SwingWorker() {
        public Object construct() {
          // This is where Duke speaks
          voice.speak(text);
          return null;
        }
      };
      worker.start();
      // Reset semaphore
      playing = false;
    }

    /**
     * @see PlayerModel#getVolume()
     */
    public float getVolume() {
      // Get volume from Voice instance
      // and convert to scale range 0-10
      float adjustedVolume = voice.getVolume();
      return (adjustedVolume < 0.5)
        ? 0f
        : (float) ((adjustedVolume - 0.5) * 20);
    }

    /**
     * @see PlayerModel#setVolume(float)
     */
    public void setVolume(float volume) {
      // Set volume in Voice instance
      // convert from scale range 0-10 to Voice range 0.5-1.0
      float adjustedVolume = (float) (volume / 20 + 0.5);
      voice.setVolume(adjustedVolume);
    }

    /**
     * @see PlayerModel#getSpeakingRate()
     */
    public float getSpeakingRate() {
      // Get speaking rate from Voice instance
      return voice.getRate();
    }

    /**
     * @see PlayerModel#setSpeakingRate(float)
     */
    public void setSpeakingRate(float wordsPerMin) {
```

Listing 5.5 (Continues)

```
    // Set speaking rate in Voice instance
    voice.setRate(wordsPerMin);
}

/**
 * @see PlayerModel#getPitch()
 */
public float getPitch() {
    // Get pitch from Voice instance
    return voice.getPitch();
}

/**
 * @see PlayerModel#setPitch(float)
 */
public void setPitch(float pitch) {
    // Set pitch in Voice instance
    voice.setPitch(pitch);
}

/**
 * @see PlayerModel#getRange()
 */
public float getRange() {
    // Get variation from Voice instance
    return voice.getPitchRange();
}

/**
 * @see PlayerModel#setRange(float)
 */
public void setRange(float range) {
    // Set variation in Voice instance
    voice.setPitchRange(range);
}
}
```

Listing 5.5 (Continued)

The Presentation

After defining the domain model you can implement the visible part of the user interface. This is done in the PlayerPanel class, which is implemented as a subclass of the Swing JPanel class in the com.bdaum.dukeSpeaks package.

To implement this class you can use the Visual Editor for Java (VE) that was already discussed in Chapter 3. After creating the PlayerPanel class in the usual way, define the instance fields and the constructor (Listing 5.6).

```
public class PlayerPanel {

    // The data model
    private PlayerModel playerModel;
```

Listing 5.6 (Continues)

```
  // The JPanel instance for the face
  private JPanel face;

  public PlayerPanel(PlayerModel playerModel, JPanel face) {
    super();
    // Save parameters into fields
    this.playerModel = playerModel;
    this.face = face;
  }
}
```

Listing 5.6 (Continued)

Visual Editor

Now you can close the Java Editor and open the same class again with the Visual Editor. Figure 5.1 shows the hierarchy of GUI elements. First, place a `JPanel` component into the design area and pull it up to 600 by 500 pixels, or enter this size in the Size entry in the Properties View. Then you can subdivide this content pane into additional `JPanels` in order to place the face and sliders for volume, speed, pitch, and variation on top of it. In addition, you need a field for text input, a few buttons, and, of course, the necessary event processing for these control elements.

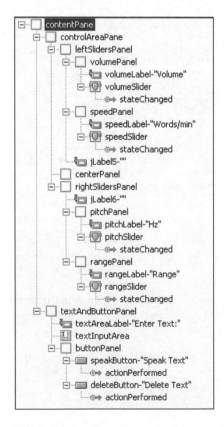

Figure 5.1

Layouts

Most of these panels use BorderLayouts or GridLayouts, but for the buttonPanel a FlowLayout is used. In the BorderLayouts the most important element is placed into the Center area; all other elements are placed into the North, South, East, or West areas. For example, each slider sits in the Center area of its panel, while the corresponding label is placed into the North area. The centerPanel component has a GridLayout of the size 1x1. The single grid field will later contain the Face component. Using the GridLayout guarantees that the Face component is correctly resized when the size of the window changes. Also the leftSlidersPanel and rightSlidersPanel panels are equipped with GridLayouts. One grid cell is filled with an empty label that acts as spacer. The following table shows which Layout is used for which component.

Panel	Layout	Row	Column
contentPanel	BorderLayout	-	-
controlAreaPanel	GridLayout	1	3
leftSlidersPanel	GridLayout	1	3
volumePanel	BorderLayout	-	-
speedPanel	BorderLayout	-	-
centerPanel	GridLayout	1	1
rightSlidersPanel	GridLayout	1	3
pitchPanel	BorderLayout	-	-
rangePanel	BorderLayout	-	-
textAreaAndButtonsPanel	BorderLayout	-	-
buttonPanel	FlowLayout	-	-

Sliders

The sliders also need some adjustments in the Properties view. First, you must set their orientation to VERTICAL. Then you must specify the minimum and maximum values and the scaling (minorTickSpacing and majorTickSpacing), and you must indicate that the track, scale, and labels must be drawn, that is, you must set the paintLabels, paintTicks, and paintTrack attributes to true. You should also specify an appropriate tooltip under toolTipText. The following table shows the bounding and scaling attributes of the various sliders.

Slider	Minimum	Maximum	minorTick	majorTick
volumeSlider	0	10	1	5
speedSlider	0	400	50	100
pitchSlider	50	200	25	50
rangeSlider	0	50	5	10

Events

In addition, you need to implement some event processing for each slider. To do so, apply the Events > stateChanged context function to each slider and replace the pregenerated instruction System.out.println() with

```
playerModel.setVolume((float) volumeSlider.getValue());
```

for the volumeSlider,

```
playerModel.setSpeakingRate((float) speedSlider.getValue());
```

for the speedSlider,

```
playerModel.setPitch((float) pitchSlider.getValue());
```

for the pitchSlider, and

```
playerModel.setRange((float) rangeSlider.getValue());
```

for the rangeSlider.

Labels

For the corresponding labels you should set an appropriate text (as discussed in Chapter 3) in the text attribute. In addition, set an appropriate mnemonic code in the displayedMnemonic attribute. However, this definition alone is not sufficient. It does not make sense that the label gets the focus when the defined mnemonic key accelerator is pressed. Instead, the corresponding slider should get the focus. You can achieve this via the setLabelFor() method, for example:

```
rangeLabel.setLabelFor(rangeSlider);
```

By doing so, you could later control the application completely without a mouse and thus improve the accessibility. However, at the moment, the above instruction does not make much sense, because you cannot be sure that the specified rangeSlider instance already exists. You should, therefore, defer the implementation of this instruction to a later time (see below in method getContentPane()).

Text

The same is true for the textAreaLabel belonging to the text input area. For the textInputArea component the number of lines should be set to five, the lineWrap attribute should be set to true, and under text an appropriate example text should be specified.

Buttons

For the buttons specify the labeling (text), a tooltip (toolTipText), a mnemonic (displayedMnemonic), and optionally a different background color (background). Here, too, you need to generate appropriate event processing via Events > actionPerformed and to replace the generated System.out.println() instructions with

```
String inputText = textInputArea.getText();
if (inputText.length() > 0)
  playerModel.play(inputText);
```

for the Speak button and

```
textInputArea.setText("");
```

for the Clear button.

Figure 5.2 shows how the finished PlayerPanel looks in the Visual Editor. The large empty area in the center is reserved for the Face component; to the left and right of this area are spacers.

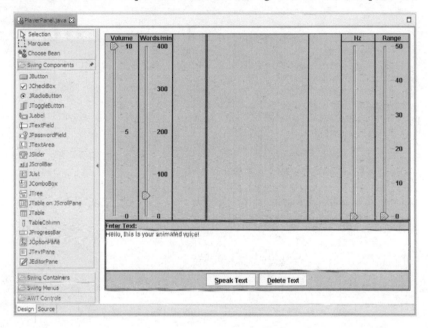

Figure 5.2

Integration

The graphical design of the user interface of your application is now nearly completed. What is still missing is the integration of the Face component, the initialization of the sliders, and making the content pane visible to the application. You need to embed the Face component into the centerPanel as follows:

```
private javax.swing.JPanel getCenterPanel() {
    if(centerPanel == null) {
        centerPanel = new javax.swing.JPanel();
        centerPanel.setLayout(new java.awt.GridLayout(1,1));
        centerPanel.add(face);
    }
    return centerPanel;
}
```

ContentPane

To make the content pane visible to the application, declare the getContentPane() method as public. In addition, insert the initialization of the sliders into this method. Also, you can now insert all setLabelFor() methods, because after the execution of the method body, you can be sure that all target objects of setLabelFor() exist.

```java
public javax.swing.JPanel getContentPane() {
  if(contentPane == null) {
    contentPane = new javax.swing.JPanel();
    contentPane.setLayout(new java.awt.BorderLayout());
    contentPane.add(getControlAreaPane(),
                    java.awt.BorderLayout.CENTER);
    contentPane.add(getTextAndButtonPanel(),
                    java.awt.BorderLayout.SOUTH);
    contentPane.setSize(new java.awt.Dimension(600,500));
    volumeLabel.setLabelFor(volumeSlider);
    speedLabel.setLabelFor(speedSlider);
    pitchLabel.setLabelFor(pitchSlider);
    rangeLabel.setLabelFor(rangeSlider);
    textAreaLabel.setLabelFor(textInputArea);
    updateSliders();
  }
  return contentPane;
}
```

The updateSliders() method is defined as follows:

```java
private void updateSliders() {
  // Volume
  int volume = (int) playerModel.getVolume();
  if (volume >= 0)
    volumeSlider.setValue(volume);
  // Speed
  int rate = (int) playerModel.getSpeakingRate();
  if (rate >= 0)
    speedSlider.setValue(rate);
  // Pitch
  int pitch = (int) playerModel.getPitch();
  if (pitch >= 0)
    pitchSlider.setValue(pitch);
  // Variation
  int range = (int) playerModel.getRange();
  if (range >= 0)
    rangeSlider.setValue(range);
}
```

Listing 5.7 contains the complete source code of the PlayerPanel class as generated by the Visual Editor, with the necessary source code modifications applied.

```java
package com.bdaum.dukeSpeaks;

import java.awt.GridLayout;
import javax.swing.JPanel;

public class PlayerPanel {

  // The data model
  private PlayerModel playerModel;
  // The JPanel instance for the face
  private JPanel face;


  private javax.swing.JPanel contentPane = null;
  private javax.swing.JPanel controlAreaPane = null;
  private javax.swing.JPanel leftSlidersPanel = null;
  private javax.swing.JPanel centerPanel = null;
  private javax.swing.JPanel rightSlidersPanel = null;
  private javax.swing.JPanel volumePanel = null;
  private javax.swing.JLabel volumeLabel = null;
  private javax.swing.JSlider volumeSlider = null;
  private javax.swing.JPanel speedPanel = null;
  private javax.swing.JLabel speedLabel = null;
  private javax.swing.JSlider speedSlider = null;
  private javax.swing.JPanel pitchPanel = null;
  private javax.swing.JLabel pitchLabel = null;
  private javax.swing.JSlider pitchSlider = null;
  private javax.swing.JPanel rangePanel = null;
  private javax.swing.JLabel rangeLabel = null;
  private javax.swing.JSlider rangeSlider = null;
  private javax.swing.JPanel textAndButtonPanel = null;
  private javax.swing.JLabel textAreaLabel = null;
  private javax.swing.JPanel buttonPanel = null;
  private javax.swing.JButton speakButton = null;
  private javax.swing.JButton deleteButton = null;
  private javax.swing.JTextArea textInputArea = null;
  private javax.swing.JLabel jLabel5 = null;
  private javax.swing.JLabel jLabel6 = null;
  /**
   *
   */
  public PlayerPanel(PlayerModel playerModel, JPanel face) {
    super();
    // Save parameters into fields
    this.playerModel = playerModel;
    this.face = face;
  }

  /**
   * Method updateSliders.
   * updates all the sliders with values from the PlayerModel.
   */
  private void updateSliders() {
    // Volume
```

Listing 5.7 (Continues)

```
        int volume = (int) playerModel.getVolume();
        if (volume >= 0)
          volumeSlider.setValue(volume);
        // Speed
        int rate = (int) playerModel.getSpeakingRate();
        if (rate >= 0)
          speedSlider.setValue(rate);
        // Pitch
        int pitch = (int) playerModel.getPitch();
        if (pitch >= 0)
          pitchSlider.setValue(pitch);
        // Variation
        int range = (int) playerModel.getRange();
        if (range >= 0)
          rangeSlider.setValue(range);
    }

    public javax.swing.JPanel getContentPane() {
        if(contentPane == null) {
          contentPane = new javax.swing.JPanel();
          contentPane.setLayout(new java.awt.BorderLayout());
          contentPane.add(getControlAreaPane(),
java.awt.BorderLayout.CENTER);
          contentPane.add(getTextAndButtonPanel(),
java.awt.BorderLayout.SOUTH);
          contentPane.setSize(new java.awt.Dimension(600,500));
          volumeLabel.setLabelFor(volumeSlider);
          speedLabel.setLabelFor(speedSlider);
          pitchLabel.setLabelFor(pitchSlider);
          rangeLabel.setLabelFor(rangeSlider);
          textAreaLabel.setLabelFor(textInputArea);
          updateSliders();
        }
        return contentPane;
    }
    /**
     * This method initializes controlAreaPane
     *
     * @return javax.swing.JPanel
     */
    private javax.swing.JPanel getControlAreaPane() {
        if(controlAreaPane == null) {
          controlAreaPane = new javax.swing.JPanel();
          controlAreaPane.setLayout(new GridLayout(1, 3));
          controlAreaPane.add(getLeftSlidersPanel());
          controlAreaPane.add(getCenterPanel());
          controlAreaPane.add(getRightSlidersPanel());
        }
        return controlAreaPane;
    }
    /**
     * This method initializes leftSlidersPanel
     *
     * @return javax.swing.JPanel
```

Listing 5.7 (Continues)

```java
    */
    private javax.swing.JPanel getLeftSlidersPanel() {
      if(leftSlidersPanel == null) {
        leftSlidersPanel = new javax.swing.JPanel();
        leftSlidersPanel.setLayout(new java.awt.GridLayout(1,3));
        leftSlidersPanel.add(getVolumePanel());
        leftSlidersPanel.add(getSpeedPanel());
        leftSlidersPanel.add(getJLabel5(), null);
      }
      return leftSlidersPanel;
    }
    /**
     * This method initializes centerPanel
     *
     * @return javax.swing.JPanel
     */
    private javax.swing.JPanel getCenterPanel() {
      if(centerPanel == null) {
        centerPanel = new javax.swing.JPanel();
        centerPanel.setLayout(new java.awt.GridLayout(1,1));
        centerPanel.add(face);
      }
      return centerPanel;
    }
    /**
     * This method initializes rightSlidersPanel
     *
     * @return javax.swing.JPanel
     */
    private javax.swing.JPanel getRightSlidersPanel() {
      if(rightSlidersPanel == null) {
        rightSlidersPanel = new javax.swing.JPanel();
        java.awt.GridLayout layGridLayout1 =
                  new java.awt.GridLayout(1, 2);
        layGridLayout1.setColumns(3);
        rightSlidersPanel.setLayout(layGridLayout1);
        rightSlidersPanel.add(getJLabel6(), null);
        rightSlidersPanel.add(getPitchPanel());
        rightSlidersPanel.add(getRangePanel());
      }
      return rightSlidersPanel;
    }
    /**
     * This method initializes volumePanel
     *
     * @return javax.swing.JPanel
     */
    private javax.swing.JPanel getVolumePanel() {
      if(volumePanel == null) {
        volumePanel = new javax.swing.JPanel();
        volumePanel.setLayout(new java.awt.BorderLayout());
        volumePanel.add(getVolumeLabel(), java.awt.BorderLayout.NORTH);
        volumePanel.add(getVolumeSlider(),
          java.awt.BorderLayout.CENTER);
```

Listing 5.7 (Continues)

```
      }
      return volumePanel;
  }
  /**
   * This method initializes volumeLabel
   *
   * @return javax.swing.JLabel
   */
  private javax.swing.JLabel getVolumeLabel() {
    if(volumeLabel == null) {
      volumeLabel = new javax.swing.JLabel();
      volumeLabel.setText("Volume");
      volumeLabel.setHorizontalTextPosition(
        javax.swing.SwingConstants.CENTER);
      volumeLabel.setHorizontalAlignment(
        javax.swing.SwingConstants.CENTER);
      volumeLabel.setDisplayedMnemonic(java.awt.event.KeyEvent.VK_V);
    }
    return volumeLabel;
  }
  /**
   * This method initializes volumeSlider
   *
   * @return javax.swing.JSlider
   */
  private javax.swing.JSlider getVolumeSlider() {
    if(volumeSlider == null) {
      volumeSlider = new javax.swing.JSlider();
      volumeSlider.putClientProperty("JSlider.isFilled",
                                     Boolean.TRUE);
      volumeSlider.setMaximum(10);
      volumeSlider.setMinorTickSpacing(1);
      volumeSlider.setMajorTickSpacing(5);
      volumeSlider.setOrientation(javax.swing.JSlider.VERTICAL);
      volumeSlider.setToolTipText("Volume");
      volumeSlider.setPaintLabels(true);
      volumeSlider.setPaintTicks(true);
      volumeSlider.addChangeListener(
       new javax.swing.event.ChangeListener() {
        public void stateChanged(javax.swing.event.ChangeEvent e) {
          playerModel.setVolume((float) volumeSlider.getValue());
        }
      });
    }
    return volumeSlider;
  }
  /**
   * This method initializes speedPanel
   *
   * @return javax.swing.JPanel
   */
  private javax.swing.JPanel getSpeedPanel() {
    if(speedPanel == null) {
      speedPanel = new javax.swing.JPanel();
```

Listing 5.7 (Continues)

```
        speedPanel.setLayout(new java.awt.BorderLayout());
        speedPanel.add(getSpeedLabel(), java.awt.BorderLayout.NORTH);
        speedPanel.add(getSpeedSlider(), java.awt.BorderLayout.CENTER);
    }
    return speedPanel;
}
/**
 * This method initializes speedLabel
 *
 * @return javax.swing.JLabel
 */
private javax.swing.JLabel getSpeedLabel() {
    if(speedLabel == null) {
        speedLabel = new javax.swing.JLabel();
        speedLabel.setText("Words/min");
        speedLabel.setHorizontalAlignment(
            javax.swing.SwingConstants.CENTER);
        speedLabel.setHorizontalTextPosition(
            javax.swing.SwingConstants.CENTER);
        speedLabel.setDisplayedMnemonic(java.awt.event.KeyEvent.VK_W);
    }
    return speedLabel;
}
/**
 * This method initializes speedSlider
 *
 * @return javax.swing.JSlider
 */
private javax.swing.JSlider getSpeedSlider() {
    if(speedSlider == null) {
        speedSlider = new javax.swing.JSlider();
        speedSlider.setOrientation(javax.swing.JSlider.VERTICAL);
        speedSlider.putClientProperty("JSlider.isFilled", Boolean.TRUE);
        speedSlider.setMaximum(400);
        speedSlider.setMinorTickSpacing(50);
        speedSlider.setMajorTickSpacing(100);
        speedSlider.setToolTipText("Speed");
        speedSlider.setPaintLabels(true);
        speedSlider.setPaintTicks(true);
        speedSlider.setPaintTrack(true);
        speedSlider.addChangeListener(
          new javax.swing.event.ChangeListener() {
            public void stateChanged(javax.swing.event.ChangeEvent e) {
                playerModel.setSpeakingRate((float) speedSlider.getValue());
            }
          });
    }
    return speedSlider;
}
/**
 * This method initializes pitchPanel
 *
 * @return javax.swing.JPanel
 */
```

Listing 5.7 (Continues)

```java
private javax.swing.JPanel getPitchPanel() {
  if(pitchPanel == null) {
    pitchPanel = new javax.swing.JPanel();
    pitchPanel.setLayout(new java.awt.BorderLayout());
    pitchPanel.add(getPitchLabel(), java.awt.BorderLayout.NORTH);
    pitchPanel.add(getPitchSlider(), java.awt.BorderLayout.CENTER);
  }
  return pitchPanel;
}
/**
 * This method initializes pitchLabel
 *
 * @return javax.swing.JLabel
 */
private javax.swing.JLabel getPitchLabel() {
  if(pitchLabel == null) {
    pitchLabel = new javax.swing.JLabel();
    pitchLabel.setText("Hz");
    pitchLabel.setHorizontalAlignment(
      javax.swing.SwingConstants.CENTER);
    pitchLabel.setHorizontalTextPosition(
      javax.swing.SwingConstants.CENTER);
    pitchLabel.setDisplayedMnemonic(java.awt.event.KeyEvent.VK_H);
  }
  return pitchLabel;
}
/**
 * This method initializes pitchSlider
 *
 * @return javax.swing.JSlider
 */
private javax.swing.JSlider getPitchSlider() {
  if(pitchSlider == null) {
    pitchSlider = new javax.swing.JSlider();
    pitchSlider.putClientProperty("JSlider.isFilled", Boolean.TRUE);
    pitchSlider.setOrientation(javax.swing.JSlider.VERTICAL);
    pitchSlider.setMinimum(50);
    pitchSlider.setMaximum(200);
    pitchSlider.setMinorTickSpacing(25);
    pitchSlider.setMajorTickSpacing(50);
    pitchSlider.setValue(50);
    pitchSlider.setToolTipText("Pitch");
    pitchSlider.setPaintTicks(true);
    pitchSlider.addChangeListener(
      new javax.swing.event.ChangeListener() {
        public void stateChanged(javax.swing.event.ChangeEvent e) {
          playerModel.setPitch((float) pitchSlider.getValue());
        }
      });
  }
  return pitchSlider;
}
/**
 * This method initializes rangePanel
```

Listing 5.7 (Continues)

```
   *
   * @return javax.swing.JPanel
   */
  private javax.swing.JPanel getRangePanel() {
    if(rangePanel == null) {
      rangePanel = new javax.swing.JPanel();
      rangePanel.setLayout(new java.awt.BorderLayout());
      rangePanel.add(getRangeLabel(), java.awt.BorderLayout.NORTH);
      rangePanel.add(getRangeSlider(), java.awt.BorderLayout.CENTER);
    }
    return rangePanel;
  }
  /**
   * This method initializes rangeLabel
   *
   * @return javax.swing.JLabel
   */
  private javax.swing.JLabel getRangeLabel() {
    if(rangeLabel == null) {
      rangeLabel = new javax.swing.JLabel();
      rangeLabel.setText("Range");
      rangeLabel.setHorizontalAlignment(
        javax.swing.SwingConstants.CENTER);
      rangeLabel.setHorizontalTextPosition(
        javax.swing.SwingConstants.CENTER);
      rangeLabel.setDisplayedMnemonic(java.awt.event.KeyEvent.VK_R);
    }
    return rangeLabel;
  }
  /**
   * This method initializes rangeSlider
   *
   * @return javax.swing.JSlider
   */
  private javax.swing.JSlider getRangeSlider() {
    if(rangeSlider == null) {
      rangeSlider = new javax.swing.JSlider();
      rangeSlider.setOrientation(javax.swing.JSlider.VERTICAL);
      rangeSlider.putClientProperty("JSlider.isFilled", Boolean.TRUE);
      rangeSlider.setMaximum(50);
      rangeSlider.setMajorTickSpacing(10);
      rangeSlider.setMinorTickSpacing(5);
      rangeSlider.setValue(0);
      rangeSlider.setToolTipText("Variation");
      rangeSlider.setPaintLabels(true);
      rangeSlider.setPaintTicks(true);
      rangeSlider.addChangeListener(
      new javax.swing.event.ChangeListener() {
        public void stateChanged(javax.swing.event.ChangeEvent e) {
          playerModel.setRange((float) rangeSlider.getValue());        }
      });
    }
    return rangeSlider;
  }
```

Listing 5.7 (Continues)

```java
/**
 * This method initializes textAndButtonPanel
 *
 * @return javax.swing.JPanel
 */
private javax.swing.JPanel getTextAndButtonPanel() {
  if(textAndButtonPanel == null) {
    textAndButtonPanel = new javax.swing.JPanel();
    textAndButtonPanel.setLayout(new java.awt.BorderLayout());
    textAndButtonPanel.add(getTextAreaLabel(),
                           java.awt.BorderLayout.NORTH);
    textAndButtonPanel.add(getTextInputArea(),
                           java.awt.BorderLayout.CENTER);
    textAndButtonPanel.add(getButtonPanel(),
                           java.awt.BorderLayout.SOUTH);
    textAndButtonPanel.setBorder(
      javax.swing.BorderFactory.createEtchedBorder(
              javax.swing.border.EtchedBorder.RAISED));
  }
  return textAndButtonPanel;
}
/**
 * This method initializes textAreaLabel
 *
 * @return javax.swing.JLabel
 */
private javax.swing.JLabel getTextAreaLabel() {
  if(textAreaLabel == null) {
    textAreaLabel = new javax.swing.JLabel();
    textAreaLabel.setText("Enter Text:");
    textAreaLabel.setDisplayedMnemonic(
      java.awt.event.KeyEvent.VK_T);
  }
  return textAreaLabel;
}
/**
 * This method initializes buttonPanel
 *
 * @return javax.swing.JPanel
 */
private javax.swing.JPanel getButtonPanel() {
  if(buttonPanel == null) {
    buttonPanel = new javax.swing.JPanel();
    buttonPanel.add(getSpeakButton(), null);
    buttonPanel.add(getDeleteButton(), null);
  }
  return buttonPanel;
}
/**
 * This method initializes speakButton
 *
 * @return javax.swing.JButton
 */
private javax.swing.JButton getSpeakButton() {
```

Listing 5.7 (Continues)

```java
    if(speakButton == null) {
      speakButton = new javax.swing.JButton();
      speakButton.setText("Speak Text");
      speakButton.setMnemonic(java.awt.event.KeyEvent.VK_S);
      speakButton.setToolTipText("Speak text in text area");
      speakButton.setBackground(new java.awt.Color(250,250,250));
      speakButton.addActionListener(
       new java.awt.event.ActionListener() {
        public void actionPerformed(java.awt.event.ActionEvent e) {
          String inputText = textInputArea.getText();
          if (inputText.length() > 0)
            playerModel.play(inputText);
        }
      });
    }
    return speakButton;
  }
  /**
   * This method initializes deleteButton
   *
   * @return javax.swing.JButton
   */
  private javax.swing.JButton getDeleteButton() {
    if(deleteButton == null) {
      deleteButton = new javax.swing.JButton();
      deleteButton.setText("Delete Text");
      deleteButton.setMnemonic(java.awt.event.KeyEvent.VK_D);
      deleteButton.setToolTipText("Delete all text in text area");
      deleteButton.setBackground(new java.awt.Color(250,250,250));
      deleteButton.addActionListener(
       new java.awt.event.ActionListener() {
        public void actionPerformed(java.awt.event.ActionEvent e) {
          textInputArea.setText("");
        }
      });
    }
    return deleteButton;
  }
  /**
   * This method initializes textInputArea
   *
   * @return javax.swing.JTextArea
   */
  private javax.swing.JTextArea getTextInputArea() {
    if(textInputArea == null) {
      textInputArea = new javax.swing.JTextArea();
      textInputArea.setLineWrap(true);
      textInputArea.setRows(5);
      textInputArea.setText("Hello, this is your animated voice!");
    }
    return textInputArea;
  }
  /**
   * This method initializes jLabel5
```

Listing 5.7 (Continues)

```
     *
     * @return javax.swing.JLabel
     */
    private javax.swing.JLabel getJLabel5() {
      if(jLabel5 == null) {
        jLabel5 = new javax.swing.JLabel();
        jLabel5.setText("");
      }
      return jLabel5;
    }
    /**
     * This method initializes jLabel6
     *
     * @return javax.swing.JLabel
     */
    private javax.swing.JLabel getJLabel6() {
      if(jLabel6 == null) {
        jLabel6 = new javax.swing.JLabel();
        jLabel6.setText("");
      }
      return jLabel6;
    }
  }  //  @jve:visual-info  decl-index=0 visual-constraint="12,9"
```

Listing 5.7 (Continued)

The Complete Application

Finally, you need a `Player` root class for the whole application. This class contains the `main()` method. Within this method you can create a new `Player` instance. This causes the `Players` constructor to create a `Face` and a `Voice` instance and to connect both with the help of the `Animator` class. Furthermore, a `PlayerModel` instance and a `PlayerPanel` instance are created and wired together.

The Player.java class

The `Player` class is implemented as an extension of the Swing `JFrame` class. When you create this class you must specify `JFrame` as a super class. In addition, you must checkmark the `public static void main(...)` option. This will generate a stub for the `main()` method.

```
package com.bdaum.dukeSpeaks;

import java.awt.BorderLayout;
import java.awt.event.WindowAdapter;
import java.awt.event.WindowEvent;
import java.net.URL;
import java.util.Locale;

import javax.swing.*;

import com.sun.speech.freetts.Age;
import com.sun.speech.freetts.Gender;
```

```
import com.sun.speech.freetts.audio.AnimatedAudioPlayer;
import com.sun.speech.freetts.en.us.AnimatedDiphoneVoice;
import com.sun.speech.freetts.en.us.CMULexicon;
import com.sun.speech.freetts.en.us.cmu_us_kal.KevinVoiceDirectory;
import com.sun.speech.freetts.relp.Animator;

public class Player extends JFrame {

  private PlayerPanel playerPanel;
```

Constructor

The following code constructs the Player frame. It sets the Look and Feel for Swing, and adds a WindowListener in order to react to window close events. It then constructs an Animator object and uses this object to connect the newly created AnimatedDiphoneVoice with the Face GUI object. Finally it constructs the PlayerPanel and creates a data model instance for the player.

```
    /**
     * @see java.awt.Frame#Frame(String)
     */
    public Player(String title) {
        super(title);
        // Set Look&Feel for Swing
        setDefaultLookAndFeelDecorated(true);
        // WindowListener for close button event handling
        addWindowListener(new WindowAdapter() {
            public void windowClosing(WindowEvent e) {
                System.exit(0);
            }
        });

        // Create new Animator object
        Animator a = new Animator();
    // Get URL of the voice database
    URL url =
KevinVoiceDirectory.class.getResource("cmu_us_kal16.bin");
    // Create Voice object
    // see com.sun.speech.freetts.en.us.cmu_us_kal.KevinVoiceDirectory
    AnimatedDiphoneVoice voice =
      new AnimatedDiphoneVoice("kevin16", Gender.MALE,
        Age.YOUNGER_ADULT, "default 16-bit diphone voice",
        Locale.US, "general", "cmu", new CMULexicon(),
        url, a);
        // Use AnimatedAudioPlayer as audio player
        // for this voice
        // Register Animator object as LineListener
        voice.setAudioPlayer(new AnimatedAudioPlayer(a));
        // Create Face object
        Face face = new Face();
        // Set face border area
        face.setBorder(BorderFactory.createEmptyBorder(30, 30, 10, 30));
        // Set face size
        face.setPreferredSize(new Dimension(400, 300));
```

```
        // Register Face object as
        // AnimationListener with Animator object
        a.addAnimationListener(face);
        // Load the voice (mainly the lexicon)
        voice.allocate();
        // Create a PlayerModel instance with the new voice
        PlayerModelImpl impl = new PlayerModelImpl(voice);
        // Create a PlayerPanel instance and pass the PlayerModel object
        // and the Face-Objekt to it.
        playerPanel = new PlayerPanel(impl,face);
        // Use the size of the PlayerPanel for the whole Player
        setSize(playerPanel.getContentPane().getSize());
        // Insert the PlayerPanel into the Player
        getContentPane().add(playerPanel.getContentPane(),
BorderLayout.CENTER);

    }
```

main()

The main() method simply creates a new Player instance and makes it visible. Before doing so it sets Swing's Look and Feel to "Metal."

```
    /**
     * Method main.
     * The main() method of the Player.
     *
     * @param args (not used)
     * @throws Exception
     */
    public static void main(String[] args) throws Exception {
        // Set Metal Look&Feel for Swing
        try {
            UIManager.setLookAndFeel(
                "javax.swing.plaf.metal.MetalLookAndFeel");
        } catch(Exception e) {
            System.err.println("Error setting look&feel: " + e);
        }
        // Create new Player instance
        Player player = new Player("Animated FreeTTS Player");
        // and display it
        player.setVisible(true);
    }
}
```

You have now completed your application. In the Package Explorer you should now select the Player class in the DukeSpeaks project and then call the Run > Run As > Java Application function. If everything was done correctly, you will now see the window shown in Figure 5.3.

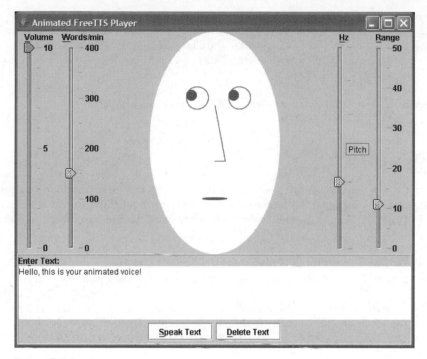

Figure 5.3

You can play around a bit with the speaking face. Change the speed, the pitch, or the variation. Copy other texts into the text input field (using Ctrl+V). Note that the lexicon is based on U.S. English. If you copy foreign language texts into the input field, expect Duke to speak these languages with a U.S. accent.

Exporting the Application

To be able to run your application outside Eclipse, export it as a JAR file. To do so, select the DukeSpeaks project and call the *Export* context function. In the dialog that appears, select the JAR File category.

In the next dialog, checkmark the Export Generated Class Files and Resources field and remove the checkmark from the Export Java Source Files and Resources field. In addition, expand the DukeSpeaks project node and checkmark all packages.

Finally, specify a target location under JAR file. Use dukeSpeaks.jar as the filename.

All binary objects of your DukeSpeaks project are now combined in a single JAR file. To run the player successfully outside Eclipse, you obviously also need the FreeTTS JARs that you previously added as external JARs to the project's Java Build Path in the Classpath of the JVM. Therefore, the Classpath must contain the dukeSpeaks.jar, cmuawb.jar, cmukal16.jar, cmukal8.jar, cmulex.jar, cmu-timelex.jar, and freetts.jar JARs.

A JRE of Version 1.4.0 or higher is required to run this program successfully.

Bibliography

The main purpose of this chapter has been to acquaint you with practical work in the Eclipse workbench. You have learned how third-party projects can be imported into the Eclipse workspace and how they can be navigated and modified. You also have also seen how the various assistants are used to create code efficiently.

In the course of this example I could only scratch the surface of the technologies used. Therefore, I want to give some pointers as to where to get more information about these technologies:

❑ There are several excellent Swing tutorials. In particular, I want to mention the chapter "User Interfaces that Swing" in the official Java tutorial from JavaSoft (www.javasoft.com). Matthew Robinson and Pavel Vorobiev have written a remarkable book about Swing, simply called *Swing*.

❑ The FreeTTS documentation contains valuable information about speech synthesis in general and FreeTTS speech synthesis in particular. You will also find some links to related articles there.

❑ The application implemented here shows only lip synchronization of the simplest kind. Also, the rendering of the face is rather minimalist. The current state of the art is 3-D animations in which each facial muscle can be moved separately. Depending on the text content it is even possible to express emotions. Searching the Web for "lip synchronization" will result in some interesting links. The DECFace project is particularly interesting: details can be found at crl.research.compaq.com/projects/facial/facial.html.

Summary

With this project you have now had your first experiences with Eclipse. Based on these experiences we can derive some "best practices" for the creation of applications with Eclipse:

❑ If the API of a module is well understood, you should create an interface before you create the implementation. This allows you to use the interface when generating the method stubs in the implementing class. At the same time, these method stubs are automatically equipped with Javadoc comments that use the Javadoc keyword @see to refer back to the method description in the interface.

If the API is not well understood or subject to change, you should create the implementation first. Later you can derive the interface from the implementation (see the "Refactoring Code" section in Chapter 2).

- ❑ If it later becomes necessary to extend the interface definition, you can pull down these extensions into the implementation by using the Source > Override Methods context function or by using the Content Assistant.

- ❑ Javadoc comments should be always created with the Source > Add JavaDoc Comment context function or by entering /**. This helps to achieve consistent and complete API documentation.

- ❑ Completing the Create a New Java Class dialog carefully is well worth the effort. By specifying super classes and interfaces and by marking the various options, you can save considerable typing, because Eclipse will generate the method and constructor stubs for you.

- ❑ After making large changes in a compilation unit you should call the Source > Organize Imports context function. This function adds missing `import` statements and removes unused ones.

- ❑ Using the Code Assistant (Ctrl+Spacebar) for program constructs, type, and fieldnames saves you a lot of typing and a lot of searching in the documentation and can possibly protect you from RSI (repetitive strain injury). At the same time, the Code Assistant can generate the necessary `import` statements (if this option was set in the preferences). Ctrl+Spacebar should become the typical gesture of an Eclipse programmer.

In the next chapter we will look at testing and debugging Java applications with Eclipse.

Project Development

In the first part of this chapter I discuss the Eclipse Java Debugger in detail. I will show how the debugger can be configured, introduce the Debug Perspective, and explain how to create and manage breakpoints and watchpoints. In the second part I will introduce the JUnit test tool, which is part of the Eclipse SDK distribution. Finally, in the third part I will show how Javadoc documentation can be exported.

Debugging

Searching for bugs in a complex application is always a time-consuming task. A powerful debugger can be of great help here. Fortunately, the Eclipse Java IDE is equipped with a full-featured debugger that leaves hardly anything to be desired.

This debugger has two operation modes: *local* and *remote*. Here, I will discuss local debugging. Later, in the "Remote Debugging" section. I will then show how the debugger is used in a remote scenario.

The Debug Configuration

Like many other parts of the Eclipse workbench, the Debugger can be configured by the user in various ways. For example, under Window > Preferences > Java > Debug > Detail Formatters, you can specify how the values of Java types are to be displayed in the Details section of the Variables View. The default formatting uses the `toString()` method for displaying the variable's value. To add a new formatter, press the Add button, enter or browse for a type, and then enter a code snippet to be applied to instances of this type. For example, if you want to display the text content of objects of type `org.eclipse.jface.text.Document` in the Details View, select this type and enter `get()` as the code snippet for detail formatting.

Under Window > Preferences > Java > Debug > Step Filtering, you can specify which classes should be skipped when stepping though a program. These settings are used during the Step with Filters operation (Figure 6.1).

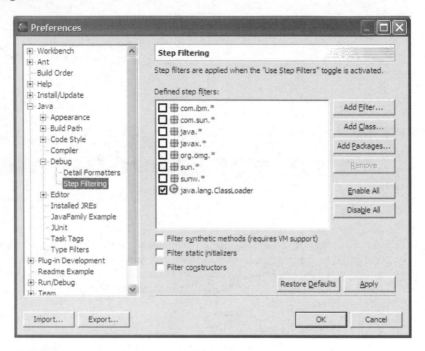

Figure 6.1

Some step filters are predefined so that you can simply activate them with a checkmark (by default only the Java class loader is skipped). You can also add other classes, packages, or generic filter expressions to the list, however.

The Debug Perspective

You can start debugging by clicking the bug symbol in the workbench's toolbar. This function is very similar to the Run function (see the "Hello World" section in Chapter 1) with the difference that execution is interrupted at breakpoints. You can also make Eclipse automatically switch to the *Debug Perspective* by specifying *Always* for the Switch to Associated Perspective When Launching option in Window > Preferences > Run/Debug > Launching. Alternatively, you can specify Always for the Switch to Associated Perspective When a Breakpoint Is Hit option in Window > Preferences > Run/Debug. The Debug Perspective contains the same windows as the Java Perspective plus two more.

Figure 6.2 shows the Debug Perspective. In the top-left corner you see the Debug window listing the active threads. Under the thread [AWT-Event-Queue-0] the execution stack with the method call hierarchy is displayed. In the top-right corner the variables of the current execution context are shown. Behind this view are three more stacked views: Breakpoints, Expressions, and Display. Variable values can be displayed, too, by hovering with the mouse over a variable name in the editor.

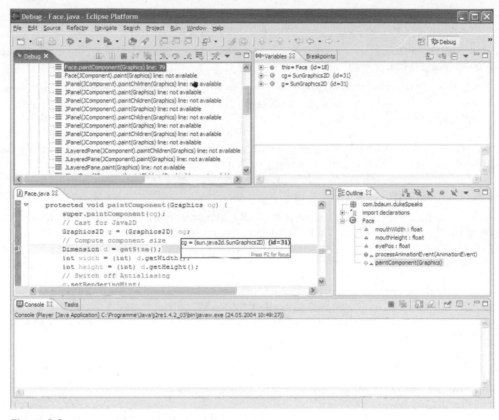

Figure 6.2

Controlling Program Execution

The toolbar of the Debug window is equipped with all the buttons needed to control the execution of the current program. Most of these functions, however, can be called via function keys, which is much faster. From left to right you see the following:

- ❑ **Resume (F8).** Continues the execution of an interrupted thread.

- ❑ **Suspend.** Interrupts the execution of a running thread. This function is especially useful when the thread is looping.

- ❑ **Terminate.** The execution of a running or interrupted program is terminated.

- ❑ **Disconnect.** This function is required to finish debugging a remote program (remote debugging).

- ❑ **Remove All Terminated Launches.** This function removes "garbage" from the Debug View.

- ❑ **Step Into (F5).** Used on a method call, this function will step into the invoked method. In program lines containing multiple method calls, however, this function steps through all of them. In such cases, it is better to select the method call in question and use the Step into Selection context function.

❑ **Step Over (F6).** Used on a method call, this function will step over the invoked method (provided the method does not contain active breakpoints).

❑ **Step Return (F7).** The current method is executed in normal mode. When the method returns, step mode is reactivated.

❑ **Step with Filters (Shift+F5).** When you use this function the step operation is influenced by the step filters defined in the preferences (see the "Debug Configuration" section). All other functions ignore the step filters.

After executing a program step by step, you can retrace the single steps backwards by pressing the Back navigation button (see the "Navigation" section in Chapter 4)!

Setting Breakpoints

How do you start a debug session? You would usually set a breakpoint at an interesting location in your program. This is easily done by double-clicking the left margin of the Java source editor. It doesn't matter if you do this in the Java Perspective or in the Debug Perspective. You can remove the breakpoint with another double-click at the same position.

Now, set a breakpoint onto the `Dimension d = getSize()` instruction in the `paintComponent()` method in the `Face` class, as shown in the previous figure. When you start the debug process by clicking the Debug button, the program will stop at this instruction. The variable values of the current object appear in the window at the right-hand side.

Testing Interactively

You have now the following possibilities:

❑ You can continue the execution of the program by pressing F8. The program will be interrupted only when it passes this breakpoint again.

❑ You can stop execution by clicking the Terminate button.

❑ You can execute the `getSize()` method step by step by pressing the F5 key.

❑ You can step over the `getSize()` method by pressing the F6 key.

❑ You can set further breakpoints, or you can remove breakpoints.

Variables

You have the following options for variables:

❑ You can view the content of variables by hovering with the cursor over a variable name in the source editor.

❑ In the Variables View you can take a closer look at the variables of the current execution environment. Complex objects can be expanded by clicking the + character (or by double-clicking the variable name) so that you can view their details.

❑ In the execution stack in the Debug window you can select a different execution environment. For example, you may select: `Player(java.awt.Container).paint(java.awt.Graphics) line 1123`.

❑ The source editor automatically shows the corresponding source code, and the Variables View shows the variables of this execution environment.

❑ You can modify variables. By double-clicking a variable in the Variables View you can open an editor for the variable's value and modify the value. Alternatively, you can edit the value in the Details section of the Variables View and then assign it by invoking the Assign Value context function.

❑ By applying the Watch context function to individual variables you can add those variables to the Expressions window. As you step through the program, the variables in the Expressions window will be updated when their value changes. This provides a way to monitor specific variables during program execution.

HotSwap

During a debug session you can apply changes to the program code and save (and compile) the changed code. In many cases—provided you run under JDK 1.4—the debug session need not be restarted but can continue with the modified module in place (HotSwap). In some cases, however—for example, when the signature of a public method is changed—using HotSwap is impossible. In this case you are prompted whether to abort or restart execution.

Testing Expressions

In the *Display* View (and also in the Details area of the Expression View), you can enter expressions that can be executed within the current execution context (see also the discussion of the "Scrapbook" in Chapter 1). To do so, select the entered expression and invoke the Inspect or Display context function. For example, if you execute the getBackground() expression while in the execution context of Player.paint() (see above), the Display function will deliver the background color of player.

Managing Breakpoints

The Breakpoints View shows an overview of all defined breakpoints. Here, you can delete breakpoints that you don't need anymore or position the source editor to a breakpoint position by double-clicking it.

With the Disable context function you can disable a breakpoint temporarily. With Enable you can activate it again. The *Properties* context function allows further customization of breakpoints (Figure 6.3).

The breakpoint properties dialog allows for detailed instrumentation of a breakpoint. By setting a hit count, the breakpoint is activated only after several passes through it. You can also specify an additional condition under which the breakpoint should become active. The breakpoint is activated either when the Boolean value of the condition is true or when the value of the condition changes, depending on the option chosen.

Another useful function of the Breakpoints View is the Add Java Exception Breakpoint function (the button with the exclamation mark). When invoking this function you can select an exception type from a list.

Usually, Eclipse aborts program execution when an uncaught exception occurs and shows you the stack trace. But with this function, you can interrupt directly at the point where the exception occurs and look into variables and so on. Better still, you can even optionally trap exceptions that are caught in a try/catch block. It is a good idea to set Java Exception Breakpoints for common uncaught exception types such as NullPointerException, ClassCastException, and IndexOutOfBoundsException.

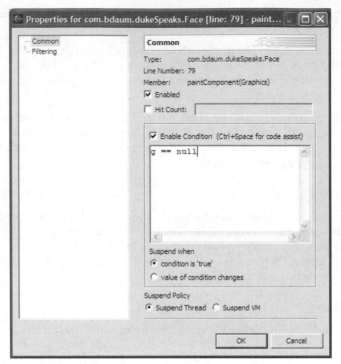

Figure 6.3

If you have trapped an exception with such a breakpoint, program execution is interrupted when the exception occurs. In the *Debug* window you now can select a method within the stack trace shown under the current thread. The *Variables* View shows you the variables of the method's execution environment, so that in most cases you can easily determine the reason for the exception.

Finally, the Skip All Breakpoints tool button in the Breakpoints window allows you to disable all break-points temporarily.

The Java Console

Although the debugger provides you with a rich arsenal of tools to find bugs in programs, you should not ignore the Java console. To find a problem, it is sometimes simpler to program a test output into a method or constructor instead of spending ages stepping through program code. You can accomplish such outputs with System.out.println() or System.err.println(). By using the Code Assistant (see the "Java Information Windows" section Chapter 2), you can simply enter sysout or syserr to create such an instruction.

In the case of a program crash, the console is a valuable source of information, too, since it displays the execution stack. Eclipse here offers additional help: double-clicking a stack entry opens the corresponding compilation unit and positions the editor window to the specified line!

Note, that each test run creates a new console instance. In the *Console View* you can select which console to display by clicking the arrow button.

Remote Debugging

Remote debugging is used for applications that run on a remote JVM, especially for an application that runs outside the Eclipse platform. Typical targets for remote debugging are servlets that have neither a GUI nor a console.

To make a Java application accessible to an external debugger, you must specify additional command-line parameters when starting the application's JVM. In the following example—assuming that this application has already been installed outside Eclipse—I demonstrate how `DukeSpeaks` can be made accessible to a remote debugger:

```
java.exe -Xdebug -Xnoagent -Djava.compiler=NONE
    -Xrunjdwp:transport=dt_socket,server=y,suspend=y, address=8787
    -classpath %LOCALCLASSPATH%
    com.bdaum.dukeSpeaks.Player
```

First, the JVM is switched into debug mode. The `sun.tools.debug` agent is switched off, as well as the JIT and HotSpot compilers. With `-Xrunjdwp` the reference implementation of the Java Debug Wire Protocols (JDWP) is loaded. A socket connection is selected as transport mode. The `server=y` parameter specifies that the application acts as a debug server, and the `suspend=y` parameter specifies that the application must not start autonomously but must wait for a connection with the debug client. Finally, the `address=8787` parameter specifies the debug port number that can be selected from the host computer's free ports.

Now, start the application and execute the command. Nothing happens. The application waits for the debug client. Now it's time to create a remote debug configuration in Eclipse. To do so, invoke the Run > Debug function. In the selection list at the left-hand side of the dialog, select Remote Java Application and press the New button.

Then enter a name for the new configuration (for example, `DukeSpeaksRemote`) and select the project (`DukeSpeaks`). This specification is actually not used to tell the Eclipse debugger the location of the binary files but to inform it about the location of the source files.

The Connection Type field remains unchanged: Standard (Socket Attach). Since the remote application runs on the same host computer, you must enter the localhost value under Host. For Port, specify exactly the same value that was used above in the `java` command. So enter `8787`. Finally, mark the Allow Termination of Remote VM checkbox. This allows you to terminate the application via remote control from the Eclipse debugger.

Now the configuration is properly set up. You can start the debugging process by clicking the Debug button. From now on, everything works just as with local debugging. You can set breakpoints, look at variables, and even modify the values of variables. The only thing that does not work with remote debugging is, of course, HotSwapping.

JUnit

JUnit is an Open Source tool that allows you to create and execute test suites quickly and systematically. The people behind JUnit are Kent Beck and Erich Gamma. Since Erich Gamma is also significantly involved in the development of Eclipse, it is no surprise that JUnit is contained in the Eclipse SDK distribution. Detailed information is available at www.junit.org or in *Professional Java Tools for Extreme Programming* by Richard Hightower, et al.

Test tools such as JUnit are used to test program modules repeatedly, especially after changes have been applied to a module. Using such automated test tools allows you to test frequently and after each small incremental development step, following the XP motto: *Code a little, test a little.*

Of course, the quality of the test results stands or falls with the quality of the test suite. A good test suite should cover the whole functional range of a program module. This is, however, easier said than done!

Setting Up JUnit

To be able to work with JUnit, the JUnit JAR file is required in the build path of your project. You could manually add junit.jar as an external JAR file to DukeSpeaks project, as described in the "Project Properties" section in Chapter 4. You can find junit.jar under \eclipse\plugins\org .junit_3.8.1. However, this is not really required, since Eclipse will do this for you when you create your first test case.

In the DukeSpeaks project you can now create a test case class (a subclass of the JUnit TestCase class), which you can call PlayerTest. You can create such a class manually, or you can use the JUnit Wizard (Figure 6.4) in which case you proceed as follows:

1. Invoke the wizard via the File > New > Other > Java > JUnit > Test Case function.

2. In the first page of the wizard, press the Browse button at the Class to Test field and select the class that you want to test (Player).

3. To name the test, enter PlayerTest in the Name field.

4. In the Package field select a target package (within your project) for the new TestCase class.

5. Additional options allow you to generate a main() method, a setUp() method, a tearDown() method, and a constructor for the new test case.

On the next page of the wizard select which of the test class test methods are to be generated (Figure 6.5).

Here I have selected only two methods. Normally you would first select all methods and then explicitly deselect all the methods that you don't want to test. Optionally, you can decorate all generated methods with the modifier "final." TODO comments can be generated into the method stubs.

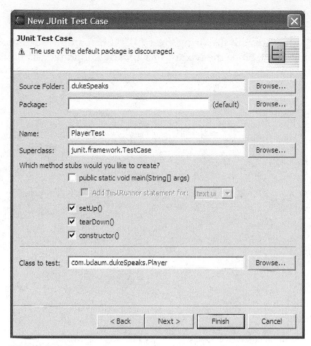

Figure 6.4

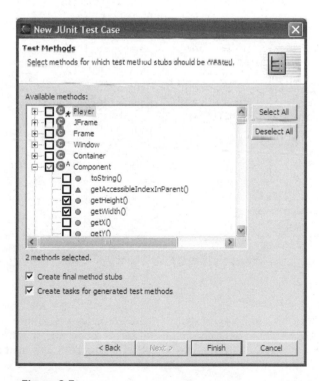

Figure 6.5

Creating a Test Suite

All generated test methods start with the string "test." JUnit recognizes such method names and executes them when running a test. Since the wizard has already generated the method stubs, you need only add the code inside the method body. If you need to initialize variables or other resources, you do this in the setUp() method. See Listing 6.1.

```java
import junit.framework.TestCase;
import com.bdaum.dukeSpeaks.Player;
public class PlayerTest extends TestCase {
    Player player;

    /**
     * Constructor for TestCase1.
     * @param arg0
     */
    public PlayerTest(String arg0) {
        super(arg0);
    }

    /**
     * Initialize the player
     */
    protected void setUp() throws Exception {
        super.setUp();
        player = new Player("Animated FreeTTS Player");
    }

    final public void testGetWidth() {
        assertTrue("width != 600: "+player.getWidth(),
            player.getWidth() == 600);
    }
    final public void testGetHeight() {
        assertTrue("height != 500: "+player.getHeight(),
            player.getHeight() == 500);
    }

    /**
     * Dispose of everything
     */
    protected void tearDown() throws Exception {
        super.tearDown();
        player = null;
    }
}
```

Listing 6.1

Here, two tests (testWidth() and testHeight()) are implemented. In these tests the JUnit assertTrue() method is used to test a condition and throw an exception if the condition is not met. Both methods use the player variable that was initialized in the setUp() method. JUnit calls this method before executing the `run()` method. Similarly, the `tearDown()` method is called after all tests are executed. This method can be used to dispose of resources.

When you have created several `TestCase` classes, it makes sense to combine these classes in a test suite. The JUnit Wizard will help you with this task, too. You only have to invoke the File > New > Other > Java > JUnit > Test Suite function. In the wizard's selection list checkmark all `TestCase` classes that you want to add to the test suite (in this example the only test case is the `PlayerTest` class); see Figure 6.6. At this point it is even possible to add other test suites to the new test suite, i.e., you may nest test suites. In the Test Suite field change the proposed name AllTests according to your requirements.

Figure 6.6

After you press the Finish button, the wizard will generate the resulting `TestSuite` class:

```
import junit.framework.Test;
import junit.framework.TestSuite;
public class AllTests {
    public static Test suite() {
        TestSuite suite = new TestSuite("Test for tests");
        //$JUnit-BEGIN$
        suite.addTest(new TestSuite(PlayerTest.class));
        //$JUnit-END$
        return suite;
    }
}
```

Here, I have created a test suite solely for demonstration purposes. If you want to run only a single `TestCase` class, creating a test suite is not really required.

Running a Test Suite

Now you can execute all tests. Invoke the Run > Run as > JUnit Test function. Eclipse opens the JUnit view (in front of the Package Explorer) and runs the test suite (Figure 6.7).

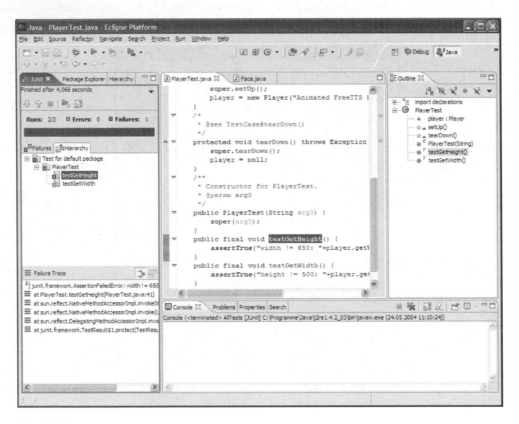

Figure 6.7

In the upper part of the JUnit View all errors are collected (to a maximum of one error per single test case). The other stacked window in the upper area shows the hierarchy of test suites and single test cases. In the lower part of the view, JUnit shows the execution stack for the currently selected error. Here, to force an error, I specified a panel width (650) in the test case that was different from the panel width specified in the application.

Documentation

In the "Java Information Windows" section in Chapter 2 you saw how Javadoc comments can be conveniently added to source code. In this section I will discuss how these comments can be exported as an HTML Javadoc documentation.

To generate the Javadoc documentation for the completed DukeSpeaks project, select the project and invoke the Export context function. On the first page of the Export Wizard, select Javadoc from the list and press the Next button. On the following page, you can specify in detail what should be exported to Javadoc (Figure 6.8). But first make sure that the Javadoc Command entry points to a valid Javadoc processor such as ...\j2sdk1.4.2\bin\javadoc.exe and that the Destination entry specifies a destination folder for the Javadoc pages. You can preset a default value by applying the Properties > Javadoc Location context function to the project. You can also specify for which packages and for which methods Javadoc is to be generated. In addition, you have the option of using a custom doclet instead of Sun Microsystems' reference implementation.

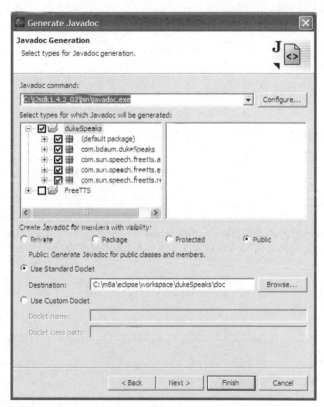

Figure 6.8

Try It Out: Javadoc Options

In the next step you can determine the content and the layout of the single Javadoc pages. The following options exist:

❑ **Generate Use Page.** This option allows you to generate a cross-reference for each class and each package.

❑ **Generate Hierarchy Tree.** When you check this option, a page is generated that displays the hierarchy of packages, classes, and interfaces.

❑ **Generate Navigator Bar.** This option generates a navigation bar at the top and at the bottom of each page.

❑ **Generate Index.** This option generates one or several index pages.

❑ **Separate Index per Letter.** Check this option to generate a separate index page for each letter in the alphabet.

❑ **@author, @version, @deprecated.** When these options are set, the corresponding key words in the Javadoc comments are evaluated and their information is included in the generated pages.

❑ **Deprecated List.** This option allows a separate page to be generated, listing all elements marked as "deprecated."

In addition, you can create links to other Javadoc documentations.

Try It Out: Command-Line Options

On the next wizard page (Figure 6.9), you can specify additional command-line options for javadoc .exe, if necessary. In addition, you can specify a file containing additional text for the Javadoc Overview page.

The JRE 1.4 Source Compatibility option must be checked if your source code contains the Java assert keyword. Without this option set, Java 1.4 programs that contain this instruction would cause errors during the Javadoc generation. Checking this option is equivalent to specifying the command-line option -source 1.4.

You can also optionally create an Ant script for Javadoc generation (Figure 6.10). I will discuss Ant in more detail in Chapter 13.

After you press Finish, the Javadoc generation is started as a batch job. The output of the batch job appears on the Eclipse Java console.

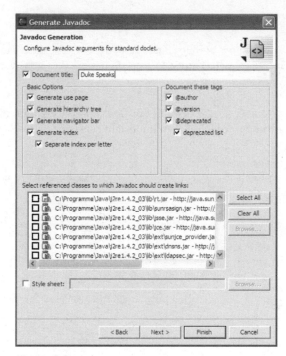

Figure 6.9

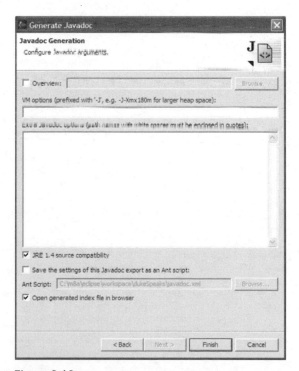

Figure 6.10

Summary

In this chapter you have learned how both local and remote Java programs can be debugged with Eclipse. You should now be able to set, remove, and configure breakpoints, to view and modify variables, and to step through a program.

I have also introduced you to the creation of JUnit test cases and the creation of Javadoc program documentation. Again, the support of JUnit is an important aspect of Eclipse's support for Extreme Programming.

In the next chapter I will explore some advanced topics such as teamwork, version management, and the embedding of external tools.

7

Advanced Topics of Project Development

In this chapter I will briefly discuss how development teams can organize their work by using a CVS repository with Eclipse. I will also show how external tools can be embedded into Eclipse.

Developing in a Team

In this book, I want to take only a short excursion into Eclipse's support for development teams. Detailed information can be found in the Eclipse help pages under Workbench User Guide > Tasks > Working in the Team Environment.

Different concepts exist for working collaboratively on the same project. These concepts range from sequential or semi-sequential workflow-oriented techniques to completely synchronous techniques such as Microsoft's NetMeeting. Eclipse uses the CVS concept (Concurrent Versions System) by default. CVS is an Open Source project that has practically become the de facto standard for the collaborative development of software projects. The CVS is based on a central repository. However, the individual members of the development team work on their own local copies of the repository content. In fact, they are able to work *only* on these local copies. For resolving clashes, the CVS uses an optimistic concept: it assumes that the same software artifact is only rarely modified simultaneously by multiple team members. Therefore, the software artifacts—even if they are currently being worked on—are not locked against the access of other team members. All team members continue to have access to the central repository, may own a local copy of any artifact in the central repository, and may modify this local copy without restrictions.

From time to time, the local copies are synchronized with the copies in the central repository. Usually, only the central repository is updated with the newest versions. Some care should be taken when doing so. Since software artifacts are usually highly dependent on each other, the global repository should be updated only when the local resources are in a consistent state, for example, when the project's test suite was executed without errors.

However, such an optimistic concept allows conflicts. Such conflicts must be resolved. For example, if the local copy of a resource and its original version in the central repository have *both* been modified since the last synchronization, simply replacing the central copy with the local copy would cause a loss of information. In such a case, the CVS offers several strategies for resolving the conflict. For example, it is possible to *merge* both copies either manually or automatically.

Another option is to open a new development *branch*. The initial code base of the project forms the *trunk*, or HEAD, of a development tree with many possible branches. Later, these different branches can be brought together with the help of the previously mentioned conflict solution strategies (see the "Working in a Team" section).

In addition, the CVS allows software artifacts to be given version numbers. Eclipse builds on this facility. Eclipse supports the version management known from Visual Age only if Eclipse collaborates with a CVS. In addition to explicit version numbers, the CVS uses internal revision numbers to uniquely identify each change in the central repository. The CVS stores the complete history of a software artifact. This allows the comparison of a given software artifact with previous versions and revisions at any time or its replacement with a previous version or revision. This feature can be very helpful, especially for maintenance and debugging.

Detailed information about the CVS can be found in the books *Open Source Projects with CVS* by Fogel and *Essential CVS* by Vesperman, and on the CVS Web site under www.cvshome.org.

Setting Up a Repository

It is a prerequisite for working in a team under Eclipse that the Eclipse workbenches of all team members have access to the central repository. Since Eclipse by default supports the CVS access protocol, direct access is possible to the following systems:

❑ Concurrent Versions System (CVS) for Linux/Unix from CVS version 1.11.1p1 onward. This CVS server is freeware and can be downloaded from www.cvshome.org.

❑ CVS for Windows is also freeware and can be downloaded from www.cvsnt.org. However, cvsnt is not officially supported by Eclipse, since it does not have the same maturity and robustness as the CVS for Linux or Unix. If you want to use it anyway, version 1.11.1.1 or later is recommended.

At the time of this writing there was no information about the compatibility of Eclipse 3 with the new CVS version 2. You can get up-to-date information about CVS versions and compatibility issues in the *Eclipse CVS FAQ* that are accessible via Help > Help Contents > Workbench User Guide > Reference > Team support with CVS > CVS.

In addition to these popular CVSs, there are some commercial systems, too, that support central code management, such as Borland StarTeam, Microsoft Visual Source Safe, and Rational ClearCase. The community page on www.eclipse.org lists on the Projects & Plugins page under the Team Repository Providers section quite a few commercial repository providers. Special plug-ins connect these repositories with Eclipse.

Now, how do you connect Eclipse with a repository? Let's assume that you have already installed a CVS. In the following scenario I assume that the root directory of the repository was created and initialized under C:\cvs\eclipse. I further assume that the repository is accessed via the pserver protocol.

Eclipse offers its own perspective for managing connected repositories (yes, there may be more than one repository connected to Eclipse). You can open the CVS Repository Exploring Perspective with Window > Open Perspective > Other > CVS Repository Exploring. In the CVS Repositories View, you can now invoke the New > Repository Location context function. In the dialog shown in Figure 7.1, you need to specify the domain name of the host computer, the access protocol, the absolute path of the repository's root directory and, if necessary, a user name and a password. In this case, the repository is located on the same host computer (localhost) as Eclipse.

After you press Finish, the new repository appears in the CVS Repositories View.

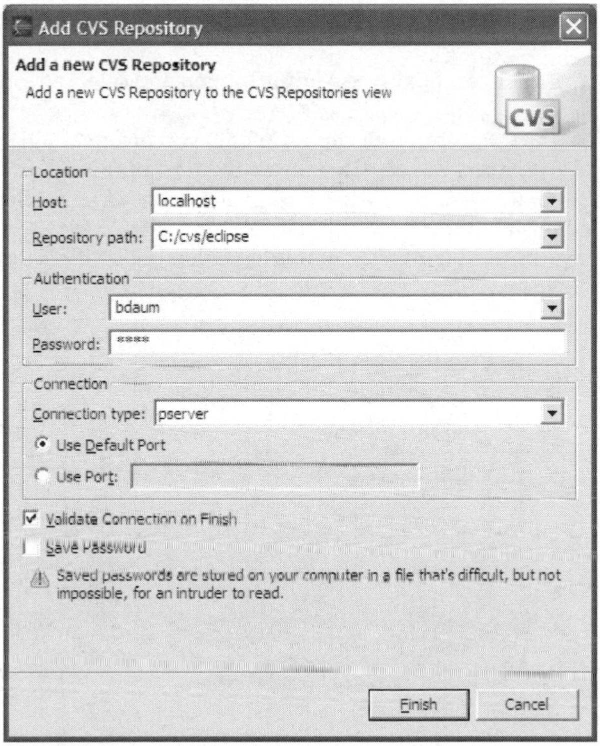

Figure 7.1

Please note that the `pserver` protocol is inherently unsafe. Eclipse also supports the safe `extssh` protocol, since Eclipse 3 also improved its implementation of the `SSH2` protocol version. The necessary controls are found under Window > Preferences >Team > CVS > Ext Connection Method and Window > Preferences > Team > CVS > SSH2 Connection Method.

In addition to these external repositories, Eclipse comes with a simple default repository based on the file system of the host platform. However, this default repository does not support version management.

Projects in the Repository

If you want to share a project with a team, you need to apply the Team > Share Project context function to the project. In the dialog that appears, select a repository from the list. After pressing the Next button, you can select a CVS module in the next step. If you leave the Use Project Name as Module Name option marked, depending on the system used it may be necessary to create such a directory beforehand by executing an appropriate command in the host operating system. For example, if you want to create a directory for the DukeSpeaks project in cvsnt, you would use the command

```
cvs import DukeSpeaks bdaum start
```

Details about this command-line syntax are found in the manuals of the respective repository systems.

Alternatively, you can mark the Use an Existing Module option and select an existing module from the list.

In the next step, just leave the HEAD entry selected. After all, you are creating a new main project and not a development branch of an existing project. Then press the *Next* button again. The project is now compared with the repository content. The next wizard page shows the changes that will be applied to the repository. Just press the Finish button to commit them. Then switch back to the CVS Repository Perspective to view the results (see Figure 7.2). In this case, the repository is located on the same host computer (localhost) as Eclipse.

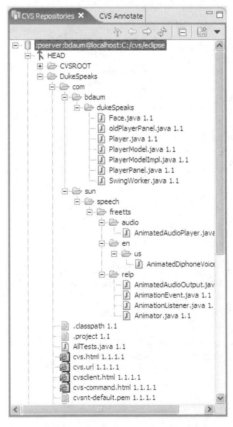

Figure 7.2

Version Management

Now you can mark the current project state as Version 1. It is this function that makes a CVS interesting even for a sole developer. Without a CVS, Eclipse cannot manage project versions.

Select all Java files from the DukeSpeaks project. Apply the Team > Tag as Version context function to this selection. Then enter the version number. You should apply this function only to files that you have previously synchronized with Team > Commit. In this case, however, you might just as well apply the function on the project itself, and thus on all source files in the project.

In principle, working on a repository-based project is no different from working on a private project. All modifications are applied to the local resources without accessing the repository. The local resources are synchronized with the resources in the repository only when you apply the Team > Commit context function to selected resources. Resources that were changed since the last synchronization with the repository are prefixed with a > character in the explorer.

Working in a Team

When several developers work on the same project, not only may the local version be newer than the central version, but the reverse situation is also possible if resources were changed and committed by other team members. You should always first import the changes made by other team members into your local project before committing your changes to the repository. You can do this import with the Team > Update function.

In cases where several team members work simultaneously with the same resource, it may happen that the resource gets changed by more than one team member. Here, we differentiate between three conflict types:

❑   **Case 1. No conflict.** Either the local or the central copy of the file was changed, but not both.

❑   **Case 2: A conflict that can be resolved by automatic merging.** This works only if the same lines of code have not been modified in both the local and the central version.

❑   **Case 3: A conflict that can only be resolved manually.** Here the resource contains lines that were modified in both the local and the central version.

The various functions for synchronization of resources react differently under these different conflict cases. The Update function, for example, replaces the local copy in any case with the central copy. However, in cases 2 and 3, the previous local version is saved under a modified name as a backup. In case 3, the function adds comments to the file to make the conflicts visible.

The Synchronize function, in contrast, opens the Compare Editor (see Figure 7.3). There is even a specific Team Synchronizing Perspective that can be opened in the usual way:

1.   After you press the Synchronize CVS tool button in the Synchronize View, the type of conflict is shown here for each resource. You may then apply an appropriate context function to a selected resource. With Override and Update you can resolve conflict cases of types 1 and 2. Type 3 cases, however, need manual treatment. For this purpose you must invoke the Open in Compare Editor function (Figure 7.3). Here, you can apply the necessary changes.

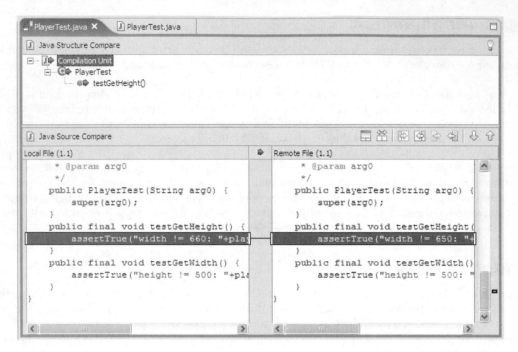

Figure 7.3

The Compare Editor shows the difference between the local workspace and the central repository. Here I have applied a modification to the `PlayerTest.java` file. In the upper window this file is embellished with an arrow to the right, indicating an outgoing change. The lower windows show the local version (left) and the repository version (right). You can edit the local version to resolve conflicts.

Generally, you have the following possibilities for resolving a conflict:

❏ Discard your own modifications and copy the new central version into the workbench. *Your own code is lost!*

❏ Force your own version on the repository (but you should ask team members for permission). *Other people's code is lost!*

❏ Manually merge the local version with the repository version.

❏ Merge the local version with the repository version using the automated merge.

❏ Open a new development branch (Team > Branch). The local version becomes the root of a new branch. Later you can merge this branch with the trunk.

❏ Finally, you have the option to extract the local changes as a *patch* and send it to another team member. This team member can apply the patch and include it in the central version. Eclipse provides the necessary functions to extract patches (Team > Create Patch) and to apply patches to resources (Team > Apply Patch). If you don't want to fall out with other team members, you should use this option (delegating work to others) only if you do not have the necessary access rights to apply the changes yourself.

2. Finally, invoke the Commit function to write the local version to the repository.

Other Functions

Besides the context functions of the Team group, there are some more context functions that refer to repositories, for example, the comparison functions Compare With > Latest From, Compare With > Another Branch or Version, Replace With > Latest From, or Replace With > Another Branch or Version. In addition, there is a Team group in the preferences (Window > Preferences > Team). Here you can set several options for the CVS. For example, you can set the content type (ASCII or binary) for different file types, and you can exclude specific file types from the repository.

Using the Export > Team Project Set and Import > Team Project Set functions, you can exchange whole sets of projects with other team members. To do so, first call the Export function. In the dialog that appears, mark all projects that you wish to pass on to others. The result is a .psf file, which must be stored in a location accessible to other team members. Your peers will then specify this file during import. Eclipse will then construct the reference projects in the workspace and will populate these projects with resources from the repository. Optionally, you can create a Working Set for these imported projects. It may be necessary to adapt the Java Build Paths of the imported projects.

External Tools

Eclipse allows you to embed external tools (i.e., tools that were not developed as plug-ins for Eclipse). All you have to do is to create a configuration for the external tool. To do so, invoke the Run > External Tools > External Tools menu function. In the dialog that appears (see Figure 7.4), you will find two configuration types: ANT-Build and Program. (Ant is discussed in more detail in Chapter 12.) Select the Program type and press the New button. Now you can enter the parameters of the new configuration, such as the name of the configuration, the location of the external tool, the working directory, and possible command-line options (arguments).

Refresh

On the Refresh page you can specify whether, and which, workspace resources should be refreshed after the tool has executed. This is necessary if the tool modifies the Eclipse workspace, that is, if it inserts, modifies, or deletes resources. You can specify in which scope the resources should be refreshed: the selected resource only, all resources in the current folder or project, and so on.

Environment

On the Environment page you can specify the operating system environment variables required by the external tool.

Associations

Another method for embedding external programs is to define file associations. In the "Associations" section in Chapter 4 I demonstrated how an external HTML editor can be embedded into the Eclipse workbench.

As an example, I have declared JavaCC as an external tool. In addition, on the Common page I have marked External Tools in the Display in Favorites Menu list. This allows you to call this tool conveniently with the Run > External Tools > Java CC function in the following calls to JavaCC. I have also removed the mark from the Launch in Background option because this tool is needed in the foreground.

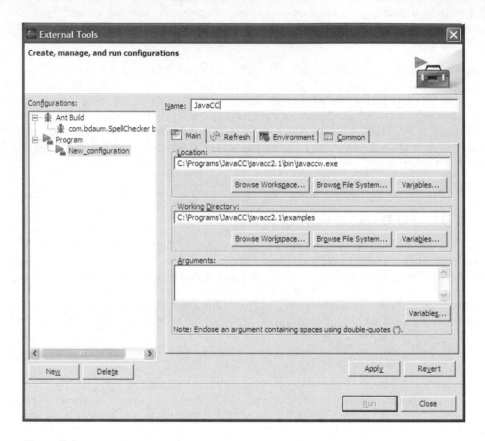

Figure 7.4

Summary

In this chapter you have learned how to connect a CVS to Eclipse. You should have an understanding of the core concepts of working with a CVS and how development in a team and version management take place in the context of Eclipse.

A second topic was the embedding of external tools into Eclipse, so that you can continue using some of your favorite development tools within the Eclipse workspace.

In the next chapter I will turn to a major component of the Eclipse platform, the Standard Widget Toolkit (SWT). By using this component within your own applications, you can implement native user interfaces with Java and forget Swing.

The SWT Library

Eclipse not only has an excellent Java IDE, but with SWT and JFace it also provides libraries that can serve as a replacement for the Java AWT and Swing. The Java AWT implements its own GUI elements and graphics operations in Java and C. Swing builds on this basis with a pure Java implementation of more advanced GUI elements. In contrast, SWT is not much more than a platform-independent interface to the host windowing system (Figure 8.1). In most cases, the SWT classes simply delegate the various method calls to the functions of this native windowing system. To do so, SWT uses the Java Native Interface (JNI), which allows C programs to be invoked from Java. Using this technology, it was possible to implement most of the SWT in Java; only a small native library is required.

The advantage of this concept is that, because of the close integration with the host operating system, the "look and feel" and the responsiveness of SWT-implemented applications are no different than in native applications. For Java this could mean a breakthrough on the desktop. Although the performance of Swing has improved with Java 1.4, Java applications that rely on Swing are still unable to match native applications in presentation quality and responsiveness.

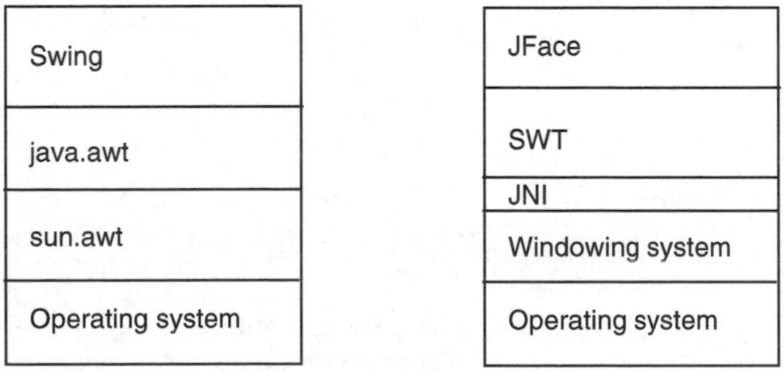

Swing
java.awt
sun.awt
Operating system

JFace
SWT
JNI
Windowing system
Operating system

Figure 8.1

In contrast to SWT, JFace does not talk directly to the native windowing system. JFace is completely written in Java and uses the classes and methods of SWT to implement complex GUI elements. Because of this, JFace components also exhibit the native "look and feel," despite the fact that JFace GUI elements do not have native siblings.

For this book, however, SWT-based applications are a problem. Because of their closeness to the host windowing system, the SWT examples in this book appear in the "look and feel" of the author's operating systems, Windows XP and Windows 2000. When you run these examples on a different operating system, they will match the appearance of that operating system.

Unlike AWT, where GUI elements are implemented in the C sun.awt library and access only low-level graphics functions of the host operating system, SWT uses the higher levels of the host windowing system.

The Standard Widget Toolkit provides a set of basic GUI classes. In this chapter I first present an overview of the SWT's function groups and discuss the pros and cons of SWT compared to Java AWT. Then I will explore the various function groups in detail.

During this exploration, however, I will refrain from presenting a full API specification. Instead, I will concentrate on the significant features of the individual function groups and how they interact. The API description for the various SWT packages is found in the Eclipse help system under Platform-Plugin Developer Guide > Reference > API Reference > Workbench.

SWT Function Group Overview

The SWT classes are organized in the following packages:

Package	Description
org.eclipse.swt	This package contains all SWT-specific constants and exceptions.
org.eclipse.swt.accessibility	This package contains all classes for the implementation of GUI support for disabled people. See the "Accessibility" section.
org.eclipse.swt.awt	This package contains the class SWT-AWT for embedding AWT elements into the SWT. See the "Widgets that Swing" section.
org.eclipse.swt.browser	This package contains the classes implementing the browser widget. See the "Browser Widget" section.
org.eclipse.swt.custom	This package contains widgets for the Eclipse platform that do not have an equivalent in the native windowing system. These widgets are implemented in Java. See the "Custom Widgets" section.

Package	Description
org.eclipse.swt.dnd	This package supports functions for data transfer, such as drag and drop or operations using the clipboard. See the "Data Transfer" section.
org.eclipse.swt.events	This package contains all SWT-specific event classes and listener interfaces. See the "Events" section.
org.eclipse.swt.graphics	This package contains classes for graphics operations. See the "Graphics" section.
org.eclipse.swt.internal	This package contains internal SWT classes. SWT applications should not directly access these classes because their API may change anytime without warning.
org.eclipse.swt.layout	This package contains various layout classes for automatic positioning of GUI elements. See the "Layouts" section.
org.eclipse.swt.ole.win32	This package supports OLE (Object Linking and Embedding) for 32-bit Windows operating systems. See the "Windows32 Support" section.
org.eclipse.swt.printing	This package implements printer support. See the "Output to Printer" section.
org.eclipse.swt.program	This package contains only the program class. Instances of this class represent file associations and support starting external programs (see the "External Tools" section in Chapter 7).
org.eclipse.swt.widgets	This package contains all widget classes of the SWT API. This is the package that implements the main functionality of the SWT. See the "Widgets" section.

SWT—Pros and Cons

The question, of course, is: when do I use SWT and when do I use Swing to implement a GUI? In the following section I discuss some pros and cons of the SWT compared to Swing.

Advantages of SWT

The main advantage of SWT is the seamless integration of an SWT-based application into the host environment. Since SWT-based widgets don't emulate the native user interface, as Swing does, but act only as an adapter to the native widgets, SWT-based user interfaces are indistinguishable from user interfaces of native applications to normal end users. Under Windows 2000 an SWT button looks exactly like a Windows 2000 button, under Windows XP exactly like a Windows XP button, and on a Mac exactly like a Mac button. With Swing this is not always the case. Of course, Swing comes with some skins that mimic native user interfaces, but the right skin is not always available.

Better Interaction

In the case of responsiveness, Eclipse also has an advantage. In this aspect SWT does not show different behavior compared to native applications, since it uses native event processing. Swing, in contrast, is a bit slower, and this can be annoying to the end user at times. In addition, SWT is less resource-hungry than Swing.

Since the Eclipse platform is completely implemented on the basis of SWT, SWT should be the first choice when implementing Eclipse plug-ins and when using GUI components of the Eclipse workbench in plug-ins.

More Robust

Finally, since most SWT-based widgets are only adapters to the native widgets of the host windowing system, you can expect SWT to be more robust and tolerant in regard to heterogeneous hardware and the various accelerator settings of the graphics subsystem. In fact, under Windows I have found that SWT-based applications run without problems, while AWT- and Swing-based applications have occasionally brought my machine to a full halt because of DirectX incompatibilities.

Disadvantages of SWT

There are also a few "lemons" that an SWT programmer has to deal with:

❑ SWT-based applications run only on platforms for which SWT is implemented. These are presently the various Windows platforms (including Windows CE), Linux with the GTK or Motif (including 64-bit GTK on AMD64), various Unix derivatives (Solaris, QNX, AIX, and HP-UX), and Mac OS X.

❑ In general, the various implementations of SWT are functionally equivalent. But as you probably know, the devil is in the detail. For some functions, the behavior of GUI elements can differ from platform to platform. If you plan to deploy a software product on multiple platforms, it is essential to test the product thoroughly on each platform.

❑ In contrast to AWT, SWT requires explicit resource management. SWT uses resources of the host windowing system for images, colors, and fonts. These resources must be released with `dispose()` when they are no longer needed. I will discuss this in detail in the "Resource Management" section.

The SWT Package

The `org.eclipse.swt` package contains only three classes: `SWT`, `SWTException`, and `SWTError`. While the last two classes support error handling (recoverable and nonrecoverable errors), the SWT class defines all SWT-specific constants, such as constants for key identifications, predefined colors, layout variations for widgets, text styles, cursor variations, mouse actions, predefined buttons, and more.

For example, the `SWT.LINE_DASHDOT` constant represents, as the name indicates, a dash-dotted line style, and `SWT.MouseDoubleClick` represents a mouse double-click event. You will meet some of these constants in the following examples.

Events

Events provide the basic means for applications to communicate with the GUI. Typically, an application registers listeners with widgets to receive events. Usually caused by user actions such as mouse clicks or key presses, events inform the application via the listener about the kind of action that happened.

The `org.eclipse.swt.events` package contains three different groups: `Listener` interfaces, `Event` classes, and `Adapter` classes. Events can be differentiated into two categories: typed events such as `ControlEvent` or `MouseEvent` and untyped events (`Event`). Similarly, the `Listener` interfaces are divided into typed and untyped ones.

Listeners

For each different event type there is also a different `Listener` class. For example, to a button (`Button`) you can add a `SelectionListener` instance via the `addSelectionListener()` method. The `widgetSelected()` method of this instance is invoked when the button is selected (clicked). The `SelectionListener` instance is passed to the method as a parameter.

Following is an example:

```
public void createButton(Composite parent) {
    Button myButton = new Button(parent, SWT.PUSH);
    myButton.addSelectionListener(new SelectionListener() {
        public void widgetSelected(SelectionEvent e) {
            System.out.println("Button pressed!");
        }
        public void widgetDefaultSelected(SelectionEvent e) {
        }
    });
}
```

Here, I have added an instance of the inner anonymous `SelectionListener` class to the new button as a listener.

As a matter of fact, there is a remove…Listener() method for each add…Listener() method. In complex systems in particular, you should deregister (remove) listening components that are currently inactive to avoid overhead. Later, when the component becomes active again, you can add it again as a listener with add…Listener().

It is precisely for this reason that you should not make assumptions about the order in which registered listeners are called. While it is true that the list of listeners is processed sequentially when an event is fired, the sequence within this list is practically unpredictable, because components can register and deregister at their own discretion.

Adapters

An adapter is a standard implementation of a given interface that does nothing. It contains empty methods for each method defined in the interface.

The only purpose of an adapter is programmer convenience. Instead of having to implement all the methods of an interface, the programmer has only to declare a subclass of the corresponding adapter and to override the methods of interest.

In the example from the previous section you can replace SelectionListener with SelectionAdapter to avoid the definition of the empty widgetDefaultSelected() method:

```
public void createButton(Composite parent) {
    Button myButton = new Button(parent, SWT.PUSH);
    myButton.addSelectionListener(new SelectionAdapter() {
        public void widgetSelected(SelectionEvent e) {
            System.out.println("Button pressed!");
        }
    });
}
```

Events

All SWT event classes, with the exception of the Event class, are subclasses of the TypedEvent class, which in turn is a subclass of the java.util.EventObject class.

> TypedEvent **is not a subclass of** Event!

Each event type has a number of public fields that contain specific data about the event represented by the event object. For example, the MouseEvent type contains the integer fields x, y, stateMask, and button. All those fields must be accessed directly (without a get…() method). In addition, each TypedEvent class contains the getSource() method. Not surprisingly, this method is used to retrieve the source of the event.

In contrast, the generic Event event class contains a field named type, from which you can retrieve the type of event. The source of the event is contained in the widget field.

Overview of Listeners, Adapters, and Events

The following tables provide you with an overview of the relationship between SWT events, listeners, and adapters. If no adapter is provided, the listener must be used instead.

This table describes typed events:

Listener	Event	Adapter
ArmListener	ArmEvent This event happens when a widget such as a menu is prepared (armed) for selection. In particular, this is the case when the mouse is moved over the widget.	–
ControlListener	ControlEvent This event happens when a GUI element is moved or modified in size.	ControlAdapter
DisposeListener	DisposeEvent This event happens when a widget is disposed.	–
FocusListener	FocusEvent This event happens when a GUI element gains or loses focus.	FocusAdapter
HelpListener	HelpEvent This event happens when help for a GUI element is requested (F1 key).	–
KeyListener	KeyEvent This event happens when a key is pressed or released.	KeyAdapter
MenuListener	MenuEvent This event happens when a menu is shown or hidden.	MenuAdapter
ModifyListener	ModifyEvent This event happens after text is modified.	–
MouseListener This listener is notified when a mouse button is pressed or released.	MouseEvent Generic mouse event.	MouseAdapter

Listener	Event	Adapter
MouseMoveListener This listener is notified when the mouse is moved.	MouseEvent Generic mouse event.	–
MouseTrackListener This listener is notified when the mouse is moved over a GUI element or hovers over a GUI element.	MouseEvent Generic mouse event.	MouseTrackAdapter
PaintListener	PaintEvent This event happens when a GUI element must be redrawn.	–
SelectionListener	SelectionEvent This event happens when a GUI element is selected.	SelectionAdapter
ShellListener	ShellEvent This event happens when the state of a shell instance changes (default, minimized, maximized).	ShellAdapter
TraverseListener	TraverseEvent This event happens when the user transfers the focus to another GUI element by pressing Tab or when the traverse() method is called.	–
TreeListener	TreeEvent This event happens when a tree node expands or collapses.	TreeAdapter
VerifyListener	VerifyEvent This event happens before text is modified. By assigning the value "false" to the doit field of the event objects, the modification can be vetoed.	–

This table describes a generic event:

Listener	Event	Adapter
–	Untyped event used internally within the SWT. This event type is generated only by non-widget objects.	–

Widgets

In this section I discuss the various GUI elements and their position in the inheritance tree (Figure 8.2 shows the inheritance tree for the most significant Widget classes). At the top is the Widget class. The inheritance tree includes, of course, the obvious control elements such as buttons (Button), text fields (Text), or sliders (Slider). Elements that are used to organize other elements into groups are also included, such as the Group and Composite classes.

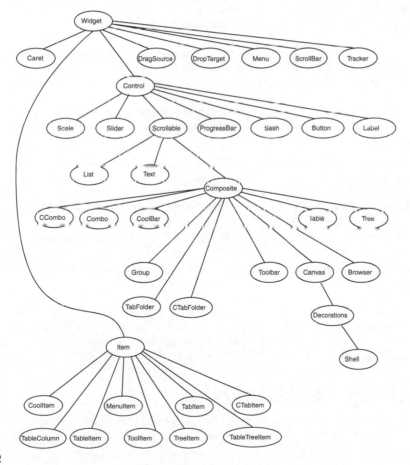

Figure 8.2

The Widget Class

All GUI elements are derived from the Widget abstract class. This class implements some of the common methods for GUI elements such as dispose() or addDisposeListener(). On execution of dispose(), a DisposeEvent object is sent to all registered DisposeListener instances.

The Control Class

The Control class is an immediate derivative of the Widget class. Instances of this class represent window-related GUI elements and correspond directly with GUI elements of the host windowing or operating system.

The Control class may send event objects of the following types to registered listeners: ControlEvent, FocusEvent, HelpEvent, KeyEvent, MouseEvent, MouseTrackEvent, MouseMoveEvent, and PaintEvent. For this purpose Control provides the necessary add...Listener() and remove...Listener() methods for the corresponding listeners.

In addition, Control provides a rich set of methods that allow the various properties of the specific GUI elements to be set and retrieved. In particular, the setVisible() and setEnabled() methods allow a GUI element to be shown or hidden, enabled or disabled.

The size of a Control instance is set initially to a default value. In many cases this is the minimum size (0x0), allowing the GUI element to remain invisible. The setBounds() method allows the size of a GUI element to be set and also its position relative to the containing Composite (see the "Composites, Groups and Canvas" section). Alternatively, the containing Composite can be equipped with a layout (see the "Layouts" section) that organizes the sizing and positioning for all Control instances contained in the Composite. The pack() method is used to recompute the size of a GUI element from the preferred size setting or from the layout.

Visual Overview

The best overview of the various native widgets in SWT is obtained with the help of one of the example applications for Eclipse. In Chapter 1 you installed the Eclipse example applications, so now you need only start the required application. To do this, invoke the Window > Show View > Other function. In the dialog select SWT Examples > SWT Controls. This view then appears in the window at the bottom-right corner. Because you need all the space you can get with this application, double-click the view's tag to maximize it.

Since this application is perfectly suited to visualize widgets in varying configurations, I will in most cases refrain from depicting widgets on the following pages. Another example application, Custom Controls, provides an overview of the non-native widgets. Both applications allow you to experiment with events and listeners.

Displays, Shells, and Monitors

The Display and Shell classes form the basis for the construction of a user interface. The Display class represents the GUI process (thread); the Shell class represents windows.

Display

The Display class connects the Java application with the operating system. Each application with an SWT-based GUI creates at least one instance of this class. Or, to be more precise, as long as only one GUI thread is needed, only one Display instance is needed. Should you want to execute GUI operations in multiple threads, you would then need a separate Display instance for each thread. With the help of the Display.getCurrent() static method, you can retrieve the active Display instance for the current thread.

Unlike the AWT and Swing, the SWT enforces an SWT object to be used only from the thread in which it was created. To allow for multithreaded applications, the Display class provides two methods that allow the execution of arbitrary code in the context of the SWT thread. A Runnable object can be passed as a parameter to the syncExec() and asyncExec() methods, which in turn execute the run() method of Runnable. In the following chapters I will make use of this technique frequently.

Figure 8.3 shows how the SWT Controls example application organizes the various native widget types in different pages. On the right you can configure the selected widget type by specifying parameters. The names of the buttons reflect the names of the corresponding SWT constants. The configured widgets are shown on the left.

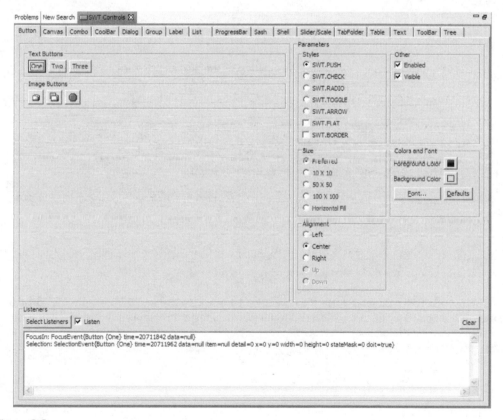

Figure 8.3

In addition to these services, the Display class provides methods that allow you to retrieve GUI properties of the host windowing system, such as getSystemFont() and getDoubleClickTime(). Display also manages the resources of the host windowing system.

Finally, the Display class provides methods for the general management of widgets, such as getActiveShell() and getFocusControl(). The map() method allows mapping the coordinates of points or rectangles from the coordinate system of one control to the coordinate system of another control.

A Display instance generates events of the Event class (see the "Events" section) and of the SWT.Open or SWT.Close type, respectively. The post() method can be used to generate events of the KeyDown, KeyUp, MouseDown, MouseUp, or MouseMove type programmatically. This feature can be used to automate user interfaces. Here is an example:

```
// Translate window coordinate (100,50) to display coordinate system
Point coord = display.map(shell, null, 100, 50);
event = new Event();
event.type = SWT.MouseMove;
event.x = coord.x;
event.y = coord.y;
display.post(event);
```

Shell

The Shell class represents a window on the desktop of the host windowing system. A Shell instance can be in one of three different operation modes: maximized, default, and minimized. When the operation mode changes, the Shell generates an event of the ShellEvent type.

> **You must not subclass Shell. (An exception is thrown at runtime in such a case.) To implement your own window types, it is better to subclass the JFace Window class (see the "Dialogs and Windows" section in Chapter 9).**

SWT supports two different shell types:

❑ Top-level shells are used to implement the main window of an application.

❑ Dialog shells are shells that are subordinate to other shells.

Which of the two types is created when a new Shell instance is created depends on the constructor's parameter: If a Display instance is passed to the constructor, a top-level shell is created; if a Shell instance is passed, a dialog shell is created.

When a shell is created, you can optionally supply one or several style parameters from the following table.

Style Parameter	Description
SWT.NONE	Default window. Layout depends on host system.
SWT.BORDER	Bordered window (depends on host platform).
SWT.CLOSE	Window has a title bar with a Close button.
SWT.MIN	Window has a title bar with a Minimize button.
SWT.MAX	Window has a title bar with a Maximize button.
SWT.NO_TRIM	Window has neither a title bar nor a border.
SWT.RESIZE	Window can be resized by using a mouse action.
SWT.TITLE	Window has a title bar.
SWT.SHELL_TRIM	Combination of styles suitable for a top-level window: (SWT.CLOSE | SWT.TITLE | SWT.MIN | SWT.MAX | SWT.RESIZE).
SWT.DIALOG_TRIM	Combination of styles suitable for a dialog window: (SWT.CLOSE | SWT.TITLE | SWT.BORDER).

There are additional constants that control the modal behavior of the window: SWT.APPLICATION_MODAL, SWT.MODELESS, SWT.PRIMARY_MODAL, and SWT.SYSTEM_MODAL. A modal window in the foreground does not allow other windows (of the same application or even of the whole system) to come to the foreground. Such a window should be instrumented with a Close button, so that the end user can close the window.

If no style parameter was specified, the default style depends on the host system and on the shell type. For example, for Windows CE the default style is SWT.NONE. For other Windows versions, however, the default style is SHELL_TRIM for top-level shells and DIALOG TRIM for dialog shells.

The setImage() method can be used to specify an icon that represents the window when it is minimized. This icon is usually displayed in the title bar, too. Images in several resolutions can be specified via the setImages() method. The platform will choose an icon from these images that fits best for a specific purpose.

Figure 8.4 shows a shell with two buttons under Windows 2000. The shell was created with the SWT.BORDER, SWT.TITLE, SWT.CLOSE, SWT.MIN, and SWT.MAX options, so it is equipped with a 3D border, a title bar, a Close button, a Minimize button, and a Maximize button.

Figure 8.4

Region

A shell does not necessarily have a rectangular outline. By assigning a region to a shell, you can mold a shell into any imaginable outline. To do so, first create a `Region` instance to which you add one or several outlines using the `add()` method. You can even use the `subtract()` method to punch holes in the region. Then assign the region to the shell with the `Shell setRegion()` method. Note that this assignment takes effect only for shells that were created with the `SWT.NO_TRIM` style. The consequence is that you must organize the closing, moving, and resizing of the shell by yourself. In the "Player Module" section in Chapter 10 I show how this is done.

Setting Up the Workbench

Before writing the first example program for a shell, you need to prepare the workbench. Create a new project called `widgets`. In this project create a new class called `widgetTest`. The SWT library is not yet known to this project. You must therefore add it as an external JAR file to the Java Build Path. I described how to do this in the "Project Properties" section in Chapter 4.

When running under Windows you will find the SWT library under

```
\eclipse\plugins\org.eclipse.swt.win32_3.0.0\ws\win32\swt.jar
```

Under Linux GTK you need two JAR files:

```
/opt/eclipse/plugins/org.eclipse.swt.gtk_3.0.0/ws/gtk/swt.jar
/opt/eclipse/plugins/org.eclipse.swt.gtk_3.0.0/ws/gtk/swt-pi.jar
```

Under other operating systems you will find the SWT libraries in similar places. Under later Eclipse versions you need to modify these paths accordingly.

The First SWT Program

You can now write your first SWT-based program (see Listing 8.1). First, create a new `Display` instance and then a new top-level shell by passing the `Display` instance to the `Shell` constructor. (For a dialog shell you would instead pass another `Shell` instance.)

```
import org.eclipse.swt.widgets.Display;
import org.eclipse.swt.widgets.Shell;

public class widgetTest {

    public static void main(String[] args) {
        // Create Display instance
```

Listing 8.1 (Continues)

```
        final Display display = new Display();
        // Create top level Shell (pass display as parent)
        final Shell toplevelShell = new Shell(display);
        // Set title line
        toplevelShell.setText("TopLevel.Titelzeile");
        // Display shell
        toplevelShell.open();
        // Create a dialog shell (pass toplevelShell as parent)
        final Shell dialogShell = new Shell(toplevelShell);
        // Set title line
        dialogShell.setText("Dialog.Titelzeile");
        // Display shell
        dialogShell.open();
        // Wait until top level shell is closed
        while (!toplevelShell.isDisposed()) {
            // Check for waiting events
            if (!display.readAndDispatch()) display.sleep();
        }
    }
}
```

Listing 8.1 (Continued)

The while loop at the end of this program is very important. Under SWT the programmer is responsible for the event loop! Without this loop, the user interface would lock up while this program is running. This problem is solved in the while loop with the readAndDispatch() method, which reads events waiting at the Display instance and passes them to the listening GUI element. If no more events are waiting, the sleep() method, which waits until a new event occurs, is invoked.

SWT Run Configuration

Now you can execute this little program. For this purpose you must create a new Run configuration of the Java Application type. To do so, invoke the Run > Run function and press the New button. Specify widgetTest as the name for the new configuration, and do the same under Main Class. Under Project specify widgets.

However, these specifications are not sufficient to run this program successfully. The SWT requires native modules, and these modules must be made known to the Java Virtual Machine. The path of the module library is specified in the Run configuration on the Arguments page under VM Arguments. In the case of a Windows host system, you have to specify the following parameters:

```
-Djava.library.path=
   C:\eclipse\plugins\org.eclipse.swt.win32_3.0.0\os\win32\x86
```

Under Linux/GTK specify

```
-Djava.library.path=
   /opt/eclipse/plugins/org.eclipse.swt.gtk_3.0.0/os/linux/x86
```

Under other host systems you will find this module library in a similar place. Under later Eclipse versions you need to modify these paths accordingly.

Then you can press the Run button and be rewarded with a new window on your desktop.

Monitor

Since Eclipse 3.0 the SWT also supports hardware setups with multiple monitors. What first sounds like a special purpose application isn't. Many professional notebook computers are able to distribute the desktop over the internal LCD monitor and a connected external monitor.

Eclipse supports such hardware with the SWT Monitor class. With the Display getMonitors() method you can obtain an array of connected monitors. The getPrimaryMonitor() method delivers a Monitor instance for the primary monitor. In particular, the Monitor class provides the getBounds() and getClientArea() methods, with which you can obtain the position and size of the monitor (or, to be precise, of the monitor's client area) within the display area. (The client area does not, for example, contain the Windows taskbar.)

SWT applications that position, move, or resize dialogs, menus, and so on should use these methods to ensure an appropriate user experience. For example, you want to make sure that dialogs and menus are not distributed over two monitors but appear completely on the primary monitor. In the "Player Module" section in Chapter 10 I show how the Monitor class can be used in a real-world application.

Dialogs

The Dialog class is an abstract class from which you can derive concrete native dialogs. The necessary code is in Listing 8.2.

```
public class MyDialog extends Dialog {
    Object result;
    // Constructor with style parameter
    public MyDialog (Shell parent, int style) {
        super (parent, style);
    }
    // Constructor without style parameter
    public MyDialog (Shell parent) {
        this (parent, 0);
        // The 0 can be replaced by own default style parameters.
    }
    public Object open () {
        // Get containing shell (as set in the constructor)
        final Shell parent = getParent();
        // Create new dialog shell
        final Shell shell = new Shell(parent, SWT.DIALOG_TRIM |

            SWT.APPLICATION_MODAL);

        // Transfer dialog title to shell title
        shell.setText(getText());
        // TODO Create all widgets here
        // Usually the result variable is set in the
        // event processing of the widgets
        shell.open();
        // Wait until dialog shell is closed
        final Display display = parent.getDisplay();
```

Listing 8.2 (Continues)

```
        while (!shell.isDisposed()) {
            if (!display.readAndDispatch())
                display.sleep();
        }
        return result;
    }
}
```

Listing 8.2 (Continued)

Predefined Dialogs

The SWT already contains some concrete subclasses of `Dialog`, such as these:

Subclass	Description
ColorDialog	Dialog for selecting a color.
DirectoryDialog	Dialog for selecting a directory in the host file system.
FileDialog	Dialog for selecting a file in the host file system. The SWT.OPEN and SWT.SAVE style parameters are used to determine the purpose for which the file is selected.
FontDialog	Dialog for selecting a text font.
MessageBox	Dialog for displaying a message. With various style parameters you can determine which buttons are used to instrument the dialog. The following combinations are possible:
	SWT.OK
	SWT.OK | SWT.CANCEL)
	SWT.YES | SWT.NO)
	SWT.YES | SWT.NO | SWT.CANCEL)
	SWT.RETRY | SWT.CANCEL)
	SWT.ABORT | SWT.RETRY | SWT.IGNORE)
	In addition, you can determine which icon is displayed with the message:
	SWT.ICON_ERROR
	SWT.ICON_INFORMATION
	SWT.ICON_QUESTION
	SWT.ICON_WARNING
	SWT.ICON_WORKING
PrintDialog	Dialog for selecting a printer and for the printer settings. See also the "Output to Printer" section.

The "look and feel" of these dialogs depends, of course, on the host system. To get an idea of what these dialogs look like on your platform, refer to the *Dialog* page in the Eclipse example application, SWT Controls.

MessageBox

In Listing 8.3 I show how you can create and use a `MessageBox` dialog in an example program of your own. Figure 8.5 shows the results.

```java
import org.eclipse.swt.SWT;
import org.eclipse.swt.widgets.Display;
import org.eclipse.swt.widgets.MessageBox;
import org.eclipse.swt.widgets.Shell;

public class widgetTest {

    public widgetTest() {
        super();
    }

    public static void main(String[] args) {
        // Create Display instance
        final Display display = new Display();
        // Create top level shell (pass display as parent)
        final Shell toplevelShell = new Shell(display);
        // Set title line
        toplevelShell.setText("TopLevel.titleLine");
        // Show shell
        toplevelShell.open();
        while (true) {
            // Create message box
            MessageBox box =
                new MessageBox(
                toplevelShell,
                SWT.RETRY
                | SWT.CANCEL
                | SWT.APPLICATION_MODAL
                | SWT.ICON_QUESTION);
            // Set title
            box.setText("Test");
            // Set message
            box.setMessage("Do you want to try again?");
            // Open message box
            if (box.open() == SWT.CANCEL)
            break;
        }
    }
}
```

Listing 8.3

Figure 8.5

Figure 8.5 shows the message box created by this example under Windows XP. You can tell from the picture that this dialog is native, indeed. Here I'm running a German language version of Windows 2000. The Retry button (Wiederholen) and the Cancel button (Abbrechen) are generated by Windows and are consequently in the German language.

However, for your own complex dialogs you will probably not use the SWT Dialog class but rather the similarly named JFace class (see Chapter 9), because the JFace version is much more convenient to use. Most of the Eclipse workbench dialogs, for example, build upon the JFace Dialog class and not on low-level SWT dialogs.

Composites, Groups, and Canvas

Usually you will not mount widgets directly into a shell but rather will put one or several hierarchies of Composite instances in between. Composites are used to organize widgets into groups. For example, you can combine the buttons of a dialog into one group with the help of a Composite. This is important for radio buttons, where pressing one button releases all other buttons in the same group. Another possibility is organizing several input fields and labels into a group to improve the layout or the navigation.

If you want to add widgets to a Composite, you will search in vain for an appropriate add() method. Instead, under the SWT, GUIs are constructed in a completely different way. Each time you create a new widget, the containing Composite is passed as a parameter to the constructor. The widgets in the Composite are ordered in the sequence of their creation.

Since Composites are widgets, too, you must specify a containing Composite instance when you create a new Composite (shells are also Composites). You will usually transfer the background and foreground color and the type font from the containing composite. Also, you can specify the position and the dimensions of the new Composite in relation to the containing Composite.

```
// Create new Composite instance
final Composite composite = new Composite(parent,0);
// Get properties from the containing composite
composite.setBackground(parent.getBackground());
composite.setForeground(parent.getForeground());
composite.setFont(parent.getFont());
// Set position and size
composite.setBounds(X,Y,WIDTH,HEIGHT);
```

You may optionally specify the constant SWT.NO_RADIO_GROUP as a second parameter in the constructor if you don't want the composite to interfere with the release mechanism of the radio buttons.

155

The Group class is a subclass of the Composite class. This class is also equipped with a border line that clearly demarcates the group area. The style of this line can be influenced with the SWT.SHADOW_ETCHED_IN, SWT.SHADOW_ETCHED_OUT, SWT.SHADOW_IN, SWT.SHADOW_OUT, and SWT.SHADOW_NONE constants, provided that the host windowing system supports this. The setText() method can be used to place a title into this border line. In many cases Groups are a better choice than Composites. When dialogs become complex, Groups allow a better navigation with the keyboard and thus are more user-friendly for disabled persons (see the "Accessibility" section).

For Composite and Group instances that contain other widgets, you usually will set a layout. I will discuss this in more detail in the Layouts section.

The Canvas class is a subclass of Composite. Its purpose is not to contain other GUI elements (although this is possible) but to serve as a canvas for drawing operations. In particular, if you want to invent your own GUI elements, you can draw them on a Canvas instance.

In addition, the Canvas class supports a caret (setCaret() and getCaret()).

Buttons

Buttons come in many faces. The button type created by the Button() constructor depends on the style constant passed to this constructor, as shown in the following table.

Style Constant	Buttons	Description
SWT.ARROW		Button with a small arrow. Normally used for drop-down menus and the like.
SWT.CHECK		Check box that can be marked. The button text is printed beside the check box.
SWT.PUSH		Pushbutton with the button text on the button face.
SWT.RADIO		Radio button. Radio buttons within the same group release one another when pressed.
SWT.TOGGLE		A toggle button is similar to a pushbutton. The difference is that the button remains pushed after the first click. The second click will release it.

In addition, the following table shows the options for controlling the look and the alignment of a button. However, not all platforms support these attributes.

Style Constant	Description
SWT.FLAT	The button is not drawn in 3D fashion but in a flat fashion.
SWT.BORDER	The button is enclosed by a frame.

Using the setText() and setImage() methods you can assign text or an image to a button. For push-buttons and toggle buttons, the text or the image appears on the button face. For check boxes and radio buttons, the text or image is shown beside the button. Buttons of the ARROW type show neither text nor image.

Both methods are mutually exclusive. Use either

```
final Button button = new Button(composite,SWT.PUSH);
button.setText("Press me!");
// React to click events
button.addSelectionListener(new SelectionAdapter() {
    public void widgetSelected(SelectionEvent e) {
        System.out.println("Key was pressed");
    }
});
```

or

```
final Button button = new Button(composite,SWT.PUSH);
Display display = composite.getDisplay();
final Image image = new Image(display, "images/button1.gif");
button.setImage(image);
// React to click events
button.addSelectionListener(new SelectionAdapter() {
    public void widgetSelected(SelectionEvent e) {
        System.out.println("Key was pressed");
    }
});
// Dispose image when button is disposed
button.addDisposeListener(new DisposeListener() {
    public void widgetDisposed(DisposeEvent e) {
        image.dispose();
    }
});
```

In the second case, additional logic was needed to dispose of the Image resource when it was no longer required. This was necessary because images allocate resources in the host operating system.

> A good source for images for buttons, toolbars, and other purposes is the icon directories in the various Eclipse plug-ins, for example, \eclipse\plugins\ org.eclipse.pde.ui_3.0.0\icons\obj16.

Sliders and Scales

Both the `Slider` and `Scale` classes support entry of a numeric value via a sliding control. Usually the `Slider` class is used for positioning window contents (scroll bar), while `Scale` is used for adjusting numeric parameters such as volume, brightness, contrast, and so on. Figure 8.6 shows an instance of each Slider and Scale, enclosed by a Group widget.

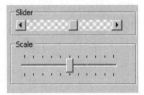

Figure 8.6

The following style constants influence the presentation of these widgets:

`SWT.HORIZONTAL` `SWT.VERTICAL`	Horizontal or vertical orientation.
`SWT.BORDER`	Scales are surrounded with a frame. This option has no effect for the `Slider` class.

The following example in Listing 8.4 creates a simple slider:

```
final Slider slider = new Slider(composite,SWT.HORIZONTAL);
// Set minimum value
slider.setMinimum(0);
// Set maximum value
slider.setMaximum(1000);
// Set increment value for arrow buttons
slider.setIncrement(50);
// Set increment value for clicks on the slider face
slider.setPageIncrement(200);
// Set current position
slider.setSelection(500);
// Set size of handle
slider.setThumb(200);
// React to slider events
slider.addSelectionListener(new SelectionAdapter() {
    public void widgetSelected(SelectionEvent e) {
        System.out.println("Slider was moved to: "
            +slider.getSelection());
    }
});
```

Listing 8.4

With the corresponding get...() methods you can retrieve these values, too. Scale provides the same methods, except the setThumb() and getThumb() methods.

ProgressBar

The ProgressBar class supports the presentation of a progress indicator. The API is very similar to that of the Slider class, except that ProgressBar does not generate events.

There are also two more style constants:

❑ SWT.SMOOTH enforces a continuous progress indicator. Otherwise, the progress indicator is broken into segments.

❑ SWT.INDETERMINATE is used to create a constantly moving progress indicator. When the progress indicator reaches the maximum size, it starts over with the minimum size. With this option set you cannot use setSelection() for indicating progress.

Using this class is not as easy as it seems, because the progress indicator is updated only when the event loop is not locked.

Scrollable and ScrollBar

Some widgets are already equipped with scroll bars. All these widgets are subclasses of Scrollable. You can control which sliders are active for a Scrollable instance with the style constants SWT.H_SCROLL and SWT.V_SCROLL. The Scrollable class, by the way, does not use Slider instances to implement the scroll bars but instead uses instances of the ScrollBar class. In contrast to Slider and Scale, ScrollBar is not a subclass of Control, that is, it is not a native widget.

Text Fields and Labels

Instances of the Text class are used to display, enter, or modify text. The following style constants can be used to configure Text instances:

SWT.MULTI SWT.SINGLE	Determines whether the text field has multiple lines or only a single line.
SWT.READ_ONLY	When this option is set, the end user cannot modify the text in the text field.
SWT.WRAP	When this option is set, automatic word wrapping is supported.

Figure 8.7 shows an example. The upper field is a Text instance; the lower field is a StyledText instance (see the "Custom Widgets" section). For both fields I set the Eras Book font, and for the lower field I applied additional formatting. In addition, for each field I specified a vertical scroll bar with SWT.VERTICAL.

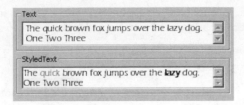

Figure 8.7

Instances of the Text class create the following event types:

SelectionEvent	When the Enter key is pressed, the widgetDefaultSelected() method is called for all registered SelectionListeners.
ModifyEvent	This event is fired after text is modified.
VerifyEvent	This event is fired before the widget's text content is modified. By assigning the value false to the event object's doit field, you can veto the modification of the text.

The example in Listing 8.5 creates a text field with a VerifyListener event to reject invalid modifications:

```
final Text text = new Text(composite,SWT.SINGLE);
text.setText("Input text");
text.addSelectionListener(new SelectionAdapter() {
    public void widgetDefaultSelected(SelectionEvent e) {
        System.out.println("Enter was pressed: "+text.getSelection());
    }
});
text.addModifyListener(new ModifyListener() {
    public void modifyText(ModifyEvent e) {
        System.out.println("Text after modification: "+text.getText());
    }
});
text.addVerifyListener(new VerifyListener() {
    public void verifyText(VerifyEvent e) {
        String s = text.getText();
        System.out.println("Text before modification: "+s);
        // Veto: Text longer than 10 characters is prohibited
        if (s.length() >= 10) e.doit = false;
    }
});
```

Listing 8.5

The Text class has a rich variety of methods for processing text input. In particular, it has methods for exchanging text content with the host system's clipboard (cut(), copy(), and paste()).

Not surprisingly, instances of the Label class are used to label other widgets. In addition, you can use labels to display an image or a horizontal or vertical line. You can control label presentation and purpose with the following style constants:

SWT.SEPARATOR	The label is displayed as a horizontal or vertical line.
SWT.HORIZONTAL SWT.VERTICAL	Determines the orientation of the label.
SWT.SHADOW_IN SWT.SHADOW_OUT SWT.SHADOW_NONE	Determines the shadowing effects of the label.
SWT.CENTER SWT.LEFT SWT.RIGHT	Determines the alignment of text or image labels.
SWT.WRAP	When the option is set, automatic word wrapping is supported for text labels.

The following code can be used to create a text label:

```
final Label label = new Label(composite, SWT.NULL);
label.setText("Enter");
```

For image labels, the image is set with the setImage() method. Just as with Buttons (see the "Buttons" section), Image instances should be released when they are no longer needed.

Tables, Lists, and Combos

Tables and lists are used to present contents in columns. Both widget types support the selection of single or multiple elements. Combos are a space-saving variant for selecting items from a list.

Tables

The Table class is responsible for the presentation of tables. In addition to the Composite style constants, Table provides these other style constants:

SWT.SINGLE SWT.MULTI	The end user can select only single or multiple table rows, respectively.
SWT.FULL_SELECTION	The whole table row is selectable. (Normally, only the first element of a row can be selected.)

SWT.CHECK	Each table row is equipped with a check box placed in front of the row. The state of the check box can be accessed with the setChecked() and getChecked() methods.
SWT.VIRTUAL	This constant indicates a virtual table, i.e., a table with table items that are created lazily when actually needed. This is to support very large tables. When using a virtual table, you should explicitly set the item count via the setItemCount() method. When a new table item is needed, the table will create it and fire an SWT.SetData event. The Event object carries the item, which then can be completed by the Listener before it is displayed.

Table instances generate SelectionEvent objects when a table element is selected. The SelectionListener widgetDefaultSelected() method is called when Enter is pressed for a table element or when a table element is double-clicked.

Figure 8.8 shows, from left to right, a table, a list, and a combo. At the right, the top widget shows the combo in its normal state; the bottom widget shows the same combo expanded after a click on the arrow button. I made the grid lines and the column headers visible for the table.

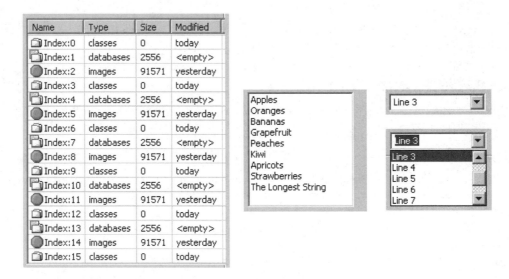

Figure 8.8

Table Columns

To configure individual table columns you can assign TableColumn to a Table instance. This is done in the same way as widgets are added to a Composite—the Table instance is passed to the

TableColumn() constructor as a parameter. In addition, you can specify a column header and a width (in pixels) for each table column, using the setText() and setWidth() methods.

The end user is still able to modify the width of table columns. In addition, the column headers act as buttons. In consequence, TableColumn instances can create a variety of events. A ControlEvent is fired when a table column is moved or modified in size. A SelectionEvent is fired when a column header is clicked.

You can specify the alignment of table columns with the help of the SWT.LEFT, SWT.CENTER, and SWT.RIGHT style constants. You can use the showColumn() method to reveal a specific column in the visible area.

Table Rows

In a similar way you can create table rows as TableItem objects. The setText() method is used to set the content of a table row. The content is passed to this method as a string or, in the case of multicolumn tables, as an array of strings. Since Eclipse V3 you can even set text color, background color, and font for each individual TableItem via the setForeground(),setBackground(), andsetFont() methods.

The Table setHeaderVisible() and setLinesVisible() methods are used to show or hide the column headers and grid lines.

The code in Listing 8.6 creates a table with three columns and two lines.

```
final Table table = new Table(composite,
    SWT.SINGLE | SWT.H_SCROLL |
    SWT.V_SCROLL | SWT.BORDER |
    SWT.FULL_SELECTION );
// Create three table columns
final TableColumn col1 = new TableColumn(table,SWT.LEFT);
col1.setText("Column 1");
col1.setWidth(80);
final TableColumn col2 = new TableColumn(table,SWT.LEFT);
col2.setText("Column 2");
col2.setWidth(80);
final TableColumn col3 = new TableColumn(table,SWT.LEFT);
col3.setText("Column 3");
col3.setWidth(80);
// Make column headers and grid lines visible
table.setHeaderVisible(true);
table.setLinesVisible(true);
// Create table rows
final TableItem item1 = new TableItem(table,0);
item1.setText(new String[] {"a","b","c"});
final TableItem item2 = new TableItem(table,0);
item2.setText(new String[] {"d","c","e"});
// Add selection listeners
table.addSelectionListener(new SelectionAdapter() {
    public void widgetDefaultSelected(SelectionEvent e) {
        processSelection("Enter was pressed: ");
    }
```

Listing 8.6 (Continues)

```
    public void widgetSelected(SelectionEvent e) {
        processSelection("Table element was selected: ");
    }
    private void processSelection(String message) {
        // Get selected table row
        TableItem[] selection = table.getSelection();
        // Because of SWT.SINGLE only one row was selected
        TableItem selectedRow = selection[0];
        // Format the table elements for output
        String s = selectedRow.getText(0)+", "+
            selectedRow.getText(1)+", "+selectedRow.getText(2);
        System.out.println(message + s);
    }
});
```

Listing 8.6 (Continued)

Lists

If you want to offer only a single-column list of string elements for selection, using the `List` class is much simpler than creating a table. List instances generate the same event types as `Table` instances, but the `widgetDefaultSelected()` method is called only in the case of a double-click on a list element. You can use the `SWT.SINGLE` and `SWT.MULTI` style constants to specify whether the end user can select only single or multiple list entries.

In Listing 8.7 I construct a list with three entries. The selection of multiple entries is allowed and processed.

```
final List list = new List(composite,SWT.MULTI);
list.add("Element1");
list.add("Element2");
list.add("Element3");
list.addSelectionListener(new SelectionAdapter() {
    public void widgetDefaultSelected(SelectionEvent e) {
        processSelection("Enter was pressed: ");
    }
    public void widgetSelected(SelectionEvent e) {
        processSelection("List entry was selected: ");
    }
    private void processSelection(String message) {
        // Get selected entries
        String[] selection = list.getSelection();
        // Format entries for output
        StringBuffer sb = new StringBuffer();
        for (int i = 0; i < selection.length; i++) {
            sb.append(selection[i]+" ");
        }
        System.out.println(message + sb);
    }
});
```

Listing 8.7

Combos

Finally, there is the Combo class, which combines a selection from a list with text input. Instances of the Combo class generate the following event types:

SelectionEvent	If the Enter key is pressed on a list entry, the SelectionListener widgetDefaultSelected() method is invoked.
	If a list entry is selected, the widgetSelected() method is called instead.
ModifyEvent	This event is fired when the text is changed via the keyboard or via list selection.

The following style constants influence the presentation and the function of Combo instances:

SWT.DROP_DOWN	The selection list is shown only after a click on the arrow button.
SWT.READ_ONLY	When this option is specified, values can be only selected from the list but not entered by the keyboard.
SWT.SIMPLE	The selection list is always visible if this option is specified.

The code in Listing 8.8 creates a Combo instance.

```
final Combo combo = new Combo(composite,SWT.DROP_DOWN);
// Create three list elements
combo.add("Element1");
combo.add("Element2");
combo.add("Element3");
// Supply default value for text field
combo.setText("Select");
// Add selection listener
combo.addSelectionListener(new SelectionAdapter() {
    public void widgetDefaultSelected(SelectionEvent e) {
        System.out.println("Enter was pressed: " + combo.getText());
        }
        public void widgetSelected(SelectionEvent e) {
            System.out.println("List entry was selected: " +
                combo.getText());
            }
        });
        // Add ModifyListener
        combo.addModifyListener(new ModifyListener() {
        public void modifyText(ModifyEvent e) {
        System.out.println("Text was modified: "+combo.getText());
    }
});
```

Listing 8.8

The non-native CCombo widget is very similar to the Combo widget but also supports borderless presentation. It is usually used within table cells.

Trees

The Tree class is responsible for the presentation of trees. The presentation and functionality of the tree can be influenced by the following style constants:

SWT.SINGLE SWT.MULTI	The end user can select only single or multiple tree nodes, respectively.
SWT.CHECK	Each tree node is equipped with a check box in front of the node. The state of the check box can be accessed via the setChecked() and getChecked() methods.

Figure 8.9 shows two trees. The tree on the left has only text nodes, while the tree on the right has images assigned to the tree nodes.

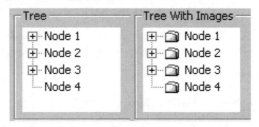

Figure 8.9

Tree instances generate the following event types:

SelectionEvent	In case of a double-click or when the *Enter* key is pressed on a tree node, the SelectionListener widgetDefaultSelected() method is called. The widgetSelected() method is invoked when a tree node is selected.
TreeEvent	The TreeListener treeExpanded() method is called when a tree node is expanded. The treeCollapsed() method is called when a tree node is collapsed. The node in question is passed in the item field in the TreeEvent object.

The individual tree nodes are implemented as TreeItem instances. When such an instance is created, you can pass either the Tree object or another TreeItem instance as the parent node via the constructor. The text content of a TreeItem instance is set via the setText() method; its text font is set with the setFont() method. In addition, you can assign an image to each tree node using the setImage() method. As already discussed with Buttons (see the "Buttons" section), you should dispose of Image instances when they are no longer needed.

The code in Listing 8.9 creates a simple tree with three nodes. The first node has two child nodes.

```
final Tree tree = new Tree(composite,SWT.SINGLE);
// Create first node level
final TreeItem node1 = new TreeItem(tree,SWT.NULL);
node1.setText("Node 1");
final TreeItem node2 = new TreeItem(tree,SWT.NULL);
node2.setText("Node 2");
final TreeItem node3 = new TreeItem(tree,SWT.NULL);
node3.setText("Node 3");
// Create second node level
final TreeItem node11 = new TreeItem(node1,SWT.NULL);
node11.setText("Node 1.1");
final TreeItem node12 = new TreeItem(node1,SWT.NULL);
node12.setText("Node 1.2");
// Add selection listener
tree.addSelectionListener(new SelectionAdapter() {
    public void widgetDefaultSelected(SelectionEvent e) {
        System.out.println("Enter was pressed: " +
            tree.getSelection()[0].getText());
    }
    public void widgetSelected(SelectionEvent e) {
        System.out.println("Tree node was selected: " +
            tree.getSelection()[0].getText());
    }
});
// Add TreeListener
tree.addTreeListener(new TreeAdapter() {
    public void treeCollapsed(TreeEvent e) {
        System.out.println("Tree node was collapsed: " +
            ((TreeItem) e.item).getText());
    }
    public void treeExpanded(TreeEvent e) {
        System.out.println("ree node was expanded. " +
            ((TreeItem) e.item).getText()),
    }
});
```

Listing 8.9

For larger trees you will usually refrain from constructing the tree completely before displaying it. A better way is to construct a tree lazily, meaning to create nodes as they become visible, that is, when their parent nodes are expanded.

Sashes

The Sash class is responsible for representing sashes. Sashes can be used to segment a Composite into separate areas. The end user is able to reposition the sashes so that the size of the areas can change. Since the sashes don't control the size of the adjoining areas themselves, the programmer is responsible for reacting to events from Sash instances and adjusting the size and position of these areas accordingly. Sash instances create events of the SelectEvent type. The orientation of a sash can be controlled via the SWT.HORIZONTAL and SWT.VERTICAL style constants.

Instead of organizing the coordination of sashes manually, you can also make use of the SashForm class (see the "Custom Widgets" section).

Tabbed Folders

The TabFolder class implements a tabbed folder, a multipage unit in which a page can be brought to the front by clicking on the page's tab. Each TabFolder instance is a Composite, which may contain one or several TabItem instances. Each TabItem object relates to a tab, and the tab's text can be set with the setText() method. With the setControl() method you can assign a Control instance (such as a Composite) to each TabItem object. The Control instance is made visible when the corresponding TabItem object is selected. The Control instance must be created as a part of the TabFolder (i.e., by specifying the TabFolder instance in the constructor when the Control is created).

TabFolder supports only the SWT.BORDER style constant.

TabFolder instances generate SelectionEvents on the selection of a TabItem.

The code in Listing 8.10 creates a tabbed folder with two tabs.

```java
import org.eclipse.swt.SWT;
import org.eclipse.swt.events.SelectionAdapter;
import org.eclipse.swt.events.SelectionEvent;
import org.eclipse.swt.layout.FillLayout;
import org.eclipse.swt.widgets.*;

public class widgetTest {

    public static void main(String[] args) {
        // Create display instance
        final Display display = new Display();
        // Create top level shell (pass display as parent)
        final Shell toplevelShell = new Shell(display);
        // Set title
        toplevelShell.setText("TopLevel.Titelzeile");
        // Fill the shell completely with content
        toplevelShell.setLayout(new FillLayout());
        // Create tabbed folder
        TabFolder folder = new TabFolder(toplevelShell, SWT.NONE);
        // Protocol selection event
        folder.addSelectionListener(new SelectionAdapter() {
            public void widgetSelected(SelectionEvent e) {
                System.out.println(
                    "Tab selected: " + ((TabItem) (e.item)).getText());
            }
        });
        // Fill tabbed folder completely with content
        folder.setLayout(new FillLayout());
        Composite page1 = createTabPage(folder, "tab1");
        // We can now place more GUI elements onto page1
        //...
        Composite page2 = createTabPage(folder, "tab2");
```

Listing 8.10 (Continues)

```
        // We can now place more GUI elements onto page2
        //...
        // Display shell
        toplevelShell.open();
        // Event loop
        while (!toplevelShell.isDisposed()) {
            if (!display.readAndDispatch())
            display.sleep();
        }
    }

    private static Composite createTabPage(TabFolder folder,
        String label) {
        // Create and label a new tab
        TabItem tab = new TabItem(folder, SWT.NONE);
        tab.setText(label);
        // Create a new page as a Composite instance
        Composite page = new Composite(folder, SWT.NONE);
        //... and assign to tab
        tab.setControl(page);
        return page;
    }
}
```

Listing 8.10 (Continued)

The non-native `CTabFolder` widget is very similar to the `TabFolder` widget but supports positioning the tabs (`CTabItem`) at the top (`SWT.TOP`) or the bottom (`SWT.BOTTOM`) of the folder and uses tabs with a curved outline.

Toolbars

The `ToolBar` class not surprisingly implements toolbars. Each `ToolBar` instance is a `Composite` that contains one or several `ToolItem` instances.

You can control the presentation of toolbars with the following style constants:

`SWT.FLAT`	Use a two-dimensional representation instead of three-dimensional presentation, provided this is supported by the host platform.
`SWT.WRAP`	Use automatic word wrapping.
`SWT.RIGHT`	Align right.
`SWT.HORIZONTAL` `SWT.VERTICAL`	Horizontal or vertical orientation, respectively.

`ToolItem` instances represent the buttons on the toolbar. You can control the button type via the following style constants:

SWT.PUSH	Normal button that releases immediately.
SWT.CHECK	Locking button (similar to toggle buttons).
SWT.RADIO	Radio button that releases other radio buttons in the same toolbar when pressed.
SWT.SEPARATOR	Passive element to separate button groups.
SWT.DROP_DOWN	Normal button with an associated arrow button.

Tool items are labeled via the `setText()` method. Image buttons can be created with the `setImage()` method. With the `setHotImage()` method you can set an additional image that appears when the mouse hovers over the button. With the `setDisabledImage()` method you can set an image that is shown when the tool item is disabled. This way, you can visualize the different operation modes of a tool item. As already discussed for `Buttons` (see the "Buttons" section), `Image` instances must be disposed of when they are no longer needed. With `setToolTipText()` you can add additional text to the tool item that is shown when the mouse is moved over the tool item.

When activated, `ToolItem` instances generate `SelectionEvent` objects. In the case of `DROP_DOWN` tool items, you have to find out whether the main button or the arrow button was pressed. You can do this by checking the condition `(event.detail == SWT.ARROW)`. The event listener can then create a menu list for the drop-down menu, allowing the selection of a function.

Moveable Tool Groups (CoolBar)

The `CoolBar` class can be used to combine several `ToolBar` instances into so-called `CoolItems`, that is, tool groups that can be repositioned by the end user. A good example of a `CoolBar` is the toolbar of the Eclipse workbench. Each single `Toolbar` instance is embedded into a `CoolItem` instance. These `CoolItem` instances are placed onto a `CoolBar` and can be moved within the area of the `CoolBar`. The association between `CoolItem` and `ToolBar` is achieved with the `CoolItem setControl()` method. Initially, you must assign a minimum size for each `CoolItem` instance. I will show how this is done in the second example that follows.

If you assign the `SWT.DROP_DOWN` style constant for a `CoolItem` instance, an arrow symbol appears when all tools within the tool group cannot be displayed. You need to implement the necessary event processing in such a case: you must construct a drop-down menu, as you had to do for drop-down tool items (see the previous section).

Menus

The `Menu` class is used to implement menus. The following style constants influence the presentation of a `Menu` instance:

SWT.BAR	The instance represents a menu bar.
SWT.DROP_DOWN	The instance represents a drop-down menu.
SWT.POP_UP	The instance represents a pop-up menu.

Menu instances generate events of the `HelpEvent` and `MenuEvent` types. When a menu appears on the screen, the `MenuListener menuShown()` method is invoked. When the menu disappears, the `menuHidden()` method is called.

Menu items are implemented by `MenuItem` instances. The type of item is controlled via a style constant:

SWT.CHECK	The menu item is equipped with a check mark. This symbol is toggled with each click on the menu entry.
SWT.CASCADE	The menu item implements a cascading menu.
SWT.PUSH	Normal menu item.
SWT.RADIO	Menu item with a check mark. When this symbol is set, other radio menu items in the same menu are reset.
SWT.SEPARATOR	Passive item implementing a separator line.

Menu items are labeled with the help of the `setText()` method.

`MenuItem` instances create events of the `SelectionEvent`, `ArmEvent`, and `HelpEvent` types. `ArmEvents` are fired when the menu item is armed, that is, when the mouse cursor is moved over the item.

If you want to create a typical menu bar, you first must create a `Menu` instance of the `SWT.BAR` type. When doing so, you must specify the `Shell` for which the menu is created as the `Composite` parent. The creation of the menu bar is not enough, however. You must also activate the menu bar for the parent shell. This is done in the `Shell` instance by calling the `setMenuBar()` method.

The individual menu titles are then created as cascading `MenuItem` instances. The submenus belonging to these instances are created as independent `SWT.DROP_DOWN` menus under the `Shell` instance. Then the `MenuItem setMenu()` method is used to assign the submenus to the cascading menu items

The example in Listing 8.11 shows the construction of a simple menu with a single menu title:

```java
// Create menu bar
Menu menuBar = new Menu(toplevelShell, SWT.BAR);
toplevelShell.setMenuBar(menuBar);
// Create menu title
MenuItem fileTitle = new MenuItem(menuBar, SWT.CASCADE);
fileTitle.setText("File");
// Create submenu for this menu title
Menu fileMenu = new Menu(toplevelShell, SWT.DROP_DOWN);
fileTitle.setMenu(fileMenu);
// Create menu item
MenuItem item = new MenuItem(fileMenu, SWT.NULL);
item.setText("Exit");
// Event processing for menu item
item.addSelectionListener(new SelectionAdapter() {
    public void widgetSelected(SelectionEvent e) {
        toplevelShell.close();
    }
});
```

Listing 8.11

In Listing 8.12 I create a `CoolBar` consisting of two moveable groups with five different buttons. There is also a drop-down button that expands a menu with two menu items when pressed.

```java
// Create CoolBar
final CoolBar coolbar = new CoolBar(composite, SWT.NULL);
// Create ToolBar as a component of CoolBar
final ToolBar toolbar1 = new ToolBar(coolbar, SWT.NULL);
// Create pushbutton
final ToolItem toolitem1 = new ToolItem(toolbar1, SWT.PUSH);
toolitem1.setText("Push");
toolitem1.setToolTipText("Push button");
// Create event processing for pushbutton
toolitem1.addSelectionListener(new SelectionAdapter() {
    public void widgetSelected(SelectionEvent e) {
        System.out.println(
            "Tool button was pressed: " + toolitem1.getText());
    }
});
// Create check button
final ToolItem toolitem2 = new ToolItem(toolbar1, SWT.CHECK);
toolitem2.setText("Check");
toolitem2.setToolTipText("Check button");
// Create CoolItem instance
final CoolItem coolitem1 = new CoolItem(coolbar, SWT.NULL);
// Assign this tool bar to the CoolItem instance
coolitem1.setControl(toolbar1);
// Compute size of tool bar
Point size = toolbar1.computeSize(SWT.DEFAULT, SWT.DEFAULT);
// Compute required size of CoolItems instance
size = coolitem1.computeSize(size.x, size.y);
// Set size for this CoolItem instance
coolitem1.setSize(size);
// The minimum size of the CoolItem is the width of the first button
coolitem1.setMinimumSize(toolitem1.getWidth(), size.y);

// Create second ToolBar instance
final ToolBar toolbar2 = new ToolBar(coolbar, SWT.NULL);
// Create two radio buttons
final ToolItem toolitem3a = new ToolItem(toolbar2, SWT.RADIO);
toolitem3a.setText("Radio");
toolitem3a.setToolTipText("Radio button a");
final ToolItem toolitem3b = new ToolItem(toolbar2, SWT.RADIO);
toolitem3b.setText("Radio");
toolitem3b.setToolTipText("Radio button b");
// Create separator
new ToolItem(toolbar2, SWT.SEPARATOR);
// Create drop-down menu button
final ToolItem toolitem5 = new ToolItem(toolbar2, SWT.DROP_DOWN);
toolitem5.setText("Drop-down-Menu");
// Add event processing to drop-down menu button
toolitem5.addSelectionListener(
    // In class DropDownSelectionListener we construct the menu
    new DropDownSelectionListener(composite.getShell()));
    // Create second CoolItem, assing Toolbar to it and set size
    final CoolItem coolitem2 = new CoolItem(coolbar, SWT.NULL);
```

Listing 8.12 (Continues)

```
        coolitem2.setControl(toolbar2);
        size = toolbar2.computeSize(SWT.DEFAULT, SWT.DEFAULT);
        size = coolitem2.computeSize(size.x, size.y);
        coolitem2.setSize(size);
        coolitem2.setMinimumSize(toolitem3a.getWidth(), size.y);
```

Listing 8.12 (Continued)

The DropDownSelectionListener class is responsible for menu construction and is defined as demonstrated in Listing 8.13.

```
class DropDownSelectionListener extends SelectionAdapter {
    private Menu menu;
    private Composite parent;

    public DropDownSelectionListener(Composite parent) {
        this.parent = parent;
    }

    public void widgetSelected(final SelectionEvent e) {
        // Create menu lazily
        if (menu == null) {
            menu = new Menu(parent);
            final MenuItem menuItem1 = new MenuItem(menu, SWT.NULL);
            menuItem1.setTcxt("Item1");
            // Set SelectionListener for menuItem1
            menuItem1.addSelectionListener(new SelectionAdapter() {
                public void widgetSelected(SelectionEvent m) {
                    processMcnuEvent(e, menuItem1);
                }
            });
            menuItem1.addArmListener(new ArmListener() {
                public void widgetArmed(ArmEvent m) {
                    System.out.println("Mouse is over menu item 1");
                }
            }),

            final MenuItem menuItem2 = new MenuItem(menu, SWT.NULL);
            menuItem2.setText("Item2");
            // Set SelectionListener foYr menuItem1
            menuItem2.addSelectionListener(new SelectionAdapter() {
                public void widgetSelected(SelectionEvent m) {
                    processMenuEvent(e, menuItem2);
                }
            });
            menuItem2.addArmListener(new ArmListener() {
                public void widgetArmed(ArmEvent m) {
                    System.out.println("Mouse is over menu item 2");
                }
            });
        }
        // Check, if it was the arrow button that was pressed
        if (e.detail == SWT.ARROW) {
```

Listing 8.13 (Continues)

173

```
            if (menu.isVisible()) {
                // Set visible menu invisible
                menu.setVisible(false);
            } else {
                // Retrieve ToolItem and ToolBar from the event object
                final ToolItem toolItem = (ToolItem) e.widget;
                final ToolBar toolBar = toolItem.getParent();
                // Get position and size of the ToolItem
                Rectangle toolItemBounds = toolItem.getBounds();
                // Convert relative position to absolute position
                Point point =
                toolBar.toDisplay(
                    new Point(toolItemBounds.x, toolItemBounds.y));
                // Set menu position
                menu.setLocation(point.x, point.y + toolItemBounds.height);
                // Make menu visible
                menu.setVisible(true);
            }
        } else {
            final ToolItem toolItem = (ToolItem) e.widget;
            System.out.println(
            "Tool button was pressed: " + toolItem.getText());
            }
        }
    private void processMenuEvent(
        final SelectionEvent e,
    final MenuItem item) {
        // Get text of menu item
        final String s = item.getText();
        // Get ToolItem
        final ToolItem toolItem = (ToolItem) e.widget;
        // Replace ToolItem label with text of the menu item
        toolItem.setText(s);
        // Hide menu
        menu.setVisible(false);
    }
}
```

Listing 8.13 (Continued)

Custom Widgets

The org.eclipse.swt.custom package contains additional widgets that are not mapped to native widgets of the host platform but are pure Java implementations.

I've already discussed the CCombo and CTabFolder widgets. The following table lists some more of these widget classes:

BusyIndicator	This class is used to replace the mouse pointer with a busy symbol (hourglass, etc.). To do this, you must call the showWhile(display, runnable) method. The second parameter must be of the java.lang.Runnable type. The run() method of this Runnable contains the processing logic to be executed while the busy symbol is shown.
ControlEditor	This class is used to attach a Composite to another GUI element. When the Composite is moved or modified in size, the position of the attached element is also changed. Normally, ControlEditor is used to attach an editor to a noneditable Composite. The Eclipse API reference documentation contains an example in which a button is attached to a Canvas instance (see the "Graphics" section). When the button is pressed, the background color of the canvas changes. When the canvas is moved, the button moves with the canvas.
PopupList	This class works similarly to the List class (see the "Tables, Lists and Combos" section). However, the list appears in its own shell in front of the Shell instance that is specified in the PopupList() constructor. Normally, this class is used to select values from a list within a table element.
SashForm	This class is implemented as a subclass of Composite and organizes its children horizontally or vertically (as specified) separated by sashes (see the "Sashes" section). Weights can be specified for each child to control the width resp. height. The setMaximizedControl() method can be used to temporarily maximize a single child and minimize the others.
StyledText	This class implements a single- or multiline text input field, similarly to the Text class. In addition, some text attributes are supported: background and foreground color, text font, bold, italic, and normal text style. This functionality is sufficient for programming program editors but insufficient for implementing word processors. The text can be formatted with the help of the getStyleRangeAtOffset(), getStyleRanges(), setStyleRange(), and setStyleRanges() methods that allow StyleRange instances to be retrieved and set. In addition, the getLineBackground() and setLineBackground() methods allow retrieving and setting the background color of a text line. As an alternative to these methods, you can implement your own text style processing as LineStyleListener and LineBackgroundListener instances. The text content model of a StyledText widget must implement the StyledTextContent interface. You can even provide your own StyledTextContent implementations. The setContent() method can be used to initialize a StyledText widget.

TableTree	This class has similar functionality to the Tree class (see the "Trees" section). However, the graphical representation is different. The tree structure appears as a series of hierarchically indented tables; lines representing the tree branches are not shown. The individual tree nodes are implemented by TableTreeItem instances.
TableEditor TreeEditor TableTreeEditor	These classes are similar to the ControlEditor class but are specialized for the Table, Tree, and TableTree target classes. The Eclipse API reference documentation contains examples that show how to attach text fields to TableItem, TreeItem, and TableTreeItem instances.

Listing 8.14 contains an example for the SashForm class. Two SashForms are created: a vertical SashForm inside a horizontal SashForm. Figure 8.10 shows the results. Both SashForms have List widgets as children.

```
// Create outer SashForm
SashForm sf1 = new SashForm(toplevelShell, SWT.HORIZONTAL);
// Create inner SashForm
SashForm sf2 = new SashForm(sf1, SWT.VERTICAL);
// Create content for vertical SashForm
List list1 = new List(sf2, SWT.NONE);
list1.setItems(new String[]{"red", "green", "blue"});
List list2 = new List(sf2, SWT.NONE);
list2.setItems(new String[]{"A", "B", "C"});
// Apply even weights
sf2.setWeights(new int[] {100,100});
// Create content for horizontal SashForm
List list3 = new List(sf1, SWT.NONE);
list3.setItems(
       new String[]{"one", "two", "three", "four", "five", "six"});
// Apply uneven weights
sf1.setWeights(new int[] {100,200});
```

Listing 8.14

Figure 8.10

In the resulting composite, both sashes can be moved with the mouse. When the window is resized, the sashes move accordingly.

The Browser Widget

Since Eclipse V3, developers can use a web browser widget within their SWT applications. This widget is implemented as a `Composite` in the `Browser` class and is located in the `org.eclipse.swt.browser` package. The Eclipse team, however, has not implemented their own complete web browser version but utilizes the native browsers of the various host platforms. Under Windows, for example, the `Browser` class implements an OLE client for the Internet Explorer. Under Linux, Mozilla is used, and under Mac OS X, the Safari browser is used. The advantage of this approach is that the browser widget exhibits the same functionality as the host platform's web browser. Security and other preferences applied to the native web browser affect the browser widget, too. On the other hand, the browser widget in many aspects does not behave like a standard widget. For example, you cannot add a context menu to the widget (because the native browser is already equipped with one); `MouseListeners` and `KeyListeners` don't receive mouse and key events; and you can neither draw on the surface of the widget nor place other widgets into the `Browser` composite.

Instead, the browser widget features a range of methods for browser-specific tasks such as `setURL()` to display a web page at a specified location, `getURL()` to retrieve the URL of the current web page, or `setText()` to display some HTML text. Navigation is supported by the `back()`, `isBackEnabled()`, `forward()`, `isForwardEnabled()`, `refresh()`, and `stop()` methods.

In addition, the browser widget can be instrumented with a variety of listeners such as `CloseWindowListener`, `LocationListener`, `OpenWindowListener`, `ProgressListener`, `StatusTextListener`, `TitleListener`, or `VisibilityWindowListener` in order to react to state and content changes of the embedded web browser.

In the "Description Window" section in Chapter 10 I show the browser widget in a practical application.

Layouts

After this *tour de force* through the land of widgets, you now have a look at layouts. Layouts are used to position GUI elements on a `Composite` in an automated way. The layout computes the size and position of each GUI element that belongs to a `Composite`. Should the size of the `Composite` change—either under program control or by user interaction—the layout of the GUI elements is recomputed automatically.

By default, all GUI elements within the `Composite` are treated as equal by the layout. However, it is possible to influence the layout process for each GUI element individually by assigning specific layout data to GUI elements. This is done with the `Control setLayoutData()` method.

Eclipse provides five predefined layout classes. In addition, it offers the possibility of creating your own layout classes. The names of the predefined layout classes all follow the pattern `*Layout`. The names of the corresponding classes for the individual layout data follow the pattern `*Data`. With the exception of the `StackLayout` class, which is part of the `org.eclipse.swt.custom` package, all predefined layout classes are contained in the `org.eclipse.swt.layout` package.

An excellent article about layouts is "Understanding Layouts in SWT" by Carolyn MacLeod and Shantha Ramachandran.

> Composite with a layout may be simpler and more user friendly, because this component allows the end user to divide the available space freely between child components.

Visual Overview

The best way to gain an overview of the different layouts and their options is to activate one of the Eclipse example applications under Window > Show View > Other. In the displayed dialog, select the SWT Examples > SWT Layouts application, which then shows up in the bottom-right corner of the workbench window (see Figure 8.11). Because you will need all the space you can get, you should maximize this application window by double-clicking its tag.

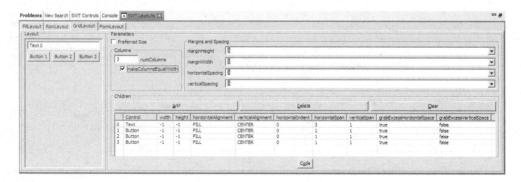

Figure 8.11

The SWT Layouts example application can be used to try the various options for FillLayout, RowLayout, GridLayout, and FormLayout. You can generate the corresponding source code with the Code button, so this example application can be used as a (very) minimal GUI designer.

Since this application is perfectly suited for visualizing the various layouts and their options, I will refrain from showing the corresponding screen shots.

The FillLayout Class

FillLayout is the simplest of the predefined layouts. The effect of a FillLayout is that the GUI elements completely fill the containing Composite. There are neither spaces nor margins between the GUI elements. Also, automatic wrapping in the event of insufficient space is not possible. All GUI elements are the same size. The height is determined by the GUI element with the largest preferred height, and the width is determined by the GUI element with the largest preferred width. FillLayouts are typically used for toolbars where the individual buttons are not separated by spaces. They are also used in cases where a single GUI element completely fills a Composite.

By default, all GUI elements are concatenated in the horizontal direction. However, you can enforce a vertical orientation by specifying the SWT.VERTICAL style constant to the layout's type field:

```
FillLayout fillLayout = new FillLayout();
fillLayout.type = SWT.VERTICAL;
composite.setLayout(fillLayout);
new Button(composite, SWT.RADIO).setText("One");
new Button(composite, SWT.RADIO).setText("Two");
new Button(composite, SWT.RADIO).setText("Three");
```

In the case of `FillLayouts` you have no option to set the size of the contained GUI elements individually.

The RowLayout Class

Similarly to `FillLayout`, the `RowLayout` positions the contained GUI elements in a row. However, `RowLayout` provides the following fields for additional options:

type	As in `FillLayout`.
wrap	If this option is set to `true` (the default), GUI elements that do not fit into a line are wrapped onto the next line.
pack	If this option is set to `true` (the default), GUI elements are displayed in their preferred size and at the left-most position. Otherwise, the GUI elements fill all the available space, similarly to `FillLayout`.
justify	If this option is set to `true`, GUI elements are distributed evenly over the available space. The default is `false`.
marginLeft marginTop marginRight marginBottom	These fields control the size of the margins in pixels.
spacing	This field controls the minimum space between the GUI elements in pixels.

The following code shows how to set the various options of a RowLayout instance:

```
RowLayout rowLayout = new RowLayout();
rowLayout.wrap = false;
rowLayout.pack = false;
rowLayout.justify = true;
rowLayout.type = SWT.VERTICAL;
rowLayout.marginLeft = 10;
rowLayout.marginTop = 5;
rowLayout.marginRight = 10;
rowLayout.marginBottom = 8;
rowLayout.spacing = 5;
composite.setLayout(rowLayout);
```

For GUI elements within a `RowLayout` instance, you can set the size of each GUI element individually by assigning a `RowData` instance to it. In the following example, two buttons are created, and height and width are assigned to both of them:

```
Button button1 = new Button(composite, SWT.PUSH);
button1.setText("70x20");
button1.setLayoutData(new RowData(70, 20));
Button button2 = new Button(composite, SWT.PUSH);
button2.setText("50x35");
button2.setLayoutData(new RowData(50, 35));
```

The GridLayout Class

The GridLayout class is the most useful and powerful of the predefined layout classes. However, it is not easy to manage, because of its many parameters and their interactions. If you have experience in the layout of HTML pages using tables, you will know what I mean.

GridLayout has, indeed, some similarity to HTML tables. Here, there are also rows and columns, and it is possible to fuse adjoining table elements horizontally or vertically.

The following options are available for GridLayouts:

numColumns	The number of columns. The number of rows is determined automatically from the number of GUI elements and the number of columns.
makeColumnsEqualWidth	If this field is set to true, all columns are laid out with the same width. The default is false.
marginHeight	This field controls the height of the upper and lower margins in pixels.
marginWidth	This field controls the width of the left and right margins in pixels.
horizontalSpacing	This field controls the minimum distance between columns in pixels.
verticalSpacing	This field controls the minimum distance between rows in pixels.

The following example shows how to set the various options of a GridLayout instance:

```
GridLayout gridLayout = new GridLayout();
gridLayout.numColumns = 3;
gridLayout.marginWidth = 10;
gridLayout.makeColumnsEqualWidth = true;
gridLayout.marginHeight = 5;
gridLayout.horizontalSpacing = 6;
gridLayout.verticalSpacing = 4;
gridLayout.makeColumnsEqualWidth = true;
composite.setLayout(gridLayout);
```

GridData

The layout options that you can set for individual GUI elements with the help of GridData instances are quite rich. GridData objects have the following public fields:

grabExcessHorizontalSpace	If this field is set to `true`, the GUI element fills all the remaining horizontal space. The default is `false`.
grabExcessVerticalSpace	If this field is set to `true`, the GUI element fills all the remaining vertical space. The default is `false`.
heightHint	This field specifies a minimum height in pixels. If a value is specified, the vertical scroll function of a corresponding scrollable GUI element is disabled.
horizontalAlignment	This field specifies how the GUI element is aligned horizontally in its table cell. The following constants can be specified: GridData.BEGINNING (default) GridData.CENTER GridData.END GridData.FILL
horizontalIndent	This field specifies how many pixels a GUI element is indented from the left.
horizontalSpan	This field specifies how many table cells the GUI element consumes in the horizontal direction (the cells are fused).
verticalAlignment	This field specifies how the GUI element is aligned vertically in its table cell. The following constants can be specified: GridData.BEGINNING GridData.CENTER (default) GridData.END GridData.FILL
verticalSpan	This field specifies how many table cells the GUI element consumes in a vertical direction (the cells are fused).
widthHint	This field specifies a minimum width in pixels. If a value is specified, the horizontal scroll function of a corresponding scrollable GUI element is disabled.

Some of these options may already be specified in the `GridData()` constructor. For this purpose, the following style constants are available:

Constant	Equivalent
GridData.GRAB_HORIZONTAL	grabExcessHorizontalSpace = true
GridData.GRAB_VERTICAL	grabExcessVerticalSpace = true

Constant	Equivalent
`GridData.HORIZONTAL_ALIGN_BEGINNING`	`horizontalAlignment = GridData.BEGINNING`
`GridData.HORIZONTAL_ALIGN_CENTER`	`horizontalAlignment = GridData.CENTER`
`GridData.HORIZONTAL_ALIGN_END`	`horizontalAlignment = GridData.END`
`GridData.HORIZONTAL_ALIGN_FILL`	`horizontalAlignment = GridData.FILL`
`GridData.VERTICAL_ALIGN_BEGINNING`	`verticalAlignment = GridData.BEGINNING`
`GridData.VERTICAL_ALIGN_CENTER`	`verticalAlignment = GridData.CENTER`
`GridData.VERTICAL_ALIGN_END`	`verticalAlignment = GridData.END`
`GridData.VERTICAL_ALIGN_FILL`	`verticalAlignment = GridData.FILL`
`GridData.FILL_HORIZONTAL`	`HORIZONTAL_ALIGN_FILL | GRAB_HORIZONTAL`
`GridData.FILL_VERTICAL`	`VERTICAL_ALIGN_FILL | GRAB_VERTICAL`
`GridData.FILL_BOTH`	`FILL_VERTICAL | FILL_HORIZONTAL`

I do not give a code example here but rather refer you to the "Player Module" section in Chapter 10, which shows the use of the `GridLayout` class in a real application.

Should all these layout options be insufficient, you still have the option of nesting `GridLayouts` by nesting `Composites`. This technique should be well known to all those who have laid out HTML pages with the help of nested tables.

The FormLayout Class

`FormLayout` was introduced with Eclipse 2.0. It allows you to position GUI elements on a two-dimensional surface in relation to another GUI element or in relation to the borders of the `Composite`. This is done by using `FormAttachment` instances.

For `FormLayouts` you have the following options:

`marginHeight`	This field controls the height of the upper and lower margins in pixels.
`marginWidth`	This field controls the width of the left and right margins in pixels.

FormData

Most of the layout options of form layouts are contained in the `FormData` and `FormAttachment` classes. `FormData` provides the following options that are applied to individual GUI elements:

`height`	The preferred height of the GUI element in pixels.
`width`	The preferred width of the GUI element in pixels.

`top`
`bottom`
`left`
`right`
	These fields accept a `FormAttachment` instance that specifies to which item the upper/lower/left/right edge of the GUI element relates.

For `FormAttachment` instances, there are two variants:

- ❑ Specification of a relative position with the `Composite`
- ❑ Specification relative to another GUI element

Composite

For the `Composite` variant, two constructors are available:

```
FormAttachment fa = new FormAttachment(percent,offset);
```

and

```
FormAttachment fa = new FormAttachment(numerator, denominator,
   offset);
```

The position p is computed from the width and height of the `Composites`, respectively, as follows:

```
p = d*numerator/denominator+offset
```

If a percent value is specified, the following formula is used:

```
p = d*percent/100+offset
```

Let's assume that the `Composite` is 400 pixels wide and 300 pixels high. When you create a `FormAttachment` instance with a `FormAttachment(30,10)` constructor and assign it to the `top` field of a `FormData` instance, you get

```
p = 30/100*300+5 = 95
```

The upper edge of the GUI element will therefore be positioned 95 pixels below the upper border of the `Composite`'s client area. If you would assign the same `FormAttachment` instance to the bottom field of the `FormData` instance, the lower edge of your GUI element would be 95 pixels above the lower border of the `Composite`'s client area.

If you would assign the same FormAttachment instance to the left field of the FormData instance, you would get a distance of

```
p = 30/100*400+5 = 125
```

The left edge of the GUI element will therefore be 125 pixels to the right of the left border of the Composite's client area. So what happens when you assign the FormAttachment instance to the right field? By now, you should be able to find the answer yourself.

Reference GUI Element

For the second variant (positioning relative to another GUI element), there are three constructors:

```
FormAttachment (control, offset, alignment)
FormAttachment (control, offset)
FormAttachment (control)
```

The control parameter accepts a Control instance (the GUI element to which you want to relate).

The offset parameter specifies the distance to the reference element. If this parameter is omitted, the distance is 0.

The alignment parameter specifies to which edge of the reference element you want to relate. When you assign this FormAttachment instance to a top or bottom field, you can use the SWT.TOP, SWT.BOTTOM, and SWT.CENTER style constants. If you assign it to a left or right field, you can use the SWT.LEFT, SWT.RIGHT, and SWT.CENTER constants. If the alignment parameter is omitted, you will relate to the closest edge of the reference element.

The StackLayout class

Unlike the previous classes, this class is not contained in org.eclipse.swt.layout but in org.eclipse.swt.custom. In contrast to the other layout classes, this layout can show only a single GUI element at a time within a Composite. The reason is that all GUI elements contained in the Composite are made equal in size and are positioned at the same spot on top of each other, so only the front-most element is visible. The StackLayout class is useful when you want to switch between GUI elements. You need only move the Control instance to be shown to the front-most position.

The StackLayout class has the following public fields:

marginHeight	This field controls the height of the upper and lower margins.
marginWidth	This field controls the width of the left and right margins.
topControl	This field accepts the top (visible) Control instance.

In Listing 8.15 two Button instances are positioned on top of each other. When one button is pressed, the other button becomes visible:

```
// Create new composite
final Composite stackComposite = new Composite(composite,SWT.NULL);
final StackLayout stackLayout = new StackLayout();
// Create text buttons
final Button buttonA = new Button(stackComposite, SWT.PUSH);
buttonA.setText("Button A");
final Button buttonB = new Button(stackComposite, SWT.PUSH);
buttonB.setText("Button B");
// React to clicks
buttonA.addSelectionListener(new SelectionAdapter() {
    public void widgetSelected(SelectionEvent e) {
        stackLayout.topControl = buttonB;
        // Enforce new layout
        stackComposite.layout();
        // Set focus to visible button
        buttonB.setFocus();
    }
});
buttonB.addSelectionListener(new SelectionAdapter() {
    public void widgetSelected(SelectionEvent e) {
        stackLayout.topControl = buttonA;
        // Enforce new layout
        stackComposite.layout();
        // Set focus to visible button
        buttonA.setFocus();
    }
});
// Initialize layout
stackLayout.topControl = buttonA;
stackLayout.marginWidth = 10;
stackLayout.marginHeight = 5;
// Set layout
stackComposite.setLayout(stackLayout);
```

Listing 8.15

Graphics

The interfaces and classes for graphical operations are contained in the `org.eclipse.swt.graphics` package. The functionality of this package is based on the graphical functionality of the supported platforms. While the functionality of the package exceeds those of the basic classes of the Java AWT, it does not match the functionality of the Java2D API. I will discuss how this functionality can be extended in the "Widgets that Swing" section.

The Graphics Context

The `GC` class contains all the methods needed for drawing, such as `drawLine()`, `drawOval()`, `drawPolygon()`, `setFont()`, `getFontMetrics()`, and many more.

You can draw onto instances of all those classes that implement the `Drawable` interface. This is in particular the case for the `Image` and `Control` classes and their subclasses such as `Canvas` and `Display`.

Usually you will draw on an `Image` when implementing *double buffering* (for a description of this technique see the "Images" section). You will draw on a `Canvas` when you want to display a drawing to the user. You will draw on a `Display` when you want to draw not inside a window but all over the screen. You can select the medium for drawing operations by passing `Drawable` to the `GC()` constructor.

When you create a graphics context with the help of a `GC()` constructor, you must dispose of the `GC` instance when it is no longer needed, because `GC` instances allocate resources in the host system. However, more often than not, you will not need to create a graphics context yourself but will instead use a context given to you by a `PaintEvent`.

The golden rule for graphics processing is this:

> **All graphical operations must be executed within the** `paintControl()` **method of a** `PaintListener` **object, that is, within the** `PaintEvent` **processing of a Control instance.**

Listing 8.16 shows how you can decorate a `Composite` with a green key line.

```
composite.addPaintListener(new PaintListener () {
    public void paintControl(PaintEvent event){
        // Get Display intsance from event object
        Display display = event.display;
        // Get a green system color object - we don't
        // need to dispose that
        Color green = display.getSystemColor(SWT.COLOR_DARK_GREEN);
        // Get the graphics context from the event object
        GC gc = event.gc;
        // Set line color
        gc.setForeground(green);
        // Get size of the Composite's client area
        Rectangle rect = ((Composite) event.widget).getClientArea();
        // Now draw an rectangle
        gc.drawRectangle(rect.x + 2, rect.y + 2,
            rect.width - 4, rect.height - 4);
    }
});
```

Listing 8.16

Colors

Within a graphics context you can set line and text colors—as shown previously—with the help of the `setForeground()` method. Fill colors are set with `setBackground()`.

To set colors, you first have to supply yourself with color objects. There are two ways to obtain colors:

- ❏ You can fetch a system color from a `Device` instance. Since `Display` is a subclass of `Device`, you can fetch a system color from the widget's `Display` instance with the help of the `getSystemColor()` method. The necessary `COLOR_...` constants for the color names are defined in the `SWT` class.

  Color objects that are obtained in this or another way from other instances must not be released with `dispose()`, because they may still be in use elsewhere!

- ❏ You can create your own color objects:

```
Color red = new Color(device, 255,0,0)
```

  or

```
Color blue = new Color(device, new RGB(0,255,0));
```

  The `device` parameter accepts objects of the `Device` type. `RGB` is a simple utility class for representing device-independent RGB color tuples.

The representation of colors is exact on all devices with a color depth of 24 bits. On devices with a lower color depth, Eclipse will approximate the color as exactly as possible. For detailed information, please see the "SWT Color Model" article by Moody and MacLeod on www.eclipse.org.

If you create `Color` instances in this way, you *must* release them with `dispose()` when they are no longer needed.

Fonts

Fonts work similarly to colors. The current font of a graphics context is set with the `setFont()` method.

- ❏ You can obtain the current system font from a `Device` instance with the help of the `getSystemFont()` method. Such a font instance must not be disposed of with the `dispose()` method.

- ❏ You can create new `Font` instances with one of the following constructors:

```
Font font = new Font(device,"Arial",12,SWT.ITALIC)
```

  or

```
Font font = new Font(device,new FontData("Arial",12,SWT.ITALIC))
```

`FontData` is a device-independent representation of a font.

If you create `Font` instances in this way, you *must* release them with `dispose()` when they are no longer needed.

In Listing 8.17 the current system font is fetched, an italic variant is created, the graphics context is configured with this new font, and the word *Hello* is drawn.

```
// Get Display instance
Display display = composite.getDisplay();
// Fetch system font
Font systemFont = display.getSystemFont();
// FontData objects contain the font properties.
// With some operating systems a font may possess multiple
// FontData instances. We only use the first one.
FontData[] data = systemFont.getFontData();
FontData data0 = data[0];
// Set the font style to italic
data0.setStyle(SWT.ITALIC);
// Create a new font
Font italicFont = new Font(display, data0);
// Set the new font in the graphics context
gc.setFont(italicFont);
// TODO: call italicFont.dispose() in the DisposeListener
// of composite
// Draw text at position (4,4) with a transparent background (true).
gc.drawText("Hello",4,4,true);
```

Listing 8.17

In the GC class there are a few more text methods for text processing. For example, the getFontMetrics() method delivers a FontMetrics object that contains the characteristic measurements of the current font. The stringExtent() and textExtent() methods allow you to compute the pixel dimensions of a string if it was drawn with the currently active font. Unlike textExtent(), the stringExtent() method ignores TAB and CR characters when computing the text extent.

Images

The Image class is responsible for the device-dependent representation of images. Image instances can be created in many ways: by specifying a java.io.Stream object, by specifying a filename (absolute or relative to the current project), or by specifying an ImageData object.

In contrast to Image, the ImageData class is responsible for the device-independent representation of images. Instances of this class can be created by specifying a java.io.Stream object or by specifying a filename. Alternatively, an ImageData instance can be obtained from an Image object via the getImageData() method.

Both Image and ImageData support images in RGB format as well as in indexed format. Transparency is possible (alpha channel for RGB images, transparent color for indexed images). The following file formats are supported when reading an image from file: .bmp, .gif, .jpg, .png, .tif, and .ico. In the "Buttons" section I have already shown how an image is read from a file.

In Listing 8.18 an Image instance is used to implement double buffering. This technique is frequently used to avoid screen flicker when drawing graphics. First, an Image instance large enough to contain the drawing is created. Then a GC instance for the Image instance is created, and all drawing operations are performed within this graphics context. Finally, the complete Image instance is painted onto the Drawable target.

```
// Create canvas
final Canvas canvas = new Canvas(composite,SWT.BORDER);
// Get white system color
Color white = canvas.getDisplay().getSystemColor(SWT.COLOR_WHITE);
// Set canvas background to white
canvas.setBackground(white);
// Add paint listener
canvas.addPaintListener(new PaintListener() {
    public void paintControl(PaintEvent e) {
        // Get Display instance from the event object
        Display display = e.display;
        // Get black and red system color - don't dispose these
        Color black = display.getSystemColor(SWT.COLOR_BLACK);
        Color red = display.getSystemColor(SWT.COLOR_RED);
        // Get the graphics context from event object
        GC gc = e.gc;
        // Get the widget that caused the event
        Composite source = (Composite) e.widget;
        // Get the size of this widgets client area
        Rectangle rect = source.getClientArea();
        // Create buffer for double buffering
        Image buffer = new Image(display,rect.width,rect.height);
        // Create graphics context for this buffer
        GC bufferGC = new GC(buffer);
        // perform drawing operations
        bufferGC.setBackground(red);
        bufferGC.fillRectangle(5,5,rect.width-10,rect.height-10);
        bufferGC.setForeground(black);
        bufferGC.drawRectangle(5,5,rect.width-10,rect.height-10);
        bufferGC.setBackground(source.getBackground());
        bufferGC.fillRectangle(10,10,rect.width-20,rect.height-20);
        // Now draw the buffered image to the target drawable
        gc.drawImage(buffer,0,0);
        // Dispose of the buffer's graphics context
        bufferGC.dispose();
        // Dispose of the buffer
        buffer.dispose();
    }
});
```

Listing 8.18

You can obtain images used by the system from the current Display instance via the getSystemImage() method. You can use the following constants to identify the respective image: SWT.ICON_ERROR, SWT.ICON_INFORMATION, SWT.ICON_QUESTION, and SWT.ICON_WARNING.

The Cursor

Also in the org.eclipse.swt.graphics package you will find the Cursor class that represents the mouse pointer. To assign a new shape to the mouse pointer, you have to explicitly create a new instance of this class. The current display is passed as a parameter and also as a style constant specifying the wanted shape. How this will finally look depends, of course, on the host platform:

CURSOR_ARROW	Arrow
CURSOR_WAIT	Waiting
CURSOR_CROSS	Crosshair
CURSOR_APPSTARTING	Application starting
CURSOR_HELP	Help
CURSOR_SIZEALL	Overall size change
CURSOR_SIZENESW	Size change on NE/SW axis
CURSOR_SIZENS	Size change on N/S axis
CURSOR_SIZENWSE	Size change on NW/SE axis
CURSOR_SIZEWE	Size change on W/E axis
CURSOR_SIZEN	Size change north direction
CURSOR_SIZES	Size change south direction
CURSOR_SIZEE	Size change east direction
CURSOR_SIZEW	Size change west direction
CURSOR_SIZENE	Size change NE direction
CURSOR_SIZESE	Size change SE direction
CURSOR_SIZESW	Size change SW direction
CURSOR_SIZENW	Size change NW direction
CURSOR_UPARROW	Upward arrow
CURSOR_IBEAM	Text cursor
CURSOR_NO	Invalid operation
CURSOR_HAND	Hand for moving

Since Eclipse V3 you can alternatively specify the cursor shape by passing an ImageData instance (see the "Images" section) to the Cursor constructor. In addition, you can pass a second ImageData instance that acts as a mask.

Please keep in mind that the cursor allocates a resource of the host windowing system. Therefore, you must dispose of the Cursor instance when it is no longer needed. The same applies for the ImageData instance(s).

Widgets That Swing

Because of its native character, the SWT provides a new approach to the implementation of the lowest layer of graphical user interfaces. However, the question remains: how do you deal with the higher layers?

As far as graphical elements such as windows, dialogs, and menus are concerned, the answer is simple. Functionality that was provided by Swing is more or less provided by the JFace libraries (see Chapter 9).

Things become difficult, however, when you look at graphical operations. Powerful graphical layers such as Java2D or Java3D, SVG processing as in Batik (www.apache.org), or bitmap manipulations such as in Java Advanced Imaging (JAI) are not provided by the SWT and JFace. All these APIs are incompatible with the SWT. Advanced functionality such as antialiasing options, transparent drawing operations, or text rotation is not available to SWT users.

However, with Eclipse 3 things have changed completely. Now it is possible to place Swing and AWT elements into SWT Composites. This allows integrating the higher-level graphical layers within SWT applications. And all of a sudden, Swing is fun again, thanks to the SWT. Under Windows, you need to run under JRE 1.3 or later to enable this functionality, while on other platforms, at least JRE 1.5 is required.

Embedded Contents

The new SWT EMBEDDED style constant makes all this possible. A Composite created with this style constant can contain contents foreign to the SWT (but nothing else). In Eclipse 3 this can be java.awt.Frame components, which can be created via the SWT_AWT.new_Frame() factory method. For example:

```
Composite awtContainer = new Composite(parent, SWT.EMBEDDED);
java.awt.Frame myFrame = SWT_AWT.new_Frame(awtContainer);
```

Now you can add AWT and Swing components to this Frame instance to your heart's desire.

In addition, the SWT_AWT class provides the new_Shell() method. This method creates a new SWT shell for a given AWT canvas, so this canvas is presented in its own window but within the SWT application.

Events

But how would you process events within such a mixed environment? Well, that isn't very difficult: listeners are added in the usual way to the AWT and Swing components, and these listeners can react to AWT events. You must use caution, however, when such a listener tries to access an SWT resource because SWT and AWT run in different threads. Therefore, these accesses must be encapsulated into a

`Runnable` and executed via an appropriate `Display` method such as `syncExec()`, `asyncExec()`, or `timerExec()`. I discussed this technique already in the "Displays, Shells, and Monitors" section.

Vice versa, when accessing AWT and Swing components from SWT event processing, these accesses should be encapsulated, too, into a `Runnable`. This `Runnable` is then executed via the static AWT `EventQueue.invokeLater()` method. This is not enforced by the AWT (as is done by the SWT) but is strongly recommended.

The following example shows these techniques in context. The example shows, too, how SWT components can be placed on top of an AWT surface (in its own shell). The example implements a Java2D canvas within an SWT shell. An SWT button allows you to clear the canvas. Clicking the canvas opens an SWT text input field on top of the canvas. Another click on the canvas hides this field again, and the text entered into the text input field is drawn on the Java2D canvas.

```java
import java.util.ArrayList;
import java.util.Iterator;

import org.eclipse.swt.SWT;
import org.eclipse.swt.awt.SWT_AWT;
import org.eclipse.swt.events.*;
import org.eclipse.swt.graphics.*;
import org.eclipse.swt.layout.*;
import org.eclipse.swt.widgets.*;

public class SWT2D {

  // Shell for pop-up editor
  Shell eShell = null;
  // Text widget for editor
  Text eText = null;
  // List of strings entered
  ArrayList wordList = new ArrayList(12);

  public static void main(String[] args) {
    SWT2D swtawt = new SWT2D();
    swtawt.run();
  }
```

First, an SWT shell is created. A `GridLayout` contains the container composited (`EMBEDDED`) for the AWT canvas and the Clear button.

```java
  private void run() {
    // Create top level shell
    final Display display = new Display();
    final Shell shell = new Shell(display);
    shell.setText("Java 2D Example");
    // GridLayout for canvas and button
    shell.setLayout(new GridLayout());
    // Create container for AWT canvas
    final Composite canvasComp = new Composite(shell,
        SWT.EMBEDDED);
    // Set preferred size
```

```
        GridData data = new GridData();
        data.widthHint = 600;
        data.heightHint = 500;
        canvasComp.setLayoutData(data);
```

Then, the SWT_AWT class is used to create an AWT Frame within the SWT Composite. An AWT Canvas is then added to the Frame in the usual way. A graphical context is retrieved from this canvas and cast to a Java2D graphical context. Later, this object will be used to perform the drawing operations. First, the initial affine transformation of the graphical context is saved, so that you can always reset the graphical context to its initial state. In addition, antialiasing is switched on—one of the beauties of Java2D.

```
    // Create AWT Frame for Canvas
    java.awt.Frame canvasFrame = SWT_AWT
        .new_Frame(canvasComp);
    // Create Canvas and add it to the Frame
    final java.awt.Canvas canvas = new java.awt.Canvas();
    canvasFrame.add(canvas);
    // Get graphical context and cast to Java2D
    final java.awt.Graphics2D g2d = (java.awt.Graphics2D) canvas
        .getGraphics();
    // Enable antialiasing
    g2d.setRenderingHint(RenderingHints.KEY_ANTIALIASING,
        RenderingHints.VALUE_ANTIALIAS_ON);
    // Remember initial transform
    final java.awt.geom.AffineTransform origTransform = g2d
        .getTransform();
```

Now, the Clear button is created. In its event processing routine, a redraw of the Canvas is enforced by invoking the redraw() method of the SWT container Composite.

```
    // Create Clear button and position it
    Button clearButton = new Button(shell, SWT_PUSH);
    clearButton.setText("Clear");
    data = new GridData();
    data.horizontalAlignment = GridData.CENTER;
    clearButton.setLayoutData(data);
    // Event processing for Clear button
    clearButton
        .addSelectionListener(new SelectionAdapter() {
          public void widgetSelected(SelectionEvent e) {
            // Delete word list and redraw canvas
            wordList.clear();
            canvasComp.redraw();
          }
        });
```

Clicking the mouse on the canvas (note that this is AWT event processing) makes the text input field visible or invisible depending on its current state. Only during the very first invocation is a new instance of this small editor created. Because SWT widgets cannot be added to AWT canvasses, the editor is created in its own shell. It's important to create this shell non-modal, so that the canvas remains accessible for mouse clicks when the shell is opened.

This technique of setting the shell visible or invisible is better than closing the shell and then creating a new one. This not only saves resources but also avoids some nasty effects. When a shell is explicitly closed, parts of the `close()` processing are executed after all AWT event processing and thus after `canvasComp.redraw()`. The result would be an ugly white area remaining at the former position of the editor. This cannot happen when using `setVisible(false)`.

```java
            // Process canvas mouse clicks
      canvas.addMouseListener(new java.awt.event.MouseListener() {
            public void mouseClicked(
                java.awt.event.MouseEvent e) {}

            public void mouseEntered(
                java.awt.event.MouseEvent e) {}

            public void mouseExited(
                java.awt.event.MouseEvent e) {}

            public void mousePressed(
                java.awt.event.MouseEvent e) {
              // Manage pop-up editor
              display.syncExec(new Runnable() {
                public void run() {
                  if (eShell == null) {
                    // Create new Shell: non-modal!
                    eShell = new Shell(shell, SWT.NO_TRIM
                        | SWT.MODELESS);
                    eShell.setLayout(new FillLayout());
                    // Text input field
                    eText = new Text(eShell, SWT.BORDER);
                    eText.setText("Text rotation in the SWT?");
                    eShell.pack();
                    // Set position (Display coordinates)
                    java.awt.Rectangle bounds = canvas.getBounds();
                    org.eclipse.swt.graphics.Point pos = canvasComp
                        .toDisplay(bounds.width / 2, bounds.height / 2);
                    Point size = eShell.getSize();
                    eShell.setBounds(pos.x, pos.y, size.x, size.y);
                    // Open Shell
                    eShell.open();
                  } else if (!eShell.isVisible()) {
                    // Editor versteckt, sichtbar machen
                    eShell.setVisible(true);
                  } else {
                    // Editor is visible - get text
                    String t = eText.getText();
                    // set editor invisible
                    eShell.setVisible(false);
                    // Add text to list and redraw canvas
                    wordList.add(t);
                    canvasComp.redraw();
                  }
                }
              });
            }
```

```
        public void mouseReleased(
            java.awt.event.MouseEvent e) {}
    });
```

Finally, here is the routine for drawing the canvas content. This happens in a `PaintListener` that has been attached to the canvas's SWT container. Java2D text rotation is employed to lay out the entered text in the form of a star. Since all of the resources used (`Color`, `Font`) are AWT resources, it is not necessary to release these resources with `dispose()`. Java garbage collection will take care of that. Figure 8.12 shows the results.

```
    // Redraw the canvas
    canvasComp.addPaintListener(new PaintListener() {
      public void paintControl(PaintEvent e) {
        // Pass the redraw task to AWT event queue
        java.awt.EventQueue.invokeLater(new Runnable() {
          public void run() {
            // Compute canvas center
            java.awt.Rectangle bounds = canvas.getBounds();
            int originX = bounds.width / 2;
            int originY = bounds.height / 2;
            // Reset canvas
            g2d.setTransform(origTransform);
            g2d.setColor(java.awt.Color.WHITE);
            g2d.fillRect(0, 0, bounds.width, bounds.height);
            // Set font
            g2d.setFont(new java.awt.Font("Myriad",
                java.awt.Font.PLAIN, 32));
            double angle = 0d;
            // Prepare star shape
            double increment = Math.toRadians(30);
            Iterator iter = wordList.iterator();
            while (iter.hasNext()) {
              // Determine text colors in RGB color cycle
              float red = (float) (0.5 + 0.5 * Math
                  .sin(angle));
              float green = (float) (0.5 + 0.5 * Math
                  .sin(angle + Math.toRadians(120)));
              float blue = (float) (0.5 + 0.5 * Math
                  .sin(angle + Math.toRadians(240)));
              g2d.setColor(new java.awt.Color(red, green,
                  blue));
              // Redraw text
              String text = (String) iter.next();
              g2d.drawString(text, originX + 50, originY);
              // Rotate for next text output
              g2d.rotate(increment, originX, originY);
              angle += increment;
            }
          }
        });
      }
    });
```

```
    // Finish shell and open it
    shell.pack();
    shell.open();
    // SWT event processing
    while (!shell.isDisposed()) {
      if (!display.readAndDispatch()) display.sleep();
    }
    display.dispose();
  }
}
```

Figure 8.12

Output to a Printer

Output to a printer is performed with the help of the PrintDialog, PrinterData, and Printer classes. PrintDialog is a subclass of the Dialog abstract class and represents the printer selection dialog of the host operating system. As a result, PrintDialog delivers either a PrinterData instance or null. The PrinterData instance contains all the specifications made in the printer selection dialog, such as the number of copies, printing scope, and so on. By accessing the corresponding fields (copyCount, scope, etc.), you can use these specifications for the resulting output process.

For the actual printing process, you need to create an instance of the Printer class, which is a Device subclass. You then use this to create a new graphics context (GC). You must perform all output operations necessary for filling the printed pages with content on this graphics context.

First, call the `Printer startJob()` method to create a new print task. Then call the `startPage()` method for each page. Next, apply all drawing operations on the printer's graphics context. After each page is filled, call the `endPage()` method. When all pages are printed, close the printing task by calling the `endJob()` method. Finally, you must dispose of the graphics context and the `Printer` object by calling their `dispose()` methods. Listing 8.19 shows how it's done.

```java
// Create button for starting printing process
final Button printButton = new Button(composite, SWT.PUSH);
printButton.setText("Print");
// React to clicks
printButton.addSelectionListener(new SelectionAdapter() {
    public void widgetSelected(SelectionEvent e) {
        // Get Shell instance
        Shell shell = composite.getShell();
        // Create printer selection dialog
        PrintDialog printDialog = new PrintDialog(shell);
        // and open it
        PrinterData printerData = printDialog.open();
        // Check if OK was pressed
        if (printerData != null) {
            // Create new Printer instance
            Printer printer = new Printer(printerData);
            // Create graphics context for this printer
            GC gc = new GC(printer);
            // Open printing task
            if (!printer.startJob("Hello"))
                System.out.println("Starting printer task failed");
            else {
                // Print first page
                if (!printer.startPage())
                    System.out.println("Printing of page 1 failed");
                else {
                    // Get green system color from printer
                    // and set it as text color
                    Color green =
                        printer.getSystemColor(SWT.COLOR_DARK_GREEN);
                    gc.setForeground(green);
                    // Draw text
                    gc.drawText("Hello World", 4, 4, true);
                    // Close page
                    printer.endPage();
                }
                // Print second page
                if (!printer.startPage())
                    System.out.println("Printing of page 2 failed");
                else {
                    // Get blue system color from printer
                    // and set it as text color
                    Color blue = printer.getSystemColor(SWT.COLOR_BLUE);
                    gc.setForeground(blue);
                    // Draw text
                    gc.drawText("Hello Eclipse", 4, 4, true);
                    // Close page
                    printer.endPage();
```

Listing 8.19 (Continues)

```
            }
            // Close printing task
            printer.endJob();
        }
        // Release operating system resources
        gc.dispose();
        printer.dispose();
    }
  }
});
```

Listing 8.19 (Continued)

In fact, this code shows only the simplest case. Processing becomes more complicated if you have to consider `PrinterData` specifications such as the number of copies, collating options, or printing scope. In addition, it makes sense to fetch the printer's resolution from the `Printer` instance via the `getDPI()` method and to scale the graphical operations accordingly.

Data Transfer

SWT data transfer includes both the exchange of data via the clipboard and the exchange of data via a drag-and-drop operation with the mouse. The classes implementing data transfer are located in the `org.eclipse.swt.dnd` package.

The Clipboard

Eclipse utilizes the system-wide native clipboard of the host platform to perform clipboard operations. The SWT provides access to this clipboard via the `Clipboard` class. This class implements the `setContents()` and `getContents()` methods, which can be used to transfer content to and from the clipboard. Since the clipboard allocates operating system resources, you must release the clipboard by calling its `dispose()` method when it is no longer needed.

A clipboard usually contains the transferred data in various formats. Text processors, for example, would transfer a copied text segment in both RTF format and plain-text format to the clipboard. Eclipse identifies these formats with the help of transfer types. These are subclasses of the `Transfer` abstract class. In particular, the following types are available: `FileTransfer`, `MarkerTransfer`, `RTFTransfer`, `TextTransfer`, and additional Eclipse-specific transfer types. Should you have your own demands for a special transfer type, you can roll your own (usually implemented as a subclass of the `ByteArrayTransfer` class). The source code of `ByteArrayTransfer` contains a short tutorial of how this is done.

These concrete transfer types serve as transformers of the type-specific data formats into the operating system data format of the clipboard. When you want to transfer data to the clipboard, just pass an array with data items (each in a specific format) and an array of corresponding transfer types to the `setContents()` method. Similarly, when reading data from the clipboard, pass a transfer type to the `getContents()` method and obtain the clipboard data in the desired data format. The `getAvailableTypes()` method delivers an array of the transfer types of the current clipboard data.

This allows you to find out quickly if a desired format is present without having to read the contents of the clipboard. An example program for clipboard operations contained in the `org.eclipse.swt` `.examples` plug-in (`Clipboard.java`).

Drag and Drop

For a drag-and-drop operation you need a data source and a data target. One or the other can be provided by a different application or by the system. Data sources are implemented in Eclipse in form of the `DragSource` class, while the `DropTarget` class implements the data target. Both classes are subclasses of the `Widget` class. An application can be equipped with several instances of both classes; however, you must uniquely assign a `Control` instance to each instance of a `DragSource` or a `DropTarget`. This is done by passing the `Control` instance to the `DragSource()` or `DropTarget()` constructor. This assignment also defines the position and size of the data transfer element. In addition, at this point you must specify, too, the operations possible for this source or target (`DND.NONE`, `DND.MOVE`, `DND.COPY`, `DND.LINK`).

During a drag-and-drop operation the instances of these classes generate corresponding events (`DragSourceEvent` resp. `DropTargetEvent`), which can be intercepted with an appropriate listener instance (`DragSourceListener` resp. `DropTargetListener`). The various methods of these listeners allow seamless control over the drag-and-drop operation. The `DragSourceListener dragStart()` method is called at the beginning of a drag-and-drop operation. When the cursor enters the `DropTarget` area, the `DropTargetListener dragEnter()` method is called. Similarly, `dragLeave()` is called when the mouse leaves this area, and `dragOver()` is called when the mouse moves over this area. When the operation mode is changed during the operation (usually by pressing Ctrl or Alt), the `dragOperationChanged()` method is called. When the mouse button is released over the drop target, the `dropAccept()` method is called. This is the last opportunity to veto the operation. Then the `DragSourceListener dragSetData()` method is called. In this method the `DragSourceListener` must provide the transfer data. This data is delivered to the `drop()` method of the `DropTargetListener`. Finally, the `DragSourceListener dragFinished()` method is called. Here you can perform cleanup tasks.

In all methods that are performed before the actual transfer of the data, you can still influence the operation. By assigning `DND.DROP_NONE` to the `DropTargetEvent` field detail, you can veto the operation. By assigning a different operation code, you can modify the mode of the operation.

The actual transfer of the data is performed via the `data` fields of the `DragSourceEvent` and `DropTargetEvent` objects. Similarly, as with the clipboard (see the "Clipboard" section) you can pass the data in various forms, which are described via transfer types. The `dataType` resp. `currentDataType` fields of the event objects contain the current transfer type.

The "Playlist Viewer" section in Chapter 10 shows the implementation of a drop target in an example application. A detailed article by Veronika Irvine about how to use SWT-based drag and drop is found on Eclipse Corner (www.eclipse.org).

Resource Management

In the course of this chapter, you have met several resource types that need to be disposed of when no longer needed. In particular, they are instances of the `Color`, `Font`, `Image`, `GC`, `Cursor`, `Printer`, `Display`, and `Shell` classes.

For all of these resources the golden rule is this:

> **If you created something, you must also dispose of it, but if you got a resource from somewhere else (for example, with** `getSystemColor()`**), you must not dispose of it.**

However, you don't need to dispose of resources at the end of a program—the host operating system will do this for you. So this rule applies only to resources that are used temporarily within an application.

This sounds quite simple, but it can become complicated in larger applications. In many cases you want to use the same color, font, or image in several places in an application. Who is responsible for disposing of the resource in such a case? And is it really necessary to dispose of a resource if it can be reused later somewhere else?

In such cases you can make use of a "store" concept. You can implement a Resource Store that manages the lifecycle of your resources. The Resource Store disposes of the managed resources when the Resource Store is itself disposed of. This allows you to reuse resources. This is useful in particular with `Image` instances, because images can be very memory hungry.

In Listing 8.20 I show a simple Resource Store for color resources. When the `ColorStore` class is asked for a `Color` object, it will return an existing `Color` object if it is already in the store; otherwise, it will create a new `Color` object. When the `ColorStore` is disposed of by calling its `dispose()` method, all `Color` objects in the store are disposed of, too.

```
import java.util.HashMap;
import java.util.Iterator;
import java.util.Map;
import org.eclipse.swt.graphics.Color;
import org.eclipse.swt.graphics.Device;

public class ColorStore {

    private static Map store = new HashMap();

    /**
     * Method getColor.
     * @param name some Color name
     * @param device Device instance
     * @param r red-value
     * @param g green-value
     * @param b blue-value
     * @return Color requested color
```

Listing 8.20 (Continues)

```
    */
    public static Color getColor(String name,Device device,
        int r, int g, int b) {
        Object obj = store.get(name);
        if (obj == null) {
            Color newColor = new Color(device,r,g,b);
            store.put(name,newColor);
            return newColor;
        }
        return (Color) obj;
    }

    /**
     * Method dispose.
     */
    public static void dispose() {
        Iterator iter = store.values().iterator();
        while (iter.hasNext()) {
            Color color = (Color) iter.next();
            color.dispose();
        }
    }
}
```

Listing 8.20 (Continued)

Here is how you can obtain a `Color` object from the store:

```
Color green = ColorStore.getColor("green",display,0,255,0);
```

Since all methods in the `ColorStore` class are static, `ColorStore` can manage all the colors of an application. Only when you need no more colors do you dispose of the whole store with

```
ColorStore.dispose();
```

In the "Resource Management" section in Chapter 9 I will discuss some predefined registries for fonts and images.

Windows32 Support (OLE)

SWT provides a special library supporting the OLE mechanism of Microsoft's Windows operating systems. The Microsoft Win32 Object Linking and Embedding (OLE) mechanism is supported by the classes in the `org.eclipse.swt.ole.win32` package. OLE allows OLE documents and other ActiveX control elements to be embedded in other (Container) applications. This allows you, for example, to use Microsoft Internet Explorer as an SWT GUI element (the `Browser` widget is implemented this way) or to embed a Microsoft Office document into an SWT user interface. Using these classes requires sufficient knowledge of the OLE API. A small example plug-in is found in the Eclipse example collection under `org.eclipse.swt.examples.ole.win32_3.0.0`.

SWT on the Pocket PC

The Microsoft Pocket PC Platform is a valid runtime environment for SWT-based applications. However, there are a number of special requirements and restrictions that must be considered when developing applications for machines running under Windows CE:

❑ PDA users usually ask for highly convenient user interfaces, more so than desktop users.

❑ Processors are slower the desktop machines.

❑ The available memory is smaller than on desktop machines.

❑ The screen size is smaller than on desktop machines.

❑ Very often there is no keyboard; the device is operated via a pen.

Often when a PDA is not equipped with a keyboard, an emulated keyboard is displayed on the screen when text is to be entered. This reduces the space left for the application windows. Pocket PC applications should therefore create `Shells` with the `SWT.RESIZE` style parameter to enable the SWT to automatically resize the shell when the emulated keyboard is opened or closed.

A special SWT library for Pocket PC platforms is available on www.eclipse.org. To reduce the size of this library, some packages have been removed. These are:

❑ `org.eclipse.swt.dnd` (drag and drop, see the "Data Transfer" section)

❑ `org.eclipse.swt.ole` (OLE, see the "Windows32 Support" section)

❑ `org.eclipse.swt.accessibility` (accessibility functions, see the "Accessibility" section)

❑ `org.eclipse.swt.custom` (special widgets, see the "Custom Widgets" section)

❑ `org.eclipse.swt.printing` (printer support, see the "Output to Printer" section)

❑ `org.eclipse.swt.program` (file associations)

Of course, you can create your own SWT library from these packages according to your requirements. In addition, it is possible to reduce the size of the library even further by removing unused classes. The Pocket PC article "A small cup of SWT" by Christophe Cornu2003 at www.eclipse.org explains in detail how this can be achieved and how the startup time for Pocket PC applications can be minimized.

Accessibility

Finally, I briefly discuss how SWT supports the creation of user interfaces that are suitable for disabled persons. Accessibility is an important topic in the context of commercial application development. Many public institutions are allowed to purchase only software conforming to certain standards regarding its usability by disabled persons.

The Eclipse documentation contains a special chapter about this topic in the Platform Plug-in Developer Guide under Reference > Other Reference Information > Tips For Making User Interfaces Accessible.

Many operating systems support special hardware devices designed for disabled persons and provide an API for these devices. Eclipse supports the Microsoft Active Accessibility (MSAA) API. This support is provided by the classes defined in the `org.eclipse.swt.accessibility` package. All SWT `Control` instances can provide an instance of the `Accessible` class via the `getAccessible()` method. This instance serves as a link to the Accessibility API.

Summary

In this chapter I have given you an introduction into the core concepts of the Standard Widget Toolkit (SWT). By now, you should have an understanding of the SWT event model and of the main widget groups found in the SWT. You should know the different layout types and how to use them (however, you'll need practice to master them). You should by now understand how basic graphics can be created with the SWT and how advanced graphics produced with Swing and Java2D can be embedded into an SWT environment. You should be able to produce output for a printer and to use the clipboard and the drag-and-drop facilities. You have also learned about the most common traps for SWT programmers: the necessity to release allocated resources and how to access the SWT thread from a non-SWT thread.

In the next chapter we move to the higher-level GUI layers of the JFace component.

JFace

The JFace API is based on the SWT API and provides the programmer with higher-level GUI components such as viewers, actions, dialogs, wizards, and much more. In the following sections I will discuss the most important function groups.

Some of the JFace components are specific to the Eclipse workbench and are packaged in the archive workbench.jar as an integral part of the Eclipse workbench plug-in. Most of the components of JFace, however, can be used independently from the Eclipse workbench and are therefore packaged in the archive jface.jar and are deployed in a separate JFace plug-in.

Resource Management

This chapter begins with the topic with which the previous chapter ended: resource management. JFace provides some classes that support the management of resources such as fonts, colors, and images. The classes of this group are contained in the package org.eclipse.jface.resource.

The FontRegistry Class

The FontRegistry class is able to manage all the fonts used within an application. A FontRegistry instance is always created for a concrete Display instance. If no Display instance is passed to the FontRegistry() constructor, the current Display instance will be used.

You don't need to specify a Display instance when adding a font to the FontRegistry with the help of the put() method, because the FontRegistry can supply the Display instance by itself if it needs to create a new font instance. It is sufficient to specify the symbolic font name and a FontData instance (see the "Fonts" section in Chapter 8). You can retrieve a font from the FontRegistry with the method get() by specifying a symbolic name.

What is convenient with a `FontRegistry` is that you don't have to care at all about the disposal of font resources. When a `FontRegistry` is created, it links itself into the `DisposeEvent()` processing of its `Display` instance. When this `Display` instance is disposed of, the `FontRegistry` and all fonts contained in the registry are disposed of as well. It is important *not* to explicitly dispose of a font contained in the `FontRegistry` by calling its `dispose()` method.

The ImageRegistry Class

The `ImageRegistry` class works quite similarly to `FontRegistry` but is responsible for the management of images. `ImageRegistry` instances are also associated with a concrete `Display` instance. Images are added to the registry with the `put()` method and are addressed with a symbolic name. They can be retrieved again with `get()`. In the section "Some Dialog Subclasses" I will show a code example of how to use the `ImageRegistry`. As with `FontRegistry`, the disposal of the `ImageRegistry` instance and of the contained images is linked to the `DisposeEvent()` processing of the corresponding `Display` instance.

In lieu of an `Image` instance, you can add an `ImageDescriptor` instance to the registry using `put()`. `ImageDescriptor` instances act as proxies for images: they contain only the image metadata and know where and how to fetch the corresponding image. The image is loaded only when it is really needed—in the case of the `ImageRegistry`, this is when it is retrieved with `get()`.

The JFaceColors Class

This class organizes consistent color management for all GUI components of JFace. Various static methods allow the retrieval of specific colors, such as the color of error messages, hyperlinks, or other GUI elements.

The JFaceResources Class

This class organizes consistent font and registry management for all JFace GUI components. Various static methods allow the retrieval of specific fonts, such as fonts for dialogs, texts, banners, and so on. You can also retrieve the current `FontRegistry` and `ImageRegistry` instances.

Dialogs and Windows

The package `org.eclipse.jface.dialogs` provides some classes that implement standard dialogs. All these classes are subclasses of the abstract JFace class `Dialog`, which is itself a subclass of the abstract class `Window`.

The class `Window` can be used to implement your own windows. The typical life cycle of a window is

```
new
create()
open()
close()
```

create() can be omitted: the open() method will then automatically execute the create() method. Among other things, create() creates the window's Shell instance. Consequently, retrieving the shell via method getShell() makes sense only after create() has been executed. The shell is disposed of automatically when close() is executed. In addition, create() invokes the methods createContents() and initializeBounds(), which may be overridden or extended by subclasses. For example, you would override createContents() to construct the window content.

With the help of the getReturnCode() method you can retrieve the current state of an opened window. You obtain the value Window.OK for a window with an opened shell and the value Window.CANCEL when the window's shell is closed.

Because the class Dialog is a subclass of Window, its life cycle is similar. But unlike with Window, you would not override the createContents() method to add content to a Dialog instance. Instead, you would override one or several of the methods createDialogArea(), createButtonBar(), and createButtonsForButtonBar(). By default, the latter method creates an OK button and a Cancel button.

To create additional buttons, the class provides the createButton() method. This also creates the necessary event processing for each button. When a button is pressed, the buttonPressed() method is called. For the OK button and the Cancel button, this method in turn invokes the methods okPressed() and cancelPressed(). Both of these methods close the dialog with close(). All of these methods can be overridden or extended using subclasses.

You can get the code of the button with which the dialog was closed with the getReturnCode() method or as the result of the open() method: this will be Window.OK for the OK button and Window.CANCEL for the Cancel button.

Some Dialog Subclasses

JFace comes with a variety of predefined special purpose Dialog subclasses, some of which I discuss in the following sections.

The InputDialog Class

This class creates a simple dialog with a text field (see Figure 9.1), an OK button, and a Cancel button. Creating such a dialog requires only a few instructions:

```
InputDialog inputDialog = new InputDialog(shell,
    "Input","Please enter text","text",null);
if (inputDialog.open() == Dialog.OK) {
    String result = inputDialog.getValue();
    System.out.println(result);
}
```

InputDialog is the simplest of the predefined JFace dialogs.

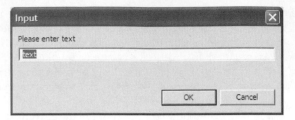

Figure 9.1

The MessageDialog Class

The class shown in Listing 9.1 generates a simple dialog for displaying messages. You can configure the number of buttons and their labeling. In addition, you can show an icon in the title bar of the dialog window. Usually, you would use a GIF image of size 16x16 pixels.

```java
// Create image registry
ImageRegistry imageRegistry = new ImageRegistry();
// Load icon for title line
final Image image = new Image(shell.getDisplay(),
    "images/envelop.gif");
// Register image
imageRegistry.put("envelope",image);
// Create message dialog
MessageDialog messageDialog = new MessageDialog(shell,
    "Message", imageRegistry.get("envelope"),
    "You have mail!", MessageDialog.INFORMATION,
    new String[] {"View", "Dispose", "Abort"}, 0);
// Open dialog and retrieve the index of the button pressed
int buttonPressed = messageDialog.open();
System.out.println("Button pressed: "+buttonPressed);
```

Listing 9.1

In the third parameter you can pass an image for the title line. (You can retrieve this image from the image registry.) If you don't want to use an image, just specify null. In the fifth parameter specify a style constant declaring the type of dialog and the icon shown in front of the message:

MessageDialog.NONE	No specification, no icon shown
MessageDialog.ERROR	Error message
MessageDialog.INFORMATION	Info message
MessageDialog.QUESTION	Question
MessageDialog.WARNING	Warning

In the sixth parameter specify a `String[]` array containing all the button labels. The seventh parameter specifies the index of the default button. Figure 9.2 shows the MessageDialog from the previous code example.

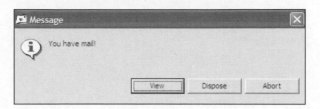

Figure 9.2

The class `MessageDialog`, in addition, provides some static methods implementing simple standard dialogs such as `openConfirm()`, `openError()`, `openInformation()`, `openQuestion()`, and `openWarning()`. Here is an example using the `openConfirm()` method:

```
if (MessageDialog.openConfirm(shell,
      "General question", "System crash!\nPlease acknowledge!")) {
      System.out.println("OK was pressed");
}
```

The TitleAreaDialog Class

This class defines a basic pattern for more complex dialogs. You would usually not instantiate this class directly, but rather you would define your own subclasses (see "Implementing Your Own Dialog Classes"). The class `TitleAreaDialog` provides the following features:

- ❑ Title line.

- ❑ Message area. This area usually contains one or two lines of text. Iit also displays an error message when present. Optionally, you may specify your own image for this area with `setTitleImage()`. Figure 9.3 shows the Eclipse default image for the `TitleAreaDialog` on the right-hand side of the message area. This image has a size of 72x72 pixels. Since this image controls the height of the message area, you can make room for additional message lines by specifying a taller image.

- ❑ An OK button and a Cancel button.

The following code shows how a `TitleAreaDialog` instance is created and initialized. Before you can set features such as title, message, or image, you must invoke the `create()` method:

```
TitleAreaDialog titleAreaDialog = new TitleAreaDialog(shell);
titleAreaDialog.create();
titleAreaDialog.setTitle("Important message");
titleAreaDialog.setMessage(
    "You have mail!\nIt could be vital for your career...");
if (titleAreaDialog.open() == Dialog.OK) {
    System.out.println("OK was pressed");
}
```

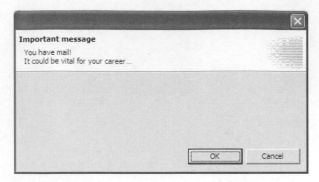

Figure 9.3

Implementing Your Own Dialog Classes

You can derive your own subclasses from the dialog classes discussed previously (and, of course, also from the mother of all JFace dialogs, the class `Dialog`). This makes sense, in particular, for the class `TitleAreaDialog`. This dialog still has a big empty space in the center that needs to be filled.

The various areas in such a dialog are all created using different methods. By overriding one or several of those methods, you can change the configuration of the dialog considerably. For example, by overriding the method `createButtonsForButtonBar()`, you can add additional buttons along with the OK button and the Cancel button or even replace those buttons.

Listing 9.2 implements the `MailDialog` class, which is based on the `TitleAreaDialog` class. The center area contains a `List` widget that displays mail messages that have arrived. The OK button and the Cancel button are replaced with the buttons Open, Delete, and Abort. The Delete button does not close the dialog but simply removes an item from the list. When no items are selected, the Open button and the Delete button are disabled, and an error message is shown in place of the normal message.

```
import org.eclipse.jface.dialogs.TitleAreaDialog;
import org.eclipse.swt.SWT;
import org.eclipse.swt.events.SelectionAdapter;
import org.eclipse.swt.events.SelectionEvent;
import org.eclipse.swt.layout.GridData;
import org.eclipse.swt.layout.GridLayout;
import org.eclipse.swt.widgets.Button;
import org.eclipse.swt.widgets.Composite;
import org.eclipse.swt.widgets.Control;
import org.eclipse.swt.widgets.List;
import org.eclipse.swt.widgets.Shell;

public class MailDialog extends TitleAreaDialog {
    // IDs for MailDialog buttons
    // We use large integers because we don't want
    // to conflict with system constants
    public static final int OPEN = 9999;
```

Listing 9.2 (Continues)

```
    public static final int DELETE = 9998;
    // List widget
    List list;
    // Initial content of the list
    String[] items;
    // Selected items
    String[] itemsToOpen;
    /**
     * Constructor for MailDialog.
     * @param shell - Containing shell
     * @param items - Mail messages passed to the dialog
     */
    public MailDialog(Shell shell, String[] items) {
        super(shell);
        this.items = items;
    }
    /**
     * @see org.eclipse.jface.window.Window#create()
     * We complete the dialog with a title and a message
     */
    public void create() {
        super.create();
        setTitle("Mail");
        setMessage(
            "You have mail!\n It could be vital for this evening…");
    }
    /**
     * @see org.eclipse.jface.dialogs.Dialog#
     * createDialogArea(org.eclipse.swt.widgets.Composite)
     * Here we fill the center area of the dialog
     */
    protected Control createDialogArea(Composite parent) {
        // Create new composite as container
        final Composite area = new Composite(parent, SWT.NULL);
        // We use a grid layout and set the size of the margins
        final GridLayout gridLayout = new GridLayout();
        gridLayout.marginWidth = 15;
        gridLayout.marginHeight = 10;
        area.setLayout(gridLayout);
        // Now we create the list widget
        list = new List(area, SWT.BORDER | SWT.MULTI);
        // We define a minimum width for the list
        final GridData gridData = new GridData();
        gridData.widthHint = 200;
        list.setLayoutData(gridData);
        // We add a SelectionListener
        list.addSelectionListener(new SelectionAdapter() {
            public void widgetSelected(SelectionEvent e) {
                // When the selection changes, we re-validate the list
                validate();
            }
        });
```

Listing 9.2 (Continues)

```
        // We add the initial mail messages to the list
        for (int i = 0; i < items.length; i++) {
            list.add(items[i]);
        }
        return area;
    }
    private void validate() {
        // We select the number of selected list entries
        boolean selected = (list.getSelectionCount() > 0);
        // We enable/disable the Open and Delete buttons
        getButton(OPEN).setEnabled(selected);
        getButton(DELETE).setEnabled(selected);
        if (!selected)
            // If nothing was selected, we set an error message
            setErrorMessage("Select at least one entry!");
        else
            // Otherwise we set the error message to null
            // to show the intial content of the message area
            setErrorMessage(null);
    }
    /**
     * @see org.eclipse.jface.dialogs.Dialog#
     * createButtonsForButtonBar(org.eclipse.swt.widgets.Composite)
     * We replace the OK and Cancel buttons by our own creations
     * We use the method createButton() (from Dialog),
     * to create the new buttons
     */
    protected void createButtonsForButtonBar(Composite parent) {
        // Create Open button
        Button openButton = createButton(parent, OPEN,
            "Open", true);
        // Initially deactivate it
        openButton.setEnabled(false);
        // Add a SelectionListener
        openButton.addSelectionListener(new SelectionAdapter() {
            public void widgetSelected(SelectionEvent e) {
                // Retrieve selected entries from list
                itemsToOpen = list.getSelection();
                // Set return code
                setReturnCode(OPEN);
                // Close dialog
                close();
            }
        });
        // Create Delete button
        Button deleteButton =
            createButton(parent, DELETE, "Delete", false);
        deleteButton.setEnabled(false);
        // Add a SelectionListener
        deleteButton.addSelectionListener(new SelectionAdapter() {
        public void widgetSelected(SelectionEvent e) {
```

Listing 9.2 (Continues)

```
                    // Get the indices of the selected entries
                    int selectedItems[] = list.getSelectionIndices();
                    // Remove all these entries
                    list.remove(selectedItems);
                    // Now re-validate the list because it has changed
                    validate();
            }
        });
        // Create Cancel button
        Button cancelButton =
            createButton(parent, CANCEL, "Cancel", false);
        // Add a SelectionListener
        cancelButton.addSelectionListener(new SelectionAdapter() {
            public void widgetSelected(SelectionEvent e) {
                setReturnCode(CANCEL);
                close();
            }
        });
    }
    /**
     * Method getItemsToOpen.
     * @return String[] - the selected items
     */
    public String[] getItemsToOpen() {
        return itemsToOpen;
    }
}
```

Listing 9.2 (Continued)

You can then use the MailDialog class as shown in Listing 9.3.

```
MailDialog mailDialog = new MailDialog(shell,
new String[] {"Carol", "Eve", "Claudia", "Alice" });
if (mailDialog.open() == MailDialog.OPEN) {
    String[] itemsToOpen = mailDialog.getItemsToOpen();
    for (int i = 0; i < itemsToOpen.length; i++) {
        System.out.println(itemsToOpen[i]);
    }
}
```

Listing 9.3

Making Dialogs Persistent

The interface IDialogSettings is used to save and restore the state of Dialog instances across sessions, such as the state of checkboxes, entries in text fields, and so on.

For this purpose `IDialogSettings` defines methods that allow you to set and retrieve name/value pairs. With `get()` and `getArray()` you can read scalar string values or string arrays, respectively, and with `put()` you can write both scalars and arrays. There is also a variety of data type–specific `get...()` methods, such as `getInt()`, `getLong()`, `getFloat()`, `getDouble()`, and `getBoolean()`.

In addition, you have the option to store and retrieve whole subsections of dialog settings with the `addSection()`, `addNewSection()`, and `getSection()` methods. Each subsection is represented by another `IDialogSettings` instance. Consequently, subsections may be nested. You can thus construct a deeply nested tree.

With the `load()` method you can read an `IDialogSettings` instance from a file or from an input stream, and with `save()` you can write an `IDialogSettings` instance to a file or to an input stream.

The class `DialogSettings` is the standard implementation for the interface `IDialogSettings`. It uses XML as the file format for persistent storage of the settings.

In Listing 9.4 the `DialogSettings` instance with two subsections is created.

```
IDialogSettings settings = new DialogSettings("dialog");
IDialogSettings section1 = new DialogSettings("dialogPage1");
settings.addSection(section1);
section1.put("volume",4.5);
section1.put("pitch",300);
IDialogSettings section2 = new DialogSettings("dialogPage2");
settings.addSection(section2);
    section2.put("Languages", new String[]{"english",
        "german","french"});
settings.save("settings/test/dialog.xml");
```

Listing 9.4

Viewers

Despite the name Viewer, the classes in the package `org.eclipse.jface.viewers` do not only support viewing contents. All ...`Viewer` classes also support the modification of contents. In fact, some of the editors in the Eclipse workbench are constructed with the help of these viewer classes. The name Viewer is derived from the Model-Viewer-Controller (MVC) design pattern. This pattern defines cooperation between three component types: the Model component manages the domain data, the Viewer component is responsible for the representation of the data on the screen, and the Controller component handles user interaction. Besides a clear separation of concerns, this design pattern has the advantage that it allows several Viewer instances for a single Model instance. This allows you to display the same data in different ways simultaneously.

The Viewer Event Model

In the context of the MVC design pattern, JFace establishes its own event model. This model features all event types that are sent from the Viewer component to the Controller. The following event types are available:

Event	Listener	Description
CheckStateChangedEvent	ICheckStateListener	This event is generated when the state of a check box within the viewer changes.
DoubleClickEvent	IDoubleClickListener	This event is generated when a data element representation in the viewer is double-clicked.
OpenEvent	IOpenListener	This event is generated when a data element shown in the viewer is opened with a double-click or by pressing the Enter key.
SelectionChangedEvent	ISelectionChangedListener	This event is generated when the selection in the viewer changes.
TreeExpansionEvent	ITreeViewerListener	This event is generated when a tree node expands or collapses.

All these event types are subclasses of class `java.util.EventObject`.

The Viewer Hierarchy

The abstract class `Viewer` is the mother of all viewer classes in JFace (Figure 9.4). Most notably, each `Viewer` instance wraps an SWT widget that is responsible for the representation of data, such as widgets of type `Table`, `Tree`, `TableTree`, and so on. The class `Viewer` provides the basis for the concrete viewer implementation but also provides some methods of general interest, such as functions supporting the help system.

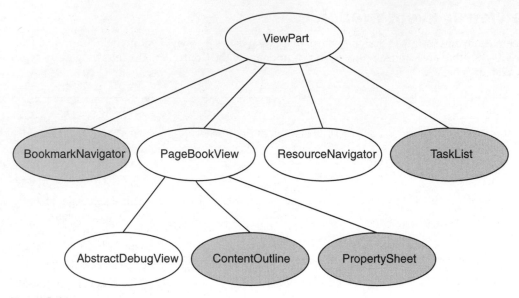

Figure 9.4

ContentViewer

The class `ContentViewer` is an immediate subclass of class `Viewer` and implements the MVC design pattern. `ContentViewer` retrieves the domain data from an `IContentProvider` instance that has been registered with the `ContentViewer` via the `setContentProvider()` method. The `IContentProvider` instance may deliver the data in its raw format: the later transformation of the individual data elements into their representational format is done via an `IBaseLabelProvider` instance that has been registered with the `ContentViewer` via the `setLabelProvider()` method. For example, if you want to display a table containing the various file attributes for a set of files, the `IContentProvider` would deliver just the `File` instances. The `IBaseLabelProvider` would retrieve for each table column the corresponding attributes from a single `File` instance and would deliver the representation of the attribute. `IBaseLabelProviders` can deliver both text and image representations.

Both `IContentProvider` and `IBaseLabelProvider` are "abstract" interfaces, that is, they don't declare methods to retrieve or transform contents. They declare only general methods such as `dispose()` or `inputChanged()`.

ILabelProvider

The definition of the actual methods for data transformation are left to "concrete" interfaces such as `ILabelProvider` with the methods `getImage()` and `getText()`, `ITableLabelProvider` with the methods `getColumnImage()` and `getColumnText()`, and `IStructuredContentProvider` with the methods `getChildren()`, `hasChildren()`, and `getParent()`.

StructuredViewer

The class `ContentViewer` is the direct parent class for the (still) abstract class `StructuredViewer`. This class is the basis for most of the concrete viewer implementations in JFace. It provides a wealth of additional methods—in particular, methods that allow you to sort and filter the dataset displayed in the viewer. The abstract classes `ViewerSorter` and `ViewerFilter` act as a basis for implementations of custom sorters and filters. In the "Playlist Viewer" section in Chapter 8 you will see a `TableViewer` as a concrete example of the `StructuredViewer` in full action.

TreeViewer

The abstract class `AbstractTreeViewer` provides the basis for all concrete tree-oriented viewer implementations such as `TreeViewer` (and its derivative `CheckboxTreeViewer`) and `TableTreeViewer`. In particular, this class provides methods for the management of trees, such as methods for expanding and collapsing tree nodes.

Cell Editors

All table-oriented viewers such as `TableViewer` and `TableTreeViewer` can be equipped with cell editors, allowing you not only to view table contents but also to edit them. Eclipse provides a variety of predefined cell editors:

`CheckboxCellEditor`	This editor allows the modification of a Boolean value.
`ColorCellEditor`	This editor supports the selection of a color.
`ComboBoxCellEditor`	This editor allows the selection of a value from a list but also the free input of an arbitrary value.
`DialogCellEditor`	This editor allows the invocation of arbitrary dialogs. The result value of the dialog is then assigned to the cell.
`TextCellEditor`	This editor allows unrestricted input into the cell.

All these editors are derivatives of the abstract class `CellEditor`. To make tables and table trees editable, several components must cooperate:

❑ You need a suitable viewer (`TableViewer` or `TableTreeViewer`).

❑ You need a suitable cell editor (as previously mentioned), too. The editor is registered with the viewer via the method `setCellEditors()`. You can register an individual editor for each column.

❑ With each editor you can register an `ICellEditorValidator` instance via the `setValidator()` method. These instances are responsible for validating the editor input.

❑ You must register an `ICellModifier` instance with the viewer via method `setCellModifier()`. This instance is responsible for the data flow between the viewer and the editor. Each `ICellModifier` instance must implement the following three methods:

    ❑ `getValue()` retrieves from the domain data the value that will appear in the editor.

    ❑ `canModify()` checks to see whether a given value can be modified.

    ❑ `modify()` gets the result data from the editor and modifies the domain data accordingly.

❑ Column properties identify each column uniquely. The `CellModifier` can recognize the column it works on with the help of these column properties. You can assign a column property to each viewer column via the method `setColumnProperties()`.

In the section "The Playlist Viewer" in Chapter 10 you will see cell editors in action.

Data Transfer

Basically, all JFace viewers are prepared to support data transfer via drag and drop. This functionality is built on top of the SWT data transfer functionality (see the "Data Transfer" section in Chapter 8). For example, you can easily add a `DragSourceListener` to a viewer via its `addDragSupport()` method. In this method call you also would define the supported operations and transfer types. Similarly, you can add a `DropTargetListener` via method `addDropSupport()`. Within these listeners, drag-and-drop events are processed as already discussed in the "Drag-and-Drop" section in Chapter 8.

However, if you want to exchange data with existing viewers, you must know which transfer types are supported by these viewers. For example, the Eclipse Navigator supports the types `FileTransfer` and `ResourceTransfer`. The Tasks View, the Problems View, and the Bookmarks View support the types `MarkerTransfer` and `TextTransfer`.

Details about the JFace data transfer are discussed in the Eclipse Corner (www.eclipse.org) article by John Arthorne.

Text Processing

Text processing is another main functional group of JFace. In particular, the various Eclipse editors are based on JFace's text processing. However, it is possible to use JFace text processing isolated from the Eclipse workbench.

The Eclipse text-processing functionality is deployed in two separate plug-ins, `org.eclipse.jface.text` with archive `jfacetext.jar` and `org.eclipse.text` with archive `text.jar`, and consists of the following packages:

```
org.eclipse.text.*
org.eclipse.jface.text.*
```

Text Processing Base Classes

The text processing function group is separated into a data domain layer and a presentation layer. The representation is done by the `TextViewer` class, while the data model is described by the interface `IDocument`. For the interface `IDocument`, Eclipse provides the standard implementations `AbstractDocument` and `Document`.

The Document Model

Classes that implement the `IDocument` interface must provide the following services:

❑ **Text manipulation.** Modifying the text content of a document is done with the help of the `replace()` method. This method can replace a specified text area with another string. Such operations generate `DocumentEvent`s that inform registered `Listeners` and `IPositionUpdaters` (see the following explanation) about the text modification.

❑ **Positioning.** `Position` instances represent a position or an area within a document. You can add any number of `Position` instances to an `IDocument` instance and can assign each

Position instance to a category. For the Java editor, for example, there are breakpoints, problem markers, and other positional categories. Remembering a document position in a Position instance, however, raises a problem. When the document changes, the real position may change, too. It is therefore necessary to update all Position instances in the case of document modification. This is done with the help of IPositionUpdate instances. (The DefaultPositionUpdater class is the standard implementation of this interface). You can add any number of these instances to a document. When a document is modified, all registered IPositionUpdate instances are invoked in their registration order via their update() method, and a DocumentEvent instance is passed to this method.

❑ **Partitioning.** Partitions are non-overlapping sections within a document. For example, a source code document could be segmented into partitions of the types comment, declaration, and instruction. Each partition is characterized by its position, its length, and its type. A document is segmented into separate partitions with the help of an associated IDocumentPartitioner instance. If a document does not have such an IDocumentPartitioner, it consists of only a single partition—the entire document. When a partition is changed, the method documentPartitioningChanged() is called for a registered IDocumentPartitioningListener instance.

❑ **Searching.** The method search() supports searching for a character string. It can search forward and backward, allows case-sensitive or case-insensitive searching, and can search for words or generic character strings.

❑ **Line tracking.** The line-tracking functions are found only in the standard implementations AbstractDocument and Document but don't belong to the IDocument interface. With an ILineTracker instance (standard implementations are AbstractLineTracker, DefaultLineTracker, and ConfigurableLineTracker), you can create a relationship between document position and line number. Initially, the whole text is parsed for line-separation characters. Later modifications are made known to the ILineTracker instance, so that this instance can update its internal line number associations. It is not the client's responsibility to register an ILineTracker instance with a document. Instead, an ILineTracker is associated with an IDocument instance by implementation, that is, when a subclass of AbstractDocument is implemented. For example, the class Document uses the standard implementation DefaultLineTracker.

IDocument implementations throw a BadLocationException or a BadPositionCategoryException when you try to access beyond the document bounds or when you use an unknown position category.

Scripts

Since Eclipse 3 it is possible to combine several text operations into a single script. To do so, you must represent each single text operation by a TextEdit instance. JFace provides a specific subclass of class TextEdit for each operation type, such as DeleteEdit, InsertEdit, and ReplaceEdit. The class MultiTextEdit can combine multiple text operations, which can be added to a MultiTextEdit instance with the help of the method addChild() or addChildren(). MultiTextEdit objects can be nested, and thus TextEdit objects form trees. You can apply such scripts with the help of the method apply() to IDocument instances. This method returns as a result an UndoEdit object with which you can undo the just-performed operations. Listing 9.5 shows this.

```
public static void main(String[] args)
              throws MalformedTreeException, BadLocationException {
   IDocument document= new Document("Eclipse 3");
   System.out.println(document.get());
   MultiTextEdit edit= new MultiTextEdit();
   edit.addChild(new InsertEdit(0, "Java Entwicklung"));
   edit.addChild(new InsertEdit(0, " mit "));
   UndoEdit undo = edit.apply(document);
   System.out.println(document.get());
   undo.apply(document);
   System.out.println(document.get());
}
```

Listing 9.5

The result is the following output on the Java console:

```
Eclipse 3
Java Entwicklung mit Eclipse 3
Eclipse 3
```

In addition to these delete, insert, and replace operations, there are also the classes `MoveSourceEdit`, `MoveTargetEdit`, `CopySourceEdit`, and `CopySourceEdit` to support the moving and copying of text within a document. When you use these classes, every `SourceEdit` must have a corresponding `TargetEdit`, and vice versa. When moving or copying text contents, you can modify these contents before inserting them into the target position. This is done by adding a suitable `ISourceModifier` instance to `MoveSourceEdit` or `CopySourceEdit` instances via the method `setSourceModifier()`.

The TextViewer

The class `TextViewer` implements the presentation layer of the text-processing function group. It uses the SWT class `StyledText` (see "Custom Widgets" in Chapter 8) for displaying and editing text. Writing a bare-bones text editor with the help of this class is almost trivial. For example:

```
Document doc = new Document("Some text");
TextViewer textViewer = new TextViewer(composite,SWT.MULTI
    | SWT.H_SCROLL | SWT.V_SCROLL);
textViewer.setDocument(doc);
```

Despite this minimalist example, the class `TextViewer` provides such rich functionality that it would require a complete book to cover the topic. Here, I want to list only the most important functions.

The event processing for class `TextViewer` is handled by four `Listener` interfaces:

Listener	Event	Description
ITextInputListener	–	The inputDocumentAboutToBeChanged() method is called before the current document is replaced by a new document. After the replacement the method inputDocumentChanged() is invoked.
ITextListener	TextEvent	The textChanged() method is invoked when text is changed. The TextEvent describes the replaced text and the replacement.
IViewportListener	–	The viewportChanged() method is invoked when text is changed within the visible window of the viewer.
VerifyKeyListener	VerifyEvent	The VerifyEvent of the StyledText widget.

Selection

The methods getSelectedRange(), setSelectedRange(), getSelection(), and setSelection() allow clients to retrieve and set text selections. These methods use TextSelection instances for parameters and results. With setTextColor() or changeTextPresentation() you can assign a different color to a selected text area. In addition, you can set and retrieve text markers with setMark() and getMark().

Viewport

The viewport describes the editor's visible window onto the text. This viewport can be managed with the getTopIndex(), setTopIndex(), getBottomIndex(), getTopIndexStartOffset(), and getBottomIndexEndOffset() methods. You can therefore get and set the line number of the top line in the viewport, the line number of the bottom line in the viewport, the text position of the top-left viewport corner, and the text position of the bottom-right corner of the viewport. With revealRange() you can position the editor window in the specified area.

Visible Text Region

The visible text region consists of all text lines that can be displayed in the editor window. Apart from these lines, a document may contain lines that always remain invisible. The following methods can be used to manage the visible region:

- ❑ getVisibleRegion()
- ❑ setVisibleRegion()
- ❑ resetVisibleRegion()
- ❑ overlapsWithVisibleRegion()

Hover

You can set or retrieve an ITextHover instance for each text partition with the methods setHover() and getHover(). These instances organize the display of explanation texts that are displayed when the mouse hovers over a text area. They implement the method getHoverInfo(), which composes the explanation text, and the method getHoverRegion(), which computes the text area for which the explanation is provided from a text position.

Apart from these basic functions, the TextViewer establishes a framework for implementing a complete text editor. This includes support for operations and support for installing plug-ins.

Operations

Instances of type ITextOperationTarget represent operations typically performed by the user. This interface is implemented by the TextViewer with the methods canDoOperation() and doOperation(). The latter method must be invoked only if canDoOperation() is successful. In addition, the TextViewer implements the method enableOperation() from the interface ITextOperationTargetExtension.

Operations can be identified with the following predefined constants (defined in interface ITextOperationTarget): COPY, CUT, DELETE, PASTE, PREFIX, PRINT, REDO, SELECT_ALL, SHIFT_LEFT, SHIFT_RIGHT, STRIP_PREFIX, and UNDO. For example, the following code deletes all text:

```
textViewer.doOperation(ITextOperationTarget.SELECT_ALL);
if (textViewer.canDoOperation(ITextOperationTarget.DELETE))
    textViewer.doOperation(ITextOperationTarget.DELETE);
```

Some of these operations are available only if you have previously created an appropriate manager for the TextViewer. In particular, this is the case for UNDO and REDO operations. Before you can perform these operations, you first must add an IUndoManager instance to the TextViewer via the setUndoManager() method. In the following code the IUndoManager standard implementation, the class DefaultUndoManager, is installed:

```
// maximum 99 Undos
 IUndoManager undoManager = new DefaultUndoManager(99);
undoManager.connect(textViewer);
textViewer.setUndoManager(undoManager);
```

The operations PREFIX and STRIP_PREFIX can be configured by setting a default prefix with the setDefaultPrefixes() method. This allows you to set a different default prefix for each text category. Similarly, you can use the method setIndentPrefix() to specify category-specific prefixes for text indentation used by the operations SHIFT_LEFT and SHIFT_RIGHT.

The indentation of text can, in addition, be automated by specifying an IAutoIndentStrategy instance. For each text modification, the customizeDocumentCommand() of this instance is called. A DocumentCommand is passed as a parameter to this method and informs you how the text was changed. The IAutoIndentStrategy instance may then decide how to indent the text. The IAutoIndentStrategy standard implementation, for example, always indents a line by left aligning it with the previous line. The following code shows how this strategy is installed:

```
try {
    textViewer.setAutoIndentStrategy(new DefaultAutoIndentStrategy(),
        doc.getContentType(0));
} catch (BadLocationException e) {}
```

Text Presentation

Since the TextViewer uses internally a widget of type StyledText (see "Custom Widgets" in Chapter 8), it is possible to apply an appropriate text presentation, for instance, displaying text sections in a different style or color. Since Eclipse 3 there are two new interfaces to support this task: ITextViewerExtension4 and ITextPresentationListener. You should use this API instead of resorting to the low-level API of the StyledText widget. If a TextViewer implements the interface ITextViewerExtension4, you can instrument it with an ITextPresentationListener instance. The applyTextPresentation() method of this instance is called whenever a new text presentation must be created or updated, receiving a TextPresentation object via its parameter. You can add StyleRange instances to this object by invoking the methods addStyleRange() and mergeStyleRanges() and thus modify the existing text presentation.

The SourceViewer Class

The SourceViewer class is a subclass of TextViewer. In addition to the TextViewer, it offers a vertical ruler on which you can place annotations and mark text areas. There are some new operations, too:

❑   CONTENTASSIST_PROPOSALS

❑   CONTENTASSIST_CONTEXT_INFORMATION

❑   FORMAT

❑   INFORMATION

The SourceViewer is, in particular, suited to implementing source code editors. An example for the application of the SourceViewer is given in Chapter 10.

Configuration

The SourceViewer combines most of its configuration settings and managers in a separate configuration object, an instance of the SourceViewerConfiguration class. Here you can specify all kinds of settings such as prefixes, UndoManager, hover behavior, or the content assistant in complete isolation from the SourceViewer. Later you can assign the configuration object to a SourceViewer instance via the configure() method. Usually you would want to create subclasses of SourceViewerConfiguration to create editors of different behavior. Instead of subclassing the class SourceViewer, you subclass SourceViewerConfiguration and use the instances of these subclasses to configure the SourceViewer.

Annotations

Annotations for a document are managed outside the IDocument instance. The package org.eclipse.jface.text.source provides the interface IAnnotationModel for this purpose with the standard implementation AnnotationModel. With the connect() method you can connect this model with the document instance. The `SourceViewer` is told about the annotation model as an additional parameter in the `setDocument()` method (together with the `IDocument` instance).

The `IAnnotationModel` interface provides a number of methods to add `Annotation` instances to the model or to remove or retrieve annotations. When it does so, the position of the annotation is specified with a `Position` instance (see "Text Processing Base Classes"). This guarantees that the annotation remains in the right position, even when the document content changes.

In addition, you have the option of adding an `IAnnotationModelListener` instance to the annotation model. The `modelChanged()` method of this instance is invoked when the model changes.

The abstract class `Annotation` defines some methods for the graphical representation of annotations. You have the option of specifying a layer for each `Annotation` instance, so you can position annotations on top of each other.

The interface `IAnnotationHover` also belongs to the annotation mechanism. Instances of type `IAnnotationHover` can be registered with the `SourceViewer` via the method `setAnnotationHover()`. Implementations of `IAnnotationHover` must implement the method `getHoverInfo()`. This method generates text that is displayed when the mouse hovers over the annotation for each given line number.

Text Formatters

Text formatters modify the content of a document. They insert characters or remove characters to mold the text into a given format. An example of a text formatter is the Java code formatter introduced in the "Formatting Code" section in Chapter 1.

Text formatters are passed from a `SourceViewerConfiguration` to a `SourceViewer` instance via method `getContentFormatter()`. All these formatters must implement the interface `IContentFormatter`. The standard implementation `ContentFormatter` can work in two operation modes: being aware of text categories or being insensitive to text categories. For each text category, you can specify a special formatting strategy via the method `setFormattingStrategy()`. The formatting strategies must implement the interface `IFormattingStrategy`. The actual formatting is done in the `format()` method. The methods `formatterStarts()` and `formatterStops()` inform the `IFormattingStrategy` instance about the start and the end of the formatting process.

Content Assistants

Content assistants (or *code assistants*) suggest content completion proposals to the end user. After the end user selects a proposal and commits to it, the content assistant modifies the document.

Content assistants are passed from a `SourceViewerConfiguration` to a `SourceViewer` instance via the method `getContentAssistant()`. All these assistants must implement the interface `IContentAssistant`. The standard implementation of this interface is the class `ContentAssistant`. Usually, instances of this class are configured appropriately before they are used. This can be done with the `enableAutoActivation()` and `setAutoActivationDelay()` methods. With these methods you can specify that the content assistant automatically appears on the screen after a specified time, even when no activation key (such as Ctrl+Spacebar) is pressed. When you want to activate the content assistant via a key press, you must explicitly call the `SourceViewer` method `doOperation(SourceViewer.CONTENTASSIST_PROPOSALS)`.

The proposals of the content assistant are compiled with the help of IContentAssistProcessor instances. Such instances can be registered for each text category separately with the ContentAssistant via the method setContentAssistProcessor(). These processors implement the method computeCompletionProposals(), which computes appropriate proposals based on the current position in the document. The method returns an array of ICompletionProposal instances. They can be simple proposals of type CompletionProposal or PositionBasedCompletionProposal. Each of these proposals contains the string to be inserted into the document, the position at which to insert the string, the length of text to be replaced, and the new position of the cursor relative to the inserted string. Another possibility is proposals of type TemplateProposal. In the "Code Assistant" section in Chapter 2 you encountered templates from the end user's view.

A simple example for a content assistant is given in the "Description Editor" section in Chapter 10. A more detailed discussion on creating content assistants is found in my article "Equipping SWT Applications with Content Assistants" at www.ibm.com/developerworks.

Text Presentation

The classes in the package org.eclipse.jface.text.presentation are responsible for presenting the text content on the screen. These operations do not modify the document. The interface IPresentationReconciler covers the presentation process when text parts are modified. Instances of this interface are passed from a SourceViewerConfiguration to a SourceViewer instance via the getPresentationReconciler() method. The standard implementation of this interface is the class PresentationReconciler. This class uses two cooperating processors: an instance of IPresentationDamager and an instance of IPresentationRepairer. The IPresentationDamager computes the document area for which the current representation has become invalid because the document was changed. The IPresentationRepairer decorates this text area with new text attributes. The standard implementation DefaultDamagerRepairer implements both interfaces.

When creating a DefaultDamagerRepairer instance, an ITokenScanner instance is passed in the constructor. Usually, a subclass of RuleBasedScanner is used here. (RuleBasedScanner implements ITokenScanner). And so we arrive at the package org.eclipse.jface.text.rules.

Since RuleBasedScanners can be programmed by supplying an ordered list of rules, they are quite flexible. They analyze the specified text area with the help of these rules and deliver a series of tokens, which can then be interpreted by the client (in this case, the DefaultDamagerRepairer). In this case, these tokens contain only TextAttribute instances that specify color and style attributes for the corresponding text sections.

All rules must implement the IPredicateRule interface. They search in the specified text area for a given pattern. You can specify such a pattern by supplying the string with which the pattern begins and the string with which it ends. When a rule finds a pattern in the text, it will return the specified token. If it does not, the RuleBasedScanner will continue the process with the next rule.

The various concrete rule types, such as SingleLineRule, WordRule, MultiLineRule, and so on, differ in how they treat space characters and line-separation characters. For example, the SingleLineRule does not search for patterns across line breaks, and the WordRule does not search across word breaks. In addition, there are special rules such as the NumberRule, which recognizes numeric values.

A simple example for rule-based text presentation is given in the "Description Editor" section in Chapter 10.

The ProjectionViewer

The class ProjectionViewer extends the class SourceViewer. Instead of a single visible text region, it supports multiple regions that can be modified dynamically. In particular, this class is used to support Folding, that is, collapsing and expanding text regions, as you've already seen in the Java editor (see "Code Folding" in Chapter 2).

The class ProjectionViewer can add another column to the vertical ruler of the SourceViewer via method addVerticalRulerColumn(). This column can be used to display the control elements for the Folding operations. The additional operations are COLLAPSE, EXPAND, EXPAND_ALL, and TOGGLE. (With operation TOGGLE you can switch the Folding mode on or off.)

Comfortable Text Fields and Combos

Since Eclipse 3 you have the option to instrument simple Text fields ("Text Fields and Labels" in Chapter 8) and Combos ("Tables, Lists and Combos" in Chapter 8) with the comfortable input aids discussed above, especially with content assistants. Input fields that you want to utilize this functionality must implement the interface IContentAssistSubject. As a matter of fact, this is not the case for the classes Text and Combo. The solution is to wrap these widgets into adapter objects. Eclipse provides for this purpose the classes TextContentAssistSubjectAdapter and ComboContentAssistSubjectAdapter. Both are subclasses of class AbstractControlContentAssistSubjectAdapter, which implements the interface IContentAssistSubject. These adapters provide the methods required by content assistants, such as getCaretOffset(), getLocationAtOffset(), getSelectedRange(), and getDocument(). Optionally, it is possible to display a visual clue at the left-hand side of an input field when the field is equipped with a content assistant.

Actions and Menus

Action instances represent abstract user actions such as "Save to file," "Search," or "Go to marker." Actions can be represented on the user interface in many ways, for example, as a menu item, a toolbar button, or both.

The IAction Interface

The IAction interface is contained in the package org.eclipse.jface.action. It defines a set of methods with which the properties of an action can be set or retrieved. For example, you can assign a unique identification (string) to an action via the method setId(). With the method setText() you can define a display text that is shown when the action is represented as menu text or a toolbar button. This text can contain display text for a keyboard shortcut, separated by an @ or \t character. If the keyboard shortcut consists of several keys, you must concatenate the key names using the + character. With the method setToolTipText(), you can specify text that appears on the screen when the mouse hovers over the action representation. In addition, you can use the method setDescription() to specify longer descriptive text. This text is shown in a status line when the action is selected.

With the setImageDescriptor() method you can set an icon that represents the action on a toolbar. With setDisabledImageDescriptor() you can specify a special variant of that icon that is shown when the action is disabled. With setHoverImageDescriptor() you can specify an icon variant that is shown when the mouse hovers over the action. You can disable or enable an action by invoking setEnabled(). With setChecked() you can set an action to checked or reset the action. How the checked state is represented on the user interface depends on the representation of the action itself: in menus a check mark is displayed; in toolbars the button remains pushed.

With the setAccelerator() method you can specify a keyboard shortcut for the action. If this short-cut consists of several keys, you must combine the key codes using the | operator for binary OR. To specify alphanumeric keys you specify just the character. Codes for other keys are defined in the class SWT. For example, you can specify SWT.CTRL | 'Z' for the keyboard shortcut Ctrl+Z.

With the method setHelpListener() you can register the action's HelpListener. This listener will receive an appropriate event object when the F1 key is pressed for the selected action.

Finally, each IAction instance must implement the run() method. This action is called when the end user activates the action.

The Managers

I discussed menus and toolbars in the "Toolbar" and "Menus" sections in Chapter 8. The question here is how to organize the cooperation between menus, toolbars, status lines, and actions. All this coopera-tion is handled by IContributionManager instances that come in various derived types such as IMenuManager, IToolBarManager, ICoolBarManager, and IStatusLineManager and their stan-dard implementations MenuManager, ToolBarManager, CoolBarManager, and StatusLineManager.

MenuManager

I will now briefly discuss the MenuManager (ToolBarManager and CoolBarManager work quite similarly) and then the StatusLineManager.

You can create a new menu manager with the constructor MenuManager(). Optionally, you may pass a text and an identification with this constructor. Then you tell the menu manager to create a menu. With the method createContextMenu() you can create a context menu, and with createMenuBar() you can create a menu bar.

The addMenuListener() method allows you to register an IMenuListener instance with the menu manager. The menuAboutToShow() method of this instance is called before the menu is displayed. You will usually construct the menu each time from scratch when this method is invoked—and especially when the menu content depends on the context. This is not difficult: you just add IAction instances (and possibly also Separator instances) to the menu manager using the add() method. One thing still remains to be done: you must tell the menu manager to remove all entries after the menu has been shown. This is achieved with the method setRemoveAllWhenShown(). Otherwise, you would create double entries the next time the method menuAboutToShow() is invoked.

In the implementation of the SpellCorrectionView class in Chapter 13 I show how to construct a context menu with the help of a menu manager as a practical example.

StatusLineManager

The StatusLineManager creates a StatusLine object when the method createControl() is called. The StatusLineManager provides several methods for the output of information messages and error messages into this status line, such as setMessage() and setErrorMessage(). With the method getProgressMonitor() you can access the progress monitor built into the status line. For this progress monitor you can allow cancellation of an operation by the end user by calling the setCancelEnabled() method. You can determine whether the end user has cancelled an operation with isCancelEnabled().

Wizards

Wizards consist of a series of dialogs that guide the user through several steps of a task. The user can step forward and backward within the task. Typical examples for such wizards are the New File Wizard, the Import Wizard, and the Export Wizard.

The package org.eclipse.jface.wizard provides four classes with which you can implement such wizards:

❑ The abstract class Wizard forms the basis on which all wizards are implemented. This class is the standard implementation of the interface IWizard.

❑ The class WizardDialog implements the dialog that presents the wizard to the end user. This dialog may have several pages.

❑ The abstract class WizardPage forms the basis on which all wizard pages can be implemented.

❑ Finally, there is the class WizardSelectionPage. This class allows the end user to select a specific wizard from a list of possible wizards.

The Wizard Class

The implementation of a new wizard begins by extending the class Wizard. This class offers various wizards that you can use to configure the concrete wizard subclass. This configuration is usually done in the method addPages(), which is called when the wizard is initialized.

addPage()	This method can be used to add new pages of type WizardPage to the wizard.
setHelpAvailable()	This method can be invoked to indicate that help is available for the wizard.
setDefaultPageImageDescriptor()	This method is called to decorate the default page with an image (ImageDescriptor).

setDialogSettings() getDialogSettings()	These methods allow you to set and retrieve instances of type IDialogSettings (see the section "Making Dialogs Persistent") to make wizard properties persistent.
setNeedsProgressMonitor()	This method is called to equip the wizard with a ProgressMonitor.
setTitleBarColor()	You can use this method to set the title bar color.
setWindowTitle()	You can use this method to set a title.

Concrete subclasses of Wizard will, in addition, override some wizard methods to implement application logic. In particular, you may want to override the methods performCancel() and performFinish(), possibly also the methods createPageControls(), addPages(), and dispose(). In the method performFinish() you will start all operations that need to be performed after the Finish button has been pressed. The method performCancel() is called when the Cancel button is pressed. In this method you may want to undo operations that have been performed on the single wizard pages. In method createPageControl() the wizard content is constructed. The construction of the single pages is done in the individual WizardPage instances, but the corresponding method calls IDialogPage.createControl() are invoked from the createPageControls() method.

The WizardPage Class

To implement a concrete wizard you construct wizard pages by subclassing the abstract class WizardPage. When a page instance is created, you pass a unique identification with the constructor and optionally a page title and a title image (ImageDescriptor).

This class also offers various methods that support the configuration of the wizard page:

setDescription()	This method can be used to supply a long explanatory text that is shown below the page title.
setErrorMessage()	With this method you can set an error message. This error message replaces an information message previously set with setMessage(). To reset the error message, supply null as a parameter.
setImageDescriptor()	With this method you can set an image (ImageDescriptor) to be displayed on the page. Here you won't use small 16x16 icons but rather images of size 48x48 pixels or larger.
setMessage()	With this method you can display an information message to the end user. Typically, you would use it to ask the end user to do something.
setPageComplete()	This method can be used to set an internal indicator when the end user completes the page. This indicator can be retrieved via the method isPageComplete().
setPreviousPage()	This method sets the page to be shown when the end user presses the Back button.
setTitle()	This method can be used to set the page title.

Here, too, the concrete subclasses can override several methods of class `WizardPage` to implement specific implementation logic. In particular, you may want to override the following methods:

`performHelp()`	This method shows the help information for the wizard page.
`canFlipToNextPage()`	This method enables the Next button.
`isPageComplete()`	This method finds out whether the end user completed the page. The standard implementation returns just the value set by the method `setPageComplete()`.
`setDescription()`	See above.
`setTitle()`	See above.
`dispose()`	This method can be extended if you need to release page-specific resources.

The WizardSelectionPage Class

The `WizardSelectionPage` class is an abstract subclass of class `WizardPage`. It is used as a basis for wizard pages that allow the selection of nested wizards. This allows you to concatenate wizards with each other. The class `WizardSelectionPage` introduces only two new methods: using `setSelectedNode()` and `getSelectedNode()` you can set or retrieve the selection on the page. When creating such a page, you would usually construct a list of available wizards. When a wizard gets selected, you would create a corresponding `IWizardNode` and set it in the `WizardSelectionPage` with `setSelectedNode()`.

The WizardDialog Class

Instances of type `WizardDialog` act as GUI containers for a wizard and support the end user in stepping through the wizard's pages. To execute a wizard, you first create a new instance of this wizard. Then you create a new instance of the class `WizardDialog` and pass the `Wizard` instance in the constructor as a parameter. Then you can open the `WizardDialog` instance via method `open()`:

```
IWizard wizard = new FancyWizard();
WizardDialog dialog = new WizardDialog(shell, wizard);
dialog.open();
```

You would usually use the class `WizardDialog` in its original form. However, in special cases it may be necessary to create subclasses and to override individual methods. In particular, it may become necessary to override the methods `backPressed()` and `nextPressed()` if you need to perform special processing during a page change.

Preferences

To manage application-specific preferences, several components need to cooperate. The package `org.eclipse.jface.preference` provides these components. First, there is the class

PreferenceStore, which can store preferences in the form of name/value pairs. Next, there is the class PreferenceConverter, which can convert popular object types into string values. The user interface can be constructed with the help of the classes PreferencePage, PreferenceDialog, PreferenceManager, and PreferenceNode. Using FieldEditors in PreferencePages can save some hard-coding.

The PreferenceStore and PreferenceConverter Classes

To be precise, PreferenceStore doesn't store preferences as name/value pairs but as triples, which consist of an identifier, a value, and a default value. The identification must be unique within the context of a PreferenceStore instance. When you read a preference from the store, you will get the previously set value (usually a value that has been set by the end user). If such a value does not exist, the default value defined by the application is returned.

The interface IPreferenceStore defines various data type–specific access methods for values and default values. The methods getDefault*xxx*() return the default value, and the get*xxx*() methods return the previously set value or the default value if no value has been set. With setDefault*xxx*() you can set the default value, and with set*xxx*() you can set the current value. All these methods have variants for the following data types: boolean, int, long, float, double, and String.

For example

```
store.setDefaultBoolean("use_animation",true);
```

or

```
double speed = store.getDouble("animation speed");
```

Of course, these data types are not sufficient by themselves. The class PreferenceConverter therefore provides a set of conversion methods, with which you can convert popular object types into string values and vice versa. In particular, the types RGB (colors), FontData (fonts), Point (coordinates), and Rectangle (areas) are supported.

Since the modification of preference values can influence the behavior and the appearance of an application, you must have a means to react to changes of preference values. It is therefore possible to register an IPropertyChangeListener instance with the PreferenceStore via the method addPropertyChangeListener(). This instance is notified immediately when a preference value within the PreferenceStore is changed: it receives an event object of type PropertyChangeEvent via the method propertyChanged(). This object passes information about the identification of the modified preference value, both the new value and the old value. You can thus react to such a modification and adapt the application's appearance accordingly.

You can specify a filename when you create a new PreferenceStore instance. Using the methods load() and save() you can load the preference store content from the specified file or save its content to the file. Only the actual values are written to file, not the default values: the default values of the preference store must always be set by the application. This is best done during the initialization of the application so that the PreferenceStore is always correctly configured.

The PreferencePage Class

The abstract `PreferencePage` is the base class for implementing your own preference pages. By default, this class is equipped with four buttons. The end user can commit the entered values with the OK button. The Cancel button is used to abort the modification of preference values. The Apply button allows the user to modify the values in the `PreferenceStore` without closing the preference dialog. The Default button can be pressed to reset all values to the default values.

The last two buttons can be suppressed by calling the method noDefaultAndApplyButton(). This method must be called before the method createControl() is invoked; it is a good idea to call it in the constructor.

Each concrete subclass of `PreferencePage` must implement the method createControl(). Here you will set up all the input fields for the preference values, usually with the help of field editors (see the following section).

In addition, you should extend or override the method doComputeSize(). This method computes the size of the area constructed in the createControl() method.

Field Editors

You could construct a `PreferencePage` manually with the help of SWT widgets and set the `PreferenceStore` values using the set*xxx*() methods. But it is far simpler to construct a preference page based on the abstract class `FieldEditorPreferencePage` and to use field editors.

To do this, just define your own preference page as a subclass of `FieldEditorPreferencePage` and override the method createFieldEditors(). Within this method add field editors, one for each preference value, to the page by using addField().

All field editors are based on the abstract class `FieldEditor`. When creating a new field editor, you must pass as parameters in the constructor the identification of the preference value (see the section "The PreferenceStore and PreferenceConverter Classes"), a display text, and the containing `Composite`. You must fetch this `Composite` with the method getParent() from the preference page for each field editor, because the `FieldEditorPreferencePage` may create a new `Composite` each time a new field editor is added.

JFace provides the following concrete subclasses of `FieldEditor`:

`BooleanFieldEditor`	A field editor for a Boolean value. This field editor is represented as a check box.
`ColorFieldEditor`	A field editor for entering a color value. By pressing a button, the end user can select the color from a host system–specific color selection dialog.
`DirectoryFieldEditor`	A field editor for selecting a directory. This field editor is a subclass of the `StringButtonFieldEditor`.
`FileFieldEditor`	A field editor for selecting a file. This field editor is a subclass of the `StringButtonFieldEditor`.

FontFieldEditor	A field editor for entering a type font. By pressing a button, the end user can select the font from a host system–specific font selection dialog.
ListEditor	An abstract field editor for entering multiple values that are organized as a list. Concrete subclasses must implement the methods parseString(), createList(), and createNewInputObject().
IntegerFieldEditor	A field editor for entering an integer value. This field editor is a subclass of StringFieldEditor.
PathEditor	This field editor is a subclass of ListEditor. With the help of this editor the end user can compile a list of file and directory paths from the host operating system. Besides New and Remove buttons, this editor features Up and Down buttons with which the order in the path list can be changed. An additional title line for the pop-up path selection dialog must be specified in the constructor of this class.
RadioGroupFieldEditor	A field editor that presents an enumeration of radio buttons for selection. This class requires some additional parameters in the constructor: the number of columns and a two-dimensional array containing all the number/value pairs available for selection. You may optionally specify an additional parameter that places the specified radio buttons into a Group widget (see section "Composites, Groups, and Canvas" in Chapter 8).
ScaleFieldEditor	A field editor employing a Scale (see section "Sliders and Scales" in Chapter 8) as an input device. Optional parameters in the constructor can be used to specify minimum and maximum, as well as simple increment and page increment.
StringButtonFieldEditor	An abstract field editor that displays a Change button next to the input field. Pressing this button will lead to a pop-up dialog in which the new value can be entered.
StringFieldEditor	A field editor for entering a string value.

An example of the use of field editors in connection with the FieldEditorPreferencePage is shown in the "Preferences" section in Chapter 13.

Preference Page Trees

The classes PreferenceNode, PreferenceManager, and PreferenceDialog can be used to organize multiple PreferencePages into a preference page tree. In a larger application (and, in particular, on an open platform such as Eclipse) it is neither possible nor desirable to place all preferences on a single page. It is better to distribute the preferences across multiple pages and to order these pages according to topic. A tree structure is best suited to support the organization of preference pages.

The PreferenceNode Class

The class PreferenceNode with the corresponding interface IPreferenceNode is used to implement such a tree structure. Each node within a preference page tree is implemented by an instance of this class. The class features all the usual methods to construct and manage trees such as add(), remove(), getSubNodes(), and findSubNode().

Each PreferenceNode has a unique identification that is specified in the constructor when an instance is created. In addition, you can specify a PreferencePage instance that belongs to this node in the constructor. Later, you can retrieve this page via the method getPage(), and you can modify the page via the method setPage().

A further variant of the constructor allows you to create PreferencePage instances lazily, that is, at the time they are first displayed. This can be achieved by specifying the class name of the concrete PreferencePage in lieu of the PreferencePage instance. Using the Java Reflection facility, the PreferenceNode will create the PreferencePage instance when it is actually needed. This makes sense for applications with many preference pages, the Eclipse workbench being one of them.

In addition to the PreferencePages, the PreferenceNode instances take care of the display information needed for the presentation of the preference page tree. This information consists of a label and an icon (ImageDescriptor). These objects can also be specified in the constructor.

The PreferenceManager Class

This class provides methods that allow you to navigate within preference page trees by just specifying a path. Each path consists of a series of PreferenceNode identifications that are separated with a separator character. This character can be specified in the constructor of the PreferenceManager.

Other methods allow the modification of preference page trees: in particular, the methods addTo(), remove(), and find() use path expressions. You can add child nodes to a node specified by a path with addTo(). Similarly, remove() removes the child node addressed by the specified path from its parent node. The method find() returns the node at the specified path. There are additional utility methods such as removeAll() or addToRoot(). All these PreferenceManager methods allow you to completely construct and manage a preference page tree.

The PreferenceDialog Class

The class PreferenceDialog is an extension of the class Dialog (see the section "Dialogs and Windows"). In addition to the Dialog methods, it features the methods setPreferenceStore() and getPreferenceStore() to set and retrieve a PreferenceStore instance. You must also specify a PreferenceManager instance as an additional parameter in the PreferenceDialog() constructor. This instance is used by the PreferenceDialog to organize the user interaction. The PreferenceDialog displays the tree managed by PreferenceManager on the left-hand side of the dialog. When the user clicks on a tree node, the attached PreferencePage is opened on the right-hand side of the dialog.

Summary

In this chapter you have become acquainted with some of the higher-level components of the JFace layer. Most of the components of this layer are used within the Eclipse workbench, but all of them—together with SWT components—can be used within your own applications. We have looked at dialogs and windows, various viewers such as table, tree, text, and source viewers, actions and menus, wizards, preferences, and drag-and-drop facilities.

In the next chapter you will apply some of these components in a larger example.

Project Two: Jukebox

In this chapter I use a longer example to demonstrate the various techniques employed in the use of SWT and JFace. The example is a Java version of a jukebox, a device that can play sound files or lists of sound files, known as playlists. The idea is to implement the player's user interface using SWT and JFace. However, I don't want to implement the player as an Eclipse plug-in but as a standalone application.

To make the jukebox a bit more interesting, I allow for the association of a background image and descriptive text with each entry in the playlist. By doing this I achieve nearly the same multimedia experience as with an old vinyl album collection, but without the crackles and hisses.

Design Goals and How to Achieve Them

Before beginning the implementation, you should first perform a short requirements analysis:

❑ The jukebox should be able to play diverse sound file formats, including MP3.

❑ It should be possible to associate a title, a background image, and descriptive text with each sound file.

❑ It should be possible to mark up descriptive texts in some way. End users should get some assistance when editing descriptions, for example, when inserting keywords into the text.

❑ It should be possible to define individual playlists, to store the playlists, and to navigate within the playlists.

During the implementation of these design goals, you must take several technological constraints into consideration:

❏ For replaying sound files you need external modules. For this project I have selected the JavaZoom sound modules (www.javazoom.net). These modules support many sound formats, including MP3, and are completely written in Java. The modules are freely available and come with source code. They also include a nice player skin. However, the player GUI is different from what is implemented here.

❏ For the storage of playlists there are different options. For example, you could store the different playlist entries in a relational database and could query this database via SQL. Another possibility is to store a whole playlist in a single XML document. You can organize access to the playlist entries via a DOM API. I suggest the latter option for this implementation.

Apart from implementing a jukebox and listening to music, there is also some real work to do—that is, applying the topics discussed in previous chapters to a real-world example. In particular, I discuss the following issues:

❏ Creation of GUI elements, layouts, and SWT event processing. This applies in particular when implementing the main window of the jukebox.

❏ Using irregular (non-rectangular) shell shapes for the main window of the jukebox.

❏ The application of a TableViewer for the presentation of playlists. This includes the implementation of custom cell editors for modifying playlists.

❏ Using drag-and-drop functionality when adding items to the playlist.

❏ Syntax highlighting in an editor based on a SourceViewer. For this editor I also demonstrate the implementation of a Content Assistant. I also equip the viewer with an Undo and Redo function.

❏ Displaying HTML contents with the help of the Browser widget.

❏ Communication between the SWT thread and other threads within the player.

Figure 10.1 shows the UML class diagram for the Jukebox application.

Installing the Project

First, you need the module for replaying sound files. You can download the module jlGui 2.2 from www.javazoom.net/jlgui/sources.html. The ZIP file found there is completely adequate for your purposes: the installer module is not required. After downloading the file, unzip it into an empty directory.

Now, you can create a new Eclipse Java project called Jukebox. You should already know how to do this. After entering the name on the first page of the New Java Project Wizard, just click Next. On the second page you need to complete the Java Build Path.

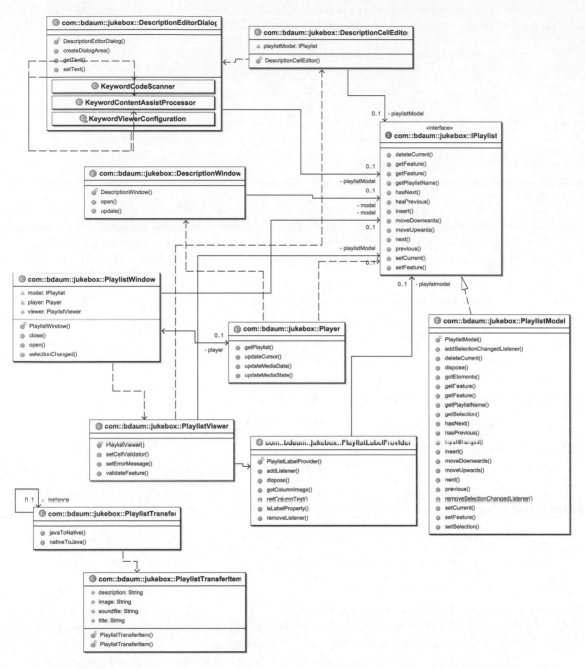

Figure 10.1

You will need to add some Eclipse JARs to the Java Build Path. Obviously, you need the JARs for SWT and for JFace, but you also need the JARs for text processing; these are:

- ❑ swt.jar (plus swt-pi.jar under Linux)
- ❑ jface.jar
- ❑ jfacetext.jar
- ❑ text.jar
- ❑ osgi.jar
- ❑ runtime.jar

The JARs `osgi.jar` and `runtime.jar` are needed by the JFace `TableViewer` used in this example.

All of these JARs are located in subfolders of the directory `\eclipse\plugins`. Because the names of these subfolders differ depending on the Eclipse version and on the platform, I give only their short names here. Your best option is to search for these JARs with the search function of your operating system.

Second, you also need to add all the JARs from the `lib` directory of the unpacked jlGui ZIP file; these are:

- ❑ jl020.jar
- ❑ jogg-0.0.5.jar
- ❑ jorbis-0.0.12.jar
- ❑ mp3sp.1.6.jar
- ❑ vorbissp0.7.jar

Figure 10.2 shows the Java Build Path for the Jukebox project.

After you have created this project, you can import (see section "Importing Files" in Chapter 4) three more files from the `src` directory of the unpacked jlGui archive:

- ❑ `javazoom/jlGui/BasicPlayer.java`
- ❑ `javazoom/jlGui/BasicPlayerListener.java`
- ❑ `javazoom/Util/Debug.java`

By now, your project should have two Java packages: `javazoom.jlGui` and `javazoom.Util`.

Finally, you need a folder for images. Directly under the project, create a new folder named `icons`. In this folder place a little warning icon that you "borrow" from Eclipse. Import the image named `alert_obj.gif` from the directory `\eclipse\plugins\org.eclipse.pde.ui_3.0.0\ full\obj16`—into the newly created folder.

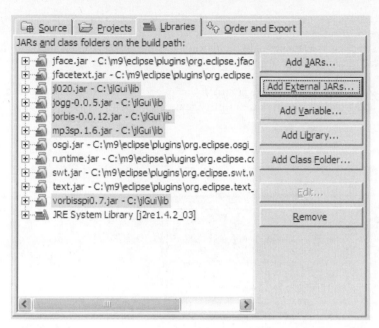

Figure 10.2

Actually, you do not necessarily have to invoke the Import Wizard to perform this task. Depending on the host operating system, you can just drag and drop the object that you want to import from the native directory into the target folder of the Eclipse navigator.

The Player Module

To get an idea of what the player should look like, I made a sketch of its layout (see Figure 10.3). The windows for the descriptive text of the current tune and the window for the playlist should be shown only on demand. So, you should include some buttons for opening and closing these windows.

Layout

For the main window, use a non-rectangular shape by applying `Region` definitions. In the main window install a `Canvas` object. You will use this canvas to display the background image. On top of the `Canvas` object mount the player's instrumentation and the status display. The instrumentation includes the usual player buttons, Start, Stop, Pause, Forward, and Backward, and the buttons for opening and closing the additional windows. Combine all the buttons in a toolbar.

In addition, install a `Scale` instance. This scale should always display the current position of the tune being played. In addition, it should allow the user to freely navigate (scroll) in the tune. However, the jlGui2.2 engine supports this functionality only for WAV files. In the case of other sound file formats, therefore, you need to lock the scale against modifications by the user.

Figure 10.3 shows a rough sketch of the layout of the jukebox. It shows the main window, the windows for the playlist, and the current tune's descriptive text.

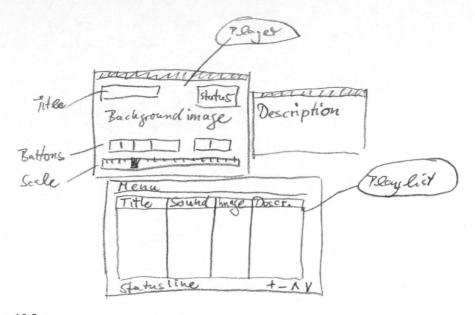

Figure 10.3

The status display includes the status panel in the upper-right corner and the title display in the upper-left corner. The status panel shows the total length of the current tune and the current operational state. Both the status display and the toolbar appear only as long as the mouse hovers over the canvas. When the mouse is gone, the background image is shown in its full beauty.

Threads

All of these GUI elements must be updated during the operation of the player. For example, the operational state changes when the current tune is finished. The scale's handle must move from left to right during the player's operation, and the push buttons for the additional windows must be released when these windows are closed.

While the player is operating, two threads are active:

❑ **The main() thread in which our player operates.** This thread also acts as the SWT thread in which all SWT operations are performed.

❑ **The thread of the jlGui engine.** This must be a separate thread; otherwise, the jukebox would be locked against user interaction as long as a tune is playing.

Of course, this setup causes some complications. The jlGui engine produces events that must be reflected in the user interface, so the SWT thread must react to those events. Unfortunately, SWT accepts method calls only from its own thread: method calls from other threads are rejected by throwing an exception.

The problem is solved by first storing the events from the jlGui engine in a field of the `Player` instance. Then the method `updateGUI()` is called. This method creates a new `Runnable` instance by calling the method `display.asyncExec()`. Within the `run()` method of this `Runnable` the GUI elements are updated and—if necessary—a new replay process is started. This is possible because this `run()` method is executed in the SWT thread (see also "Displays, Shells, and Monitors" in Chapter 8).

In the following sections we walk step by step through the player's source code.

The Player.java Class

Listing 10.1 contains the Player class which starts, of course, with the necessary `package` and `import` declarations, followed by the class declaration and the declarations of all instance variables. Here the fields holding the various GUI elements such as buttons, scale, and windows are defined. In addition, there are a few fields for storing the current state of the player.

```
package com.bdaum.jukebox;

import java.io.File;
import java.io.IOException;
import javax.sound.sampled.LineUnavailableException;
import javax.sound.sampled.UnsupportedAudioFileException;
import javazoom.jlGui.BasicPlayer;
import javazoom.jlGui.BasicPlayerListener;
import org.eclipse.swt.SWT;
import org.eclipse.swt.events.*;
import org.eclipse.swt.graphics.*;
import org.eclipse.swt.layout.GridData;
import org.eclipse.swt.layout.GridLayout;
import org.eclipse.swt.layout.RowLayout;
import org.eclipse.swt.widgets.*;

/**
 * Player module. This module demonstrates the various techniques
 * of the SWT, in particular the coordination between SWT thread
 * and other threads.
 */
public class Player implements BasicPlayerListener {

    // Operation states
    private static final int PLAY = 1;
    private static final int PAUSE = 2;
    private static final int STOP = 3;
    private static final int EOM = 4;
    // Text representation of operation state
    private static final String PLAYING = "Playing";
    private static final String PAUSED = "Paused";
    private static final String IDLE = "Idle";
    // Features in the playlist data model
```

Listing 10.1 (Continues)

```
  public final static String TITLE = "title";
public final static String SOUNDFILE = "soundfile";
public final static String IMAGEFILE = "image";
public final static String DESCRIPTION = "description";
  /* Data model of the player model */

  // Current operation state
  private int state = STOP;
  // The player engine
  private BasicPlayer soundPlayer;
// The playlist's data model
private IPlaylist playlistModel;
// Duration of current tune
private double lengthInSec = 0;
// Current position
private int currentPosition = 0;
// Maximum position
private int maxPosition = 0;
// Text representation of current operation state
private String mediaState = "Stopped";
// Current background image
private String currentImage;
// Title of current tune
private String currentTitle = "";

  /*** GUI elements ***/
  /* Widgets of player windows */

  // Player shell
  private Shell toplevelShell;
// Outline of shell
private static final int[] OUTLINE = new int[]{
                5, 0,
                355, 0,
                360, 5,
                360, 20,
                330, 295,
                325, 300,
                15, 290,
                10, 285,
                0, 5};
// The hole in the shell
private static final int[] HOLLOW = new int[]{
                13, 10,
                247, 10,
                250, 13,
                255, 27,
                252, 30,
                13, 30,
                10, 27,
                10, 13};
// Current Display instance
private Display display;
// Canvas for background image
```

Listing 10.1 (Continues)

```
   private Canvas canvas;
   // Taste zum Schließen der Shell
   private Button closeButton;
   // Status Panel
   private Composite statusPanel;
   private Label statusLabel, lengthLabel;
   // Toolbar with buttons
   private ToolBar toolbar;
   private ToolItem backButton, playButton, pauseButton,
                  stopButton, forwardButton, playlistButton,
                  descriptionButton;
   // Scale
   private Scale scale;
   // Additional windows
   private DescriptionWindow descriptionWindow;
   private PlaylistWindow playlistWindow;


   /**
    * main method for starting the player
    *
    * @param args - unused
    */
   public static void main(String args[]) {
     Player player = new Player();
     player.run();
   }
```

Listing 10.1 (Continued)

The method run() is similar to the SWT programs shown in Chapter 8. A shell instance is created and the content of this shell is constructed in the constructPlayer() method. After opening the shell, the process stays in the event loop, thus ensuring that the GUI is supplied with all occurring events.

In the case of multiscreen displays, the shell is opened on the primary monitor. You set the outline of the shell by applying Region objects to the shell. These Region objects are created from the array constants OUTLINE and HOLLOW, which were declared previously. Since such a shell must always be created with the style constant SWT.NO_TRIM, you must organize all window management yourself. For example, you can enable the user to reposition the window on the desktop by creating a Listener object in a listener variable. This listener is the registered with the shell for the events SWT.MouseUp, SWT.MouseDown, and SWT.MouseMove. Later, you must care for the window's Close button as well.

In addition, you must initially create the domain model of the playlist (see section "The Playlist Domain Model"). Before the shell is opened, create an instance of the jlGui engine by calling new BasicPlayer(). During its creation the player instance registers as a BasicPlayerListener with the engine. See Listing 10.2.

```
   /**
    * Initialize Player
    */
```

Listing 10.2 (Continues)

```
private void run() {
  // Create Playlist domain model
  playlistModel = new PlaylistModel();
  // Create Display instance
  display = new Display();
  // Create top level shell with the usual controls
  toplevelShell = new Shell(display, SWT.NO_TRIM);
  // Set title (appears in tasks bar)
  toplevelShell.setText("Jukebox");
  // Hintergrundfarbe setzen
  Color bgColor = new Color(display, 160, 160, 255);
  toplevelShell.setBackground(bgColor);
  // Create region for the player shell outline
  Region region = new Region();
  region.add(OUTLINE);
  region.subtract(HOLLOW);
  // Apply region to shell
  toplevelShell.setRegion(region);
  // Retrieve size of region
  Rectangle size = region.getBounds();
  // Position shell on the primary monitor
  Monitor mon1 = display.getPrimaryMonitor();
  Rectangle r = mon1.getClientArea();
  toplevelShell.setBounds(r.x + 20, r.y + 20, size.width,
                size.height);
  // Since the shell does not have a trim
  // we must handle the repositioning of the window ourselves
  Listener listener = new Listener() {
    Point origin;

    public void handleEvent(Event e) {
      switch (e.type) {
        case SWT.MouseDown :
                    // Remember mouse position
          origin = new Point(e.x, e.y);
                    break;
        case SWT.MouseUp :
                    // Indicate operation stopped
          origin = null;
          break;
        case SWT.MouseMove :
          if (origin != null) {
                          // Shift shell by difference to origin
            Point p = display.map(toplevelShell, null, e.x,
                        e.y);
            toplevelShell.setLocation(p.x - origin.x, p.y
                        - origin.y);
          }
          break;
      }
    }
  };
  toplevelShell.addListener(SWT.MouseDown, listener);
  toplevelShell.addListener(SWT.MouseUp, listener);
```

Listing 10.2 (Continues)

246

```
      toplevelShell.addListener(SWT.MouseMove, listener);
      // Create rest of Player GUI
      constructPlayer(toplevelShell);
      // Create the jlGui-engine
      soundPlayer = new BasicPlayer(this);
      // Display shell
      toplevelShell.open();
      // Event loop
      while (!toplevelShell.isDisposed()) {
        // Check for waiting events
        if (!display.readAndDispatch()) display.sleep();
      }
      // If necessary stop playing
      stop();
      // Force session exit -
      // otherwise the Java audio system would remain active
      System.exit(0);
  }

  /**
   * Retrieves the playlist
   *
   * @return IPlaylist - the playlist model
   */
  public IPlaylist getPlaylist() {
    return playlistModel;
  }
```

Listing 10.2 (Continued)

Create the GUI

Now the surface of the player is instrumented in the method constructPlayer(). First, the Composite for the status display and the window's Close button is created. These elements are constructed in the methods createStatusPanel() and createCloseButton().

Then a Canvas instance is created. This instance will contain the background image and will serve as a surface for graphical operations. On this Canvas instance the controls are placed with the help of the methods createToolbar() and createScale(). A PaintListener is registered with the Canvas instance, because the correct method for drawing something onto a Canvas is to do this in the paintCanvas() method of a PaintListener.

In addition, a MouseTrackListener is registered with the Canvas. The listener allows you to hide the control elements when the mouse leaves the canvas area. When you move the mouse back to the canvas, the control elements reappear. The additional tests in the method mouseExit() are required to check that the mouse has really left the canvas area, because this method is also called when the mouse is moved over controls that hide the canvas area. See Listing 10.3.

```
/** * GUI erzeugen ** */
/**
```

Listing 10.3 (Continues)

```
 * Constructs the Player-GUI.
 *
 * @param parent - containing Composite
 */
private void constructPlayer(Composite parent) {
  // We use a GridLayout for the containing Composite
  GridLayout gridLayout = new GridLayout();
  gridLayout.marginHeight = 0;
  parent.setLayout(gridLayout);
  // Composite for CloseButton and StatusPanel
  Composite comp = new Composite(parent, SWT.NONE);
  gridLayout = new GridLayout(2, false);
  gridLayout.marginWidth = 10;
  comp.setLayout(gridLayout);
  comp.setBackground(parent.getBackground());
  // Layoutdaten for Composite
  GridData data = new GridData();
  data.horizontalAlignment = GridData.END;
  data.verticalAlignment = GridData.BEGINNING;
  data.grabExcessHorizontalSpace = true;
  comp.setLayoutData(data);
    // Create status panel
  createStatusPanel(comp);
  // Create button for closing the window
  createCloseButton(comp);
    // Create canvas
  canvas = new Canvas(parent, SWT.NONE);
  // Set preferred canvas size
  data = new GridData();
  data.widthHint = 355;
  data.heightHint = 235;
  canvas.setLayoutData(data);
    // The Canvas instance acts as a Composite, too.
    // So we apply a GridLayout to it, too.
    gridLayout = new GridLayout();
  gridLayout.marginHeight = 2;
  gridLayout.verticalSpacing = 0;
  canvas.setLayout(gridLayout);
    // Construct Toolbar
  createToolbar(canvas);
  // Construct scale
  createScale(canvas);
    // Add PaintListener to Canvas to support drawing
    canvas.addPaintListener(new PaintListener() {
    public void paintControl(PaintEvent e) {
      paintCanvas(e.gc);
    }
  });
  // Add MouseTrackListener to Canvas
  canvas.addMouseTrackListener(new MouseTrackAdapter() {
    public void mouseEnter(MouseEvent e) {
      setCanvasControlsVisible(true);
    }
```

Listing 10.3 (Continues)

```
      public void mouseExit(MouseEvent e) {
        Rectangle rect = canvas.getClientArea();
        // Check if mouse has really left the canvas area
        if (!rect.contains(e.x, e.y))
          setCanvasControlsVisible(false);
      }
    });
    setCanvasControlsVisible(false);
  }

  /**
   * Create window close button
   *
   * @param parent - the containing Composite
   */
  private void createCloseButton(Composite parent) {
    closeButton = new Button(parent, SWT.PUSH | SWT.FLAT);
    closeButton.setText("x");
    closeButton.addListener(SWT.Selection, new Listener() {
      public void handleEvent(Event e) {
        toplevelShell.close();
      }
    });
  }

  /**
   * Shows or hides the control elements on top of the canvas.
   *
   * @param v - true for showing, false for hiding
   */
  private void setCanvasControlsVisible(boolean v) {
    toolbar.setVisible(v);
    scale.setVisible(v);
  }
```

Listing 10.3 (Continued)

Graphics Operations

Let's now look at paintCanvas(), which is always invoked when the canvas needs to be redrawn. If you have an image file, just create from this image file a new Image instance. Then draw this image onto the graphics context (GC) of the Canvas instance. Immediately afterward, dispose of the Image instance (see also the "Graphics" section in Chapter 8).

Then draw the title line over this background. System colors are used for the background color and the text color, so you don't need to dispose of these colors. See Listing 10.4.

```
/** * Graphic Operations ** */
/**
 * Draw all graphical elements on the canvas.
 *
```

Listing 10.4 (Continues)

```
  * @param gc - The graphics context
  */
private void paintCanvas(GC gc) {
  Rectangle area = canvas.getClientArea();
  // Check if we have an image file
  if (doesFileExist(currentImage)) {
    // Scale and draw image
    Image image = new Image(display, currentImage);
    Rectangle bounds = image.getBounds();
    gc.drawImage(image, bounds.x, bounds.y, bounds.width,
                 bounds.height, area.x, area.y, area.width,
                 area.height);
    // Dispose image
    image.dispose();
  } else {
    // Otherwise fill background with gray color
    gc.setBackground(toplevelShell.getBackground());
    gc.fillRectangle(area);
  }
  // Draw title of current sound file
  if (currentTitle != null && currentTitle.length() > 0) {
    gc.setBackground(display
                  .getSystemColor(SWT.COLOR_DARK_GRAY));
    gc.setForeground(display.getSystemColor(SWT.COLOR_WHITE));
    gc.drawText(" " + currentTitle + " ", 5, 12, false);
  }
}

/**
 * Checks if a file with the specified name exists.
 *
 * @param filename - File name
 * @return boolean - true, if the file exists
 */
private static boolean doesFileExist(String filename) {
  return (filename != null && filename.length() > 0 && openFile(
                filename).exists());
}

/**
 * Convert file name into File instance
 *
 * @param file - File name
 * @return File - File instance
 */
private static File openFile(String file) {
  return new File(file);
}
```

Listing 10.4 (Continued)

Instrumentation

Now, place the control element onto the `Canvas` instance. The scale is used to display the current position in the sound file. In case of WAV files, it is possible to scroll within the sound file by moving the scale's handle. For this purpose add a `SelectionListener` to the `Scale` instance. You can perform the positioning within a tune in the `widgetSelected()` method of this listener by invoking the `seek()` method. See Listing 10.5.

```
/** * Instrument Canvas ** */
/**
 * Creates a scale that shows the current position
     * in the sound file.
 *
 * @param parent - the containing Composite
 */
private void createScale(Composite parent) {
  scale = new Scale(parent, SWT.NONE);
  // Set scale size
  GridData data = new GridData();
  data.horizontalIndent = 18;
  data.widthHint = 300;
  data.heightHint = 20;
  scale.setLayoutData(data);
  // Event processing for scale handle movements
  scale.addSelectionListener(new SelectionAdapter() {
    public void widgetSelected(SelectionEvent e) {
      seek();
    }
  });
}
```

Listing 10.5

The toolbar contains the usual buttons for operating a player (Listing 10.6). In addition, two more buttons are implemented, allowing the end user to open and close the playlist and description windows. These buttons are created with the style constant `SWT.CHECK` to achieve a toggling behavior. You can separate these two buttons from the rest of the buttons with another button that has the style constant `SWT.SEPARATOR`.

The event processing for all buttons is done in the method `processButton()`. Depending on the button—and in case of the last two buttons, also depending on the state of the button—this method calls the appropriate methods for controlling the player and opening and closing the windows, respectively.

By specifying a `GridData` instance appropriately, you can position the toolbar at the lower border of the player area.

```
/**
 * Create toolbar with all buttons
 *
```

Listing 10.6 (Continues)

```
      * @param parent - the containing Composite
      */
    private void createToolbar(Composite parent) {
      // Create Toolbar instance
      toolbar = new ToolBar(parent, SWT.NONE);
      // Create all buttons
      backButton = makeToolItem(toolbar, SWT.PUSH, "<<", "Previous");
      playButton = makeToolItem(toolbar, SWT.PUSH, ">", "Play");
      pauseButton = makeToolItem(toolbar, SWT.PUSH, "||", "Pause");
      stopButton = makeToolItem(toolbar, SWT.PUSH, "[]", "Stop");
      forwardButton = makeToolItem(toolbar, SWT.PUSH, ">>", "Next");
      makeToolItem(toolbar, SWT.SEPARATOR, null, null);
      playlistButton = makeToolItem(toolbar, SWT.CHECK,
                      "PlayList", "Show Playlist");
      descriptionButton = makeToolItem(toolbar, SWT.CHECK,
                      "ShowText", "Show Description");
      // Create layout data for toolbar
      GridData data = new GridData();
      data.horizontalIndent = 5;
      data.verticalAlignment = GridData.END;
      data.grabExcessHorizontalSpace = true;
      data.grabExcessVerticalSpace = true;
      toolbar.setLayoutData(data);
    }

    /**
     * Convenience method for creating a toolbar button.
     *
     * @param bar - the ToolBar instance
     * @param style - the button type
     * @param text - text for button label
     * @param tip - tool tip
     * @return ToolItem - the created toolbar button
     */
    private ToolItem makeToolItem(ToolBar bar, int style,
                    String text, String tip) {
      ToolItem item = new ToolItem(bar, style);
      if (style != SWT.SEPARATOR) {
        item.setText(text);
        item.setToolTipText(tip);
        // Add event processing for button clicks
        item.addSelectionListener(new SelectionAdapter() {
          public void widgetSelected(SelectionEvent e) {
            processButton(e);
          }
        });
      }
      return item;
    }

    /**
     * This method processes all ToolItem events.
     *
     * @param e - the event object
```

Listing 10.6 (Continues)

```
    */
    private void processButton(SelectionEvent e) {
      Widget widget = e.widget;
      if (widget == playButton) {
        play();
      } else if (widget == stopButton) {
        stop();
      } else if (widget == pauseButton) {
        pause();
      } else if (widget == forwardButton) {
        forward();
      } else if (widget == backButton) {
        back();
              // The following buttons are of type CHECK.
              // We must retrieve their state to react correctly.
        } else if (widget == descriptionButton) {
      if (descriptionButton.getSelection())
        showDescription();
      else
        hideDescription();
      } else if (widget == playlistButton) {
      if (playlistButton.getSelection())
        showPlaylist();
      else
        hidePlaylist();
      }
    }
```

Listing 10.6 (Continued)

Finally in Listing 10.7, create a small status panel that displays the current operating mode of the player and the total length of the current sound file. With the help of a vertical RowLayout, the display elements are arranged in a vertical column.

```
    /**
     * Create status panel with total duration and operating mode.
     *
     * @param parent - the containing Composite
     */
    private void createStatusPanel(Composite parent) {
      // Create panel as a new Composite
      statusPanel = new Composite(parent, SWT.NONE);
      statusPanel.setBackground(parent.getBackground());
      // Use a vertical row layout for the panel
      RowLayout rowLayout = new RowLayout();
      rowLayout.type = SWT.VERTICAL;
      rowLayout.wrap = false;
      rowLayout.pack = false;
      statusPanel.setLayout(rowLayout);
      // Now create the widgets of the status panel
      lengthLabel = createStatusLabel(statusPanel, timeFormat(0));
```

Listing 10.7 (Continues)

```
      statusLabel = createStatusLabel(statusPanel, IDLE);
    }

    private Label createStatusLabel(Composite panel, String text) {
      Label label = new Label(panel, SWT.RIGHT);
      label.setBackground(panel.getBackground());
      label.setForeground(display.getSystemColor(SWT.COLOR_WHITE));
      label.setText(text);
      return label;
    }

    /**
     * Converts the duration into an appropriate display format.
     *
     * @param sec
     *                          Seconds
     * @return String mm:ss.s
     */
    private static String timeFormat(double sec) {
      int sec10 = (int) (sec * 10);
      return twoDigitFormat(sec10 / 600) + ":"
                    + twoDigitFormat((sec10 / 10) % 60) + "."
                    + (sec10 % 10);
    }

    /**
     * Format an integer into a two-digit string with leading zeros.
     *
     * @param n
     *                          the integer value
     * @return String - the result string
     */
    private static String twoDigitFormat(int n) {
      if (n < 10) return "0" + n;
      return String.valueOf(n);
    }
```

Listing 10.7 (Continued)

The method `updateGUI()` shown in Listing 10.8 is intended to make state changes in the jlGui engine visible on the player's GUI. Since the engine runs in a different thread and this method is invoked from the thread, you cannot directly access the GUI elements because they run in the SWT thread. Therefore, you must encapsulate all these accesses into a `Runnable`, which you pass to the `Display` instance via the `asyncExec()` method. For each event, the status panel (see the previous code) is updated. When the engine reaches the end of a sound file, the next sound file in the playlist is played.

```
    /** * Update SWT-Thread ** */
    /**
       * Updates SWT-Widgets, caused by events from other threads, are
       * executed via this method. By performing the updates under the
       * SWT-thread (display.asyncExec()) we avoid an SWT thread error.
```

Listing 10.8 (Continues)

```
      */
    private void updateGUI() {
      display.asyncExec(new Runnable() {
        public void run() {
          if (!toplevelShell.isDisposed()) {
            // Update scale
            scale.setMaximum(maxPosition);
            scale.setSelection(currentPosition);
            // Update operation mode
            updateText(statusLabel, mediaState);
            // Update total length
            updateText(lengthLabel, timeFormat(lengthInSec));
            // Check if we have to start the next sound file
            if (state == EOM) {
              state = STOP;
              forward();
            }
          }
        }
      });
    }

    /**
     * Updates the text of a label
     *
     * @param c - the Label instance
     * @param s - the new text
     */
    private void updateText(Label c, String s) {
      // test against current content to avoid screen flicker
      if (!c.getText().equals(s)) c.setText(s);
    }
```

Listing 10.8 (Continued)

Now it's time to implement some player functions that are invoked by pressing a button. All you have to do in such a case is to update the player mode, update the status panel via the method `updateGUI()`, and pass the invoked function to the jlGui engine.

Only the `play()` method is more elaborate. Here you need to fetch the data from the playlist model (title, image, name of the sound file, and description). The `Canvas` instance is updated with a new background image, and the window with the descriptive text is updated. Then, initialize the jlGui engine and—depending on the file type of the sound file—disable or enable the scale. See Listing 10.9.

```
/** ** Button actions *** */
/**
     * Positions in the sound file when the scale is modified
     * by the end user (only for .WAV files).
     */
private void seek() {
  try {
```

Listing 10.9 (Continues)

```
        double position = ((double) scale.getSelection())
                       / ((double) scale.getMaximum());
      soundPlayer.setSeek(position);
      updateGUI();
    } catch (IOException e) {
      System.out.println(e.toString());
    }
  }

  /**
   * Stops playing.
   */
  private void stop() {
    if (state != STOP) {
      soundPlayer.stopPlayback();
      state = STOP;
      mediaState = IDLE;
      lengthInSec = 0;
    }
    updateGUI();
  }

  /**
   * Pauses the playing process.
   */
  private void pause() {
    switch (state) {
      case PLAY :
        soundPlayer.pausePlayback();
        state = PAUSE;
        mediaState = PAUSED;
        break;
      case PAUSE :
        soundPlayer.resumePlayback();
        state = PLAY;
        mediaState = PLAYING;
    }
    updateGUI();
  }

  /**
   * Starts playing.
   */
  private void play() {
    if (state == PLAY)
    // Current play processes are stopped
      stop();
    try {
      switch (state) {
        case PAUSE :
          // If the playing process was paused, we resume it.
          soundPlayer.resumePlayback();
          break;
        case STOP :
```

Listing 10.9 (Continues)

```
                            // Otherwise we start all over again.
                            // Fetch name of background image and title
                    currentImage = playlistModel.getFeature(IMAGEFILE);
            currentTitle = playlistModel.getFeature(TITLE);
            // Update description window
            updateDescription();
            // Fetch name of sound file
            String filename = playlistModel.getFeature(SOUNDFILE);
            // Enforce a redraw of the canvas
            canvas.redraw();
            // Do nothing if the sound file does not
                    // exist any more.
            if (!doesFileExist(filename)) return;
            // Otherwise configure the engine
            soundPlayer.setDataSource(openFile(filename));
            soundPlayer.startPlayback();
            soundPlayer.setGain(0.5f);
            soundPlayer.setPan(0.5f);
            // Fetch the total duration of the sound file
            lengthInSec = soundPlayer.getTotalLengthInSeconds();
            maxPosition = (int) lengthInSec;
            // If the sound format is not WAV we deactivate
                    // disable the scale (no scrolling possible).
            boolean canSeek = ((soundPlayer.getAudioFileFormat() != null)
                                        && (soundPlayer
                        .getAudioFileFormat().getType()
                        .toString().startsWith("WAV")));
            scale.setEnabled(canSeek);
        }
    // Now set the operation modus and update the GUI.
    state = PLAY;
    mediaState = PLAYING;
    updateGUI();
  } catch (UnsupportedAudioFileException e) {
    System.out.println(e.toString());
  } catch (LineUnavailableException e) {
    System.out.println(e.toString());
  } catch (IOException e) {
    System.out.println(e.toString());
  }
}


/**
 * If the playlist has a next element, we stop playing
  * the current sound file and start again with the next.
 */
private void forward() {
  if (playlistModel.next()) {
    stop();
    play();
  }
}

/**
```

Listing 10.9 (Continues)

```
     * If the playlist has a previous element, we stop playing
      * the current sound file and start again with the previous.
   */
  private void back() {
    if (playlistModel.previous()) {
      stop();
      play();
    }
  }
}
```

Listing 10.9 (Continued)

Managing Windows

The three methods shown in Listing 10.10 are used to open a window for the descriptive text, update this text, and close the window. The description window is implemented as the class DescriptionWindow, a subclass of Window. You need to create and initialize an instance of the class, get its Shell instance, position the window to an appropriate location, and instrument the Shell instance with a ShellListener that informs you when the window is closed. When the window is closed, you must also reset the corresponding button on the toolbar.

```
/** ** Manage windows ** */
/**
   * Creates a new DescriptionViewer if it not yet exists.
   * Supplies the DescriptionViewer with new text content.
   */
  private void showDescription() {
    if (descriptionWindow == null) {
      // Create window
      descriptionWindow = new DescriptionWindow(toplevelShell,
                      playlistModel);
      // Initialize window
      descriptionWindow.create();
      // Fetch Shell instance
      Shell shell = descriptionWindow.getShell();
      Rectangle bounds = toplevelShell.getBounds();
      // Position at the right hand side of the main window
      shell.setBounds(bounds.x + bounds.width - 5,
                      bounds.y + 10, 320, 240);
      // React to shell's close button
      shell.addShellListener(new ShellAdapter() {
        public void shellClosed(ShellEvent e) {
          // Update toolbar button
          hideDescription();
        }
      });
      // Open the window
      descriptionWindow.open();
    }
  }
```

Listing 10.10 (Continues)

```
/**
 * Closes the description window
 */
private void hideDescription() {
  // Reset the description toolbar button
  descriptionButton.setSelection(false);
  // Close window
  if (descriptionWindow != null) {
    descriptionWindow.close();
    descriptionWindow = null;
  }
}

/**
 * Updates the window with new text
 */
private void updateDescription() {
  if (descriptionWindow != null) descriptionWindow.update();
}
```

Listing 10.10 (Continued)

Managing the playlist window is very similar (see Listing 10.11).

```
/**
 * Creates a new playlist window
 */
private void showPlaylist() {
  if (playlistWindow == null) {
    // Create new PlaylistWindow instance
    playlistWindow = new PlaylistWindow(toplevelShell,
                  playlistModel);
    // Initialize the window to allow us to retrieve
          // the shell instance
    playlistWindow.create();
    Shell shell = playlistWindow.getShell();
    shell.addShellListener(new ShellAdapter() {
      public void shellClosed(ShellEvent e) {
        hidePlaylist();
      }
    });
    // Position the shell below the main window
    Rectangle bounds = toplevelShell.getBounds();
    shell.setBounds(bounds.x + bounds.width / 8, bounds.y
                  + bounds.height - 5, 400, 240);
    // Open the window.
    playlistWindow.open();
  }
}

/**
 * Closes playlist window
```

Listing 10.11 (Continues)

```
      */
    private void hidePlaylist() {
      // Reset playlist toolbar button.
      playlistButton.setSelection(false);
      // Close window
      if (playlistWindow != null) {
        playlistWindow.close();
        playlistWindow = null;
      }
    }
}
```

Listing 10.11 (Continued)

BasicPlayerListener

Finally, in this section are the methods that implement the interface `BasicPlayerListener`. These methods accept the events from the jlGui engine. The `updateGUI()` method (shown previously) is used to update the user interface accordingly. See Listing 10.12.

```
/** * Methods of the BasicPlayerListener interface ** */
/**
 * @see javazoom.jlGui.BasicPlayerListener#updateMediaData(byte)
 */
public void updateMediaData(byte[] data) {}

/**
 * @see javazoom.jlGui.BasicPlayerListener#
 *      updateMediaState(java.lang.String)
 */
public void updateMediaState(String newState) {
  // At file end set operation mode to IDLE
  if (newState.equals("EOM") && state != STOP) {
    this.state = EOM;
    mediaState = IDLE;
    // Update GUI
    updateGUI();
  }
}

/**
 * @see javazoom.jlGui.BasicPlayerListener#updateCursor(int, int)
 */
public void updateCursor(int cursor, int total) {
  // Save maximum position and current position; update GUI
  maxPosition = total;
  currentPosition = cursor;
  updateGUI();
}
}
```

Listing 10.12

The Playlist Domain Model

The domain model of the playlist has nothing to do with the user interface. It simply contains the data and the current state of the playlist. I have separated this model into an interface IPlaylist and an implementation PlaylistModel. While the interface is completely independent of the underlying storage method for the playlist, my implementation uses XML files as the storage method. If you would rather use a relational database to store your playlist, all you have to do is to rewrite the class PlaylistModel.

The Interface

The concept of the playlist domain model is quite generic. You can decorate entries within the playlist with any kind of features that can be configured through the API. In class Player (see "The Player Module") the playlist model was configured with the feature identifications TITLE, SOUNDFILE, IMAGEFILE, and DESCRIPTON. The functions of the playlist domain model include setting and retrieving the values of these features, the positioning within the playlist, and adding or removing playlist entries.

In addition to these basic functions, the playlist model includes the methods of the ISelectionProvider interface. These methods allow adding and removing SelectionListener instances in the playlist model. The model can inform these listeners when its content or state changes. The methods of the IStructuredContentProvider interface such as getElements(), inputChanged(), and dispose() are also included. The PlaylistViewer uses the PlaylistViewer getElements() method to fetch the playlist entries to be displayed. The PlaylistViewer signals to the model that a new playlist is opened via the method inputChanged(). Finally, dispose() is called when the PlaylistViewer is disposed of. Here the model implementation could, for example, close open files.

Listing 10.13 shows the The IPlaylist.java interface.

```
package com.bdaum.jukebox;

import org.eclipse.jface.viewers.ISelectionProvider;
import org.eclipse.jface.viewers.IStructuredContentProvider;

public interface IPlaylist
    extends IStructuredContentProvider, ISelectionProvider {

    /**
     * Returns the name of the current playlist
     * or null if no playlist active
     * @return String - Name of current playlist
     */
    public String getPlaylistName();
    /**
     * Returns the specified feature of the current playlist entry.
     * @param feature - Feature identification
     * @return String - Feature value
     */
    public String getFeature(String feature);
```

Listing 10.13 (Continues)

```
/**
 * Returns the specified feature of the specified playlist element.
 * @param record - Playlist element
 * @param feature - Feature identification
 * @return String - Feature value
 */
public String getFeature(Object record, String feature);
/**
 * Sets the specified feature of the specified playlist element
 * to the specified value.
 * @param record - Playlist element
 * @param feature - Feature identification
 * @param value - new Feature value
 */
public void setFeature(Object record, String feature,
    String value);
/**
 * Positions to the next playlist entry.
 * @return boolean - true if successfull
 */
public boolean next();
/**
 * Tests if we have a next entry in the playlist
 * @return boolean - true if successfull
 */
public boolean hasNext();
/**
 * Positions to the previous playlist entry.
 * @return boolean - true if successfull
 */
public boolean previous();
/**
 * Tests if we have a previous entry in the playlist
 * @return boolean - true if successfull
 */
public boolean hasPrevious();
/**
 * Sets the current position of the playlist onto
 * the specified playlist element.
 * @param current - The new current playlist entry
 */
public void setCurrent(Object current);

/**
 *    Deletes the current playlist entry.
 * The next playlist entry becomes the current entry.
 * If none exists, the previous playlist entry becomes the
 * current entry. If this does not exist, too, the
 * current playlist entry is undefined (null).
 */
public void deleteCurrent();

/**
```

Listing 10.13 (Continues)

```
        * Creates a new playlist entry in front of the current playlist
        * entry. The new playlist entry becomes the current
        * playlist entry.
        * @return Object - The new playlist element
        */
       public Object insert();

       /**
        * Moves the current playlist entry one position
        * towards the beginning
        * of the playlist.
        * @return boolean - true if successfull
        */
       public boolean moveUpwards();

       /**
        * Moves the current playlist entry one position towards the end\
        * of the playlist.
        * @return boolean - true if successfull
        */
       public boolean moveDownwards();
    }
```

Listing 10.13 (Continued)

The Implementation

The following code shows how this interface can be implemented. I selected XML as the file format. The schema (DTD) used for playlists is defined as follows:

```
<?xml version="1.0" encoding-"UTF-8"?>
<!ELEMENT playlist (record*)>
<!ELEMENT record (soundfile | title | image | description)*>
<!ELEMENT description (#PCDATA)>
<!ELEMENT image (#PCDATA)>
<!ELEMENT soundfile (#PCDATA)>
<!ELEMENT title (#PCDATA)>
```

When creating an interface and its implementation, you always can choose what you would like to do first. You can create the interface first and specify it as an implemented interface when you create the implementation. Eclipse will then generate all method stubs for you.

Alternatively, you can create the implementation first. Later, after the code has matured, you can always extract an interface by applying the context method Refactor > Extract Interface.... This way, you can, at least in the beginning, avoid some double work when modifying the API. Also, navigation in the code is easier.

Listing 10.14 shows the PlaylistModel.java implementation.

```
package com.bdaum.jukebox;

import java.io.*;
import java.util.Properties;

import javax.xml.parsers.DocumentBuilder;
import javax.xml.parsers.DocumentBuilderFactory;
import javax.xml.transform.OutputKeys;

import org.apache.crimson.jaxp.DocumentBuilderFactoryImpl;
import org.apache.xalan.serialize.SerializerToXML;
import org.eclipse.jface.util.ListenerList;
import org.eclipse.jface.viewers.*;
import org.w3c.dom.*;
import org.xml.sax.ErrorHandler;
import org.xml.sax.InputSource;
import org.xml.sax.SAXException;
import org.xml.sax.SAXParseException;

/**
 * This class implements the playlist domain model. XML is used as
 * file format to make the model data persistent. Access to the
 * XML data is organized via the JAXP DOM.
 */
public class PlaylistModel implements IPlaylist {

  // Name of INI file
  private final static String INIFILE = "jukebox.ini";

  // XML prolog
  private final static String XMLPROLOG =
"<?xml version=\"1.0\" encoding=\"UTF-8\"?>";
  // Empty playlist
  private final static String XMLROOT = XMLPROLOG
                  + "<playlist></playlist>";
  // Tag for playlist entries
  public final static String RECORD = "record";

  // INI file
  private File iniFile;
  // current playlist file name
  private String currentPlaylistFile;
  // current playlist DOM
  private Document playlistDoc;
  // current playlist entry DOM node
  private Node currentElement;
  // Listeners to be informed about changes
  private ListenerList selectionChangedListeners = new ListenerList();
```

Listing 10.14

INI File

To produce a user-friendly player it makes sense to maintain an INI file that stores the name of the most recently used playlist. So, if you construct a new `PlaylistModel` instance, just read the INI file, get the playlist name, and open the playlist. See Listing 10.15.

```java
/**
 * Constructor for PlaylistModel.
 */
public PlaylistModel() {
  super();
  try {
    // Try to read the INI file
    iniFile = new File(INIFILE);
    InputStream stream = new FileInputStream(iniFile);
    byte[] buffer = new byte[1024];
    int l = stream.read(buffer);
    // If it exists, read the name of the most recent
    // playlist and open this playlist
    openPlaylist(new String(buffer, 0, l));

  } catch (FileNotFoundException e) {
  } catch (IOException e) {
  }
}
```

Listing 10.15

Parsing

The method `openPlayList()` is called in two situations: opening an existing playlist file or creating a new playlist. If a file with the specified name does not exist, a new empty playlist document is created. The resulting stream is then parsed by a DOM parser. Finally, the first `<record>` element is searched for, and if one exists, the pointer for the current record is set to this element.

When a new DOM parser is created, it is configured to the requirements of the player. For example, lazy instantiation is used to keep the overhead low, and ignorable whitespace is ignored. Also, the SAX error handling is modified to avoid having the standard SAX error message appear on the console. See Listing 10.16.

```java
/**
 * Opens the playlist file
 *
 * @param name - Name of playlist file
 */
private void openPlaylist(String name) {
  if (name == null) return;
  currentPlaylistFile = name;
  File playlistFile = new File(name);
  // Input stream of playlist file
```

Listing 10.16 (Continues)

```
      InputStream stream;
      try {
        stream = new FileInputStream(playlistFile);
      } catch (FileNotFoundException e) {
        // File does not exist
        // Create an empty playlist document
        stream = makeStream(XMLROOT);
      }
      if (stream != null) try {
        // Parse the file content, creating a DOM
        playlistDoc = parseStream(stream, false);
      } catch (Throwable e) {
        playlistDoc = null;
        System.err.println("XML parsing error: " + e);
      }
      if (playlistDoc != null) {
        // Look for <record>-elements and set the first one
        // as current song
        NodeList nl = playlistDoc.getElementsByTagName(RECORD);
        if (nl.getLength() > 0) currentElement = nl.item(0);
      }
    }


  /**
    * Convert string into InputStream
    *
    * @param input - Input string
    * @return InputStream - resulting InputStream instance
    */
  public static InputStream makeStream(String input) {
      try {
        return new ByteArrayInputStream(input.getBytes("UTF8"));
      } catch (UnsupportedEncodingException x) {
        // should never happen
        return null;
      }
    }


/**
    * Convert serialized XML stream into DOM tree.
    *
    * @param stream - input stream
    * @param silent -
    *          don't show error messages on the console if set to true
    * @return Document - the resulting DOM document
    * @throws Throwable - various Throwables from Parser
    */
  private static Document parseStream(
      InputStream stream, boolean silent) throws Throwable {
      // Create InputSource from stream
      InputSource source = new InputSource(stream);
      // Create a document builder factory
      DocumentBuilderFactory factory = new DocumentBuilderFactoryImpl();
      // Create a document builder
```

Listing 10.16 (Continues)

```
      DocumentBuilder builder = factory.newDocumentBuilder();
      // When "silent" is set we override the SAX error handler and
      // suppress the output of error message to the Java console.
      if (silent) {
        builder.setErrorHandler(new ErrorHandler() {
          public void error(
            SAXParseException exception) throws SAXException {
            throw exception;
          }
          public void fatalError(
            SAXParseException exception) throws SAXException {
            throw exception;
          }
          public void warning(
            SAXParseException exception) throws SAXException {
            throw exception;
          }
        });
      }
      // Everything is configured - let's parse.
      return builder.parse(source);
    }
```

Listing 10.16 (Continued)

Serializing

Vice-versa, when a playlist is closed and it was modified, it must be rewritten to file. This is done with the help of an XML serializer. This serializer is configured so that it does not produce extra whitespace and produces an XML prologue only when needed (see Listing 10.17).

```
/**
 * Save current playlist to file.
 */
private void savePlaylist() {
  if (playlistDoc == null || currentPlaylistFile == null)
    return;
  File playlistFile = new File(currentPlaylistFile);
  try {
    // Create new file and set output stream to this file.
    playlistFile.createNewFile();
    OutputStream stream = new FileOutputStream(playlistFile);
    // Serialize DOM and write to output stream
    stream.write(serializeNode(playlistDoc, true)
                    .toByteArray());
  } catch (IOException e) {
    System.err.println("IO-exception during save: " + e);
  }
}

/**
 * Convert whole DOM document or subtree into XML stream.
```

Listing 10.17 (Continues)

```
     *
     * @param nod - DOM document or DOM node
     * @param prolog - "true" if an XML prolog is required
     * @return ByteArrayOutputStream - serialized XML text
     */
    public static ByteArrayOutputStream serializeNode(
        Node nod, boolean prolog) {
        // Set output formats
        // (no identation, XML prolog depending on option)
        SerializerToXML serializer = new SerializerToXML();
        Properties props = new Properties();
        props.setProperty(OutputKeys.METHOD, "xml");
        props.setProperty(OutputKeys.INDENT, "no");
        props.setProperty(OutputKeys.OMIT_XML_DECLARATION,
                (prolog) ? "no" : "yes");
        serializer.setOutputFormat(props);
        // Create OutputStream and Serializer instances.
        ByteArrayOutputStream outstream = new ByteArrayOutputStream();
        serializer.setOutputStream(outstream);
        try {
          // Serialize.
          serializer.serialize(nod);
        } catch (IOException e) { // should never happen
        }
        return outstream;
    }
```

Listing 10.17 (Continued)

Implementing IPlayList

After implementing the logic for opening (reading) and closing (writing) playlists, you may want to implement the IPlayList methods. As far as the navigational methods are concerned, this is almost trivial. You just need to translate the playlist navigation into DOM tree navigation. See Listing 10.18.

```
    /** *** IPlayList methods **** */

    /**
     * @see IPlayList#getPlaylistName()
     */
    public String getPlaylistName() {
      return currentPlaylistFile;
    }

    /**
     * @see IPlayList#next()
     */
    public boolean next() {
        // fetch next entry
        Node nod = getNext();
        if (nod == null) return false;
```

Listing 10.18 (Continues)

```java
    // in case of success set current entry to this value
    setCurrent(nod);
    return true;
}

/**
 * Searches from current entry onwards for next entry.
 *
 * @return Node - the next entry
 */
private Node getNext() {
  Node nod = currentElement;
  // search next element with tag <record>
  while (nod != null) {
    nod = nod.getNextSibling();
    if (nod instanceof Element
                  && ((Element) nod).getTagName().equals(
                                    RECORD)) return nod;
  }
  return null;
}

/**
 * @see IPlayList#previous()
 */
public boolean previous() {
  // fetch previous entry
  Node nod = getPrevious();
  if (nod == null) return false;
  // in case of success set current entry to this value
  setCurrent(nod);
  return true;
}

/**
 * Searches from current entry onwards for previous entry.
 *
 * @return Node - the previous entry
 */
private Node getPrevious() {
  Node nod = currentElement;
  // search previous element with tag <record>
  while (nod != null) {
    nod = nod.getPreviousSibling();
    if (nod instanceof Element
                  && ((Element) nod).getTagName().equals(
                                    RECORD)) return nod;
  }
  return null;
}

/**
 * @see IPlayList#hasNext()
 */
```

Listing 10.18 (Continues)

```
public boolean hasNext() {
  return getNext() != null;
}

/**
 * @see IPlayList#hasPrevious()
 */
public boolean hasPrevious() {
  return getPrevious() != null;
}
```

Listing 10.18 (Continued)

Accessing Features

Getting and setting a feature of a playlist entry requires a bit more work. To retrieve a feature, the text content of the corresponding XML element must be read. Since this content can be distributed over several chunks of text, it is necessary to concatenate these chunks. See Listing 10.19.

```
/**
 * @see IPlayList#getFeature(org.w3c.dom.Node,
 *      java.lang.String, boolean)
 */
public String getFeature(String tag) {
  return getFeature(currentElement, tag);
}

/**
 * @see IPlayList#getFeature(org.w3c.dom.Node,
 *      java.lang.String, boolean)
 */
public String getFeature(Object record, String tag) {
  if (record == null) return "";
  // Find all child elements with specified name
  NodeList nl = ((Element) record).getElementsByTagName(tag);
  if (nl.getLength() == 0) return "";
  // Should be the only one
  Node nod = nl.item(0);
  // Now get all text child elements and concatenate them
  StringBuffer sb = new StringBuffer();
  nl = nod.getChildNodes();
  for (int i = 0; i < nl.getLength(); i++) {
    if (nl.item(i) instanceof Text)
      sb.append(((Text) nl.item(i)).getData());
  }
  return sb.toString();
}

/**
 * @see IPlayList#setFeature(org.w3c.dom.Node,
 *      java.lang.String, java.lang.String)
```

Listing 10.19 (Continues)

```
     */
    public void setFeature(Object record, String tag, String value) {
      // Assuming that playlist elements are XML elements
      Element el = (Element) record;
      // Get corresponding DOM document
      Document doc = el.getOwnerDocument();
      NodeList nl = ((Element) record).getElementsByTagName(tag);
      // Remove existing elements with same name
      for (int i = 0; i < nl.getLength(); i++)
        el.removeChild(nl.item(i));
      if (value == null || value.length() == 0)
      // Deletion of feature - finished.
        return;
      // Create child element, append to parent, and fill with content.
      Node nod = doc.createElement(tag);
      el.appendChild(nod);
      nod.appendChild(doc.createTextNode(value.trim()));
    }
```

Listing 10.19 (Continued)

Managing Entries

Apart from modifying entry features, you can replace, delete, or insert whole entries or change the sequence of entries. This is done in the methods setCurrent(), deleteCurrent(), insert(), moveDownwards(), and moveUpwards() (Listing 10.20).

```
    /**
     * @see IPlayList#setCurrent(org.w3c.dom.Node)
     */
    public void setCurrent(Object current) {
      // To avoid event avalanches check if
      // the new entry is different from the current entry.
      if (currentElement != current) {
        // yes, update current entry and notify listeners.
        currentElement = (Element) current;
        fireSelectionChanged(getSelection());
      }
    }

    /**
     * Notify all listeners about change of current entry
     *
     * @param selection - the current entry wrapped into an ISelection
     *        instance
     */
    private void fireSelectionChanged(ISelection selection) {
      Object[] listeners = selectionChangedListeners
                  .getListeners();
      SelectionChangedEvent event = new SelectionChangedEvent(
                  this, selection);
```

Listing 10.20 (Continues)

```
    for (int i = 0; i < listeners.length; i++)
        ((ISelectionChangedListener) listeners[i])
                        .selectionChanged(event);
}

/**
 * @see IPlayList#deleteCurrent()
 */
public void deleteCurrent() {
    if (currentElement == null) return;
    // When deleting the current element position to the next
    // element. If this does not exist position to the previous
    // element.
    Node nod = getNext();
    if (nod == null) getPrevious();
    // Remove from playlist.
    Element playlist = playlistDoc.getDocumentElement();
    playlist.removeChild(currentElement);
    // Update current element.
    setCurrent(nod);
}

/**
 * @see IPlayList#insert(java.lang.String, java.lang.String)
 */
public Object insert() {
    // Create a new <record> element
    Element newRecord = playlistDoc.createElement(RECORD);
    // Insert the new element in front of the current element...
    Element playlist = playlistDoc.getDocumentElement();
    playlist.insertBefore(newRecord, currentElement);
    // ...and update the current element.
    setCurrent(newRecord);
    return newRecord;
}

/**
 * @see IPlayList#moveDownwards()
 */
public boolean moveDownwards() {
    Node next = getNext();
    if (next == null) return false;
    // If there is a next element, remove the current element
    // and insert it again behind the next element.
    Element playlist = playlistDoc.getDocumentElement();
    playlist.removeChild(currentElement);
    playlist.insertBefore(currentElement, next.getNextSibling());
    return true;
}

/**
 * @see IPlayList#moveUpwards()
 */
public boolean moveUpwards() {
```

Listing 10.20 (Continues)

```
      Node previous = getPrevious();
      if (previous == null) return false;
      // If there is a previos element, remove the current
      // element and insert it again in front of the previos element.
      Element playlist = playlistDoc.getDocumentElement();
      playlist.removeChild(currentElement);
      playlist.insertBefore(currentElement, previous);
      return true;
   }
```

Listing 10.20 (Continued)

Content Provider

The following method getElements() implements the interface IStructuredContentProvider. This method is required by the table viewer used in the playlist window. It returns all the entries in the playlist. See Listing 10.21.

```
/** *** IStructuredContentProvider methods *** */

/**
 * @see org.eclipse.jface.viewers.IStructuredContentProvider#
 *       getElements(java.lang.Object)
 */
public Object[] getElements(Object inputElement) {
   // Fetch all <record> elements from the playlist...
   NodeList nl = playlistDoc.getElementsByTagName(RECORD);
   // ...and write them into an array
   Object[] result = new Object[nl.getLength()];
   for (int i = 0; i < result.length; i++)
      result[i] = nl.item(i);
   return result;
}
```

Listing 10.21

Playlist Switch

Also, the table viewer requires the method inputChanged() because IStructuredContentProvider is a subinterface of IContentProvider. When the table's input changes, the current playlist must be saved and a new playlist must be opened. At the end of the session (when the parameter newInput is null) the INI file is updated. If none exists, it is created. See Listing 10.22.

```
/** *** IContentProvider methods *** */

/**
 * @see org.eclipse.jface.viewers.IContentProvider#
```

Listing 10.22 (Continues)

```
 *        inputChanged(org.eclipse.jface.viewers.Viewer,
 *        java.lang.Object, java.lang.Object)
 *
 * We trust that this method is called, too, when the
 * application is closed.
 */
public void inputChanged(Viewer viewer, Object oldInput,
                Object newInput) {
  // First save the current playlist
  savePlaylist();
  if (newInput == null) {
    // The application is closed and sets the input to null
    if (currentPlaylistFile != null) {
      // A playlist was open. Save its name into the INI-file
      try {
        OutputStream stream = new FileOutputStream(iniFile);
        stream.write(currentPlaylistFile.getBytes());
      } catch (FileNotFoundException e) {
      } catch (IOException e) {
      }
    }
    return;
  }
  if (currentPlaylistFile == null
                 || !currentPlaylistFile.equals(newInput))
    // Open a new playlist
    openPlaylist((String) newInput);
}

/**
 * @see org.eclipse.jface.viewers.IContentProvider#dispose()
 */
public void dispose() {}
```

Listing 10.22 (Continued)

Selections

Finally, Listing 10.23 contains the methods for the ISelectionProvider interface. When you implement this interface, the PlaylistModel can notify listeners that have registered via the method addSelectionChangedListener() about selection changes. The method getSelection() is responsible for constructing an IStructuredSelection instance as required by the playlist's table viewer, and the method setSelection() accepts IStructuredSelection instances to update the current selection in the model.

```
/** *** ISelectionProvider methods **** */

/**
 * @see IPlayList#addSelectionChangedListener(
```

Listing 10.23 (Continues)

```
 *          org.eclipse.jface.viewers.ISelectionChangedListener)
 */
public void addSelectionChangedListener(
                ISelectionChangedListener listener) {
  selectionChangedListeners.add(listener);
}


/**
 * @see org.eclipse.jface.viewers.ISelectionProvider#getSelection()
 */
public ISelection getSelection() {
  return new StructuredSelection((currentElement == null)
                ? new Object[0]
                : new Object[]{currentElement});
}


/**
 * @see org.eclipse.jface.viewers.ISelectionProvider#
 *      removeSelectionChangedListener(
 *      org.eclipse.jface.viewers.ISelectionChangedListener)
 */
public void removeSelectionChangedListener(
                ISelectionChangedListener listener) {
  selectionChangedListeners.remove(listener);
}


/**
 * @see org.eclipse.jface.viewers.ISelectionProvider#
 *      setSelection(org.eclipse.jface.viewers.ISelection)
 */
public void setSelection(ISelection selection) {
  if (selection instanceof IStructuredSelection) {
    Object selected = ((IStructuredSelection) selection)
                      .getFirstElement();
    currentElement = (Element) selected;
  }
}
}
```

Listing 10.23 (Continued)

The Description Window

The description window is based on the JFace class `Window` (see the section "Dialogs and Windows" in Chapter 9). It shows the descriptive text of the current playlist entry as long as the entry is being played. The window is positioned at the right-hand side of the player window and is updated with each new playlist entry that is played.

Since the description may contain HTML markup, the Browser widget is used to display the description. Nevertheless, the keywords should be displayed in a different color. You can achieve this by scanning the text for keywords, removing the $ character at the front, and adding additional markup for coloring.

The DescriptionWindow Class

The DescriptionWindow class (Listing 10.24) starts with the necessary package and import declarations, followed by the class declaration and the declarations of all instance variables. Here the fields holding the Browser instance, the playlist data model, and the Display instance are defined.

```
package com.bdaum.jukebox;

import java.util.StringTokenizer;

import org.eclipse.jface.window.Window;
import org.eclipse.swt.SWT;
import org.eclipse.swt.browser.Browser;
import org.eclipse.swt.layout.FillLayout;
import org.eclipse.swt.layout.GridData;
import org.eclipse.swt.widgets.Composite;
import org.eclipse.swt.widgets.Control;
import org.eclipse.swt.widgets.Display;
import org.eclipse.swt.widgets.Shell;

public class DescriptionWindow extends Window {

  // The browser widget responsible for displaying the text
  private Browser browser;
  // The playlist model
  private IPlaylist model;
  // The current display
  private Display display;
```

Listing 10.24

When you instantiate the DescriptionWindow instance, the playlist domain model is passed to this instance. It is used when the window is opened or updated: the text is retrieved from the DESCRIPTION feature of the current playlist entry and replaces the content of the Browser widget. This widget was created in the method createContents(), which is called by the parent class Window when create() is executed. See Listing 10.25.

```
/**
 * Constructor.
 *
 * @param parent - the containing shell
 * @param model - the player model
 */

public DescriptionWindow(Shell parent, IPlaylist model) {
```

Listing 10.25 (Continues)

```
    super(parent);
    display = parent.getDisplay();
    this.model = model;
}

/**
 * This method is called form superclass Window.
 * It constructs the window contents.
 */
protected Control createContents(Composite parent) {
    parent.setLayout(new FillLayout());
    Composite composite = new Composite(parent, SWT.NONE);
    composite.setLayout(new FillLayout());
    // Create a browser widget
    browser = new Browser(composite, SWT.NONE);
    GridData data = new GridData(GridData.FILL_BOTH);
    browser.setLayoutData(data);
    return composite;
}

/**
 * Prepare HTML-text and display it Browser widget
 */
public void update() {
    String description = model.getFeature(Player.DESCRIPTION);
    if (description == null)
        browser.setText("");
    else {
        // Coloring for keywords
        StringBuffer html = new StringBuffer(
                    "<html><small><font color='green'>");
        StringTokenizer tokenizer = new StringTokenizer(
                    description, "<> \n\t", true);
        while (tokenizer.hasMoreTokens()) {
            String token = tokenizer.nextToken();
            if (token.length() == 1) {
                html.append(token);
            } else if (token.startsWith("$")) {
                html.append("<font color='red'>");
                html.append(token.substring(1));
                html.append("</font>");
            } else
                html.append(token);
        }
        html.append("</font></small></html>");
        // Display in browser
        browser.setText(html.toString());
    }
}

/**
 * Override open() method of superclass Window to
 * update the displayed text.
 */
```

Listing 10.25 (Continues)

```
public int open() {
  update();
  return super.open();
}
}
```

Listing 10.25 (Continued)

The Playlist Viewer

The playlist viewer runs in its own window (`PlaylistWindow`) and allows the user to open, create, and modify a playlist. The viewer is equipped with specialized cell editors for the individual playlist entries. The playlist domain model serves as a Content Provider for the playlist viewer.

To illustrate the cooperation between player, playlist viewer, playlist window, and playlist domain model, the event processing for the playlist is shown as an interaction diagram in Figure 10.4.

In principle, there is a possibility of event loops. However, you can avoid these loops by passing events only when an event means a real change (for example, in the playlist model).

An interesting problem occurs when performing the `insert()` operation. This method causes a change of selection. Consequently, the model sends a `selectionChanged` event to the playlist window, which passes it on to the viewer via the method `setSelection()`. The viewer performs this selection. However, at this time, the new element has not yet been inserted into the `Table` widget. Consequently, setting the selection for this element results in a `null` selection. This, again, is sent as a `selectionChanged` event to the playlist viewer. The viewer then sets the selection in the model to `null` by calling the method `setCurrent()`! This is certainly not our intention. You can solve the problem by invoking the viewer's `refresh()` method from the `selectionChanged()` method before calling `setSelection()`. By doing this, you can force an update of the `Table` instance according to the content of the playlist model.

The PlaylistWindow Class

The PlaylistWindow class (Listing 10.26) starts with the necessary `package` and `import` declarations, followed by the class declaration and the declarations of all instance variables. Here the fields holding the PlaylistViewer, the Player, and the playlist data model are defined.

```
package com.bdaum.jukebox;

import org.eclipse.jface.viewers.ISelectionChangedListener;
import org.eclipse.jface.viewers.IStructuredSelection;
import org.eclipse.jface.viewers.SelectionChangedEvent;
import org.eclipse.jface.window.Window;
import org.eclipse.swt.SWT;
import org.eclipse.swt.layout.FillLayout;
import org.eclipse.swt.widgets.Composite;
import org.eclipse.swt.widgets.Control;
import org.eclipse.swt.widgets.Shell;
```

Listing 10.26 (Continues)

```
public class PlaylistWindow extends Window
        implements ISelectionChangedListener {

    PlaylistViewer viewer;
    Player player;
    IPlaylist model;

    /**
     * Constructor.
     * @param parent - The containing shell
     * @param player - The player
     */
    public PlaylistWindow(Shell parent, IPlaylist model) {
        super(parent);
        this.model = model;
    }
```

Listing 10.26 (Continued)

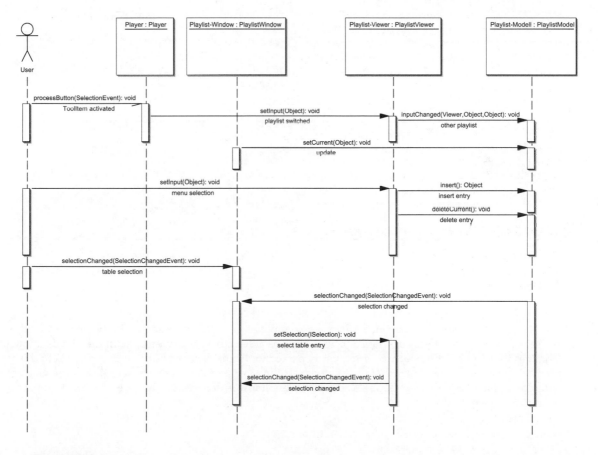

Figure 10.4

In the `createContents()` method that is called from the parent class `Window` (see the section "Dialogs and Windows" in Chapter 9), `PlaylistWindow` constructs the window content. In particular, an instance of the class `PlaylistViewer` (a subclass of `TableViewer`) is created. This viewer is configured with the help of style constants: horizontal and vertical scrolling is allowed, only single table rows can be selected, and the whole table row appears selected.

Then the viewer is equipped with event processing. When a row is selected, the `selectionChanged()` method is invoked. This method retrieves the selection object from the event object. The selected table entry is the first element in the selection object. This table entry is passed, via the method `setCurrent()`, to the playlist model to update the selection there.

Finally, the viewer is initialized by fetching the filename of the current playlist from the playlist model and passing this name to the viewer via the `setInput()` method. See Listing 10.27.

```
protected Control createContents(Composite parent) {
    parent.setLayout(new FillLayout());
    Composite composite = new Composite(parent, SWT.NONE);
    composite.setLayout(new FillLayout());
    viewer = new PlaylistViewer(composite,
    SWT.SINGLE | SWT.VERTICAL | SWT.H_SCROLL
        | SWT.V_SCROLL | SWT.BORDER | SWT.FULL_SELECTION, model);
    // Add event processing for selection events
    viewer.addSelectionChangedListener(new
        ISelectionChangedListener() {
        public void selectionChanged(SelectionChangedEvent e) {
            IStructuredSelection selection =
                (IStructuredSelection) e.getSelection();
            // Get selected table entry
            Object selected = selection.getFirstElement();
            // and pass to playlist model
            model.setCurrent(selected);
        }
    });
    // Get current playlist
    String playlistFile = model.getPlaylistName();
    // and set as input data
    viewer.setInput(playlistFile);
    return composite;
}
```

Listing 10.27

In Listing 10.28 the two `Window` methods `open()` and `close()` are overridden. In the `open()` method the selection of the viewer is updated and registered as a `SelectionListener` with the playlist model. Changes in the playlist model are consequently passed to the method `selectionChanged()`. In this method the viewer's `Table` widget is updated by calling `refresh()`. Then the selection of the viewer is updated. Finally, in method `close()` the playlist window is deregistered as a `SelectionListener` from the playlist model.

```
    /*
     * Open window and register with the model
     */
    public int open() {
        // Update the viewers selection
        viewer.setSelection(model.getSelection());
        // Register as a SelectionChangedListener
        model.addSelectionChangedListener(this);
        // Open window
        return super.open();
    }


    /*
     * Close window and deregister from the model
     */
    public boolean close() {
        // deregister as a SelectionChangedListener
        model.removeSelectionChangedListener(this);
        // Close window
        return super.close();
    }


    /*
     * Model has changed - we have to update the viewer
     */
    public void selectionChanged(SelectionChangedEvent event) {
        // Force table update
        viewer.refresh();
        // Update selection
        viewer.setSelection(model.getSelection());
    }
}
```

Listing 10.28

The PlaylistViewer Class

The playlist viewer is defined as a subclass of the JFace class TableViewer. First, the PlaylistViewer instance is instrumented with a ContentProvider, a LabelProvider, cell editors, modifiers, and column identifications. For a cell editor, the standard TextCellEditor is used, but with the following exceptions: filenames are edited with the FileCellEditor that follows, and descriptions are edited with the DescriptionCellEditor discussed later in "The Description Editor" section.

Then the layout and the presentation of the table are modified somewhat, and a menu, status line, and toolbar are added. For the layout a nested GridLayout is used. First, the status line and the toolbar are placed into a two-column GridLayout (which results in one row). Then the Composite is placed together with the Table instance into a one-column GridLayout.

The menu is added directly to the shell of the playlist window. The menu functions bring up file-selection dialogs for opening existing playlists and for creating new playlists.

The toolbar contains functions for creating, deleting, and moving playlist elements. The `ToolItem` events directly result in the invocation of the corresponding operations in the playlist model. Such operations may, of course, change the current element in the playlist model. The model therefore creates an appropriate `SelectionChangedEvent`, which is received by the playlist window. The window instance then uses the method `setSelection()` to update the selection in the `PlaylistViewer`. See Listing 10.29.

```java
package com.bdaum.jukebox;

import java.io.File;
import org.eclipse.jface.dialogs.MessageDialog;
import org.eclipse.jface.viewers.*;
import org.eclipse.swt.SWT;
import org.eclipse.swt.dnd.*;
import org.eclipse.swt.dnd.DropTarget;
import org.eclipse.swt.dnd.DropTargetListener;
import org.eclipse.swt.dnd.FileTransfer;
import org.eclipse.swt.dnd.Transfer;
import org.eclipse.swt.events.SelectionAdapter;
import org.eclipse.swt.events.SelectionEvent;
import org.eclipse.swt.layout.GridData;
import org.eclipse.swt.layout.GridLayout;
import org.eclipse.swt.widgets.*;

/**
 * This class implements a viewer for playlists.
 */
public class PlaylistViewer extends TableViewer {

  // File extension for for playlists
  public final static String PLS = ".jpl";
  // Filter for the selection of playlist files
  public final static String[] PLAYLISTEXTENSIONS = new String[]{"*"
                  + PLS};
  // Filter for the selection of sound files
  public final static String[] SOUNDEXTENSIONS =
    new String[]{"*.m3u;*.wsz;*.mpg;*.snd;*.aifc;*.aif;*.wav;"
                  +"*.au;*.mp1;*.mp2;*.mp3;*.ogg", "*.*"};
  // Filter for the selection of image files
  public final static String[] IMAGEEXTENSIONS =
    new String[]{"*.gif; *.jpg; *.jpeg; *.png; *.bmp; *.tif", "*.*"};

  // the playlist model instance
  private IPlaylist playlistModel;
  // the label provider for the table
  private ITableLabelProvider labelProvider;

  // Widgets
  private MenuItem newPlaylistItem, openPlaylistItem;
  private Label statusLine;
  private ToolItem insertButton, deleteButton, upButton, downButton;
```

Listing 10.29

CellModifier

In Listing 10.30 a single instance of type ICellModifier is defined. This instance organizes the data transfer between the model and the table cells. To set the value of a table cell, the method getValue() is called. The parameter property contains the feature identification that corresponds to the appropriate column of the table cell. This identification is used to fetch the cell value from the playlist model.

Vice versa, when the end user modifies a cell value, it is also necessary to set it in the model. Here again, the feature identification is received in the parameter property. The feature value is passed in the value parameter. However, the use of this method is not consistent in regard to the element parameter. In some cases, the data element of the table row is passed in this parameter; in other cases, the TableItem instance of the table row is passed instead. Therefore, you need to check the type of the parameter value and act accordingly. In addition, all entered values are validated: empty titles and empty sound filenames are not allowed.

```java
private ICellModifier cellModifier = new ICellModifier() {
  // Get value from model
  public Object getValue(Object element, String property) {
    return playlistModel.getFeature(element, property);
  }

  // All elements may be modified by the end user
  public boolean canModify(Object element, String property) {
    return true;
  }

  // Set value in the model
  public void modify(Object element, String property,
                     Object value) {
    // ATTENTION: A TableItem instance may be passed as element
    // In this case we retrieve the playlist entry from the TableItem
    if (element instanceof Item)
      element = ((Item) element).getData();
    // To be safe we validate the new value
    if (validateFeature(property, (String) value) == null) {
      // OK, we set the new value in the model
      playlistModel.setFeature(element, property,
                    (String) value);
      // Refresh the viewer so that the new value is
      // shown in the table
      PlaylistViewer.this.refresh();
    }
  }
};

/**
 * Validates a feature
 *
 * @param tag - Feature name
 * @param value - Value
 * @return String - Error message or null
 */
```

Listing 10.30 (Continues)

```
   public String validateFeature(String tag, String value) {
     if (tag == Player.TITLE) {
       // Empty titles are not valid
       if (value == null || value.length() == 0)
         return "Must specify a title";
     } else if (tag == Player.SOUNDFILE) {
       // Empty sound file names are not valid
       if (value == null || value.length() == 0)
         return "Must specify a sound file";
     }
     return null;
   }
}
```

Listing 10.30 (Continued)

The viewer instance is configured in the constructor of the `PlaylistViewer`. The playlist model is registered as a `ContentProvider` (the instance that provides the table entries). A new `PlaylistLabelProvider` (see the following code) instance is created as a `LabelProvider` (the instance that is responsible for formatting the table elements).

Then the viewer's table object is fetched. A special cell editor and a validator are attached to each column of the table. The individual columns are identified by the feature identifications. A `TextCellEditor` is created for the column containing the song titles, `FileCellEditor` instances are created for the columns with the sound files and the image files, and a `DescriptionCellEditor` is created for the column containing the descriptions. While the `TextCellEditor` already belongs to the JFace functionality, you must implement the other two editors. The validators are created as anonymous inner classes of type `ICellEditorValidator` with the help of the `setCellValidator()` method.

Finally, the `CellModifier` created previously is registered, column headers are created, column headers and grid lines are made visible, and the menu, the drag-and-drop support, and the status line are added to the viewer. See Listing 10.31.

```
/**
 * Constructor for PlaylistViewer.
 *
 * @param parent - containing Composite
 * @param style - Style constants
 * @param model - Playlist domain model
 */
public PlaylistViewer(Composite parent, int style,
                 IPlaylist model) {
  // Create viewer (TableViewer)
  super(parent, style);
  playlistModel = model;
  // Create LabelProvider
  labelProvider = new PlaylistLabelProvider(playlistModel);
  // Set Content- and LabelProvider
  setContentProvider(playlistModel);
  setLabelProvider(labelProvider);
```

Listing 10.31 (Continues)

```
        // Create cell editors and validators
        // First the editor for song titles
        Table table = getTable();
        TextCellEditor titleEditor = new TextCellEditor(table);
        setCellValidator(titleEditor, Player.TITLE);
        // Then the editor for the sound file
        FileCellEditor soundFileEditor = new FileCellEditor(table,
                    "Select sound file", SOUNDEXTENSIONS);
        setCellValidator(soundFileEditor, Player.SOUNDFILE);
        // Then the editor for the image file
        FileCellEditor imageFileEditor = new FileCellEditor(table,
                    "Select image file", IMAGEEXTENSIONS);
        setCellValidator(imageFileEditor, Player.IMAGEFILE);
        // Then the editor for the description
        DescriptionCellEditor descriptionEditor =
                new DescriptionCellEditor(table, playlistModel);
        setCellValidator(descriptionEditor, Player.DESCRIPTION);
        // Now we pass all editors to the viewer
        // The sequence corresponds with the column sequence
        setCellEditors(new CellEditor[]{titleEditor,
                    soundFileEditor, imageFileEditor,
                    descriptionEditor});
        // Set cell modifier
        setCellModifier(cellModifier);
        // Set column identifiers
        setColumnProperties(new String[]{Player.TITLE,
                    Player.SOUNDFILE, Player.IMAGEFILE,
                    Player.DESCRIPTION});
            // Create column headers
        createColumn(table, "Title", 80);
        createColumn(table, "Sound file", 120);
        createColumn(table, "Image file", 100);
        createColumn(table, "Description", 240);
        // Make column headers and grid lines visible
        table.setHeaderVisible(true);
        table.setLinesVisible(true);
        // We still need a menu, a toolbar, and a status line
        constructMenu(parent.getShell());
        // Add status line
        addStatusLineAndButtons(table);
        // Add support for drag and drop
        addDropSupport(table);
    }
```

Listing 10.31 (Continued)

Validator for Cell Editors

To validate the cell content of a CellEditor, an anonymous class of type ICellEditorValidator is created. In its isValid() method the cell content is passed via the value parameter and checked with the help of the validateFeature() method. See Listing 10.32.

```
/**
 * Set validators for cell editors
 *
 * @param editor - The cell editor
 * @param feature - The feature identification
 */
public void setCellValidator(CellEditor editor,
                final String feature) {
  editor.setValidator(new ICellEditorValidator() {
    // isValid is called by the cell editor when the
    // cell content was modified
    public String isValid(Object value) {
      // We validate the cell content
      String errorMessage = validateFeature(feature, (String) value);
      // and show the error message in the status line
      setErrorMessage(errorMessage);
      // The cell editor wants the error message
      // What it does with it is unknown
      return errorMessage;
    }
  });
}
```

Listing 10.32

Column Headers

Column headers are created in the convenience method `createColumn()`. In Listing 10.33 a new `TableColumn` instance is created for the given Table and then configured with the header text and the column width.

```
/**
 * Create column header
 *
 * @param table - Table
 * @param header - Label
 * @param width - Column width
 */
private void createColumn(Table table, String header, int width) {
  TableColumn col = new TableColumn(table, SWT.LEFT);
  col.setText(header);
  col.setWidth(width);
}
```

Listing 10.33

DropTarget

In the method `addDropSupport()` the viewer is configured as a target for a drag-and-drop operation. This will allow users to add new sound files to the playlist by simply dragging them to the playlist area.

To do so, you construct a new `DropTarget` instance and associate it with the playlist table. Valid operations are `MOVE` and `COPY`, and only files (`FileTransfer`) are accepted as valid transfer types.

The drag-and-drop operation itself is performed by the `DropTargetListener`. When the mouse pointer enters the drop area (the playlist area), the method `dragEnter()` checks to see if a valid operation type and a valid transfer type are used. `MOVE` operations are converted into `COPY` operations because the original sound file should persist. You make all of these adjustments by assigning appropriate values to the event object.

The method `dragOver()` determines the behavior when the mouse pointer is moved over the target area. Assigning `DND.FEEDBACK_SELECT` to `event.feedback` causes those table elements that are under the mouse pointer to become selected. Assigning `DND.FEEDBACK_SCROLL` causes the table to be scrolled up or down when the mouse pointer reaches the upper or lower border of the visible playlist area.

The method `dragOperationChanged()` reacts to changes of the operation modus, for example, when the Ctrl key is pressed during the dragging action. The method rejects invalid operations and converts `MOVE` operations into `COPY` operations.

Finally, the method `drop()` reacts when a sound file is dropped onto the playlist area. The filename is retrieved from the event object and inserted into the playlist. This is done at the position of the currently selected playlist entry. See Listing 10.34.

```java
/**
 * Adds Drop-Support to the view.
 *
 * @param table - table widget
 */
private void addDropSupport(final Table table) {
    // Valid operations
    final int ops = DND.DROP_MOVE | DND.DROP_COPY;
    // Allow both moving and copying
    DropTarget target = new DropTarget(table, ops);
    // Only files are accepted
    final FileTransfer fileTransfer = FileTransfer
                    .getInstance();
    Transfer[] types = new Transfer[]{fileTransfer};
    target.setTransfer(types);
    // Add DropListener to DropTarget
    target.addDropListener(new DropTargetListener() {
        // Mouse pointer has entered drop area
        public void dragEnter(DropTargetEvent event) {
            // Only files are accepted
            for (int i = 0; i < event.dataTypes.length; i++) {
                if (fileTransfer.isSupportedType(event.dataTypes[i])) {
                    event.currentDataType = event.dataTypes[i];
                    if ((event.detail & ops) == 0)
                        // Inhibit invalid operations
                        event.detail = DND.DROP_NONE;
                    else
                        // Force copy operation
```

Listing 10.34 (Continues)

```
        event.detail = DND.DROP_COPY;
        return;
      }
    }
  }
  // Invalid transfer type
  event.detail = DND.DROP_NONE;
}


// The mouse pointer moves within the DropTarget area
public void dragOver(DropTargetEvent event) {
  event.feedback = DND.FEEDBACK_SELECT
                 | DND.FEEDBACK_SCROLL;
}


// Operation was changed
// (for example by pressing the Crtl key)
public void dragOperationChanged(DropTargetEvent event) {
  // Only files are accepted
  if (fileTransfer
               .isSupportedType(event.currentDataType)) {
    // Check for invalid operations
    if ((event.detail & ops) == 0)
      // Inhibit invalid operations
      event.detail = DND.DROP_NONE;
    else
      // Force copy operation
      event.detail = DND.DROP_COPY;
  } else
    // Invalid transfer type
    event.detail = DND.DROP_NONE;
}


// Mouse pointer has left DropTarget area
public void dragLeave(DropTargetEvent event) {}

// The dragged object is about to be dropped
public void dropAccept(DropTargetEvent event) {}
// The dragged object has been dropped
public void drop(DropTargetEvent event) {
  if (fileTransfer.isSupportedType(event.currentDataType)) {
    String[] filenames = (String[]) event.data;
    for (int i = 0; i < filenames.length; i++) {
      // Insert file into playlist
      if (insertSoundFile(filenames[i]) != null)
        refresh();
    }
  }
}
});
}
```

Listing 10.34 (Continued)

Nested Grid Layout

Since the inherited `TableViewer` contains only a table, you need to improve it a bit. In addition to the table, you need to add the status line and the toolbar. To do so, fetch the parent `Composite` of the table. On this `Composite` apply a one-column `GridLayout` via the `setLayout()` method (see the "Layouts" section in Chapter 8). Then add a new `Composite` (statusGroup) to this `Composite`. This new `Composite` will appear below the table. Now apply a two-column `GridLayout` to statusGroup. Then add a new `Label` to statusGroup, which will appear at the left-hand side. This new label acts as a status line. Finally, add a `ToolBar` to statusGroup. This toolbar will appear at the right-hand side of statusGroup. By using different `GridData` instances, you can make the table as big as possible, give statusGroup and the status line the maximum width, and align the toolbar to the right. Finally, set the text color of the status line to red. See Listing 10.35.

```java
/**
 * Adds a status line and a toolbar
 * @param table - the viewers Table instance
 */
private void addStatusLineAndButtons(Table table) {
    // Fetch parent Composite
    Composite parent = table.getParent();
    // Use a one-column GridLayout for this Composite.
    GridLayout gridLayout = new GridLayout();
    gridLayout.marginHeight = 0;
    gridLayout.marginWidth = 2;
    gridLayout.verticalSpacing = 3;
    parent.setLayout(gridLayout);
    // Create Composite for statusline and toolbar
    Composite statusGroup = new Composite(parent, SWT.NONE);
    // For this Composite we use a two-column GridLayout
    gridLayout = new GridLayout();
    gridLayout.numColumns = 2;
    gridLayout.marginHeight = 0;
    gridLayout.marginWidth = 0;
    statusGroup.setLayout(gridLayout);
    // Create status line
    statusLine = new Label(statusGroup, SWT.BORDER);
    // Create toolbar
    ToolBar toolbar = createToolbar(statusGroup);
    // Set table to maximum size
    GridData data = new GridData();
    data.horizontalAlignment = GridData.FILL;
    data.verticalAlignment = GridData.FILL;
    data.grabExcessHorizontalSpace = true;
    data.grabExcessVerticalSpace = true;
    table.setLayoutData(data);
    // Set statusGroup to maximum width
    data = new GridData();
    data.horizontalAlignment = GridData.FILL;
    data.grabExcessHorizontalSpace = true;
    statusGroup.setLayoutData(data);
    // Set status line to maximum width
    data = new GridData();
```

Listing 10.35 (Continues)

```
        data.horizontalAlignment = GridData.FILL;
        data.grabExcessHorizontalSpace = true;
        statusLine.setLayoutData(data);
        data = new GridData();
        // Align the toolbar to the right
        data.horizontalAlignment = GridData.END;
        toolbar.setLayoutData(data);
        // Set status line text color to red
        statusLine.setForeground(parent.getDisplay()
                    .getSystemColor(SWT.COLOR_RED));
    }


    /**
     * Displays an error message in the status line.
     *
     * @param errorMessage - error message or null
     */
    public void setErrorMessage(String errorMessage) {
        statusLine.setText((errorMessage == null)
                    ? "" : errorMessage);
    }
```

Listing 10.35 (Continued)

Toolbar

The toolbar (see the "Toolbar" section in Chapter 8) is equipped with four buttons for adding new songs to the playlist, deleting songs, and moving entries upward or downward. The event processing for these buttons is done in the processToolEvent() method. Depending on the button pressed, the appropriate operation is performed. See Listing 10.36.

```
    /**
     * Method createToolbar. Creates toolbar with all buttons
     *
     * @param parent - containing Composite
     * @return ToolBar - created ToolBar instance
     */
    private ToolBar createToolbar(Composite parent) {
        ToolBar toolbar = new ToolBar(parent, SWT.VERTICAL
                        | SWT.FLAT);
        // Create buttons
        insertButton = makeToolItem(toolbar, "+",
                        "Insert new entries");
        deleteButton = makeToolItem(toolbar, "-",
                        "Delete selected entry");
        upButton = makeToolItem(toolbar, "^",
                        "Move selected entry one step up");
        downButton = makeToolItem(toolbar, "v",
                        "Move selected entry one step down");
        return toolbar;
    }
```

Listing 10.36 (Continues)

```
    /**
     * Check if a playlist is open. If yes, enable all buttons.
     * If no, issue an error message
     */
    private void updateToolBar() {
      boolean enabled = (getInput() != null);
      statusLine.setText((enabled)
                      ? "" : "No playlist open");
      insertButton.setEnabled(enabled);
      deleteButton.setEnabled(enabled);
      upButton.setEnabled(enabled);
      downButton.setEnabled(enabled);
    }


    /**
     * Create button.
     *
     * @param parent - the toolbar
     * @param text - label
     * @param toolTipText - the hover text
     * @return ToolItem - the created ToolItem instance
     */
    private ToolItem makeToolItem(ToolBar parent, String text,
                    String toolTipText) {
      ToolItem button = new ToolItem(parent, SWT.PUSH);
      button.setText(text);
      button.setToolTipText(toolTipText);
      // Add event processing
      button.addSelectionListener(new SelectionAdapter() {
        public void widgetSelected(SelectionEvent e) {
          processToolEvent(e);
        }
      });
      return button;
    }


    /**
     * Process an event from a tool button.
     *
     * @param e - The event object
     */
    private void processToolEvent(SelectionEvent e) {
      // Get ToolItem instance form event object
      ToolItem item = (ToolItem) e.widget;
      if (item == insertButton) {
        // Create new playlist entries
        getSoundFiles(item.getParent().getShell());
      } else if (item == deleteButton) {
        // Delete playlist entry
        playlistModel.deleteCurrent();
      } else if (item == upButton) {
        // Move playlist entry upwards
        playlistModel.moveUpwards();
```

Listing 10.36 (Continues)

```
    } else if (item == downButton) {
      // Move playlist entry downwards
      playlistModel.moveDownwards();
    }
    refresh();
  }
```

Listing 10.36 (Continued)

File-Selection Dialogs

In Listing 10.37 a `FileDialog` (see the "Dialogs" section in Chapter 8) is used to add new sound files to a playlist. It allows the selection of one or several sound files from the file system. The option to select more than one file in one step is explicitly enabled. The selection list is restricted to the sound file types declared in constant `SOUNDEXTENSIONS` with the method `setFilterExtensions()`. Finally, a new entry in the playlist model is created for each selected file. The required song title is initially derived from the filename.

```
/**
 * Obtains a sound file from user input.
 *
 * @param shell - Parent shell of dialog
 */
private void getSoundFiles(Shell shell) {
  // Create file selection dialog
  FileDialog dialog = new FileDialog(shell, SWT.OPEN
                      | SWT.MULTI);
  dialog.setFilterExtensions(SOUNDEXTENSIONS);
  dialog.setText("Select sound files");
  if (dialog.open() != null) {
    String root = dialog.getFilterPath()
                      + File.separatorChar;
    String[] filenames = dialog.getFileNames();
    for (int i = filenames.length - 1; i >= 0; i--) {
      // Compute the absolute file name
      String filename = root + filenames[i];
      insertSoundFile(filename);
    }
  }
}

/**
 * Insert new soundfile into playlist
 *
 * @param filename - the name of the new file
 * @return - the currently selected entry in the playlist
 */
private Object insertSoundFile(String filename) {
  // Check if file exists
  File file = new File(filename);
```

Listing 10.37 (Continues)

```
    if (!file.exists()) return null;
    // Derive the default title from the file name
    String title = file.getName();
    int p = title.lastIndexOf('.');
    if (p > 0) title = title.substring(0, p);
    // Insert new element into model
    Object record = playlistModel.insert();
    playlistModel.setFeature(record, Player.TITLE, title);
    playlistModel.setFeature(record, Player.SOUNDFILE, filename);
    return record;
}
```

Listing 10.37 (Continued)

Menu

Finally, in Listing 10.38 a menu for the playlist viewer (see the "Menu" section in Chapter 8) is created. The menu functions enable you to create new playlists or to open existing playlists. The menu instance is added directly to the shell. The single File menu title is created as a `MenuItem` instance for the menu using the style constant `SWT.CASCADE`. A submenu is attached to this menu title with `setMenu()`. This submenu is created directly under the shell but with the style constant `SWT.DROP_DOWN`. Then the two menu items are added to the submenu as `MenuItem` instances.

The event processing for these `MenuItem` instances takes place in the method `processMenuSelection()`.

```
/**
 * Constructs the menu
 *
 * @param shell - the parent shell
 */
private void constructMenu(Shell shell) {
    // This menu is used to create new playlists
    // and to open existing playlists
    Menu menuBar = new Menu(shell, SWT.BAR);
    shell.setMenuBar(menuBar);
    // Create File menu title
    MenuItem fileTitle = new MenuItem(menuBar, SWT.CASCADE);
    fileTitle.setText("File");
    // Create Submenu and attach it to the menu title
    Menu fileMenu = new Menu(shell, SWT.DROP_DOWN);
    fileTitle.setMenu(fileMenu);
    // Create menu items for the File menu title
    newPlaylistItem = createMenuItem(fileMenu, "New Playlist...");
    openPlaylistItem = createMenuItem(fileMenu,
                    "Open Playlist...");
}

/**
 * Creates a menu item
 *
```

Listing 10.38 (Continues)

```
 * @param menu - The menu
 * @param text - Label for the menu item
 * @return MenuItem - the new MenuItem instance
 */
private MenuItem createMenuItem(Menu menu, String text) {
  MenuItem item = new MenuItem(menu, SWT.NULL);
  item.setText(text);
  // Add event processing
  item.addSelectionListener(new SelectionAdapter() {
    public void widgetSelected(SelectionEvent e) {
      processMenuSelection(e);
    }
  });
  return item;
}
```

Listing 10.38 (Continued)

Once again, a `FileDialog` instance of type `SWT.OPEN` is used to open an existing playlist. The selected filename is then set as a new input source for the playlist model via the `setInput()` method. The viewer will notify the playlist model about this event via `inputChanged()`. This is possible because the playlist model implements the `IContentProvider` interface.

If you want to create a new playlist, you need to use a `FileDialog` of type `SWT.SAVE`. This dialog allows the end user to enter the filename explicitly. However, a check for the existence of the specified file is necessary. If the file already exists, a `MessageDialog` is used to ask the end user whether the file should be overwritten. If the user answers positively, the existing file is first deleted, and then the filename is passed to the viewer via the method `setInput()`. The playlist model then automatically creates a new playlist file with the specified name and signals this via the `inputChanged()` method. See Listing 10.39.

```
/**
 * Process menu events
 *
 * @param e - The event object
 */
private void processMenuSelection(SelectionEvent e) {
  // Retrieve MenuItem instance from event object
  Widget widget = e.widget;
  // Retrieve shell
  Shell shell = e.display.getShells()[0];
  if (widget == openPlaylistItem) {
    // Open playlist: Create and open file selection dialog
    FileDialog dialog = new FileDialog(shell, SWT.OPEN);
    dialog.setFilterExtensions(PLAYLISTEXTENSIONS);
    dialog.setText("Open Playlist ");
    String filename = dialog.open();
    // Set this file as new input for TableViewer
    if (filename != null) setInput(filename);
  } else if (widget == newPlaylistItem) {
    // New playlist: Create and open file selection dialog
    while (true) {
```

Listing 10.39 (Continues)

```
            FileDialog dialog = new FileDialog(shell, SWT.SAVE);
            dialog.setFilterExtensions(PLAYLISTEXTENSIONS);
            dialog.setText("Create new Playlist");
            String filename = dialog.open();
            if (filename == null) return;
            // Add file extension if necessary
            if (!filename.endsWith(PLS)) filename += PLS;
            // Check if file already exists
            File file = new File(filename);
            if (!file.exists()) {
              // Set this file as new input for TableViewer
              setInput(filename);
              break;
            } else if (
            // File already exists.
            // Asks user if file is to be overwritten.
            MessageDialog.openQuestion(shell, "New Playlist",
                            "File already exists.\nOverwrite?")) {
              file.delete();
              setInput(filename);
              break;
            }
          }
        }
      updateToolBar();
    }
  }
}
```

Listing 10.39 (Continued)

The PlaylistLabelProvider Class

PlaylistLabelProvider is responsible for deriving the table cell contents from the playlist entries. It retrieves the corresponding feature value from a specified playlist entry and a specified column number by using the access methods of the playlist domain model.

In the case of sound and image files, the class checks to see if these files exist. If not, the cell content is prefixed with a warning icon via the method getColumnImage(). See Listing 10.40.

```
package com.bdaum.jukebox;

import java.io.File;
import org.eclipse.jface.viewers.ILabelProviderListener;
import org.eclipse.jface.viewers.ITableLabelProvider;
import org.eclipse.swt.graphics.Image;
import org.eclipse.swt.widgets.Display;
import org.w3c.dom.Node;

/**
 * This class provides the table of the playlist viewer
```

Listing 10.40 (Continues)

```
 * with cell contents.
 */
public class PlaylistLabelProvider implements ITableLabelProvider {

    // Playlist domain model
    private IPlaylist playlistmodel;
    // Here we store the warning icon
    private Image alertImage;

    /**
     * Constructor.
     */
    public PlaylistLabelProvider(IPlaylist playlistmodel) {
        super();
        this.playlistmodel = playlistmodel;
    }
```

Listing 10.40 (Continued)

Returning a Warning Icon

The method getColumnImage() is called by the Table instance when rows have to be redrawn. For the first and second columns of the table, the method getFileAlert() is used to test whether the files specified in the table cells still exist. If not, the warning icon is returned as an Image instance. The method caches this Image instance in the instance field alertImage, so this image needs to be loaded only the first time it is used.

If the PlayListLabelProvider is no longer needed, the image is released by calling its dispose() method.

When loading the image from file, a Display instance is needed to convert it into an Image instance. Because this method does not have access to a widget from which you could obtain such a Display instance, you need to use a different approach. You need to fetch the Display instance from the current SWT thread via the static method Display.getCurrent(). This is possible because this method is executed within the SWT thread (otherwise, you would obtain the value null). See Listing 10.41.

```
/**
 * Returns warning icons for missing files
 * @see org.eclipse.jface.viewers.ITableLabelProvider#
 *                 getColumnImage(java.lang.Object, int)
 */
public Image getColumnImage(Object element, int columnIndex) {
    Node nod = (Node) element;
    // For the features <soundfile> and <image> we test for
    // the existence of the specified files. If the file does not
    // exist we return a warning icon
    switch (columnIndex) {
    case 1 :
        return getFileAlert(playlistmodel.getFeature(nod,
            Player.SOUNDFILE));
    case 2 :
```

Listing 10.41 (Continues)

```
        return getFileAlert(playlistmodel.getFeature(nod,
                Player.IMAGEFILE));
        default :
            return null;
        }
}

/**
 * Load a warning icon from file
 * @param string
 *                    File name
 * @return Image - A warning icon if the specified does not exist
 * null otherwise.
 */
private Image getFileAlert(String name) {
    if (name == null || name.length() == 0) return null;
    // Test if file exists
    File file = new File(name);
    if (file.exists()) return null;
    // No, let's return the warning icon
    // If the icon is not yet loaded, we load it now.
    if (alertImage == null)
        alertImage = new Image(Display.getCurrent(),
            "icons/             alert_obj.gif");
        return alertImage;
}

/**
 * @see org.eclipse.jface.viewers.IContentProvider#dispose()
 */
public void dispose() {
    // Release the warning icon again
    if (alertImage != null) {
        alertImage.dispose();
        alertImage = null;
    }
}
```

Listing 10.41 (Continued)

Cell Text

The text content of the table cells is provided by the getColumnText() method. This is quite simple: the corresponding feature values are retrieved from the playlist model. In the case of filenames, a bit of formatting is also applied. See Listing 10.42.

```
/**
 * Returns the column text
 * @see org.eclipse.jface.viewers.ITableLabelProvider#
 *              getColumnText(java.lang.Object, int)
 */
public String getColumnText(Object element, int columnIndex) {
```

Listing 10.42 (Continues)

```
            Node nod = (Node) element;
            // In case of file names we only return the short name
            switch (columnIndex) {
                case 0 :
                    return playlistmodel.getFeature(nod, Player.TITLE);
                case 1 :
                        return getShortName(playlistmodel.getFeature(nod,
                            Player.SOUNDFILE));
                case 2 :
                    return getShortName(playlistmodel.getFeature(nod,
                        Player.IMAGEFILE));
                case 3 :
                    return playlistmodel.getFeature(nod, Player.DESCRIPTION);
            }
            return null;
        }


    /**
     * Convert file path into short file name
     * @param filename - File path
     * @return String - Short file name
     */
    private String getShortName(String filename) {
        if (filename == null)
            return "";
        File file = new File(filename);
        return file.getName();
    }
```

Listing 10.42 (Continued)

The next two methods (see Listing 10.43) are required for implementing the interface
IBaseLabelProvider. Here, you have the option of informing possible
ILabelProviderListeners about changes in the state of the PlaylistLabelProvider.
(This could require a refresh of the viewer table.) However, you don't need this functionality,
and therefore you should leave these methods empty.

The method isLabelProperty() is used for optimization. Here you have the option to return the
value false if the cell representation of a feature is independent of the value of the feature. You can
thus avoid unnecessary updates of table elements. In this case, however, all cell representations depend
solely on the corresponding feature values—therefore, you should always return the value true.

```
    /**
     * @see org.eclipse.jface.viewers.IBaseLabelProvider#
     * addListener(org.eclipse.jface.viewers.ILabelProviderListener)
     */
    public void addListener(ILabelProviderListener listener) {
    }

    /**
     * @see org.eclipse.jface.viewers.IBaseLabelProvider#
     * removeListener(org.eclipse.jface.viewers.ILabelProviderListener)
```

Listing 10.42 (Continues)

```
        */
      public void removeListener(ILabelProviderListener listener) {
      }

      /**
       * @see org.eclipse.jface.viewers.IBaseLabelProvider#
       * isLabelProperty(java.lang.Object, java.lang.String)
       */
      public boolean isLabelProperty(Object element, String property) {
          return true;
      }
  }
```

Listing 10.43 (Continued)

The FileCellEditor Class

Now the missing cell editors for the table of the viewer (see the section "Cell Editors" in Chapter 9) are implemented. The class FileCellEditor is based on the JFace class DialogCellEditor. When such an editor is clicked twice (but not a double-click), a small button appears on the right-hand side of the cell. A further click on this button opens a dialog. In this case, it is a file-selection dialog.

Since the class FileCellEditor should be used for two different features (sound files and image files), it should be possible to configure this class via its constructor. The constructor accepts a parameter for the dialog's title line and a filter list for the file selection.

Then the method openDialogBox() of the parent class DialogCellEditor is overridden. The contents (filename) of the table cell are fetched via the method getValue() and passed to the FileDialog instance. This is to make sure that the file-selection dialog is already positioned to the current file named in the table cell. The specified title is set, too, and also the list of file extensions for the file-selection filter. When the FileDialog is closed, a test is applied to see if a filename has been returned (null is returned if the dialog was canceled). Using the method setValueValid() the state of the cell editor is set accordingly. Then the filename received from the FileDialog is returned to the caller: the DialogCellEditor will replace the current cell contents with this value provided that it was marked as valid. See Listing 10.44.

```
    package com.bdaum.jukebox;

    import org.eclipse.jface.viewers.DialogCellEditor;
    import org.eclipse.swt.SWT;
    import org.eclipse.swt.widgets.Composite;
    import org.eclipse.swt.widgets.Control;
    import org.eclipse.swt.widgets.FileDialog;

    public class FileCellEditor extends DialogCellEditor {

        // Filter for the file selection
        private String[] extensions;
        // Title for pop-up dialog
```

Listing 10.43 (Continues)

```
        private String title;
        /**
         * Constructor for FileCellEditor.
         * @param parent - containing Composite
         * @param title - Title for pop-up dialog
         * @param extensions - Filter for file selection
         */
        public FileCellEditor(Composite parent, String title,
            String[] extensions) {
            super(parent);
            // Save parameters
            this.extensions = extensions;
            this.title = title;
        }
        /**
         * @see org.eclipse.jface.viewers.DialogCellEditor#
         * openDialogBox(org.eclipse.swt.widgets.Control)
         */
        protected Object openDialogBox(Control cellEditorWindow) {
            // Create file selection dialog
            FileDialog dialog =
                new FileDialog(cellEditorWindow.getShell(), SWT.OPEN);
            // Position dialog to current file
            dialog.setFileName((String) getValue());
            // Set filter and title
            dialog.setFilterExtensions(extensions);
            dialog.setText(title);
            String filename = dialog.open();
            // Indicate if file name is valid
            setValueValid(filename != null);
            return filename;
        }
    }
```

Listing 10.44 (Continued)

The Description Editor

The description editor consists of the class DescriptionCellEditor (which acts as its root class), and the class DescriptionEditorDialog which implements most of the functionality of the description editor.

The DescriptionCellEditor Class

The DescriptionCellEditor (Listing 10.45) is also based on the class DialogCellEditor. In this case, clicking the cell's Edit button will bring up a pop-up dialog for the convenient input of descriptive text. This dialog is implemented as a DescriptionEditorDialog instance, to which the playlist model is passed as a parameter. After the dialog is constructed, it is initialized with the current cell contents. When the dialog is closed, a check is applied to determine whether it was closed with the

OK button. If so, the modified text is fetched from the dialog and returned to the caller, after it has been declared as valid.

```
package com.bdaum.jukebox;

import org.eclipse.jface.dialogs.Dialog;
import org.eclipse.jface.viewers.DialogCellEditor;
import org.eclipse.swt.widgets.Composite;
import org.eclipse.swt.widgets.Control;

public class DescriptionCellEditor
    extends DialogCellEditor {

    // The playlist domain model
    IPlaylist playlistModel;

    /**
     * Constructor.
     * @param parent
     *                      Containing Composite
     * @param playlistModel
     *                      The playlist domain model
     */
    public DescriptionCellEditor(Composite parent,
                      IPlaylist playlistModel) {
        super(parent);
        // Save parameters
        this.playlistModel = playlistModel;
    }
    /**
     * Opens the window for description editing
     * @see org.eclipse.jface.viewers.DialogCellEditor#
     *              openDialogBox(org.eclipse.swt.widgets.Control)
     */
    protected Object openDialogBox(Control cellEditorWindow) {
        // Create new DescriptionEditorDialog instance
        DescriptionEditorDialog dialog = new DescriptionEditorDialog(
            cellEditorWindow.getShell(), playlistModel);
        // Create the dialogs GUI-elements
        dialog.create();
        // Initialize with current cell content
        dialog.setText((String) getValue());
        if (dialog.open() == Dialog.OK) {
            // Indicate that value is valid
            setValueValid(true);
            // Return new text
            return dialog.getText();
        }
        return null;
    }
}
```

Listing 10.45

301

The DescriptionEditorDialog Class

We go into the final round with the implementation of this class. However, it still offers you something to learn. It implements a pop-up dialog for entering descriptive text and is based on the JFace class `TitleAreaDialog` (see "Some Dialog Subclasses" in Chapter 9). A `SourceViewer` instance (see "The SourceViewer Class" in Chapter 9) is used as the editor for the descriptive text.

During this editing process, syntax-driven text coloring is needed: HTML tags and keywords that begin with the $ character will be displayed in a different color. To support the input of HTML markup and of keywords, a Content Assistant that can be invoked by pressing Ctrl+Spacebar is offered.

In addition, an Undo Manager is configured for the `SourceViewer`. This Undo Manager can be called via the keyboard shortcuts Ctrl+Z and Ctrl+Y for undo and redo. Copying, deleting, and pasting text via the keyboard shortcuts Ctrl+C, Ctrl+X, and Ctrl+V are already supported by the predefined `SourceViewer`. See Listing 10.46.

```
package com.bdaum.jukebox;

import java.util.ArrayList;
import java.util.List;
import org.eclipse.jface.dialogs.TitleAreaDialog;
import org.eclipse.jface.text.*;
import org.eclipse.jface.text.contentassist.*;
import org.eclipse.jface.text.presentation.IPresentationReconciler;
import org.eclipse.jface.text.presentation.PresentationReconciler;
import org.eclipse.jface.text.rules.*;
import org.eclipse.jface.text.source.ISourceViewer;
import org.eclipse.jface.text.source.SourceViewer;
import org.eclipse.jface.text.source.SourceViewerConfiguration;
import org.eclipse.swt.SWT;
import org.eclipse.swt.custom.VerifyKeyListener;
import org.eclipse.swt.events.KeyAdapter;
import org.eclipse.swt.events.KeyEvent;
import org.eclipse.swt.events.VerifyEvent;
import org.eclipse.swt.graphics.Point;
import org.eclipse.swt.layout.GridData;
import org.eclipse.swt.widgets.Composite;
import org.eclipse.swt.widgets.Control;
import org.eclipse.swt.widgets.Display;
import org.eclipse.swt.widgets.Shell;

public class DescriptionEditorDialog extends TitleAreaDialog {

    /**
     * This class allows editing descriptions in a separate
     * window. Key words starting with '$' and HTML tags are
     * coded in a different color. In addition, a content
     * assistant is implemented. This assistant is activated via
     * Ctrl+Spacebar, and automatically after entering a '$'. In
     * case of a '$' the content assistant makes proposals for
```

Listing 10.46 (Continues)

```
 * keywords. If text is selected, the content assistant
 * makes proposals for HTML character formatting. Also undo
 * functions are implemented( Ctrl+Z for Undo, Ctrl+Y for Redo).
 */
```

Listing 10.46 (Continued)

Code Scanner

The inner class KeywordCodeScanner (Listing 10.47) is responsible for the syntax highlighting of the displayed text. The class is based on a RuleBasedScanner (see the section "The SourceViewer Class" in Chapter 9). In our example, only two SingleLineRules are necessary to recognize keywords and HTML markup. In the first case, $ is specified as the start character and a space as the end character, while HTML markup is enclosed by < and >. (The last parameter specifies the escape character \.) These syntactical elements (keywords and HTML markup) are then decorated with the created Token instance. The array with these two rules is then passed to the scanner via the setRules() method.

```
public class KeywordCodeScanner extends RuleBasedScanner {

  // This class implements a specific RuleBasedScanner.
  // It assigns specific colors to keywords.
  public KeywordCodeScanner() {
    // We fetch the current Display instance
    // for later retrieval of system colors
    Display display = Display.getCurrent();
    // We create a token for keywords and paint it green
    IToken keyToken = new Token(new TextAttribute(display
                   .getSystemColor(SWT.COLOR_DARK_GREEN)));
    // We create a token for HTML tags and paint it red
    IToken htmlToken = new Token(new TextAttribute(display
                   .getSystemColor(SWT.COLOR_DARK_RED)));
    // We only need a single rule to recognize a keyword
    IRule[] rules = new IRule[2];
    // By using a SingleLineRule we make sure that
    // the keyword does not stretch across line breaks
    rules[0] = new SingleLineRule("$", " ", keyToken, '\\');
    rules[1] = new SingleLineRule("<", ">", htmlToken, '\\');
    // We set this rule for the scanner
    setRules(rules);
  }
}
```

Listing 10.47

Content Assistant

The inner class `KeywordContentAssistProcessor` implements a Content Assistant (see the section "The SourceViewer Class" in Chapter 9) that makes proposals for keywords and HTML character formatting. This assistant is automatically called when a $ is entered. This is controlled via the `getCompletionProposalAutoActivationCharacters()` method.

All proposals are compiled in the method `computeCompletionProposals()`. This method first retrieves the current document from the viewer and checks to see if text is selected. If so, it assumes that the user wants to apply character formatting to the selected text and calls the method `computeHtmlProposals()` to compile a list of HTML character formatting proposals.

Otherwise, it will call the method `computeKeywordProposals()` in order to compile a list of keyword proposals. In this case, the method `getQualifier()` is called, too, to determine whether a part of the keyword has already been entered. This knowledge is used to restrict the set of possible proposals. Finally, all `CompletionProposal` instances are returned in an array. Each of these instances contains the proposed character string, the position at which to insert it (the current cursor position minus the length of the keyword part already entered), the length of the text area that should be replaced by the proposal (the length of the keyword part already entered), and the new cursor position. In this case, the cursor is always positioned behind the proposal.

In the method `getQualifier()` the document is read from the current position backwards, character by character, and these characters are stored into a `StringBuffer`. If the process arrives at a space character or a line break, the empty string is returned—obviously, no keyword part was entered. If it arrives at a $ character, the contents of the `StringBuffer` are reversed and the reversed string is returned as the result. This result is then used in the method `computeProposals()` to restrict the set of possible keywords to only those keywords that start with the string already entered.

The method `computeHtmlProposals()` works in a similar way. However, here an extended form of the constructor `CompletionProposal()` is used. This form allows the display of specific labels for the proposals, that is, the string inserted when the proposal is applied and the label representing the proposal need not be identical. This allows displaying the proposals under labels such as "bold" or "italic" instead of "..." and "<i>...</i>".

The rest of this class contains standard implementations of the `IContentAssistProcessor` methods. These methods are not needed for this application. See Listing 10.48.

```java
// All keywords
private final static String[] KEYWORDS = new String[]{
                "performers", "producer", "publisher",
                "pubDate", "title"};
// HTML style tags proposed for character formatting
private final static String[] HTMLTAGS = new String[]{"b",
                "em", "i", "strong"};
// Display text for HTML style tags
private final static String[] STYLELABELS = new String[]{
                "bold", "emphasis", "italic", "strong"};

public class KeywordContentAssistProcessor
                implements IContentAssistProcessor {
    /**
```

Listing 10.48 (Continues)

```
 * Compiles an array of CompletionProposal instances.
 *
 * @param viewer - The viewer, from which this method is called
 * @param documentOffset - The current position in the document
 */
/**
 * Make automatic proposals after a $-character
 */
public char[] getCompletionProposalAutoActivationCharacters() {
  return new char[]{'$'};
}

public ICompletionProposal[] computeCompletionProposals(
               ITextViewer viewer, int documentOffset) {
  IDocument doc = viewer.getDocument();
  // Get text selection
  Point selectedRange = viewer.getSelectedRange();
  List propList;
  try {
    propList = (selectedRange.y == 0)
        ? computeKeywordProposals(getQualifier(doc,
                                  documentOffset), documentOffset)
        : computeHtmlProposals(selectedRange.x, doc.get(
                               selectedRange.x, selectedRange.y));
    // Convert into Array
    return (CompletionProposal[])
        propList.toArray(new CompletionProposal[propList.size()]);
  } catch (BadLocationException e) {
    return new CompletionProposal[0];
  }
}
/**
 * Compiles proposals for HTML mark-up.
 *
 * @param documentOffset - the current position in the text
 * @param selectedText - the currently selected text
 * @return - list of proposals
 */
private List computeHtmlProposals(int documentOffset,
               String selectedText) {
  List propList = new ArrayList();
  for (int i = 0; i < HTMLTAGS.length; i++) {
    // Compute the string that will replace the selection
    String insert = "<" + HTMLTAGS[i] + ">" + selectedText
                    + "</" + HTMLTAGS[i] + ">";
    int cursor = insert.length();
    // Construct proposal with replacement string and
    // display label
    CompletionProposal proposal = new CompletionProposal(
          insert, documentOffset, selectedText.length(), cursor,
            null, STYLELABELS[i], null, insert);
    propList.add(proposal);
  }
  return propList;
```

Listing 10.48 (Continues)

305

```
    }
/**
 * Retrieves qualifying user input.
 *
 * @param viewer - The viewer under which we work
 * @param documentOffset - The current position in the document
 * @return String - Keyword part that already has been entered
 */
private String getQualifier(IDocument doc, int documentOffset) {
  // Read the document backwards
  // until whitespace or a $-character is encountered
  StringBuffer buf = new StringBuffer();
  while (true) {
    try {
      // Get character in front of cursor
      char c = doc.getChar(--documentOffset);
      if (Character.isWhitespace(c)) {
        // Begin of line or begin of word -
        // no keyword was found.
        break;
      }
      buf.append(c);
      if (c == '$')
        // Keyword was found.
        // Revert the string and return it.
        return buf.reverse().toString();
    } catch (BadLocationException e) {
      // Begin of document - no keyword found
      break;
    }
  }
  return "";
}
/**
 *
 * Compiles a list with keyword proposals
 *
 * @param qualifier - Significant characters entered by the user to
 *         restrict the number of proposals
 * @param documentOffset - the current position in the document
 * @return list of proposals
 */
private List computeKeywordProposals(String qualifier,
                int documentOffset) {
  List propList = new ArrayList();
  for (int i = 0; i < KEYWORDS.length; i++) {
    String insert = "$" + KEYWORDS[i] + " ";
    if (insert.startsWith(qualifier)) {
      // Only allow the keywords that start with the qualifier
      int cursor = insert.length();
      CompletionProposal proposal =
            new CompletionProposal(insert,
                      documentOffset - qualifier.length(),
                      qualifier.length(), cursor);
```

Listing 10.48 (Continues)

```
            propList.add(proposal);
        }
    }
    return propList;
}

/**
 * Standard implementation for display of contexts
 */
public IContextInformation[] computeContextInformation(
                ITextViewer viewer, int documentOffset) {
    return null;
}

/**
 * Standard implementation for activation of contexts
 */
public char[] getContextInformationAutoActivationCharacters() {
    return null;
}

/**
 * Standard implementation for validation of contexts
 */
public IContextInformationValidator
        getContextInformationValidator() {
    return null;
}

/**
 * Standard implementation for error messages
 */
public String getErrorMessage() {
    return null;
}
}
```

Listing 10.48 (Continued)

SourceViewer Configuration

Now, you must tell the SourceViewer about the syntax highlighting and the Content Assistant. This happens in the following code, where a new SourceViewer-Configuration (see the section "The SourceViewer Class" in Chapter 9) under the name KeywordViewerConfiguration is created. Using the KeywordCodeScanner declared previously, a new DefaultDamagerRepairer that is responsible for the presentation of the text is created. This DefaultDamagerRepairer is then registered with a new PresentationReconciler instance as both a Damager and a Repairer. This is done for the content category IDocument.DEFAULT_CONTENT_TYPE, which is the only content category used here.

A new ContentAssistant instance is created in the method getContentAssistant(). For this instance set the KeywordContentAssistProcessor declared previously as the processor. Switch to automatic activation of the Content Assistant and specify 500 milliseconds as the delay.

Finally, add an Undo Manager to this configuration, too. Use the Eclipse standard implementation `DefaultUndoManager` and allow nine undo steps. See Listing 10.49.

```java
// SourceViewer Configuration
class KeywordViewerConfiguration extends SourceViewerConfiguration {

  // Configure Presentation
  public IPresentationReconciler getPresentationReconciler(
                  ISourceViewer sourceViewer) {
    // Create new PresentationReconciler instance
    PresentationReconciler reconciler = new PresentationReconciler();
    // We use a DefaultDamagerRepairer as both Damager and Repairer
    DefaultDamagerRepairer dr = new DefaultDamagerRepairer(
                  new KeywordCodeScanner());
    reconciler.setDamager(dr,IDocument.DEFAULT_CONTENT_TYPE);
    reconciler.setRepairer(dr, IDocument.DEFAULT_CONTENT_TYPE);
    return reconciler;
  }

  // Configure Content Assist
  public IContentAssistant getContentAssistant(
                  ISourceViewer sourceViewer) {
    // Create new ContentAssistant instance
    ContentAssistant assistant = new ContentAssistant();
    // Set the ContentAssistProcessor for the
    // default content category
    assistant.setContentAssistProcessor(
                  new KeywordContentAssistProcessor(),
                  IDocument.DEFAULT_CONTENT_TYPE);
    // Allow automatic activation after 500 msec
    assistant.enableAutoActivation(true);
    assistant.setAutoActivationDelay(500);
    return assistant;
  }
  // We use the DefaultUndoManager as Undo Manager
  public IUndoManager getUndoManager(ISourceViewer sourceViewer) {
    // A maximum of 9 undo steps
    return new DefaultUndoManager(9);
  }
}
```

Listing 10.49

SourceViewer

Now you can begin to implement the `DescriptionEditorDialog`. The constructor accepts the parent shell and the playlist domain model.

Add a title and a message text to the dialog. Then in the method `createDialogArea()` add the `SourceViewer` to the dialog.

The `SourceViewer` is then configured with the `KeywordViewerConfiguration` declared previously. In addition, equip the `SourceViewer` with a document instance. To make the `SourceViewer` fill the dialog area completely, fetch the `SourceViewer`'s `StyledText` widget and apply an appropriate `GridData` instance to it.

Then look after the keyboard event. Add a `VerifyKeyListener` to the `SourceViewer`. With this listener, trap all key presses that are modified with the Ctrl key: in this case, set the variable `doit` in the event object to `false`. Thus, the event is vetoed and the key press is ignored.

In the `KeyListener` that you added to the `SourceViewer`'s `StyledText` widget, however, all key presses modified with Ctrl get special treatment. Depending on the key combination pressed, an appropriate `ITextOperationTarget` operation is selected. Then you need to ask the `SourceViewer` with the method `canDoOperation()` if the operation can be performed: if so, execute it via the `doOperation()` method. This test with `canDoOperation()` is absolutely necessary! See Listing 10.50.

```java
// Widgets
private SourceViewer sourceViewer;
// The SourceViewers Document instance
private Document doc = new Document();
// The playlist domain model
private IPlaylist playlistModel;

/**
 * Constructor DescriptionEditorDialog.
 *
 * @param parentShell - Containing Shell
 * @param playlistModel - The playlist domain model
 */
public DescriptionEditorDialog(Shell parentShell,
                IPlaylist playlistModel) {
  // Save parameters
  super(parentShell);
  this.playlistModel = playlistModel;
}
/**
 * @see org.eclipse.jface.dialogs.Dialog#
 *      createDialogArea(org.eclipse.swt.widgets.Composite)
 */
public Control createDialogArea(Composite parent) {
  // Set title
  setTitle("Description");
  // Set message
  setMessage("Enter description text.\n"
    + "Press Ctrl-Spacebar to invoke the Content Assistant.");
  // Create Composite
  Composite composite = (Composite) super
                .createDialogArea(parent);
  // Create SourceViewer
  sourceViewer = new SourceViewer(composite, null, SWT.MULTI
                | SWT.BORDER | SWT.WRAP | SWT.H_SCROLL
                | SWT.V_SCROLL);
  // Configure SourceViewer
```

Listing 10.50 (Continues)

```java
    sourceViewer.configure(new KeywordViewerConfiguration());
    // Set Document instance
    sourceViewer.setDocument(doc);
    // Get StyledText widget
    Control styleTextWidget = sourceViewer.getControl();
    // Set the widget to maximum size
    styleTextWidget.setLayoutData(new GridData(
            GridData.GRAB_HORIZONTAL
          | GridData.GRAB_VERTICAL
          | GridData.HORIZONTAL_ALIGN_FILL
          | GridData.VERTICAL_ALIGN_FILL));
    // Avoid hotkeys appearing in the text
    sourceViewer.appendVerifyKeyListener(new VerifyKeyListener() {
      public void verifyKey(VerifyEvent event) {
        if ((event.stateMask & SWT.CTRL) != 0) {
          // Veto, if CTRL was pressed
          event.doit = false;
        }
      }
    });
    // Event processing for hotkeys
    styleTextWidget.addKeyListener(new KeyAdapter() {
      public void keyPressed(KeyEvent e) {
        // Only if CTRL was pressed
        if ((e.stateMask & SWT.CTRL) == 0) return;
        int operation = 0;
        if (e.character == ' ') {
          // Ctrl+Spacebar: Content Assist
          operation = SourceViewer.CONTENTASSIST_PROPOSALS;
        } else if ((e.character | '\u0040') == 'Z') {
          // Ctrl+Z: Undo
          operation = ITextOperationTarget.UNDO;
        } else if ((e.character | '\u0040') == 'Y') {
          // Ctrl+Y: Redo
          operation = ITextOperationTarget.REDO;
        }
        // Check if operation is possible
        if (operation != 0 && sourceViewer.canDoOperation(operation))
          // Perform operation
          sourceViewer.doOperation(operation);
      }
    });
    return composite;
}

/**
 * Return the edited text.
 *
 * @return String - Edited text
 */
public String getText() {
  return doc.get();
}
```

Listing 10.50 (Continues)

```
/**
 * Initialize document with text.
 *
 * @param input - Default text for text field
 */
public void setText(String input) {
    doc.set((input == null) ? "" : input);
}
}
```

Listing 10.50 (Continued)

Deploying the Jukebox

It is not very difficult to deploy the jukebox as a standalone application. You only have to take care that all the required JAR files and the required native SWT libraries are included in the deployment.

First, export the whole project into a directory of your choice as a JAR file. Please make sure that you remove the check mark from file jukebox.ini when selecting the files to be exported. This file is created automatically by the playlist model implementation when the application is executed for the first time.

When invoking the Jukebox, you must make sure that all JAR files included in the Java Build Path are also included into the Java Classpath. In addition, it is necessary to specify the native SWT library in the -D option of the java command.

On the Macintosh, however, things are much simpler. Eclipse 3 offers in the Package Explorer the context function Export > Mac OS X Application Bundle. This function allows you to deploy an SWT project as an Application Bundle that can be executed on the Mac with just a double mouse click.

Summary

The player implemented on these pages is, of course, miles away from a really convenient and powerful Jukebox. However, it can be used as the basis for your own extensions. My goal was to demonstrate core concepts of the SWT and the JFace libraries in the context of a nontrivial application.

As expected, this application looks like a native application of the host's operating system (here Windows 2000). The windows and dialogs behave like native windows and dialogs—in fact, they *are* native windows and dialogs.

What is more difficult, as with a pure Java application, is deployment. Because the SWT archives and the native SWT library are platform-specific, you need a different deployment package for each platform. Alternatively, you can pack all platform-specific SWT archives and libraries into a single installation, but this then becomes large. Another option is using Sun Microsystems's Java Web Start to deploy SWT applications. An detailed discussion about this topic is found in the article "Deploy an SWT application using Java Web Start" by Jeff Gunther on www.ibm.com/developerworks.

What remains in the wish list is better deployment support for Windows and Linux, such as the possibility to automatically generate command files for running deployed applications on the target platform.

Figure 10.5 shows the various windows of the jukebox. At the top left you see the main window with a background image; on the right is the window with the descriptive text. At the bottom left is the playlist window, and to the right of this window is the editor for the descriptive text.

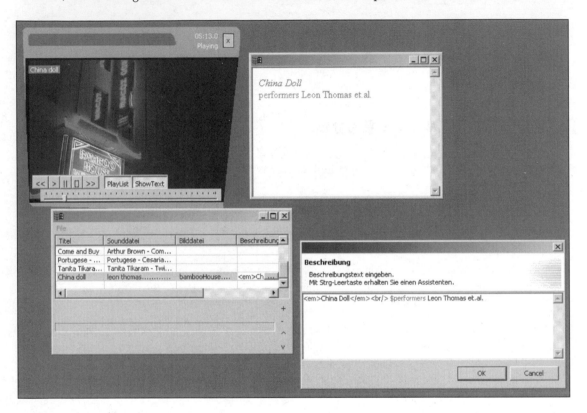

Figure 10.5

In fact, the layout of the player could be improved considerably. The control elements are currently somewhat minimalist. One idea would be to implement sliders for volume and balance and to allow for different operational modes (single pass, loop, shuffle).

The management of the playlists could also be more user friendly. If the same song is used in multiple playlists, repeatedly entering the song data becomes tiring. An option would be to scan all existing playlists for a song when it is inserted into a playlist and to derive the features (title, background image, description) from existing entries. It should also be possible to nest playlists. Another option would be to add other features such as a transition time for cross-fading into the next song. This could be done by using two jlGui engine instances.

However, all this must be left to the interested reader. In the next chapter we discuss plug-in development.

11

Developing Plug-ins for the Eclipse Platform

Plug-in development sounds at first like a topic for Eclipse specialists. However, this feature quickly proves to be one of the main selling points of the Eclipse platform. To understand this, we must briefly discuss the architecture of the Eclipse platform (see the following section, "The Architecture of the Eclipse Platform"). Eclipse consists of a fairly small core application whose functionality is mainly restricted to the execution of plug-ins. In fact, every function the Eclipse workbench has to offer has been added to this core in the form of a plug-in.

To learn which plug-ins your current Eclipse SDK contains, just invoke the menu function Help > About Eclipse Platform > Plug-in Details. Another way to get an overview of the installed plug-ins is the Plug-in Browser that you can open via Window > Show View > Plug-ins. Finally, the Search function supports the search for plug-ins, provided that it is used under the Plug-in Development perspective (see "The Plug-in Development Perspective" section).

This plug-in-oriented architecture has two consequences:

❑ First, the Eclipse SDK can be extended almost indefinitely. Most of the third-party plug-ins currently offered for Eclipse deal with some aspect of application development. For example, there are plug-ins for modeling with UML or AOM, and plug-ins for special Java tools such as JavaCC (see Appendix A). Other plug-ins provide IDEs for programming languages such as C++ or AspectJ.

❑ Second, it is possible to remove features from the Eclipse SDK. Theoretically, you can build on the "naked" Eclipse core to construct applications that have very little to do with program development. In particular, this makes sense for applications that require a certain degree of variability and so need to be implemented using a plug-in concept. Such applications are found in areas like graphics and imaging applications, video editing, prepress, content management, sound studios, and many others.

When developing such applications and plug-ins, you can use the functionality of existing Eclipse plug-ins. In particular, the plug-ins for the Eclipse workspace resource management (projects, views, and files) and for the GUI components of the Eclipse workbench (editors, views, wizards, preferences, help system, and much more) are worth mentioning. Despite the steep learning curve of the Eclipse architecture, the time and effort saved by reusing these components by far outweighs the effort necessary to get acquainted with the architecture.

In this chapter I discuss the principles of the Eclipse plug-in architecture and give an introduction into plug-in development. I refrain from presenting runnable example programs at this point because the classes and interfaces discussed here make sense only within the context of a complete plug-in. Instead, larger example plug-ins will be shown in Chapters 13 and 15.

The Architecture of the Eclipse Platform

The only purpose of the tiny Eclipse core is to load and execute plug-ins. All the other functionality of the Eclipse platform is provided by plug-ins. In most cases—but not always—such a plug-in consists of a Java archive. In addition, it may contain other files such as images or help texts. An absolute requirement for each plug-in, however, is the plug-in manifest file `plugin.xml`, which describes the configuration of the plug-in and its integration into the platform. I will discuss this manifest in more detail in the section "Configuring Plug-ins."

Extension Points

Extension Points are a core concept of the plug-in architecture. Plug-ins can define their own extension points to which other plug-ins can connect. In the manifest file `plugin.xml` each plug-in describes to which existing extension points it connects and which new extension points it adds to the platform.

OSGi

Until version 2.1 Eclipse used proprietary formats for the core and for the plug-ins. With version 3 this has changed. Internally, plug-ins are based on the OSGi (Open Service Gateway Initiative) specification. The Eclipse core now fulfills the role of an OSGi server. A compatibility layer ensures that older plug-ins can be executed on this platform without problems.

The Open Service Gateway Initiative was founded in 1999. Its mission was the standardization of services for local networks and embedded devices. Services conforming to the OSGi specifications can be executed on OSGi complying servers such as IBM's SMF server or Sun Microsystems's Java Embedded Server. In particular, the automotive and electrical appliances industries are part of this initiative. What is relevant currently for Eclipse is that Eclipse plug-ins are now based on an open standard.

OSGi-conforming services (also called OSGi *bundles*) must implement the interface `BundleActivator` and must provide an OSGi manifest file. A `BundleActivator` registers the service with the OSGi server in its `start()` method and deregisters it in its `stop()` method. In Eclipse this is done by the abstract class `Plugin`, which implements a `BundleActivator`. So, normally you should not have to deal with OSGi matters at all. In the future, however, Eclipse will utilize more of the OSGi functionality to make Eclipse plug-ins more versatile. One advantage of the OSGi architecture is that plug-ins can be added and removed from the Eclipse platform without having to restart Eclipse after such an operation.

A Minimal Platform

The whole plug-in game begins with the platform core runtime `org.eclipse.core.runtime`. This is formally a plug-in, too, and consists of a Java library `runtime.jar` and a manifest file `plugin.xml`. This platform, along with the plug-in `org.eclipse.core.runtime.compatibility` for the Java archive `compatibility.jar` and the plug-in `org.eclipse.core.boot` for the Java archive `boot.jar`, is part of the absolute minimum number of plug-ins required for each Eclipse-based application. The `boot.jar` archive is, among other things, also responsible for completing the installation of a freshly installed Eclipse platform.

Later, in "The Core Classes of the Eclipse Platform," I will discuss the platform core in more detail.

Rich Client Platform vs. IDE

In Eclipse 2 all applications that wanted to utilize the Eclipse workbench were restricted to the IDE (Integrated Development Environment) concept. Such applications were required to manage the Eclipse workspace and to work with workspace resources. This is, however, a severe restriction, inhibiting the widespread use of the Eclipse platform as a universal application framework.

Consequently, this restriction was loosened with Eclipse 3. It is now possible to implement generic applications on the basis of the Rich Client Platform (RCP). In particular, the RCP does not use the Eclipse workspace and its resources. Since the Eclipse workbench also made extensive use of the workspace concept, it was refactored into a workspace-agnostic part called the generic workbench and a workspace-specific part called the IDE. The generic workbench is implemented in the plug-in `org.eclipse.ui.workbench`, while the workspace-specific part has been moved to the new plug-in `org.eclipse.ui.ide`.

Resource Management

Resources in Eclipse are projects, folders, and files of the Eclipse workspace. The plug-in `org.eclipse.core.resources` provides the necessary functionality for accessing and managing resources independently of the host file system. In addition, it implements some services that are usually not provided by the host file system. Such services include a mechanism for managing resource annotations (Marker) and an event management for resource changes. In "Configuring Plug-ins" I will discuss resource management in more detail.

The resource management plug-in is based on a further plug-in: `org.eclipse.ant.core`. This plug-in organizes the support for the Ant tool. Ant (`www.apache.com`) is a Java-based tool supporting the Make process (that is, the assembly) of projects (see also "Embedded Ant" in Chapter 12). The reason why this tool is used for resource management lies in Eclipse's support for the assembly of projects at the resource level. The Ant functionality is therefore available virtually everywhere in the platform. The Eclipse plug-ins for resource management may be included in and deployed with your own applications. However, since some components (for example, Ant) are covered by the Apache Software License 1.1, products based on these plug-ins must refer explicitly to the Apache copyright and liability regulations.

User Interface

Several plug-ins are available for the implementation of user interfaces. These include SWT and JFace, which I've already discussed in Chapters 8 and 9, but also higher-level components such as views, text editors, and forms. This functionality is divided into several plug-ins, such as the following:

```
org.eclipse.ui
org.eclipse.swt
org.eclipse.text
org.eclipse.jface
org.eclipse.jface.text
org.eclipse.ui.views
org.eclipse.ui.workbench
org.eclipse.ui.workbench.compatibility
org.eclipse.ui.workbench.texteditor
org.eclipse.ui.ide
org.eclipse.ui.editors
org.eclipse.ui.forms
```

The Eclipse workbench is implemented with the help of these plug-ins. By using them in your own applications, you can achieve high-quality and consistent user interfaces with relatively little effort. Also, there are no difficulties in terms of licenses—all the plug-ins in the Eclipse SDK are covered by the Common Public License Version 1.0. This allows you to use these plug-ins in your own applications and to deploy them with your own applications. The section "Components of the Eclipse User Interface" introduces several components of these GUI plug-ins.

Help System

The following plug-ins implement a complete system for end-user help:

```
org.eclipse.help
org.eclipse.help.base
org.eclipse.help.ui
org.eclipse.help.ide
org.eclipse.help.appserver
org.eclipse.help.webapp
```

The help functions of the Eclipse workbench are also based on these plug-ins. The complete help system is implemented as a Web server; the HTML help pages can be displayed with a standard Web browser such as Internet Explorer or Mozilla. Eclipse is able to use Web browsers found on the host system for this purpose. I will discuss the help system in more detail later.

Team Support

Several plug-ins support the development of software artifacts in a team:

```
org.eclipse.team.core
org.eclipse.team.cvs.core
org.eclipse.team.cvs.ssh
org.eclipse.team.cvs.ssh2
org.eclipse.team.cvs.ui
org.eclipse.team.ui
```

These plug-ins also implement development team support (see "Developing in a Team" in Chapter 7) for the Eclipse workbench. The support they provide is based on a client/server architecture with a central repository that contains the team's artifacts, and on clients that implement the user interface. These plug-ins feature a relatively generic architecture. For example, it is possible to implement various user-specific workflow strategies. Several repositories can coexist in one application, and several clients are possible for a single repository. This allows for quite flexible workflow strategies.

Other Plug-in Groups

The plug-ins I just mentioned are well suited for generic application development. Besides these plug-ins, the Eclipse SDK contains various other plug-in groups, such as plug-ins for Java development, for debugging, and for plug-in development itself (the creation of the manifest and other configuration files). In this book I will not discuss the APIs of these plug-ins in detail, since they are of interest for only very specific applications.

Architecture Summary

When you want to implement a new Eclipse-based application, besides the core components you will usually use the plug-ins for the SWT and JFace, for the generic workbench, and for text processing and the help system. When implementing plug-ins for the Eclipse SDK, you will also use the plug-ins for the IDE functionality and some other optional plug-ins, such as those for team support (see Figure 11.1).

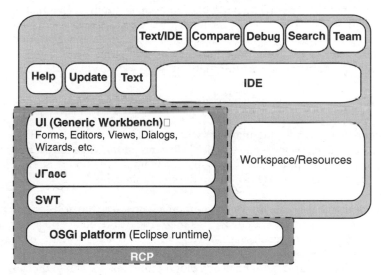

Figure 11.1

The components contained in the Eclipse SDK cover most of the functions that are necessary for running the Eclipse platform and the IDE. If you implement an application from outside this application spectrum, you may occasionally find that some required component is missing. For example, the Eclipse SDK contains neither a state-of-the-art graphics editor nor a spreadsheet component. Here you have to make use of third-party plug-ins, which appear in ever-increasing numbers on the market. Of course, you must check the individual license conditions of these plug-ins before you integrate them into your own applications. Appendix A lists some of the most important third-party plug-ins for Eclipse-based application development.

The Core Classes of the Eclipse Platform

As I already have mentioned, the nucleus of the Eclipse platform is very small and contains only the functionality required to load and execute Eclipse plug-ins. In addition, it contains some interfaces and classes that are of general interest. All these interfaces and classes are contained in the package `org.eclipse.core.runtime`.

The Platform Class

The `Platform` class is of general significance. It cannot be instantiated, and it contains only static methods. It manages all the installed plug-ins, takes care of the access authorization to Eclipse workspace resources, and maintains the Eclipse protocol (URLs used in Eclipse make use of the Eclipse-specific `platform://` prefix). In particular, you can obtain the location of the workspace root directory via the method `getLocation()`. Using the `getCommandLineArgs()` method you can get the command-line options that were specified when the Eclipse platform was started. This allows you to configure plug-ins by command-line options. You can search a particular plug-in in the plug-in registry with `getPlugin()` by specifying its identification.

The Plugin Class

The implementation of an Eclipse plug-in begins with a subclass of the abstract class `Plugin`. In the constructor of the new subclass you must create a single instance of this class (singleton) and store this instance into a static field. In addition, you need to implement the methods `getInstance()` and `getDefault()`, from which you can later obtain the created instance.

In the constructor you will also initialize the plug-in preferences (see the next section) and any resource bundles that you may need (see the "Summary" section). The API reference documentation provides a code example for such a `Plugin` subclass under Help > Help Contents > Platform Plug-in Developer Guide > Reference > API Reference > org.eclipse.core.runtime > Plugin. This example program also shows how to use an INI file to save the state of a plug-in from one session to the next.

Most of the methods of the `Plugin` class deal with low-level resource management and the management of preferences. For example, the methods `setPluginPreferences()` and `getPluginPreferences()` store and retrieve the current preferences. With `find()` you can obtain the URL of a specified workspace resource, and with `openStream()` you can open an input stream on a specified workspace resource.

The method getDialogSettings() is equally important, and with it you can retrieve the settings of all persistent dialogs of a plug-in (see also the section "Making Dialogs Persistent" in Chapter 9). Best practice is to create an individual section for each dialog. The plug-in automatically loads and saves the settings.

The Preferences Class

This class implements a persistent preference store. A single instance of this class contains all the preferences of a given plug-in. Each individual preference entry consists of a name/value pair. The name is a non-empty character string that is unique within the context of the plug-in. The value can be of type boolean, double, float, int, long, or String. Using the methods getBoolean(), getDouble(), and setValue(), you can retrieve the single preference values or set new preference values, respectively. Changes in the preference store cause events of type Preferences.PropertyChangeEvent.

If a value was not previously set, querying that value returns the default value. For preferences of type String, this is normally the empty string; for all other preference types, the default value is zero. It is possible to preset the default value of each preference entry via setDefault(). Note that these default values are not persistent and must always be set when the plug-in is initialized.

To initialize preferences, you must override the method initializeDefaultPluginPreferences() in your Plugin subclass. All default preference values can be preset in this method. Examples are given in the section "The Plugin Class and Preferences" in Chapter 13.

This initialization happens in several steps: the invocation of the method initializeDefaultPluginPreferences() is only the first step. In the second step, Eclipse evaluates the contents of the file preference.ini if such a file exists in the plug-in directory. The default values defined in this file will override the default values set in step one.

Here is an example of an entry in preferences.ini:

```
SPELL_THRESHOLD=99
```

Defining such a file allows you to modify the preference default values without recompiling the plug-in. A typical use for this is debug switches for testing output.

In the third step, the plugin_customization.ini files defined in other Eclipse features are evaluated (see "The Plug-in Manifest" section). The entries defined here will override the entries set in the first and second initialization steps.

Path Specifications

The interface IPath and its standard implementation Path represent resource path specifications for both workspace resources and resources outside the Eclipse workspace. The representation of these path is independent from the host system: The character / is always used as the separator between path steps. The specification of a device such as c: or server/disk1: is also possible. IPath and Path are equipped with a variety of methods that allow evaluation, synthesis, or modification of path specifications.

Monitoring Long-Running Processes

The interface `IProgressMonitor` and the classes `NullProgressMonitor`, `ProgressMonitorWrapper`, and `SubProgressMonitor` allow the monitoring of long-running processes (see "Managing Long-Running Processes"). During such a process you can display a progress bar and provide a button for aborting the process. Each `IProgressMonitor` object is informed about the start and the end of the process and about the steps in between so that it can display the progress of the process accordingly.

The `NullProgressMonitor` does—guess what—nothing. You would use it in those cases when you don't want to display the processes' progress. Should you actually want to show a progress bar, you can use two existing JFace classes:

```
org.eclipse.jface.dialogs.ProgressMonitorDialog
org.eclipse.jface.wizard.ProgressMonitorPart
```

While the latter implements a progress bar widget that can be embedded into other `Composites`, the first implements a complete dialog from which you can obtain an `IProgressMonitor` object via the method `getProgressMonitor()`. You can initialize such an object via the method `beginTask()`. With the `worked()` method you can update the progress bar after each step. The end of the process is indicated via the method `done()`. Using the method `isCanceled()` you can check whether the process has been canceled by the end user or by another program unit (via the method `cancel()`).

The Eclipse Workspace

I introduced the various resources of the Eclipse workspace in the section "Resources" in Chapter 4: projects, folders, and files. In this section I am going to discuss the resource management's API.

Unlike the Eclipse predecessor Visual Age, which stored resources in a central repository, Eclipse uses the file system of the host operating system directly. Projects, folders, and files are mapped onto the corresponding items in the host's file system: projects and folders onto directories and files onto files. The advantage is that you may still access these resources when Eclipse is no longer installed or if it is not functional.

Eclipse does have an internal repository, of course. This sits in the workspace in the subdirectory `.metadata` and stores all kind of metadata, such as preferences for the various plug-ins, the configuration and current state of the Eclipse platform, markers and annotations for problems, tasks, and breakpoints, the Local History of resources (see "Local History" in Chapter 2), specific resource properties, and much more. Programmers do not have direct access to this metadata.

Resources

Resources of the Eclipse workspace are described by the `IResource` interface. This interface, together with other resource management interfaces and classes, resides in the package `org.eclipse.core.resources`. The complete functionality of the resource management unit is deployed as a separate Eclipse plug-in.

The most common resources are projects, folders, and files. Projects may contain folders and files. Folders may contain subfolders and files. Figure 11.2 shows the resource type hierarchy.

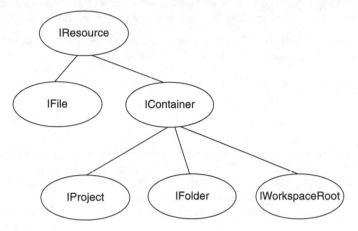

Figure 11.2

Since each resource in the workspace corresponds with a resource in the host file system, each resource has two addresses: the address within the workspace and the location in the host file system. (Consequently, there are two different ways to open files, depending on the location of the file: inside the workspace or outside the workspace.) You can retrieve the workspace address of a resource via its method getFullPath(), and the location within the host file system can be retrieved via the method getLocation(). Both of these addresses are represented as IPath instances (see the "Path Specifications" section).

Normally, the address obtained with getLocation() consists of the concatenation of Platform.getLocation() (see the "The Platform Class" section) and getFullPath()— but only normally. In the case where a whole project is imported into the workspace (via the menu function Import > Existing Project into Workspace), the imported files are *not* moved into the workspace directory. Instead, Eclipse creates only a mapping of workspace addresses to the imported project, so these files are not contained physically in the workspace folder. This is one of the reasons why you should never try to manually construct file system locations from workspace addresses but should always use the IResource method getLocation().

IResource defines a rich arsenal of methods. Here are the major function groups:

❑ Methods for classical resource management such as exists(), move(), copy(), and delete().

❑ Methods for the implementation of the Visitor design pattern. You can pass an IResourceVisitor instance to a resource via the accept() method. This resource then invokes the visit() method of the visitor instance. If it is successful, the IResourceVisitor instance is also passed to the child resources of the current resource via their respective accept() methods.

❑ Methods for managing markers. Eclipse provides a concept for adding markers such as problems, tasks, or breakpoints to resources. The methods `createMarker()`, `findMarker()`, `findMarkers()`, `getMarker()`, and `deleteMarkers()` belong to this group. Markers and the corresponding interface `IMarker` will be examined more closely in the next section.

❑ Methods for managing Resource Properties. This group allows the addition of an unlimited number of properties to each resource. The methods

```
setPersistentProperty()
setSessionProperty()
getPersistentProperty()
getSessionProperty()
```

allow the setting and retrieval of single properties. The concept is quite similar to the WebDAV standard (`www.webdav.org`). Each property consists of a unique name and a string value. Usually, you would want to use an XML expression for the string value to allow for more complex structured values. What you write into such a property depends on the application. For example, you could remember the current state of a resource in such a property and could thus organize a workflow. Session properties are not persistent—they vanish when the session is closed. Persistent properties, in contrast, live across sessions because they are stored on disk (`.metadata`).

Containers

The interface `IContainer` is derived from `IResource`. Interfaces of resources that can contain other resources are based on this interface, such as `IProject`, `IWorkspaceRoot`, and `IFolder`. In addition to the `IResource` methods, the interface provides methods for localizing and retrieving child resources, such as `findMember()`, `getFile()`, `getFolder()`, and `members()`.

The Workspace Root

The interface `IWorkspaceRoot` represents the root directory of the Eclipse workspace. With `getProject()` and `getProjects()` you can obtain a specific project in the workspace and a list of all projects, respectively. You can obtain the root directory from the current `Plugin` instance via `getWorkspace().getRoot()`.

Projects and Project Natures

Projects are units that contain all the resources of a software product. Projects may contain other folders and files. The project acts as a root directory for these folders and files. In addition, a project may control how the final software product is assembled from its components. Projects may not contain other projects, although they can refer to other prerequisite projects. This information is stored in the project folder in a file named `.project`.

Projects can be equipped with one or several plug-in–specific project natures. Each nature describes a specific behavioral aspect of a project. For example, a Java project has a Java nature. Natures can be defined and selected freely. However, it is also possible to restrict the selection of natures for a given project. You may even specify natures that rely on other natures as prerequisites. New natures can be implemented as subtypes of the interface `IProjectNature`. How project natures can be created and assigned to projects is described in detail under Help > Help Contents > Platform Plug-in Developer Guide > Programmer's Guide > Resources Overview > Project Natures.

In order to support all this additional functionality, the interface `IProject` offers—besides the methods inherited from `IResource` and `IContainer`—additional methods such as `build()` for the assembly of a software product, `getReferencedProjects()` and `getReferencingProjects()` for retrieving the dependencies between projects, and `getNature()`, `hasNature()` and `isNatureEnabled()` for the retrieval of project natures.

With `create()` you can create a new project. But to do so, you must first own an `IProject` instance. You can obtain such an instance from the `IWorkspaceRoot` instance with the help of `getProject()`. For example:

```
IWorkspace workspace = ResourcesPlugin.getWorkspace();
IWorkspaceRoot root = workspace.getRoot();
IProject project = root.getProject("newProject");
try {
    // progressMonitor=null
    project.create(null);
} catch (CoreException e) {
    e.printStackTrace();
}
```

In this example you first fetch an `IWorkspace` instance from the resources plug-in. From this instance you get the workspace root instance, and from there you can fetch an `IProject` instance with the specified name. Finally, you can create the project. For simplicity's sake, in this example I have specified the value `null` for the `IProgressMonitor` instance requested by the `create()` method.

Folders

The interface `IFolder` does not offer much more functionality than that inherited from the interface `IContainer`. New folders are created via `create()` in the same way that projects are created. You can get an `IFolder` instance from an `IWorkspaceRoot` instance via `getFolder()`.

Files

Files are described by the interface `IFile`. You can get an `IFile` instance from the workspace root via `getFile()`. New files are created with the `IFile` method `create()`. The `IFile` interface offers the following methods to manipulate the contents of a file: `setContents()` to overwrite the contents, `appendContents()` to append additional contents to a file, and `getContents()` to retrieve the complete contents of a file. In all these methods you can specify an `IProgressMonitor` instance as parameter to visualize the progress of the operation.

All these methods are history-aware: When the contents of a file are changed or when a file is deleted, you can optionally keep a copy of the old file version in the Local History (see the section "Local History" in Chapter 2). `getHistory()` allows you to get a list of all previous versions of a file. This list is provided in the form of an `IFileState` array. From such an `IFileState` instance you get the previous contents of the file via `getContents()`, and you can get the time stamp of this version using `getModificationTime()`. Only file contents are subject to the Local History, not the file's properties (see the Resources section).

In the following example I create a new file by concatenating two existing files. I also keep a copy of the intermediate versions in the Local History. I set the parameter `force` to `false` because I don't want the file to be modified when the workspace entry (metadata) of the file does not match the file version in the host file system.

```
IFile file1 = project.getFile("hello.txt");
IFile file2 = project.getFile("world.txt");
if (file1.exists() && file2.exists()) {
    try {
        InputStream is1 = file1.getContents();
        InputStream is2 = file2.getContents();
        IFile file3 = project.getFile("helloWorld.txt");
        // force=false, no ProgressMonitor
        file3.create(is1, false, null);
        // force=false, keepHistory=true, no ProgressMonitor
        file3.appendContents(is2, false, true, null);
    } catch (CoreException e) {
        e.printStackTrace();
    }
}
```

Markers

As I demonstrated in the section "Tasks and Markers" in Chapter 1, Eclipse offers the option of attaching annotations to resources. The interface `IMarker` describes a general interface for creating and managing such annotations. However, it is not expected that programmers implement this interface. Instead, `IMarker` instances are obtained via the `IResource` method `createMarker()`. This method accepts a string describing the marker type as a parameter. Eclipse already defines five standard marker types:

`org.eclipse.core.resources.marker`	Generic marker type
`org.eclipse.core.resources.taskmarker`	Markers for tasks
`org.eclipse.core.resources.problemmarker`	Markers for problems
`org.eclipse.core.resources.bookmark`	Markers for book marks
`org.eclipse.core.resources.textmarker`	Other text markers

Each `IMarker` instance has an identifier that uniquely identifies the marker within a resource. You can obtain this identification via the method `getID()`. In addition, you may equip any marker with an arbitrary number of attributes. Each attribute must be identified uniquely via a name and has a value of type `boolean`, `int`, `String`, or `Object`. With `setAttribute()` and `getAttribute()` you can set and retrieve such attributes individually. With `setAttributes()` and `getAttributes()` you can set and retrieve all attributes of a marker in one operation. Eclipse predefines the following standard attributes: `CHAR_START`, `CHAR_END`, `DONE`, `LINE_NUMBER`, `LOCATION`, `MESSAGE`, `PRIORITY`, `SEVERITY`, `TRANSIENT`, and `USER_EDITABLE`. In the case of `PRIORITY`, you can choose between the attribute values `PRIORITY_HIGH` and `PRIORITY_LOW`, and in the case of `SEVERITY`, you can choose between the attribute values `SEVERITY_INFO`, `SEVERITY_WARNING`, and `SEVERITY_ERROR`.

Shortly I will discuss how plug-ins can be configured. During this configuration it is possible to declare your own marker types and to construct marker hierarchies in which child marker types inherit attributes from ancestor marker types. For this reason, the `IMarker` interface provides the method `isSubtypeOf()`, which allows you to query the inheritance relationships between marker types.

You can declare individual marker types as persistent in the plug-in configuration. Such markers live across sessions. Normally, you would use persistent markers to implement end-user–created task markers. Problem markers, in contrast, will usually be updated when a resource is opened. Nevertheless, it can make sense to make problem markers persistent, too. This allows the Package Explorer to decorate the corresponding resource with a problem indicator.

Reacting to Resource Changes

In some cases, it may be necessary for an application to react to changes of workspace resources caused by other plug-ins. This is particularly true when the currently opened resources depend in some way on the modified resource, or when the end user reverts the currently opened resources to a previous version via the Replace… function.

If you want to react to such changes, you must implement the interface IResourceChangeListener and register an instance of this interface with the workspace. First you need a workspace instance, which you get from the resources plug-in:

```
IWorkspace workspace = ResourcesPlugin.getWorkspace();
```

Then you can register an IResourceChangeListener with the IWorkspace instance:

```
IResourceChangeListener listener = new IResourceChangeListener() {
    public void resourceChanged(IResourceChangeEvent event) {
        System.out.println("A resource was changed!");
    }
};
workspace.addResourceChangeListener(listener);
```

Since changes to resources happen frequently, and consequently create some overhead, you should deregister the listener as soon as possible via the method removeResourceChangeListener(). ResourceChangeListener should work as effectively as possible to avoid performance problems.

The interface IResourceChangeListener features only the single method resourceChanged(), which accepts IResourceChangeEvent objects. Using the method getType() you can get information about the type of event. Normally, you would want to react to events of type POST_CHANGE. When registering an IResourceChangeListener, you can optionally specify an event mask, so that the listener method is invoked only for the selected event types.

IResourceChangeEvent objects do not necessarily represent a single resource change but possibly a whole series of resource changes. All of these changes are represented in the form of an IResourceDelta instance, which forms the root node of an IResourceDelta tree. This tree mirrors the resource tree in the Eclipse workspace but contains only the modified resources and their parent containers. All of these resources are represented as IResourceDelta instances. To analyze all these changes you must therefore walk through the entire tree. For this purpose, IResourceDelta offers the accept() method, to which you may pass an IResourceDeltaVisitor instance. The visit() method of this instance is then called for each node of the tree. (However, if you are interested in only a single resource, the method findMember() offers a quicker way to get there.)

Usually, you would first retrieve the kind of change (ADDED, REMOVED, CHANGED) for the specific resource delta in the visitor's accept() method. This can be done with the IResourceDelta method getKind(). With getFlags() you can obtain details, for example, whether the contents or the type of the resource was changed or whether, in the case of REMOVED, the resource was deleted or moved to another location. In the latter case, you can obtain the new location via getMovedToPath(). The corresponding resource instance is obtained via the method getResource().

If you want to represent such resource changes in the user interface, you have to be cautious. The resourceChanged() method does not necessarily run in the SWT thread. The required changes in the GUI must therefore by wrapped into a suitable Display method such as asyncExec() or syncExec(). In the previous example application (see "The Player Module" section in Chapter 10), I showed you how this is done.

In addition, you should be aware of the fact that all resources are locked against modification while the resourceChanged() method is active, to avoid avalanches and loops. The event types PRE_AUTO_BUILD and POST_AUTO_BUILD are excluded from this rule, however.

I will leave this short overview about resource changes at this stage. If you are interested in details, you should refer to the excellent article about resource changes by John Arthorne in the Eclipse Corner (www.eclipse.org). However, some of the details in this article do not apply to Eclipse 3, since in Eclipse 3 Auto-Build processes can run asynchronously in the background.

Managing Long-Running Processes

Since version 3, Eclipse supports the asynchronous execution of long-running processes in the background. Since such processes are typically related to the Eclipse workspace, it is the workspace plug-in that provides adequate support.

In particular, the IWorkspace method run() is used to start a long-running process, which must be implemented in the form of an IWorkspaceRunnable. The run() method of IWorkspaceRunnable is executed when the process is started, and an IProgressMonitor instance (see the section "Monitoring Long-Running Processes") is passed to it.

However, managing asynchronous processes can be tricky, since several of these processes can be active at the same time and may influence each other by modifying shared resources. To avoid conflicts, you can specify scheduling rules (ISchedulingRule) with each IWorkspaceRunnable. When a process is started and its scheduling rule conflicts with the scheduling rules of the other processes already running, it fails.

When a long-running process modifies resources, it will notify IResourceChangeListener (see the previous section) about these changes. Other than in Eclipse 2 where all changes were collected until the process had finished and were posted in one event, long-running processes in Eclipse 3 will by default periodically notify listeners about resource changes.

Configuring Plug-ins

After a look into the basics of the Eclipse resource management, it's now time to turn your attention to creating plug-ins. You will discover that some things here are quite different from the creation of independent Java applications. First, you must define how the plug-in is embedded into the Eclipse workbench. For example, you may need to add additional editors and views to the workbench as well as new menus and tool items to the workbench's menu and toolbar. The debugging phase of a plug-in is also different than that of a conventional application: to test a plug-in, you must start a second Eclipse platform under which the test plug-in is executed. In the meantime, the first workbench controls the execution of the debug process.

The Plug-in Development Perspective

To support this development process, Eclipse provides a special perspective. Of course, it is possible to create plug-ins under the Java perspective, but the Plug-in Development perspective makes life much easier (Figure 11.3). In the same way, as shown in the section "The First Application: Hello World" in Chapter 1, you can open the Plug-in Development perspective with the Open Perspective tool button.

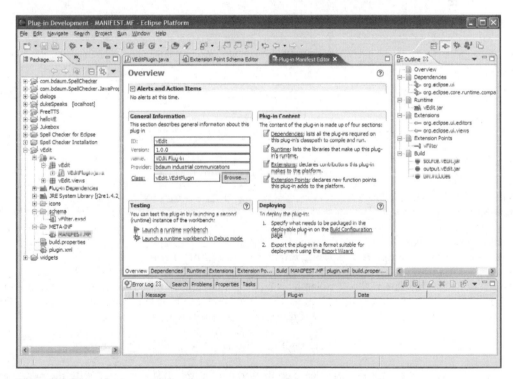

Figure 11.3

In addition to the familiar components from the Java perspective, this perspective features a browser for installed plug-ins, a window for showing the properties of selected items, and (under the Tasks window) windows for the error log file and the Java console. The last two windows are important for debugging: the error messages produced by the plug-in being tested are shown there.

A special function in the Plug-in Development perspective is the wizard for the creation of new plug-in development projects. Click the New button, and then select the Plug-in Project shortcut (instead of Java). On the following wizard pages, enter the project name and leave all other entries at their default value. Finally, you get to the selection of the plug-in template (Figure 11.4).

Figure 11.4

Several templates are available for creating a new plug-in. All of these templates result in plug-ins that can be immediately executed and tested. Try some of these templates and look at the generated code to learn about the construction of the standard plug-in types!

Select an appropriate template depending on your requirements. For example, if your planned plug-in is based on a text editor, select the Plug-in template *with an editor*. By removing the check mark from the Create a Plug-in with One of the Templates option, you can create a minimal plug-in containing just the Plugin class and the manifest file plugin.xml, which you can build on later. Once you press Finish, the necessary folder structures and files of the new plug-in are created.

You can invoke this plug-in immediately via Run > Run as... > Run-time Workbench.

After a while, a second workbench appears on the screen (Figure 11.5), equipped with the new plug-in to be tested. Of course, there is currently nothing to debug—you first have to add a few custom functions to the new plug-in. In the following sections I will call this workbench the Test Platform and the workbench from which we started the new workbench the Development Platform. I will also call them by the nicknames Little Eclipse and Big Eclipse. The following figure shows the workbench with a newly created plug-in. Besides the windows that are usually present in the Resource Perspective (Navigator, Outline, Tasks), there is a large empty space that may eventually be filled by the new plug-in.

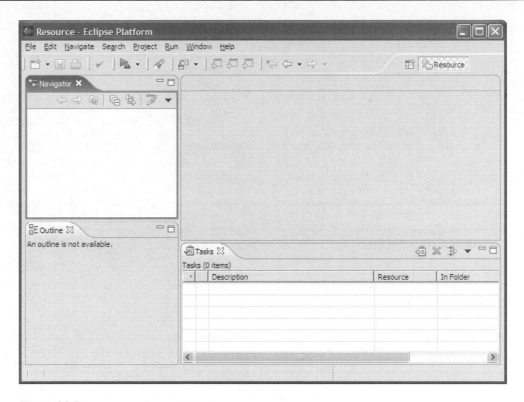

Figure 11.5

One more word about the debug process: since the invocation of a new workbench requires time, the debugging process can become a bit tiresome at times. Fortunately, however, Eclipse supports hot swapping: while the test platform is running, you can modify the plug-in code in the development platform and recompile it using the Save function. These changes are carried through to the test platform. You can therefore avoid stopping and restarting the test platform in many cases. However, hot swapping works only in Debug mode, not in Run mode, and requires at least JRE 1.4.0.

The Plug-in Manifest

Now, let's close the test platform and return to the development platform. In Figure 11.6, you see the overview of the plug-in manifest plugin.xml. This file is the central instance for plug-in development. It controls how the plug-in is embedded into the workbench and controls the assembly of the plug-in from its components. The file extension .xml indicates that this file is stored in XML format. For your minimal plug-in, the source of this file should look similar to Listing 11.1.

```
<?xml version="1.0" encoding="UTF-8"?>
<?eclipse version="3.0"?>
<plugin
    id="vEdit"
    name="VEdit Plug-in"
    version="1.0.0"
```

Listing 11.1 (Continues)

```
    provider-name=""
    class="vEdit.VEditPlugin">
    <runtime>
        <library name="vEdit.jar">
            <export name="*"/>
        </library>
    </runtime>
    <requires>
        <import plugin="org.eclipse.ui"/>
        <import plugin="org.eclipse.core.runtime.compatibility"/>
    </requires>
</plugin>
```

Listing 11.1 (Continued)

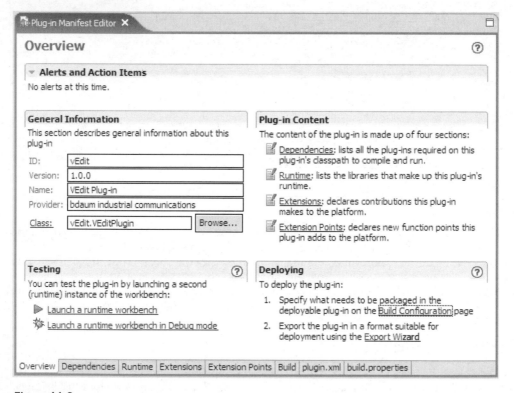

Figure 11.6

However, only in rare cases do you need to edit the raw XML source code. It is much easier to edit this file with the manifest editor. The various sections of the manifest file are distributed over several editor pages.

The Overview Page

This page (shown in Figure 11.6) provides a summary of the most important properties of the plug-in. In addition, this page serves as a central point for testing and deploying a plug-in. With the hyperlinks in the Testing section, you can start a test platform in Run or Debug mode. In the Deploying section, you can determine what goes into a deployment, and you can start deployment by invoking the Export Wizard. I described this wizard in detail in the section "The Plug-in Development Perspective."

All the information from the other pages is repeated here in condensed form. Clicking one of the More… buttons leads to a more detailed page.

The Dependencies Page

This page lists all the plug-ins that are required to successfully execute the current plug-in. For your minimal plug-in there are only two: the plug-in `org.eclipse.core.runtime.compatibility` and the plug-in for the user interface, `org.eclipse.ui`. You can easily add other plug-ins to the list with the Add button. For example, if you want to provide end-user help functions within your plug-in, you would add the help-related plug-ins such as `org.eclipse.help`. As soon as you save the manifest file (via Ctrl+S), the JAR files of these plug-ins appear in the Package Browser. Your own classes and interfaces can now use the classes and interfaces contained in these JAR files.

On the right-hand side of the Dependencies page you can make further specifications for a selected plug-in. For example, you can specify that the dependency from the selected plug-in also becomes visible for plug-ins using the current plug-in (Reexport the Dependency). In addition, you can specify rules for selecting a specific version of the required plug-in, and you can declare a dependency as optional. You can search for cyclic dependencies, for plug-ins that refer to your current plug-in, and for unused dependencies.

The Runtime Page

All the JAR files that contain binaries of the current plug-in (`.class` files, `.properties` files, etc.) and that belong to the plug-in's Classpath are declared on this page in the Run-time Libraries section. The first archive, named `projectname.jar`, is already pregenerated here.

In the Library Exporting section you can specify Export rules for each archive. The classes and interfaces of an exported archive are visible to foreign plug-ins; other archives are private to the current plug-in.

Finally, in the Plug-in Activation section you can generate an OSGi manifest, MANIFEST.MF, for plug-ins that are targeted at Eclipse 3 platforms only. Once such a manifest is generated, you can add activation rules to improve the performance.

The Extensions Page

This page provides an overview of the extension points used by the current plug-in. Since your minimal plug-in offers no functionality at all, this page is empty. You can add new functionality such as editors, views, menu items, or tool buttons to your plug-in with the Add button. When you do, you obtain a list of the extension points currently installed in the platform. All of these extension points are described with the help of Extension Point Schemas that augment the completion of the extension definition. If a plug-in symbol is decorated with a magic wand, additional templates are defined for this extension point. When you select such an extension point, the templates will appear in the Available Templates section (a synopsis of these templates is found on the Extension Wizards page). When you select such a template, Eclipse will pregenerate large parts of the new extension. Otherwise, without the help of the template, you would have to write most of the classes generated by the wizard by yourself.

I will discuss these extension points shortly in more detail in "The Most Important SDK Extension Points."

The Extension Points Page

On this page you can define which extension points the current plug-in provides for other plug-ins. By specifying such extension points, you can prepare your plug-in for later extensions (even from third parties). You can specify a new extension point with the Add button.

You need to specify three values:

❑ **Extension Point ID.** Here you must specify an identification that is unique within the scope of the current plug-in. Other plug-ins may refer to the extension point by specifying its fully qualified extension point ID (that is, the ID defined in the manifest prefixed with the plug-in ID). For example, if you specify the extension point `vFilter` within the plug-in `vEdit`, other plug-ins may refer to this extension point via the ID `vEdit.vFilter`.

Since larger plug-ins may define hundreds or even thousands of extension points, you should avoid very long identification strings. Short identifications are processed faster and need fewer resources.

❑ **Extension Point Name.** The name of an extension point used for display purposes, such as `Video Effect Filter`.

❑ **Extension Point Schema.** Finally, you need to provide a schema for each defined extension point. This schema will guide the user of the extension point and prompt for the required parameters when configuring a plug-in. Here, you may specify an existing schema or enter the name of a new schema. For the previous example, Eclipse will suggest the schema `schema/vFilter.exsd`.

After you specify these three values, the Schema Editor can be started automatically. Later, I will discuss the Schema Editor in detail.

The Build Page

This page lets you define the configuration file `build.properties`. The source code of this file is contained on the `build.properties` page. I discussed this page in more detail previously in the section "The Plug-in Development Perspective."

The Most Important SDK Extension Points

As I have already mentioned, all components of the Eclipse SDK are implemented as plug-ins. You can use this functionality in your own plug-in by using the extension points of the existing plug-ins, or you can add your own plug-in to an existing plug-in.

Schema-Based Extension Points

When using the wizard for schema-based extension points, you should acquaint yourself about the particular extension point. All extension points defined in the Eclipse SDK are documented in detail under Help > Help Contents > Platform Developer Guide > Reference > Extensions Points Reference. For third-party plug-ins, however, you need the corresponding documentation from the plug-in's manufacturer.

In the manifest editor, go to the Extensions page, press the Add button, and select an extension point, such as `org.eclipse.ui.editors`. After you click the Finish button, the selected extension appears in the All Extensions section. In the Extension Element Details area, you can optionally define your own identification and a name for the new extension.

The schema belonging to the extension point will now guide you through the definition of the new extension.

1.   Select the extension `org.eclipse.ui.editors` and invoke the context function New > Editor. In the Extension Element Details area, you will now see all the parameters of the new editor. Identification and Name are already predefined, as shown in Figure 11.7.

2.   Now you need only apply the right entries at the right places of the Extension Element Details area. Let's begin with the attribute `class`. Here you enter the name of the class that implements the new editor. This can be the name of an existing class (use the Browse button to select one). In most cases, however, you will enter the name of a not-yet-existent class (click the Class hyperlink). In this case, Eclipse generates a stub for the new class. Here, this is a subclass of the abstract class `EditorPart`.

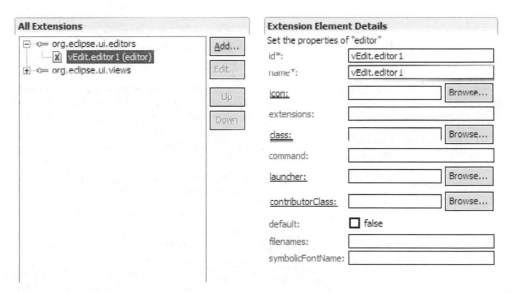

Figure 11.7

Java Classes

Most extension points have attributes that require the specification of Java classes. These classes must be specified with their fully qualified name. You may even prefix this name with a plug-in identification separated by a slash so that you can call classes from other plug-ins. If the specified class implements the interface `IExecutableExtension`, you can even append—separated by a colon—initialization data. This data can be retrieved with the `IExecutableExtension` method `setInitializationData()`. In particular, views and editors implement this interface.

In the case of the editor extension, there are three attributes that demand the specification of a Java class: `class`, `contributorClass`, and `launcher`. The other parameters consist of Boolean values, character strings, or file paths. You can find a description of all these parameters in the help section Platform Developer Guide > Reference > Extensions Points Reference > Workbench > org.eclipse.ui.editors. Later I'll take a closer look at the editors of the Eclipse SDK.

GUI Extension Points

In the following table I have listed the most important extension points for creating user interfaces. For a complete listing, see the help section Platform Developer Guide > Reference > Extensions.

`~.core.runtime.applications`	This extension can be used to define entry points into an application. Usually this is the Eclipse IDE, but for applications running on the Eclipse Rich Client Platform (see Chapter 14) different entry points must be specified. These entry points are specified in the element `application/run` in the attribute `class` and must be a class of type `IPlatformRunnable`. In addition, you may specify one or several `parameter` child elements in element `run`.
`~.core.runtime.products`	With this extension point you can define one or several product descriptions for products that are implemented with the current plug-in. Each product is identified by the `id` attribute of the `extension` element. When the software is deployed, a product is selected by specifying a product identification in the file `config.ini` (see the section "Advanced Product Customization" in Chapter 14).
	Each extension may define a product in a static or dynamic way. When using the static method, you specify the product name, the application (see above), and the description as attributes of the element `product`. Furthermore, additional `property` child elements consisting of name/value pairs may be specified. The definitions made here correlate (and complete or replace) the definitions made in file about.ini (see the section "Customizing Products" in Chapter 12).

	In case of the dynamic method, you specify an `IProductProvider` class in the `provider` element. This class would deliver `IProduct` product descriptions at runtime.
`~.ui.actionSets` `~.ui.actionSetPartAssociations`	`actionSets` defines actions and action groups. An `action` in Eclipse is an abstract user action. This action can appear in various presentations such as menus, menu items, or tools buttons on a toolbar (see the "Actions" section). End users can activate or deactivate individual action groups. `actionSetPartAssociations` can assign action groups to selected components of the workbench. If that component is no longer active, the corresponding actions vanish from the menu and the toolbar.
`~.ui.activities`	This extension point allows defining specific user activities such as Java Development or Plug-in Development. Each activity can correlate with a set of workbench plug-ins. Only if the end user activates an activity the correlated plug-ins will become visible in the workbench. Activities may rely on other activities, so that if one activity is activated, the other required activities are activated as well.

`~.ui.cheatsheets.`
    `cheatSheetContent`
`~.ui.cheatsheets.`
    `cheatSheetItemExtension`
	`cheatSheetContent` allows the declaration of Cheat Sheets that can be invoked by the end user under Help > Cheat Sheets.... Later in this chapter I will discuss how Cheat Sheets are authored. `cheatSheetItemExtension` supports the definition of GUI controls for Cheat Sheets.

`~.ui.commands`	In Eclipse a command is an abstract user command without a defined semantic. To each command you can attach one or several keyboard shortcuts (`keyBinding`). Many of these keyboard shortcuts are already predefined in the manifest file `org.eclipse.ui_3.0.0/plugin.xml`. The correlation between commands and actions (see above) happens via the ID of the command. This ID must be identical with the `definitionID` of the corresponding action.
	It is possible to restrict the scope of such a correlation. Besides predefined `scopes` (global, text editor, Java editor), it is also possible to define custom scopes.
	Keyboard shortcuts can be assigned for specific configurations. You can use one of the predefined configurations (Standard, Emacs) or provide your own `keyConfiguration`.

	Finally, you can assign the individual commands to existing or new categories to organize them into groups on the preferences page (Window > Preferences > Workbench > Keys).
`~.ui.dropActions`	`dropActions` define possible drag-and-drop actions between the components of the workbench. By specifying a `dropAction` and implementing an `IDropActionDelegate`, existing components can be converted into transfer targets. A generic transfer format is provided by the class `PluginTransferData` with the corresponding transfer type `PluginTransfer` (see also the section "Drag and Drop" in Chapter 8). More details can be found in the article "Drag and Drop in the Eclipse UI" by John Arthorne on www.eclipse.org.
`~.ui.editors` `~.ui.editorActions`	The extension point `editors` adds new editors to the workbench. Here you can build on the standard text editor implementation contained in the Eclipse SDK. You also use this extension point to invoke external editors. With `editorActions` you can equip existing editors with additional actions such as menu items or tool buttons (discussed later in this chapter).
`~.ui.editors.templates`	With this extension point you can add templates (see "Automatic Code Completion" in Chapter 2) to editors. Templates can be associated with specific contexts. An example for this extension point is found in the manifest `plugin.xml` of plug-in `org.eclipse.jdt.ui`.
`~.ui.exportWizards` `~.ui.importWizards`	These extension points allow you to add new choice points into the Import and Export wizards.
`~.ui.ide.markerHelp` `~.ui.ide.markerResolution`	`markerHelp` allows you to attach help texts to markers, such as problems or tasks. With the extension point `markerResolution` you can attach a `MarkerResolutionGenerator` to markers. These generators are used to generate correction suggestions (QuickFix).
`~.ui.ide.resourceFilters`	This extension point allows you to equip views displaying resources (such as the Navigator View) with additional file filters.

`~.ui.intro`	This extension point defines in its `intro` elements classes that are responsible for creating and managing the Eclipse Welcome Screen. These classes must subclass the class `IntroPart`. Several of these elements are possible to support product customization. In `introProductBinding` elements these `intro` elements can be bound to specific product identifications. An example is found in Chapter 15.
`~.ui.newWizards`	This extension point allows you to add new choice points to the New Wizard.
`~.ui.perspectives` `~.ui.perspectiveExtensions`	The extension point `perspectives` is used to define new workbench perspectives. The class specified here defines the initial layout of the perspective. The extension point `perspectiveExtensions` allows you to add additional components to existing perspectives.
`~.ui.popupMenus`	This extension point allows you to add new menu items to existing context menus.
`~.ui.preferencePages`	This extension point allows you to add new pages to the workbench's Preferences.
`~.ui.propertyPages`	This extension point allows you to define new pages in the Properties dialog box. This is the dialog that appears when you invoke the context function Properties for a selected resource.
`~.ui.ide.resourceFilters`	This extension point allows you to equip views that display resources (such as the Navigator View) with additional file filters.
`~.ui.startup`	This extension point allows you to specify the plug-ins that should be started when the platform is started.
`~.ui.themes`	This extension point allows you to influence the appearance of the user interface. In particular, it is possible to modify the default colors and fonts for particular uses (text, background, etc.)
`~.ui.views` `~.ui.viewActions`	The extension point `views` allows you to add new views to the workbench. The extension point `viewActions` enables new actions, such as menu items and tool buttons (discussed later), to be added to existing views.

`~.ui.workingSets`	This extension point allows you to create new wizards for the definition of working sets. Working sets are used in various views such as the Navigator to restrict the displayed set of resources. Eclipse understands several working set types. For each type you can define your own wizard.

`~.help.base.browser`
`~.help.base.luceneAnalyzer`
`~.help.contentProducer`
`~.help.contexts`
`~.help.toc`
	The extension point `browser` can be used to specify a browser for displaying the HTML help texts.
	
	Eclipse uses Apache's Lucene engine for indexing help texts. With the extension point `luceneAnalyzer` you can equip Lucene with a custom program for text analysis.
	
	The extension point `contentProducer` is used to provide dynamic help content that is generated at runtime.
	
	The extension point `contexts` allows you to define context-sensitive help for the current plug-in.
	
	The extension point `toc` specifies a help text table of contents for the current plug-in.

`~.search.searchPages` `~.search.searchResultSorters`	The extension point `searchPages` allows you to add additional pages to the search dialog in order to support specialized search operations. With the extension point `searchResultSorters` you can define specific sort strategies for the search results.

A documentation of all schema-based extension points defined in the Eclipse SDK is found under Help > Help Contents > Platform Plug-in Developers Guide > Reference > Extension Points Reference.

Extension Point Templates

Predefined templates are available for some extension points. These templates offer very extensive configuration possibilities and can generate almost complete applications or function groups, saving you a lot of coding. Figure 11.8 shows how templates can be accessed.

First, you select an extension point equipped with templates, say `org.eclipse.ui.views`, then a template from the list, say Sample View. On the following wizard pages (Figures 11.9 and 11.10) you can configure this view according to your requirements.

In Figure 11.9 the Sample View component is configured. The package name and the class of the view implementation are specified. Specifying a View Category Id allows you to combine several views into groups when they are displayed under the function Window > Show View. Finally, you can determine the contents of a view—either a table or a tree—and whether you want to add the view to the Resource perspective. I will discuss workbench views in more detail later in this chapter.

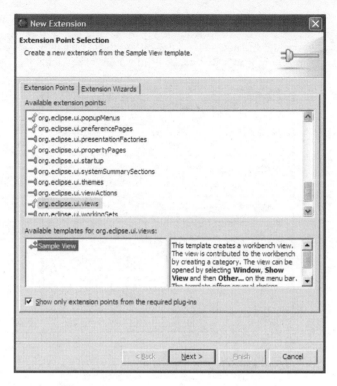

Figure 11.8

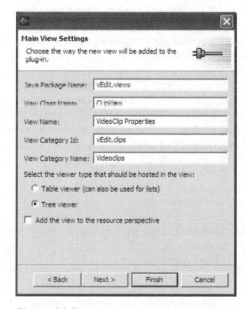

Figure 11.9

After you enter all the options and press the Finish button, the necessary classes and packages are generated, and the necessary entries are added to the manifest file plugin.xml. In this case, these are entries for the new category and the new view. After saving these files (Ctrl+S), you can execute the plug-in immediately by invoking Run > Run as... > Run-time Workbench.

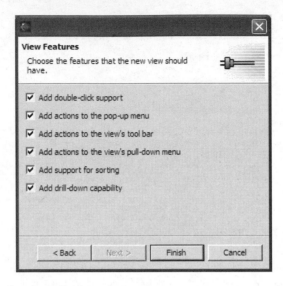

Figure 11.10

On the third wizard page you can specify additional options for the new view. I will discuss actions in the Actions section and event processing in the section "Event Processing in the Eclipse Workbench."

First, the new view is invisible (if you did not check the option Add the View to the Resource Perspective). With the function Window > Show View > Other... you can select the new view in the Videoclips category and open it.

This gives you a relatively well-instrumented tree-based view, as shown in Figure 11.11. What remains is to equip this view with an application-specific domain model. Template-based extension points thus offer the possibility of producing premanufactured application components with just a few mouse clicks. Instead of having to hunt through dozens of APIs, you can obtain well-functioning code that you need only modify according to your requirements.

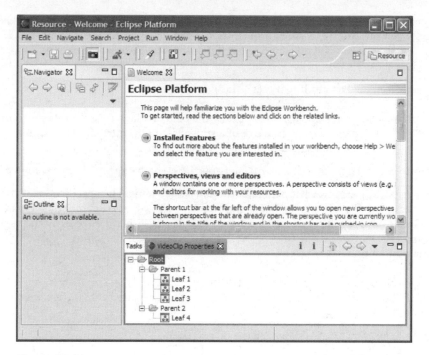

Figure 11.11

The Schema Editor

If you want to define your own extension points (as discussed previously), it makes sense to define schemas with these extension points, too. These schemas can guide programmers through the specification of extension point parameters, as you have already had seen in the section "The Most Important SDK Extension Points."

Eclipse uses a subset of the XML Schema language to define such schemas. In some respects, however, such as namespace usage or the spelling of some tags, the dialect used in Eclipse differs from the standard defined by the World Wide Web Consortium (W3C). For this reason, Eclipse schemas have the file extension .exsd instead of the usual .xsd extension.

Fortunately, Eclipse provides a Schema Editor that you can use to create schemas without detailed knowledge of the schema language syntax. With the help of this schema editor, you can easily create arbitrarily complex descriptions of extension points.

Schema Elements

A schema consists of one or several named *elements*. In addition, it is possible to decorate these elements with *attributes*. Elements are first defined independently of each other in the left-hand part of the

Schema Editor. Here you must specify the name of each element. You can also add icons to them. Under Label Attribute you can specify which of the element's attributes specifies the display label of the element.

Attributes

You have the choice between attribute types (Kind):

❑ An attribute of type `java` will later specify the path of a Java class. In this case, you should specify the full path of an interface or of a superclass in the attribute `BasedOn`. Eclipse can later use this information to generate the method stubs of such a class.

❑ An attribute of type `resource` will later specify the path of a workspace resource.

❑ An attribute of type `string` will later contain a data value. The specification "string" is a bit misleading at this point. In fact, this attribute type allows two different data types: Boolean attributes (`boolean`) can accept the values true and false, and string attributes (`string`) can accept any character string. It is possible to restrict the possible values by specifying an enumeration under `Restriction`.

Under the `Use` entry, you can determine whether the attribute must be specified (`required`) or is optional. In addition, you can specify a default value in the `Value` entry if you specified the value `default` under the `Use` entry.

Schema Structure

If you defined several elements, you must organize them into a tree structure. This is done in the right-hand part of the Schema Editor (see Figure 11.12). Each schema must consist of a single root element—the first element in the element list in the left-hand-side window of the editor—to which the other elements are connected directly or indirectly.

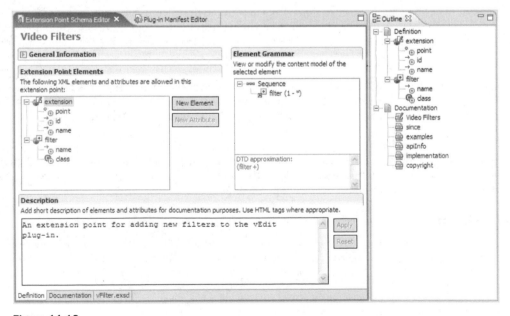

Figure 11.12

Each element within this tree represents either a tree node with child elements or a leaf node. For each tree node with child elements, you can specify a branching type by selecting from four connectors:

❑ **Sequence.** This connector organizes its child nodes into an ordered list. Schema instances must follow the sequence of child nodes in this node.

❑ **All.** This connector organizes the child nodes in an unordered list. Schema instances may use a different order of child nodes as specified for this node.

❑ **Choice.** This connector describes an alternative. In a concrete instance of the schema, only one child node from the Choice list must be specified.

❑ **Group.** This connector is not available in the W3C standard and seems to be quite superfluous. Sequence, All, and Choice are sufficient for the construction of schema trees.

All of these connectors can be nested to an arbitrary depth. In addition, you may specify a repetition factor for each connector and each element. You can specify a lower bound (minOccurs) and an upper bound (maxOccurs) for repetitions. By specifying minOccurs="0" you can define optional tree nodes. If a node can be repeated without an upper bound, you can specify maxOccurs="unbounded".

The previous figure shows the schema editor with the opened schema file vFilter.exsd. At the left you see a list of XML elements with their attributes. The window on the right shows the child elements for the element extension. The Description window at the bottom allows you to specify element-specific and attribute-specific documentation. You can enter additional documentation on the Documentation page.

New Schema File

When you create a new schema file (File > New > Other > Plug-in Development > Extension Point Schema), the wizard first prompts you for four values:

❑ The ID of the plug-in for which the schema file is created

❑ The ID of the extension point relative to the plug-in

❑ The name of the extension point for display purposes

❑ The name of the new schema file

The new schema file already contains the root element extension with the attributes point, id, and name. You will usually leave this element unmodified, since it only describes general properties of the extension point. Application-specific elements are created by pressing New Element and then connecting the new element directly or indirectly to the root element.

Documentation

The Schema Editor is able to generate an HTML reference document from the defined schema. You can get a preview of this document with the context function Preview Reference Document.

Components of the Eclipse User Interface

Applications written as Eclipse plug-ins that want to use the Eclipse user interface (UI) will in one form or the other use components of the Eclipse UI as clients. These components are deployed in the plug-ins that begin with `org.eclipse.ui`. You can use all of these components in your own programs as long as they are not contained in packages with the name part "internal."

The Eclipse UI consists on the one hand of plug-ins that provide a certain infrastructure such as the support for forms (discussed next) and for Cheat Sheets (discussed later) and on the other hand of plug-ins that implement the workbench itself (discussed previously). In addition, there are the plug-ins for the help system (see the section "The Help System"). The workbench itself is divided into a generic, resource-independent part and an IDE-specific part that relates to the components of the Eclipse Workspace. All resource-dependent plug-ins and packages have the name part "ide." These parts cannot be used in the context of the Rich Client Platform (see Chapter 14).

Forms

Eclipse 2 already had components for a forms-based user interface, but these components were used only internally for implementing the manifest and schema editors. With Eclipse 3 this functionality has been packaged into the separate plug-in `org.eclipse.ui.forms` and the API was published. Application programmers have now a powerful means of creating forms-based views and editors. An example is found in Chapter 15.

Basics

Forms mostly use SWT GUI elements, which we have already discussed in Chapter 8. However, these elements are configured in a different way, and additional elements have been added (such as two new layout managers and a hyperlink element). Since the correct configuration is essential for the consistent construction of a form, you should refrain from creating SWT GUI elements using constructors when using them for a form. Instead, the forms plug-in provides via its `FormToolkit` class various factory methods. In Listing 11.2 you will see how the working area of a view (see the "Views" section) can be filled with a form.

```
public void createPartControl(Composite parent) {
    // Create FormToolkit instance
    toolkit = new FormToolkit(parent.getDisplay());
    // Create ScrolledForm instance
    form = toolkit.createScrolledForm(parent);
    // Create title
    form.setText("Forms in Eclipse");
    // Use a Gridlayout with two columns
    GridLayout layout = new GridLayout(2, false);
    // Fetch the form's container with getBody()
    // (Composite)
    form.getBody().setLayout(layout);
    // Create Hyperlink and add Listener
    Hyperlink link = toolkit.createHyperlink(form.getBody(),
        "I want a click!", SWT.WRAP);
    GridData gd = new GridData();
    gd.horizontalSpan = 2;
    link.setLayoutData(gd);
```

Listing 11.2 (Continues)

```
      link.addHyperlinkListener(new HyperlinkAdapter() {
        public void linkActivated(HyperlinkEvent e) {
          System.out.println("Hyperlink was activated!");
        }
      });
      // Create Label
      Label label1 = toolkit.createLabel(form.getBody(),
                                   "Input field 1:");
      // Create text element and place behind label
      Text text1 = toolkit.createText(form.getBody(), "Default text");
      text1.setLayoutData(new GridData(GridData.FILL_HORIZONTAL));
      // Create Label
      Label label2 = toolkit.createLabel(form.getBody(),
                                   "Input field 2:");
      // Create text element with right alignment
      Text text2 = new Text(form.getBody(), SWT.RIGHT);
      // and adapt to forms conventions
      toolkit.adapt(text2, true, true);
      text2.setText("475");
      text2.setLayoutData(new GridData(GridData.FILL_HORIZONTAL));
      // Enforce a tree border instead of a text border
      text2.setData(FormToolkit.KEY_DRAW_BORDER,
                                   FormToolkit.TREE_BORDER);
      // Create button
      Button button = toolkit.createButton(form.getBody(),
                            "check me", SWT.CHECK);
      gd = new GridData();
      gd.horizontalSpan = 2;
      button.setLayoutData(gd);
      // Make sure that borders are drawn on all platforms
      toolkit.paintBordersFor(form.getBody());
  }
```

Listing 11.2 (Continued)

Here I have demonstrated quite a few techniques. First, I created a ScrolledForm, that is, a form that shows a scrollbar when space becomes scarce. If you don't want scrollbars, just use the class Form. Here I have used a GridLayout in the usual way. I have added a Hyperlink element and defined some event processing. Hyperlinks behave just like normal buttons (pushbuttons) but look like text (as a matter of fact, they can be equipped with images, too). The Hyperlink, the following Labels, and the first Text object are all created with the factory methods of the FormToolkit. The Composite contained in the ScrolledForm is specified as a parent container. This container can be retrieved via the method getBody(). For a change, I have created the second Text object in usual way via its constructor. In this case, it was necessary to call the FormToolkit method adapt() for this object to configure it according to the forms standards. For this Text object I have also enforced a different border style. Since borders are not drawn natively on some platforms, I have made sure by calling the method paintBordersFor() that the borders are drawn by the FormToolkit itself with the help of a PaintListener.

Figure 11.13 shows how the form looks. If you reduce the size of the window sufficiently, scrollbars will appear automatically.

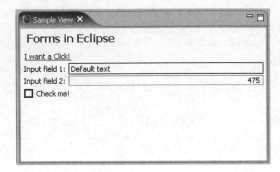

Figure 11.13

Layouts

The forms package provides two additional layout classes that are better suited to the specific requirement of a form than the standard layouts from the SWT plug-in.

TableWrapLayout

Using a GridLayout for forms has a disadvantage: long labels and hyperlinks are not wrapped if space becomes scarce. To solve this problem, the class TableWrapLayout was introduced. This layout manager works similarly to the GridLayout (see the section "The GridLayout Class" in Chapter 8), except that it is able to wrap long elements. TableWrapLayout cooperates with the class TableWrapData with which you can configure the single GUI elements within a layout. For the layout algorithms, the class TableWrapLayout follows the W3C recommendations for the layout of tables in HTML pages.

ColumnLayout

Another new layout manager is the class ColumnLayout. This class works similarly to a vertical RowLayout (see section "The RowLayout Class" in Chapter 8) but is able to distribute its elements dynamically into several columns, keeping these columns at approximately the same height. You can specify a minimum and maximum number of columns for a ColumnLayout. The default is one to three columns. A good example for ColumnLayout is the Overview page in the manifest editor (see "The Plug-in Manifest" section).

Collapsible GUI Elements

Two classes enable the end user to collapse and expand parts of a form: ExpandableComposite and Section.

ExpandableComposite

Instances of class ExpandableComposite are created in the usual way with the factory class FormToolkit and are used as a container for collapsible contents:

```
ExpandableComposite ec = toolkit.createExpandableComposite(form
                    .getBody(), ExpandableComposite.TREE_NODE);
```

Such an `ExpandableComposite` has a control element for collapsing and expanding it, and usually it has a title line, too.

```
ec.setText("This is the title");
```

Clicking the title line has the same effect as clicking the control element. The behavior and the appearance of an `ExpandableComposite` can be influenced with the following style constants:

TREE_NODE	The control element looks like the control element of a tree node (+).
TWISTIE	A small triangle is used as a control element.
EXPANDED	The `ExpandableComposite` is initially in an expanded state.
COMPACT	The size of the content is considered only for computing the width of the `ExpandableComposite` when it is expanded.
NO_TITLE	The title line is not displayed.
TITLE_BAR	The background of the title line is filled with decoration.
FOCUS_TITLE	The title line can get the focus.
CLIENT_INDENT	The content of the `ExpandableComposite` is left-aligned with the title line.

Its content is assigned to an `ExpandableComposite` with the help of the method `setClient()`:

```
Label client = toolkit.createLabel(ec, someText, SWT.WRAP);
ec.setClient(client);
```

When the end user clicks the control element of an `ExpandableComposite`, an `ExpansionEvent` is created. This event must be processed with an `ExpansionListener` or an `ExpansionAdapter`. When doing so, it is necessary to force the form to reposition its contents by calling its method `reflow()`:

```
ec.addExpansionListener(new ExpansionAdapter() {
   public void expansionStateChanged(ExpansionEvent e) {
      form.reflow(true);
   }
});
```

Section

The class `Section` is a subclass of the class `ExpandableComposites`. This class also allows you to use a separator and to define a description text that is displayed below the separator. The following example demonstrates the usage of the class `Section`:

```
Section section = toolkit.createSection(form.getBody(),
     Section.DESCRIPTION | Section.TWISTIE | Section.EXPANDED);
section.addExpansionListener(new ExpansionAdapter() {
   public void expansionStateChanged(ExpansionEvent e) {
```

```
            form.reflow(true);
      }
   });
   section.setText("The Question");
   toolkit.createCompositeSeparator(section);
   section.setDescription("Select the one or the other");
   Composite content = toolkit.createComposite(section);
   content.setLayout(new GridLayout());
   toolkit.createButton(content, "to be", SWT.RADIO);
   toolkit.createButton(content, "not to be", SWT.RADIO);
   section.setClient(content);
```

Figure 11.14 shows the section implemented, first in its initial state and then after the user clicked the control element.

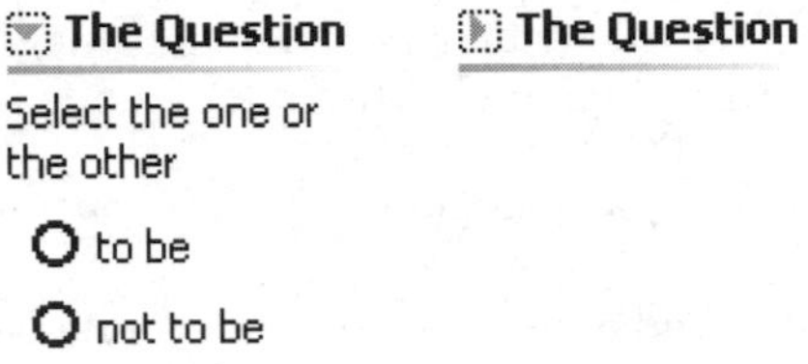

Figure 11.14

Text Markup

The class FormText by far exceeds the text representation functionality achievable with Labels. There are three operation modes that can you can control via the parameters of the method setText():

❑   Normal text (Label mode)

❑   Automatic transformation of URLs into Hyperlink objects

❑   Text with XML mark-up

The last mode is the most powerful, so I want to discuss it in more detail. The following example shows the application of class FormText using XML markup:

```
FormText rtext = toolkit.createFormText(form.getBody(), true);
String data =
   "<form><p>You can find some more information about <b>Eclipse</b>"
      + " at the <a href=\"http://www.eclipse.org\">eclipse.org</a>"
      + " web site.</p></form>";
rtext.setText(data, true, false);
rtext.addHyperlinkListener(new HyperlinkAdapter() {
  public void linkActivated(HyperlinkEvent e) {
    System.out.println("URL was activated: "
                     + e.getLabel() + ", " + e.getHref());
  }
});
```

As you can see, the marked-up text must be included in the <form>...</form> tags. Individual paragraphs are separated from each other via <p>...</p> or <li>...</li>. <li> denotes list elements and can be configured with the following attributes:

style	Specify "text" or "bullet" or "image."
value	Specifies in the case of "bullet" the text to be used as a bullet point. In the case of "image" the image key is specified.
vspace	If "false" is specified, no distance is inserted between list entries. The default value is "true."
indent	Horizontal body indent in pixels.
bindent	Horizontal indent of bullet point in pixels.

For `<p>` paragraphs only the attribute `vspace` can be specified. Within a paragraph the following markup is possible:

`<b>...</b>`	Bold text.
`<span>...</span>`	Text color and text font can be specified with the attributes `color` and `font`.
`<a href="href">` `...</a>`	Hyperlink. The target is specified in the attribute `href`.
`<img href="ikey"/>`	An image specified by the key defined in the `href` attribute.

As shown here, images are identified via key values. The same is true for colors and fonts. The particular keys must be associated with suitable `Image`, `Color`, and `Font` instances via the `FormText` methods `setImage()`, `setColor()`, and `setFont()`. Colors used by the forms subsystem can be obtained from the `FormToolkit`:

```
toolkit.getColors().getColor(FormColors.TITLE));
```

As you can see, the class `FormText` provides some powerful text-representation functions, but by far it cannot reach the representational power of HTML. The number of markup elements is restricted, and it is not possible to nest markup elements. If you require advanced HTML functionality, you should use the Browser widget discussed in the section "The Browser Widget" in Chapter 0.

Resource Management

If you use several forms within an application, you should share the resources (colors and fonts) used in these forms for reasons of efficiency. In such a case it is recommended to use a repository for colors, an instance of the class `FormColors`. When you create a `FormToolkit`, you pass the `FormColors` instance to the `FormToolkit` as a parameter, so that the `FormToolkit` leaves the management of colors to the central `FormColors` instance. In addition, you don't need a separate `FormToolkit` for each form—you should always share a `FormToolkit` instance between forms with a similar lifecycle. If a `FormToolkit` instance is no longer required, you should release it with its `dispose()` method. You should also dispose of the `FormColors` instance when the lifecycle of the plug-in ends.

As far as fonts are concerned, you should use only fonts used by the Eclipse platform itself (`JFaceResources`). This prevents problems with fonts that might not be available on all platforms.

Separation between Data Model and Representation

In Chapter 9 you saw how the different viewers (TableViewer, TreeViewer, etc.) can separate a data model from its representation. For form-based user interfaces this is achieved with the class ManagedForm. When a ManagedForm instance is created, a ScrolledForm instance and a FormToolkit are passed to it. If not, it will itself create such objects. With the method addPart() you can the add form parts in the form of IFormPart instances to the ManagedForm. With the method setInput() you can set the input data, which is then passed on to the registered form parts. Depending on their state, these form parts are then redrawn, and the method reflow() is executed automatically for the form.

For implementing IFormPart instances you can subclass the class AbstractFormPart. A specialized class SectionFormPart is available for form parts that consist of only a Section instance.

The Master-Details-Block

A popular design pattern for forms-based user interfaces is the Master-Details-Block. This block is horizontally or vertically separated into two areas: the master area and the details area. Depending on the selection in the master area, the content of the details area changes. Eclipse provides for this purpose the abstract class MasterDetailsBlock, which separates its client area with a Sash. To create a user interface based on the above design pattern, it is necessary to implement a concrete subclass of MasterDetailsBlock. To create the master area, you must implement the method createMasterPart(). By implementing the method createToolBarActions() it is possible to create extra control elements for the block. You can register several detail pages for the detail area by implementing the method registerPages(). Detail pages must implement the interface IDetailPage.

The Eclipse Workbench

The Eclipse workbench features various workbench views as well as text-based editors. Graphical editors such as diagram editors or bitmap editors are not available in the Eclipse SDK. If such components are required you can find appropriate third-party plug-ins (see Appendix A).

In particular, when using editors you would either use the class TextEditor or implement your own editor by extending one of the abstract or concrete editors from the editor hierarchy shown in the "Editors" section. Since Eclipse 3 there is also a forms-based editor called FormEditor (discussed in the "Actions" section) on which the various PDE editors such as the manifest editor and the schema editor are based. For workbench views the situation is somewhat different. Several concrete view components such as TaskList, BookmarkNavigator, and ResourceNavigator are already active within the workbench. You can use these view instances from your own application; you gain access to these views by specifying the view identification to the workbench. If you want to implement your own view components, you can extend the existing abstract view classes such as `ViewPart` or `PageBookView`.

All concrete workbench components implement the `IAdaptable` interface with the method `getAdapter()`. `getAdapter()` is a factory method; from a class specification (a `Class` instance) it can create an instance of that class.

This allows Eclipse to generate concrete instances from the class names specified in the manifest file `plugin.xml` (see the section "The Plug-in Manifest"). In addition, it becomes possible to save the current workbench state when the workbench is closed and to open the workbench again with the same components active.

The Architecture of the Eclipse Workbench

The Eclipse workbench is represented by an `IWorkbench` instance. This is the root object for the whole Eclipse user interface. You obtain this instance by invoking the static method `PlatformUI.getWorkbench()`.

The Eclipse workbench has a clear hierarchical structure. At the top are the workbench instances; the lowest level is constituted from various workbench components (IWorkbenchPart) such as editors or views. "I…Site" instances allow access to the manifest declarations and other information of the runtime environment.

Workbench Window

The workbench may consist of one or several workbench windows. By default, when Eclipse is started, the workbench is started with a single window. Optionally, it is possible to open each perspective in its own workbench window (Window > Preferences > Workbench > Perspectives). Consequently, the `IWorkbench` instance can own several workbench windows (`IWorkbenchWindow`) that you can retrieve via `getWorkbenchWindows()`. When the last workbench window is closed, the workbench is also closed.

The Workbench Page

Each workbench window can own one or several workbench pages (`IWorkbenchPage`). These pages are used to display the various perspectives of a workbench window. Only one page per workbench window is active and visible to the end user at a time. You can retrieve the list of all pages by calling the `IWorkbenchWindow` method `getPages()`. The currently active page is obtained via the method `getActivePage()`.

Workbench Components

Each workbench page is constituted from one or several workbench components (`IWorkbenchPart`). These are either editors or views (both discussed later in this chapter). Workbench pages offer a series of methods for managing these editors and views. For example, you can obtain a list of references of all editors available in the current workbench page with `getEditorReferences()`. With `getActiveEditor()` you get the currently active editor; with `getDirtyEditors()` you get all those editors where the content has been changed and must be saved when the workbench is closed. With `openEditor()` you can open an editor, and with `closeEditor()` or `closeAllEditors()` you can close the editors.

Managing views is simpler: with getViewReferences() you obtain a list of references of all views available in the current workbench page. You can get a view instance with findView() by specifying its identification (as defined in the manifest file plugin.xml). You can make a view visible with showView(), while you can make it invisible with hideView(). You can get all views stacked with a given view by calling the method getViewStack().

Besides managing editors and views, workbench pages are also responsible for managing Action Sets. With showActionSet() and hideActionSet() you can make Action Sets visible or invisible, respectively.

Workbench pages are also able to manage the navigation history. You can retrieve INavigationHistory instances with getNavigationHistory().

Perspectives

It is the responsibility of the end user to determine how the single components are placed onto a workbench page. However, an application may define the initial layout of a workbench page by specifying a perspective. The Eclipse platform provides some predefined perspectives, such as the Resource perspective or the Java perspective. Of course, applications are free to define their own perspectives.

You can get a reference (IPerspectiveDescriptor) to the currently active perspective of a workbench page using getPerspective(). With setPerspective() you can set a new active perspective for a workbench page, while resetPerspective() allows you to cancel the layout changes made by the end user.

Manifest Information

To the interfaces IWorkbench and IWorkbenchPart belong the corresponding interfaces IWorkbenchSite and IWorkbenchPartSite. With these interfaces you can get access to the runtime environment of the workbench and of each workbench component. The declarations made in the manifest file plugin.xml belong to this environment, as do registered context menus (see the section "Actions" section). You can gain access to instances of type IWorkbenchSite and IWorkbenchPartSite via the method getSite().

Two subtypes, IEditorSite and IViewSite, are available for the type IWorkbenchPartSite. These types provide extended environment information for editors and views.

Event Processing in the Eclipse Workbench

Each application implemented on the basis of the Eclipse platform usually consists of several workbench components. An application may implement its own components, such as special editors or views, or it may use existing components such as a text editor, the Navigator View, or the Tasks View.

The coordination of these various components is organized via event processing, a common technique in object-oriented programming. Usually, each component observes state changes in other components and reacts accordingly. To do so, the observing component registers with the observed component as a listener. The observed component then notifies it when an event occurs via a call to a listener method. I have already demonstrated this kind of event processing in the example given in Chapter 10.

In an open architecture such as the Eclipse platform, however, this concept is not flexible enough. Since the platform can be extended at any time with new plug-ins, you cannot assume a fixed configuration; by using "hard-wired" event processing between components, you would prevent further extensions of a given configuration.

For this reason, the Eclipse platform provides central event management. Components that create events register with the central event management as an event provider and inform the central management whenever events occur. All components that have registered with the central event management as listeners are then informed about the events accordingly. This strategy ensures that the platform remains extensible: new components must register with the central event management only as event providers or listeners.

Now let's have a look at the various event types.

Window Events

IWorkbench events occur when a workbench window is opened (windowOpened()), activated (windowActivated()), deactivated (windowDeactivated()), or closed (windowClosed()).

Components that wish to receive these events must register with the IWorkbench instance as an IWindowListener via addWindowListener().

Component Events

Component events, that is, events that are caused by state changes of IWorkbenchPart instances, are obtained from the component service of the Eclipse platform. You can obtain an IPartService instance from a IWorkbenchWindow instance via the method getPartService(). The concrete IPartService instance will usually be a workbench page, since IWorkbenchPage is a subtype of IPartService.

From this IPartService instance you can fetch the currently active component or a reference to the active component via the methods getActivePart() and getActivePartReference(), respectively. In addition, you can register as an observer via addPartListener(). These observers are represented by two interfaces: IPartListener and IPartListener2. The latter interface is an extension of the first and reports about a few more event types.

partActivated()	Component was activated.
partBroughtToTop()	Component was brought to the top.
partClosed()	Component was closed.
partDeactivated()	Component was deactivated.
partHidden()	Component was made invisible (IPartListener2).
partOpened()	Component was opened.
partVisible()	Component was made visible (IPartListener2).

Selection Events

Selection events occur when a GUI element in the workbench is selected, for example, when a resource is selected in the Navigator. You can obtain selection events from the selection service (ISelectionService). ISelectionService instances can be obtained from an IWorkbenchWindow instance via getSelectionService(). Usually, this will be a workbench page, since IWorkbenchPage is a subtype ISelectionService.

You can retrieve the current selection from such an ISelectionService instance via the method getSelection(). With the help of the methods addSelectionListener() and addPostSelectionListener() you can register observers of type ISelectionListener. The difference between these two methods is that the latter method supports only events from StructuredViewer instances (see "The Viewer Hierarchy" in Chapter 9) and that the event is fired after a short delay if it was caused by a keyboard event. ISelectionListener instances are notified about selection events via selectionChanged(). The event object contains information about the component that caused the event (IWorkbenchPart) and about the selection (ISelection). If you want to get access to the selection details, you must first typecast the generic ISelection object to a more concrete type such as IMarkSelection, IStructuredSelection, or ITextSelection.

How can a component register with the selection service to notify it about selection events? To do this, the component needs only to implement the interface ISelectionProvider with the methods addSelectionListener(), removeSelectionListener(), getSelection(), and setSelection(). When a component is activated, the workbench always checks automatically to see if the component implements this interface. If this is the case, it registers the appropriate selection service with the activated component as an observer via addSelectionListener(). The central selection service is thus notified about selection events caused by this component when the component calls the method selectionChanged() as required. When the component is deactivated, the workbench automatically deregisters the selection service with the component.

Processing Events Correctly

It is normally not sufficient just to register with the selection service as a listener and wait for the event to arrive. For example, when a view is opened, it is not yet informed about the current selection state. Consequently, it cannot display information relating to the selection. The view would be updated only when the end user changes the selection.

This problem also occurs when the workbench is started. The programmer has no influence over the order in which the components of a workbench page are initialized. For example, if you have a view that displays properties that depend on the selection state of an editor and the editor is initialized before the view is initialized, the view is not notified about the selection state of the editor. This is because it was not registered as a selection listener when the editor was started, and therefore it was not informed about the editor's selection state.

Initialization

When you initialize a component, you must therefore fetch the currently active component from the part service via getActivePart() and the current selection from the selection service via getSelection(). This is usually done at the end of the method createPartControl(), where the component is initialized.

When processing events, you cannot make assumptions about the sequence in which components are notified about these events. Components should therefore be implemented in such a way that they can act autonomously without relying on the state of other components. Their behavior should depend only on received events and not make assumptions that other components already have processed such events.

Sequence

However, it can sometimes become necessary to do exactly that, for example, to avoid costly recomputations for performance reasons. In such a case, you can force a specific sequence in event processing by starting event processing after a short delay. This can be done via the method `Display.timerExec()`. With this trick, event processing is performed after all other components have processed an event— provided that these components don't use the same trick! You can then call methods from other components without running the risk of obtaining outdated information.

However, you must execute some caution when using the method `timerExec()`. The processing scheduled in this method can still be executed when the component that scheduled this task is already closed and its widgets are disposed. If you access widgets in such a delayed method, therefore, you must play it safe:

```
if (widget != null && !widget.isDisposed)
```

Editors

All workbench editors are based on the abstract class `EditorPart`. This class mainly implements the `IEditorInput` concept. The interface `IEditorInput` describes the data source of an editor in abstract form. This may be a file, but it may be also a byte stream.

Figure 11.15 shows the hierarchy of editor input sources. IPathEditorInput describes an input source form the local file system. IFileEditorInput describes a generic file-based input source.

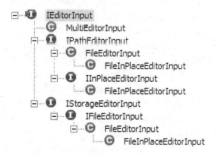

Figure 11.15

The input source for an editor is set by the workbench via `init()` shortly after the `EditorPart` instance has been created. It can be retrieved with `getEditorInput()`. Figure 11.16 shows the hierarchy of text-based editors. Other editor types such as graphical editors can be implemented on the basis of `EditorPart`.

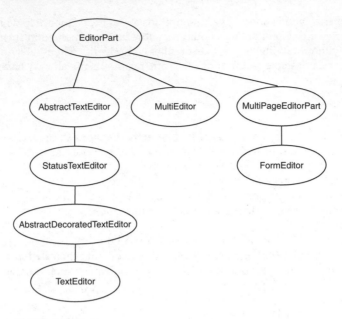

Figure 11.16

Editor classes that subclass `EditorPart` usually override the method `createPartControl()`. Within that method they create the concrete appearance of the editor by creating the necessary SWT widgets and JFace components.

Toolbars and Menus

Usually, you don't need to construct toolbars and menus manually, because Eclipse does this automatically by interpreting the definitions made in the manifest file `plugin.xml` (refer back to the section "The Plug-in Manifest"). However, the option exists to create menus and toolbars manually. To do so, first use the method `getEditorSite()` to fetch an `IEditorSite` instance. From this instance you can obtain an `IEditorActionBarContributor` instance with the help of `getActionBarContributor()`. This instance manages the menus, toolbars, and the status line. These tasks—managing menus, toolbars, and status line—cannot be left to the editor, because actions and menus would appear multiple times if several editors of the same type were opened in the same workbench page. The `IEditorActionBarContributor`, in contrast, can be shared among several editor instances. The standard implementation `EditorActionBarContributor` features the method `getActionBars()` with which you can fetch an `IActionBars` instance. From this instance you can obtain the menu manager (`IMenuManager`) via `getMenuManager()` and the toolbar manager (`IToolManager`) via `getToolManager()`. If you want to construct a toolbar or a drop-down menu, you can just add actions (`IAction` instances) to these managers via their respective `add()` methods. Further details about menu managers are given in the "Actions" section. This section also describes how to construct context menus for editors.

Keyboard Shortcuts

Access to the key-binding service (`IKeyBindingService`) is obtained from the `IEditorSite` instance via `getKeyBindingService()`. Here you can restrict the scope for keyboard shortcuts to the current editor using `setScopes()`. This is necessary if you want to introduce a new editor type that uses key scopes that differ from the scopes defined for the standard editors (text editor). Such scopes can be declared in the extension point `org.eclipse.ui.commands` (discussed previously in the section "The Most Important SDK Extension Points").

Status Line

The `IActionBars` instance also provides access to the workbench's `StatusLineManager` (see the section "The Managers" in Chapter 9) via the method `getStatusLineManager()`.

Saving Files

In addition, the `EditorPart` API contains a method group for saving the modified editor content:

```
doSave()
doSaveAs()
isDirty()
isSaveAsAllowed()
isSaveOnCloseNeeded()
```

All of these methods can be overridden by `EditorPart` subclasses to implement the required functionality. The Eclipse SDK already contains four abstract subclasses of `EditorPart`: `AbstractTextEditor`, `AbstractDecoratedTextEditor`, `MultiEditor`, and `MultiPageEditorPart` (see Figure 11.16).

The AbstractTextEditor Class

The `AbstractTextEditor` class is the standard implementation of the interface `ITextEditor` and represents the common basis for all text-based editors in the Eclipse workbench. The standard text editor in Eclipse (the class `TextEditor`), among others, is a subclass of this class, as are the various program editors. To implement concrete editors, you will usually use the text-processing classes defined in JFace, which was already discussed in the "Text Processing" section in Chapter 9.

`AbstractTextEditor` implements some of the standard functions that are common to text-based editors, such as:

❑ Standard functions for text processing, such as cut, copy, paste, find, and replace

❑ Management of context menus

❑ Reaction to resource changes in the workbench, for example, when a resource is refreshed, when projects are closed, or when a resource is deleted that is currently open in an editor

A class that wants to extend `AbstractTextEditor` must first configure this editor. The Eclipse workbench must be notified about the extension points of the various context menus. This is done with the help of the methods `setEditorContextMenuId` and `setRulerContextMenuId`. The manifest file `plugin.xml` (see section "The Most Important SDK Extension Points") can now refer to these identifications and link Action Sets to the editor's context menus.

Layout

You can change the appearance of the editor if desired. By default, the `AbstractTextEditor` consists of a `SourceViewer` and a vertical `Ruler` for markers at the left-hand side of the `SourceViewer`. You can easily add further widgets by overriding or extending the method `createPartControl()`.

With the method `setStatusField()` you can determine a status field in which the status messages of the editor are shown. You can assign different status fields for different categories of status messages. The editor's status fields are displayed in the status line of the workbench when the editor becomes active. Status fields are described by the interface `IStatusField`. The default implementation of this interface is the class `StatusLineContributionItem`.

Document Model

`ITextEditor` separates the document model from the user interface. The current document is given to the editor by an `IDocumentProvider` instance. This allows several editors to access the same document. `IDocumentProvider` manages documents of type `IDocument`, as discussed in "Text Processing Base Classes" section in Chapter 9. `IDocumentProviders` are responsible for saving and restoring the managed documents. The `AbstractTextEditor` uses the methods of the registered `IDocumentProvider` instance when performing editor operations such as `doSave()` or `doRevertToSaved()`.

These and other operations are usually invoked by user actions (choosing a menu function, clicking a tool button, using the context menu). How does the communication between actions and editor functions work?

Actions

You can install an action (discussed later in the "Actions" section) of type `IAction` with the editor using the method `setAction()`. When doing so, you must assign an identification string to each `IAction` instance. Using this string, you can query the editor for a specific action via `getAction()`, and you can assign keyboard shortcuts to actions via `setActionActivationCode()` and remove them again with `removeActionActivationCode()`. To implement a specific action, you would extend the standard implementation `Action` rather than implement the interface `IAction`. Its subclasses override the `run()` method to implement specific behavior. With the following editor methods

```
markAsContentDependentAction()
markAsPropertyDependentAction()
markAsSelectionDependentAction()
markAsStateDependentAction()
```

you can organize the various actions according to their behavior. This is important when actions must be updated after editor events.

Selection

The `AbstractTextEditor` also provides methods for setting and retrieving emphasized text ranges ((`setHighlightRange()`, `resetHighlightRange()`, and `getHighlightRange()`) and for retrieving the `ISelectionProvider` (`getSelectionProvider()`). This `ISelectionProvider` instance allows you to set and retrieve selections (`ISelection`) and to set and remove `ISelectionChangedListeners`.

Extending the AbstractTextEditor

Subclasses that extend the class `AbstractTextEditor` can override several method of this class to adapt their behavior as required. In particular, you may want to override the following methods:

`createActions()`	Creates the standard actions of the `AbstractTextEditor`:
	Undo, Redo, Cut, CutLine, CutLineToEnd, Copy, Paste, Delete, DeleteLine, DeleteLineToBeginning, DeleteLineToEnd, SetMark, ClearMark, SwapMark, SelectAll, ShiftRight, ShiftLeft, Print, FindReplace, FindNext, FindPrevious, FindIncremental, FindIncrementalReverse, Save, Revert, GotoLine, MoveLinesUp, MoveLinesDown, CopyLinesUp, CopyLinesDown, UpperCase, SmartEnter, and SmartEnterReverse.
`createPartControl()`	Creates the vertical `Ruler`, at the left-hand border of the editor area, and the `SourceViewer`.
`dispose()`	This method must be extended when the subclass needs to release resources (colors, fonts, printer, etc.) when the editor is disposed of.

`doSave()`
`doSaveAs()`
`doRevertToSaved()`
	These methods save the current editor document and restore it to its last saved state.

`editorContextMenuAboutToShow()`	This method is invoked before the editor's context menu is to be shown. The context menu must be constructed in this method.
`init()`	Initializes the editor with an `IEditorSite` instance and an `IEditorInput` instance.
`isSaveAsAllowed()`	The standard implementation always returns the value `false` for this method. Subclasses can override it as required.

The StatusTextEditor Class

This class implements a concrete editor that can handle editor input sources with associated status information.

The AbstractDecoratedTextEditor Class

The abstract class `AbstractDecoratedTextEditor` serves as a basis for implementing feature-rich editors. In particular, concepts such as vertical rulers for displaying changes and overviews, print margins, and highlighting of the current line are supported. Other than the `AbstractTextEditor`, this editor is not independent from the Eclipse workspace and the Eclipse resource model and therefore supports working with resource markers.

The TextEditor Class

The class TextEditor is the standard text editor of the Eclipse workbench and is based on the class AbstractDecoratedTextEditor. In many cases, you may want to extend this class instead of the AbstractTextEditor class. This editor has the identification org.eclipse.ui.DefaultTextEditor.

An example for the extension of the class TextEditor is the ReadmeTool example program, which is found in the plug-in directory:

```
\eclipse\plugins\org.eclipse.ui.examples.readmetool_3.0.0
```

The class ReadmeEditor adds an Outline window to the text editor, that is, a view in which a summary of the editor's contents is displayed. To implement this, the ReadmeEditor overrides the method getAdapter(). In the overridden getAdapter() it generates a suitable ReadmeContentOutlinePage from a received IFileEditorInput instance. It also overrides the method doSave() in order to update the content of the Outline page after saving the editor content, and it overrides the method editorContextMenuAboutToShow() to display an example context menu.

The MultiEditor Class

A MultiEditor combines several editors in a single GUI component. To manage these editors (known as inner editors), the following methods are necessary:

createInnerPartControl()	This method creates the GUI of an inner editor.
getActiveEditor()	This method returns the currently active editor.
getInnerEditors()	This method returns all inner editors.

The MultiPageEditorPart Class

The abstract class MultiPageEditorPart implements an editor with several pages. Each page can contain its own editor, consisting of arbitrary SWT control elements.

Subclasses that extend this class must implement the following methods:

createPages()	This method creates all the editor pages. The method addPage() can also be used to do this.
IEditorPart.doSave() IEditorPart.doSaveAs()	These methods save the contents of the whole editor.
IEditorPart.isSaveAsAllowed()	This method returns the value true if Save As is allowed.

The FormEditor Class

The abstract FormEditor class extends the class MultiPageEditorPart. It is used to implement form-based editors (such as the manifest editor). Subclasses must implement the method addPages() to furnish this editor with pages. All pages are constructed lazily, that is, shortly before they are displayed. For creating such pages, three addPage() methods are provided: page construction with plain SWT elements, page construction with an inner editor (`IEditorPart`), and forms-based page construction with an `IFormPage` instance. Such instances must be derived from the class `FormPage`. If such an instance is created, a `ScrolledForm` instance is created internally and wrapped into a `ManagedForm` (see the "Forms" section). Subclasses of `FormPage` must implement the method `createFormContent()`. This method receives the `ManagedForm` instance as a parameter and can thus fill the page with content by adding form parts to this instance.

Working with Markers

`IMarker` instances were discussed previously in the "Markers" section in connection with resources. Here I am going to discuss how you can declare your own marker types in the manifest file and how markers can be used in the context of an editor.

Declaring Markers

The declaration of a new marker type is achieved by specifying a new `extension` element at the extension point `org.eclipse.core.resources.markers`. The attribute `id` of this extension identifies the marker type, while the attribute `name` specifies a marker name for display purposes. The `extension` element can be equipped with several child elements:

❑ The element `attribute` declares a marker attribute. The attribute `name` specifies the name of that attribute.

❑ The element `persistent` declares whether the marker is persistent or not. The attribute `value` takes the values `true` for persistent markers and `false` for transient markers.

Inheritance

The element `super` declares the parent marker type. In the `type` attribute you specify the identification of the parent marker type. The current marker inherits all attributes from the parent marker except the ones it overrides. It is possible to specify several `super` elements (multiple inheritance). The persistency property is *not* inherited. For example:

```
<extension id="diagramProblem"
    name="Diagram Problem"
    point="org.eclipse.core.resources.markers">
    <super type="org.eclipse.core.resources.problemmarker"/>
    <super type="com.bdaum.myApplication.diagramMarker"/>
    <persistent value="false"/>
    <attribute name="item"/>
    <attribute name="flags"/>
</extension>
```

Here I have defined a new marker type `diagramProblem`. This marker type inherits all attributes from the predefined marker type `org.eclipse.core.resources.problemmarker` and from the marker type `diagramMarker`, from which you can assume that it has been declared previously. The new marker type is declared as transient and is equipped with the additional attributes `item` and `flags`.

Earlier in this chapter I discussed how `IMarker` instances can be created and how attributes are set and retrieved. These are just the methods used when you want to implement the method `gotoMarker()` for a given editor. Editors supporting positioning by marker selection must implement the interface `IGotoMarker` with its `gotoMarker()` method.

GotoMarker

If a new marker is created, the Tasks View or Problems View automatically appears on the screen, depending on the marker type and provided that the Tasks View filter does not inhibit this. If you double-click an entry in these views, the resource to which the marker belongs is opened with its current default editor and the `gotoMarker()` method of this editor is invoked, provided the editor implements the interface `IGotoMarker`. What happens next depends on the editor type and the marker type. In the case of a text editor, the attribute `IMarker.LINE_NUMBER` or the attributes `IMarker.CHAR_START` and `IMarker.CHAR_END` are evaluated. The editor viewport is positioned to the corresponding text area, and this text area is selected. A diagram editor would rather store the identification of a graphical element in a suitable attribute `item` (as indicated above). Double-clicking the marker would select the element.

Marker Lifecycle

When you work with markers, you should be aware that `IMarker` instances are not really "first-class citizens," that is, they don't contain the marker data. Instead, they contain only a handle to a data record that itself contains the marker attributes. It may therefore happen that the data record belonging to a given `IMarker` instance does not exist, for example, if the resource to which the marker belongs has been deleted in the meantime. You should therefore safeguard all marker operations by first querying the marker's `exists()` method.

Views

Besides editors, views are the other basic ingredient of the Eclipse workbench. All views are based on the abstract class `ViewPart`. Unlike editors, views don't have their own input source. Instead, they show the state information of the active editor or of the workbench.

Figure 11.17 shows the hierarchy of view types. The grayed-out components cannot be instantiated or subclassed.

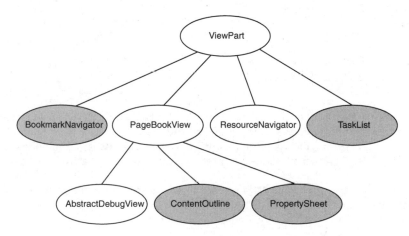

Figure 11.17

The Eclipse SDK comes with a variety of predefined view types. Of course, is it possible to implement your own view types as well, based on `ViewPart` or one of its subclasses. I give an example of such a custom view in the section "The Correction Window" in Chapter 13. By overriding the `ViewPart` method `init()` you can implement a specific initialization for a custom view.

Persistency

This is necessary when you want to maintain the state of a view across sessions. You can archive the state by overriding the method `saveState()`. A parameter of type `IMemento` is passed to this method. In the next session the same `IMemento` instance is received by the `init()` method. Mementos are hierarchical structures—each memento can contain other mementos as child node—in which the state information of a view can be preserved. The Eclipse SDK provides a concrete implementation of the `IMemento` interface with the class `XMLMemento`. As its name indicates, this class stores the view's state information in the form of an XML file.

View Toolbars

In contrast to editors, each view instance has its own toolbar, which can also be equipped with a view-specific drop-down menu. You can obtain this toolbar from the `IViewSite` instance via `getActionBars()`. (The `IViewSite` instance can be retrieved from the `ViewPart` via the method `getViewSite()`.) The method `getActionBars()` delivers an `IActionBars` instance, from which you can obtain the menu manager (`IMenuManager`) via `getMenuManager()` and the toolbar manager (`IToolManager`) via `getToolManager()`. If you want to construct a toolbar or a drop-down menu, just add `IAction` instances to these managers with the help of their respective `add()` methods. Further information about menu managers can be found in the "Actions" section. That section also describes how to construct context menus for views, just as it is done for editors.

The ResourceNavigator Class

The `ResourceNavigator` class implements the navigator for the Eclipse workspace resource (see Figure 11.18). Clients can configure the navigator via the `IResourceNavigator` interface.

Figure 11.18

The following methods can be used to configure the resource navigator:

getFrameList()	This method delivers a FrameList instance that contains the user's navigation history. For example, you can navigate to a previous resource view by calling the back() method of this instance (see also the section "Navigation" in Chapter 4).
getPatternFilter()	This method delivers the active filter of the resource navigator. The class ResourcePatternFilter manages string arrays that contain the filter patterns. Each pattern specifies resources that are *not* to be shown in the navigator.
getSorter()	This method delivers the current ResourceSorter. ResourceSorter allows the displayed IResource instances to be sorted by name or type.
getViewer()	This method delivers the TreeViewer instance used by the ResourceNavigator to display the resources.
getWorkingSet()	This method delivers the currently active IWorkingSet instance or null if no Working Set is currently active.
setFiltersPreference()	This method allows you to set new filter patterns. The end user can activate a filter pattern by selecting it from this list.
setSorter()	Using this method you can set a new ResourceSorter and thus modify the sort strategy.
setWorkingSet()	With this method you can set an IWorkingSet instance as a new active Working Set.

Various other navigators, such as the Java Package Explorer, are based on the ResourceNavigator and use the methods listed here to achieve their individual configurations.

The PageBookView Class

The abstract class PageBookView serves as a basis for the implementation of the classes AbstractDebugView, ContentOutline, and PropertyView. The latter two classes are discussed in more detail shortly. You can also use the PageBookView as a basis for the implementation of custom views.

The class PageBookView supports views that display state information from particular workbench components (IWorkbenchPart) such as state information from the active editor. As the name indicates, a PageBookView instance can be equipped with several pages. The standard page usually shows state information from the currently active component. Additional pages may display state information from other workbench components.

Each subclass of `PageBookView` must implement the following methods:

`createDefaultPage()`	In the implementation of this method you must construct the default page. This page is always shown when no specific `PageBookView` page can be found for the currently active workbench component.
`getBootstrapPart()`	This method is used for determining the currently active workbench component. By overriding this method, clients can determine an active component that differs from the currently active component of the `WorkbenchPage`.
`isImportant()`	This method must return the value `true` if a `PageBookView` page is to be constructed for the received `IWorkbenchPart` component.
`doCreatePage()`	In the implementation of this method you can construct the `PageBookView` pages for specific workbench components. The method is invoked only when the previously called method `isImportant()` returns the value `true`.
`doDestroyPage()`	In the implementation of this method you can dispose of `PageBookView` pages for specific workbench components.

Subclasses of `PageBookView` can override further methods, such as `partActivated()`, `partBroughtToTop()`, `partClosed()`, `partDeactivated()`, and `partOpened()`. By doing so, you can vary the page order—and, of course, the page contents—according to the state of the workbench page.

The Outline View

The class `ContentOutline` implements a view that displays an outline for editor contents. The Outline view of the Java perspective (discussed previously) is an example of such a view.

You cannot instantiate or subclass the `ContentOutline` class—its (only) instance is created and managed by the workbench when needed. This singleton can be displayed by calling the `IWorkbenchPage` method:

```
showView("org.eclipse.ui.views.ContentOutline");
```

Despite the fact that this class cannot be extended via subclasses, it supports the creation of outlines for all possible editor types. This works as follows: when the `ContentOutline` discovers that a component of type `IEditorPart` is activated, it asks that component if it can provide an Outline page. If the response is yes, the Outline page is included in the view. (Remember that `ContentOutline` is a subclass of `PageBookView`).

Editors that wish to contribute an Outline must provide a suitable adapter (see the section "Editors"). The `ContentOutline` instance will fetch the Outline page with the following method call:

```
editor.getAdapter(IContentOutlinePage.class);
```

An example of this technique is found in the Readme editor contained in the Eclipse SDK as an example application.

The Property View

Property views are used to display and edit specific properties of selected objects.

The `PropertyView` class works very similarly to the `ContentOutline` class. `PropertyView` can also not be instantiated or subclassed—its (only) instance is created and managed by the workbench when needed. This instance can be displayed by calling the `IWorkbenchPage` method:

```
showView("org.eclipse.ui.views.PropertySheet");
```

When the `PropertyView` discovers that a component is activated, it asks that component if it can provide a `PropertySheetPage` instance. If the response is yes, the page is included in the view.

Components that wish to contribute a `PropertySheetPage` must provide a suitable adapter (see the section "Editors"). The `PropertyView` instance will fetch the `PropertySheetPage` instance with the following method call:

```
part.getAdapter(IPropertySheetPage.class);
```

The Bookmark Manager

The class `BookmarkManager` implements a view that displays bookmarks (see the "Bookmarks" section in Chapter 1). If the end user double-clicks a bookmark, the corresponding editor is opened and its viewport is positioned to the bookmark.

This class can also not be instantiated or subclassed—its (only) instance is created and managed by the workbench when needed. This instance can be displayed by calling the `IWorkbenchPage` method:

```
showView("org.eclipse.ui.views.BookmarkNavigator");
```

New bookmarks are not explicitly added to the bookmark manager but are added as `IMarker` objects to the corresponding resource (see the "Markers" section). They then appear automatically, depending on the filter settings in the bookmark manager.

The Tasks View

Things are quite similar for the `TaskList` class, which can display the current problems and tasks (see "The Plug-in Manifest" section). Again, this class cannot be instantiated or subclassed—its instance is created and managed by the workbench when needed. This instance can be displayed by calling the `IWorkbenchPage` method:

```
showView("org.eclipse.ui.views.TaskList");
```

New tasks and problems are not explicitly added to `TaskList` but are added as `IMarker` objects to the corresponding resource (see the "Markers" section). They then appear automatically, depending on the filter settings in the task list. Note that Eclipse 3 does not use this class for its own Tasks View and Problems View but instead uses the internal classes `TaskView` and `ProblemView`.

Actions

From time to time, I have mentioned the concept of *actions*. In Eclipse, this idea represents an abstract user action, such as writing to a file, searching for a string in text, or jumping to a marker. Actions are represented in Eclipse by the JFace interface IAction (see the section "The IAction Interface" in Chapter 9). This interface abstracts the action's semantics from the representation of the action in the workbench. When you execute the action, it makes no difference whether the action was represented as a menu item, as a toolbar button, or as both.

Local and Global Actions

Eclipse offers two different action types: local actions and global actions. Global actions are useful if several editors have actions with the same name, such as Undo, Save, or Find. To prevent menus and toolbars from becoming overcrowded with the individual actions from all active editors, it is possible to combine similarly named actions into global actions. The implementation of global actions is, in fact, quite different from local actions. The Eclipse SDK already defines a set of constants in the interface org.eclipse.ui.IWorkbenchActionConstants that can be used as identifiers for global actions.

In particular, the following actions can be shared among different editors and views:

View				Editor	
File	**Edit**	**Navigate**	**Project**	**File**	**Edit**
move	cut	go into	open	revert	find
rename	copy	go to	close	print	cut
refresh	paste	resource	build		copy
properties	delete	sync with			paste
	select all	editor			delete
	undo	back			select all
	redo	forward			undo
		up			redo
		next			
		previous			

When implementing an action you have two main options:

❑ You can specify the action in an Action Set in the manifest file plugin.xml (see "The Most Important SDK Extension Points" section). In this case, the IAction instances are instantiated by the workbench—the programmer does not need to implement IAction. However, you must implement an action delegate (IActionDelegate). The manifest editor will generate an IActionDelegate stub for each new action.

❑ You can explicitly implement the IAction interface in your own application. In this case, the application is also responsible for creating IAction instances. This is required for actions whose enabling does not depend on workbench selection but rather on other criteria. It is also required for context menus that cannot yet be declared in the manifest.

Defining Actions in the Manifest

Let's deal with the first case first. Here you need only describe the action sufficiently in the manifest. This is usually the best practice because it allows you to easily extend the plug-in's functionality later. Figure 11.19 shows the manifest attributes defined for the action `CheckSpelling` from Chapter 13.

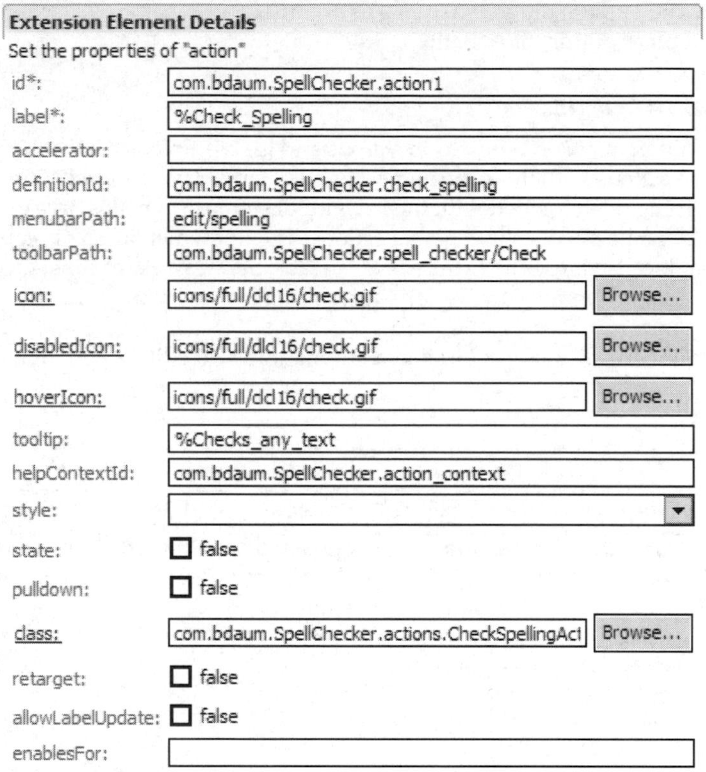

Extension Element Details

Set the properties of "action"

id*:	com.bdaum.SpellChecker.action1
label*:	%Check_Spelling
accelerator:	
definitionId:	com.bdaum.SpellChecker.check_spelling
menubarPath:	edit/spelling
toolbarPath:	com.bdaum.SpellChecker.spell_checker/Check
icon:	icons/full/dcl16/check.gif Browse...
disabledIcon:	icons/full/dlcl16/check.gif Browse...
hoverIcon:	icons/full/dcl16/check.gif Browse...
tooltip:	%Checks_any_text
helpContextId:	com.bdaum.SpellChecker.action_context
style:	
state:	☐ false
pulldown:	☐ false
class:	com.bdaum.SpellChecker.actions.CheckSpellingActi Browse...
retarget:	☐ false
allowLabelUpdate: ☐ false	
enablesFor:	

Figure 11.19

Actions can be defined in various extension points, such as `org.eclipse.ui.actionSets`, `org.eclipse.ui.editorActions`, and `org.eclipse.ui.viewActions` (see "The Most Important SDK Extension Points").

For each action you can specify the following attributes:

`id`	A unique identifier of the action.
`label`	A display text for the action, to be shown, for example, in the menu item or the tool button. You can emphasize one letter of the text by prefixing it in the usual way with the character &. This letter will then act as a mnemonic code for the action. In addition, you may append a keyboard shortcut in the form of a text string separated by the character @. Several key names can be concatenated with the help of the character +, as in @Ctrl+Shift+S.

accelerator	The code for the keyboard shortcut as defined in the class SWT. If the shortcut consists of several keys, their code values are summed.
definitionId	The identification for an action definition. This is needed only when the key assignment is performed dynamically via the Key Binding Service. In this case, the definitionId must match the id used in the action definition and the id used for the action in the corresponding Action Set.
menubarPath	A path expression describing where the action should appear in the workbench menu. If this attribute is omitted, the action is not represented as a menu item.
	Each section in the path specification (except the last section) must specify the valid identifier of an existing menu item. The last section specifies either the name of a new group or an existing group to which the action is to be added.
	The necessary menu item identifiers are found in the interface org.eclipse.ui.IWorkbenchActionConstants.
toolbarPath	A path expression describing where the action should appear in the workbench toolbar. If this attribute is omitted, the action is not represented as a tool item.
	The first section of this path specification identifies the toolbar. (Normal stands for the default workbench toolbar.) The second section specifies either the name of a new group or an existing group to which the action is to be added.
icon	The path, relative to the location of plugin.xml, of an icon that represents the action in toolbars.
disabledIcon	Another icon that represents the action when it is disabled. If this icon is omitted, a gray version of the icon specified under the icon attribute is used.
hoverIcon	The icon that should appear when the mouse hovers over the enabled action. This icon is also used to represent enabled actions in menus. If this attribute is omitted, the icon specified under the icon attribute is used instead.
tooltip	A message that is displayed on the screen when the mouse hovers over the toolbar representation of the action.
helpContextId	A unique identifier of the action for context-sensitive help. See the section "The Help System" for details.
state	If this value is specified, the action can be toggled. The specified value (true or false) determines the initial state.
pulldown	An alternative to the state attribute, this attribute can specify that the action be equipped with a drop-down menu. In toolbars, a pull-down arrow appears at the right-hand side of the action's representation.

class	The fully qualified name of a class implementing the interface org.eclipse.ui.IWorkbenchWindowActionDelegate (see below).
retarget	An alternative to the class attribute, it can specify the value true for this attribute if the action is a global action (see below).
allowLabelUpdates	This attribute is used only when true is specified for the attribute retarget. If the attribute allowLabelUpdates is set to true, clients can modify the display label and the tool tip of the global action.
enablesFor	This attribute specifies when the action is enabled: ! Nothing selected. ? Nothing or only a single element selected. + One or more elements selected. 2+ Two or more elements selected. n Exactly n elements selected. * Enabling is independent of selection. If the attribute is omitted, the action's enabling depends solely on program logic. In addition, actions can be enabled or disabled by the application.

In addition to the quite basic enablesFor attribute, you can make further specifications for enabling, disabling, and notification of actions. To do so, select the action in the manifest editor and invoke the context function New. You then have the choice between selection and enablement.

Selection

Under the element selection specify the fully qualified name of a class or an interface (for example, org.eclipse.core.resources.IResource) in the attribute class. By doing so, you enforce the selected objects to be sent only to the IActionDelegate when all selected elements are of the specified type. In all other cases, the IActionDelegate method selectionChanged() will obtain the empty selection. Under the attribute name you can specify a filter pattern (such as *.txt). The names of all selected objects must match this pattern to enable the action.

Enabling and Disabling Actions

Further control about the enabling of actions is possible via the enablement element. Here you can declare the enabling of an action as a function of the type and current state of the selected object and also of the state of the plug-in and the state of the whole system. These individual conditions can be combined with Boolean expressions. The various criteria and Boolean operators are declared as child elements of the enablement element (via the context function New).

objectClass	Under the attribute name you can specify the fully qualified name of a class or an interface. If all selected objects belong to this type, the condition has the value true.
objectState	Under the attribute name you can specify the name of an object property, and under the attribute value the value of that property. If all selected objects have properties with such a value, the condition has the value true.
	To support the workbench in the evaluation of this condition, the selected objects must implement the interface IActionFilter or must be able to provide an IActionFilter instance via getAdapter(). If this is not the case, the condition results in false. The workbench uses the testAttribute() method of the IActionFilter interface to test the state of an object.
	If you want to introduce new, selectable objects into the workbench, you should always implement the IActionFilter interface. This allows for actions that are added later by plug-ins to react to state changes of selected objects.
	The Eclipse SDK already implements action filters for the object types IResource, IMarker, and IProject. Which properties may be queried for these object types is described in the interfaces IResourceActionFilter, IMarkerActionFilter, and IProjectActionFilter.
systemProperty	Under the attribute name you can specify the name of a system property. The workbench will use this name to query the corresponding system property via System.getProperty() and will compare the result with the value specified under the attribute value. If equal, the condition returns true.
pluginState	Under the attribute id you can specify the identification of a plug-in. When you specify the value installed under the attribute value, the workbench will test whether the specified plug-in is installed. If the value activated is specified, the workbench will test whether the plug-in is active.

Delegates

How do you connect an action with the application? This depends on whether the action is local or global. For local actions you must specify a class of type org.eclipse.ui.IWorkbenchWindowActionDelegate under the attribute class. The section "The Class SpellCheckingTarget" in Chapter 13 shows an example of such a delegate. The init() method here is invoked when the workbench is started. When the selection within the workbench changes, the method selectionChanged() is called. The method run() is invoked when the end user activates the action.

Global actions are defined by specifying the value true under the attribute retarget. In this case, the class attribute is not specified. It is the application that is responsible for creating a concrete RetargetAction instance (or a LabelRetargetAction instance when allowLabelUpdates is set to `true`). Usually this is done in the `createPartControl()` method of the respective editor or view. The new action instance is then registered via

```
getViewSite().getActionBars().setGlobalActionHandler(
    id, retargetAction);
```

In this code, first the view's runtime environment is fetched via `getViewSite()`. From this view site the view's toolbar is fetched via `getActionBars()` (see the "Views" section). Then the action is registered with the help of `setGlobalActionHandler()` by specifying the identification of the action (`id`) and the `RetargetAction` instance (`retargetAction`). The code for registering editor actions is similar. However, in this case an intermediate step via an `IEditorActionBarContributor` instance is required (see the "Editors" section).

The example Readme editor contained in the Eclipse SDK demonstrates how to work with global actions quite explicitly.

Implementing Actions Manually

As an alternative to declaring actions in the manifest file `plugin.xml` you can, of course, implement actions the hard way in Java code. For global actions, you have already seen that the application is responsible for creating the respective `IAction` instances (such as `RetargetAction` or `LabelRetargetAction` instances).

You will usually not implement the `IAction` interface from scratch, but rather you will extend one of the classes from the package `org.eclipse.ui.actions`. You can find a variety of actions for standard tasks in this package.

If you don't define an action within `plugin.xml`, you must ensure that the action appears in the appropriate toolbars and menus. This is, in particular, the case for context function actions, because context functions cannot be declared in `plugin.xml`.

In Chapter 13 I will show how to hard-code actions for a view in an example plug-in. First, individual action instances are created, and then a toolbar, a drop-down menu, and a context menu are constructed with these actions. `Separator` instances are created, too, that act as anchor points, allowing other plug-ins to add actions to the so-created menus.

I have already discussed how actions can be added to the toolbar of a view. For context menus you must do a bit more work, making use of the respective JFace components, as discussed in the section "Actions and Menus" in Chapter 9.

Dialogs

You can find a set of ready-made `Dialog` classes that can be used within plug-ins in the package `org.eclipse.ui.dialogs`. Using these classes can save you a lot of work and help you to achieve a consistent "look and feel" in an application. Further resource-specific dialogs and dialogs for IDE functions are contained in the package `org.eclipse.ui.ide.dialogs`.

Figure 11.20 shows the hierarchy of `Dialog` classes in the package org.eclipse.ui.dialog.

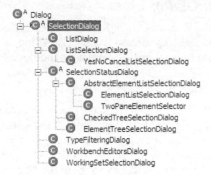

Figure 11.20

All of these `Dialog` classes are based on the abstract class `SelectionDialog`, which is itself based on the JFace class (and therefore, too, on the JFace class `Window`), which has already been discussed in the section "Dialogs and Windows" in Chapter 9. Consequently, this class is equipped with the methods inherited from `Dialog`, such as `create()`, `open()`, `close()`, and so on. It implements additional methods, such as `setInitialElementSelections()` and `setInitialSelections()`, with which an initial selection of dialog elements is possible. The methods `setTitle()` and `setMessage()` allow you to set a title and longer text for the message area of the dialog. These methods must be used between the method calls `create()` and `open()`.

The result of a dialog is obtained with the help of the method `getResult()`. If the dialog was not closed with the OK button, this method returns the value `null`.

We will now take a closer look at some of the concrete dialog classes of the package `org.eclipse .ui.dialogs`.

The CheckedTreeSelectionDialog and ElementTreeSelectionDialog Classes

These dialogs support the selection of elements from a tree. You can supply the viewer of these dialogs with input data using the method `setInput()`, and you can determine which elements are initially expanded via the method `setExpandedElements()`. With `addFilter()` you can set a `ViewerFilter` instance. This instance determines which elements of the input data are shown in the tree. With `setSorter()` you can set a sorter for the tree elements. A validator can be specified with `setValidator()`. In the case of selection changes, this validator checks to determine whether all selected elements are valid and enables or disables the OK button accordingly. Finally, you can set the size of the tree area in characters via `setSize()`.

`ElementTreeSelectionDialog` features, in addition, the methods `setAllowMultiple()` and `setDoubleClickSelects()` for allowing and disallowing multiple selection of tree elements and determining the behavior in the case of double-clicks. Since both classes are derivatives of `SelectionStatusDialog`, they also have methods for managing the status line. Among these methods are the method `setStatusLineAboveButtons()` for determining the position of the status line and the method `updateStatus()`, with which the status line can be updated. In addition, you can control the state of the OK button with the method `updateButtonsEnableState()`.

The ElementListSelectionDialog Class

This dialog implements a simple list from which the end user can select elements. You can set the elements of this list via the method setElements(). This dialog, too, is a derivative of SelectionStatusDialog and thus inherits the previous methods for status-line management.

The ListSelectionDialog Class

This dialog also implements a list from which elements can be selected by the end user. However, this dialog works with arbitrary domain models. The contents of the selection list are retrieved from an IContentProvider instance, and the representation is computed with the help of an ILabelProvider instance. You can pass the input object, an IStructuredContentProvider instance, the ILabelProvider instance, and a message in the ListSelectionDialog() constructor.

The ContainerSelectionDialog Class

This dialog allows the end user to select a workspace container (project or folder). You can specify the root directory of the selection tree in the constructor of this class. In addition, you can specify whether new containers may be created.

The ResourceListSelectionDialog Class

This dialog allows the end user to select workspace resources. You specify the root directory of the selection tree in the constructor of this class, and you can specify an initial selection with setInitialSelections().

The SaveAsDialog Class

This dialog can be used to prompt the end user for the location and name for a file to be stored. You can set a default selection with the method setOriginalFile(). This method must be executed before create(). The specified file location is obtained as an IPath object via getResult().

The NewFolderDialog Class

You can prompt the end user for the name of a new directory with this dialog. The parent container is specified in the constructor of this class. The dialog will immediately create the new directory when the OK button is pressed.

The ContainerGenerator Class

This class is not a dialog but is nevertheless useful. It creates all missing resource containers along a specified path. The path is specified in the constructor of the class. You can then create all missing containers using generateContainer().

Workbench Wizards

In the section "Wizards" in Chapter 9 I discussed how wizards can be implemented with JFace classes. Here I discuss how the existing wizards of the Eclipse workbench can be extended. In particular, this is required when an application needs to create new files or new projects. In this case, you should not create your own eccentric solution but rather link into the New Wizard of the Eclipse workbench.

The newWizard Extension Point

Integration into the New Wizard is quite easy to achieve: you simply define the extension in the manifest file plugin.xml. The extension point identification for the New Wizard is org.eclipse .ui.newWizards. You can add three elements to this extension point:

❑ **category.** You can define a new category for the new wizard in this element. The attribute id identifies the category uniquely. Under the attribute name a display name for the new category is defined. You can define the identification of an existing category to which the new category is added as a child with the optional attribute parentCategory.

❑ **wizard.** This element is required to declare the new wizard. The attribute id identifies the wizard uniquely. A display name for the new wizard is defined under the attribute name. With the optional attribute category you can assign the new wizard to a category. If this attribute is not specified, the wizard is by default assigned to the Others category. You can specify the relative path of an icon that represents the wizard in the selection list under icon. The implementation of the wizard is specified in the attribute class. The class specified here must implement the interface INewWizard.

If the optional attribute project is set to true, the new wizard will not be used to create new files but to create new projects—the wizard appears in the New Project dialog. In this case, you can specify the attribute finalPerspective (see the section "Defining Perspectives"). This attribute specifies the identification of the perspective that should be opened when the new project is created.

Finally, the child element description can be added to the wizard element. This element can contain a description text for the wizard.

❑ **selection.** Under the attribute class you can specify the fully qualified name of a class or interface (for example, org.eclipse.core.resources.IResource). If all selected elements of the workbench belong to this type, the selection will be passed to the wizard when it is initialized. Otherwise, it will obtain the empty selection. Under the attribute name you can specify a filter pattern (for example, *.txt) that must be satisfied by the names of all selected elements for the selection to be passed to the wizard.

Here is an example for a (fictitious) wizard for creating a new jukebox playlist (see the section "The Description Window" in Chapter 10). First, a new category called Jukebox is created. In this category a new wizard called Playlist is created. When the wizard is activated, an instance of the class PlaylistCreationWizard is created and the run() method of this instance is invoked. Workbench selections are passed to the wizard only when all elements of the selection are workspace resources.

```
<extension
    point="org.eclipse.ui.newWizards">
    <category
        name="Jukebox"
        id="com.bdaum.jukebox.newWizard">
    </category>
    <wizard
        name="Playlist"
        icon="icons/basic/obj16/playlist.gif"
        category="com.bdaum.jukebox.newWizard"
        class="com.bdaum.jukebox.wizards.PlaylistCreationWizard"
```

```
            id="com.bdaum.jukebox.newPlaylistWizard">
        <description>
            Creates new Jukebox playlist file
        </description>
        <selection
            class="org.eclipse.core.resources.IResource">
        </selection>
    </wizard>
</extension>
```

The IWorkbenchWizard Interface

Wizards that are created for the Eclipse workbench should implement the interface
IWorkbenchWizard. The interface INewWizard is an extension of this interface. IWorkbenchWizard
is based on the JFace interface IWizard but specifies an additional method, init(). This is invoked
when the wizard is started and passes the Workbench instance and the current workbench selection to
the wizard, provided that the selection satisfies the conditions specified in the selection element.

The WizardNewFileCreationPage Class

When creating a New File Wizard, you can in many cases save yourself some work if you base the wizard's default page on the class WizardNewFileCreationPage. This class prompts the end user for the
required input and creates the new file based on that input. You can use this class in its original form or
you can create your own subclasses. In particular, you may want to override or extend the methods
getInitialContents(), getNewFileLabel(), and handleEvent(). The method
getInitialContents() returns the initial contents of the new file in form of an InputStream—
these contents will be written into the new file. The method getNewFileLabel() returns the display
label for the input field of the filename. The method handleEvent() is called for any events caused by
this wizard page. You can react adequately to user actions by extending this method.

For example, if you want to create a default page PlayListCreationWizardPage for your wizard
PlaylistCreationWizard, it could look like this:

```java
public class PlayListCreationWizardPage extends
    WizardNewFileCreationPage {
    private final static String XMLPROLOG =
        "<?xml version=\"1.0\" encoding=\"UTF-8\"?>";

    protected InputStream getInitialContents() {
        try {
            String input = XMLPROLOG + "<playlist></playlist>"
            return new ByteArrayInputStream(input.getBytes("UTF8"));
        } catch (UnsupportedEncodingException x) {
            return null;
        }
    }

    protected String getNewFileLabel() {
        return "Playlist name";
    }
}
```

The method getInitialContents() here creates an empty playlist in XML format.

Preferences and Property Pages

I discussed preference pages and preference trees in the "Preferences" section in Chapter 9. You don't need to deal with the classes PreferenceNode, PreferenceManager, and PreferenceDialog in the context of the Eclipse workbench. The workbench already constructs a preference tree that can be opened by the end user via Window > Preferences. All you have to do is to add the preference pages provided by your plug-in to this tree.

This is done by declaring an appropriate extension in the manifest file plugin.xml. The extension point in question is org.eclipse.ui.preferencePages. This extension point is quite simple and consists of only the single element page. You need to specify the identification of the new node in the preference tree under the attribute id. Under name specify the display text for this node, and under the attribute class specify the fully qualified class name of the respective PreferencePage implementation. The workbench will later create an instance of this class when required. Finally, you can specify the path for the identification of the parent node of the new node under category. If this attribute is not specified, the new node is appended directly to the root node of the preference tree.

I will give some examples for the declaration of preference pages in plugin.xml in "The Plug-in Configuration" and the "A Plug-in for Java-Properties" sections in Chapter 13.

As already mentioned in Chapter 9 and in "The Core Classes of the Eclipse Platform" section in this chapter, it is necessary to initialize the PreferenceStore with default values when an application is started, because default values are not persistent. In the context of a plug-in, the best place for doing so is the Plugin class or a special class that represents the preferences' domain model. Initializing the preference default values in the PreferencePage class is *not* recommended, because this would increase the startup time of the Eclipse platform. In "The Plugin Class" and the "Configuring the Spell Checker" sections in Chapter 13 I show how plug-in preferences can be initialized and modified.

In addition to preference pages, the package org.eclipse.ui.dialogs provides a subclass of PreferencePage: the class PropertyPage. This class serves as a superclass for dialogs that pop up when the user applies the context function Properties to a workspace resource. In addition to the methods inherited from PreferencePage, the class PropertyPage provides the methods setElement() and getElement(). These methods allow you to set and retrieve the resource associated with a specific property page. Of course, all property pages must be declared in the manifest file plugin.xml.

A standard application of property pages is to override workbench-wide preferences on the project level. Instead of implementing these pages from scratch, it is sometimes better to derive the pages from the corresponding property pages. My article "Mutatis mutandis–Using Preference Pages as Property Pages" on www.eclipse.org shows how this can be done.

Defining Perspectives

Perspectives define the initial layout of a workbench page: they define where editors and views are placed and which Action Sets are visible.

Plug-ins may (but are not required to) add one or several perspectives to the workbench. This is recommended when the existing perspectives are not suitable for the tasks that are to be performed with the specific plug-in. Another thing to consider is that a plug-in may be installed in the minimal Eclipse Runtime Environment, and this environment understands only the Resource perspective. The Rich Client Platform (RCP) (see Chapter 14) does not even provide such a perspective, so at least one plug-in must provide a perspective when an application is based on the RCP.

The definition of a new perspective begins with an entry in the manifest file `plugin.xml`. The corresponding extension point is `org.eclipse.ui.perspectives` with the element `perspective`. This element may possess a child element `description` containing a description text for the perspective. The attribute `id` contains the identification of the perspective. The attribute `name` specifies the display text. The attribute `icon` refers to an icon that is displayed on the Open Perspective button of the perspective, on the left border of the workbench. Finally, the attribute `class` specifies the fully qualified name of a class that implements the interface `IPerspectiveFactory`. This class is responsible for the construction of the initial layout.

This is done in the only method of this interface, `createInitialLayout()`. This method accepts an instance of type `IPageLayout` as a parameter, representing the layout of a workbench page. In the API documentation of this interface you can also find an example of the implementation of the method `createInitialLayout()`.

Perspective Layout

Initially, a perspective consists of a single area, occupied by the editor. You get the identification of this area from the `IPageLayout` object with the help of `getEditorArea()`. Starting from this area, you can then add additional folder areas of type `IFolderLayout` with the help of `createFolder()`. Such a folder area can contain one or several views, stacked on top of each other. The parameters needed for this method are the identification of the new area, the orientation (TOP, BOTTOM, LEFT, RIGHT), the size ratio to the reference area, and the identification of the reference area. The reference area can be the editor area or another previously created folder area. It is possible to construct deeply nested layouts.

You can now attach an arbitrary number of views to each folder. This is done with `addView()`. This method accepts the identification of the respective view (as defined in `plugin.xml`) as a parameter. Alternatively, you can use the method `addPlaceholder()` to reserve space for a not-yet-visible view. When the end user opens this view at a later time with Window > Show View, the view will appear in the reserved area. You have the option of adding a view to the primary Show View list via `addShowViewShortcut()`. Without doing so, the view would appear only under Window > Show View > Others.

FastViews

As you saw in Chapter 4, you have the option of using views as FastViews instead of stacking them in a folder area. When defining a perspective, you may also initialize a view as a FastView: the method `addFastView()` is used for this purpose.

Action Sets

Finally, you have the option of activating Action Sets defined in the manifest file `plugin.xml` when initializing the perspective. This is done with `addActionSet()`.

You can place the Open Perspective button with the specified icon onto the workbench's perspective bar with the method `addPerspectiveShortcut()`.

The Help System

I have already mentioned the Eclipse help system in various sections of this book. While JFace still requires you to code help functions explicitly (for example, by registering a help listener), things are quite different in the context of plug-in programming. Here, help pages are associated with GUI elements in the higher software layers.

There are two different ways to offer help. One way is to offer it via the help function of the Eclipse workbench (Help > Help Contents). Each plug-in can provide a help table of contents (toc) that can be embedded into the global table of contents. It may appear there as a separate chapter or may be added further below in the tree of help pages.

The other way is to offer context-sensitive help. When the user presses the F1 key, the GUI element that has the focus determines the help page to be displayed. The central mechanism here is the help identification. It links the respective GUI element or the respective program function to one or several help pages.

Both the table of contents and the association of help pages with help identifications are encoded into separate XML files. The advantage is that the help system can be developed quite independently from the application. It is even possible to deploy the help system of a given plug-in as a separate plug-in.

Creating a Help Table of Contents

The table of contents of the help pages of a plug-in is defined in a file that is usually called `toc.xml` and stored in the project directory of the plug-in.

As the file extension indicates, the table of contents is an XML file. No special editor for this file type exists in the Eclipse SDK, but you can use the text editor. Another possibility is to create a simple XML editor. This is done with just a few mouse clicks.

First, create a new plug-in project (see the section "Configuring Plug-ins"). On the Plug-in Code Generators page of the New Project Wizard, select Plug-in with an Editor. This will generate a complete XML editor with syntax highlighting. You can install this editor by copying the plug-in directory from the `workspace` directory into the directory `plugins` and then restarting Eclipse.

If you want more features, there are some "grown-up" XML editors available as third-party plug-ins (see Appendix A).

The file `toc.xml` must contain a root element named `toc`. Usually, such a `toc` element contains one or several `topic` elements that can be nested.

Here is the help table of contents from "The Help Table of Contents" section in Chapter 13 as an example:

```
<?xml version="1.0" encoding="UTF-8"?>
<toc label="Spell Checker" topic="html/spelling.html">
    <topic label="Correction View" href=
        "html/SpellCheckerView.html"/>
```

```
        <topic label="Default Preferences"
            href="html/SpellCheckerPreferences.html">
            <anchor id="postPreferences"/>
        </topic>
        <topic label="Other Information">
        <topic label="Acknowledgements" href=
            "html/Acknowledgements.html"/>
                <topic label="Dictionaries" href="html/Dictionaries.html"/>
        </topic>
    </toc>
```

The label attributes define the display text shown in the help page tree. Clicking on this text will display the help page referenced by the attribute href. (If this attribute is not defined, nothing will happen, of course.) If topic elements are nested, the inner elements appear as a subsection of the other elements. It is possible to expand or collapse the outer elements depending on the browser used and on the browser preferences.

As you can see in the previous code, it is also possible to assign a help page to the toc element. This is done in abbreviated form with the attribute topic.

The path expression in the href attributes and the topic attribute do not necessarily need to remain within the boundaries of your own plug-in. However, the reference point is always your own plug-in directory. By using appropriate path expressions, however, you can also point to help pages in other plug-in directories. For example:

```
href="../org.eclipse.jdt.doc.user_3.0.0/tips/jdt-tips.html"
```

A specialty is the anchor element shown in the previous example. Such an element allows other plug-ins to link into this table of contents or to organize a table of contents in the form of several modules. I will show how this is done in the section "A Plug-in for Java-Properties" in Chapter 13.

Of course, it is still necessary to declare the help table of contents in the manifest file plugin.xml. This is done with the extension point org.eclipse.help.toc in the element toc. Here you need to specify under the attribute file the name of the XML file containing the table of contents (for example, toc.xml) The attribute primary="true" identifies this table of contents as an autonomous table of contents (primary="false" would indicate a table of contents that is to be embedded into another table of contents). You can specify the relative path of a directory containing all help pages that cannot be reached via the table of contents (that is, pages that can be reached only via context-sensitive help or via the index) in the attribute extradir. When the help subsystem computes the help index, it will analyze all pages that are referenced in the table of contents and all pages contained in the directory referenced by extradir.

The sections "The Plug-in Configuration" and "A Plug-in for Java-Properties" in Chapter 13 show what such manifest declarations look like.

Creating Help Context Associations

The association of help pages with help identifications for a plug-in is done in a file usually called contexts.xml. This file is stored in the project directory of the plug-in. The file must contain a root element named contexts. This element usually contains one or several context child elements. Each of these context elements corresponds to an Infopop (a little window that appears when the F1 key is pressed). The section "Context-Sensitive Help" in Chapter 13 shows an example of such a context association.

Each context has an attribute id, which declares the help identification with which the element is associated. In addition, a context element may contain a description child element and one or several topic child elements. Both of these have already been discussed.

It is also necessary to declare the help–context association in the manifest file plugin.xml. This happens via the extension point org.eclipse.help.contexts with the element contexts. You must specify the name of the context association file (for example, contexts.xml) under the attribute file.

Setting Context Identifications

Help identifications can be assigned to individual GUI elements using the static method setHelp() of the class WorkbenchHelp. The respective GUI element and the help identification string are passed as parameters. The following GUI element types can be equipped with context-sensitive help: Control, IAction, MenuItem, and Menu.

For example:

```
Button button = new Button(parent, SWT.PUSH);
WorkbenchHelp.setHelp(button, "example.plugin.button1_context");
```

You must specify the fully qualified context identification (including the plug-in identification) in this method.

For some abstract constructs you have the option of declaring context identification in the manifest. In particular, this is possible for actions in Action Sets, by specifying the helpContextId attribute (see the "Actions" section). An example is found in section "The Plug-in Configuration" in Chapter 13.

Also, for markers of all kinds, you can declare help identification in the manifest file. This is done in the extension point org.eclipse.ui.markerHelp with the element markerHelp. Here you can define an association between the marker type (specified in the attribute markerType) and a help identification (specified in the attribute helpContextId).

Instead of the attribute markerType, or in combination with this attribute, you can specify one or several attribute child elements. Each of these elements specifies a marker attribute name (name) and an attribute value (value). With this specification you can associate a help identification to markers that have at least one attribute that matches the specified attribute value. If several markerHelp declarations match a marker in such a case, the help identification of the markerHelp declaration with the most matching attributes is used, allowing the help information to depend on the content of the marker. For example, for a problem marker you could show a specific help text for each different problem type.

Packaging Help for Deployment

Help pages are implemented as HTML pages. They are located, together with the other resources (images, etc.), in a separate appropriately named folder (for example, html or doc). The href references in the topic elements in the table of contents and in the help-context association file refer to these files.

In the case of large help systems, however, this storage method wastes a lot of disk space. Help pages are usually quite small but allocate a full block (for example, 64 KB) on the disk. Eclipse therefore allows you to package all help resources in a Zip archive. This archive must have the name doc.zip. If the Eclipse help subsystem finds such an archive, it will search there first for requested help pages. Only if the page is not found is it searched for among the unpacked help pages.

Active Help

Eclipse even allows workbench functions or plug-in functions to be offered in help pages. Instead of asking the user to perform a specific action, you can embed a hyperlink in the help page that performs the action for the user when it is clicked.

To offer this functionality, Eclipse uses the central JavaScript file livehelp.js. This must be declared in all help pages that wish to use this functionality. For example:

```
<script language=
    "JavaScript" src="../../org.eclipse.help/livehelp.js"/>
```

You can then use this script in all HTML elements that accept scripts, for example, in a hyperlink:

```
<a href='javascript:liveAction(
    "com.bdaum.SpellChecker",
    "com.bdaum.SpellChecker.actions.ActiveHelpAction",
    "start"
)'>Check Spelling</a>
```

The first parameter specifies the plug-in identification. The second parameter specifies the class that implements the action, and the third parameter is a string value that is transmitted to the action.

The class that represents the action must implement the interface ILiveHelpAction. Two methods must be implemented:

❑ The method setInitializationString() accepts the value of the third parameter in the JavaScript call. This allows using this class in different places with different parameter values and to react differently depending on those values.

❑ The method run() must perform the requested action.

An example of such a class and its invocation can be found in section "Active Help" in Chapter 13.

Dynamic Help

The extension point org.eclipse.help.contentProducer allows you to register a Java class as a content provider for the help system. This class must implement the interface IHelpContentProducer with its only method getInputStream(). The plug-in identification and URL of the requested help page are passed as parameters. The class may return a help page in the form of an InputStream or may return null. If it returns null, the help page is searched among the non-dynamic help pages (see the previous sections).

Cheat Sheets

In addition to help pages, each plug-in may define an arbitrary number of Cheat Sheets. Cheat Sheets are an ideal means for authoring tutorials. They are similar in structure to the `welcome.xml` files known from Eclipse 2.1. Cheat Sheets lead the end user step-by-step through a series of work items (`item`). Each item contains a title and a description, an option reference to a help page, and an optional action with which the user may invoke system functions.

Also, for Cheat Sheets there is no dedicated editor. You can edit them with the built-in text editor or with an XML editor (see "The Help System" section).

The root element of each Cheat Sheet is named `cheatsheet` and has a `title` attribute. It contains one `intro` element and an arbitrary number of `item` elements.

Each item element has a `title` attribute. Both the `intro` and `item` elements may specify an optional `href` attribute pointing to an HTML help page. The reference consists of the plug-in identification, suffixed by the relative path of the help page, for example, `/com.bdaum.SpellChecker/html/Acknowledgements.html`.

The main text of `intro` and `item` elements is contained in the child element `description`. Within this description it is possible to enclose text to be printed in bold style with `<b> ... </b>`.

In addition, each `item` element allows for an `action` child element. These elements produce a button below the item's description. When the end user clicks that button, the corresponding action is performed. The `action` element specifies the following attributes:

- ❑ **pluginId.** The identification of the plug-in containing the action.
- ❑ **class.** The fully qualified name of the class implementing the action. The class must implement the JFace interface `IAction`. For example, it may be implemented as a subclass of class `Action`. When activated, its `run()` method is executed.

  In cases where the user might abort the action, the action should report success or failure via the method `notifyResult()`.

- ❑ **confirm.** If the value `true` is specified here, another button is displayed below the description. The end user must press this button as soon as she has finished her task. Only then does the Cheat Sheet step to the next item.

- ❑ **param1, param2, ...** Additional parameters that are passed to the class specified under attribute `class` can be supplied with these attributes. In this case the class must implement the interface `ICheatSheetAction`.

Listing 11.3 contains a complete Cheat Sheet.

```
<?xml version="1.0" encoding="UTF-8"?>
<cheatsheet title="Eclipse Multimedia Studio">

  <intro>
    <description>This page introduces you to the <b>Eclipse Multimedia
Studio</b>. Please read it. After each step press the action button.
  </description>
```

Listing 11.3 (Continues)

```
      </intro>

      <item title="Eclipse Multimedia Studio Perspective">
        <action
           pluginId="com.bdaum.vedit"
           class="com.bdaum.vedit.actions.OpenPerspectiveAction"
           confirm="true"/>
        <description>To experience the full comfort of the studio, please open
the
<b>Eclipse Multimedia Studio Perspective</b> with Window > Open Perspective >
Other ... > Multimedia Studio.
        </description>
      </item>

      <item
        href="/org.com.bdaum.vedit.doc.user/guide/installing_examples.htm"
         title="Install Example">
        <action
           pluginId="com.bdaum.vedit"
           class="com.bdaum.vedit.actions.InstallFirstProjectAction"
           confirm="false"/>
        <description>To populate the workspace with an example project and
example
files, please click here.
        </description>
      </item>
</cheatsheet>
```

Listing 11.3 (Continued)

However, the definition of such a Cheat Sheet alone is not sufficient to list it under the menu item Help > Cheat Sheets.... In addition, in the manifest file plugin.xml you need to extend the extension point org.eclipse.ui.cheatsheets.cheatSheetContent:

```
    <extension point="org.eclipse.ui.cheatsheets.cheatSheetContent">
        <cheatsheet
             name="Multimedia Studio Installation"
             contentFile="cheatsheets/vedit.xml"
             id="com.bdaum.vedit">
          <description>Step-by-step tutorial for the installation of the
Multimedia
Studio</description>
        </cheatsheet>
    </extension>
```

Summary

As a core concept of Eclipse, plug-ins are the essential concept when you develop applications on the basis of the Eclipse framework. Since Eclipse V3, the plug-in concept is based on the OSGi standard. In this chapter I have given an introduction into the architecture of the Eclipse platform. By now, you should know which components (in addition to the components from SWT and JFace) are available and can be used within your own applications. I have discussed editors, views, dialogs, forms, actions, preferences, the help system, and Cheat Sheets in detail.

You should also know how plug-ins can be configured via a manifest file, that the concept of extension points and extensions is essential to plug-ins, and where to find information about the extension points defined in the platform.

In the next chapter I will discuss what else is needed to implement a plug-in–based application.

12

Developing Your Own Eclipse-Based Products

From the implementation and testing of a plug-in to its deployment, there are quite a few steps to cover. Fortunately, Eclipse offers support in this area, but some steps may require manual intervention.

Before you can deploy a product, you must decide how you will segment the product into modules. Eclipse offers three different deployment constructs: features, plug-ins, and fragments. Eclipse uses the Ant assembly tool for all of these constructs when creating the deployment archives and automatically creates the scripts used to control Ant. However, manual modifications are possible.

Features combine several plug-ins into one deployment unit (Figure 12.1). *Plug-ins* can be enhanced and augmented by additional *fragments* deployed as a separate feature. In this chapter I will discuss each of these constructs in detail.

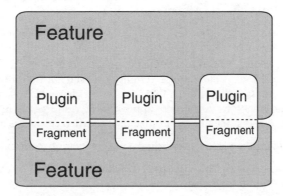

Figure 12.1

You have several options for the installation format. For example, you can deliver a plug-in as a ZIP file. Your customer then simply unpacks the file into the `eclipse/plugins` directory. Remember that the installation of the Eclipse SDK was quite similar. A further option is to use a commercial installation manager such as InstallAnyWhere or InstallShield. Finally, Eclipse offers its own elegant installation function, the Eclipse Update Manager. However, this function can be used only when deploying Eclipse add-ons, not for deploying standalone products. I will discuss these options in this chapter.

For standalone products the issue of customization is also important. For example, such a product should start with its own splash screen. The configuration of the About pages and the Help pages will also differ from the standard solution provided by the Eclipse SDK. Applications based on the Rich Client Platform (see Chapter 14) also need a different installation configuration.

In this chapter I will also discuss the localization of an application. Eclipse offers several ways to adapt applications to different national or cultural contexts.

Finally, I will discuss feature patches for deploying bug fixes.

Embedded Ant

Ant is an Apache project (`ant.apache.org`). Ant offers similar functionality to `make` and other tools that assemble deployment archives from development artifacts. The big difference between Ant and `make` and other such tools is that Ant does not use shell commands to perform tasks—all actions are performed with the help of Java classes. The Ant script is merely an XML file. The advantage is that Ant scripts are completely platform independent, as is the Ant system itself.

Ant is already embedded in the Eclipse SDK. To run an Ant script, you simply select the script file in the Navigator (the file must have the extension `.xml`) and then invoke the context function Run Ant… or the menu function Run > External Tools > Run As > Ant Build.

Configuration

If no Ant configuration currently exists, you must create a new configuration. This is done in a similar fashion to creating a Run configuration (see the "External Tools" section in Chapter 7). Just invoke the function Run > External Tools > External Tools….

The Configuration dialog (Figure 12.2) offers various options spread over several pages:

❑ On the Refresh page of the Configuration dialog, you can determine the resources for which a Refresh function should be executed after running Ant. The reason for this setting is that Ant is executed as an external tool. This means that it runs outside the Eclipse workspace. By default, the resource changes caused by Ant do not appear in the resource navigator of the Eclipse workbench. Therefore, it is necessary to synchronize the modified resources after running Ant.

❑ On the Targets page, you can select individual Ant targets for execution.

❑ On the Classpath page, you can modify the classpath under which Ant is running. Changes are required only if you have added your own Java classes to Ant.

- ❑ On the Properties page, you can assign values to Ant variables. Alternatively, you can specify property files that contain name/value pairs for Ant variables.

- ❑ On the JRE page, you can specify an alternate JRE for executing Ant.

- ❑ If you're running an alternate JRE, you can specify environment variables for the Ant build task on the Environment page.

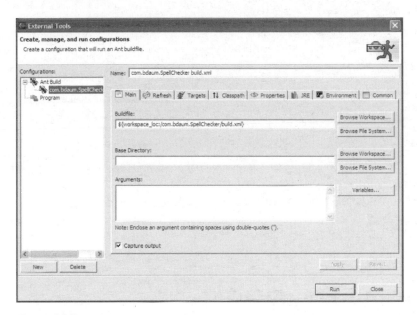

Figure 12.2

For typical Eclipse tasks, such as the assembly of deployment archives for features, plug-ins, and fragments, Eclipse generates the required Ant scripts automatically and removes them after usage. You can control the generation of these scripts via the build.properties file (see the section "Deploying a Feature"). If you have explicit requirements for an Ant script, you can manually generate it by selecting a manifest file (such as plugin.xml, fragment.xml, or feature.xml) and then invoking the context function PDE Tools > Create Ant Build File. The generated script targets are then stored in a file named build.xml.

If you want to modify generated scripts or create your own Ant scripts, you should, of course, learn the Ant script language. Detailed information about Ant can be found on the Apache Web site at ant.apache.org. Some comprehensive books about Ant are also available, such as those by Erik Hatcher and Jesse Tilly.

Editing Ant Scripts

You can open Ant scripts with the Ant editor (simply double-click the Ant script to open it). The Ant editor provided by Eclipse (Figure 12.3) is quite useful. It features syntax coloring, an Outline View, and a content assistant that you can invoke by pressing Ctrl+Spacebar.

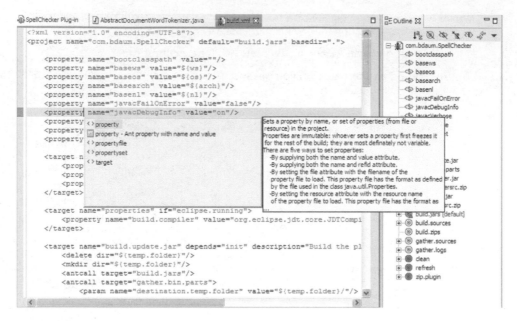

Figure 12.3

Plug-ins and Fragments

At minimum, a plug-in consists of just the manifest file `plugin.xml`. Normally, however, a plug-in contains additional binary Java files—in particular, the class `Plugin`—as well as help pages, a help table of contents, context associations, icons, schemas, and other resources.

In some cases it makes sense to subdivide a plug-in into several fragments. This allows you to develop the core functionality of a plug-in as early as possible. You can then separately deploy additional components later, such as support for a national language or support for other host operating systems. Fragments make this possible.

Fragments are created in a similar way to plug-ins via the New Wizard. However, instead of selecting Plug-in Project as the project type, you select Fragment Project. The wizard will then create a `fragment.xml` file instead of the `plugin.xml` file. The fragment manifest file `fragment.xml` is quite similar to `plugin.xml`, but it must specify the identification and version of the corresponding plug-in. In addition, the wizard does not generate a `Plugin` class, because fragments are not allowed to have their own `Plugin` class.

The fragment can be developed independently from the rest of the plug-in and can also be deployed separately. During installation it is merged into the corresponding plug-in, allowing the plug-in to access the functionality of the fragment. The end user will be unable to distinguish between the fragment and the corresponding plug-in. Of course, plug-ins should always be implemented such that they can be executed without the additional fragments.

Features

Features consist of one or several plug-ins that are deployed as a single functional unit. For example, the Eclipse Java IDE is a single feature consisting of several plug-ins. The feature description also contains copyright information and licensing conditions.

Creating and Editing Features

Features are created as separate projects. Again, you use the New Wizard to create a feature. The wizard leads you through the specification of the project name, the feature name, the feature identification, the version, and the feature provider. Finally, you need to mark all plug-ins that you want to belong to the feature. The wizard creates the manifest file `feature.xml` from these specifications, which is then opened in the Feature Editor (Figure 12.4). Here, you can include additional specifications.

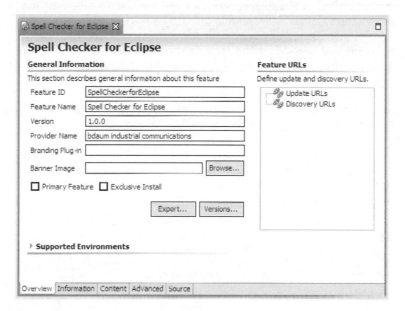

Figure 12.4

The Overview page shows all the specifications that you entered when you created the feature. You must make sure that the identification of the feature matches the identification of the main plug-in. You can also specify two types of URL on this page: a Discovery URL can point to a Web page that offers information about other products or technical support. An Update URL points to a Web address where the Update Manager can find new versions of the feature.

You should mark the Primary Feature check box if the current feature is not an add-on to already installed Eclipse platforms but represents (together with the Eclipse platform itself) a standalone product. By marking the Exclusive Install check box, you can ensure that no other features will be installed on the same platform. You can also specify a Banner Image, which will appear when the plug-in is activated the very first time in a session.

391

In the Supported Environments section, you can restrict the feature to certain host operating and windowing systems, to certain national language environments, and to certain processor architectures. If you specify nothing here, the feature can be installed anywhere.

The Versions button offers several options for version numbering. You have the option of determining the version number of the feature from the plug-ins or of forcing the version number of the feature onto the plug-ins. It is important that you press this button again after changing the version number of a plug-in to update the feature manifest! (The Export… button is discussed shortly in the section "Deploying a Feature.")

The next page, Information, can contain auxiliary information such as description text, a copyright notice, and license conditions. In addition to the explicitly defined text, you can also specify URLs that point to HTML pages that contain the required information. However, the license conditions should always be given both explicitly and as a URL. The explicit text appears during the installation of the feature, whereas the URL target is displayed when the end user invokes the function Help > About Eclipse Platform > Feature Details > More Info.

On the Advanced page, you can add existing features and external archive files to the current feature. You also may specify custom Install Handlers (see the section "Installing from an Update Site").

The window on the left side of the Content page in the Feature Editor (Figure 12.5) shows the plug-ins that belong to the feature. The window on the right shows the plug-ins that are necessary for executing the feature. It is not necessary to create this list manually—clicking the Compute button is sufficient.

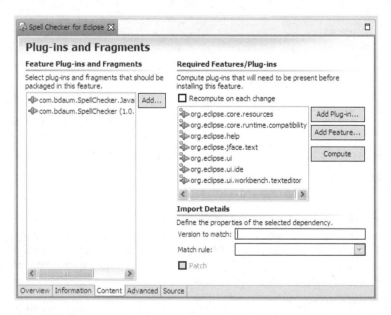

Figure 12.5

Deployment

Usually, you will deploy your product in one of the following formats:

❑ As an extension to existing Eclipse platforms. Such an extension comes usually in the form of a feature. I will discuss the deployment of single features next and the deployment of update sites (collections of features) shortly.

❑ As a complete product that includes the Eclipse runtime environment. I will discuss this type of deployment in the "Deploying Complete Products" section.

In both cases, you may deploy binaries only or you may include the source files, for example, when you want to deliver an SDK.

Deploying a Feature

To create a deployment package for a feature, click the Export... button on the Overview page of the Feature Editor. You have the option of creating a single ZIP file at the specified destination (such a file is installed by simply unpacking it into the `eclipse` directory) or creating individual JAR files for an update site (discussed in the next section). A third possibility is to export the deployed files into a specified directory structure. Optionally, the source code of the feature plug-ins can be exported along with the binaries.

When the Export function is executed, Eclipse will internally create an Ant script (discussed previously), perform the Ant build process to create the deployment archive, and delete the Ant script afterward. If you would rather keep this script, just check the option Save This Export Operation as an Ant Build Script and specify a suitable filename. Later, you can easily repeat the export operation even from outside Eclipse by running this Ant script.

The question is, how do you determine what goes into the deployment archive? The answer is quite simple, because you can control the creation of the Ant scripts—and thus the content of the deployment archives—by modifying the `build.properties` file. Such files exist for the feature project, for all plug-in projects, and for all fragment projects.

Eclipse provides a special Build page in the manifest editor for editing this file, which you can invoke simply by double-clicking the manifest file `plugin.xml`. Here you can add Java libraries (JAR files) and other files and folders to the build. You can even differentiate between binary builds and source builds. You will see an example of this in the "Defining the Spell Checker Feature" section of Chapter 13.

If you want to use a custom Ant script to perform a build for your project, you should mark the Custom Build option on the Build page. This will prevent Eclipse from overwriting your build script when the Export... function is used.

Now, what goes into such a build? You don't have to mark binary files, because they are already included in the JAR files that you have added to the build. Metafiles such as `.project`, `.classpath`, `.template`, `build.xml`, and `build.properties` are not required either. Those that are required are such files as icons, help pages, help control files (such as `toc.xml` and `contexts.xml`), license pages, the product customization files (`about.ini`), and so on.

Deploying Complete Products

A product based on Eclipse needs, of course, the Eclipse runtime environment. It is not necessary to deploy the whole Eclipse SDK. It is sufficient to deploy the minimal Eclipse runtime environment, plus the plug-ins required by your application. Minimal Eclipse runtime environments are available as separate downloads on the Eclipse Web site at www.eclipse.org.

Per ZIP

The Dependencies page of the manifest file plugin.xml provides a good overview of the plug-ins that must be deployed with any given plug-in. You therefore must include the product's feature manifest, your own plug-ins, and the plug-ins required by your plug-ins.

In the simplest case, you can zip everything together (using the Export... function of the Feature Editor) and leave the installation to the user. The installation is as simple as installing the Eclipse SDK. This works well as long as you provide a different deployment archive for each supported host platform.

Installation Aids

In more complex cases—for example, if you want to combine files for different host operating systems or national languages into one deployment archive, or if you want to include a Java runtime environment—you should make use of an installation tool such as InstallShield or InstallAnyWhere. Such tools, of course, need scripts, and you have to create these scripts. The best way to extract the deployed resources from Eclipse is to use the Export... function of the Feature Editor but select a directory structure as the output format (Deploy As). Detailed instructions about working with installers can be found in the Eclipse help system under Platform Plug-in Developer Guide > Programmer's Guide > Packaging and Delivering Eclipse Based Products > Product Installation Guidelines.

Customizing Products

If you deliver your product in this form, however, it does not look like your own product but like the Eclipse workbench with an installed plug-in. To really make it look like a product in its own right, you must make a few more customizations. You can do this in a few extra files listed in the table below. All of these files (except splash.bmp) are stored in the feature plug-in folder, that is, the plug-in that has the same identification as the feature that constitutes the product, and are referenced by the about.ini file.

about.ini	This file describes feature properties. The file format is the same as in a properties file (java.io.Properties). The following properties may be specified:
	aboutText. The text to be shown in the About dialog.
	windowImage. Refers to an icon of 16x16 pixels. The icon will appear at the top-left corner of all windows. This specification is necessary only for primary features.
	featureImage. Refers to an icon of 32x32 pixels. The icon will appear in the Feature Description section of the About dialog.

	about Image. Refers to an image of 500x330 or 115x164 pixels. The image will appear in the Product Description section of the About dialog.
	appName. Contains the application name. This specification is necessary only for primary features.
	welcomePerspective. Contains the identification of the perspective (see "Defining Perspectives" in Chapter 11) to be opened after installation of the feature.
	tipsAndTricksHref. Refers to a "tips and tricks" HTML page. This page is listed on the target platform under Help > Tips and Tricks.
	By the way, the same definitions can be made by adding properties elements to extension point org.eclipse.core.runtime .products (see "The Most Important SDK Extension Points" in Chapter 11).
about.html	HTML page with additional text about the plug-in or about the feature. This page is displayed by pressing the More Info button in the About dialog.
about.mappings	This page may contain parameter values that are inserted into the About texts. The file format is the same as in a Java properties file (java.io .Properties).
	For example, the property aboutText in the about.ini file might contain the text "This product has the registration number {0}." about.mappings could then contain the text "0=2342-8A8S-234B," resulting in the final text "This product has the registration number 2342-8A8S-234B."
about.properties	Contains translations for about.ini. This is necessary only for multilingual deployment; see "Internationalizing Products."
plugin_customization.ini	This file can contain the default preferences for other plug-ins (see Plug-ins and Fragments). The file format is the same as in a Java properties file (java.io.Properties). The condition is, of course, that the preference identifications of the target plug-ins are public. For example, you could start the Eclipse workbench under a different perspective:

	`org.eclipse.ui/`
	`defaultPerspectiveId=`
	`com.us.prod.ourPerspective`

`plugin_customization.properties`	Contains translations for `plugin_customization.ini`. This is necessary only for multilingual deployment; see Internationalizing Products.
`splash.bmp`	The splash screen is shown while the platform is being loaded. This image should be a 24-bit BMP file with a size of about 500x330 pixels. The file is used in the plug-ins `org.eclipse.platform` and `org.eclipse.core.boot`. A copy of this file is stored in the corresponding plug-in directories.

I will discuss advanced possibilities of product customization in the context of the Eclipse Rich Client Platform in Chapter 14.

Populating the Workspace

If you want to deploy example projects and files as well, you should refrain from populating the workspace directory during installation, because these projects and files would not normally appear in the Eclipse workspace: the necessary metadata is missing. In addition, you should never include the `.metadata` directory in a deployment; the files contained in this directory depend on the configuration, platform, version, and session history.

A better way is to install all example files in the plug-in directory. But how do you get them into the workspace? One idea would be to make the `Plugin` class transfer these files to the Eclipse workspace during its very first activation. Unfortunately, however, this class is activated only when it is actually needed, such as when the first resource belonging to this plug-in is opened. It would not be very helpful to users to show the example files in the Navigator at such a late stage.

Another possibility would be to leave the initiative to the end user. For example, you can give the end user the option of whether to populate the workspace with example files on a Cheat Sheet (see "The Help System" section in Chapter 11). Listing 12.1 shows how the implementation of a corresponding action might look.

```
package com.bdaum.multimedia.studio.actions;

import java.io.FileInputStream;
import java.io.FileNotFoundException;
import java.io.IOException;
import java.net.URL;
import org.eclipse.core.resources.IFile;
import org.eclipse.core.resources.IProject;
import org.eclipse.core.resources.IWorkspace;
import org.eclipse.core.resources.IWorkspaceRoot;
import org.eclipse.core.resources.ResourcesPlugin;
```

Listing 12.1 (Continues)

```java
import org.eclipse.core.runtime.CoreException;
import org.eclipse.core.runtime.IPath;
import org.eclipse.core.runtime.Path;
import org.eclipse.core.runtime.Platform;
import org.eclipse.jface.action.Action;
import com.bdaum.multimedia.studio.StudioPlugin;

public class InstallFirstProjectAction extends Action {

    private static String EXAMPLE_PROJECT = "firstStudio";
    private static String EXAMPLE_FILE = "HipHopStudio.mms";

    // Constructor
    public InstallFirstProjectAction() {
    }

    // Override run-Methode
    public void run() {
        // Fetch workspace instance
        IWorkspace workspace = ResourcesPlugin.getWorkspace();
        // Get workspace root
        IWorkspaceRoot root = workspace.getRoot();
        // Create IProject instance with specified name
        IProject firstModel = root.getProject(EXAMPLE_PROJECT);
        if (!firstModel.exists()) {
            try {
                // Create project if it does not exist
                firstModel.create(null);
            } catch (CoreException e) {
                System.err.println(e);
            }
        }
        if (!firstModel.isOpen()) {
            try {
                // Open project if it is not open
                firstModel.open(null);
            } catch (CoreException e) {
                System.err.println(e);
            }
        }
        // Construct path of workspace file
        IPath path = new Path(EXAMPLE_PROJECT + "/" + EXAMPLE_FILE);
        // Create IFile instance with specified path
        IFile mFile = root.getFile(path);
        if (!mFile.exists()) {
            // If file does not yet exist, we fetch the URL
            // of the example file in the plug-in directory
            URL url =
            StudioPlugin.getDefault().getBundle().
                        getEntry(EXAMPLE_FILE);
            try {
                // Resolve the Eclipse pseudo URL
                url = Platform.resolve(url);
                // Extract file path
```

Listing 12.1 (Continues)

```
                String urls = url.getPath();
                try {
                    // Get file in plug-in directory
                    java.io.File input = new java.io.File(urls);
                    // Create new file in workspace and fill with content
                    mFile.create(new FileInputStream(input), true, null);
                } catch (FileNotFoundException e) {
                    System.err.println(e);
                } catch (CoreException e) {
                    System.err.println(e);
                }
            } catch (IOException e) {
                System.err.println(e);
            }
        }
    }
}
```

Listing 12.1 (Continued)

Creating Update Sites

Features whose purpose is to upgrade existing platforms in the field are best deployed in the format supported by the Update Manager. Don't be misled by the name of this manager—you can use it to deploy even brand-new plug-ins and features. The term *update* relates to the Eclipse platform being updated, not to the individual plug-ins and features.

You can, of course, also deploy a feature or plug-in in the form of a ZIP file, but using the Update Manager does have some advantages. During the installation, the Update Manager checks to see if all required plug-ins do exist and if their versions are compatible. In addition, it can check to determine whether the host operating system, the windowing system, and the processor architecture match the installation requirements. Before performing the installation, the Update Manager can prompt the end user with the license conditions and will perform the installation only when the end user accepts them. The Update Manager also supports installation over the Web via an installation URL, to avoid a separate download.

To support installation via the Update Manager, you must create an *update site*. Such a site consists of two directories—the `features` directory and the `plugins` directory—and a site manifest `site.xml`. An update site can contain several features that can be installed selectively.

You can create such a site quickly with the help of the New Wizard. Open the New Wizard and then select Plug-in Development > Update Site Project. Enter the name of the project. On the next page you can change the names of the plug-in and feature folders. Optionally, you may generate an `index.html` page to advertise the features on your update site. When you press the Finish button, the manifest file `site.xml` is created and the Site Editor opens (see Figure 12.6). You can now enter additional specifications using the pages of the Site Editor.

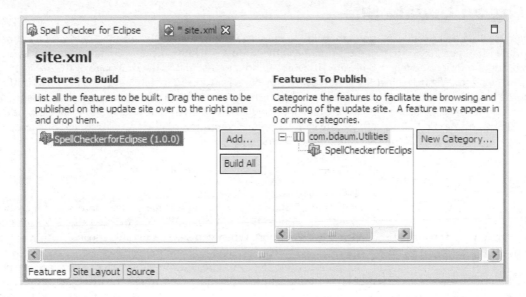

Figure 12.6

❏ On the Features page, you can specify the features that are to be built by the Update Manager (left-hand side) and the features to be published (right-hand side). To add features to the left-hand side, press the Add button and mark the features in the list that you want to include in the update site. On the right-hand side you can create categories by pressing the New Category button. Categories are useful for organizing your published features into groups. To create a subcategory, select a category and press the New Category button again. You can add features to categories by dragging them from the left-hand side onto a category. A feature can appear in several categories. If you drag a feature to the right-hand side but not onto a category, it will end up in the default category, Other. To build or rebuild all features listed on the left side, press the Build All button.

❏ On the Site Layout page, you can enter some descriptive text and a URL pointing to the published update site on the Web. At this address you should always place an index.html file containing installation instructions, for example, the index.html file generated during creation of the update site. You can also specify different names for the folders containing the feature and plug-in files. If you want to add extra files not contained in these folders to the update site, you can do so by specifying the path-to-URL mapping for each archive that you want to add.

Installing from an Update Site

The Eclipse Update Manager offers functions for installing and removing new features, updating existing features, and managing the current platform configuration. You can access it via the menu item Help > Software Updates.

Adding an Update Site

After creating an update site, you can install the new feature immediately with the help of the Eclipse Update Manager. To do so, you must first make the update site known to the Update Manager by invoking the function Help > Software Updates > Find and Install. On the first page of the Install/Update Wizard, select the option Search for New Features to Install and press the Next button. On the next page, all update sites known to Eclipse are listed. You can add another site by pressing one of three buttons. Click Add Update Site and specify the URL of an update site on the Web; click Add Local Site and navigate to an update site stored on your computer; or click Add Archived Site and navigate to a ZIP or JAR file that contains an update site.

Installing Features

After you have added the new site, you must mark all sites in the list that you want to scan for installable features. Then press the Next button. Eclipse will go through all of the marked sites step-by-step and present the features offered there for installation. When you select a feature, its description will be displayed in the text field below the listed features. For more information such as license conditions, copyright notices, and general information, press the Properties button. To install one or more features, mark these features and click the Next button. Eclipse will walk you through the installation process. Once the installation is complete, you will be asked if you want to restart the workbench. The Eclipse developers intend to make the installation of plug-ins and features dynamic so that you will not need to restart in order to activate an installed feature, but currently restarting the workbench is recommended.

If you have installed a feature and it does not show up in the workbench after a restart, it may well be that Eclipse has not enabled the feature because some prerequisites (either prerequisite features or prerequisite plug-ins) are missing. Unfortunately, there is no easy way to gather this information during installation. In such a case, you should check with the feature provider about required features and plug-ins.

Updating Features

Once you have installed a feature, it is quite easy to check for new versions and to install them. Just invoke the function Help > Software Updates > Find and Install again, but this time select the option Search for Updates of the Currently Installed Features. Press the Next button, and Eclipse will scan all known update sites and look for newer versions of the installed features. If newer versions exist, they will appear in a list. By marking features in this list you can install them in the usual way.

You can even automate the task of keeping your platform up-to-date. Under Window > Preferences > Install/Update > Automatic Updates you can specify that the known update sites should be scanned with each start of the Eclipse platform or regularly controlled by a specified schedule.

Managing the Configuration

If you want to deactivate a feature or if you want to return to a previous platform configuration, you find the required function under Help > Software Updates > Manage Configuration. On the left side of the window you will find the current configuration tree. You can view the details by expanding the tree nodes (by clicking the + icon). To disable a feature, select it and then click the Disable hyperlink at the right side. Afterward, you may either enable it again or remove it completely.

When the root node Eclipse Platform is selected, you will see some additional functions listed on the right side of the window. By clicking the Revert to Previous hyperlink you can return to the state of the platform before you applied the last change to the configuration. If you have previously added features by simply unpacking them into the \eclipse\ root folder, the Process Detected Changes hyperlink appears. By clicking this hyperlink you can perform the missing installation steps for such a feature.

Install Handlers

The Eclipse Update Manager can be extended via so-called *install handlers*. These are Java classes that implement the interface IInstallHandler from the package org.eclipse.update.core (usually they extend the standard implementation BaseInstallHandler). The methods of such a class are called at specific points of the installation or update process and can perform specific actions.

You can predefine an install handler as a global install handler. This is done in the manifest file plugin.xml of a suitable plug-in at the extension point org.eclipse.update.core .installHandlers. Alternatively, you can include an install handler in the installation archive. However, in this case, they can be used only within the current installation (a local install handler).

If you want to use an install handler during the installation of a feature, you must declare it on the Advanced page of the feature manifest feature.xml (see the section "Creating and Editing Features"). There you specify, in the Library field, the name of the archive containing the install handler. In the Handler field, you specify the name of the IInstallHandler class. If you use a global instead of a local install handler, the Library field remains empty and the Handler field specifies the identification under which the global install handler was installed.

A typical application of install handlers is for the installation of resources outside the Eclipse platform, for example, if you want to deploy a specific Java Runtime Environment.

Internationalizing Products

I am wary of writing anything about this topic, because there is an excellent article about internationalization by Dan Kehn, Scott Fairbrother, and Cam-Thu Le on www.eclipse.org. A short overview should therefore be sufficient. A practical example is given in the section "Internationalizing the Spell Checker" of Chapter 13.

Internationalization is often understood as merely translating texts presented to the end user into a national language. This is certainly an important aspect of internationalization, but it is not the only one. For example, the meaning of images may differ from culture to culture and so the images should also be adapted to the target culture. You probably are aware of the confusion that date formats (European vs. U.S.) can cause. But the placement of GUI elements may also differ from culture to culture. Countries such as the Arabic nations and Israel, for example, read from right to left, and many Asiatic countries read from top to bottom. A good example of how things can go wrong was an advertisement for a new detergent in Arabic countries. It read: "Big effect in very little time" and displayed the dirty laundry on the left and the clean laundry on the right!

Similarly, people may have different expectations of where important form elements should be positioned. The various lengths of text constants in different languages may also influence the layout of screen masks.

Despite these layout problems, I will concentrate here on text elements in different languages. Internationalizing other items such as images and icons as well as currency and date formats can often be achieved by mapping them onto text strings (image name, format string).

Text Constants in Programs

The simplest case is the internationalization of text constants in programs. In the Java source editor, Eclipse offers excellent support for this with the context function Source > Externalize Strings. This wizard creates a list with all string constants used in a compilation unit. Afterward, you can sort these string constants into three different categories:

❑ **Translate.** In this case the string constant is moved to a properties file. In the source code, the string constant is replaced with a call to an access method. This method fetches the string constant at runtime from the properties file with the help of a specified key. In addition, the source line is suffixed with a comment that looks like this:

```
//$NON-NLS-1$
```

This comment indicates that the string constant (now the key) must not be analyzed when the function Externalize Strings is executed again. For example, the instruction

```
replaceAction.setText("Replace");
```

is translated into

```
replaceAction.setText
  Messages.getString("SpellCorrectionView.Replace_5")); //$NON-NLS-1$
```

❑ **Never Translate.** The string constant is equipped with a // $NON-NLS-...$ comment, so that it is not analyzed in future invocations of the function Externalize Strings. For example

```
manager.add(new Separator("Additions"));
```

is translated into

```
manager.add(new Separator("Additions")); //$NON-NLS-1$
```

❑ **Skip.** Nothing is changed. The string constant is offered for externalization in future invocations of the function Externalize Strings.

The wizard performs all the selected replacements in the source file. It also creates a properties file within the current package that contains the externalized string constants. It also creates a Messages class that organizes access to the file via the getString() method.

All that remains to do is to translate the properties file into the target language. If you use the Java naming convention `basename_lang_region_variant.properties` for the properties file, the `Message` class will automatically use the correct properties file, depending on the national language of the target host platform. You can then add new languages in the form of new properties files without recompiling a single Java class.

In some cases, it may be necessary to embed program-generated values into the string constants. This can be done with the help of parameters. These are defined in the string literals in the properties file, in the following way:

```
Editor.save.SVG.error=Error saving SVG file {0} in folder {1}
```

If you use such parameters, it is a good idea to extend the `Messages` class with a parameterized variant of the method `getString()`:

```
public static String getString(String key, Object[] params) {
    if (params == null)
        return getString(key);
    try {
        return java.text.MessageFormat.format(getString(key), params);
    } catch (Exception e) {
        return "!"+key+"!";
    }
}
```

Text Constants in Manifest Files

To internationalize the various manifest files such as `plugin.xml`, `feature.xml`, `fragment.xml`, `site.xml`, `about.ini`, etc. requires a bit more work, because there is no tool support for this task.

Here, you need to create a corresponding properties file for each of these files: `plugin.properties`, `feature.properties`, `site.properties`, `about.properties`, etc. The exception is `fragment.xml`. Instead of `fragment.properties`, the file `plugin.properties` is used.

In the original file, replace the translatable string constants with key strings that are identified via a prefixed % character. In the corresponding properties file, specify the key definition. You can translate these files into the target language afterward, as discussed in the previous section.

Here is an example of the definition of an Action Set in the manifest file `plugin.xml`:

```
label="Check spelling"
```

You would change this into

```
label="%checkSpelling"
```

and include in the `plugin.properties` file the line

```
checkSpelling=Check spelling
```

Help Texts and Cheat Sheets

In the case of help pages and Cheat Sheets this approach is not suitable. Instead, you need to translate the whole page. You must create a separate folder for each language in which to store the translated pages.

At runtime, the correct folder is selected by evaluating substitution variables. Eclipse understands four different substitution variables that can modify library paths:

`os`	This variable is replaced by a token representing the current operation system (`linux`, `macosx`, `qnx`, `solaris`, `win32`).
`ws`	This variable is replaced by a token representing the current windowing system (`carbon`, `gtk`, `motif`, `photon`, `win32`).
`nl`	This variable is replaced by the current Java locale.
`arch`	This variable is replaced by a token representing the current processor architecture (`PA_RISC`, `ppc`, `sparc`, `x86`).

When you want to test a plug-in that uses these variables, you can set the variables under Window > Preference > Plug-in Development > Target Environment.

For example, if you specify a Cheat Sheet (see the section "The Help System" in Chapter 11) in `plugin.xml`, you can use a substitution variable for the folder name:

```
contentFile="$nl/vedit.xml"
```

During execution, the variable $nl is replaced by the current locale, for example by `DE_de`. The Cheat Sheet is then fetched from `DE_de/vedit.xml`.

This works quite similarly for help pages, too. Here you would translate not only the HTML pages but also the table of contents (`toc.xml`) and the context associations (`contexts.xml`), since these files contain references as well as display texts. References to `toc.xml` and `contexts.xml` (for example, from `plugin.xml`) would then be prefixed with $nl/. This is normally not required for the references specified in `toc.xml` and `contexts.xml`, since these references are usually specified relative to the current location.

Unfortunately, this approach has a severe disadvantage: if a specific language package is not available, Eclipse will simply show nothing instead of the standard English version. Fortunately, there is an alternative, which works without substitution variables. This alternative approach relies solely on naming conventions. If you want, for example, to create help pages and Cheat Sheets in the German language, you would store them under the directory `nl/de` (for all German language areas) and `nl/de/DE` (for Germany only). At runtime, Eclipse evaluates the Locale information of the JVM and tries to find an appropriate folder under the `nl/` directory. If such a folder is not found, the standard help pages and Cheat Sheets (usually in English) are used. These pages are not stored under the `nl/` directory.

Deploying National Language Resource Bundles

The best method is to deploy language bundles as separate fragments (see "Plug-ins and Fragments"). To do so, just create a package structure within the new fragment that mirrors the package structure of the corresponding plug-in. However, the fragment packages contain only the properties files that have been translated into the target language. The translated nl/ folders are also included in the fragment. You must mark these folders on the Build page of the manifest editor for inclusion into the deployment archive (see the section "Deploying a Feature"). An exception to the rule is the plugin_*locale*.xml files, which must be stored in the src/ directory instead of the project folder.

Patches

When a product is deployed and then bugs are later discovered, it is often unacceptable for the customer to reinstall the whole product, especially if the product is large. Download times are lengthy in such cases, and sometimes an online update is impossible. Fixing bugs by sending CDs to customers is expensive. Fortunately, Eclipse-based applications have a modular structure that enables a partial update.

The Eclipse Feature Patch allows exactly that. Instead of redeploying the entire updated feature, you can create a feature patch that contains only the modified plug-ins. The Eclipse Update Manager is intelligent enough to merge the patch into the installed feature.

To create a Feature Patch, create a new project by choosing File > New > Other > Plug-in Development > Feature Patch. In the wizard enter a project name, and continue to the next page. There define a patch ID, a patch name, and the patch provider. Then select the feature to be patched. On the Included Plug-ins and Fragments page, select the plug-ins and fragments that go into the patch. Then press Finish. The Feature Patch project is now ready for deployment. It can be deployed like any other feature project.

Summary

In this chapter I have discussed additional concepts required for creating Eclipse-based products. You should now know what fragments and features are and how they relate to plug-ins. You should be able to internationalize and customize your application and to deploy such an application.

In the next chapter you will apply the knowledge gained in Chapter 11 and this chapter in a larger example.

Project Three: A Spell Checker as an Eclipse Plug-in

The third example application is a fully functional spell checker for the Eclipse SDK. An early version of this example was published in my book *Eclipse 2 for Java Developsers*, and the (enhanced) plug-in that was offered as a separate download became quite popular—so popular that in Eclipse 3 the Java editor was equipped with an integrated spell checker.

The spell checker presented here, however, is more versatile. It can perform spell checking not only in Java sources but in any editor and text widget. And it can be extended with plug-ins so that it can intelligently spell-check text formats such as Java, C++, JavaScript, HTML, PHP, JSP, and so on. For the purpose of this book, I present a stripped-down version (no checking while typing, no overriding of preferences on the project level) due to space limitations. The full version, including source code, is available at www.wrox.com (see also Appendix C).

During the implementation of this spell checker I demonstrate the following plug-in development techniques:

- ❑ Definition of a plug-in manifest
- ❑ Integration of third-party JARs into your own plug-ins
- ❑ Use of the API for the ITextEditor interface and the MultiEditor class
- ❑ Addition of menu items to the menu structure of the Eclipse workbench
- ❑ Addition of menu items to the context menu of editors
- ❑ Addition of tool buttons to the toolbar of the Eclipse workbench
- ❑ Association of actions with keyboard shortcuts
- ❑ Implementation of a workbench view (for correction proposals)

Chapter 13

- ❑ Creation of a view toolbar and a view menu

- ❑ Location and opening of view instances

- ❑ Creation of new preference pages

- ❑ Creation of a help system, including table of contents, context-sensitive help (InfoPops), and active help

- ❑ Internationalization of a plug-in

I also show how to write a plug-in that can be extended by others. The spell-checking functionality will not be implemented in the form of a single plug-in but as a group of cooperating plug-ins. Different spell-checking strategies for different document types can be implemented as required and installed separately. To do this, the spell checker base plug-in defines its own extension points. These points allow the addition of file type–specific plug-ins. As an example I will show the implementation of an extension plug-in for spell checking in JavaScript source files. This gives the end user the optional ability to perform spell checking in Javadoc comments, non-Javadoc comments, and string literals. When I implement this plug-in, I will demonstrate the following techniques:

- ❑ Definition of an extension point, including a schema

- ❑ Definition of dependencies between plug-ins

- ❑ Integration of help systems from several plug-ins

The Spell Checker Core Classes

The core classes of the spell checker consist of the a spell checking engine (which we take from an existing Open Source project), and classes that construct a framework in which later add-ons may plug in. This framework is, in particular, responsible for implementing a GUI (Spell Correction View, actions, preference pages), for controlling the spell-checking engine, and for managing additional plug-ins.

The Engine

I don't implement the core spell checking classes myself but instead use the engine of the jazzy spell checker. This engine is completely implemented in Java and is available as an Open Source project at `sourceforge.net/projects/jazzy`. The algorithms used in this engine belong to the most effective current spell-checking algorithms.

I use version 0.5 of jazzy here. The archive `jazzy-0.5-bin.zip` also contains the source code. In addition, the dictionary `english.0.zip` is required, which is also available on the SourceForge Web site.

The jazzy archive also contains the JAR file `jazzy-core.jar`. This is the archive that you will need for your project. It contains the packages `com.swabunga.spell.engine` and `com.swabunga.spell.event`.

Overview

Figure 13.1 shows the most important classes in the spell checker and how they interact (the numbers in parentheses indicate the sequence of method calls). In addition, there are the `Plugin` class, the classes for managing the preferences, and the classes for configuring the spell-checking engine. The spell-checking process is initiated by the `CheckSpellingActionDelegate` class. The `SpellCheckManager` class acts as a central controller. The `SpellCheckCorrectionView` class displays spelling errors and interacts with the end user. The `DocumentWordTokenizer` class is used by the jazzy engine to tokenize a document into single words. The `SpellCheckingTarget` class acts as a common view on editors and text widgets. It provides the text content of these objects in the form of `IDocument` instances to the other classes and is concerned with text selection and text replacement.

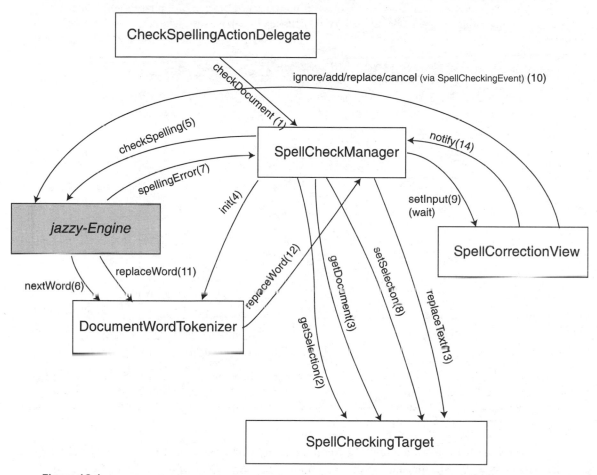

Figure 13.1

Setting Up the Project

First, you want to make sure that the functions for plug-in development are enabled in your Eclipse platform. Go to Window > Configure Activities… and mark Plug-in Development.

Next, you must set up the target platform. Testing and debugging a plug-in does not happen in the development platform but in a separate Eclipse session. The configuration of this platform can differ considerably from the configuration of the development platform. For example, you may want to run the new plug-in in the minimal Eclipse runtime environment, that is, in a platform that does not have a Java IDE or a PDE. So you must first determine with which plug-ins your target platform is equipped. You can do this with the function Window > Preferences > Plug-in Development > Target Platform (Figure 13.2). You can exclude certain plug-ins during the configuration of the target platform, and you can include other plug-ins that are not in the Eclipse workspace by clicking the Not In Workspace button.

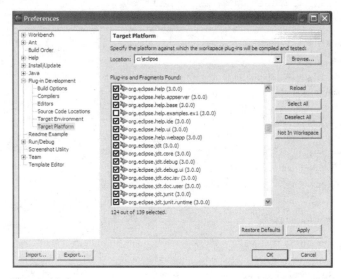

Figure 13.2

In this case, you may want to test the spell checker plug-in in an environment that is equipped with a Java IDE and a PDE, since you want to use the spell-checking facility in the editors of those features. Therefore, you need to checkmark all plug-ins of the target platform with the exception of the example plug-ins and the source code plug-ins.

If you have already installed the spell checker plug-in into your development platform, you should also disable all of the plug-ins that start with `com.bdaum.SpellChecker` in order to avoid conflicts.

Instead of modifying the global preferences for the target platform, another possibility is to later create a special Run configuration for the new plug-in. To do so, invoke Run > Run… and press the New button to create a new configuration for a runtime workbench. On the Plug-ins page, you may select from various options. When you mark the Choose Plug-ins and Fragments to Launch option from the list, you may select individual plug-ins for inclusion into the test platform. If you want to use the minimum number of plug-ins for running your plug-in, proceed as follows:

1. Press the Deselect All button.

2. Now mark the Workspace Plug-ins check box (or only the plug-ins that you want to test).

3. Press the Add Required Plug-ins button. This will mark all plug-ins that are required for running the plug-ins selected in the previous step.

But now let's return from this excursion and create the project. In contrast to the first two example applications, you don't create a Java project for this example. Instead, you need to switch to the Plug-in Development perspective and select File > New > Plug-in Project. This wizard leads you step-by-step through the creation of a plug-in project:

1. On the second wizard page, enter the project's name. This will also be the identification of the plug-in. You should therefore choose a name that is not being used by the manufacturers of other plug-ins. Common practice is to prefix the plug-in with the identification of the authoring organization. I have named the plug-in `com.bdaum.SpellChecker` in this case.

2. On the next page, select Java Project and leave all other controls at their default values.

3. On the next page, enter a provider name. Make sure that the options Generate the Java Class That Controls the Plug-in's Life Cycle and This Plug-in Will Make Contributions to the UI are checked.

4. On the next page, checkmark the option Create a Plug-in Using One of the Templates and select Custom Plug-in Wizard. This will allow you to generate large parts of the new plug-in from existing templates.

5. On the next page, checkmark the options Hello World Action Set, Help Table of Contents, Preference Page, and View. Remove the check marks from all other options.

Now you need to configure the generators for these templates. On the following pages, enter the details:

❑ On the Sample Action Set page, change Action Class Name to `CheckSpellingActionDelegate`.

❑ On the Sample Help Table of Contents page, change Label of Table of Contents to `Spell Checker`. Checkmark the Primary option because this is the main table of contents for the spell checker feature. Remove the check marks of all categories because you want to create only a single table of contents with no nested tocs.

❑ On the Sample Preference Page page, change Page Class Name to `DefaultSpellCheckerPreferencePage`. Under Page Name enter `%Spelling`. The % character indicates that this is not display text but a key that still needs to be resolved into display text when the project is internationalized (see "Text Constants in Manifest Files" later in this chapter).

❑ On the Main View Settings page, change View Class Name to `SpellCorrectionView`. Under View Name, enter `%Spell`. Under View Category Id, enter `com.bdaum.SpellChecker.views`, and under View Category Name, enter `%Spell_Checker`. (The view category identifies the group under which the new view appears when the function Window > Show View is invoked.) Select Table Viewer as the viewer type (this table will later contain the correction proposals). In addition, uncheck the option Add the View to the Resource Perspective. The view therefore remains invisible initially—it will appear only when the spell checker is in use.

❑ On the View Features page, uncheck the option Add Support for Sorting.

When you press the Finish button, Eclipse opens the new plug-in the `plugin.xml` manifest in the PDE editor. Eclipse has also generated the packages `com.bdaum.SpellChecker`, `com.bdaum.SpellChecker.actions`, `com.bdaum.SpellChecker.preferences`, and `com.bdaum.SpellChecker.views` with the classes `SpellCheckerPlugin`, `CheckSpellingActionDelegate`, `DefaultSpellCheckerPreferencePage`, and `SpellCorrectionView`. You now have the base classes for the new plug-in, and you may now modify and complete these classes.

The Plug-in Configuration

Next you need to describe some more details of the new plug-in in the manifest file `plugin.xml`. If this file is not yet open, you can double-click it to open it. Figure 13.3 shows the Overview page of the plug-in manifest. Since you are going to define your own extension point for this plug-in, you will also need to define a schema (see the section "The Schema documentTokenizer.exsd").

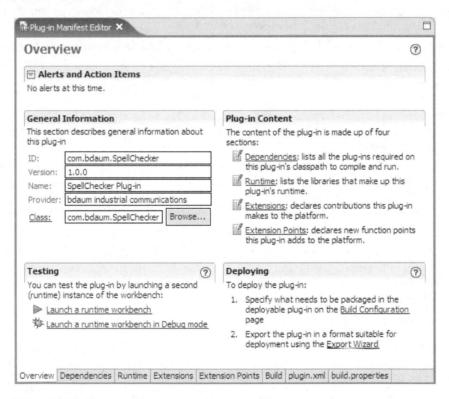

Figure 13.3

The Manifest plugin.xml

The following source code shows the manifest in its nearly final state. All changes and additions applied manually are printed in bold. Now, what do you need to change?

```
<?xml version="1.0" encoding="UTF-8"?>
<?eclipse version="3.0"?>
<plugin
    id="com.bdaum.SpellChecker"
    name="SpellChecker Plug-in"
    version="1.0.0"
    provider-name="bdaum industrial communications"
    class="com.bdaum.SpellChecker.SpellCheckerPlugin">
```

On the Runtime page of the PDE editor, change the suggested archive name to SpellChecker.jar. Also add the imported JAR file jazzy-core.jar to the list of required libraries. On the lower-right section of this page, checkmark the option Export the Whole Library for Both Libraries. This allows later extensions to use the classes defined in these libraries.

```
<runtime>
    <library name="SpellChecker.jar">
        <export name="*"/>
    </library>
    <library name="jazzy-core.jar">
        <export name="*"/>
    </library>
</runtime>
```

The spell checker plug-in requires a few other plug-ins for its operation. You can add these plug-ins to the Dependencies page. First, there are the basic plug-ins for the Eclipse runtime: org.eclipse.core.resources and org.eclipse.core.runtime. Second, you will need the basic plug-ins for the user interface of the Eclipse IDE, org.eclipse.ui and org.eclipse.ui.ide. Third, because the plug-in deals with text editors and text processing, you will also need the plug-ins org.eclipse.jface.text and org.eclipse.ui.workbench.texteditor. And finally, the plug-in for help support, org.eclipse.help, is required, too, because the spell checker plug-in will offer help to the end user.

For the plug-ins org.eclipse.core.runtime, org.eclipse.ui, org.eclipse.jface.text, and org.eclipse.help mark the option Re-export the Dependency. This will make these plug-ins available to all plug-ins that specify com.bdaum.SpellChecker as a required plug-in.

```
<requires>
    <import plugin="org.eclipse.core.resources"/>
    <import plugin="org.eclipse.core.runtime"
           export="true"/>
    <import plugin="org.eclipse.ui" export="true"/>
    <import plugin="org.eclipse.ui.ide"/>
    <import plugin="org.eclipse.jface.text" export="true"/>
    <import plugin="org.eclipse.ui.workbench.texteditor"/>
    <import plugin="org.eclipse.help" export="true"/>
</requires>
```

On the Extension Points page, you need to define a new extension point, documentTokenizer. This extension point will allow you and others to add extensions for specific text formats later, such as a plug-in for Java source code spell checking (see the section "A Plug-in for Java Properties"). The name of this extension point is chosen on the basis that later extensions will consist more or less of specific tokenizers that break the text into single words following file type–specific rules.

```
<extension-point    id="documentTokenizer"
                        name="Document Tokenizer"
                        schema="schema/documentTokenizer.exsd"/>
```

Now turn your attention to the Extensions page. You need to make the generated example action more concrete. The current spell-checking plug-in contains only a single action, Check Spelling.

❑   In particular, you need to set a display text (label), an explanation text (tooltip), an icon for the disabled state (disabledIcon), and an icon for the enabled state (hoverIcon). It is easier to define these settings when the referenced icons already exist in an appropriate folder (see the section "Managing Images"). Also, the Action Set gets a new name.

❑   Define a new toolbarPath com.bdaum.SpellChecker.spell_checker, so that the action will appear in a separate group in the workbench's toolbar.

❑   For menubarPath specify the value edit/spelling. Consequently, the action will appear under the Edit menu.

❑   By not specifying a value for the enablesFor attribute, you ensure that the action's enabling does not depend on the number of selected resources but is controlled programmatically.

❑   Specify a definitionId to establish a reference to the following command extension.

❑   Under helpContextId define the anchor point for context-sensitive help (InfoPop).

```
<extension point="org.eclipse.ui.actionSets">
    <actionSet id="com.bdaum.SpellChecker.actionSet"
                        label="%Spell_Checker" visible="true">
      <action id="com.bdaum.SpellChecker.action1" class=
          "com.bdaum.SpellChecker.actions.CheckSpellingActionDelegate"
          label="%Check_Spelling"
          tooltip="%Checks_any_text"
          disabledIcon="icons/full/dlcl16/check.gif"
          hoverIcon="icons/full/clcl16/check.gif"
      icon="icons/full/clcl16/check.gif"
          toolbarPath="com.bdaum.SpellChecker.spell_checker/Check"
          menubarPath="edit/spelling"
          definitionId="com.bdaum.SpellChecker.check_spelling"
          helpContextId="com.bdaum.SpellChecker.action_context">
      </action>
    </actionSet>
</extension>
```

The specification of command extensions (org.eclipse.ui.commands) allows end users to configure the perspectives of the workbench with actions contributed by plug-ins. In addition, command extensions allow you to define key bindings that may later be modified by the end user.

First, define a command and associate it with the `org.eclipse.ui.category.textEditor`
category. Thus, the command will later be listed under the Text Editing category when the function
Window > Preferences > Workbench > Keys is invoked. Note that the ID of the command must match
the `definitionId` of the action defined previously.

Second, define two key bindings: one for the global context and one for the text editor context. This will
assign the F9 function key to the spell-checking action both in generic windows and during text editing.
If you want, you may define additional key bindings for other configurations such as the emacs configuration (`org.eclipse.ui.emacsAcceleratorConfiguration`).

```xml
<extension id="com.bdaum.SpellChecker.commands"
        name="%Spell_Checker_Command"
        point="org.eclipse.ui.commands">
    <command name="%Check_Spelling"
            category="org.eclipse.ui.category.textEditor"
            description="%Starts_spell_checking"
            id="com.bdaum.SpellChecker.check_spelling">
    </command>
    <keyBinding keySequence="F9"
            contextId="org.eclipse.ui.globalScope"
            commandId="com.bdaum.SpellChecker.check_spelling"
            keyConfigurationId=
                "org.eclipse.ui.defaultAcceleratorConfiguration">
    </keyBinding>
    <keyBinding keySequence="F9"
            contextId="org.eclipse.ui.textEditorScope"
            commandId="com.bdaum.SpellChecker.check_spelling"
            keyConfigurationId=
                "org.eclipse.ui.defaultAcceleratorConfiguration">
    </keyBinding>
</extension>
```

The spell-checking function should also be accessible via the context menu of the editors. You can do this
by defining an extension for the extension point `org.eclipse.ui.popupMenus` and adding
`viewerContributions` to this extension. Unfortunately, there is no way to add a function to any editor type that may later be installed into the platform by other plug-ins. The only thing you can do is to
define viewer contributions to the most common editor types. You associate viewer contributions to editors by specifying a `targetId`. When an editor is initialized, it sets this menu ID with the method
`setEditorContextMenuId()`. The mother of all text editors, the `AbstractTextEditor` class, sets
the menu ID `#EditorContext`. The subclass `TextEditor` overrides this with
`#TextEditorContext`, and the subclass `CompilationUnitEditor`, which acts as an ancestor of
source code editors such as the Java editor, overrides this menu ID with
`#CompilationUnitEditorContext`. By specifying these three IDs, you should cover a wide range of
editors, indeed.

```xml
<extension point="org.eclipse.ui.popupMenus">
    <viewerContribution id="com.bdaum.SpellChecker.editorContextMenu"
            targetID="#CompilationUnitEditorContext">
        <action id="com.bdaum.SpellChecker.check_spelling_in_context1"
                label="%Check_Spelling"
                icon="icons/full/clcl16/check.gif"
```

```
                    helpContextId="com.bdaum.SpellChecker.action_context"
          class="com.bdaum.SpellChecker.actions.CheckSpellingActionDelegate"
                    menubarPath="additions">
        </action>
    </viewerContribution>
    <viewerContribution id="com.bdaum.SpellChecker.editorContextMenu"
            targetID="#TextEditorContext">
        <action id="com.bdaum.SpellChecker.check_spelling_in_context2"
            label="%Check_Spelling"
            icon="icons/full/clcl16/check.gif"
            helpContextId="com.bdaum.SpellChecker.action_context"
          class="com.bdaum.SpellChecker.actions.CheckSpellingActionDelegate"
            menubarPath="additions">
        </action>
    </viewerContribution>
    <viewerContribution targetID="#EditorContext"
            id="com.bdaum.SpellChecker.editorContextMenu">
        <action id="com.bdaum.SpellChecker.check_spelling_in_context3"
                label="%Check_Spelling"
                icon="icons/full/clcl16/check.gif"
                helpContextId="com.bdaum.SpellChecker.action_context"
          class="com.bdaum.SpellChecker.actions.CheckSpellingActionDelegate"
                menubarPath="additions">
        </action>
    </viewerContribution>
</extension>
```

Of course, the spell-checking action should appear in the Resource perspective as soon as the spell-checking feature is installed into an Eclipse platform. You can achieve this by defining a perspective extension (`org.eclipse.ui.perspectiveExtensions`) for the Resource perspective, as shown in the following code.

In addition, the code defines the position and the size of the Spell Correction View relative to the Tasks View.

```
<extension point="org.eclipse.ui.perspectiveExtensions">
    <perspectiveExtension targetID="org.eclipse.ui.resourcePerspective">
        <actionSet id="com.bdaum.SpellChecker.actionSet">
        </actionSet>
    </perspectiveExtension>
    <perspectiveExtension targetID="org.eclipse.ui.resourcePerspective">
        <view id="com.bdaum.SpellChecker.views.SpellCorrectionView"
                ratio="0.5"
                relative="org.eclipse.ui.views.TaskList"
                relationship="right">
        </view>
    </perspectiveExtension>
</extension>
```

For the Spell Correction View itself, you need only add an icon definition.

```
<extension point="org.eclipse.ui.views">
    <category id="com.bdaum.SpellChecker.views"
            name="%Spell_Checker">
    </category>
    <view name="%Spell"
            icon="icons/basic/correction_view.gif"
            category="com.bdaum.SpellChecker.views"
            class="com.bdaum.SpellChecker.views.SpellCorrectionView"
            id="com.bdaum.SpellChecker.views.SpellCorrectionView">
    </view>
</extension>
```

No changes are required for the preferences extension and the help table of contents extension.

```
<extension point="org.eclipse.ui.preferencePages">
    <page id="com.bdaum.SpellChecker.preferences.defaultPreferences"
        name="%Spelling"
        class=
"com.bdaum.SpellChecker.preferences.DefaultSpellCheckerPreferencePage">
    </page>
</extension>

<extension point="org.eclipse.help.toc">
    <toc file="toc.xml" primary="true">
    </toc>
</extension>
```

Finally, add an extension for the support of context-sensitive help. The help associations are defined in the `contexts.xml` file, as explained in Context-Sensitive Help.

```
<extension point="org.eclipse.help.contexts">
    <contexts file="contexts.xml">
    </contexts>
</extension>

</plugin>
```

The Schema documentTokenizer.exsd

The schema `documentTokenizer.exsd` describes the extension point `documentTokenizer`, which was created in the previous section. It was generated by the manifest editor; now you need only complete it. The completed schema is shown in Listing 13.1 (I shortened it a bit by removing the documentation sections).

First, the schema consists of the usual extension root element. Besides the attributes point, id, and name, such an extension may—in this case—contain an unlimited number of tokenizer elements.

These tokenizer elements are equipped with the following attributes:

Element	Attribute
name	Name of the tokenizer.
id	Identification of the tokenizer.
class	A class that must extend the class AbstractDocumentWordTokenizer.
preferences	The class implementing the tokenizer's preferences. This class must extend the class SpellCheckerPreferences. If this attribute is omitted, the default spell-checking preferences will be used for this tokenizer.
extensions	A list of file extensions for which this tokenizer should be activated.

```xml
<?xml version='1.0' encoding='UTF-8'?>
<!-- Schema file written by PDE -->
<schema targetNamespace="SpellChecker">
    <annotation>
        <appInfo>
            <meta.schema plugin="SpellChecker"
                    id="documentTokenizer"
                    name="Document Tokenizer"/>
        </appInfo>
    </annotation>
    <element name="extension">
        <complexType>
            <sequence>
                <element ref="tokenizer" minOccurs="1"
maxOccurs="unbounded"/>
            </sequence>
            <attribute name="point" type="string" use="required">
            </attribute>
            <attribute name="id" type="string">
            </attribute>
            <attribute name="name" type="string">
            </attribute>
        </complexType>
    </element>
    <element name="tokenizer">
        <complexType>
            <attribute name="name" type="string" use="required">
            </attribute>
```

Listing 13.1 (Continues)

```
            <attribute name="id" type="string" use="required">
            </attribute>
            <attribute name="class" type="string" use="required">
                <annotation>
                    <appInfo>
                        <meta.attribute kind="java" basedOn=
"com.bdaum.SpellChecker.AbstractDocumentWordTokenizer"/>
                    </appInfo>
                </annotation>
            </attribute>
            <attribute name="preferences" type="string">
                <annotation>
                    <appInfo>
                        <meta.attribute kind="java"/>
                    </appInfo>
                </annotation>
            </attribute>
            <attribute name="extensions" type="string" use="required">
            </attribute>
        </complexType>
    </element>
</schema>
```

Listing 13.1 (Continued)

Imported Files

Before continuing with the plug-in's Java classes, you should make the spell checker engine, `jazzy-core.jar`, available to your project. This time, you don't add the JAR as an external JAR to the project but import the complete JAR into the project (Import from File System). Then invoke the project's Properties context function and add this JAR to the Java Build Path by pressing the Add Jars… button. This approach makes it easier to later integrate this JAR file into the deployment archive. On the Order and Export page, checkmark the `jazzy-core.jar` file to make it available to later plug-ins.

In addition, you need a dictionary. Directly under the project, create a new folder called `dict`. Then unpack the `english.0.zip` file that you downloaded from the SourceForge site and import the `english.0` file into the new folder. You can do this with a drag-and-drop mouse action.

The Plugin Class

The generated `SpellCheckerPlugin` class serves as the Java representation of the plug-in. On initialization of the plug-in, a single instance of this class is created. This instance can be obtained via the static method `getDefault()`. This class is therefore well suited to be a central registry that can be accessed from anywhere in the plug-in. It also provides methods for obtaining information about the plug-in.

```
package com.bdaum.SpellChecker;

import java.io.IOException;
import java.net.URL;

import org.eclipse.core.runtime.IStatus;
import org.eclipse.core.runtime.Platform;
import org.eclipse.core.runtime.Status;
import org.eclipse.jface.preference.IPreferenceStore;
import org.eclipse.ui.plugin.AbstractUIPlugin;

import com.bdaum.SpellChecker.actions.CheckSpellingActionDelegate;
import com.bdaum.SpellChecker.preferences.SpellCheckerPreferences;

/**
 * This class cares for the initialization of preferences and
 * acts as a central registry for core components such as
 * SpellCheckManager and CheckSpellingActionDelegate.
 */
public class SpellCheckerPlugin extends AbstractUIPlugin {
```

The DEFAULTDICT and USERDICT constants describe the storage location of the English default dictionary and the user dictionary relative to the storage location of the plug-in. Then you need a few fields to hold instances of SpellCheckerPreferences, SpellCheckerManager, and CheckSpellingActionDelegate. Also, the field spThread is used to hold an instance of the spell-checking thread. By registering the spell-checking thread in a central location, you can later easily control the proper serialization of competing spell-checking actions.

```
// Default dictionaries
private static final String DEFAULTDICT = "dict/english.0";
private static final String USERDICT = "dict/user.dict";

// The singleton
private static SpellCheckerPlugin plugin;
// Default preferences
private SpellCheckerPreferences preferences;
// Active SpellCheckManager
private SpellCheckManager manager;
// Active ActionDelegate
private CheckSpellingActionDelegate spellCheckingActionDelegate;
// Spell checking thread
private Thread spThread;
```

The constructor of this class, SpellCheckerPlugin(), must set the system property jazzy.config to the value com.bdaum.SpellChecker.SpellCheckConfiguration. This tells the configuration model of the jazzy engine to fetch the configuration data not from the jazzy.properties files but instead from the class SpellCheckConfiguration, which you will implement later.

```
/**
 * The Constructor.
 */
public SpellCheckerPlugin() {
  super();
  plugin = this;
```

```
    // Set configuration for jazzy engine. We make jazzy fetch
    // the configuration from our own configuration
    // implementation.
    System.setProperty("jazzy.config",
                "com.bdaum.SpellChecker.SpellCheckConfiguration");
}

/**
 * Returns the plug-in singleton
 */
public static SpellCheckerPlugin getDefault() {
  return plugin;
}
```

The utility method `getId()` fetches the plug-in identification string from the plug-in descriptor as it was defined in the manifest file `plugin.xml`.

```
/**
 * Fetches the plug-in identification.
 *
 * @return String - the identification.
 */
public static String getId() {
  return getDefault().getBundle().getSymbolicName();
}
```

The following methods are used to resolve the relative dictionary paths just defined into absolute path names. Please note that the dictionary is not in the Eclipse workspace but belongs to the installation files located in the plug-in directory.

To retrieve the location of these files, you must first fetch the OSGi bundle. This bundle contains general information about the plug-in, as well as the URLs of its various components. However, this URL is given in a format that only Eclipse can interpret correctly: it starts with the protocol specification `platform:`. To resolve this URL into a conventional file URL (a URL beginning with `file:`), you must first apply the `resolve()` method.

Dictionary URL

The `getPreferences()` method returns the one and only instance of the `SpellCheckerPreferences` class. If it does not exist yet, a new instance is created.

```
/**
 * Returns the absolute
 * path of the default dictionary file.
 *
 * @return String - Default dictionary file path
 */
public static String getDefaultDictionaryFileName() {
  return getDefaultDictionaryFileName(DEFAULTDICT);
}
```

```
/**
 * Returns the absolute
 * path of the default user dictionary file.
 *
 * @return String - Default dictionary file path
 */
public static String getDefaultUserDictFileName() {
  return getDefaultDictionaryFileName(USERDICT);
}

private static String getDefaultDictionaryFileName(
    String filename) {
  // First, fetch the URL of the plug-in.
  URL pluginURL = getDefault().getBundle().getEntry(filename);
  // This URL starts with the pseudo protocol "plugin:"
  // Therefore resolve this URL into a real URL
  try {
    URL resolvedURL = Platform.resolve(pluginURL);
    // Extract the path information
    return resolvedURL.getPath();
  } catch (IOException e) {
          logError(4,                        Messages.getString(
                    "SpellCheckerPlugin.Error_resolving_dictionary_URL"),
e);
  }
  return null;
}
```

You must also provide some code to initialize the default values of the preferences. Remember that when the Eclipse platform is started, only the manifest files of the various plug-ins are interpreted, but no plug-in–specific code is executed. The preference store is therefore not initialized at that time.

However, the `Plugin` class invokes `initializeDefaultPreferences()` during the very first call of the `getPluginPreferences()` method. You can override this method to apply the necessary initializations. It delegates the initialization of the preference values to the `SpellCheckerPreferences` class.

Initializing Preferences

The `getManager()` method returns the one and only instance of the spell-checking manager. If it does not exist yet, a new instance is created.

```
/**
 * Returns the preferences of this plug-in
 */
public SpellCheckerPreferences getPreferences() {
  if (preferences == null)
    preferences = new SpellCheckerPreferences();
  return plugin.preferences;
}

/**
```

```
 * Initialization of the PreferenceStore
 *
 * @param store - the plug-in's preference store
 */
protected void initializeDefaultPreferences(
                             IPreferenceStore store) {
   getPreferences().initializeDefaults(store);
}
```

The Manager

The manager mediates the communication between the user interface and the spell-checking engine. To be able to access this manager from all classes, an instance of the manager is stored here in the plug-in instance. During its very first call, getManager() creates an instance of the SpellCheckManager class. This lazy creation ensures that this component is created only when it is actually needed.

```
/**
 * Returns the manager.
 *
 * @return SpellCheckManager
 */
public static SpellCheckManager getManager() {
  // Create SpellCheckManager instance if necessary
  if (plugin.manager == null)
    plugin.manager = new SpellCheckManager();
  return plugin.manager;
}
```

The spellCheckingActionDelegate field with its get...() and set...() access methods acts as a registry for the ActionDelegate instance created by the workbench. You will need these methods later in the context of active help (see the section "Active Help").

```
/**
 * Registers the active SpellCheckingActionDelegate.
 *
 * @param delegate   active SpellCheckingActionDelegate
 */
public static void setSpellCheckingActionDelegate(
             CheckSpellingActionDelegate delegate) {
  plugin.spellCheckingActionDelegate = delegate;
}

/**
 * Returns the currently active SpellCheckingActionDelegate.
 *
 * @return CheckSpellingActionDelegate - active action
 *         delegate
 */
public static CheckSpellingActionDelegate

getSpellCheckingActionDelegate() {
   return plugin.spellCheckingActionDelegate;
}
```

The static methods `isPending()` and `startThread()` are used to determine whether the spell-checking thread is currently active and to start a new thread.

```
/**
 * Checks if there is a pending spell checking thread
 *
 * @return - true if a thread is pending
 */
public static boolean isPending() {
  return (plugin.spThread != null && plugin.spThread.isAlive());
}

/**
 * Starts a new synchronous spell checking thread
 *
 * @param thread - the new thread
 */
public static void startThread(Thread thread) {
  plugin.spThread = thread;
  thread.start();
}
```

Finally, the static method `logError()` is used to write error messages into the log file of the Eclipse platform. Within a plug-in scenario, this should always be the preferred way to report internal errors instead of writing to the Java console `System.err`. You can obtain the log file instance from the plug-in singleton via the `getLog()` method.

```
/**
 * Writes internal errors to log file.
 *
 * @param code - Plug-in specific error code
 * @param message - message text
 * @param ex - Throwable that caused the error or null.
 */
public static void logError(
  int code, String message, Throwable ex) {
  getDefault().getLog().log(
        new Status(IStatus.ERROR, getId(), code, message, ex));
}

}
```

The Check Spelling Action

The Check Spelling action can be applied to editor text areas as well as to other editable text widgets of the type `Text` or `StyledText`. This chapter discusses the `CheckSpellingActionDelegate` class that acts as a proxy for the Check Spelling action and the `SpellCheckingTarget` class that acts as an umbrella class for the various concrete targets of the action.

The SpellCheckingTarget Class

The Eclipse platform hosts a wide variety of editors such as simple text editors and the Java editor but also more complex editors such as the PDE manifest editor and the PDE schema editor. In Chapter 11, the section "The Architecture of the Eclipse Workbench" shows the hierarchy of editor types used in Eclipse. The common root type, IEditorPart, has only a tiny API that does not offer enough functionality for spell-checking purposes, while the various concrete editor implementations have differing APIs for accessing the editor contents. For this reason, I opted to introduce the umbrella class SpellCheckingTarget, which implements a consistent API for the editor functions required for spellchecking purposes. An additional benefit is that this class can even represent editor-less spell-checking targets such as text fields in dialog boxes.

```java
package com.bdaum.SpellChecker;

import java.lang.reflect.Method;

import org.eclipse.jface.text.*;
import org.eclipse.jface.viewers.ISelection;
import org.eclipse.jface.viewers.ISelectionProvider;
import org.eclipse.swt.custom.StyledText;
import org.eclipse.swt.events.ModifyEvent;
import org.eclipse.swt.events.ModifyListener;
import org.eclipse.swt.graphics.Point;
import org.eclipse.swt.widgets.Control;
import org.eclipse.swt.widgets.Text;
import org.eclipse.ui.IEditorInput;
import org.eclipse.ui.IEditorPart;
import org.eclipse.ui.IWorkbenchPart;
import org.eclipse.ui.texteditor.IDocumentProvider;
import org.eclipse.ui.texteditor.ITextEditor;


public class SpellCheckingTarget implements ModifyListener {

    private static final Class[] NOPARMS = new Class[0];
    private static final Object[] NOARGS = new Object[0];
    private static final Point NOSELECTION = new Point(0, 0);
```

A SpellCheckerTarget instance maintains references to the target editor (which may be null), to the target widget, and to the tokenizer used to analyze the text. For editor spell-checking targets, it determines the selection provider and the document provider from the target editor. For spell-checking targets without a document provider, an auxiliary document instance is created.

```java
    // The target editor or null
    public IEditorPart editor;
    // The target widget or null
    public Control textArea;
    // Indicated if target is editable
    public boolean isEditable = true;
    // The document tokenizer associated with this target
    public AbstractDocumentWordTokenizer tokenizer;
```

```
// The targets selection provider
private ISelectionProvider selectionProvider;
// The target document provider
private IDocumentProvider documentProvider;
// If we have no document provider we create an auxiliary document
private IDocument auxDocument;
```

Factory Method

SpellCheckingTarget instances are not created via a public constructor but by the factory method getInstance(). This method differentiates between three cases. In the case of a target editor of type ITextEditor, the methods defined in this interface are used to derive the necessary information, such as the selection provider and the document provider. In case of the more general type IEditorPart, Java reflection is used to determine the selection provider. A document provider is not set in this case. Finally, if there is no target editor, information is retrieved directly from the widget.

```
/**
 * Constructor should not be used outside this class
 */
private SpellCheckingTarget() {}

/**
 * Factory method.
 *
 * @param part - currently active workbench part or null
 * @param control - Text or StyledText control that currently has the
 *          focus or null
 */
public static SpellCheckingTarget getInstance(IWorkbenchPart part,
Control control) {
  SpellCheckingTarget instance = null;
  if (part instanceof ITextEditor) {
    // Special treatment for text editor
    instance = new SpellCheckingTarget();
    ITextEditor textEditor = (ITextEditor) part;
    instance.editor = textEditor;
    instance.isEditable = textEditor.isEditable();
    instance.documentProvider = textEditor.getDocumentProvider();
    instance.selectionProvider = textEditor.getSelectionProvider();
    instance.textArea = control;
  } else if (control != null) {
    // No text editor - just use the text control
    instance = new SpellCheckingTarget();
    instance.textArea = control;
    instance.isEditable = control.isEnabled();
    if (part instanceof IEditorPart) {
      // Find selection provider for generic editors
      instance.editor = (IEditorPart) part;
      if (part instanceof ISelectionProvider)
        // The editor is an selection provider itself
        instance.selectionProvider = (ISelectionProvider) part;
      else {
        // Find the editors selection provider by using reflection
```

```
        try {
          Method getSelectionProvider = part.getClass()
                  .getMethod("getSelectionProvider", NOPARMS);
          instance.selectionProvider = (ISelectionProvider)
                        getSelectionProvider.invoke(part, NOARGS);
        } catch (Exception e1) {
        }
      }
    }
  }
  return instance;
}
```

Selections

To perform spell-checking only within a selected text block, the SpellCheckingTarget class implements the getSelection() method. If a selection provider was set, the selection is retrieved from this selection provider. Otherwise, the selection is retrieved directly from the widget. The selection provider method is preferred because it is more reliable. For some editors, the length of the text in the widget differs from the length of the text in the document. This is the case, for example, for HTML and XML editors. Character entities such as " are represented as a single character in the widget but appear in the document in their serialized form.

```
/**
 * Get the targets text selection
 *
 * @return - point with start and end of selection
 */
public Point getSelection() {
  if (selectionProvider != null) {
    // use the selection provider
    ISelection sel = selectionProvider.getSelection();
    if (sel instanceof ITextSelection) {
      int pos = ((ITextSelection) sel).getOffset();
      return new Point(pos, pos
              + ((ITextSelection) sel).getLength());
    }
  }
  // otherwise retrieve selection from text control
  if (textArea instanceof Text)
    return ((Text) textArea).getSelection();
  if (textArea instanceof StyledText)
    return ((StyledText) textArea).getSelection();
  return NOSELECTION;
}
```

It is necessary to set a new selection for highlighting a misspelled word and for restoring the original selection when spell-checking is finished. The logic is quite similar to the previous method. In the case of a target editor of type ITextEditor, the selectAndReveal() method is used to select a text block and to position the editor window at that location. Otherwise, the widget's methods are used to select a text block. Only if there is no valid widget is the selection set via the selection provider. The reason why the widget method is preferred over the selection provider method is that some selection providers don't support the setting of a selection.

```
/**
 * Set the targets text selection
 *
 * @param start - start of selection
 * @param end - end of selection
 */
public void setSelection(int start, int end) {
  // Special treatment for ITextEditor
  if (editor instanceof ITextEditor)
    ((ITextEditor) editor).selectAndReveal(start, end - start);
  // if we have a text control set selection directly in control
  else if (textArea instanceof Text)
    ((Text) textArea).setSelection(start, end);
  else if (textArea instanceof StyledText)
    ((StyledText) textArea).setSelection(start, end);
  // for other editors use standard way
  else if (selectionProvider != null)
    selectionProvider.setSelection(new TextSelection(start,
         end - start));
}
```

Document Management

Retrieving the underlying document is quite simple when the spell-checking target has a document provider. The editor input object is passed to the document provider, and the corresponding document is returned. If there is no document provider, an auxiliary document is created and the SpellCheckingTarget instance is registered as a ModifyListener with the text widget. When this widget is modified, the auxiliary document is updated accordingly in the modifyText() method. Because the getDocument() method can be called from the spell-checking thread, all SWT accesses must be encapsulated into a syncExec() block.

```
/**
 * Get the underlying document instance
 *
 * @return - the text document
 */
public IDocument getDocument() {
  if (hasLiveDocument())
    return documentProvider.getDocument(getEditorInput());
  // Create auxiliary document and store it for further use
  if (textArea != null && auxDocument == null) {
    textArea.getDisplay().syncExec(new Runnable() {
      public void run() {
        if (textArea instanceof Text)
          ((Text) textArea)
                 .addModifyListener(SpellCheckingTarget.this);
        else
          ((StyledText) textArea)
                 .addModifyListener(SpellCheckingTarget.this);
```

```java
            auxDocument = new Document(getWidgetText());
          }
        });
      }
      return auxDocument;
    }


    /**
     * Tests if the underlying document is not auxiliary
     *
     * @return - true if the underlying document is not auxiliary
     */
    public boolean hasLiveDocument() {
      return (documentProvider != null);
    }


    /**
     * Get the targets editor input
     *
     * @return - the editor input or null
     */
    public IEditorInput getEditorInput() {
      return (editor != null) ? editor.getEditorInput() : null;
    }


    /**
     * Reacts to text widget modifications
     *
     * @param e - event object (ignored)
     */
    public void modifyText(
      ModifyEvent e) {
      auxDocument.set(getWidgetText());
    }


    /**
     * Retrieves the text from the text widget
     *
     * @return - the text content of the focus widget
     */
    private String getWidgetText() {
      return (textArea instanceof Text) ?
             ((Text) textArea).getText() :
             ((StyledText) textArea).getText();
    }
```

Text Replacement

When a spelling error is corrected, the misspelled word must be replaced in the spell-checking target with the corrected word. Before this is done, the corrected word is serialized with the help of the tokenizer. For a plain text editor this is a null operation; however, for other text types the text representation in the document may differ from the text representation in the user interface (and the dictionary).

If the document is auxiliary, the change in the document is not reflected automatically by the corresponding text widget. In such a case, the widget must be updated explicitly.

```java
/**
 * Replace text in the target
 *
 * @param pos - the replacement position
 * @param len - the length of the text part to be replaced
 * @param replacement - the replacement string
 * @return - length change of document
 */
public int replaceText(int pos, int len, String replacement) {
  try {
    IDocument document = getDocument();
    String oldWord = document.get(pos, len);
    if (!oldWord.equals(replacement)) {
      // True change - replace word in document
      String rawString = (tokenizer != null) ?
              tokenizer.serializeWord(replacement) :
              replacement;
      document.replace(pos, len, rawString);
      // In case of auxiliary document apply change to
      // Text or StyleText widget, too.
      if (!hasLiveDocument()) {
        if (textArea instanceof Text) {
          ((Text) textArea).setSelection(pos, pos + len);
          ((Text) textArea).insert(replacement);
        } else if (textArea instanceof StyledText)
          ((StyledText) textArea).replaceTextRange(pos, len,
                  replacement);
      }
      return replacement.length() - len;
    }
  } catch (BadLocationException ex) {
  }
  return 0;
}
```

Disposal

Finally, if this `SpellCheckingTarget` instance is no longer needed, it must be disposed of. If the instance was previously registered with the target widget as a `ModifyListener`, it is now deregistered. If a tokenizer was set, the tokenizer is disposed of, too.

```java
/**
 * Dispose this target
 */
public void dispose() {
  if (textArea != null) {
    // Can be called from outside the SWT-thread
    textArea.getDisplay().syncExec(new Runnable() {
      public void run() {
        if (textArea instanceof Text)
```

```
                ((Text) textArea)
                        .removeModifyListener(SpellCheckingTarget.this);
            else
                ((StyledText) textArea)
                        .removeModifyListener(SpellCheckingTarget.this);
        }
    });
    }
    if (tokenizer != null) tokenizer.dispose();
  }
}
```

The CheckSpellingActionDelegate Class

The CheckSpellingActionDelegate class was also generated by the Plug-in Creation Wizard.
The run() method of this class is called when the end user invokes the spell-checking function. Because
this class keeps track of the focus, it knows which widget will be checked for the correct spelling.

```
package com.bdaum.SpellChecker.actions;

import org.eclipse.jface.action.IAction;
import org.eclipse.jface.viewers.ISelection;
import org.eclipse.swt.custom.StyledText;
import org.eclipse.swt.events.FocusEvent;
import org.eclipse.swt.events.FocusListener;
import org.eclipse.swt.widgets.Control;
import org.eclipse.swt.widgets.Display;
import org.eclipse.swt.widgets.Shell;
import org.eclipse.swt.widgets.Text;
import org.eclipse.ui.IEditorActionDelegate;
import org.eclipse.ui.IEditorPart;
import org.eclipse.ui.IPartListener;
import org.eclipse.ui.IPartService;
import org.eclipse.ui.IWorkbenchPage;
import org.eclipse.ui.IWorkbenchPart;
import org.eclipse.ui.IWorkbenchWindow;
import org.eclipse.ui.IWorkbenchWindowActionDelegate;
import org.eclipse.ui.PartInitException;
import org.eclipse.ui.PlatformUI;
import org.eclipse.ui.part.MultiEditor;

import com.bdaum.SpellChecker.Messages;
import com.bdaum.SpellChecker.SpellCheckManager;
import com.bdaum.SpellChecker.SpellCheckerPlugin;
import com.bdaum.SpellChecker.SpellCheckingTarget;
import com.bdaum.SpellChecker.views.SpellCorrectionView;

/**
 * This class implements the workbench action "Check Spelling".
 * It also starts a tracking mechanism that keeps it informed
 * about the focus control and the currently activated
 * workbench part.
 *
```

```
 * @see IWorkbenchWindowActionDelegate
 */
public class CheckSpellingActionDelegate
    implements IWorkbenchWindowActionDelegate,
               IEditorActionDelegate, FocusListener, IPartListener {

    private IWorkbenchWindow window;
    /** The current IAction instance **/
    private IAction action;
    /** The current focus control element **/
    private Control currentFocusControl;
    /** The most recent spell checking target under the focus **/
    private Control recentFocusControl;
    /** Cache for part service **/
    private IPartService partService;
    /** The most recent active workbench part **/
    private IWorkbenchPart activePart;
```

The workbench calls the init() method before the first activation of this action. The workbench window that is passed via a parameter is stored in an instance variable so that it can be used in other method calls. The method registers this CheckSpellingActionDelegate instance as a PartListener with the Eclipse part service to keep track of the currently active part. When another workbench part is activated, it is remembered in an instance field (the Spell Correction View is ignored), and the action is enabled or disabled depending on the current state.

The method also starts a tracking mechanism that monitors which SWT control currently has the focus.

Furthermore, the current CheckSpellingActionDelegate instance is registered with the SpellCheckerPlugin instance.

```
/**
 * Initialize this action delegate
 * @see IWorkbenchWindowActionDelegate#init
 */
public void init(IWorkbenchWindow window) {
    this.window = window;
    // Register with the PartService as a listener
    partService = window.getPartService();
    activePart = partService.getActivePart();
    partService.addPartListener(this);
    // Start focus tracking
    setCurrentFocusControl();
    // Register with the Plugin class.
    SpellCheckerPlugin.setSpellCheckingActionDelegate(this);
}

/** * IPartListener methods ** */

public void partActivated(IWorkbenchPart part) {
    if (!(part instanceof SpellCorrectionView))
        activePart = part;
    updateActionEnablement(action);
```

```
}

public void partBroughtToTop(
  IWorkbenchPart part) {}

public void partClosed(
  IWorkbenchPart part) {}

public void partDeactivated(
  IWorkbenchPart part) {}

public void partOpened(
  IWorkbenchPart part) {}
```

Focus tracking is done in the setCurrentFocusControl() method. This method first asks the current Display instance which control currently has the focus. A FocusListener is registered with this focus owner that tells you when the owner loses the focus. In such a case, the next focus owner is retrieved. If this is not possible, a retry is started 100 milliseconds later. In particular, this can happen during the first call of this method from init(). At this time, a focus may not yet be assigned to a Control element.

```
// Tracking the focus
private void setCurrentFocusControl() {
  Shell shell = window.getShell();
  if (shell == null || shell.isDisposed()) return;
  Display display = shell.getDisplay();
  Control newFocusControl = display.getFocusControl();
  // Remove and set listeners if focus control has changed
  if (newFocusControl != currentFocusControl) {
    if (currentFocusControl != null)
      currentFocusControl.removeFocusListener(this);
    if (newFocusControl != null)
      newFocusControl.addFocusListener(this);
    currentFocusControl = newFocusControl;
  }
  if (currentFocusControl != null) {
    // Filter events by removing events from SpellCorrectionView.
    // This avoids that the SpellChecker action disables
    // when the focus moves to the SpellCorrectionView
    if (!(partService.getActivePart() instanceof
                                 SpellCorrectionView))
      recentFocusControl = currentFocusControl;
    return;
  }
  // Lost track - retry later
  recentFocusControl = null;
  display.timerExec(100, new Runnable() {
    public void run() {
      setCurrentFocusControl();
    }
  });
}
```

433

```
/* FocusListener methods */
public void focusGained(FocusEvent e) {
  updateActionEnablement(action);
}

public void focusLost(FocusEvent e) {
  setCurrentFocusControl();
}
```

After each focus change (and also after each change of the active workbench part or of workbench selections), the action's enabled status must be recomputed. If there is no valid spell-checking target, the action is disabled. This is done not only for the action itself (that is, for the workbench's toolbar button and menu item) but also for the buttons and menu items of the Spell Correction View.

The `indicateBusy()` method is used to disable the action while the spell-checking process is active.

```
/**
 * Enable or disable action
 *
 * @param action - the action to be enabled or disabled
 */
private void updateActionEnablement(IAction action) {
  // The action is only enabled if there is a valid spell
  // checking target
  updateActionEnablement(action, getSpellCheckingTarget() != null);
}

/**
 * Enable or disable action
 *
 * @param action - the action to be enabled or disabled
 * @param enabled - new enablement state
 */
private void updateActionEnablement(IAction action,
                                    boolean enabled) {
  if (action != null) {
    action.setEnabled(enabled);
    IWorkbenchPage activePage = window.getActivePage();
    // Update correction view actions
    if (activePage != null) {
      SpellCorrectionView view = (SpellCorrectionView) activePage
          .findView(
              "com.bdaum.SpellChecker.views.SpellCorrectionView");
      if (view != null) view.updateActionEnablement();
    }
  }
}

/**
 * Disables the action when process is busy
 *
 * @param busy - true if process is busy
```

```
  */
  public void indicateBusy(
    final boolean busy) {
    window.getShell().getDisplay().syncExec(new Runnable() {
      public void run() {
        if (busy)
          updateActionEnablement(action, false);
        else
          updateActionEnablement(action);
      }
    });
  }


  /**
   * Retrieves the enablement state of the action
   *
   * @return - true if enabled
   */
  public boolean isEnabled() {
    return (action != null && action.isEnabled());
  }
```

All IActionDelegates react to workbench events: the selectionChanged() method is invoked when another item is selected in the workbench. The method receives the IAction instance (the CheckSpellingActionDelegate class is only a delegate of that action) and, of course, the selection, as parameters.

In the selectionChanged() method, the IAction instance is simply remembered in an instance field so that it is possible to refer to it later. Also, the action enablement is updated.

```
  /**
   * The current workbench selection has changed.
   *
   * @see IWorkbenchWindowActionDelegate#selectionChanged
   */
  public void selectionChanged(IAction action, ISelection selection) {
    // Remember action
    this.action = action;
    // Update action and view
    updateActionEnablement(action);
  }
```

When the user activates the action, the run() method is invoked. Here, the spell-checking task starts. First, the currently active spell-checking target that currently has the focus is fetched via the getSpellCheckingTarget() method. If such a target is present, the SpellCorrectionView is opened via the showCorrectionView() method. In this method the currently active page of the workbench window is fetched. Then the view is opened via the showView() method by passing the view identification defined in the manifest file plugin.xml. Then the spell-checking process is started in a new thread via the SpellCheckManager. While this process is running, the action is disabled via the indicateBusy() method.

Why start a new thread? The spell-checking process may generate a whole series of spelling error events. `SpellCorrectionView` must process these events event by event. In this implementation, this is organized in such a way that the spell-checking process waits until an event is processed by the `SpellCorrectionView`, at which time the next event can be fired. If this would be done (waiting) in the SWT thread, the whole user interface would lock up.

Before a new thread is started, existing spell-checking threads are first canceled via the `SpellCheckManager` method `abortSpellChecking()`. Otherwise, an unlimited number of pending threads would come into existence if the spell-checking action were executed repeatedly without completing the previous spell-checking processes. Of course, this should not happen because the spell-checking action is disabled while it is running, but you want to be on the safe side.

```java
/**
 * Execute the spell checking action.
 *
 * @see IWorkbenchWindowActionDelegate#run
 */
public void run(IAction action) {
  // skip if not enabled
  if (this.action == null || !this.action.isEnabled())
    return;
  // Get spell checking target
  final SpellCheckingTarget target = getSpellCheckingTarget();
  if (target != null) {
    // Get current Display instance
    final Display display = window.getShell().getDisplay();
    if (display == null) return;
    try {
      // Now find the SpellCorrectionView and open it
      final SpellCorrectionView view = showCorrectionView();
      if (view == null) return;
      // Disable action when busy
      indicateBusy(true);
      // Get the SpellCheckManager
      final SpellCheckManager manager = SpellCheckerPlugin
              .getManager();
      // First cancel any pending spell checking processes.
      if (SpellCheckerPlugin.isPending())
        manager.abortSpellChecking();
      // Start spell checking process in new thread
      SpellCheckerPlugin.startThread(new Thread("SpellCheckThread") {
        public void run() {
          manager.checkDocument(target, display, view);
          // Enable action when done
          indicateBusy(false);
        }
      });
    } catch (PartInitException e) {
      SpellCheckerPlugin.logError(6,
        Messages.getString(
 "CheckSpellingActionDelegate.Cannot_initialize_SpellCorrectionView"),
 e);
    }
```

```
    }
}

/**
 * Finds and shows the spell checker correction view
 *
 * @return - the view part
 * @throws PartInitException
 */
public SpellCorrectionView showCorrectionView()
        throws PartInitException {
  // get active page
  IWorkbenchPage activePage = window.getActivePage();
  // show view
  return (activePage == null) ? null
          : (SpellCorrectionView) activePage.showView(
            "com.bdaum.SpellChecker.views.SpellCorrectionView");
}
```

The spell-checking process can, of course, be executed only if there is a valid spell-checking target.
The getSpellCheckingTarget() method tries to find such a target. First, it tests to see if the current
focus control is a valid target for spell-checking. This is the case only if the control is a Text or
StyledText widget and if this text widget is editable. Then it tests to see if the current focus control is
in the currently active workbench window. If so, it tries to get the currently active workbench part
(which could be an editor). In case of a MultiEditor, it drills down to the currently active inner editor.
Then a new SpellCheckingTarget instance is constructed from both the widget and the workbench
part. If the widget is not located in the current workbench window, it must be in a dialog box or similar
window. In this case, it constructs a new SpellCheckingTarget instance from the widget only.

```
/**
 * Returns SpellCheckingTarget with active editor and
 * a Text or StyledText instance that has the focus
 *
 * @return - a new SpellCheckingTarget.
 */
private SpellCheckingTarget getSpellCheckingTarget() {
  // First determine if the control that has the focus is a
  // valid text control
  Control validControl =
    ( (  (recentFocusControl instanceof Text &&
          ((Text) recentFocusControl).getEditable())
      || (recentFocusControl instanceof StyledText &&
          ((StyledText) recentFocusControl).getEditable()))
    && !recentFocusControl.isDisposed())
    ? recentFocusControl : null;
  // Check if focus is in workbench window
  if (validControl == null || validControl.isDisposed()
          || validControl.getShell() == window.getShell()) {
    // Get workbench component
    IWorkbenchPart part = window.getPartService().getActivePart();
    // Update active part just to make sure we have the
    // current one
    if (!(part instanceof SpellCorrectionView))
```

437

```
        activePart = part;
      // Is it a MultiEditor?
      // If yes, get the active inner editor.
      while (activePart instanceof MultiEditor)
        activePart = ((MultiEditor) activePart).getActiveEditor();
      // Now create a SpellCheckingTarget
      return SpellCheckingTarget.getInstance(activePart,
              validControl);
    }
    // Must be in a dialog box, use text field only.
    return SpellCheckingTarget.getInstance(null, validControl);
  }
```

When the IActionDelegate is disposed of, it must be deregistered as a FocusListener and from the Plugin instance and the platform's part service.

```
  /**
   * Dispose action
   */
  public void dispose() {
    // Deregister as focus listener
    if (currentFocusControl != null
            && !currentFocusControl.isDisposed())
      currentFocusControl.removeFocusListener(this);
    currentFocusControl = null;
    // Deregister from the part service
    partService.removePartListener(this);
    // also deregister from the Plugin class
    SpellCheckerPlugin.setSpellCheckingActionDelegate(null);
  }
```

The setActiveEditor() method is called before the spell-checking action is called from an editor's context menu. The action instance and the editor are passed as parameters. The method remembers the action and calls the init() method to perform the initialization of this action delegate.

```
  /**
   * Action called from editor context menu
   *
   * @param action - the action
   * @param targetEditor - the target editor
   */
  public void setActiveEditor(
    IAction action, IEditorPart targetEditor) {
    this.action = action;
    if (targetEditor != null)
      init(targetEditor.getSite().getWorkbenchWindow());
    else
      init(PlatformUI.getWorkbench().getActiveWorkbenchWindow());
  }
}
```

The Correction Window

This section shows the implementation of the Spell Correction View and, in this context also, the management of image files (for the toolbar buttons).

The SpellCorrectionView Class

The SpellCorrectionView class is quite large. In addition to the pregenerated table, the text field above the table is created, too. This field will contain the erroneous word or a replacement for the word.

A toolbar is also required, as are a drop-down menu, a context menu (all with six actions), and a special action for handling double-clicks. I opted to hard-code these actions instead of defining them in the plug-in manifest. The reason for this is that the enabling of these actions does not depend on workbench selections but on other criteria that are difficult to specify via the manifest.

```
package com.bdaum.SpellChecker.views;

import java.util.List;

import org.eclipse.jface.action.*;
import org.eclipse.jface.viewers.*;
import org.eclipse.swt.SWT;
import org.eclipse.swt.events.KeyAdapter;
import org.eclipse.swt.events.KeyEvent;
import org.eclipse.swt.events.ModifyEvent;
import org.eclipse.swt.events.ModifyListener;
import org.eclipse.swt.graphics.Image;
import org.eclipse.swt.layout.GridData;
import org.eclipse.swt.layout.GridLayout;
import org.eclipse.swt.widgets.Composite;
import org.eclipse.swt.widgets.Display;
import org.eclipse.swt.widgets.Menu;
import org.eclipse.swt.widgets.Text;
import org.eclipse.ui.IActionBars;
import org.eclipse.ui.help.WorkbenchHelp;
import org.eclipse.ui.part.ViewPart;

import com.bdaum.SpellChecker.SpellCheckManager;
import com.bdaum.SpellChecker.SpellCheckerImages;
import com.bdaum.SpellChecker.SpellCheckerPlugin;
import com.bdaum.SpellChecker.actions.CheckSpellingActionDelegate;
import com.bdaum.SpellChecker.actions.CorrectionViewAction;
import com.swabunga.spell.engine.Word;
import com.swabunga.spell.event.SpellCheckEvent;
import com.bdaum.SpellChecker.Messages;

public class SpellCorrectionView extends ViewPart {
```

The SpellCorrectionView class defines instance fields for holding the widgets of the view, the various actions, and the references to the spell-checking manager and the current spell checker event (spelling error).

```
        // Text constant for cases where we have no correction proposals
        private static final String[] NOPROPOSALS = new String[]
                {Messages.getString("SpellCorrectionView.No_suggestions")};

        /* Widgets */
        // The current Display instance
        private Display display;
        // The Text widget for displaying the bad word
        private Text badWord;
        // The TableViewer of this view
        private TableViewer viewer;

        /* View actions */
        // Toolbar and menu actions
        private IAction ignoreAction;
        private IAction ignoreAllAction;
        private IAction cancelAction;
        private IAction replaceAction;
        private IAction replaceAllAction;
        private IAction addToDictionaryAction;
        // The double click action
        private Action doubleClickAction;

        /* The manager */
        private SpellCheckManager spellCheckManager;
        /* The current spelling error event */
        private SpellCheckEvent currentEvent;
        /* Indicator if replacements are allowed */
        private boolean documentIsEditable;
```

These definitions are followed by the definitions of two inner classes: ViewContentProvider and
ViewLabelProvider. These classes support the display table elements. The ViewContentProvider
class supplies the table with the table entries. This is done in the getElements() method. In this case,
these entries are correction proposals. A list of such correction proposals—wrapped in a
SpellCheckEvent object—is passed to the view via setInput(). This event is then signaled from the
table to the ViewContentProvider by calling the inputChanged() method. This list is then trans-
formed into a suitable format using the getElements() method. If the list of correction proposals is
empty, only the default message defined previously is returned as the sole table element.

```
    /**
     * The ViewContentProvider creates the table content from the
     * spelling error event.
     */
    class ViewContentProvider implements IStructuredContentProvider {

        // Current spelling error event
        private Object spEvent;

        /**
         * This method is called by the TableViewer after
         * setInput() was called.
```

```
  */
  public void inputChanged(Viewer v, Object oldInput,
                                      Object newInput) {
    spEvent = newInput;
  }


  /**
   * This method is called when the table is refreshed
   */
  public Object[] getElements(Object parent) {
    // Fetch correction proposals from the spelling error event
    if (spEvent instanceof SpellCheckEvent) {
      List suggestions = ((SpellCheckEvent) spEvent)
                                      .getSuggestions();
      int s = suggestions.size();
      // Check if we have proposals
      if (s > 0) {
        // Return correction proposals as an array to the TableViewer
        Word[] sugArray = new Word[s];
        suggestions.toArray(sugArray);
        return sugArray;
      }
    }
    return NOPROPOSALS;
  }

  public void dispose() {}
}
```

The ViewLabelProvider is responsible for delivering text and images for each table element. Here, no images are used within the table, so the corresponding methods deliver a null value. The column text is obtained by calling the getText() method.

```
/**
 * The ViewLabelProvider creates the individual table entries
 */
class ViewLabelProvider extends LabelProvider implements
                                      TableLabelProvider {

  /*
   * Process text for table entry
   */
  public String getColumnText(Object obj, int index) {
    return getText(obj);
  }

  public Image getColumnImage(Object obj, int index) {
    return null;
  }

  public Image getImage(Object obj) {
    return null;
  }
}
```

For the Spell Correction View, Eclipse has already pregenerated the createPartControl() method. You just need to extend this method by adding the Text widget badWord above the table. This text field will be used to display the erroneous word. To combine the text field with the table, you should use Composite parent as the parent control and apply a GridLayout to it.

The text field gets a ModifyListener, too. When the content of this field changes, the actions must be updated. For example, when the field still contains the original bad word, the replacement actions should be disabled.

In addition, you need to implement the event handling for the table viewer. If a proposal is selected from the table, it must be copied to the text field badWord. The exception is the string NOPROPOSALS, which you don't want to copy into the text field. This string is not a Word instance, so you may use its type as a knockout criterion.

The KeyListener allows the invocation of some of the menu and toolbar actions via keyboard short-cuts.

The following pregenerated calls create the actions and construct the menus and the toolbar. You need only complete this code with method calls for updating the actions and for registering the view with the help system.

The implementation of the setFocus() method is a requirement from the parent class ViewPart. In the following code I set the focus to the table.

```
public void createPartControl(Composite parent) {
  // Fetch Display instance for later usage
  display = parent.getDisplay();
  // Set GridLayout
  parent.setLayout(new GridLayout());
  // Create Text widget for display of bad word
  badWord = new Text(parent, SWT.BORDER);
  badWord.setLayoutData(new GridData(
        GridData.FILL_HORIZONTAL));
  // Disable/Enable actions when content of text field changes
  badWord.addModifyListener(new ModifyListener() {
    public void modifyText(ModifyEvent e) {
      updateActionEnablement();
    }
  });
  // Create table viewer
  viewer = new TableViewer(parent, SWT.H_SCROLL
        | SWT.V_SCROLL | SWT.BORDER);
  viewer.getControl().setLayoutData(
        new GridData(GridData.FILL_BOTH));
  // Set ContentProvider and LabelProvider
  viewer.setContentProvider(new ViewContentProvider());
  viewer.setLabelProvider(new ViewLabelProvider());
  // Listener for selection of table elements
  // Selected elements are copied to text field badWord.
  viewer.addSelectionChangedListener(new ISelectionChangedListener()
      {
```

```java
                    public void selectionChanged(
                      SelectionChangedEvent event) {
                      ISelection sel = event.getSelection();
                      if (sel instanceof IStructuredSelection) {
                        Object obj = ((IStructuredSelection) sel)
                               .getFirstElement();
                        // Check for Word type to exclude NOPROPOSALS
                        // from selection
                        if (obj instanceof Word)
                          badWord.setText(obj.toString());
                      }
                    }
                  });
            // Add KeyListener to support keyboard shortcuts
            viewer.getControl().addKeyListener(new KeyAdapter() {
              public void keyPressed(KeyEvent e) {
                if (e.character == '+')
                  addToDictionaryAction.run();
                else
                  switch (e.keyCode) {
                    case 13 :
                      if ((e.stateMask & SWT.CTRL) != 0) {
                        if ((e.stateMask & SWT.SHIFT) != 0)
                          replaceAllAction.run();
                        else
                          replaceAction.run();
                      } else {
                        if ((e.stateMask & SWT.SHIFT) != 0)
                          ignoreAllAction.run();
                        else
                          ignoreAction.run();
                      }
                      break;
                    case SWT.ESC :
                      cancelAction.run();
                      break;
                  }
              }
            });


        // Create actions
        makeActions();
        // Add the context menu
        hookContextMenu();
        // Add the double click action
        hookDoubleClickAction();
        // Create the toolbar
        contributeToActionBars();
        // Initialize the actions
        updateActionEnablement();
        // Create help context
        WorkbenchHelp.setHelp(parent,
            "com.bdaum.SpellChecker.correctionView_context");
      }

    /**
      * Set focus to TableViewer
```

```
  */
public void setFocus() {
  viewer.getControl().setFocus();
}
```

The construction of the menus, the toolbar, and the double-click action are almost completely pregenerated. An anonymous `DoubleClickListener` is registered for the double-click action. This listener invokes the action's `run()` method in the case of an event. The menu manager is equipped with a `MenuListener`. Every time the menu is to be displayed, this listener constructs a new menu in the `fillContribution()` method.

To construct the toolbar, the `contributeToActionBars()` method fetches the managers for the drop-down menu and for the toolbar from the `ViewSite`. Then the `fillContribution()` method is invoked to add the required actions to these managers. Eclipse originally generated separate methods for menus and toolbars, but here I have combined both methods into a single `fillContribution()` method.

```
// Add double click action
private void hookDoubleClickAction() {
  viewer.addDoubleClickListener(new IDoubleClickListener() {
    public void doubleClick(
      DoubleClickEvent event) {
      doubleClickAction.run();
    }
  });
}

// Add context menu
private void hookContextMenu() {
  // Create new menu manager
  MenuManager menuMgr = new MenuManager("#PopupMenu"); //$NON-NLS-1$
  // Remove all menu items before building the menu
  menuMgr.setRemoveAllWhenShown(true);
  // Event processing for context menu
  menuMgr.addMenuListener(new IMenuListener() {
    public void menuAboutToShow(
      IMenuManager manager) {
      SpellCorrectionView.this.fillContribution(manager);
    }
  });
  // Create menu
  Menu menu = menuMgr.createContextMenu(viewer.getControl());
  viewer.getControl().setMenu(menu);
  // Register context menu with workbench site
  getSite().registerContextMenu(menuMgr, viewer);
}

private void contributeToActionBars() {
  // Fetch action bar from workbench site
  IActionBars bars = getViewSite().getActionBars();
  // Create the drop-down menu
  fillContribution(bars.getMenuManager());
```

```
      // Create the toolbar
      fillContribution(bars.getToolBarManager());
  }

  // Fill menus or toolbar with actions
  private void fillContribution(
    IContributionManager manager) {
    manager.add(replaceAction);
    manager.add(replaceAllAction);
    manager.add(new Separator());
    manager.add(addToDictionaryAction);
    manager.add(new Separator());
    manager.add(ignoreAction);
    manager.add(ignoreAllAction);
    manager.add(cancelAction);
    // Other plug-ins can insert new actions here
    manager.add(new Separator("Additions"));
  }
```

All actions are created in the makeActions() method. The icons are fetched from the
SpellCheckerImages class, which is listed in the "Managing Images" section. The convenience
method createAction() is used to create an action. This method creates instances of type
CorrectionViewAction, which are quite simple (see the following section of code). The run()
method of these actions just calls the view's performOperation() method. There the main processing
is performed, depending on the operation code. Finally, the signalEventProcessed() method is
called to indicate to the SpellCheckManager that the processing of the current event has finished and
that a new event can be sent.

The CANCEL action can trigger two different operations, depending on the state of the spell checker. If
the spell checker is idle (no spell-checking event is waiting), the action is used to restart the spell checker.
If the spell checker is still busy, the action cancels the spell-checking process.

```
// Create actions
  private void makeActions() {
    replaceAction = createAction(CorrectionViewAction.REPLACE,
        Messages.getString("SpellCorrectionView.Replace"),
        Messages.getString("SpellCorrectionView.Replace_occurrence"),
        SpellCheckerImages.IMG_REPLACE);
    replaceAllAction = createAction(CorrectionViewAction.REPLACEALL,
        Messages.getString("SpellCorrectionView.Replace_all"),
        Messages.getString(
                "SpellCorrectionView.Replace_all_occurrences"),
        SpellCheckerImages.IMG_REPLACEALL);
    addToDictionaryAction = createAction(CorrectionViewAction.ADD,
        Messages.getString("SpellCorrectionView.Add_to_dictionary"),
        Messages.getString(
                "SpellCorrectionView.Add_word_to_dictionary"),
        SpellCheckerImages.IMG_ADDTODICTIONARY);
    ignoreAction = createAction(CorrectionViewAction.IGNORE,
        Messages.getString("SpellCorrectionView.Ignore"),
        Messages.getString(
                "SpellCorrectionView.Ignore_spelling_problem"),
```

```
                    SpellCheckerImages.IMG_IGNORE);
    ignoreAllAction = createAction(CorrectionViewAction.IGNOREALL,
        Messages.getString("SpellCorrectionView.Ignore_all"),
        Messages.getString(
                "SpellCorrectionView.Ignore_for_all_occurrences"),
        SpellCheckerImages.IMG_IGNOREALL);
    cancelAction = createAction(CorrectionViewAction.CANCEL,
        Messages.getString("SpellCorrectionView.StartCancel"),
        Messages.getString(
                "SpellCorrectionView.StartCancel_spell_checking"),
        SpellCheckerImages.IMG_CANCEL);
    doubleClickAction = new CorrectionViewAction(this,
        CorrectionViewAction.DOUBLECLICK);
}

// Create a single action
private IAction createAction(
    int operation, String label, String toolTip, String imageID) {
    IAction action = new CorrectionViewAction(this, operation);
    action.setText(label);
    action.setToolTipText(toolTip);
    SpellCheckerImages.setImageDescriptors(action, "lcl16", imageID);
    return action;
}

/**
 * Perform operation for an action
 *
 * @param operation - the operation code
 */
public void performOperation(int operation) {
    if (currentEvent == null) {
        if (operation == CorrectionViewAction.CANCEL)
            // Start spell checking via action delegate
            SpellCheckerPlugin.getSpellCheckingActionDelegate().run(null);
        return;
    }
    switch (operation) {
        case CorrectionViewAction.DOUBLECLICK :
            if (!documentIsEditable) return;
            ISelection selection = viewer.getSelection();
            Object obj = ((IStructuredSelection) selection)
                    .getFirstElement();
            if (!(obj instanceof Word)) return;
            currentEvent.replaceWord(obj.toString(), false);
            break;
        case CorrectionViewAction.REPLACE :
            currentEvent.replaceWord(badWord.getText(), false);
            break;
        case CorrectionViewAction.REPLACEALL :
            if (!documentIsEditable) return;
            currentEvent.replaceWord(badWord.getText(), true);
            break;
        case CorrectionViewAction.ADD :
```

```
        String newWord = badWord.getText();
        String originalBadWord = currentEvent.getInvalidWord();
        if (!documentIsEditable
                && !originalBadWord.equals(newWord)) return;
        currentEvent.addToDictionary(newWord);
        break;
    case CorrectionViewAction.IGNORE :
        currentEvent.ignoreWord(false);
        break;
    case CorrectionViewAction.IGNOREALL :
        currentEvent.ignoreWord(true);
        break;
    case CorrectionViewAction.CANCEL :
        currentEvent.cancel();
        break;
    }
    signalEventProcessed();
}

// Signal end of event processing
private void signalEventProcessed() {
    // Release waiting manager
    spellCheckManager.continueSpellChecking();
    // Reset current event
    currentEvent = null;
    // Update viewer
    updateView();
}
```

The updateActionEnablement() method is used to enable or disable actions. If no more events are waiting, you disable all actions. If at least one event is waiting, the actions are enabled. However, the actions replaceAction and replaceActionAll are enabled only when the current document is editable and if the content of the badWord text field was modified. Because the CANCEL action is a toggle action, its icon, its checked state, and its tooltip are exchanged, depending on the state of the spell-checking process.

```
/**
 * Update actions. Most of the
 * actions are disabled when no more events are pending. The
 * cancel action, however, now acts as a start action.
 */
public void updateActionEnablement() {
    boolean pendingEvent = (currentEvent != null);
    // Enable or disable actions
    if (pendingEvent & documentIsEditable) {
        boolean modified = !currentEvent.getInvalidWord()
                .equals(badWord.getText());
        replaceAction.setEnabled(modified);
        replaceAllAction.setEnabled(modified);
    } else {
        replaceAction.setEnabled(false);
        replaceAllAction.setEnabled(false);
```

```
    }
    ignoreAction.setEnabled(pendingEvent);
    ignoreAllAction.setEnabled(pendingEvent);
    addToDictionaryAction.setEnabled(pendingEvent);
    // Update cancel action
    if (pendingEvent) {
      SpellCheckerImages.setImageDescriptors(cancelAction, "lcl16",
            SpellCheckerImages.IMG_CANCEL);
      cancelAction.setChecked(true);
      cancelAction.setToolTipText(Messages.getString(
              "SpellCorrectionView.Cancel_spell_checking"));
cancelAction.setEnabled(true);
    } else {
      SpellCheckerImages.setImageDescriptors(cancelAction, "lcl16",
            SpellCheckerImages.IMG_CHECK);
      cancelAction.setChecked(false);
      cancelAction.setToolTipText(Messages.getString(
              "SpellCorrectionView.Start_spell_checking"));
CheckSpellingActionDelegate delegate =
            SpellCheckerPlugin.getSpellCheckingActionDelegate();
      cancelAction.setEnabled(delegate != null
            && delegate.isEnabled());
    }
  }
```

Other modifications to the user interface are applied via the updateView() method. Here all of these updates are executed in the familiar way within a syncExec() method (see the section "Displays, Shells, and Monitors" in Chapter 8). This is necessary because some of these changes come from a different thread—the spell-checking thread. In particular, the TableViewer is updated via its setInput() method, whose event in turn is signaled to the ContentProvider of the TableViewer via the inputChanged() method. In addition, the text field and the view title are updated.

The indicateLoading() method is used to display a message when a dictionary is loaded because this may take a little while. Again, this is performed in a syncExec() block.

```
  // Update view
  private void updateView() {
   // Execute via syncExec as we are called from other thread
    display.syncExec(new Runnable() {
      public void run() {
        // Update TableViewer
        viewer.setInput(currentEvent);
        // Update Text field and title
        if (currentEvent == null) {
          badWord.setText("");
          setContentDescription(spellCheckManager.getCurrentName()
            + Messages.getString("SpellCorrectionView.done"));
        } else {
          badWord.setText(currentEvent.getInvalidWord());
          setContentDescription(spellCheckManager.getCurrentName()
            + Messages.getString("SpellCorrectionView.in_progress"));
        }
```

```
        // Update actions
        updateActionEnablement();
    }
  });
}

/**
 * Indicate that we are loading a dictionary
 */
public void indicateLoading(final String name) {
  display.syncExec(new Runnable() {
    public void run() {
      setContentDescription(name
          + Messages.getString("SpellCorrectionView.loading"));
    }
  });
}
```

The setInput() method supplies the whole view with input data. In this case, this is a
SpellCheckEvent containing the correction proposals from the jazzy engine. The method accepts this
data and updates the view accordingly.

```
/**
 * Supplies the Spell Correction View with a
 * new spelling error event
 *
 * @param event - the spelling error event
 * @param manager - the manager to be notified when finished
 * @param documentIsEditable - true, if document may be modified
 */
public void setInput(SpellCheckEvent event,
                     SpellCheckManager manager,
                     boolean documentIsEditable) {
  // Accept event, manager, and flag
  this.currentEvent = event;
  this.spellCheckManager = manager;
  this.documentIsEditable = documentIsEditable;
  // Update the view
  updateView();
}
}
```

View Actions

The CorrectionViewAction class (Listing 13.2) implements all of the SpellCorrectionView
actions and is almost trivial. In its constructor it accepts the view and the operation code of the concrete
action. This data is then used in the run() method to invoke the view's performOperation() with
the corresponding operation code.

```
package com.bdaum.SpellChecker.actions;

import org.eclipse.jface.action.Action;
import com.bdaum.SpellChecker.views.SpellCorrectionView;

public class CorrectionViewAction extends Action {

    public static final int DOUBLECLICK = 0;
    public static final int REPLACE = 1;
    public static final int REPLACEALL = 2;
    public static final int IGNORE = 3;
    public static final int IGNOREALL = 4;
    public static final int ADD = 5;
    public static final int CANCEL = 6;

    private SpellCorrectionView view;
    private int operation;

    public CorrectionViewAction(SpellCorrectionView view,
        int operation) {
        this.view = view;
        this.operation = operation;
    }

    /*
     * Perform action
     */
    public void run() {
        view.performOperation(operation);
    }
}
```

Listing 13.2

Managing Images

Icons for all of the actions of the `SpellCorrectionView` are fetched from the `SpellCheckerImages` class (Listing 13.3). The advantage of this technique is that you can easily keep an overview of the images used, because they are managed by a central instance. You could also extend this class into a central image repository for storing images for reuse. However, this is not necessary in this case, because all icons are used only once when the actions are created via `makeActions()`. Caching images to reduce repeated image loading is therefore not required.

For the various images, the following organizing principles are used.

All images are stored in subfolders of the folder `icons`. Each action can accept three states: disabled, enabled, and hot (when the mouse hovers over the icon). The enabled and hot states use the same icon.

You therefore need two different icons for each action:

❑ Colored icons for hot and enabled actions are set with the method
`setHoverImageDescriptor()`. These icons are stored in the `icons/full/clcl16` folder.

450

❑ Gray icons for disabled actions are set with the method setDisabledImageDescriptor(). These icons are stored in the icons/full/dlcl16 folder.

The number 16 refers to the size of the icons: they are all 16x16 pixels in size.

The icon correction_view.gif is a special case. It is used only in the manifest file plugin.xml; a specification in the SpellCheckerImages class is therefore not necessary. This icon is also independent of state changes, so only a single version is needed. Such icons are stored in the basic folder rather than the full folder.

In principle, this is possible for all icons. If you don't want to create different icons for each action, it is sufficient to create a single colored icon and to specify it in the setImageDescriptor() method. Eclipse then automatically computes the gray variants. You will usually arrive at graphically more satisfying solutions by creating each of the state icons manually, however.

```java
package com.bdaum.SpellChecker;

import java.net.MalformedURLException;
import java.net.URL;

import org.eclipse.jface.action.IAction;
import org.eclipse.jface.resource.ImageDescriptor;

/**
 * Compilation of the images used in com.bdaum.SpellChecker
 * plug-in.
 */
public class SpellCheckerImages {

  // Get URL for icon folder
  private static URL fgIconBaseURL = SpellCheckerPlugin
          .getDefault().getBundle().getEntry("icons/");

  /**
   * Filenames for the images in this registry
   */

  public static final String IMG_IGNORE = "ignore.gif";
  public static final String IMG_IGNOREALL = "ignoreAll.gif";
  public static final String IMG_CANCEL = "cancel.gif";
  public static final String IMG_REPLACE = "replace.gif";
  public static final String IMG_REPLACEALL = "replaceAll.gif";
  public static final String IMG_ADDTODICTIONARY =
                                  "addToDictionary.gif";
  public static final String IMG_CHECK = "check.gif";

  /**
   * Supply action with icons
   *
   * @param action - Action to be decorated
   * @param type - icon type
   * @param relPath - relative path of icon
   */
```

Listing 13.13 (Continues)

```
public static void setImageDescriptors(IAction action, String type,
                                       String relPath) {
  try {
    ImageDescriptor id = ImageDescriptor.createFromURL(
      makeIconFileURL("full/d" + type, relPath));
    if (id != null) action.setDisabledImageDescriptor(id);
  } catch (MalformedURLException e) {
    SpellCheckerPlugin.logError(8,Messages.getString(
     "SpellCheckerImages.Bad_URL_when_loading_disabled_image"), e);
  }
  try {
    ImageDescriptor id = ImageDescriptor.createFromURL(
      makeIconFileURL("full/c" + type, relPath));
    if (id != null) action.setHoverImageDescriptor(id);
  } catch (MalformedURLException e) {
    SpellCheckerPlugin.logError(9, Messages.getString(
     "SpellCheckerImages.Bad_URL_when_loading_hover_image"), e);
    action.setImageDescriptor(ImageDescriptor
                              .getMissingImageDescriptor());
  }
}

// Construct URL for icon file
private static URL makeIconFileURL(
  String prefix, String name) throws MalformedURLException {
  if (fgIconBaseURL == null)
    throw new MalformedURLException();
  return new URL(fgIconBaseURL, prefix + "/" + name);
}
}
```

Listing 13.3 (Continued)

As you have probably already discovered, you don't work here directly with Image instances but with ImageDescriptor instances. These image descriptors work as proxies for images and don't allocate resources in the host operating system. The workbench evaluates these descriptors and loads the images only when needed. Since the workbench also takes care of the required disposal of these Image instances, you don't have to.

Coordinating Core Classes with GUI Classes

Now it is time to take care of the interaction between the spell-checking engine and the user interface (actions and views). This interaction is organized by the SpellCheckManager class.

The Manager

When a `SpellCheckManager` instance is initialized, it creates a new configuration instance (`SpellCheckConfiguration`). This instance is responsible for managing the preferences from the various `PreferencePages` and for passing these preferences to the spell-checking engine. (Remember that there may be several plug-ins implementing different spell-checking strategies, and each may have its own preference page.)

```java
package com.bdaum.SpellChecker;

import java.io.File;
import java.io.FileNotFoundException;
import java.io.IOException;
import java.io.RandomAccessFile;
import java.util.HashMap;
import java.util.Map;
import java.util.StringTokenizer;

import org.eclipse.core.runtime.*;
import org.eclipse.jface.text.IDocument;
import org.eclipse.swt.graphics.Point;
import org.eclipse.swt.widgets.Display;
import org.eclipse.ui.IEditorInput;
import org.eclipse.ui.IFileEditorInput;

import com.bdaum.SpellChecker.actions.CheckSpellingActionDelegate;
import com.bdaum.SpellChecker.preferences.SpellCheckerPreferences;
import com.bdaum.SpellChecker.views.SpellCorrectionView;
import com.swabunga.spell.engine.GenericSpellDictionary;
import com.swabunga.spell.engine.SpellDictionary;
import com.swabunga.spell.engine.SpellDictionaryDichoDisk;
import com.swabunga.spell.event.SpellCheckEvent;
import com.swabunga.spell.event.SpellCheckListener;
import com.swabunga.spell.event.SpellChecker;

/**
 * This class organizes the interaction between the SpellChecker, the
 * user interface, and the spell checker configuration.
 */
public class SpellCheckManager implements SpellCheckListener {

    // File extension for phonetic dictionaries
    private static final String PHONETICEXTENSION = ".phon";
    // File extension for user dictionary
    private static final String USEREXTENSION = ".user";
    // Tuple representing an empty text selection
    private static final Point NOSELECTION = new Point(0, 0);

    /* The engines for the spell checker */
    private Map engineMap = new HashMap(10);
    private SpellChecker currentEngine;

    /* The spell checking view */
```

```
    private SpellCorrectionView correctionViewer;

    /* Currently active preferences */
    private SpellCheckerPreferences currentPreferences;

    /* The configuration */
    private SpellCheckConfiguration config =
                        new SpellCheckConfiguration();

    /* The curent spell checking target */
    private SpellCheckingTarget currentTarget;

    /* The current selection */
    private Point currentSelection = NOSELECTION;

    /* current Display */
    private Display display;

    /* Indicator for aborting the current spell checking process */
    private boolean abort = false;

    /* Current tokenizer name */
    private String currentName;
```

Selecting the Plug-in

The checkDocument() method prepares the spell-checking process. First, it determines whether some text is selected. In this case, the selection is remembered in order to restrict spell-checking to the selected text. Then, the tokenizer and the set of preferences to be applied to the spell-checking process are determined. It is the tokenizer's responsibility to break a document into words. Consequently, it has a big influence on the spell-checking function.

Basically, there are two situations:

❑   You deal with a spell-checking target that is associated with some editor input. In this case, the input type can be determined and an appropriate tokenizer and a specific set of preferences can be selected. This is done in the getWordTokenizer() method.

❑   In all other cases, the default tokenizer and the default set of preferences are used.

```
    /**
     * Checks the document content. This method is thread safe.
     *
     * @param target - the spell checking target
     * @param display - the current Display instance
     * @param correctionViewer - the spell checking view
     */
    public synchronized void checkDocument(SpellCheckingTarget target,
   Display display, SpellCorrectionView correctionViewer) {
        this.display = display;
        // First reset the current preferences to the default preferences
        currentPreferences = SpellCheckerPlugin.getDefault()
```

```
                                                    .getPreferences();
    // Save parameters
    this.correctionViewer = correctionViewer;
    this.currentTarget = target;
    // Reset tokenizer name and selection
    currentName = Messages
            .getString("SpellCheckManager.Default_Spell_Checker");
currentSelection = NOSELECTION;
    // This following must be done in the SWT thread to avoid
    // thread conflicts
    display.syncExec(new Runnable() {
      public void run() {
        // Retrieve current text selection
        currentSelection = currentTarget.getSelection();
      }
    });
    // Get preferences and find tokenizer
    IEditorInput input = target.getEditorInput();
    if (input != null) {
      // We deal with a editor input object and retrieve an input
      // specific tokenizer
      currentTarget.tokenizer = getDocumentWordTokenizer(input);
      if (currentTarget.tokenizer != null)
        performCheck();
    } else {
      // We cannot determine the text type
      // and use the default preferences
      currentPreferences = SpellCheckerPlugin.getDefault()
              .getPreferences();
      currentTarget.tokenizer = new DocumentWordTokenizer();
      performCheck();
    }
  }


  /**
   * Returns the current spell check target
   *
   * @return - Target object
   */
  public SpellCheckingTarget getCurrentTarget() {
    return currentTarget;
  }


  /**
   * Returns the current tokenizer name
   *
   * @return - tokenizer name
   */
  public String getCurrentName() {
    return currentName;
  }
```

To determine the tokenizer and the preference set, the `getDocumentWordTokenizer()` method first fetches the file extension from the editor input and searches for a suitable plug-in. To do so, it fetches the extension point `documentTokenizer` from the plug-in registry and searches through the tree structure of this extension point. It then compares the file extensions that are defined in the extensions to this extension point with the file extension of the editor input (are you still with me?).

If a matching plug-in is found, it first tries to create a plug-in–specific instance, which gives you access to the plug-in–specific preference settings. If such a `Preferences` class is not defined in the plug-in manifest, the default preferences are used instead. The `Preferences` instance that was determined in that way can be retrieved via the `getPreferences()` method.

Similarly, a specific tokenizer is created as defined in the respective plug-in.

```java
/**
 * Retrieves a suitable tokenizer for a given input
 *
 * @param input - the current editor input
 * @return - the tokenizer configured for this input type
 */
private AbstractDocumentWordTokenizer getDocumentWordTokenizer(
    IEditorInput input) {
    // Get file extension form editor input
    String doctype = (input instanceof IFileEditorInput)
            ? ((IFileEditorInput) input).getFile()
                    .getFullPath().getFileExtension()
            : "*";
    // Search for extensions to extension point "documentTokenizer"
    // First get the plug-in registry
    IExtensionRegistry reg = Platform.getExtensionRegistry();
    // Now get the extension point
    IExtensionPoint exPoint = reg.getExtensionPoint(
            SpellCheckerPlugin.getId(), "documentTokenizer");
    // Fetch all installed extensions for this extension point.
    // This can be more than one if several plug-ins were installed.
    IExtension[] tokenizers = exPoint.getExtensions();
    for (int i = 0; i < tokenizers.length; i++) {
        IExtension extension = tokenizers[i];
        // Now fetch all tokenizer specifications
        // Each extension can define several of these specifications
        IConfigurationElement[] configurations = extension
                .getConfigurationElements();
        for (int j = 0; j < configurations.length; j++) {
            IConfigurationElement element = configurations[j];
            // For each tokenizer we step through the list
            // of declared file extensions
            StringTokenizer st = new StringTokenizer(element
                                .getAttribute("extensions"));
            while (st.hasMoreElements()) {
                String ext = st.nextToken();
                if (ext.equalsIgnoreCase(doctype)) {
                    // Positive
                    try {
                        // Now fetch the plug-in specific preferences
                        currentPreferences = (SpellCheckerPreferences) element
                                .createExecutableExtension("preferences");
```

```
            } catch (CoreException e) {
              // No luck, we use the default preferences
            }
            currentName = element.getAttribute("name");
            try {
              // Try to create a tokenizer instance
              return (AbstractDocumentWordTokenizer) element
                          .createExecutableExtension("class");
            } catch (CoreException e) {
              SpellCheckerPlugin.logError(1, Messages.getString(
                "SpellCheckManager.Could_not_create_tokenizer"), e);
            }
          }
        }
      }
    }
    // No matching extension found. Use the default tokenizer.
    return new DocumentWordTokenizer();
  }


  /**
   * Returns the current SpellCheckerPreference.
   *
   * @return - current SpellCheckerPreferences
   */
  public SpellCheckerPreferences getPreferences() {
    return currentPreferences;
  }
```

Running the Engine

The performCheck() method first fetches the document to be checked from the text from the spell-checking target, It initializes the tokenizer with the document and the current selection. (A length of zero indicates that the whole document is to be checked.)

It then fetches a suitable engine via getEngine() and executes the spell check via checkSpelling(). The engine will then use the tokenizer to analyze the document and fire a series of SpellCheckEvents if spelling errors are found. Because the manager was registered with the engine as a SpellCheckListener when the engine was created, the events now arrive in the spellingError() method (see the following section of code).

When the spell-checking process has ended, the current spell-checking target is disposed of, the SpellCorrectionView is reset, and the original selection in the document is restored, because this selection may have been destroyed previously by highlighting a bad word.

```
/**
 * Runs the jazzy engine
 */
private void performCheck() {
  // Initialize the tokenizer
  IDocument document = currentTarget.getDocument();
  currentTarget.tokenizer.init(document, currentSelection.x,
```

```
                currentSelection.y - currentSelection.x, config);
    // Reset the abort flag
    abort = false;
    // Fetch the engine
    SpellChecker engine = getEngine();
    if (engine != null) {
      // Run the engine
      engine.checkSpelling(currentTarget.tokenizer);
      // Reset the spell checking view
      correctionViewer.setInput(null, this,
                currentTarget.isEditable);
      // Restore original selection
      setSelection(currentSelection.x, currentSelection.y);
      // Done - dispose the target
      currentTarget.dispose();
    }
}
```

Managing Engines

The getEngine() method is able to manage several engines. This is to support dictionaries in different languages. When another dictionary is used, a new engine is required. To avoid excessive dictionary loading time in multilingual environments, the engines are cached and reused. As a matter of fact, when engines are switched, the manager must also register as a SpellCheckListener with the new engine and deregister with the old engine.

This method will automatically attach a user dictionary to each dictionary if a user dictionary suffix is defined in the preferences. This user dictionary will accept new words learned during the spell-checking process.

```
/**
 * Finds a suitable spell check engine
 *
 * @return - the spell check engine
 */
private SpellChecker getEngine() {
  // Get default dictionary file name
  String dict = config
        .getString(SpellCheckerPreferences.SPELL_DICTIONARY);
  // Create key for engine map
  String key = dict;
  String user = config
        .getString(SpellCheckerPreferences.USER_DICTIONARY);
  if (user != null && user.length() > 0) key += "." + user;
  // Try to get engine for this dictionary from map
  SpellChecker newEngine = (SpellChecker) engineMap.get(key);
  if (newEngine == null) {
    // Not yet created
    // Create a new engine
    newEngine = createNewEngine(dict);
    if (newEngine == null) return currentEngine;
    // Store the engine in the map for next time
```

```
        engineMap.put(key, newEngine);
    }
    if (newEngine != currentEngine) {
        // If the engine has changed we must modify the listener
        // registration
        if (currentEngine != null)
        // Deregister with the previous engine
          currentEngine.removeSpellCheckListener(this);
        // and register with the new engine
        newEngine.addSpellCheckListener(this);
        currentEngine = newEngine;
    }
    return currentEngine;
}
```

Creating Engines

The `createEngine()` method is a factory method for creating engine instances. Here the dictionary is loaded, and then a new engine for this dictionary is created. The loading process is indicated to the Spell Correction View in order to inform the end user about the short delay.

In addition, this method contains logic to determine the type of dictionary and whether there is a phonetic dictionary available. By convention, a phonetic dictionary has the same filename as the main dictionary but with the extension `.phon`. A simple test determines whether a file with such a qualified name exists.

Dictionaries can be either compressed or uncompressed. Uncompressed dictionaries are simple word lists with one word per line. The engine will load these dictionaries completely into memory. Compressed dictionaries are recognized by an asterisk in the very first line and are treated differently. The engine will open these dictionaries in random access mode and read only relevant parts of the dictionary as required.

If a user dictionary was specified in the preferences, it is attached to the new engine. If this dictionary does not exist yet, a new file with that name is created. User dictionaries are always created as uncompressed dictionaries (word lists).

```
/**
 * Creates a new jazzy engine
 *
 * @param dict - Dictionary file name
 * @return - the new engine
 */
private SpellChecker createNewEngine(String dict) {
    try {
        if (dict != null) {
            // Indicate load operation
            if (correctionViewer != null)
              correctionViewer.indicateLoading(getCurrentName());
            // Load dictionary file
            String phonetic = dict;
            // First look if we have a phonetic file
```

```
              int p = phonetic.lastIndexOf('.');
              if (p >= 0) phonetic = phonetic.substring(0, p);
              phonetic += PHONETICEXTENSION;
              File phFile = new File(phonetic);
              if (!phFile.exists()) phFile = null;
              // Now read first line in dictionary file and check for '*'
              RandomAccessFile dictFile = new RandomAccessFile(dict, "r");
              String firstLine = dictFile.readLine();
              dictFile.close();
              File dFile = new File(dict);
              SpellDictionary dictionary;
              SpellChecker spellchecker;
              // A '*' in the first line signals a compressed file
              if (firstLine.indexOf('*') > 0) {
                // Create engine with compressed dictionary
                dictionary = new SpellDictionaryDichoDisk(dFile, phFile);
                spellchecker = new SpellChecker(dictionary);
              } else {
                // Create engine with uncompressed dictionary
                dictionary = new GenericSpellDictionary(dFile, phFile);
                spellchecker = new SpellChecker(dictionary);
              }
              // Get suffix for user dictionary
              String user = config
                      .getString(SpellCheckerPreferences.USER_DICTIONARY);
              String userdict = USEREXTENSION;
              if (user != null && user.length() > 0)
                userdict = "." + user + userdict;
              File uFile = new File(dict + userdict);
              // Create user dictionary file if it does not exist
              uFile.createNewFile();
              spellchecker.setUserDictionary(
                          new GenericSpellDictionary(uFile));
              return spellchecker;
          }
        SpellCheckerPlugin.logError(5,Messages.getString(
            "SpellCheckManager.No_dictionary_file_declared"), null);
      } catch (FileNotFoundException e) {
        SpellCheckerPlugin.logError(2,
            Messages.getString(
                "SpellCheckManager.Dictionary_file_not_found",
                new Object[] {dict}),
            e);
      } catch (IOException e) {
        SpellCheckerPlugin.logError(3,
            Messages.getString(
                "SpellCheckManager.Error_reading_dictionary_file",
                new Object[] {dict}),
            e);
      }
      return null;
    }
```

Processing Bad Words

The spelling error events fired by the engine arrive in the spellingError() method. First, the position and the length of the bad word are retrieved from the SpellCheckEvent object. With these values a new text selection is set to highlight the bad word via the setSelection() method.

Then the event object is passed as input to the SpellCorrectionView, which then constructs a table with correction proposals. The spell-checking thread then goes into the waiting state. It returns from this state upon notification from the SpellCorrectionView. Because of this, the spellingError() method must be executed as a synchronized method.

The SpellCorrectionView performs this notification by invoking the continueSpellChecking() method. There the waiting thread is released again via notifyAll()—spell-checking can now resume and can possibly result in another event. If no more events are present, the Spell Correction View is reset, the original selection is restored, and the performCheck() method returns.

```java
/**
 * Event processing for the jazzy engine
 *
 * @see com.swabunga.spell.event.SpellCheckListener
 *       #spellingError(com.swabunga.spell.event.SpellCheckEvent)
 */
public synchronized void spellingError(SpellCheckEvent event) {
  // Select bad word
  int pos = event.getWordContextPosition();
  setSelection(pos, pos
          + ((currentTarget.hasLiveDocument())
                  ? currentTarget.tokenizer.getCurrentWordLength()
                  : event.getInvalidWord().length())));
  // Inform the spell checking view about the event
  correctionViewer.setInput(event, this, currentTarget.isEditable);
  // Enable action while thread is waiting
  CheckSpellingActionDelegate action = SpellCheckerPlugin
          .getSpellCheckingActionDelegate();
  action.indicateBusy(false);
  try {
    // Wait until the event was processed by the view
    wait();
  } catch (InterruptedException e) {
  }
  // If view asks to abort, tell jazzy (via the event object)
  if (abort) event.cancel();
}

/**
 * Set selection in spell checking target - must happen in SWT thread
 *
 * @param start - start of selection
 * @param end - end of selection
 */
private void setSelection(
  final int start, final int end) {
  display.syncExec(new Runnable() {
```

```
      public void run() {
         currentTarget.setSelection(start, end);
      }
   });
}

/**
 * Notification that event processing was finished.
 */
public synchronized void continueSpellChecking() {
   // Disable action while busy
   CheckSpellingActionDelegate action = SpellCheckerPlugin
           .getSpellCheckingActionDelegate();
   action.indicateBusy(true);
   // Release waiting thread
   notifyAll();
}
```

Operations

The current spell-checking process can be canceled via the `abortSpellChecking()` method To do so, the method just sets a flag. Then the `spellingError()` method is awakened once again and simply terminates itself after canceling the spell-checking process by calling the event object's `cancel()` method.

```
/**
 * Cancels the current spell checking process.
 */
public void abortSpellChecking() {
   abort = true;
   continueSpellChecking();
}
```

The `replaceWord()` method is used to apply the end user's corrections to the current document. This is done via the spell-checking target's `replaceText()` method. This method returns the change in text length caused by the replacement. This value is added to the length of the current selection, so that the selection shrinks and grows with text replacements. All of this logic is encapsulated into a `syncExec()` call to avoid SWT thread errors (see the section "Displays, Shells, and Monitors" in Chapter 8).

```
/**
 * Replace word in the current document
 *
 * @param pos - Absolute position in the document
 * @param count - Number of characters to be replaced
 * @param newWord - The replacement string
 */
public void replaceWord(final int pos, final int count,
                                  final String newWord) {
   // Execute this via syncExec,
   // since it originates from the spell checking thread.
   display.syncExec(new Runnable() {
      public void run() {
```

```
        currentSelection.y += currentTarget.replaceText(pos,
                count, newWord);
    }
  });
}
```

Analyzing Documents

The jazzy spell-checking engine uses the tokenizer to break documents into single words. The tokenizer used in this plug-in is loosely based on the original jazzy word tokenizer but was extended with additional functionality and refactored into two classes:

❑   The abstract class `AbstractDocumentWordTokenizer` serves as a base class for all tokenizer implementations within the spell checker.

❑   The default tokenizer `DocumentWordTokenizer` is based on this class. This tokenizer is used for plain text files and for all text whose type is unknown.

Later, in a further plug-in, I will present another tokenizer class based on `AbstractDocumentWordTokenizer`.

Since these classes are fairly irrelevant in the context of Eclipse plug-in implementation, I refrain from discussing them here. Interested readers can find their source code on this book's Web site (www.wrox.com). See also Appendix C.

Configuring the Spell Checker

In this section I discuss how preference pages are implemented and how the settings in these preference pages are evaluated. Eclipse already generated the `DefaultSpellCheckPreferencePage` class during project setup. Of course, a few changes are necessary to represent the spell-checking options as Eclipse preferences.

In addition, the generated class `DefaultSpellCheckerPreferencePage` has been split into the separate domain model `SpellCheckerPreferences` and two GUI classes `SpellCheckPreferencePage` and `DefaultSpellCheckerPreferencePage`. This offers the advantage that the relatively large GUI classes need not be loaded when the preferences are initialized, thus shortening startup time.

Preferences

Which options need to be implemented? All the options of the jazzy engine are listed in the `configuration.properties` file. There are two option groups: the options with the prefix `EDIT_` are used for fine-tuning the spell-checking algorithm, while the options with the prefix `SPELL_` represent user options. To achieve consistent management for these configuration parameters, I have adopted both groups into the `PreferenceStore` (and initialized their default values), but I provide field editors only for the values starting with the prefix `SPELL_`.

I have also introduced a few options by myself: the dictionary path (`SPELL_DICTIONARY`), the suffix for the user dictionary (`USER_DICTIONARY`), and the options `IGNOREONELETTERWORDS` and `COMPOUNDCHARACTERS`. The default value for the dictionary path is the default dictionary defined in the `SpellCheckerPlugin` class.

Domain Model

All options are combined in class `SpellCheckerPreferences` (Listing 13.4) which implements the preference's domain model. The GUI part (the Preference Pages) will be implemented in a separate class. This concept will lead to shorter start-up times, since only the domain model needs to be initialized when the plug-in becomes active.

The `getPluginPreferences()` method is used to load the whole set of plug-in–specific preferences. Note that each plug-in has its own set of preferences. This allows the end user to configure the spell checker individually for each file type. For example, Java source files may have a different spell-checking configuration than plain text files.

```java
package com.bdaum.SpellChecker.preferences;

import org.eclipse.core.runtime.Preferences;
import org.eclipse.jface.preference.IPreferenceStore;

import com.bdaum.SpellChecker.SpellCheckerPlugin;
import com.swabunga.spell.engine.Configuration;

public class SpellCheckerPreferences {

  // Key for dictionary path
  public static final String SPELL_DICTIONARY = "SPELL_DICTIONARY";
  // Key for user dictionary suffix
  public static final String USER_DICTIONARY = "USER_DICTIONARY";
  // Key for option to ignore one letter words
  public static final String IGNOREONELETTERWORDS =
                                        "ignoreOneLetterWords";
  // Key for characters in compound words
  public static final String COMPOUNDCHARACTERS =
                                        "compoundCharacters";

  /**
   * Sets the defaults for all preferences
   *
   * @param store - the PreferenceStore instance
   */
  public void initializeDefaults(IPreferenceStore store) {
    // Only initialize if not already initialized
    // Otherwise preference.ini and plugin_customization.ini
    // would not work.
    if (store.getDefaultString(SPELL_DICTIONARY).length() == 0) {
      initializePublicPreferences(store);
```

Listing 13.4 (Continues)

```java
        initializeHiddenPreferences(store);
    }
  }

  /**
   * Public configuration data for spell check algorithm
   *
   * @param store - the PreferenceStore instance
   */
  protected void initializePublicPreferences(IPreferenceStore store) {
    store.setDefault(SPELL_DICTIONARY,
        SpellCheckerPlugin.getDefaultDictionaryFileName());
    store.setDefault(Configuration.SPELL_THRESHOLD, 140);
    store.setDefault(Configuration.SPELL_IGNOREDIGITWORDS, true);
    store.setDefault(Configuration.SPELL_IGNOREINTERNETADDRESSES,
            false);
    store.setDefault(Configuration.SPELL_IGNOREMIXEDCASE,
            false);
    store.setDefault(Configuration.SPELL_IGNOREMULTIPLEWORDS,
            false);
    store.setDefault(Configuration.SPELL_IGNORESENTENCECAPITALIZATION,
            false);
    store.setDefault(Configuration.SPELL_IGNOREUPPERCASE,
            false);
    store.setDefault(IGNOREONELETTERWORDS, false);
    store.setDefault(COMPOUNDCHARACTERS, ".:/@\\");
  }

  /**
   * Non-public configuration data for spell check algorithm
   *
   * @param store - the PreferenceStore instance
   */
  protected void initializeHiddenPreferences(IPreferenceStore store) {
    store.setDefault(Configuration.COST_REMOVE_CHAR, 95);
    store.setDefault(Configuration.COST_INSERT_CHAR, 95);
    store.setDefault(Configuration.COST_SWAP_CHARS, 90);
    store.setDefault(Configuration.COST_SUBST_CHARS, 100);
    store.setDefault(Configuration.COST_CHANGE_CASE, 10);
  }

  /**
   * Retrieve plug-in specific preferences
   *
   * @return Preferences
   */
  public Preferences getPluginPreferences() {
    return SpellCheckerPlugin.getDefault().getPluginPreferences();
  }
}
```

Listing 13.4 (Continued)

The GUI

The GUI part of the spell checker preferences consists of an abstract class SpellCheckerPreferencePage which can be utilized by all later add-ons to the spell checker. The class DefaultSpellCheckerPreferencePage extends this class and implements the basic options for operating the spell checker. With class ShortIntegerFieldEditor I show how field editors for preference pages can be extended and modified.

The SpellCheckerPreferencePage Class

The implementation of the SpellCheckerPreferencePage class closely follows the pregenerated pattern. The generated class DefaultSpellCheckerPreferencePage is renamed to SpellCheckerPreferencePage and completed, while a new version of DefaultSpellCheckerPreferencePage will be created from scratch as a subclass of SpellCheckerPreferencePage.

```
package com.bdaum.SpellChecker.preferences;

import org.eclipse.jface.preference.*;
import org.eclipse.swt.widgets.Composite;
import org.eclipse.ui.IWorkbench;
import org.eclipse.ui.IWorkbenchPreferencePage;
import org.eclipse.ui.help.WorkbenchHelp;

import com.bdaum.SpellChecker.Messages;
import com.swabunga.spell.engine.Configuration;

/**
 * This class implements the common parts of spell checker preference
 * pages.
 */

public abstract class SpellCheckerPreferencePage extends
        FieldEditorPreferencePage
        implements IWorkbenchPreferencePage {
```

Because only letters or digits are allowed in the user dictionary suffix, a special field editor is needed to allow strings containing letters and digits. This is achieved by subclassing the StringFieldEditor class and overriding the doCheckState() method. In addition, the text length is restricted to 15 characters.

```
    /**
     * Subclass of StringFieldEditor in order to check the user
     * dictionary suffix for invalid characters
     */
    public class UserSuffixFieldEditor extends StringFieldEditor {

      public UserSuffixFieldEditor(String name,
              String labelText, Composite parent) {
        super(name, labelText, 15, parent);
      }
```

```java
/**
 * Checks if entered values are valid
 *
 * @return - true if valid
 */
protected boolean doCheckState() {
  String txt = getTextControl().getText();
  for (int i = 0; i < txt.length(); i++) {
    if (!Character.isLetterOrDigit(txt.charAt(i))) {
      setErrorMessage(Messages.getString(
        "SpellCheckerPreferencePage.Invalid_character_in_suffix"));
      return false;
    }
  }
  return super.doCheckState();
}
```

The constructor specifies a grid layout. The `init()` method just adds a descriptive text to the preference page. I have also extended the `createControl()` method to set help identification for context-sensitive help (InfoPops).

```java
public static final String SPELLCHECKERPREFERENCESCONTEXT =
"com.bdaum.SpellChecker.preferences_context";

/* Constructor */

public SpellCheckerPreferencePage() {
  super(GRID);
}

/**
 * Initialization
 */
public void init(IWorkbench workbench) {
  setDescription(Messages.getString(
    "SpellCheckerPreferencePage.All_changes_will_take_effect"));
}

/**
 * Get Plug-in specific workspace PreferenceStore instance
 *
 * @return - preference store instance
 */
public abstract IPreferenceStore doGetPreferenceStore();

/**
 * Construct page content
 */
public void createControl(Composite parent) {
  super.createControl(parent);
  WorkbenchHelp.setHelp(parent.getParent(),
        getPreferenceHelpContextID());
```

```
}

/**
 * Get Help context id for this preference page
 *
 * @return String - the ID for context sensitive help.
 */
protected String getPreferenceHelpContextID() {
  return SPELLCHECKERPREFERENCESCONTEXT;
}
```

A field editor for each (public) spell-checking option is constructed in the createFieldEditors() method. Because I did not like the long and unlimited fields produced by the IntegerFieldEditor class, I implemented the ShortIntegerFieldEditor class with a configurable number of digits (see the following code).

```
/**
 * Create field editors
 */

public void createFieldEditors() {
  Composite composite = getFieldEditorParent();
  addField(new FileFieldEditor(
          SpellCheckerPreferences.SPELL_DICTIONARY,
          Messages.getString(
              "SpellCheckerPreferencePage.Spell_Dictionary_File"),
              composite));
  addField(new UserSuffixFieldEditor(
          SpellCheckerPreferences.USER_DICTIONARY,
          Messages.getString(
          "SpellCheckerPreferencePage.User_Dictionary_File_Suffix"),
              composite));
  ShortIntegerFieldEditor thresholdEditor =
          new ShortIntegerFieldEditor(Configuration.SPELL_THRESHOLD,
              Messages.getString(
                "SpellCheckerPreferencePage.Spell_Threshold"),
                composite, 4);
  thresholdEditor.setValidRange(0, 9999);
  addField(thresholdEditor);
  addField(new BooleanFieldEditor(
          Configuration.SPELL_IGNOREDIGITWORDS,
          Messages.getString(
              "SpellCheckerPreferencePage.Ignore_Numbers"),
              composite));
  addField(new BooleanFieldEditor(
          SpellCheckerPreferences.IGNOREONELETTERWORDS,
          Messages.getString(
              "SpellCheckerPreferencePage.Ignore_one_letter_words"),
              composite));
  addField(new BooleanFieldEditor(
          Configuration.SPELL_IGNOREMIXEDCASE,
          Messages.getString(
```

```
                "SpellCheckerPreferencePage.Ignore_Mixed_Case"),
                composite));
        addField(new BooleanFieldEditor(
            Configuration.SPELL_IGNORESENTENCECAPITALIZATION,
            Messages.getString(
        "SpellCheckerPreferencePage.Ignore_Sentence_Capitalization"),
                composite));
        addField(new BooleanFieldEditor(
            Configuration.SPELL_IGNOREUPPERCASE,
            Messages.getString(
                "SpellCheckerPreferencePage.Ignore_Upper_Case"),
                composite));
        addField(new StringFieldEditor(
            SpellCheckerPreferences.COMPOUNDCHARACTERS,
            Messages.getString(
                "SpellCheckerPreferencePage.CompoundCharacters"),
                15, composite));
    }
}
```

The DefaultSpellCheckerPreferencePage Class

The class DefaultSpellCheckerPreferencePage is very simple (see Listing 13.5). As a subclass of SpellCheckerPreferencePage it implements only the abstract method doGetPreferenceStore(). This method simply fetches the plug-in's preferences store and returns it.

```java
package com.bdaum.SpellChecker.preferences;

import org.eclipse.jface.preference.IPreferenceStore;

import com.bdaum.SpellChecker.SpellCheckerPlugin;

/**
 * This class implements the preference page for the basic spell
 * checker options.
 */

public class DefaultSpellCheckerPreferencePage extends
                                    SpellCheckerPreferencePage {

  /**
   * Returns the preference store of the default preferences
   *
   * @return - the default preference store
   */
  public IPreferenceStore doGetPreferenceStore() {
    return SpellCheckerPlugin.getDefault().getPreferenceStore();
  }
}
```

Listing 13.5

The ShortIntegerFieldEditor Class

The ShortIntegerFieldEditor class (Listing 13.6) is based on the standard field editor StringFieldEditor. In addition, it sets the number of allowed characters to the specified width and checks the input for nonnumeric characters and for violation of the specified limits.

```java
package com.bdaum.SpellChecker.preferences;

import org.eclipse.jface.preference.StringFieldEditor;
import org.eclipse.jface.resource.JFaceResources;
import org.eclipse.swt.widgets.Composite;
import org.eclipse.swt.widgets.Text;

public class ShortIntegerFieldEditor extends StringFieldEditor {
  private int minValidValue = 0;
  private int maxValidValue = Integer.MAX_VALUE;

  /**
   * Default constructor.
   */
  public ShortIntegerFieldEditor() {
    super();
  }

  /**
   * Qualified constructor.
   *
   * @param name - preference key
   * @param labelText - label text string
   * @param parent - parent composite
   * @param textLimit - maximum text width
   */
  public ShortIntegerFieldEditor(String name,
          String labelText, Composite parent, int width) {
    super(name, labelText, width, parent);
    setTextLimit(width);
    setEmptyStringAllowed(false);
    setErrorMessage(JFaceResources
            .getString("IntegerFieldEditor.errorMessage"));

  }

  /**
   * Sets the range of valid values for this field.
   *
   * @param min - he minimum allowed value (inclusive)
   * @param max - the maximum allowed value (inclusive)
   */
  public void setValidRange(int min, int max) {
    minValidValue = min;
    maxValidValue = max;
  }

  /**
```

Listing 13.6 (Continues)

```
    * Checks for valid field content
    *
    * @return - true if valid
    */
  protected boolean checkState() {
    Text text = getTextControl();
    if (text == null) return false;
    String numberString = text.getText();
    try {
      int number = Integer.valueOf(numberString).intValue();
      if (number >= minValidValue && number <= maxValidValue) {
        clearErrorMessage();
        return true;
      }
    } catch (NumberFormatException e1) {
    }
    showErrorMessage();
    return false;
  }
}
```

Listing 13.6 (Continued)

Reading from the PreferenceStore

What is needed now is a method to pass the options set in the preferences pages to the spell-checking engine. In the `SpellCheckerPlugin` class (see the section "The Plugin Class") the jazzy engine was already told to fetch its configuration parameters from the `SpellCheckConfiguration` class (by setting the system property `jazzy`).

Passing the preference values is quite simple. The `SpellCheckConfiguration` class (Listing 13.7) extends the jazzy class `Configuration` and overrides the methods `getBoolean()`, `setBoolean()`, `getInteger()`, and `setInteger()`. In addition, the `getString()` method was added to be able to fetch the dictionary path and the user dictionary suffix. When a `get...()` method is invoked, the value belonging to the specified key is fetched from the plug-in preferences. Which plug-in preferences are selected is determined by the `SpellCheckManager` depending on the type of file to be checked.

The `set...()` methods do nothing, because all preferences are modified via the `PreferencePages` and not via the `Configuration` class.

```
package com.bdaum.SpellChecker;

import org.eclipse.core.runtime.Preferences;

import com.bdaum.SpellChecker.preferences.SpellCheckerPreferences;
import com.swabunga.spell.engine.Configuration;

public class SpellCheckConfiguration extends Configuration {

  private static final String TRUE = "true";
```

Listing 13.7 (Continues)

```
/**
 * Fetch integer value from Preferences
 *
 * @param key - identification of value
 * @return - value belonging to the key
 */
public int getInteger(String key) {
  try {
    return Integer.parseInt(getString(key));
  } catch (NumberFormatException e) {
    return 0;
  }
}

/**
 * Fetch Boolean value from Preferences
 *
 * @param key - identification of value
 * @return - value belonging to the key
 */
public boolean getBoolean(String key) {
  return TRUE.equals(getString(key));
}

/**
 * Fetch string value from Properties or Preferences
 *
 * @param key - identification of value
 * @return - value belonging to the key
 */
public String getString(String key) {
  SpellCheckerPreferences preferences =
      SpellCheckerPlugin.getManager().getPreferences();
  Preferences prefs = preferences.getPluginPreferences();
  return prefs.getString(key);
}

/**
 * All preferences are set via the PreferencePages.
 * Therefore, the setXXX() implementation do nothing here.
 */
public void setInteger(
  String key, int value) {}

public void setBoolean(
  String key, boolean value) {}
}
```

Listing 13.7 (Continued)

The Help System

The Eclipse help system is designed in such a way that allows the implementation of help pages independently from the application, using a standard HTML editor. The association of the individual help pages to help topics (or in a context-sensitive way to GUI components) is defined via XML files.

For space reasons I will not show the HTML pages here.

The Help Table of Contents

The path of the help table of contents has already been declared in the manifest file `plugin.xml` (see the section "The Plug-in Configuration"). The file `toc.xml` is shown in Listing 13.8.

```
<?xml version="1.0" encoding="UTF-8"?>
<toc label="Spell Checker" topic="html/spelling.html">
  <topic label="Correction View" href="html/SpellCheckerView.html"/>
    <topic label="Dictionaries" href="html/Dictionaries.html"/>
    <topic label="Preferences">
    <topic label="Default Preferences"
           href="html/SpellCheckerPreferences.html"/>
    <anchor id="postPreferences"/>
  </topic>
  <topic label="Other Information">
    <topic label="Acknowledgements"
           href="html/Acknowledgements.html"/>
    <topic label="Source code" href="html/SourceCode.html"/>
  </topic>
</toc>
```

Listing 13.8

An HTML page is assigned to each `topic` element and also to the root element of the table of contents (`toc`). Topics may branch into subtopics, that is, topics may be nested. You can define a display text for each topic with the attribute `label`. The topics are displayed as a tree structure on the left-hand side of the help browser. The end user can open the associated HTML page by clicking on a topic.

The definition of the `anchor` element under the `Default Preferences` topic is a special case. Here an extension point is created to which the help systems of other plug-ins can refer. Thus, the help systems of several plug-ins can merge.

Context-Sensitive Help

The path of the file containing the associations of help pages with GUI elements has also already been declared in the manifest file `plugin.xml` (see the section "The Plug-in Configuration").

The `contexts.xml` file is shown in Listing 13.9.

```
<?xml version="1.0" encoding="UTF-8"?>
<contexts>
  <context id="action_context">
    <description>Help for Spell Checker Action Set</description>
    <topic href="html/spelling.html"  label="Spell Checker"/>
  </context>
  <context id="preferences_context">
    <description>Help for Spell Checker Preferences</description>
    <topic href="html/SpellCheckerPreferences.html"
           label="Spell Checker Preferences"/>
  </context>
  <context id="correctionView_context">
    <description>Help for Spell Checker Correction View</description>
    <topic href="html/SpellCheckerView.html"
           label="Spell Checker Correction View"/>
  </context>
</contexts>
```

Listing 13.9

All of the individual context associations are listed in the element `contexts`. Each `context` definition refers to a context ID that identifies the corresponding GUI element. This ID is always specified here relative to the plug-in. Each context definition contains a description element, which later appears in the InfoPop, and a topic element that refers to the associated HTML page.

Where do the context IDs come from? This is not handled very consistently in Eclipse. In some cases, context IDs are defined in the manifest for `plugin.xml` (for example, for actions), while in other cases, the context IDs must be set in the Java code. You have already seen this in the classes `SpellCheckPreferencePage` and `SpellCorrectionView`. In these cases, the context IDs are set in the Eclipse help system with the help of the static `WorkbenchHelp` method `setHelp()`.

Active Help

At the end of this section on help I want to demonstrate how active help works. The main help page `spelling.html` contains two hyperlinks labeled Edit > Check Spelling and Window > Customize Perspective.... By activating these hyperlinks, the end user can start spell-checking directly from the help page or can configure the current perspective, for example, add the spell-checking function to the toolbar and the menu.

Here is an HTML fragment of this page. The link to the script `livehelp.js` and the invocation of the script in the hyperlinks are printed in bold type:

```
<head>
<script language="JavaScript"
        src="../../org.eclipse.help/livehelp.js"></script>
</head>

<h1><font color="#0099FF">Spell Checker Help</font></h1>
<hr color="#66FFFF">
<h4><font color="#0099FF">Spell checking on demand</font></h4>
<p>The spell checker is started by placing the cursor inside of a text or
```

```
editor area, then invoking the function
<i><b><a href='javascript:liveAction("com.bdaum.SpellChecker",
"com.bdaum.SpellChecker.actions.ActiveHelpAction", "start")'>Edit&gt;Check
Spelling</a></b></i> or pressing the spell checker tool button (<img
border="0" src="../icons/basic/correction_view.gif" width="16" height="16">).
Alternatively, you may select a text area and then press the spell checker
button.</p>
<p>To add this function to the workbench toolbar and to the menu go to <i><a
href='javascript:liveAction("com.bdaum.SpellChecker",
"com.bdaum.SpellChecker.actions.ActiveHelpAction",
"install")'><b>Window&gt;Customize
Perspective...</b></a></i>, open the <i><b>Commands</b></i> page, and
checkmark <i><b>SpellChecker</b></i>.</p>
```

The `ActiveHelpAction` class is specified as the second parameter of the script invocation.

The ActiveHelpAction Class

The `setInitializationString()` method accepts the third parameter of the JavaScript invocation (in this case, the value `start` or `install`). This allows you to implement different help actions depending on the parameter value.

```java
package com.bdaum.SpellChecker.actions;

import org.eclipse.help.ILiveHelpAction;
import org.eclipse.swt.widgets.Display;
import org.eclipse.swt.widgets.Shell;
import org.eclipse.ui.IWorkbench;
import org.eclipse.ui.IWorkbenchWindow;
import org.eclipse.ui.IWorkbenchWindowActionDelegate;
import org.eclipse.ui.PlatformUI;
import org.eclipse.ui.internal.WorkbenchPage;

import com.bdaum.SpellChecker.SpellCheckerPlugin;

/**
 * Invoking spell checking via active help
 */
public class ActiveHelpAction implements ILiveHelpAction {
  // JavaScript invocation parameter
  String data;

  /**
   * Accepts the third parameter of the script invocation
   */
  public void setInitializationString(
    String data) {
    // Remember the parameter
    this.data = data;
  }
```

Running the Help Action

The run() method first tries to find a suitable workbench window. If there is an active window, this window is used. Otherwise, the first available window is used. If none exists, the help function will not work.

Then the current Display instance is fetched from this window instance. The rest of the action is performed in the SWT thread in order to avoid thread conflicts. The window is brought to the foreground, and, depending on the parameter of the script invocation, either the function Window > Customize Perspective... is executed via page.editActionSets() or the spell-checking action is started by fetching the spell-checking action delegate from the plug-in class and calling the run() method of the SpellCheckingActionDelegate instance.

```java
/**
 * Runs help action
 */
public void run() {
  IWorkbench wb = PlatformUI.getWorkbench();
  final IWorkbenchWindow window =
      (wb.getActiveWorkbenchWindow() == null) ?
          wb.getWorkbenchWindows()[0] :
          wb.getActiveWorkbenchWindow();
  if (window == null) return;
  Display display = window.getShell().getDisplay();
  if (display == null) return;
  // Active help does not run in the SWT thread.
  // Therefore we must encapsulate all GUI accesses into
  // a syncExec() method.
  display.syncExec(new Runnable() {
    public void run() {
      // Bring the workbench window into the foreground
      Shell shell = window.getShell();
      shell.setMinimized(false);
      shell.forceActive();
      if (data.equals("install")) {
        // Fetch workbench page
        WorkbenchPage page = (WorkbenchPage) window.getActivePage();
        if (page == null) return;
        // Call Perspective Configuration function
        page.editActionSets();
      } else if (data.equals("start")) {
        // Get the SpellCheckingActionDelegate
        IWorkbenchWindowActionDelegate delegate =
            SpellCheckerPlugin.getSpellCheckingActionDelegate();
        if (delegate == null) return;
        // Execute the spell checking action
        delegate.run(null);
      }
    }
  });
}
}
```

A Plug-in for Java Properties

After having finished the implementation of the main spell-checker plug-in, you are now going to implement a specialized spell checker plug-in for Java properties files in this section. This plug-in connects to the previous plug-in via the extension point `documentTokenizer`. Since this plug-in is aware of the syntax of properties files, it can check exactly those portions of the file content that are of interest in terms of orthography (Figure 13.4).

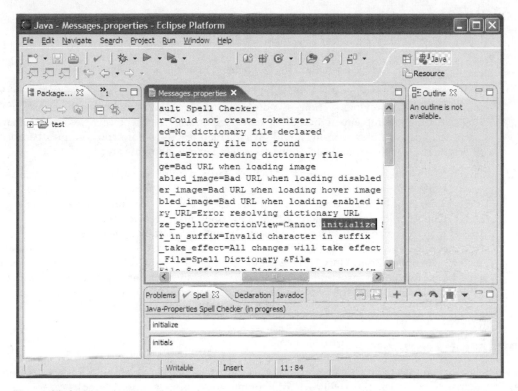

Figure 13.4

Since this specialized spell checker is implemented on the basis of the previous plug-in, only four Java classes are required: a small `Plugin` class, a tokenizer specialized for the Java properties syntax, a class for the specialized `Preferences`, and the corresponding `PreferencePage`. Additional pages are added to the help system, too.

Setting Up the Project

The Java properties spell checker is implemented as a separate project. Again, invoke the New Wizard with the function File > New > Plug-in Project. On the following wizard page, enter the name of the project: `com.bdaum.SpellChecker.JavaProperties`.

On the next wizard page, select Java Project and change the name of the Runtime Library to JavaPropertiesTokenizer.jar. On the following page, make sure that the option Generate the Java Class That Controls the Plug-in's Life Cycle is checked, make sure that the name of this class is set to JavaPropertiesPlugin, and enter a suitable Provider Name. On the following page, leave the option Create a Plug-in Using One of the Templates unchecked, and press Finish. The wizard now generates the manifest file plugin.xml and the class JavaPropertiesPlugin in the new project.

The Manifest

In this plug-in you have to create most of the manifest file by yourself:

❑ On the Overview page, change the Plug-in Name to Spellchecker for Java Properties.

❑ On the Dependencies page, it is sufficient to mark the plug-in com.bdaum.SpellChecker that you created in the previous sections as a prerequisite. This allows you to use the classes of this plug-in during the implementation of the new plug-in. All other dependencies are automatically computed from this plug-in. You should save the manifest file before you continue, because otherwise these inclusions would not be considered in the following steps.

❑ On the Extensions page, add extensions to the extension points com.bdaum.SpellChecker .documentTokenizer, org.eclipse.ui.PreferencePages, org.eclipse.help.toc, and org.eclipse.help.contexts. For all these points use schema-based extensions. The corresponding schemas, among which is the previously created schema documentTokenizer.exsd for the extension point com.bdaum.SpellChecker .documentTokenizer, help you in completing the extension point specification. You must uncheck the option Show Only Extension Points from the Required Plug-ins when you want to add the extension points org.eclipse.help.toc and org.eclipse.help.contexts. You must also first create the toc.xml and contexts.xml files to be able to add these extension points (see "The Help System"). See the following listing for details.

Tokenizer Extension

Let's step, as an example, through the specification of the extension point com.bdaum.SpellChecker .documentTokenizer. The ID for this extension point is com.bdaum.SpellChecker .JavaProperties and its name is Java-Properties Spell Checker. Now right-click on this extension point and select the menu item New > Tokenizer. A new element called com.bdaum .SpellChecker.JavaProperties.tokenizer1 is now created as a child element of com.bdaum.SpellChecker.documentTokenizer. When you select this element, you will see the individual attributes of this element in the details area as they were defined in the documentTokenizer.exsd schema.

In the Class entry, click the small button at the right-hand side of the entry and select Create a New Java Class. In the dialog that appears, enter com.bdaum.SpellChecker.JavaProperties under Package Name and JavaPropertiesTokenizer under Class Name. This will automatically generate a stub for the new class.

Under the Entry Extensions, enter the file extension `properties`, and under the Entry ID, enter `com.bdaum.SpellChecker.Java.JavaPropertiesWordTokenizer`. Under Name, enter `Java-Properties Spell Checker`. Also, under Preferences, press the little button at the right-hand side and create a new Java class called `JavaPropertiesPreferences` in the `com.bdaum.SpellChecker.JavaProperties` package. In this case, too, a stub is generated immediately.

Manifest

Listing 13.10 shows the complete plug-in manifest for the Java-Properties spell checker add-on.

```xml
<?xml version="1.0" encoding="UTF-8"?>
<?eclipse version="3.0"?>
<plugin
    id="com.bdaum.SpellChecker.JavaProperties"
    name="Spellchecker for Java-Properties"
    version="1.0.0"
    provider-name="bdaum industrial communications"
    class="com.bdaum.SpellChecker.JavaProperties.JavaPropertiesPlugin">

    <runtime>
        <library name="JavaPropertiesTokenizer.jar">
        </library>
    </runtime>
    <requires>
        <import plugin="com.bdaum.SpellChecker"/>
    </requires>

    <extension id="com.bdaum.SpellChecker.documentTokenizer"
            name="Java-Properties Spell Checker"
            point="com.bdaum.SpellChecker.documentTokenizer">
        <tokenizer id=
"com.bdaum.SpellChecker.Java.JavaPropertiesWordTokenizer"
            preferences=
"com.bdaum.SpellChecker.JavaProperties.JavaPropertiesPreferences"
            name="Java-Properties Spell Checker"
            extensions="properties"
            class=
"com.bdaum.SpellChecker.JavaProperties.JavaPropertiesTokenizer">
        </tokenizer>
    </extension>
    <extension point="org.eclipse.ui.preferencePages">
        <page id="com.bdaum.SpellChecker.JavaProperties.preferencePage"
            name="%Java_Properties"
            category=
                "com.bdaum.SpellChecker.preferences.defaultPreferences"
            class=
"com.bdaum.SpellChecker.JavaProperties.JavaPropertiesPreferencePage">
        </page>
    </extension>
    <extension point="org.eclipse.help.toc">
        <toc file="toc.xml">
        </toc>
```

Listing 13.10 (Continues)

```
      </extension>
      <extension point="org.eclipse.help.contexts">
         <contexts file="contexts.xml">
         </contexts>
      </extension>
   </plugin>
```

Listing 13.10 (Continued)

The Plugin Class

The `JavaPropertiesPlugin` class is minimal (see Listing 13.11). The only extension is the initialization of the preferences. This is delegated to the `JavaPropertiesPreferences` class (see the next section).

```java
package com.bdaum.SpellChecker.JavaProperties;

import org.eclipse.jface.preference.IPreferenceStore;
import org.eclipse.ui.plugin.AbstractUIPlugin;

import com.bdaum.SpellChecker.preferences.SpellCheckerPreferences;

/**
 * The main plug-in class
 */
public class JavaPropertiesPlugin extends AbstractUIPlugin {
  // The shared instance
  private static JavaPropertiesPlugin plugin;

  /**
   * The constructor
   */
  public JavaPropertiesPlugin() {
    super();
    plugin = this;
  }

  /**
   * Returns the shared instance
   */
  public static JavaPropertiesPlugin getDefault() {
    return plugin;
  }

  /**
   * Initialize PreferenceStore
   */
  protected void initializeDefaultPluginPreferences() {
    IPreferenceStore store = getPreferenceStore();
    SpellCheckerPreferences preferences =
                       new JavaPropertiesPreferences();
    preferences.initializeDefaults(store);
  }
}
```

Listing 13.11

The Preferences

The preferences of this plug-in are built on top of the preferences of the previous plug-in. The `JavaPropertiesPlugin` class inherits all the preferences from `SpellCheckerPreferences` but uses a plug-in–specific `PreferenceStore`.

The preferences for Java-Properties files and text files can therefore be identically named but may have different values. Some options specific to properties files are added, and different default settings are used for the inherited options; therefore, the `initializePublicPreferences()` method is overridden. See Listing 13.12.

```
package com.bdaum.SpellChecker.JavaProperties;

import org.eclipse.core.runtime.Preferences;
import org.eclipse.jface.preference.IPreferenceStore;

import com.bdaum.SpellChecker.SpellCheckerPlugin;
import com.bdaum.SpellChecker.preferences.SpellCheckerPreferences;
import com.swabunga.spell.engine.Configuration;

public class JavaPropertiesPreferences extends
                                    SpellCheckerPreferences {

  // Additional options
  public static final String CHECKCOMMENTS = "checkComments";
  public static final String CHECKKEYS = "checkKeys";

  /**
   * Set default preference values
   *
   * @param store - the preference store
   */
  protected void initializePublicPreferences(IPreferenceStore store) {
    store.setDefault(SPELL_DICTIONARY, SpellCheckerPlugin
                                .getDefaultDictionaryFileName());
    store.setDefault(Configuration.SPELL_THRESHOLD, 140);
    store.setDefault(Configuration.SPELL_IGNOREDIGITWORDS, true);
    store.setDefault(
            Configuration.SPELL_IGNOREINTERNETADDRESSES, true);
    store.setDefault(Configuration.SPELL_IGNOREMIXEDCASE, false);
    store.setDefault(Configuration.SPELL_IGNOREMULTIPLEWORDS, false);
    store.setDefault(
            Configuration.SPELL_IGNORESENTENCECAPITALIZATION, false);
    store.setDefault(Configuration.SPELL_IGNOREUPPERCASE, true);
    store.setDefault(IGNOREONELETTERWORDS, false);
    store.setDefault(COMPOUNDCHARACTERS, ".:/@\\");
    store.setDefault(CHECKCOMMENTS, false);
    store.setDefault(CHECKKEYS, false);
  }

  /**
   * Get plug-in specific preferences
   *
```

Listing 13.12 (Continues)

```
     * @return Preferences
     */
    public Preferences getPluginPreferences() {
      return JavaPropertiesPlugin.getDefault().getPluginPreferences();
    }
}
```

Listing 13.12 (Continued)

The Preference Page

The `JavaPropertiesPreferencePage` class (Listing 13.13) is similar to the default preference page, so it is defined as a subclass of the `SpellCheckerPreferencePage` class. Of course, you must add the additional options to the GUI. A different context ID for the help pages is used, too. A different `PreferenceStore` instance is retrieved from the current plug-in with the `doGetPreferenceStore()` method and to guarantee that the plug-in works with its own set of preference values.

```
package com.bdaum.SpellChecker.JavaProperties;

import org.eclipse.jface.preference.BooleanFieldEditor;
import org.eclipse.jface.preference.IPreferenceStore;
import org.eclipse.swt.widgets.Composite;
import com.bdaum.SpellChecker.preferences.SpellCheckerPreferencePage;

public class JavaPropertiesPreferencePage extends
                                      SpellCheckerPreferencePage {

  /**
   * Get Plug-in specific PreferenceStore instance
   */
  public IPreferenceStore doGetPreferenceStore() {
    return JavaPropertiesPlugin.getDefault().getPreferenceStore();
  }

  /**
   * Get Help context id for this preference page
   *
   * @return String - the ID for context sensitive help.
   */
  protected String getPreferenceHelpContextID() {
   return "com.bdaum.SpellChecker.JavaProperties.preferences_context";
  }

  /**
   * Add field editors specific for Java Properties
   */
```

Listing 13.13 (Continues)

```
public void createFieldEditors() {
  // Create standard field editors
  super.createFieldEditors();
  // Create additional field editors
  Composite composite = getFieldEditorParent();
  addField(new BooleanFieldEditor(
          JavaPropertiesPreferences.CHECKCOMMENTS,
          Messages.getString(
        "JavaPropertiesSpellCheckerPreferencePage.Check_Comments"),
          composite));
  addField(new BooleanFieldEditor(
          JavaPropertiesPreferences.CHECKKEYS,
          Messages.getString(
        "JavaPropertiesSpellCheckerPreferencePage.Check_Keys"),
          composite));
  }
}
```

Listing 13.13 (Continued)

The Java-Properties Tokenizer

The Java-Properties tokenizer is also implemented as a subclass of
`AbstractDocumentWordTokenizer`. This class consists mainly of a small parser that scans the Java-Properties file and identifies comments, keys, and values. Depending on the preferences—which are fetched via the `SpellCheckConfiguration` class—the corresponding text section is admitted to the spell-checking process or not.

Since this tokenizer does not contain Eclipse-specific code, I don't list it here. Interested readers can find the complete code at www.wrox.com).

The Help System

This plug-in also needs the help control files `toc.xml` and `contexts.xml`, along with the corresponding HTML pages. Here is the code for `toc.xml`. Note the attribute `link_to` in the `toc` element. This attribute creates a link to the anchor point defined previously in the section "The Help Table of Contents."

```
<?xml version="1.0" encoding="UTF-8"?>
<toc link_to="../com.bdaum.SpellChecker/toc.xml#postPreferences"
    label="Java Properties">
  <topic label="Java Properties"
          href="html/JavaPropertiesPreferences.html"/>
</toc>
```

The `contexts.xml` file defines only a single new context (for the Java-Properties preference page):

```
<?xml version="1.0" encoding="UTF-8"?>
<contexts>
  <context id="preferences_context">
    <description>Help for Spell Checker JavaProperties Preferences
    </description>
    <topic href="html/JavaPropertiesPreferences.html"
           label="Spell Checker Preferences for Java Property files"/>
  </context>
</contexts>
```

Internationalizing the Spell Checker

Internationalizing the spell checker involves several tasks. First, you need to deal with text constants within Java programs. Then there are the manifest files that contain text constant in national languages. And finally, there are help pages and help control files that need to be translated.

Text Constants in Java Code

The Java code given throughout this chapter occasionally contained a call to `Messages.getString()`. Every time text was to be displayed to the end user, the text was not given in its literal form, but rather the text was fetched from the `Messages` class by specifying a key. In some cases, additional parameters were specified that were to be inserted into the text delivered by the method `getString()`.

Here now is the definition of the `Messages` class for the main spell-checking plug-in (Listing 13.14). Note that each plug-in needs its own `Messages` class with the constant `BUNDLE_NAME` appropriately set.

```java
package com.bdaum.SpellChecker;

import java.text.MessageFormat;
import java.util.MissingResourceException;
import java.util.ResourceBundle;

public class Messages {

  private static final String BUNDLE_NAME =
"com.bdaum.SpellChecker.Messages";

  private static final ResourceBundle RESOURCE_BUNDLE =
                ResourceBundle.getBundle(BUNDLE_NAME);

  /**
   * Fetches a message for the specified key
   *
   * @param key - key to be translated
   * @return - the message
   */
  public static String getString(String key) {
    try {
      return RESOURCE_BUNDLE.getString(key);
```

Listing 13.14 (Continues)

```
      } catch (MissingResourceException e) {
        return '!' + key + '!';
      }
    }

    /**
     * Fetches a message for the specified key and inserts parameters
     *
     * @param key - key to be translated
     * @param params - parameters to be inserted into the message
     * @return - the message
     */
    public static String getString(String key, Object[] params) {
      if (params == null) return getString(key);
      try {
        return MessageFormat.format(getString(key), params);
      } catch (Exception e) {
        return "!" + key + "!";
      }
    }
  }
```

Listing 13.14 (Continued)

A similar class is needed for the Java-Properties plug-in but with the constant BUNDLE_NAME set to com.bdaum.SpellChecker.JavaProperties.Messages.

Of course, the file with the display texts is also needed. This file is named Messages.properties and is shown in Listing 13.15.

```
SpellCheckManager.Default_Spell_Checker=Default Spell Checker
SpellCheckManager.Could_not_create_tokenizer=\
Could not create tokenizer
SpellCheckManager.No_dictionary_file_declared=\
No dictionary file declared
SpellCheckManager.Dictionary_file_not_found=\
Dictionary file {0} not found
SpellCheckManager.Error_reading_dictionary_file=\
Error reading dictionary file {0}
SpellCheckerImages.Bad_URL_when_loading_disabled_image=\
Bad URL when loading disabled image
SpellCheckerImages.Bad_URL_when_loading_hover_image=\
Bad URL when loading hover image
SpellCheckerPlugin.Error_resolving_dictionary_URL=\
Error resolving dictionary URL
CheckSpellingActionDelegate.Cannot_initialize_SpellCorrectionView=\
Cannot initialize SpellCorrectionView
SpellCheckerPreferencePage.Invalid_character_in_suffix=\
Invalid character in suffix
SpellCheckerPreferencePage.All_changes_will_take_effect=\
All changes will take effect for the next spell checking pass.\n\n
SpellCheckerPreferencePage.Spell_Dictionary_File=\
```

Listing 13.15 (Continues)

```
Spell Dictionary &File
SpellCheckerPreferencePage.User_Dictionary_File_Suffix=\
User Dictionary File Suffi&x
SpellCheckerPreferencePage.Spell_Threshold=Spell &Threshold
SpellCheckerPreferencePage.Ignore_Numbers=&Ignore Numbers
SpellCheckerPreferencePage.CompoundCharacters=\
Ignore Com&pounds containing these Characters
SpellCheckerPreferencePage.Ignore_one_letter_words=\
I&gnore one letter words
SpellCheckerPreferencePage.Ignore_Mixed_Case=Ignore &Mixed Case
SpellCheckerPreferencePage.Ignore_Sentence_Capitalization=\
Ignore &Sentence Capitalization
SpellCheckerPreferencePage.Ignore_Upper_Case=Ignore &Upper Case
SpellCorrectionView.No_suggestions=(No suggestions)
SpellCorrectionView.Replace=Replace
SpellCorrectionView.Replace_occurrence=Replace single occurrence
SpellCorrectionView.Replace_all=Replace all
SpellCorrectionView.Replace_all_occurrences=Replace all occurrences
SpellCorrectionView.Add_to_dictionary=Add to dictionary
SpellCorrectionView.Add_word_to_dictionary=Add word to dictionary
SpellCorrectionView.Ignore=Ignore
SpellCorrectionView.Ignore_spelling_problem=Ignore spelling problem
SpellCorrectionView.Ignore_all=Ignore all
SpellCorrectionView.Ignore_for_all_occurrences=\
Ignore for all occurrences
SpellCorrectionView.StartCancel=Start/Stop
SpellCorrectionView.Start_spell_checking=Start spell checking
SpellCorrectionView.Cancel_spell_checking=Stop spell checking
SpellCorrectionView.Check=Check
SpellCorrectionView.done=\ (done)
SpellCorrectionView.in_progress=\ (in progress)
SpellCorrectionView.loading=\ (loading...)
SpellCorrectionView.aborted=\ (Aborted)
```

Listing 13.15 (Continued)

For the Java properties file, of course, different texts are required in the Messages.properties file:

```
JavaPropertiesSpellCheckerPreferencePage.Check_Comments=\
Ch&eck Comments
JavaPropertiesSpellCheckerPreferencePage.Check_Keys=\
Check &Keys
```

As a matter of fact, these files (and also the Messages.java classes) were not created manually. Instead, all display constants were first hard-coded into the different classes of the spell checker. Then, the function Source > Externalize Strings... was used to extract these text constants into the Messages.properties files, as discussed in the section "Text Constants in Programs" in Chapter 12.

Text Constants in Manifest Files

A similar logic applies to translatable text constants in the manifest file plugin.xml. In the Imported Files section you probably wondered why some of the text constants in the manifest file started with the % character. The % character indicates a key value that is to be translated via the plugin.properties file. This file is placed directly into the project folder com.bdaum.SpellChecker. Listing 13.16 shows the content of this file.

```
Spell_Checker=Spell Checker
Check_Spelling=Check Spelling
Checks_any_text=Checks the spelling of any text
Spell=Spell
Spelling=Spelling
Spell_Default=Spell Default
SpellChecker_Preferences=SpellChecker Preferences
Starts_spell_checking=Starts spell checking
Spell_Checker_Command=Spell Checker Command
```

Listing 13.16

A similar file is needed for the Java-Properties plug-in. The content of the plugin.properties file in this plug-in is

```
Java_Properties=Java-Properties
```

Creating a Language Fragment

The best way to add foreign language support for a given plug-in is to create a fragment. For the spell checker, you will need to create foreign language fragments for both plug-ins: the basic spell checker and the Java-Properties plug-in.

Fragment Project

To create foreign language fragments, invoke the function File > New > Fragment Project. On the first page of the Fragment Wizard, enter com.bdaum.SpellChecker.de as the project name. On the next wizard page, make sure that the option Create a Java Project is marked, and change the Runtime Library to SpellChecker.de.jar. On the following page, enter a suitable provider name and specify SpellChecker German Fragment as the fragment name. Then press the Browse button to the right of the Plug-in ID field and select the plug-in com.bdaum.SpellChecker. This will associate the fragment with the plug-in. As the Match Rule select Greater or Equal. This will ensure that the fragment will work for the specified version and all later versions. Then press the Finish button to generate the fragment manifest file fragment.xml. The resulting source code of this file should look like Listing 13.17.

```
<?xml version="1.0" encoding="UTF-8"?>
<?eclipse version="3.0"?>
<fragment id="com.bdaum.SpellChecker.de"
    name="SpellChecker German Fragment"
    version="1.0.0"
    provider-name="bdaum industrial communications"
```

Listing 13.17 (Continues)

```
    plugin-id="com.bdaum.SpellChecker"
    plugin-version="1.0.0"
    match="greaterOrEqual">
    <runtime>
        <library name="SpellChecker.de.jar">
            <export name="*"/>
        </library>
    </runtime>
</fragment>
```

Listing 13.17 (Continued)

Program Texts

After you have created the fragment in this way, you can start to add foreign language resources. For example, a German version of the `Messages.properties` file is needed. To create such a file, first create the `com.bdaum.SpellChecker` package in the folder `src`. Then go back to the plug-in project `com.bdaum.SpellChecker` and select the `Messages.properties` file. Then press Ctrl+C to copy it to the clipboard. Return to the fragment project and select the new package. Press Ctrl+V to paste the file into the package. Then rename the file as `Messages_de.properties` by applying the context function Refactor > Rename. Now you can edit this file and translate English text into German.

```
SpellCheckManager.Default_Spell_Checker=Standardrechtschreibeprÿfung
SpellCheckManager.Could_not_create_tokenizer=\
Tokenizer konnte nicht erzeugt werden
SpellCheckManager.No_dictionary_file_declared=\
Kein W?rterbuch deklariert
SpellCheckManager.Dictionary_file_not_found=\
W?rterbuchdatei {0} nicht gefunden
SpellCheckManager.Error_reading_dictionary_file=\
Fehler beim Lesen des W?rterbuchs {0}
SpellCheckerImages.Bad_URL_when_loading_image=\
UngŸltiger URL beim Laden eines Bildes
...
```

Manifest Texts

The next step is to do the same for the `plugin.properties` file. Just copy the file from the plug-in project into the fragment project directly beneath the project folder and rename it as `plugin_de.properties`. Then edit it and perform the translation.

```
Spell_Checker=Rechtschreibeprÿfung
Check_Spelling=Check Spelling
Checks_any_text=Prÿft die Rechtschreibung in allen Textfeldern
Spell=Rechtschreibung
Spelling=Rechtschreibung
Spell_Default=Standardrechtschreibeprÿfung
SpellChecker_Preferences=Einstellungen der Rechtschreibeprÿfung
Starts_spell_checking=Beginnt Rechtschreibeprÿfung
Spell_Checker_Command=Rechtschreibeprÿfungskommando
```

Help Files

The help files must be translated, too. Create a new folder named nl directly under the project folder. In this new folder create a subfolder called de. Then copy the files toc.xml and contexts.xml from the plug-in project into this folder. Finally copy the folder html from the plug-in project into the folder nl/de.

Now you can translate the descriptions and labels in the toc.xml and contexts.xml files and also, of course, the help pages. Here is the German version of the toc.xml file:

```xml
<?xml version="1.0" encoding="UTF-8"?>
<toc label="Rechtschreibeprüfung" topic="html/spelling.html">
  <topic label="Korrekturfenster" href="html/SpellCheckerView.html"/>
    <topic label="Wörterbücher"  href="html/Dictionaries.html"/>
    <topic label="Einstellungen">
    <topic label="Standardeinstellungen"
                         href="html/SpellCheckerPreferences.html"/>
    <anchor id="postPreferences"/>
  </topic>
  <topic label="Weitere Informationen">
    <topic label="Danksagungen" href="html/Acknowledgements.html"/>
    <topic label="Quellcode" href="html/SourceCode.html"/>
  </topic>
</toc>
```

And here is the German version of the contexts.xml file:

```xml
<?xml version="1.0" encoding="UTF-8"?>
<contexts>
  <context id="action_context">
    <description>
      Hilfe für die Aktionsgruppe der Rechtschreibeprüfung
    </description>
    <topic href="html/spelling.html"  label="Rechtschreibeprüfung"/>
  </context>
  <context id="preferences_context">
    <description>
      Hilfe für die Einstellungen der Rechtschreibeprüfung
    </description>
    <topic href="html/SpellCheckerPreferences.html"
          label="Rechtschreibeprüfung-Einstellungen"/>
  </context>
  <context id="correctionView_context">
    <description>
      Hilfe für das Korrekturfenster der Rechtschreibeprüfung
    </description>
    <topic href="html/SpellCheckerView.html"
          label="Rechtschreibeprüfung-Korrekturfenster"/>
  </context>
</contexts>
```

The translation of the help pages is left to your imagination.

Java-Properties

To create a foreign language fragment for the Java-Properties plug-in, just repeat the above steps. Create a new fragment project with the project name `com.bdaum.SpellChecker.JavaProperties` for the plug-in `com.bdaum.SpellChecker.JavaProperties`, and then create the package `com.bdaum.SpellChecker.JavaProperties.de` and German-language versions of the `Messages.properties`, `plugin.properties`, `toc.xml`, and `contexts.xml` files and the help pages as shown previously.

Deploying the Spell Checker

Deploying a software project such as the spell checker as a product involves several tasks. For easy installation, I recommend that you wrap the plug-ins that make up the product into a feature or a set of features. In this example, two features are created: one for the English version of the spell checker, and another for the German language fragments. Additional customization is performed in an `about.ini` file to deliver a finished and polished product. Auxiliary documentation (such as license files) is added.

Defining the Spell Checker Feature

The best deployment form for the spell checker is as an installable feature for the Eclipse platform. This feature should contain the default spell checker plug-in plus the spell checker plug-in for Java-Properties files.

Feature Project

To deploy the spell checker in this manner, create a new feature project. Invoke the function File > New > Feature Project. Under Project Name enter a suitable name, such as Spell Checker for Eclipse. On the next wizard page, replace the proposed Feature ID with `com.bdaum.SpellChecker`. This feature identification matches the identification of your spell checker plug-in. The Feature Provider should also be completed, for example, `bdaum`.

On the next page, you can specify a custom install handler. This is not required for the spell checker feature, so leave the option The Feature Will Contain a Custom Install Handler unchecked.

On the following page, you can determine which plug-ins should be added to the feature. Checkmark both plug-ins `com.bdaum.SpellChecker` and `com.bdaum.SpellChecker.JavaProperties`. When you press the Finish button, the Feature Editor opens. The information on the Overview page is already complete. The Primary Feature field is not marked—this is required only for standalone products. In terms of Eclipse, however, the spell checker is not a standalone product but an add-on to the Eclipse platform.

On the Information page, you can complete the Feature Description, Copyright Notice, and License Agreement sections directly using text, or you may refer to a relevant document via a URL. For example, you may create an HTML file called `license.html` describing the license conditions in this feature project. In the License Agreement section, you then specify the value `license.html` in the Optional URL field. However, it is sensible to specify important license conditions as text, too, because the end user is prompted with this text information only during the installation of the feature.

On the Content page, just press the Compute button. This will determine all the plug-ins that are required on the target platform for running the feature successfully.

Feature Manifest

This completes the definition of the feature manifest. Listing 13.18 shows the complete code of the feature.xml file.

```xml
<?xml version="1.0" encoding="UTF-8"?>
<feature id="com.bdaum.SpellChecker"
     label="Spell Checker for Eclipse"
     version="1.0.0"
     provider-name="bdaum industrial communications">
  <install-handler/>
  <description>
     This feature provides a general purpose spell checker for Eclipse.
In addition a special purpose spell checker for Java-Properties
files is provided.
  </description>
  <copyright>
     (c) 2003-2004 Berthold Daum
  </copyright>
  <license url="license.html">
     License
This Plug-in is provided to you under the terms and conditions
of the Common Public License Version 1.0. A copy of the CPL is
available at http://www.eclipse.org/legal/cpl-v10.html.
Third Party Content
The Content includes items that have been sourced from third
parties as follows:
Jazzy 0.5
Jazzy is licensed under the LGPL.
  </license>
  <requires>
     <import plugin="org.eclipse.core.runtime"/>
     <import plugin="org.eclipse.core.resources"/>
     <import plugin="org.eclipse.ui"/>
     <import plugin="org.eclipse.ui.ide"/>
     <import plugin="org.eclipse.jface.text"/>
     <import plugin="org.eclipse.ui.workbench.texteditor"/>
     <import plugin="org.eclipse.help"/>
  </requires>
  <plugin id="com.bdaum.SpellChecker"
       download-size="0"
       install-size="0"
       version="1.0.0"/>
  <plugin id="com.bdaum.SpellChecker.JavaProperties"
       download-size="0"
       install-size="0"
       version="1.0.0"/>
</feature>
```

Listing 13.18

491

about.ini

To add product-relevant information, you may want to specify an about.ini file (see the "Deployment" section in Chapter 12). In case of the spell checker, the main purpose of the about.ini file is to make the spell checker visible when you invoke the function Help > About Eclipse Platform. The spell checker icon shown there must be defined in the about.ini file. This file must not be located in the feature project but in the main plug-in project, that is, in the com.bdaum.SpellChecker project.

```
aboutText=eSpell - Spell Checker\n\
\n\
Version: 1.0.0\n\
\n\
(c) Copyright bdaum industrial communications and others 2000-2004.\n\
All rights reserved.\n\
\n\
Visit http://www.bdaum.de
featureImage=eSpell.gif
appName=eSpell
```

about.html

Additional information for the functions Help > About Eclipse Platform > Feature Details and Help > About Eclipse Platform > Plug-in Details can be provided by adding about.html files to the feature project Spell Checker for Eclipse and the plug-in projects com.bdaum.SpellChecker and com.bdaum.SpellChecker.JavaProperties. Such a file can contain references to license information, as shown here:

```
<h1>License</h1>
<hr color="#66FFFF">
<p>This Plug-in is provided to you under the terms and conditions of the
Common Public License Version 1.0.
</p>
<p>A copy of the CPL is available at <a
href="http://www.eclipse.org/legal/cpl
v10.html">http://www.eclipse.org/legal/cpl-v10.html</a>.
</p>
<h2>Third Party Content</h2>
<p>The Content includes items that have been sourced from third parties as
follows:
</p>
<p><b>Jazzy 0.5</b><br>
Jazzy is licensed under the LGPL.<br>
</p>
<hr color="#66FFFF">
<address>
   <font SIZE="4">© 2003 berthold.daum@bdaum.de</font>
</address>
```

Configuring Ant Scripts

You can now start to prepare the feature for deployment (see "Deploying a Feature" in Chapter 12). To do so, modify the build.properties files in their respective plug-in projects.

build.properties

Open the manifest editor by double-clicking the plugin.xml file and go to the Build page (Figure 13.5). For the main plug-in project com.bdaum.SpellChecker, proceed as follows:

❏ For the Binary Build, mark the following files and folders: about.html, about.ini, bin, contexts.xml, dict, html, icons, jazzy-core.jar, plugin.properties, plugin.xml, schema, toc.xml.

❏ For the Source Build, mark the following files and folders: about.html, about.ini, contexts.xml, dict, html, icons, plugin.properties, plugin.xml, schema, src, toc.xml.

The source code should then look like Listing 13.19.

```
bin.includes = plugin.xml,\
               SpellChecker.jar,\
               bin/,\
               contexts.xml,\
               dict/,\
               html/,\
               icons/,\
               jazzy-core.jar/,\
               schema/,\
               toc.xml,\
               about.ini,\
               about.html,\
               plugin.properties
jars.compile.order = SpellChecker.jar
output.SpellChecker.jar = bin/
source.SpellChecker.jar = src/
src.includes = about.html,\
               about.ini,\
               contexts.xml,\
               dict/,\
               html/,\
               icons/,\
               plugin.properties,\
               plugin.xml,\
               schema/,\
               src/,\
               toc.xml
```

Listing 13.19

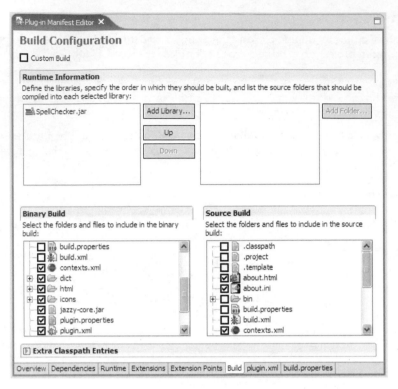

Figure 13.5

For the plug-in project com.bdaum.SpellChecker.JavaProperties, proceed as follows:

❑ For the Binary Build, mark the following files and folders: about.html, bin, contexts.xml, html, plugin.properties, plugin.xml, toc.xml.

❑ For the Source Build, mark the following files and folders: about.html, contexts.xml, html, plugin.properties, plugin.xml, src, toc.xml.

The source code should then look like Listing 13.20.

```
bin.includes = plugin.xml,\
               JavaPropertiesTokenizer.jar,\
               about.html,\
               bin/,\
               contexts.xml,\
               toc.xml
source.JavaPropertiesTokenizer.jar = src/
output.JavaPropertiesTokenizer.jar = bin/
src.includes = about.html,\
               contexts.xml,\
               plugin.xml,\
               src/,\
               toc.xml
```

Listing 13.20

For the feature project Spell Checker for Eclipse, proceed as follows:

❑ For both the Binary Build and the Source Build, mark the following files: about.html, feature.xml, license.html.

The source code should then look like Listing 13.21.

```
bin.includes = feature.xml,\
               about.html,\
               license.html
src.includes = about.html,\
               feature.xml,\
               license.html
```

Listing 13.21

Defining the Language Feature

The additional foreign-language fragments that you implemented in the section "Internationalizing the Spell Checker" should be deployed as a separate feature. To do so, create a new feature project by invoking the function File > New > Feature Project. Under Project Name, enter a suitable name such as Spell Checker - German Language Pack. On the next wizard page, replace the proposed Feature ID with com.bdaum.SpellChecker.de. This feature identification matches the identification of the foreign language fragment belonging to the spell checker's main plug-in. You should also complete the Feature Provider.

On the next page, leave the option The Feature Will Contain a Custom Install Handler unchecked.

On the following page, checkmark both fragments com.bdaum.SpellChecker.de and com.bdaum.SpellChecker.JavaProperties.de. When you press the Finish button, the Feature Editor opens. The information on the Overview page is already complete.

On the Information page, you can complete the Feature Description, Copyright Notice, and License Agreement sections. You may need to add an appropriate license.html file to the project. The resulting feature manifest should look like Listing 13.22.

```
<?xml version="1.0" encoding="UTF-8"?>
<feature
      id="com.bdaum.SpellChecker.de"
      label="Spell Checker - German language pack"
      version="1.0.0"
      provider-name="bdaum industrial communications">
   <install-handler/>
   <description>
      German language pack for Spell Checker.
   </description>

   <copyright>
      (c) 2003-2004 Berthold Daum
   </copyright>
   <license url="license.html">
      License
```

Listing 13.22 (Continues)

```
This Feature is provided to you under the terms and conditions
of the Common Public License Version 1.0. A copy of the CPL is
available at http://www.eclipse.org/legal/cpl-v10.html.
    </license>
    <plugin
        id="com.bdaum.SpellChecker.de"
        download-size="0"
        install-size="0"
        version="1.0.0"
        fragment="true"/>
    <plugin
        id="com.bdaum.SpellChecker.JavaProperties.de"
        download-size="0"
        install-size="0"
        version="1.0.0"
        fragment="true"/>
</feature>
```

Listing 13.22 (Continued)

Now you can start to prepare the foreign-language feature for deployment. To do so, modify the `build.properties` files in their respective foreign language projects.

build.properties

For both fragment projects `com.bdaum.SpellChecker.de` and `com.bdaum.SpellChecker.JavaProperties.de`, proceed as follows:

❑ For the Binary Build, mark the following files and folders: `bin`, `fragment.xml`, `nl`, `plugin_de.properties`.

❑ For the Source Build, mark the following files and folders: `fragment.xml`, `nl`, `plugin_de.properties`, `src`.

The source code of both `build.properties` files should look like Listing 13.23.

```
bin.includes = fragment.xml,\
               de.jar,\
               nl/,\
               plugin_de.properties,\
               bin/
source.de.jar = src/
output.de.jar = bin/
src.includes = fragment.xml,\
               nl/,\
               plugin_de.properties,\
               src/
```

Listing 13.23

For the feature project Spell Checker - German Language Pack, proceed as follows:

❏ For both the Binary Build and the Source Build, mark the following files: `feature.xml`, `license.html`.

The source code of the `build.properties` file should look like Listing 13.24.

```
bin.includes = feature.xml,\
               license.html
src.includes = feature.xml,\
               license.html
```

Listing 13.24

Defining the Update Site

Now you can offer the spell checker feature on an update site. To create such a site, Eclipse provides a simple wizard that generates the update site in a format understood by the Eclipse Update Manager. Invoke the function File > New > Project > Plug-in Development > Update Site Project. (Make sure to have the option Show All Wizards set when you invoke the New Wizard.) On the next wizard page, enter as a name Spell Checker Installation, and press Next. On the next page, mark the option Generate a Sample Web Page. This will create an HTML page `index.html` and an XSL stylesheet `site.xsl`. This stylesheet will dynamically create a web page from `index.html` and the manifest file `site.xml` (see the next section) that displays the features of this update site (see Figure 13.6). Then press the Finish button. The wizard then creates the `site.xml` file and opens it in the PDE editor.

Figure 13.6

In this editor enter a short description of the site on the Archives page. If you want to place this site on the Web, enter the Web location in the URL field.

On the Features page, press the Add button and select the features `com.bdaum.SpellChecker` and `com.bdaum.SpellChecker.de`. These features then appear in the Features to Build section. Then click the New Category... button and enter `com.bdaum.Utilities` as name of the new category and General Purpose Utilities as the label. The new category appears in the right-hand section of the Features page. Now drag both features onto the new category.

Site Manifest

Listing 13.25 shows the code for the manifest file `site.xml`.

```xml
<?xml version="1.0" encoding="UTF-8"?>
<site>
    <description url="http://www.bdaum.de/eclipse/eSpell">
This site contains the installation files for the Eclipse Spell Checker.
    </description>
    <feature url="features/com.bdaum.SpellChecker_1.0.0.jar"
            id="com.bdaum2.SpellChecker" version="1.0.0">
      <category name="com.bdaum.Utilities"/>
    </feature>
    <feature url="features/com.bdaum.SpellChecker.de_1.0.0.jar"
            id="com.bdaum2.SpellChecker.de" version="1.0.0">
      <category name="com.bdaum.Utilities"/>
    </feature>
    <category-def name="com.bdaum.Utilities"
                label="General Purpose Utilities"/>
</site>
```

Listing 13.25

Generating a Site

By pressing the Build All button on the Features page, you can start generating the update site. During this process two new folders, `plugins` and `features`, are created. These folders contain the installation archives that were created with the `build.xml` Ant scripts that you configured in the section "Defining the Spell Checker Feature" by editing the `build.properties` files.

Installation

Now you can invoke the Update Manager via the function Help > Software Updates > Find and Install.... On the first page of the Install Wizard, select the Search for New Features to Install option. On the next page, press the Add Local Site... button. Navigate to the location of your update site project (`\eclipse\workspace\Spell Checker Installation`) and press OK. Back in the wizard, uncheck all other sites but check the new update site you just added.

Now press the Next button and check both features of this site. Press Next to start the installation. Once you accept the license conditions, the installation is executed. Afterward, you should restart Eclipse.

Once Eclipse has restarted you may not see any trace of the spell checker, depending on the active perspective. In this case, you must first activate the spell checker's Action Set for the current perspective. To do so, invoke the function Window > Customize Perspective > Other and check the Spell Checker field. If everything is working correctly, you should see the spell checker icon in the toolbar. You can now start spell-checking!

Summary

In this chapter you have implemented a fully working spell checker that integrates into the Eclipse workbench. What experiences—negative and positive—did you have with Eclipse during the development of this tool?

If you have anything to criticize, it should be only minor issues. What I personally do not like is the inconsistent treatment of help context IDs, for example.

My very positive experiences include the extremely short time needed to implement this feature. From the first idea, though discovering, downloading, and exploring the jazzy package, to running the first working prototype, did not take me more than one working day. The fine-tuning of this plug-in was done when I wrote this chapter (which did take more than one working day!). The option to pregenerate plug-in parts was very useful. This not only saves a lot of typing, but, even more important, it saves a lot of exploring and browsing the documentation and a lot of trying and testing until the first plug-in is executable. Using this function, I could start with a plug-in template that could be executed right "out of the box" and could add the spell-checking functionality bit by bit.

In the next chapter you will have a close look at the Rich Client Platform introduced with Eclipse 3.

The Rich Client Platform

The *Rich Client Platform* (RCP) is probably the most important new feature in Eclipse 3. At least, many Eclipse users see it this way, according to opinion polls. Also the various client implementations of IBM's new Lotus versions is based on the Eclipse RCP. Generally speaking, the RCP allows you to create a wide class of applications based on the Eclipse framework.

In this chapter I will introduce the architecture of the RCP and discuss the various possibilities for application development.

In Chapter 15 I will present a board game (Hex) as a large example of an RCP application.

Definition and Motivation

A *rich client* is a piece of software that implements application-specific functionality directly at the client site (for example, the desktop or mobile platform). Its counterpart is not the *poor client* but the *thin client*, which contains no application-specific functionality but where all application-specific functions are controlled by the server. A typical example of a thin client is a web browser. The application-specific functions are in this case implemented in the form of Web pages that are loaded from the server.

As a matter of fact, there are no application-neutral standard solutions (such as a web browser) for rich clients because the rich client contains application-specific code. However, it is possible to identify function groups that are common to all rich client solutions. These function groups can be combined in a framework—this is a *Rich Client Platform*.

Although Eclipse 2 allowed you to develop applications on the basis of the Eclipse platform, the scope of possible applications was restricted to IDE-like applications, that is, applications that had to deal with the Eclipse workspace. Since many of the workbench functions related to the Eclipse workspace, the workspace concept was mandatory for applications utilizing the Eclipse workbench. With Eclipse 3, however, the workbench was refactored into a workspace-independent part (generic workbench) and a workspace-specific part (IDE). The generic parts remained in the plug-in `org.eclipse.ui_3.0.0`, while the workspace-dependent parts went into the new plug-in `org.eclipse.ui.ide_3.0.0`.

So, with the new Rich Client Platform, Eclipse now offers four options for application development with Java:

- ❑ **Classical application development with AWT and Swing.** No Eclipse components are used with this option (see Part 1).

- ❑ **Application development with SWT and JFace only (see Part 2).** You should choose this option if the memory footprint is a problem and when no other components such as the help system are needed. This option also requires you to implement your own installers.

- ❑ **Application development under the Eclipse IDE (see Part 3).** This option should be used if the application uses the metaphor of a studio and is based on a closed workspace concept.

- ❑ **Application development under the Eclipse RCP.**

Plug-ins and the RCP

Even under the RCP, application functionality is implemented in the form of plug-ins. The RCP itself is nothing more than the usual Eclipse platform with some plug-ins stripped off. In particular, all plug-ins are removed whose name carries the term `ide`, such as `org.eclipse.ui.ide_3.0.0` or `org.eclipse.help.ide_3.0.0`.

However, since the plug-in `org.eclipse.ui.ide_3.0.0` is concerned with such things as starting an application (in fact, this plug-in implements the IDE application), there are some particularities that I will discuss in the following sections.

Like all other plug-ins, the plug-in that implements a specific rich client application must have a manifest file `plugin.xml`, as we have already discussed in "The Plug-in Manifest" section of Chapter 11. A `Plugin` class (see the section "The Plug-in" in Chapter 11) is not an absolute requirement, but in most cases the implementation of such a class makes sense. In particular, it allows access to the plug-in's environment (installation URL, plug-in identification, provider, resource bundle, etc.) via the `IPluginDescriptor` interface. In addition, it allows access to the Eclipse log file and to the plug-in's preference management.

The manifest file, however, must specify extensions for the extension points `org.eclipse.core.runtime.applications` and `org.eclipse.ui.perspectives`. At least one perspective must be specified because an RCP application cannot rely on the Resource perspective normally provided by the Eclipse IDE. The extensions for the extension point `org.eclipse.core.runtime.applications` must specify in their `run` element a class that represents the application and implements the interface `IPlatformRunnable` (see the section "The IPlatformRunnable Interface" later in this chapter). Here is an example for both extension points:

```
<extension id="RcpApplication"
           point="org.eclipse.core.runtime.applications">
    <application>
```

```
        <run class="com.bdaum.RcpApplication">
        </run>
    </application>
</extension>
<extension point="org.eclipse.ui.perspectives">
    <perspective id="com.bdaum.RcpPerspective"
                name="Perspective1"
                class="com.bdaum.RcpPerspective">
    </perspective>
</extension>
```

Creating an Application

Each Rich Client Application consists of a minimal set of classes: a main class of type IPlatformRunnable, a WorkbenchAdvisor class that defines hooks for the events within the Rich Client GUI, and a class of type IPerspectiveFactory for defining the intial GUI-layout.

The IPlatformRunnable Interface

Each application must be equipped at least with one class that implements the IPlatformRunnable interface. This interface is used to identify its implementers as application entry points to Eclipse.

However, this interface has only temporary relevance. It will be replaced by a new interface as soon as Eclipse is completely adapted to an OSGi-based runtime environment (see the "OSGi" section in Chapter 11).

Classes that implement this interface must provide a run() method. A typical implementation of such a method looks like this:

```
public Object run(Object args) {
    WorkbenchAdvisor workbenchAdvisor = new RcpWorkbenchAdvisor();
    Display display = PlatformUI.createDisplay();
    int returnCode = PlatformUI.createAndRunWorkbench(display,
        workbenchAdvisor);
    return (returnCode == PlatformUI.RETURN_RESTART) ?
        IPlatformRunnable.EXIT_RESTART :
        IPlatformRunnable.EXIT_OK;
}
```

First, a new WorkbenchAdvisor instance (see the next section) is created. Then a new Display instance is created by the PlatformUI class. Finally, the workbench is started via the PlatformUI method createAndRunWorkbench(). After the workbench has terminated, its response code is translated into the IPlatformRunnable protocol.

The WorkbenchAdvisor Class

The abstract class WorkbenchAdvisor provides the means to configure the generic workbench at several points in the lifecycle of an application. To do so, you just subclass the WorkbenchAdvisor class and override some or all methods provided by `WorkbenchAdvisor`. You then specify this subclass as a parameter when starting the workbench.

Application Hooks

Now, let's examine which methods are called within the lifecycle of an RCP application:

`initialize`	Within this method you can analyze the command line that was specified when the platform was started. In addition, you can set up the application, for example, register adapters or load images.
	When this method is invoked, an `IWorkbenchConfigurer` instance is passed as a parameter. This instance should be stored for later use. By calling `IWorkbenchConfigurer`-methods, you can configure the workbench.
`preStartup`	This method is invoked after initialization but before opening the first window. Here you can determine which editors and views should be opened initially.
`postRestore`	This method is invoked after a window has been restored. It is called only for windows whose state is stored permanently.
`postStartup`	This method is invoked after all windows have been opened but before the main event loop is started. Here you can start processes that should run automatically or you can show tips or open other windows.
`preShutdown`	This method is invoked after leaving the main event loop but before closing the windows.
`postShutdown`	This method is called after all windows have been closed. Here you can store the internal state of the windows persistently or release allocated resources.

The `IWorkbenchConfigurer` instance passed as a parameter during the invocation of the `initialize()` method provides the necessary method for configuring the workbench. For example, the `setSaveAndRestore()` method can be used to determine whether the state of the workbench should be stored persistently when the workbench is closed (in order to restore the workbench to its former state when restarting it). The methods `setData()` and `getData()` can be used to associate generic objects with a key and to store and retrieve these objects under the associated key. The `declareImage()` method is used to declare the symbolic names of images that are used during the workbench's lifecycle. Finally, the `IWorkbenchConfigurer` provides the `emergencyClose()` method with which an application can be forced to shut down in case of emergencies (for example, Out of Memory). The `emergencyClosing()` method can be used to determine whether the current shutdown process is such a forced process. All `IWorkbenchConfigurer` methods should use this method to test for an emergency shutdown before they perform a user interaction and should avoid this interaction in such a case.

Window Hooks

There is also a set of methods that are called during the lifecycle of single workbench windows:

`preWindowOpen`	This method is invoked when a window instance is created. At this point you can configure the window. For example, you can specify whether the window has a menu. Remember, that the window contents are not available at this time.
`fillActionBars`	This method is invoked directly after `preWindowOpen()`. Here you can create menus and toolbars. (Usually you don't do that but rather have these elements generated from the definitions made in the manifest file `plugin.xml`.)
`postWindowRestore`	This method is invoked after a window is restored whose state was stored permanently.
`postWindowOpen`	This method is invoked after a window is opened. Here you can modify the window contents. Typically, you can set the window title and the window size at this point.
`preWindowShellClose`	This method is invoked when a window is closed but before the window's shell is closed. This method allows you to veto the closing of the window.
`postWindowClose`	This method is invoked after a window is closed. Typically, you would release resources at this time.

All of these methods except the `fillActionBars()` method receive an instance of type `IWorkbenchWindowConfigurer` on invocation. By using the appropriate `IWorkbenchWindowConfigurer` methods, you can configure the individual windows (the window is obtained via the `getWindow()` method). For example, you can use the `setTitle()` method to set the window title. The `setShowTitleBar()` method allows you to switch the title bar on or off. Similarly, the methods `setShowMenuBar()`, `setShowCoolBar()`, `setShowFastViewsBars()`, `setShowPerspectiveBar()`, and `setShowProgressIndicator()` do the same for the menu bar, the toolbar, the bars containing the Fast Views, the perspective bar, and the integrated progress bar. Of course, for all of these methods a corresponding `get...()` method exists.

The appearance of the window shell can be influenced with the `setShellStyle()` method (see the section "Displays, Shells, and Monitors" in Chapter 8). Of course, this method must be called out of the `preWindowOpen()` method. The `setData()` and `getData()` methods can be used to set and retrieve generic objects under a specified key for each individual window. Finally, the editor area of a workbench window can be equipped as a drag-and-drop area with the help of the `addEditorAreaTransfer()` and `configureEditorAreaDropListener()` methods (see the section "Drag and Drop" in Chapter 8). For example, if you register the transfer type `EditorInputTransfer` via the `addEditorAreaTransfer()` method, objects of type `IEditorInput` can be moved via drag-and-drop to and from the editor area.

The `fillActionBars()` method receives an instance of type `IActionBarConfigurer` on invocation. With the help of the `getMenuManager()`, `getStatusLineManager()`, and `getCoolBarManager()` methods, you can obtain the managers for the menu bar, the status line, and the toolbar from this instance. The `registerGlobalAction()` method can be used to register certain actions as global actions, that is, actions that can be shared by several editors (see the "Editors" section in Chapter 11).

Welcome Screen

Another hook is provided for opening the welcome screen:

openIntro	This method opens the welcome screen but only if this was specified in the preferences and if the welcome screen was not closed at the last shutdown. The method can be overridden as required.

Event Loop Hooks

The event loop also calls two methods that can be overridden to implement specific behavior:

eventLoopException	This method is invoked in the case of an uncaught exception. The default implementation writes the exception into the Eclipse log file.
eventLoopIdle	This method is invoked when there are no more events left in the event loop. Here you can perform tasks that can run in the background.

Information Providers

Finally, there is a set of methods that the platform invokes in order to gather information about the application. By overriding these methods, you can provide the platform with the necessary information. The most important of these methods is the `getInitialWindowPerspectiveId()` method, which always must be overridden.

getDefaultPageInput	This method provides input values for workbench pages that were just opened. The standard implementation delivers the `null` value.
getInitialWindowPerspectiveId	This method provides the identification of the perspective that should be opened initially.
getMainPreferencePageId	This method provides the identification of the preference page that should be shown first. The standard implementation delivers the `null` value, meaning that the pages are to be sorted alphabetically.

| isApplicationMenu | This method supports OLE (Object Linking and Embedding) in Windows 32 platforms. The method returns the value `true` if the menu functions of the application should be maintained when embedded into a foreign application. It delivers the value `false` if the menu should be ignored during embedding. The default value is `false`. |

Testing a Rich Client Application

If you take a closer look at the workbench's launch configuration under Run > Run... > Run-time Workbench > Run-time Workbench, you will see the entry `org.eclipse.ui.ide.workbench` in the Run an Application field in the Program to Run group on the Arguments page. If the Run command is executed with such a configuration, the "normal" IDE workbench is started. But if you want to start an RCP application, you will need to create a new launch configuration.

To do so, in the Configurations window select the Run-time Workbench category and press the New button. In the new configuration, enter a suitable configuration name. Then change the entry in the Application Name field. Press the arrow button at the right of the field and select an entry point for your application from the list, that is, a class that implements the interface `IPlatformRunnable` (see the section "The IPlatformRunnable Interface"). Then press the Run button, and the `run()` method of this class will be called.

> It's a good idea to add the parameter `consoleLog` to the Program Arguments entry in the launch configuration. This will save you from hunting around for log files in case of an error.

Deploying a Rich Client Application

An RCP application is deployed just like any other Eclipse-based application. If you want to deploy the application-specific part in the form of a ZIP file, just select the corresponding plug-in or feature project in the explorer and call the Export context function. In the Export Wizard, select Deployable Plug-ins and Fragments. On the following wizard page, select A Single Deployable ZIP File and specify the path of the ZIP file in the Destination field.

A ZIP file created in such a way can be easily installed on the target platform. Simply unpack it into the Eclipse root directory `\eclipse\`. Thereafter, the application can be started immediately by starting the Eclipse executable `eclipse.exe`. However, a special command-line parameter is required. The complete syntax of calling an RCP application is

```
eclipse -application ApplicationID
```

The `ApplicationID` is a composite consisting of the plug-in ID and the value of the attribute `id` in the extension point `org.eclipse.core.runtime.applications` (manifest file). For example, if your plug-in's ID is `com.myCorp.myPlugin` and the ID of the extension point `applications` is `myApplication`, the complete command line would look like this:

```
eclipse -application com.myCorp.myPlugin.myApplication
```

Of course, this is not very user friendly, because end users are required to invoke the application from a command shell or to manually create a desktop link to `eclipse.exe`, where the command-line parameters are specified. For this reason, Eclipse lets you modify its startup behavior by modifying the `config.ini` file. This file is located in the directory `\eclipse\configuration\` and can be deployed with your application. Most of the key/value pairs in the file deal with the OSGi behavior of the platform, but the last two entries deal with the specification of the product and the application. You need only specify one of these entries, or you can specify the parameter `eclipse.product`. In this case, the referenced product description `org.eclipse.core.runtime.products` (see the section "The Most Important SDK Extension Points" in Chapter 11) in the manifest file `plugin.xml` defines the application's entry point. Or you can define the parameter `eclipse.application`, where you specify the application ID of your application's entry point.

```
osgi.splashPath = platform:/base/plugins/org.eclipse.platform
#eclipse.product=com.myCorp.myProduct
eclipse.application=com.myCorp.myPlugin.myApplication
eof=eof
```

Advanced Product Customization

The most elegant option for customizing a product based on Eclipse, however, is the combination of the `config.ini` file with defining an extension for extension point `org.eclipse.core` `.runtime.products` (see the section "The Most Important SDK Extension Points" in Chapter 11). Each of these extensions can specify a whole product description and refers to a corresponding `org.eclipse.core.runtime.applications` entry. The advantage of this technique is that you can specify descriptions for several product variants, each identified by the `id` attribute of the corresponding `extension` element. You can test such product variants by checking the Run a Product option in the Program to Run group on the Arguments page of the launch configuration and then replacing the value `org.eclipse.platform.ide` with the appropriate product ID.

When you deploy the software, you can select a `product` variant simply by setting the appropriate product identification with the `eclipse.product` entry in the `config.ini` file. In Chapter 15 I will show this technique in a practical example.

The Global Welcome Screen

Another advantage of using product identifications is the possibility of changing the global welcome screen, which is an important element for the user's out-of-the-box experience with a product. In Eclipse this screen also functions as a central point of information for the end user. It can be invoked at any time via Help > Welcome. However, for a customized product, you should replace this page with one of your own creation. You can do this via the extension point `org.eclipse.ui.intro`. Here you can link in your own Java classes (which must be based on the `IntroPart` class) and associate them with product identifications. So, by swapping product descriptions, you can swap welcome screens, too. In Chapter 15 I will show how to implement an alternate welcome screen.

Summary

This chapter gave an overview of the Rich Client Platform (RCP) that was introduced with Eclipse 3. You have learned how the main aspects of such a platform can be configured and how applications based on the RCP can be implemented, debugged, and deployed.

In the next chapter you will learn how to implement such an application.

Project 4: The Hex Game as a Rich Client Application

The fourth and final large example in this book is the game Hex that we are going to implement as a rich client application. Hex was invented in 1942 by the Danish mathematician and poet Piet Hein, and it quickly became popular under the name Polygon. In 1948 it was reinvented under the name Nash by the American mathematician and economist John Nash, who did not know of Hein's invention. Today there is no commercial version of this game, but it enjoys a growing popularity. It is one of those games that you can learn in two minutes but you need a whole lifetime to master. In the context of Eclipse, it has an additional benefit: it gives you a chance to apply all the time that you saved through Eclipse's productivity gains to something useful.

The implementation presented here is a man-against-machine version that is based on an implementation by MazeWorks (www.mazeworks.com). MazeWorks offers a whole series of free games as Java applets that can be played directly out of the web browser. Here I use the Hex game engine from MazeWorks but present a different GUI that is implemented with SWT. And of course, the game is implemented here not as an applet but on the basis of the Eclipse Rich Client Platform (RCP).

Overview

As discussed in the previous chapter, an RCP application requires the implementation of some special classes such as RcpApplication, RcpPerspective, and RcpWorkbenchAdvisor. The classes configure the platform and are not directly connected with the other classes of the plug-in (Figure 15.1). The composition of the whole application is achieved by the plug-in manifest plugin.xml.

The main "business" logic is contained in the classes HexView, Game, AI, Board, StaticEval, and BestMove. The HexView class implements the one and only view within the application and creates instances of the other classes. Basically, it serves as the root class for the business logic. The game-specific logic, in contrast, is contained in the Game class. The simulation of the game board is done by the Board class. The AI class computes the moves of the computer. The StaticEval and BestMove classes are utility classes that are used by AI.

In addition, I have provided a welcome screen, which is implemented in the HexIntro class (not shown in Figure 15.1).

Setting Up the Project

As already exercised in Setting Up the Project in Chapter 13, you set up a new plug-in project by switching to the Plug-in Development perspective and invoking the function File > New > Plug-in Project. Then go step-by-step through the pages of the New Wizard:

1. First, enter the project name (which also serves as the plug-in identification), for example, com.bdaum.Hex.

2. On the following page, select Java Project and leave the other settings untouched.

3. On the Plug-in Content page, enter a suitable provider name. Also uncheck the option Generate the Java Class That Controls the Plug-in's Life Cycle. This inhibits the generation of a Plugin-class. Such a class is not required in this very simple RCP application.

4. Finally, press the Finish button. Eclipse now generates the manifest file plugin.xml and opens the manifest editor on the new file.

The Manifest plugin.xml

The generated manifest file is minimal, indeed, and should look like this:

```
<?xml version="1.0" encoding="UTF-8"?>
<?eclipse version="3.0"?>
<plugin id="com.bdaum.Hex"
    name="Hex Plug-in"
    version="1.0.0"
    provider-name="bdaum industrial communications">
  <runtime>
    <library name="Hex.jar">
      <export name="*"/>
    </library>
  </runtime>
</plugin>
```

In the following sections, you will complete this manifest file.

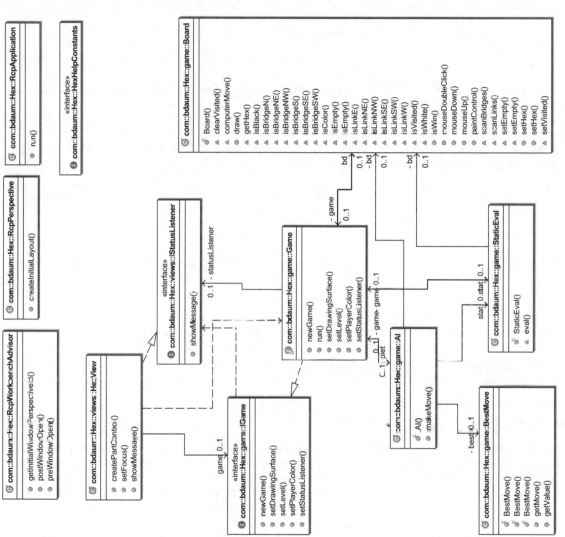

Figure 15.1

Required Eclipse Plug-ins

Next, you should determine the Eclipse plug-ins that are required for your new project. First, you need the plug-in for running the core platform:

```
org.eclipse.core.runtime
```

Then you need the plug-in for the generic workbench:

```
org.eclipse.ui
```

For the welcome screen, which will be implemented based on forms, the forms plug-in is required:

```
org.eclipse.ui.forms
```

In addition, you may want to equip your game with a help function. Therefore, you need the plug-ins for the Eclipse help system:

```
org.eclipse.help
org.eclipse.help.base
```

The plug-in `org.eclipse.help.ide` is not required; it belongs to the Eclipse IDE workbench.

To add all these plug-ins to your platform, open the Dependencies page in the manifest editor and press the Add button. In the dialog that appears, select all the plug-ins listed previously and press the OK button.

> **When you have finished these steps, you should press Ctrl+S to save the manifest file. This will make the added plug-ins known to your project, and the following steps that rely on this information will work properly.**

Declaring the Application

In an RCP application you must declare in the manifest file whose class is used as the entry point into the application. This is done via the extension point `org.eclipse.core.runtime.applications`. To create such an extension, open the Extensions page in the manifest editor and press the Add button. In the dialog that opens, select Generic Wizards and Schema-based Extensions. In the list of extension points that appears, select `org.eclipse.core.runtime.applications`.

The new extension now appears in the All Extensions window. Select this extension and enter the value RcpApplication in the Id entry in the Details section. Then apply the context function New > Application. The child element `application` is created. Select this element and apply the context function New > Run. Then select the child element `run`. You can now declare a new `IPlatformRunnable` class in the Class entry in the Details section. To do so, click the Class hyperlink to create a new class. In the following dialog, enter the value RcpApplication under Class Name. Eclipse now generates this class, but you must complete it later (see the section "Defining a View").

Defining a Perspective

In contrast to the Eclipse IDE that is equipped with at least the Resource perspective, rich client applications cannot rely on a default perspective. Therefore, it is always necessary to define your own perspective for such an application.

The Hex game needs only a single perspective—and this perspective contains only a single view. You will now create such a perspective. This is done in a similar fashion as in the previous section, except that the extension point `org.eclipse.ui.perspectives` does not require an identification. Then apply the context function New > Perspective to the new entry. In the details section, enter the value Hex in the Name field, and enter the value `com.bdaum.Hex.RcpPerspective` in the Id field. Again, create a new Java class in the Class field and call this class `RcpPerspective`.

Defining a View

The next step is to define the one and only view in this perspective. As before, create an extension for the extension point `org.eclipse.ui.views`. Apply the context function New > View to the new entry. In the Properties View, enter the value Hex 7 in the Name field, and enter the value `com.bdaum.Hex.views.HexView` in the Id field. In the Class field create another new Java class called `HexView`, but this time modify the entry in the Package Name field to `com.bdaum.Hex.views`.

Product Customization

If you want to deploy the game as a stand-alone product, some additional customization seems to be advisable. You can add the necessary definition via extension point `org.eclipse.core.runtime.products`. Just create an extension for this point and specify the value product for its Id attribute. Then create a `product` child element for the new extension. For this child element enter the value Hex Game Machine for the name attribute, and the value The game of Hex for the `description` attribute. By supplying the value com.bdaum.Hex.RcpApplication for attribute `application` you refer to the application already defined in the manifest (see the section "Declaring the Application").

Now you can modify the appearance of your product by adding some `property` child elements to the `product` element. In particular, you should add the following name/value pairs: appName=Hex and windowImage=hexWindow.gif. In addition, create a corresponding icon hexWindow.gif of size 16x16 pixels in the project folder.

Linking the Welcome Screen

The welcome screen also requires an entry in the manifest, so you need to create an extension for the extension point `org.eclipse.ui.intro`. For this extension, first create an `intro` element via New > Intro. For this element enter the Id value com.bdaum.Hex.intro. In the Class field create a new Java class called `HexIntro`. This class will implement the welcome screen.

Next, you have to connect this class to the product identification with New > introProductBinding. Under `introId`, enter the value defined previously, `com.bdaum.Hex.intro`. For the `productId`, use the product identification defined above in the `org.eclipse.core.runtime.products` extension prefixed with the plug-in identification: `com.bdaum.Hex.product`.

Adding Help

What remains to be done is to add the entries for the help table of contents and for the help context associations. However, it is better to postpone this until you have created the necessary XML files `toc.xml` and `contexts.xml`. I already showed you how to do this in the section "The Help System" in Chapter 13, so I will skip this step in this chapter.

The Completed Manifest

The completed manifest file is shown in Listing 15.1.

```xml
<?xml version="1.0" encoding="UTF-8"?>
<?eclipse version="3.0"?>
<plugin
    id="com.bdaum.Hex"
    name="Hex Plug-in"
    version="1.0.0"
    provider-name="bdaum industrial communications">

    <runtime>
        <library name="Hex.jar">
            <export name="*"/>
        </library>
    </runtime>
    <requires>
        <import plugin="org.eclipse.core.runtime"/>
        <import plugin="org.eclipse.help"/>
        <import plugin="org.eclipse.help.base"/>
        <import plugin="org.eclipse.ui"/>
        <import plugin="org.eclipse.ui.forms"/>
    </requires>

    <extension
        id="RcpApplication"
        point="org.eclipse.core.runtime.applications">
        <application>
            <run
                    class="com.bdaum.Hex.RcpApplication">
            </run>
        </application>
    </extension>
    <extension
        point="org.eclipse.ui.perspectives">
        <perspective
            name="Hex"
            class="com.bdaum.Hex.RcpPerspective"
            id="com.bdaum.Hex.RcpPerspective">
        </perspective>
    </extension>
    <extension
        point="org.eclipse.ui.views">
        <view
            name="Hex 7"
```

Listing 15.1 (Continues)

```
                class="com.bdaum.Hex.views.HexView"
                id="com.bdaum.Hex.views.HexView">
        </view>
    </extension>
    <extension
        point="org.eclipse.help.toc">
        <toc
            file="toc.xml"
            primary="true">
        </toc>
    </extension>
    <extension
        point="org.eclipse.help.contexts">
        <contexts
            file="contexts.xml">
        </contexts>
    </extension>
    <extension
        id="product"
        point="org.eclipse.core.runtime.products">
        <product
            name="Hex Game Machine"
            application="com.bdaum.Hex.RcpApplication"
            description="The game of Hex">
        <property name="appName" value="Hex"/>
        <property name="windowImage" value="hexWindow.gif"/>
        </product>
    </extension>
    <extension
        point="org.eclipse.ui.intro">
        <intro
            class="com.bdaum.Hex.HexIntro"
            id="com.bdaum.Hex.intro">
        </intro>
        <introProductBinding
            introId="com.bdaum.Hex.intro"
            productId="com.bdaum.Hex.product">
        </introProductBinding>
    </extension>
</plugin>
```

Listing 15.1 (Continued)

The RcpApplication Class

The RcpApplication class was pregenerated in the section "Declaring the Application" in this chapter; you need only complete it. In the section "The IPlatformRunnable Interface" in Chapter 14, I showed you how a basic IPlatformRunnable-class is constructed:

```
package com.bdaum.Hex;

import org.eclipse.core.runtime.IPlatformRunnable;
import org.eclipse.swt.widgets.Display;
import org.eclipse.ui.PlatformUI;
import org.eclipse.ui.application.WorkbenchAdvisor;

public class RcpApplication implements IPlatformRunnable {
  public Object run(Object args) {
    WorkbenchAdvisor workbenchAdvisor = new RcpWorkbenchAdvisor();
    Display display = PlatformUI.createDisplay();
    int returnCode = PlatformUI.createAndRunWorkbench(display,
            workbenchAdvisor);
    return (returnCode == PlatformUI.RETURN_RESTART)
            ? IPlatformRunnable.EXIT_RESTART
            : IPlatformRunnable.EXIT_OK;
  }
}
```

The RcpWorkbenchAdvisor Class

The RcpWorkbenchAdvisor class that is used in the RcpApplication class must still be implemented. This class is based on the abstract class WorkbenchAdvisor (see the section "The WorkbenchAdvisor Class" in Chapter 14). For the purpose of this application, however, you need only to override the methods getInitialWindowPerspectiveId(), preWindowOpen(), and postWindowOpen(). See Listing 15.2.

The getInitialWindowPerspectiveId() method returns just the identification of the perspective created in Defining a Perspective.

The preWindowOpen() method hides the workbench's toolbar, the bar for fast views, and the perspective bar. These bars are not required in the current application.

The postWindowOpen() method supplies the workbench window with a title.

The openIntro() method, however, requires some clarification. In this application the end user doesn't have a chance to open a welcome screen that has been closed. But if the application is shut down with a closed welcome screen, it will, by default, be started the next time with a closed welcome screen. That is not what you want, and so you must override the openIntro() method to force the welcome screen open.

```
package com.bdaum.Hex;

import org.eclipse.ui.IWorkbench;
import org.eclipse.ui.IWorkbenchWindow;
import org.eclipse.ui.application.IWorkbenchWindowConfigurer;
import org.eclipse.ui.application.WorkbenchAdvisor;
import org.eclipse.ui.intro.IIntroManager;

public class RcpWorkbenchAdvisor extends WorkbenchAdvisor {
```

Listing 15.2 (Continues)

```
      public String getInitialWindowPerspectiveId() {
        return "com.bdaum.Hex.RcpPerspective";
      }

      public void preWindowOpen(
        IWorkbenchWindowConfigurer configurer) {
        super.preWindowOpen(configurer);
        // Hide the various action bars
        configurer.setShowCoolBar(false);
        configurer.setShowFastViewBars(false);
        configurer.setShowPerspectiveBar(false);
        configurer.setShowMenuBar(false);
      }

      public void postWindowOpen(
        IWorkbenchWindowConfigurer configurer) {
        super.postWindowOpen(configurer);
        // Set window title
        configurer.setTitle("The Hex Game");
      }

      public void openIntro(IWorkbenchWindowConfigurer configurer) {
        super.openIntro(configurer);
        // Fetch intro manager and force intro open
        IWorkbenchWindow window = configurer.getWindow();
        IWorkbench workbench = window.getWorkbench();
        IIntroManager manager = workbench.getIntroManager();
        manager.showIntro(window, false);
      }
    }
```

Listing 15.2 (Continued)

The RcpPerspective Class

The RcpPerspective class was pregenerated in the section "Linking in the Welcome Screen." In Listing 15.3 you need only add the one and only view, hide the editor area, and set the layout to Fixed to stop the view from being closed.

```
    package com.bdaum.Hex;

    import org.eclipse.ui.IPageLayout;
    import org.eclipse.ui.IPerspectiveFactory;

    public class RcpPerspective implements IPerspectiveFactory {

      public void createInitialLayout(IPageLayout layout) {
        // Set layout fixed (parts cannot be closed or moved)
        // Must be set before adding views.
```

Listing 15.3 (Continues)

```
      layout.setFixed(true);
      layout.addView("com.bdaum.Hex.views.HexView",
                     IPageLayout.LEFT, 1.0f,
                     IPageLayout.ID_EDITOR_AREA);
      layout.setEditorAreaVisible(false);
   }
}
```

Listing 15.3 (Continued)

The IGame and IStatusListener Interfaces

Now all RCP-specific components are implemented. You can turn your attention to the implementation of the game itself. This consists of a GUI (represented by the view) and the game engine.

When you implement the game, it is good practice to separate the game engine as much as possible from the implementation of the user interface. This makes it easy to swap game engines when necessary, for example, to implement a different game. Therefore, I have defined two interfaces that describe the communication between the HexView class and the game engine.

The IStatusListener Interface

The IStatusListener interface enables the game engine to display a message in the status line. It features only the single method showMessage(). See Listing 15.4.

```
package com.bdaum.Hex.views;

public interface IStatusListener {
   /**
    * Show message in status line
    *
    * @param message - the message to be displayed
    */
   public void showMessage(String message);
}
```

Listing 15.4

The IGame Interface

The IGame interface describes the game engine (Listing 15.5). It defines the various methods for configuring the game engine and for informing the game engine about the drawing surface and the IStatusListener instance. Other methods are used to inform the game engine about the color chosen by the player and the playing level and to start the game. In addition, this interface defines the constants for the colors of the playing buttons and for the playing levels.

```java
package com.bdaum.Hex.game;

import org.eclipse.swt.widgets.Canvas;

import com.bdaum.Hex.views.IStatusListener;

public interface IGame {
  public static final int EMPTY = 0, WHITE = 1, BLACK = 2;
  public static final int LEVEL1 = 1, LEVEL2 = 2;

  /**
   * Set drawing surface
   *
   * @param canvas - Drawing surface
   */
  public void setDrawingSurface(Canvas canvas);

  /**
   * Set StatusListener
   *
   * @param listener - StatusListener
   */
  public void setStatusListener(IStatusListener listener);

  /**
   * Start game
   */
  public void newGame();

  /**
   * Set the player's color
   *
   * @param color - new player color
   */
  public void setPlayerColor(int color);

  /**
   * Set game level
   *
   * @param level - Game level
   */
  public void setLevel(int level);
}
```

Listing 15.5

The HexView Class

After this preparation you can implement the graphical user interface of the game, which is represented by the view. The HexView class was pregenerated in the section "Defining a View." You simply need to complete it as follows.

```
package com.bdaum.Hex.views;

import org.eclipse.jface.action.Action;
import org.eclipse.jface.action.IStatusLineManager;
import org.eclipse.jface.action.IToolBarManager;
import org.eclipse.jface.action.Separator;
import org.eclipse.swt.SWT;
import org.eclipse.swt.widgets.Canvas;
import org.eclipse.swt.widgets.Composite;
import org.eclipse.ui.IActionBars;
import org.eclipse.ui.help.WorkbenchHelp;
import org.eclipse.ui.part.ViewPart;

import com.bdaum.Hex.HexHelpConstants;
import com.bdaum.Hex.game.Game;
import com.bdaum.Hex.game.IGame;

public class HexView extends ViewPart implements IStatusListener {
```

For enabling user interaction, you need to implement a few tool buttons on the view's title line. These buttons allow the player to choose a color (black or white), to select the playing level (basic or advanced), to start a new game, and to invoke the help function.

These tool buttons are implemented in form of `Actions`. Some of these `Actions` must lock in, so they need to be configured appropriately with the style constant `AS_CHECK_BOX`. Unfortunately, the `Action()` constructor that allows this is defined as protected, so it cannot be accessed by this class. The solution is to define a subclass of `Action`, the class `ToggleAction`. Then you need to define the instance fields for these actions and constants to identify the individual actions. In addition, you need to define the `canvas` field for the drawing surface and the `game` field, which holds the game engine.

```
private class ToggleAction extends Action {
  public ToggleAction(String title, boolean init) {
    super(title, AS_CHECK_BOX);
    setChecked(init);
  }
}

/* Action IDs */
private static final int WHITE_ACTION = 0;
private static final int BLACK_ACTION = 1;
private static final int BASIC_ACTION = 2;
private static final int ADVANCED_ACTION = 3;
private static final int NEWGAME_ACTION = 4;
private static final int HELP_ACTION = 5;

/* Widgets and Actions */
private Action blackAction, whiteAction, basicAction,
        advancedAction, newGameAction, helpAction;
private Canvas canvas;

/* The game engine */
private IGame game;
```

The workbench invokes the createPartControl() method when the view is initialized. Here, you must first create a Canvas, set its background color, and assign a key for context-sensitive help to it. The HexHelpConstants interface is listed here. Then you need to create instances of the actions defined previously and to add these actions as tool buttons to the title bar of the view. Finally, you must create an instance of the game engine and configure it, and then you start the first game.

```
/**
 * Constructs the view content
 */
public void createPartControl(Composite parent) {
  canvas = new Canvas(parent, SWT.NO_BACKGROUND);
  canvas.setBackground(parent.getDisplay().getSystemColor(
        SWT.COLOR_GRAY));
  WorkbenchHelp.setHelp(canvas, HexHelpConstants.HELP_BOARD);
  makeActions();
  contributeToActionBars();
  game = new Game();
  game.setStatusListener(this);
  game.setDrawingSurface(canvas);
  game.newGame();
}
```

When you create a single action, its identification, the display label, a tool tip, and a key for the context-sensitive help are specified to construct the instance. The actions for color and level selection are constructed as toggle actions, the others as normal actions.

```
/**
 * Create actions
 */
private void makeActions() {
  newGameAction = createAction(NEWGAME_ACTION, "New Game",
        "Starts new game",
        HexHelpConstants.HELP_NEWGAME_ACTION);
  whiteAction = createToggleAction(WHITE_ACTION, "White",
        "Player plays white",
        HexHelpConstants.HELP_COLOR_ACTION, true);
  blackAction = createToggleAction(BLACK_ACTION, "Black",
        "Player plays black",
        HexHelpConstants.HELP_COLOR_ACTION, false);
  basicAction = createToggleAction(BASIC_ACTION, "Basic",
        "Basic Level", HexHelpConstants.HELP_LEVEL_ACTION,
        true);
  advancedAction = createToggleAction(ADVANCED_ACTION,
        "Advanced", "Advanced Level",
        HexHelpConstants.HELP_LEVEL_ACTION, false);
  helpAction = createAction(HELP_ACTION, "Help",
        "Help for Hex", null);
}

/**
 * Create single action
 *
 * @param id - Identification
```

```
 * @param label - Display label
 * @param tip - Tooltip
 * @param helpId - ID for context sensitive help
 * @return - the created action instance
 */
private Action createAction(final int id, String label,
        String tip, String helpId) {
  Action action = new Action() {
    public void run() {
      runAction(id);
    }
  };
  action.setText(label);
  action.setToolTipText(tip);
  if (helpId != null) WorkbenchHelp.setHelp(action, helpId);
  return action;
}

/**
 * Create single toggle action
 *
 * @param id - Identification
 * @param label - Display label
 * @param tip - Tooltip
 * @param helpId - ID for context sensitive help
 * @param init - initial state
 * @return - the created action instance
 */
private Action createToggleAction(final int id, String label,
        String tip, String helpId, boolean init) {
  Action action = new ToggleAction(label, init) {
    public void run() {
      runAction(id);
    }
  };
  action.setToolTipText(tip);
  if (helpId != null) WorkbenchHelp.setHelp(action, helpId);
  return action;
}
```

When an action is invoked, its corresponding operation (identified by the action's ID) is executed. In case of toggle actions, the invoked action is locked via the setChecked() method and its counterpart is released.

The game engine then performs the operation. An exception is the help action, which simply calls the displayHelp() method of the Eclipse help system.

```
/**
 * Run action
 *
 * @param id - Action identification
 */
protected void runAction(int id) {
```

```
    switch (id) {
      case NEWGAME_ACTION :
        game.newGame();
        break;
      case WHITE_ACTION :
        game.setPlayerColor(IGame.WHITE);
        whiteAction.setChecked(true);
        blackAction.setChecked(false);
        break;
      case BLACK_ACTION :
        game.setPlayerColor(IGame.BLACK);
        whiteAction.setChecked(false);
        blackAction.setChecked(true);
        break;
      case BASIC_ACTION :
        game.setLevel(IGame.LEVEL1);
        basicAction.setChecked(true);
        advancedAction.setChecked(false);
        break;
      case ADVANCED_ACTION :
        game.setLevel(IGame.LEVEL2);
        basicAction.setChecked(false);
        advancedAction.setChecked(true);
        break;
      case HELP_ACTION :
        WorkbenchHelp.displayHelp();
        break;
    }
  }
```

Then, the actions are added to the view's title bar. To do this, you must first fetch the ViewSite. From this site you can obtain the action bars, and from the action bars you obtain the toolbar manager. Then you can add the individual actions to the toolbar manager. In addition, you can separate the different action groups with the help of separators.

```
/**
 * Construct menu and tool bar
 */
private void contributeToActionBars() {
  IActionBars bars = getViewSite().getActionBars();
  fillLocalToolBar(bars.getToolBarManager());
}

/**
 * Construct tool bar
 *
 * @param manager - the tool bar manager
 */
private void fillLocalToolBar(IToolBarManager manager) {
  manager.add(newGameAction);
  manager.add(new Separator());
  manager.add(whiteAction);
  manager.add(blackAction);
```

```
      manager.add(new Separator());
      manager.add(basicAction);
      manager.add(advancedAction);
      manager.add(new Separator());
      manager.add(helpAction);
   }
```

Finally, you need to implement the methods required by the superclass and the implemented interfaces. First, the setFocus() method: If the view gets the focus, it has to pass it to its drawing surface, the Canvas instance.

Then you need to implement the showMessage() method from the IStatusListener interface. From the action bars of the ViewSite, fetch the StatusLineManager and pass the message to this manager via its setMessage() method. This needs to be performed in an asyncExec() block since this method can be called from the thread of the game engine. You probably remember this technique from the previous example applications.

```
   /**
    * Pass focus to Canvas-Widget
    */
   public void setFocus() {
      canvas.setFocus();
   }

   /**
    * Display message in status line
    *
    * @param message - the message to be displayed
    */
   public void showMessage(final String message) {
      canvas.getDisplay().asyncExec(new Runnable() {
         public void run() {
            IStatusLineManager sManager = getViewSite()
                    .getActionBars().getStatusLineManager();
            sManager.setMessage(message);
         }
      });
   }
}
```

And here are the required keys for the context-sensitive help. They are defined in the separate interface HexHelpConstants:

```
package com.bdaum.Hex;

public interface HexHelpConstants {

   static final String PREFIX = "com.bdaum.Hex.";

   public static final String HELP_COLOR_ACTION = PREFIX
           + "colorAction";
   public static final String HELP_LEVEL_ACTION = PREFIX
           + "levelAction";
```

```
    public static final String HELP_NEWGAME_ACTION = PREFIX
            + "newGameAction";
    public static final String HELP_BOARD = PREFIX + "board";
}
```

The Game Engine

The game engine consists of the classes AI, BestMove, Board, Game, and StaticEval. I refrain from presenting these classes here to their full extent since this code has nothing at all to do with Eclipse. Readers interested in the implementation of the game can find the source code at www.wrox.com.

Of interest in the context of Eclipse is only the Board class, which I will discuss here in sections. This class is responsible for drawing the game board and for processing the mouse actions. The data model of the game board is represented by the two-dimensional array cells, whose elements can take the values IGame.EMPTY, IGame.WHITE, and IGame.BLACK. It is the responsibility of the drawing routine to convert this abstract model into a graphical representation.

First, some fields are defined. These fields are initialized in the constructor. The current Board instance is assigned to the Canvas as both a MouseListener and a PaintListener.

```
    private int cells[][] = new int[Game.SIZE][Game.SIZE];
    private Canvas canvas;
    private Game game;
    private Display display;
    private Color white, black, gray, green, cyan;

    // Constructor
    public Board(Canvas canvas, Game game) {
        this.game = game;
        this.canvas = canvas;
        display = canvas.getDisplay();
        white = display.getSystemColor(SWT.COLOR_WHITE);
        black = display.getSystemColor(SWT.COLOR_BLACK);
        gray = display.getSystemColor(SWT.COLOR_GRAY);
        green = display.getSystemColor(SWT.COLOR_DARK_GREEN);
        cyan = display.getSystemColor(SWT.COLOR_DARK_CYAN);
        canvas.addPaintListener(this);
        canvas.addMouseListener(this);
    }
```

The redrawing of the canvas can occur in two different situations. First, if a view must be redrawn, then the canvas must also be redrawn, for example, when the application moves from the desktop background to the foreground. Second, the canvas must be redrawn when a player or the computer has made a move. This case is handled by the draw() method. Since this method is called from the thread of the game engine, its accesses to the SWT are encapsulated again into an syncExec() block.

```
    /**
     * Redraw game board
     */
    public void draw() {
```

```
      canvas.getDisplay().syncExec(new Runnable() {
        public void run() {
          // Signal partial redraw
          canvas.redraw(1, 1, 10000, 10000, false);
        }
      });
}
```

In this case, it is necessary to redraw not the whole canvas but only the game board, so you have to indicate to the `paintControl()` given in the following code that only a partial redraw is required. You can do this by specifying a redraw from position (1,1). This trick is not very nice, but it works. You probably will have noticed in the section "The HexView Class" that the `Canvas` instance was created with the style constant `SWT.NO_BACKGROUND`. This style constant enforces that the canvas background is not automatically redrawn. I specified this constant in order to avoid flicker. The consequence was that I had to organize the drawing of the canvas background myself, and I redraw the canvas background only when the whole view is redrawn but not after a game move. This is controlled by specifying the redraw position of (1,1).

In the following code section, I specify the geometry of the game board by defining appropriate constants:

```
    // Edge length of a hexagon (= outer radius)
    private static final int OUTER_RAD = 30;
    // Inner radius of a hexagon
    private static final int INNER_RAD =
            (int) (Math.sqrt(0.75d) * OUTER_RAD);
    // Outline of a hexagon
    private static final int[] CELL = new int[]{
        -OUTER_RAD,        0,
        -OUTER_RAD/2,    -INNER_RAD,
        OUTER_RAD/2,     -INNER_RAD,
        OUTER_RAD,         0,
        OUTER_RAD/2,      INNER_RAD,
        -OUTER_RAD/2,     INNER_RAD};
    // Horizontal distance between cells
    private static final int XDIST = OUTER_RAD * 3 / 2;
    // Horizontal offset of the game board
    private static final int XOFF = Game.SIZE * OUTER_RAD
            + 150;
    // Vertical offset of the game board
    private static final int YOFF = 100;
    // Horizontal border width of game board
    private static final int XMARGIN = 20;
    // Vertical border width of game board
    private static final int YMARGIN = 15;
    // Radius of a game button
    private static final int BUTTON_RAD = OUTER_RAD / 2;
    // Corner positions of the game board
    private static final Point TOP = hexToPixel(0, 0);
    private static final Point BOTTOM = hexToPixel(Game.SIZE,Game.SIZE);
    private static final Point RIGHT = hexToPixel(Game.SIZE, 0);
    private static final Point LEFT = hexToPixel(0, Game.SIZE);
    // Outlines of the game board edges
```

```java
    private static final int[] WHITEBORDER = new int[]{
        LEFT.x - XMARGIN, LEFT.y - INNER_RAD,
        RIGHT.x + XMARGIN, RIGHT.y - INNER_RAD,
        TOP.x, TOP.y - YMARGIN - INNER_RAD,
        BOTTOM.x, BOTTOM.y + YMARGIN - INNER_RAD};
    private static final int[] BLACKBORDER = new int[]{
        LEFT.x - XMARGIN, LEFT.y - INNER_RAD,
        TOP.x, TOP.y - YMARGIN - INNER_RAD,
        BOTTOM.x, BOTTOM.y + YMARGIN - INNER_RAD,
        RIGHT.x + XMARGIN, RIGHT.y - INNER_RAD};
```

The following method converts the rows and columns into pixel coordinates:

```java
/**
 * Convert rows and columns into pixel values
 * @param i - row
 * @param j - column
 * @return - (x,y)-coordinate
 */
private static Point hexToPixel(int i, int j) {
  return new Point(
      ((i - j) * XDIST) + XOFF,
      ((i + j) * INNER_RAD) + YOFF);
}
```

Now you can draw the game board. If the indicator `totalRedraw` is set, you first fill the complete background with the background color (gray). Then the black-and-white game board edges are drawn, which are later overdrawn by the game board cells.

Next you can draw the game board cell by cell. First, the cell background is drawn. You use a different background color for the cell in the center because this cell has a special meaning. Then you can draw the game button belonging to the cell—provided the cell is not empty.

```java
/**
 * Draw Canvas
 *
 * @param e - Event object
 */
public void paintControl(PaintEvent e) {
  GC gc = e.gc;
  if (e.x != 1 || e.y != 1) {
    // Draw background
    gc.setBackground(gray);
    gc.fillRectangle(canvas.getClientArea());
    // Draw game board edges
    gc.setBackground(white);
    gc.fillPolygon(WHITEBORDER);
    gc.setBackground(black);
    gc.fillPolygon(BLACKBORDER);
  }
  // Draw all hexagon cells
  for (int i = 0; i < Game.SIZE; i++)
    for (int j = 0; j < Game.SIZE; j++)
```

```
      drawCellWithButton(gc, i, j, cells[i][j]);
}


/**
 * Draw single cell
 * @param gc - Graphic Context
 * @param i - Row
 * @param j - Column
 * @param buttonColor - Color of game button
 */
private void drawCellWithButton(GC gc, int i, int j, int buttonColor) {
  Point p = hexToPixel(i, j);
  if (i == Game.SIZE / 2 && j == Game.SIZE / 2)
    drawCell(gc, p.x, p.y, cyan, black);
  else
    drawCell(gc, p.x, p.y, green, black);
  switch (buttonColor) {
    case Game.BLACK :
      drawButton(gc, p.x, p.y, black, white);
      break;
    case Game.WHITE :
      drawButton(gc, p.x, p.y, white, black);
      break;
  }
}


/**
 * Draw cell background
 * @param gc - Graphic Context
 * @param x - X-offset
 * @param y - Y-offset
 * @param cellColor - fill color
 * @param outlineColor - outline color
 */
private void drawCell(GC gc, int x, int y,
                      Color cellColor, Color outlineColor) {
  int[] points = new int[CELL.length];
  for (int k = 0; k < CELL.length; k += 2) {
    points[k] = x + CELL[k];
    points[k + 1] = y + CELL[k + 1];
  }
  gc.setBackground(cellColor);
  gc.setForeground(outlineColor);
  gc.fillPolygon(points);
  gc.drawPolygon(points);
}

/**
 * Draw game button
 * @param gc - Graphic Context
 * @param x - X-offset
 * @param y - Y-offset
 * @param bgColor - fill color
```

```
 * @param fgColor - outline color
 */
private void drawButton(GC gc, int x, int y,
                        Color bgColor, Color fgColor) {
  gc.setBackground(bgColor);
  gc.fillOval(x - BUTTON_RAD, y - BUTTON_RAD,
        2 * BUTTON_RAD, 2 * BUTTON_RAD);
  gc.setForeground(fgColor);
  gc.drawOval(x - BUTTON_RAD, y - BUTTON_RAD,
        2 * BUTTON_RAD, 2 * BUTTON_RAD);
}
```

This concludes the drawing operations. What is still missing is the processing of the mouse events. Only the single mouse down event is processed; the release of the mouse button and the double-click are ignored. On a mouse click, the mouse coordinates are converted into board coordinates. The game engine is informed about this event via the selectHex() method.

```
/*
 * Mouse button pressed
 *
 * @param e - Event object
 */
public void mouseDown(MouseEvent e) {
  Point p = pixelToHex(e.x, e.y);
  game.selectHex(p.x, p.y);
}

/**
 * Convert pixels into row and column
 * @param x - X-offset
 * @param y - Y-offset
 * @return - (row, column)-tuple
 */
private static Point pixelToHex(int x, int y) {
  int dist2 = INNER_RAD * INNER_RAD;
  for (int i = 0; i < Game.SIZE; i++) {
    for (int j = 0; j < Game.SIZE; j++) {
      Point p = hexToPixel(i, j);
      int dx = p.x - x;
      int dy = p.y - y;
      if (dx * dx + dy * dy < dist2) return new Point(i, j);
    }
  }
  return new Point(-1, -1);
}
```

The Welcome Screen

The HexIntro class is also generated during the definition of the plug-in manifest (Listing 15.6). However, it is better and easier to write this class from scratch and to subclass the IntroPart class instead of implementing the IIntroPart interface. The only thing that remains to do is to complete the setFocus() method and to construct the welcome screen in the createPartControl() method.

Here, I have decided to use forms technology. Forms are well suited for presenting some instructions for the game. In addition, I have provided a hyperlink for starting the game. The example demonstrates how different colors and fonts can be used in forms texts. The colors and fonts are referenced via symbolic names within the marked-up text, and then further down these names are defined via setColor() and setFont(). Also, for the hyperlink I have chosen a special representation: it is underlined only when the mouse hovers over it. Events produced by this hyperlink are captured by the hyperlink listener. If the user clicks on the hyperlink, the welcome screen closes and the game can begin.

```java
package com.bdaum.Hex;

import org.eclipse.jface.resource.JFaceResources;
import org.eclipse.swt.SWT;
import org.eclipse.swt.graphics.Color;
import org.eclipse.swt.graphics.Font;
import org.eclipse.swt.widgets.Composite;
import org.eclipse.ui.IWorkbench;
import org.eclipse.ui.IWorkbenchWindow;
import org.eclipse.ui.forms.HyperlinkSettings;
import org.eclipse.ui.forms.events.HyperlinkAdapter;
import org.eclipse.ui.forms.events.HyperlinkEvent;
import org.eclipse.ui.forms.widgets.Form;
import org.eclipse.ui.forms.widgets.FormText;
import org.eclipse.ui.forms.widgets.FormToolkit;
import org.eclipse.ui.forms.widgets.TableWrapLayout;
import org.eclipse.ui.intro.IIntroManager;
import org.eclipse.ui.part.IntroPart;

public class HexIntro extends IntroPart {

  // The Form-Widget
  Form introForm;

  /* (non-Javadoc)
   * @see org.eclipse.ui.part.IntroPart#setFocus()
   */
  public void setFocus() {
    introForm.setFocus();
  }

  /* (non-Javadoc)
   * @see org.eclipse.ui.part.IntroPart
   *      #createPartControl(org.eclipse.swt.widgets.Composite)
   */
  public void createPartControl(Composite parent) {
    // Fetch Toolkit
    FormToolkit tk = new FormToolkit(parent.getDisplay());
    // Create Form and set Layout
    introForm = tk.createForm(parent);
    TableWrapLayout layout = new TableWrapLayout();
    introForm.getBody().setLayout(layout);
```

Listing 15.6 (Continues)

```
    // Create forms text, more space between paragraphs
    FormText tx = tk.createFormText(introForm.getBody(), true);
    tx.setParagraphsSeparated(true);
    // Set hyperlink appearance
    // (must be done before setting the text)
    HyperlinkSettings settings = new
                HyperlinkSettings(parent.getDisplay());
    settings.setHyperlinkUnderlineMode(
                HyperlinkSettings.UNDERLINE_HOVER);
    tx.setHyperlinkSettings(settings);
    // Marked-up text
    String text = "<form><p><span font=\"title\">Hex 7</span></p>" +
        "<p><span color=\"subtitle\" font=\"subtitle\">" +
        "The game of Hex</span></p>" +
        "<p><a href=\"http://startGame\">Start game</a></p></form>";
    tx.setText(text,true,false);
    // Set Fonts
    Font titleFont = JFaceResources.getFont(JFaceResources.HEADER_FONT);
    tx.setFont("title", titleFont);
    Font subtitleFont =
            JFaceResources.getFont(JFaceResources.BANNER_FONT);
    tx.setFont("subtitle", subtitleFont);
    // Set color for subtitle
    Color col =
            parent.getDisplay().getSystemColor(SWT.COLOR_DARK_GREEN);
    tx.setColor("subtitle", col);
    // Process hyperlink events
    tx.addHyperlinkListener(new HyperlinkAdapter() {
      public void linkActivated(HyperlinkEvent e) {
        // Fetch IntroManager, close welcome screen
          IWorkbenchWindow window =
                  getIntroSite().getWorkbenchWindow();
          IWorkbench workbench = window.getWorkbench();
          IIntroManager manager = workbench.getIntroManager();
          manager.closeIntro(HexIntro.this);
      }
    });
  }

  /* (non-Javadoc)
   * @see org.eclipse.ui.intro.IIntroPart#standbyStateChanged(boolean)
   */
  public void standbyStateChanged(boolean standby) {
  }
}
```

Listing 15.6 (Continued)

Test

In order to run the game Hex from the workbench (i.e., to test it within the Eclipse platform before deploying it as a stand-alone product), just proceed as follows:

1. Invoke function Run > Run.

2. Create a new configuration of type Run-time Workbench. In the `Name` field enter the value Hex.

3. On the `Arguments` page check the `Run a Product` option in group `Program to Run`, and select there the product identification com.bdaum.Hex.product from the drop down list.

4. On the `Plug-ins` page first press the Deselect All button. Then check the plug-in `com.bdaum.Hex` in the `Workspace Plug-ins` group and press the Add Required Plug-ins button. Using this procedure, you just make sure that the game Hex will run on a platform that contains only the required plug-ins. Proper operation will not be disturbed by unnecessary plug-ins.

5. Now you can start the game by pressing the Run button.

Deployment

If you want to deploy this application in form of a ZIP file, just select the project com.bdaum.Hex in the explorer and invoke the context function Export. In the Export Wizard select the Deployable Plug-ins and Fragments option. On the following wizard page, select the option A Single Deployable ZIP File and enter the target path of the ZIP file in the Destination field. After you have created the ZIP file in this way, you still have to add the configuration\config.ini file. This is necessary because you want this file to be installed into the directory \eclipse\configuration\ when the ZIP file is unpacked into the directory \eclipse\. The content of config.ini looks like this:

```
osgi.splashPath = platform:/base/plugins/org.eclipse.platform
eclipse.product=com.bdaum.Hex.product
eclipse.buildId=I200425061208
eof=eof
```

This file sets the product identification for the deployed software. Should you later want to apply changes to the config.ini or plugin.xml files of an already installed product, you must delete all files except config.ini in the \eclipse\configuration\ folder before restarting Eclipse.

The value eclipse.buildId identifies the installed version of the Eclipse platform and must be adapted accordingly when using a version of Eclipse later than 3.0.0. It can be retrieved from the config.ini file that comes with the Eclipse product.

The installation of the Hex game consists of simply unpacking the ZIP file into an existing Eclipse installation in the Eclipse root directory \eclipse\. But be warned: afterward, this Eclipse installation won't be good for anything other than playing Hex! The required Eclipse installation doesn't need to be the full Eclipse SDK. The Eclipse RCP Runtime Binary, which is less than a 5MB download, is sufficient. You want to make sure that all plug-ins listed under Dependencies (see the section "Required Eclipse Plug-ins") are present. For example, you would need to add the plug-in org.eclipse.ui.forms, which can be taken from the full Eclipse SDK.

Summary

As shown in Figure 15.2, the application that you have created in this chapter looks like any other native application. Even experts will hardly notice that this application is running on an Eclipse platform. Only the help function exhibits some Eclipse inheritance.

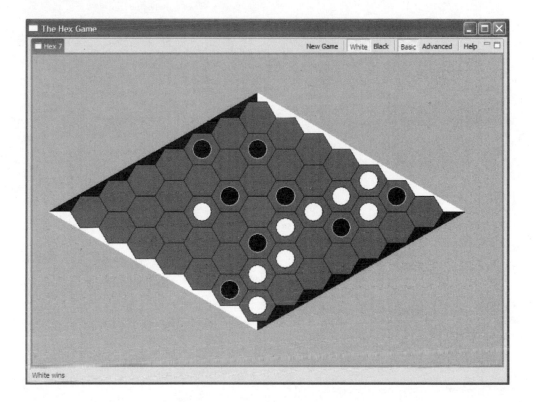

Figure 15.2

Actually, everything works quite nicely. Only the edges of the game buttons are a little bit rough because they were drawn using SWT functions that don't support anti-aliasing. Alternatively, you could implement the drawing using Java2D functions. In the section "Widgets that Swing" in Chapter 8, I showed how this can be done within an SWT application.

What is a bit disturbing, though, is the tab on top of the Hex View. However, you can turn this into an advantage if you offer more games, each on a separate page of a tabbed notebook. But in this case, you would be better off separating the individual games from the game platform and implementing them as separate plug-ins. Wouldn't that be a nice exercise?

This chapter concludes the introduction into the functionality of Eclipse. In the next chapter I will discuss how the various facilities found in Eclipse may influence your programming style.

16

Conclusions and Outlook

In this chapter I want to draw a few conclusions about the impact of Eclipse on programming style. As you will see, Eclipse supports programming techniques that are advertised under the name *Extreme Programming* or *Agile Programming*. This is not surprising because some people (such as Kent Beck) who play a prominent role in this area also have a leading role in the development of Eclipse.

The other issue is the support for Java 1.5. For the Java community Java 1.5 means the biggest breakthrough since the introduction of Java 1.2, and it will seriously influence the way in which you write programs. Eclipse 3.0, however, will not support Java 1.5 in its official release version, but experimental Java 1.5 support is available as a plug-in.

Programming Style

Considering the advances made with programming under Eclipse so far, you will probably remember programming techniques that made headlines a few years ago under the name of Extreme Programming or Agile Programming. However, only the branding of those techniques was new at the time; techniques such as Pair Programming, the early construction of test beds for the components of a software system, or the specification of user stories and the continuous feedback with customers had been previously employed by experienced programmers. The branding of those techniques under the aforementioned name, however, had some positive effects: it made those techniques more popular, encouraged managers to utilize them, and encouraged tool manufacturers to provide support for the techniques within their tools. This evolution also applies to eclipse.org. In this chapter I will show how Eclipse supports these new (old) programming techniques. In addition, I will discuss a few other effects that Eclipse has had on programming style. You can get further information about the aforementioned techniques at www.extremeprogramming.org and www.agilealliance.org.

Executable Prototypes

One of the most essential principles of Extreme Programming is the close feedback with the customer. Just shortly after a *user story* (an informal description of the application functions) is written, the programmer should be able to show a prototype to the customer. Of course, it is not necessary to implement all of the application's functions at that time. Usually it will be sufficient to be able to demonstrate a GUI or parts of the GUI. After the discussion with the customer comes the next step in the iteration: refining or extending the functions.

Eclipse is well suited for this approach, provided you are programming on the basis of the Eclipse platform, meaning that you are developing your application either as a plug-in for the Eclipse IDE or on the basis of the Rich Client Platform (see Chapters 14 and 15). When you work in this manner, you can almost always launch your application immediately after creating the first plug-in project and the manifest file. You have the entire Eclipse GUI at your disposal and don't need to implement all the GUI components usually needed in an application manually. Experience shows that for a small application, you can create the first executable prototype within hours. Eclipse can generate large parts of a plug-in, for example, views with tables or trees, editors, and much more.

An extra benefit with this approach is that you can test new functions immediately within your application prototype. This provides immediate feedback and allows you to detect bugs and deficiencies early. And if a member of the customer's staff is part of the development team, so much the better: you can immediately demonstrate new functions within the live application and discuss them with the customer's representative.

The development of Eclipse itself is a good example of this approach. During the development of Eclipse 3 (and also during the development of Eclipse 2), a new prototype (a milestone) was produced each month. Of course, some functions were still missing in these milestones or they were only partly implemented or still buggy. But the users' experiences with these milestones provided valuable input for the development of the subsequent milestones and release candidates. Thus, the Eclipse team made sure that each milestone met the requirements and needs of its users more closely and more completely.

Automated Tests

In the "JUnit" section in Chapter 6, I showed how JUnit is integrated into the Eclipse IDE. Test tools such as JUnit belong in any Extreme Programmer's toolbox. Even before a component or a class is written, a `TestCase` should be implemented. This sounds like considerable overhead, but it isn't. The `TestCases` must be written anyway—if not early, then later—before the integration tests are performed and the software is packaged and deployed. Creating these `TestCases` early will help considerably during the implementation of the corresponding components. Bugs that are detected early are found much quicker, and creating `TestCases` will help the programmer to understand the functionality of the component. An alternative is for the customer to create the `TestCases`. This is not a bad idea, since it ensures that the customer has a clear understanding of the required functionality .

Of course, after deploying milestones or official releases, you will almost certainly encounter bug reports. For each of these bug reports you should create a new test case that makes sure that this bug will be detected in a future version.

Refinements

There is another issue related to programming style under Eclipse that doesn't really belong under the umbrella of Extreme Programming. While large software systems are constructed from components, that is, constructed in a *bottom-up* fashion, the implementation of single functions happens in most cases in the opposite direction (*top-down*). First, you determine which rough steps must be implemented in order to realize the required function. Then you can begin to refine these steps into smoother steps. This is performed in an iterative manner until you reach the instruction level. Each step is implemented in the form of methods.

Eclipse supports this approach via its Quick Fix function (see "The Correction Assistant" section in Chapter 2). When you implement a method, you first specify the individual steps in the form of method calls to nonexisting methods. Eclipse will automatically decorate these calls with the Quick Fix symbol because they are considered to be source code errors. When you click on such a symbol, Eclipse generates the missing method, and the only thing that remains for you to do is to refine it.

Let's step through the following example (Figure 16.1). This example tries to compute the reproduction rate of rabbits within the course of a year. (The mathematicians among you will probably guess that the growth rate of rabbit populations is about equal to the growth rate of Fibonacci numbers.)

```java
public class Rabbits {

    private static int young_couples = 1;
    private static int fertile_couples = 0;
    private static int baby_couples = 0;

    public static void main(String[] args) {
        for (int month = 0; month <= 12; month++) {
            rabbits_are_born();
            youngster_become_mature();
            babies_become_youngsters();
            report(month);
        }
    }
}
```

Figure 16.1

First you need to implement the main() method. Then click the Quick Fix symbol at the left of rabbits_are_born() and select Create Method.... Eclipse generates the method stub rabbits_are_born() (Figure 16.2).

```java
public class Rabbits {

    private static int young_couples = 1;
    private static int fertile_couples = 0;
    private static int baby_couples = 0;

    public static void main(String[] args) {
        for (int month = 0; month <= 12; month++) {
            rabbits_are_born();
            youngster_become_mature();
            babies_become_youngsters();
            report(month);
        }
    }
    /**
     *
     */
    private static void rabbits_are_born() {
        // TODO Auto-generated method stub

    }
```

Figure 16.2

Then you can fill the method body with content (Figure 16.3).

```
public class Rabbits {

    private static int young_couples = 1;
    private static int fertile_couples = 0;
    private static int baby_couples = 0;

    public static void main(String[] args) {
        for (int month = 0; month <= 12; month++) {
            rabbits_are_born();
            youngster_become_mature();
            babies_become_youngsters();
            report(month);
        }
    }
    /**
     *
     */
    private static void rabbits_are_born() {
        baby_couples = fertile_couples;
    }
```

Figure 16.3

Continue the implementation in this way until all the method calls are resolved and refined. You can use similar techniques to create variables, fields, or new class definitions. You don't need to know in advance which of these elements you will need, because you can easily create and refine these elements as they are needed.

Embrace Change

The maxim "Embrace Change" was coined by Kent Beck, one of the subscribers of the Manifesto for Agile Software Development and one of the principal architects of the Eclipse platform. For further reading I recommend *Extreme Programming Explained: Embrace Change* by Beck and *Contributing to Eclipse: Principles, Patterns, and Plugins* by Gamma, et al. What is meant by this phrase is that modifying code should be nothing extraordinary but should be everyday business. As you have already seen in the section "Refactoring Code" in Chapter 2, Eclipse provides powerful functions for code refactoring. Therefore, you needn't be too afraid of introducing new bugs into an application by restructuring its code, because the refactoring transformations provided by Eclipse work quite reliably.

The good news is that you are not required to write code from the first version onward that is designed to last for all eternity. No matter what your personal style is, if you program by refinement, as shown in the previous section, or if you write spaghetti code with methods that stretch across many pages, there is practically nothing that you cannot fix with Refactoring functions. Methods that are too small can be inlined via the function Refactor > Inline..., and large methods can be decomposed into smaller methods via the function Refactor > Extract Method....

Keeping in mind that there is always a remedy for poor coding style, so you can go about coding in a much more relaxed way and concentrate on solving the business problem. Then, when the implemented function runs properly, you can start to think about restructuring the code to make it more maintainable, organized, aesthetically pleasing, conforming to object-oriented principles, and so on.

Just one word of advice at this point: If you tend to write spaghetti code, you should not prematurely exit your methods with `return`. A method should terminate only at its very end. The reason for this is that methods with interspersed `return` statements are hard to decompose via the function Refactor > Extract Method....

Save Energy

Finally, I have one more suggestion for the design of user interfaces that are implemented on basis of the SWT, JFace, and GUI components of the workbench. When you implement such an interface, you will save yourself a lot of development effort if you first analyze what Eclipse has to offer and then design your user interface with maximum reuse of the Eclipse components. Working in this way, you will quickly arrive at interfaces that are both robust and easy for the end user to operate. On the other hand, if you stubbornly hold onto your preconceived ideas, you will achieve less with a much greater effort.

Java 1.5

Java 1.5 means a major break for Java programmers, because it introduces a wide array of new programming concepts. Sun Microsystems has therefore adopted a new numbering system for Java: Java 1.5 is now called J2SE 5.0! I see Java 1.5 as the result of Sun Microsystems's effort to conceptually keep up with Microsoft's C# language. In particular, Java 1.5 introduces the following new concepts:

❑ **Generic types.** Generics are probably the most notable change within Java 1.5. Basically they mean that the type definition of a variable, parameter, or method return type need not be a fixed type. Instead, a type variable can be used in its place. When you use a method or class with a type variable, you must specify a concrete type to parameterize the construct. The application and benefit of this concept are most obvious in the collection classes, although it can be applied to other scenarios as well. For example, consider the generic form of the classes `List` and `ArrayList`. You can use them as lists that contain only integer values:

```
List<Integer> intList = new ArrayList<Integer>();
```

You can now retrieve integer values from such a list without a type cast:

```
Integer i = intList.get(0);
```

Clearly, this adds considerably to type safety.

❑ **Enhanced for loops.** This concept provides a more compact syntax for looping across an array. For example, the following code computes the sum of all array elements:

```
double[] a = ...
double t = 0;
for ( double n : a )
  t += n;
```

❑ **Autoboxing.** This saves you from converting primitive data types into first-class objects and vice versa in situations where only objects are allowed. For example:

```
List<Integer> intList = new ArrayList<Integer>();
intList.add(55);
int i = intList.get(0);
```

❑ **Enumerations.** Enumerations replace the lengthy definition of integer constants that are typically used to introduce symbolic names for integer values. For example, instead of

```
static final int WHITE_ACTION = 0;
```

```
static final int BLACK_ACTION = 1;
```

you can now write

```
enum ACTION { WHITE, BLACK };
```

and use the values as `ACTION.WHITE` and `ACTION.BLACK`.

❑ **Static imports.** These allow you to use static methods from external packages without the class name. For example, by importing the static methods from `java.lang.Math` you can simplify an arithmetic expression.

```
import static java.lang.Math.max;
...
double r2 = sqrt(2.0d);
```

❑ **Metadata facility.** This allows you to mark up (annotate) Java programs with tags. These tags can be evaluated by other tools and thus serve the purpose of tool integration. Depending on the configuration, they can even be stored in the binary class file. Tags consist of Java names prefixed with @. Parameters in parentheses can be appended.

I'll leave it at this short overview. You can find detailed information on Java 1.5 on `http://java .sun.com/developer/technicalArticles/releases/j2se15/` or in the numerous Java books that are now being updated for Java 1.5.

The new features have a tremendous impact on an IDE such as Eclipse. Not only is a new compiler version required, but such areas as code assistants, refactoring, outlining, syntax coloring, and so on are also affected.

In its 3.0 release, Eclipse does not support Java 1.5, and JRE 1.5 is not an official platform for running Eclipse. However, under the codename Cheetah, there is an experimental version for Java 1.5 support, which you can download from the Eclipse development CVS. At the time of writing, this is at `http://dev.eclipse.org/viewcvs/index.cgi/jdt-core-home/update-site/`. The Cheetah homepage is located at `http://dev.eclipse.org/ viewcvs/index.cgi/ %7Echeckout%7E/jdt-core-home/r3.0/main.html#updates`.

Summary

In this final chapter, I reexamined some outstanding features of the Eclipse platform. The use of Eclipse as both an IDE and a framework may have a huge impact on your programming style. In general, it will support a more agile programming style that leans toward Extreme Programming. As an open platform, Eclipse encourages such an agile work style not only for Java programming but also for other tasks. So it might be exciting to take a look at some of the third-party plug-ins, too. Appendix A lists a small but essential collection of such plug-ins.

The next big change for Java programming will come with support for J2SE 5.0 (perhaps in Eclipse 3.1?) that will lead to both a more compact and safer programming style. Eclipse has taken a steep path from version 1.0 to version 3.0 and will certainly not stop there. It will be exciting to see what the future brings.

Useful Plug-ins for Eclipse

Many useful plug-ins have been created for Eclipse, and many of them are freely available on the Web. I have listed some of these plug-ins here. I refrained from presenting plug-ins that are only in the planning stage or are at a pre-alpha stage. It may be worth visiting the listed Web sites from time to time to look for new developments.

Good starting points for searching plug-ins are, of course, the official Eclipse Web site at www.eclipse.org and SourceForge at sourceforge.net. In addition, there are some Web sites dedicated to Eclipse plug-ins, such as www.eclipse-plugins.info and www.eclipse-plugincentral.com.

Name	Description	Home Page
Databases		
Attrezzo per Xindice	A graphical user interface for the Xindice XML database. Free.	attrezzo.sourceforge.net
easysql	SQL editor and executor. Free.	sourceforge.net/projects/easysql
JFaceDbc	A JDBC client. Free.	sourceforge.net/projects/jfacedbc
Graphics		
GEF	Graphical Editor Framework. A framework for implementing diagram editors. Free.	www.eclipse.org/gef

Name	Description	Home Page
GUI design		
JellySWT	An XML-based script language for SWT-based user interfaces. Free	`jakarta.apache.org/ commons/jelly/jellyswt.html`
W4Eclipse	Visual web-GUI designer for the SWT, manufactured by INNOOPRACT (`www.innoopract.de`). Commercial product, but free for the first 5000 objects.	`w4toolkit.com`
SWT-Designer	Visual GUI designer for SWT and JFace. Commercial product.	`www.swt-designer.com`
Jigloo	Visual GUI designer for SWT/JFace and Swing. Can convert between SWT and Swing, and can import GUIs created with NetBeans. Commercial product, but free community version.	`cloudgarden.com`
VE	Official Eclipse GUI designer project. Currently supports Swing only. SWT is in preparation. Free.	`www.eclipse.org`
Modeling		
EMF	Eclipse Modeling Framework.	`www.eclipse.org/emf`
KLEEN	Graphical editor for Asset Oriented Modeling (AOM). Free.	`www.aomodeling.org`
MagicDraw	A UML design tool. Commercial product.	`www.magicdraw.com`
Omondo	A UML design tool. Integrates with the Eclipse Java IDE. Free for noncommercial use.	`www.eclipseuml.com`

Name	Description	Home Page
Modeling		
Slime UML	A UML design tool. Commercial product.	`www.mvmsoft.de/content/ plugins/slime/slime.htm`
Azzurri Clay	Graphical editor for modeling relational databases. Commercial product but free core version.	`www.azzurri.jp/en/software/clay`
Software Management		
Various team repositories	The community page on www.eclipse.org lists under the Team Repository Providers section various manufacturers that provide plug-ins for connecting their repositories to Eclipse.	
Transcoder	A useful plug-in for transforming source code from one encoding into another.	`www.qanyon.com/TechZone/ TechZoneTranscoder`
Programming Languages and Compiler-Compilers		
AspectJ	AspectJ IDE. AspectJ is an aspect-oriented programming language based on Java. Free.	`sourceforge.net/projects/ ajc-for-eclipse`
CDT	C/C++ IDE. For C and C++ development (currently only under Linux). Free.	`www.eclipse.org/cdt`
Eiffel for Eclipse	Eiffel editor and compiler. Compile into Java byte code, C, and machine code. Free.	www.eclipse.audaly.com
Improve	C# Plugin C# editor and builder. Free.	`www.improve-technologies.com/ alpha/esharp`
xored WebStudio	PHP IDE. Free.	`www.xored.com`
JavaCC	A popular compiler-compiler implemented as an Eclipse plug-in. Free.	`sourceforge.net/projects/ eclipse-javacc`
ANTLR	A powerful compiler-compiler implemented as an Eclipse plug-in. Free.	`sourceforge.net/projects/ antlreclipse`

Name	Description	Home Page
Lifecycle		
Profiler	Tuning instrument for performing measurements in Java programs.	`eclipsecolorer.sourceforge.net/index_profiler.html`
Rational	ClearCase A UML-based CASE tool. Commercial product.	`www.rational.com`
Together Edition for Eclipse	A UML-based CASE tool. Commercial product.	`www.borland.com/together`
XML		
X-Men	An XML editor for Eclipse. Supports XML Schema and DTDs. Offers source view, table view. Good navigation via outline view. Free.	`sourceforge.net/projects/xmen`
XML Buddy	An XML editor with content assist, outline, DTD generator, and much more. Free.	`www.xmlbuddy.com`
Web Projects		
Sysdeo Eclipse Tomcat Launcher	Starting, stopping, and configuring Tomcat from within the Eclipse workbench. Supports comfortable debugging of JSP and servlet-based projects. Free.	`www.sysdeo.com/eclipse/tomcatplugin.html`
Systinet WASP Server for Java	Creates Web services from Java classes. Supports the execution and debugging of Web services from within Eclipse. Free for end users.	`www.systinet.com`
MyEclipse	Various tools for J2EE development, in particular, a JSP editor and debugger. MyEclipse is the product of a joint venture between Genuitec (`www.genuitec.com`) and the Saxonian startup BebboSoft (`www.bebbosoft.de`). Commercial license.	`www.myeclipseide.org`

Name	Description	Home Page
Embedded Systems		
TimeStorm 2.0	Cross-platform IDE for embedded-Linux target platforms. Commercial product.	`www.timesys.com`
SpellChecker for Eclipse	The spell checker developed in this book, and enhanced versions. Free.	`www.bdaum.de/eclipse`

Migrating Projects to a New Eclipse Version

The migration of projects to a new version of the Eclipse platform is a special situation.

Projects

The best way is to install the new Eclipse version into a different directory and then import the projects and your own or third-party plug-ins into this new version.

When doing so, you have the following options:

❑ **Import the complete workspace into the new version.** Here you need only modify the command-line parameter -data accordingly when invoking Eclipse. For example:

```
eclipse.exe -data C:\eclipseSDK2.1.2\eclipse\workspace
```

Alternatively, you may enter the path of the old workspace into the Workspace Launcher as shown in the "Installing Eclipse" section in Chapter 1.

The existing workspace remains at its old location and becomes the workspace of the new Eclipse platform.

❑ **Import single projects from the old workspace with the help of the Import function.** To do so, select the Import category Existing Project into Workspace.

Here, too, the physical location of the imported project is not changed—the project remains in the old workspace directory!

In both cases it may be necessary to adapt the Java Build Path of the imported projects. In particular, if JAR files of the Eclipse distribution were specified as external JARs, you must make some adjustments:

❑ If the JAR file was specified relative to the environment variable ECLIPSE_HOME, this variable now points to the storage location of the new Eclipse version. However, the JAR files in the new Eclipse version usually have different version numbers, so you will have dangling references.

❑ If the JAR file was specified via an absolute path expression, this path expression is still pointing to the JAR file in the old Eclipse version. If you want to update this to the new version, you must modify the corresponding path expression.

In both cases, you must first remove the existing references to external JARs and then add them back with the Add External JARs function.

Plug-ins

In the case of plug-in projects, however, you don't have to update the JAR references manually. Instead, you use the context function PDE Tools > Update Classpath....

If your plug-in is already in an installable state, the migration to a new platform version is even simpler. In this case, you would first install the plug-in (including the source files) on the old platform. By doing so you ensure that the plug-in resources appear in the directory's plugins and features sections.

Now you can migrate the plug-in to the new platform with the help of the Import > External Plug-ins and Features function. On the second page of the wizard, select all plug-ins required by the imported plug-in from the list. Based on this selection, the Java Build Path is adapted automatically. The workspace of the new platform now contains the complete development project for the imported plug-in.

Migration to Eclipse 3

Plug-in projects that were developed under Eclipse versions prior to Eclipse 3 and are now deployed on Eclipse 3 platforms, or where development is to be continued under the Eclipse 3 SDK, require special treatment. In many cases, but not in every case, Eclipse 3 can successfully run older plug-ins, so individual tests are required.

The reason for this lies in the introduction of the Rich Client Platform (see Chapter 14) and the generic workbench. The introduction of these features required a complete reorganization of the workbench's code basis. In particular, the workbench was separated into a generic, resource-agnostic part and a resource-specific IDE part. Since plug-in projects often relate to function groups of the workbench and some of these function groups have been relocated into new plug-ins or have been renamed, changing the plug-in manifest in the "Dependencies" section may be necessary. You can perform these changes automatically by applying the context function PDE Tools > Migrate to 3.0... to a plug-in project.

However, this may not be sufficient, and changes to the Java code of some classes may be required. In particular, those classes that relate to workbench components such as editors and views and that utilize IDE-specific functions (such as markers and annotations) are affected. Since these functions have been separated from the generic workbench components, changes are necessary. For example, the IDE-specific functions of the `AbstractTextEditor` class have been relocated to the IDE-specific `ExtendedTextEditor` class, while the `AbstractTextEditor` class has become completely workspace and resource agnostic.

Also, the event processing for resource changes (see the section "Reacting to Resource Changes" in Chapter 11) has changed, since Eclipse 3 works in a more concurrent fashion than Eclipse 2. For example, Build processes can now run in the background. Of course, this has consequences for the resource change event model. Classes that react to such events may need adaptations

SWT-based projects may also need smaller code changes, since some APIs have been changed to improve the compatibility with Linux and to provide better support for the Key Binding Service.

The *Eclipse 3.0 Porting Guide* explains the required changes in detail. This guide is found under Help > Help Contents > Platform Plug-in Developer Guide > 3.0 Plug-in Migration Guide.

Important Downloads

This appendix lists the web addresses for all the third-party software used in the context of this book.

Project One: Duke Speaks

FreeTTS (version 1.2.0) can be found at `sourceforge.net/projects/freetts`. Make sure you use version 1.2.0, because the API may have been changed in later versions!

Project Two: Jukebox

The source files for playing sound files (jlGui 2.2) can be found at `www.javazoom.net/jlgui/sources.html`. Make sure you use version 2.2, because the API was changed in later versions!

Project Three: A Spell Checker as an Eclipse Plug-In

The spell checker engine (version 0.5) can be found at `sourceforge.net/projects/jazzy`. Make sure you use version 0.5, because the API may have been changed in later versions!

Book Web Site

All the required resources are replicated on a special Web site dedicated to this book. This Web site is located at www.wrox.com.

There you can find the source code for the four projects and other examples.

Bibliography

Arthorne, John. *"How You've Changed! Responding to resource changes in the Eclipse workspace."* Eclipse Corner, www.eclipse.org, 2002.

Arthorne, John. *"Drag and Drop in the Eclipse UI."* Eclipse Corner, www.eclipse.org, 2003.

Beck, Kent. *Extreme Programming Explained: Embrace Change.* Harlow: Addison-Wesley, 1999.

Cornu, Christophe. *"A Small Cup of SWT."* IBM OTI Labs, Eclipse Corner, www.eclipse.org, 2003.

Daum, Berthold. *Modeling Business Objects with XML Schema.* San Francisco: Morgan Kaufman Publishing, 2003.

Daum, Berthold. *"Mutatis mutandis – Using Preference Pages as Property Pages."* Eclipse Corner, www.eclipse.org, 2003.

Daum, Berthold. *"Equipping SWT Applications with Content Assistants."* IBM developerWorks, www106.ibm.com/developerworks/opensource/library/os-ecca/, Nov 25, 2003.

Daum, Berthold. *Eclipse 2 for Java Developers.* Chichester: John Wiley & Sons, 2003.

Daum, Berthold, Stefan Franke, and Marcel Tilly. *Webentwicklung mit Eclipse.* Heidelberg: dpunkt verlag, 2004.

Fogel, Karl and Bar Moshe. *Open Source Projects with CVS.* Phoenix: Paraglyph Publishing, 2003.

Fowler, Martin, Kent Beck, John Brant, William Opdyke, and Don Roberts. *Refactoring: Improving the Design of Existing Code.* Harlow: Addison-Wesley, 1999.

Gamma, Erich, Richard Helm, Ralph Johnson, and John Vlissides. *Design Patterns*, Harlow: Addison-Wesley, 1995.

Gamma, Erich and Kent Beck. Contributing to Eclipse: *Principles, Patterns, and Plugins*. Harlow: Addison-Wesley; 2003.

Gunther, Jeff. *"Deploy an SWT Application Using Java Web Start."* IBM developerworks, www106.ibm.com/developerworks/opensource/library/os-jws/, June 19, 2003.

Hatcher, Erik and Steve Loughran. *Java Development with Ant*. Manning Publications Company, 2002.

Hightower, Richard and Nicholas Lesiecki. *Java Tools for Extreme Programming: Mastering Open Source Tools Including Ant, JUnit, and Cactus*. Chichester: John Wiley & Sons, 2001.

Irvine, Veronika. *"Drag and Drop – Adding Drag and Drop to an SWT Application."* Eclipse Corner, www.eclipse.org, 2003.

Kehn, Dan, Scott Fairbrother, and Cam-Thu Le. *"How to Internationalize Your Eclipse Plug-In,"* Eclipse Corner, www.eclipse.org, 2002.

MacLeod, Carolyn and Shantha Ramachandran. *"Understanding Layouts in SWT,"* Eclipse Corner, www.eclipse.org, 2002.

Moody, James and Carolyn MacLeod. *"SWT Color Model." Eclipse Corner*, www.eclipse.org, 2001.

Robinson, Matthew and Pavel Vorobiev. *Swing*. Greenwich: Manning Publications, 2000.

Steams, Beth. *"Java Beans 101."* Sun Microsystems, http://java.sun.com/developer/onlineTraining/Beans/bean01/index.html, 2000.

Tilly, Jesse and Eric M. Burke. *Ant: The Definitive Guide*. Sebastopol : O'Reilly & Associates, 2002.

Vesperman, Jennifer. *Essential CVS*. Sebastopol : O'Reilly & Associates, 2003.

Index